Dictionary of
PREMILLENNIAL THEOLOGY

Dictionary of
PREMILLENNIAL THEOLOGY

Mal Couch
General Editor

Dictionary of Premillennial Theology
Mal Couch, General Editor

Published by Kregel Publications, a division of Kregel, Inc., P.O. Box 2607, Grand Rapids, MI 49501. Kregel Publications provides trusted, biblical publications for Christian growth and service. Your comments and suggestions are valued.

Cover photos: Dallas Theological Seminary and Scofield Memorial Church, Dallas, Texas
Cover design: Alan G. Hartman
Book design: Nicholas G. Richardson

Library of Congress Cataloging-in-Publication Data
Couch, Mal.
Dictionary of premillennial theology / Mal Couch, gen. ed.
p. cm.
Includes bibliographical references and index.
1. Eschatology—Dictionaries. 2. Millennialism—Dictionaries. I. Couch, Mal.
BT821.2.D53 1996 236'.9—dc20 96-22346
CIP

ISBN 0-8254-2351-1

Printed in the United States of America
1 2 3 4 5 / 00 99 98 97 96

This dictionary is dedicated to the following scholars who, through their classroom lectures at Dallas Theological Seminary and through their publications, profoundly influenced the contributors of this book. Their writings helped us cultivate a passion for the return of our Savior, Jesus Christ. As faithful teachers of the Word, they have left to each of us an enduring legacy.

J. Dwight Pentecost
Charles C. Ryrie
John F. Walvoord

TABLE OF CONTENTS

FOREWORD

Not all premillennialists are dispensationalists, but all dispensationalists are premillennialists. Both schools of thought matured together through the nineteenth century, and this union of a theological system and prophetic viewpoint brought about a new understanding of the Scriptures that is unparalleled in the past two centuries of Christianity.

At the beginning of the twentieth century, dispensationalism was one of the most important forces in fundamentalism and evangelicalism. The "blessed hope"— the visible, physical return of Jesus Christ for His church— became the central theme of this movement. Teachings on the rapture of the church, the coming of a worldwide tribulation, and the arrival of the kingdom cut across all denominational lines. Pastors and laypersons alike were studying the *Scofield Reference Bible*, despite the resistance of their church associations and denominational leaders. Following its first publication in 1909, Scofield's annotated Bible provided millions of readers around the world with a new understanding of the Bible, of God's plan for the world, and of their own place in that plan.

One outgrowth of this movement was an energetic love for Jesus Christ and the Bible that expressed itself in the explosive growth of Bible institutes, colleges, and seminaries. Missionaries and pastors by the thousands marched out from these prophecy-teaching centers to carry the Gospel to the ends of the earth. Schools such as Moody Bible Institute and Philadelphia College of the Bible became leading dispensationalist institutions. Not only were multitudes converted, but the Scriptures, as seen from a dispensational perspective, took on a new clarity. Laypersons became more spiritually motivated and capable of sharing their faith with others. Prophecy conferences and summer camp meetings focused on the regathering of Israel to Palestine and the imminent return of the Lord.

What, then, are the distinctives of dispensational teaching?

First, dispensationalists believe in the inspiration and inerrancy of the Bible. One has to embrace such a view of Scripture, especially when believing in a prophetic plan yet to be fulfilled in history by a God who will keep His Word.

Second, dispensationalists are consistent in studying the Scriptures from a historical–grammatical methodology or "literal" hermeneutic. From Genesis to Revelation, the Bible is interpreted by the same rules of grammar and language that govern the interpretation of literature in general.

Third, dispensationalists believe that God set forth His plan of the ages progressively; that is, not everything is explained at once. For example, the doctrines of the Trinity and the church were revealed "line upon line." The succeeding biblical generations were given an unfolding revelation until a doctrine was fully developed.

Fourth, God has dealt differently with mankind at distinct times in history. The Lord worked differently with Abraham than He did with Moses and Israel. He now works differently with His church than He did with the Jews under the Law. Dispensationalism is the recognition of these distinct economies in biblical history.

Fifth, world history will not end suddenly with the return of Christ. For His own divine purposes, the Lord laid out a plan for end time events. This plan involves the rapture of the church, the restoration of the Jews to their promised King and kingdom, and the Tribulation judgment of the nations. Then follows a judgment of the lost and a new heaven and new earth. Dispensationalism recognizes these and other prophetic events and holds to them in their proper order.

Finally, although the salvation of the elect is part of the merciful plan of God, dispensationalists believe that the Scriptures teach that the outworkings of His providence will bring glory to Himself, not simply the salvation of the lost. What God has purposed for the angels, the lost, the nation of Israel, and creation itself will ultimately bring honor and glory to Himself.

After the 1970s, interest in dispensationalism began to decline within the mainstream of conservative evangelicalism. Along with this de-emphasis on the teaching of the rapture and Bible prophecy in general, a paradigm shift took place in many churches and Bible schools. Many pastors became more "sophisticated" in their preaching. Prophecy was out, and psychology was in. The teaching of doctrine was replaced by sermons on current social issues and the emotional life of the believer. Although it is difficult to establish what was the cause and what was the effect, many dispensationalists would argue that either way the result was a loss of clear biblical teaching.

This dictionary has been compiled in order to explain the major tenets of dispensationalism as it has been taught historically and to show that certain false accusations against the system are nothing more than straw men. In some cases, such accusations against dispensationalism have been based upon awkward sentences pulled from their context. For instance, some claim dispensationalists believe in various ways of salvation or that they believe the Sermon on the Mount cannot be applied to believers during this age of grace. Nothing could be further from the truth, and the contributors to this work pray that critics who study this volume with an open mind will have a better grasp of what dispensationalism actually teaches.

Many of the articles in this dictionary cover the history and development of dispensationalism. Some historic persons are featured who may not be considered dispensationalists *per se* but who were in the process of developing their prophetic beliefs. Although the early church Fathers did not expound Scripture in a systematic and dispensational fashion, we can observe flashes of their understanding about prophetic issues. We all wish they had written more!

Many thanks are due to Dr. Tim LaHaye, who in 1992 called together thirty Bible prophecy scholars and urged them to speak out concerning the pretribulational rapture of the church. From this first meeting, the Pre Trib Study Center developed, which is now a think tank of some two hundred scholars, writers, broadcasters, and professors. They are continually in the process of researching, restating, and refining dispensationalism and meet yearly to share their findings

Since the founding of the group, dozens of pamphlets, books, journal articles, videos, and radio broadcasts have again proclaimed the Blessed Hope. Most (but not all) of the contributors to this dictionary belong to the Pre Trib Research Center of Washington, D.C. Another word of thanks is due Dr. Thomas Ice, who is presently the Executive Director of the Pre Trib Study Center. Dr. Ice is a church history scholar whose encouraging advice helped launch this dictionary project.

Finally, as general editor of this project, I was personally motivated by the words of the apostle Paul that I believe characterize how believers should balance a love for Bible prophecy along with a life of service to our Master—no matter how long we are on this earth. Paul commended the Thessalonian believers who, although under severe persecution, had turned to God from idols "*to serve* a living and true God, and *to wait* for His Son from heaven" (1 Thess. 1:9). Paul also encouraged them by saying that God raised Jesus from the dead "who rescues us from the coming wrath" (1:10, my translation).

Maranatha, Lord Jesus!

MAL COUCH
General Editor

ABOUT THE CONTRIBUTORS

Robert G. Anderson, Th.M., is academic dean of Houston College of Biblical Studies in Houston, Texas.

Roy E. Beacham, M.Div., Th.M., Th.D., is chairman and professor of Old Testament at Central Baptist Theological Seminary in Minneapolis, Minnesota.

Rick Bowman, D.Min., is a researcher, writer, and editor at Tyndale Theological Seminary and Biblical Institute in Ft. Worth, Texas.

Joseph R. Chambers, D.D., is founder and president of Paw Creek Radio and Media Ministry in Charlotte, North Carolina.

Mal O. Couch, M.A., Th.M., Th.D., Ph.D., is founder and president of Tyndale Theological Seminary and Biblical Institute in Ft. Worth, Texas.

Larry V. Crutchfield, Phil.M., M.A., Ph.D., is a mentor at Faraston Theological Seminary. He lives in Colorado Springs, Colorado.

Rodney Decker, M.Div., Th.D. candidate, is a professor of Bible at Calvary Theological Seminary in Kansas City, Missouri.

Timothy J. Demy, M.A., M.A., Th.M., Th.D., is a military chaplain, author, and Bible teacher. He lives in Springfield, Virginia.

Thomas Edgar, Th.M., Th.D., is professor of New Testament Literature at Capital Bible Seminary in Lanham, Maryland.

Floyd S. Elmore, Th.M., Th.D., is professor of Bible at Cedarville College in Cedarville, Ohio.

Paul P. Inns, Th.M., Th.D., is an author, founding dean of Tampa Bay Theological Seminary, and dean of the Institute of Biblical Training in Tampa, Florida.

Gary Fisher is an author and the founder and director of Lion of Judah Ministry in Franklin, Tennessee.

Harold D. Foos, Th.M., Th.D., is professor of Bible and Theology and chairman of the Department of Theology at Moody Bible Institute in Chicago, Illinois.

Arnold G. Fruchtenbaum, Th.M., Ph.D., is an author, international Bible teacher, and the founder and director of Ariel Ministries in Tustin, California.

Alden Gannett, Th.M., Th.D., is an author and conference speaker. He lives in Birmingham, Alabama.

Michael P. Gendron, M.A.B.S., M.A.S., is the founder and president of Proclaiming the Gospel Ministry in Dallas, Texas.

Robert G. Gromacki, Th.M., Th.D., is a pastor, author, and distinguished professor of Bible and Greek at Cedarville College, Cedarville, Ohio.

George A. Gunn, M.Div., is the chairman of Bible and Theology at Shasta Bible College in Reading, California.

John D. Hannah, Th.M., Ph.D., is an author and the chairman and professor of Historical Theology at Dallas Theological Seminary in Dallas, Texas.

Bobby Hayes, M.A., Ph.D. candidate, is an associate professor at Tyndale Theological Seminary and Biblical Institute in Ft. Worth, Texas.

Edward E. Hindson, M.A., Th.M., Th.D., D.Phil., is an author, the vice president of There's Hope Ministry in Atlanta, Georgia, and distinguished adjunct professor at Liberty University in Lynchburg, Virginia.

H. Wayne House, M.A., Th.M., M.Div., J.D., Th.D., is a visiting professor of Theology at various institutions, a freelance writer, and a dean and professor at Michigan Theological Seminary in Plymouth, Michigan.

Tommy D. Ice, Th.M., Ph.D., is an author, former pastor, and the executive director of the PreTrib Research Center in Washington, D.C.

Elliott Johnson, Th.M., Th.D., is an author and professor of Bible Exposition at Dallas Theological Seminary in Dallas, Texas.

Gordon Johnston, Th.M., Th.D., is associate professor of the Biblical Division at Lancaster Bible College in Lancaster, Pennsylvania.

Tim F. LaHaye, D.Min., D.D., is an author and the director of Family Life Seminars in Washington, D.C.

G. Harry Leafe, Th.M., D.Min., is professor and chairman of Bible and Theology at Houston Bible Institute in Houston, Texas.

Dale F. Leschert, M.Div., Th.M., Ph.D., is an independent researcher and writer who lives in New Westminster, British Columbia, Canada.

Robert P. Lightner, Th.M., Th.D., is an author and professor of Theology at Dallas Theological Seminary in Dallas, Texas.

Eugene J. Mayhew, Th.M., Th.D., is professor of Old Testament at Michigan Theological Seminary in Plymouth, Michigan.

Stephen L. McAvoy, Th.M., Th.D., is the director of the Institute for Biblical Studies in Lake Oswego, Oregon.

Thomas S. McCall, Th.M., Th.D., is an author, conference speaker, and researcher for Levitt Ministries. He lives in Bullard, Texas.

John A. McLean, Th.M., M.A., Ph.D., is president of Michigan Theological Seminary in Plymouth, Michigan.

George E. Meisinger, Th.M., D.Min., is president of Chafer Theological Seminary and pastor of Grace Church in Huntington Beach, California.

Charles W. Missler, M.S., is the founder of Koinonia House, Coeur d'Alene, Idaho.

John H. Mulholland, Th.M., Th.D., is professor of Systematic Theology at Capital Bible Seminary in Lanham, Maryland.

David R. Nicholas, M.S., Th.M., Th.D., is president and professor of Theology at Shasta Bible College in Reading, California.

Jerry Neuman, M.Div., is professor of Bible and Theology at Berean Baptist Institute in Natal, Brazil.

Russell L. Penney, M.A., D.Sc., Th.D. candidate, is associate professor of Biblical Studies at Tyndale Theological Seminary and Biblical Institute in Ft. Worth, Texas.

Donald Perkins is founder and president of According to Prophecy Ministries in Lemon Grove, California.

J. Randall Price, Th.M., Ph.D., is professor of Theology and Bible at Liberty Baptist Theological Seminary and is founder and president of World of the Bible Ministries, Inc. in San Marcos, Texas.

Clifford Rapp, Th.M., is professor of Theology at Chafer Theological Seminary in Huntington Beach, California.

Brian K. Richards, M.A.,is a Th.M. candidate at Tyndale Theological Seminary and Biblical Institute in Ft. Worth, Texas.

Charles C. Ryrie, Th.M., Th.D., Ph.D., is Professor of Systematic Theology, Emeritus at Dallas Theological Seminary. He is an author, lecturer, and editor of the *Ryrie Study Bible*. He lives in Dallas, Texas.

Lonnie L. Shipman, M.A., is an author and music evangelist living in Dallas, Texas.

Renald E. Showers, Th.M., Th.D., is an author on the staff of The Friends of Israel Gospel Ministry, Inc. He lives in Willow Street, Pennsylvania.

Michael D. Stallard, Th.M., Th.D., is professor of Old Testament at Baptist Bible Seminary in Clarks Summit, Pennsylvania.

Gerald B. Stanton, Th.M., Th.D., is president of Ambassadors International and professor at Asia Graduate School of Theology. He lives in Palm Beach Gardens, Florida.

Irvin R. Starwalt, M.Div., S.T.M., Ph.D. candidate, is a researcher for Tyndale Theological Seminary and Biblical Institute in Ft. Worth, Texas.

Gary P. Stewart, M.Div., Th.M., D.Min. candidate, is a chaplain in the United States Navy. He lives in Hammond, Oregon.

Kevin Stilley, M.Div., M.A., Ph.D. and D.Min. candidate, is a professor at Tyndale Theological Seminary and Biblical Institute in Ft. Worth, Texas.

Steve P. Sullivan, Th.M., D.Min. candidate, is a pastor and teacher of Bible and Theology at Houston Bible Institute in Houston, Texas.

Paul L. Tan, Th.M., Th.D., is an author and the founder and president of Bible Communications, Inc., Dallas, Texas.

Robert L. Thomas, Th.M., Th.D., is an author and professor of New Testament Language and Literature at The Master's Seminary in Stanton, California.

Elmer Towns, Th.M., M.A., M.R.E., D.Min., is dean of Religion at Liberty University in Lynchburg, Virginia.

William Varner, M.Div., S.T.M., M.A., is the dean of the Institute of Biblical Studies, a ministry of The Friends of Israel Gospel Ministry, Inc., Bellmawr, New Jersey.

ACKNOWLEDGMENTS

Because of the growing confusion over Bible prophecy, I felt this volume needed to be written and published as soon as possible. The fifty-four contributors were equally concerned and finished their assignments in record time. For this effort, I acknowledge the sacrifice and dedication these godly teachers gave to the project.

A special thanks goes also to Dennis Hillman, senior editor at Kregel Publications, and editorial assistant, Rachel Warren. While concerned about accuracy and detail, they helped finish in one year a project that could have taken three years to complete. A special thanks also goes to Kregel Publication's editors and proofreaders. As well, a warm and grateful appreciation goes to Tyndale Theological Seminary and Biblical Institute staff, Registrar John Baze and Dr. Russell Penney who contributed many hours of final proofreading to the project.

TRANSLITERATION

HEBREW

Consonants

א	’
ב	*b*
ג	*g*
ד	*d*
ה	*h*
ו	*w*
ז	*z*
ח	*ḥ*
ט	*ṭ*
י	*y*
כ, ך	*k*
ל	*l*
מ, ם	*m*
נ	*n*
ס	*s*
ע	‘
פ, ף	*p*
צ, ץ	*ṣ*
ק	*q*
ר	*r*
שׂ	*ś*
שׁ	*š*
ת	*t*

Vowels

ָ	*ā*
ַ	*a*
ֶ	*e*
ֵ	*ē*
ִ	*i*
ָ	*o*[1]
ֹ	*ō*
ֻ	*u, ū*[2]
הָ	*â*
ֶי	*ê*
ֵי	*ê*
וֹ	*î*
וּ	*û*
ֳ	*ŏ*
ֲ	*ă*
ֱ	*ĕ*
ְ	*ĕ*[3]

GREEK

α	*a*	ν	*n*
β	*b*	ξ	*x*
γ	*g, n*	ο	*o*
δ	*d*	π	*p*
ϵ	*e*	ρ	*r*
ζ	*z*	σ, ς	*s*
η	*ē*	τ	*t*
θ	*th*	υ	*y, u*
ι	*i*	φ	*ph*
κ	*k*	ψ	*ch*
λ	*l*	ω	*ō*
μ	*m*	῾	*h*

1. *qāmeṣ ḥāṭûp*
2. *u=short, ū=long defective*
3. *vocal šĕwâ*

ABBREVIATIONS

BETL	*Bibliotheca Ephemeridum Theologie*
BV	*Biblical Viewpoint*
CBQ	*The Catholic Biblical Quarterly*
CTM	*Concordia Theological Monthly*
GTJ	*Grace Theological Journal*
HUCA	*Hebrew Union College Annual*
ISBE	*The International Standard Bible Encyclopedia,* ed. J. Orr
JETS	*Journal of the Evangelical Theological Society*
JSOT	*Journal for the Study of the Old Testament*
OTWSA	*Ou testamentiese werkgemeenskap Suid-Afrika*
RExp	*Review and Expositor*
SJT	*Scottish Journal of Theology*
TB	*Tyndale Bulletin*
TDNT	*Theological Dictionary of the New Testament,* ed. G. Kittel and G. Friedrich
VT	*Vetus Testamentum*
WJT	*Westminster Journal of Theology*
ZAW	*Zeitschrift für die alttestamentliche Wissenschaft*

Dictionary of PREMILLENNIAL THEOLOGY

A

ABRAHAMIC COVENANT

God's covenant with Abraham is first set forth and initiated in Genesis 12:1–3. It is later reiterated in Genesis 13:14–17, ratified in Genesis 15, and signified in Genesis 17. It is again reiterated in Genesis 22:15–18. In each case it is enlarged upon. It is later confirmed to Isaac (Gen. 26:3–5, 24) and Jacob (Gen. 28:13–15; 35:9–12; cf. 46:1–4), and is subsequently spoken of as God's "covenant with Abraham, Isaac, and Jacob" (2 Kings 13:23).

Concept of Covenant in Scripture

Covenant means an agreement or contract between two parties that binds one or both parties to certain obligations and commitments. Scripture contains many types of covenants involving legal agreements between nations, individuals, kings and their subjects, individuals and small groups, husband and wife, and between people and God. This last type of covenant can be initiated by the people (2 Kings 11:17; Ezra 10:2–3), or by God. The Abrahamic covenant is a divine covenant in that it was initiated by God.

Biblical covenant forms resemble almost exactly Hittite treaty forms, specifically the suzerain-vassal type. Biblical covenant texts usually contain components similar to the Hittite treaty texts, such as a preamble, historical prologue, stipulations, provisions for deposit and reading of the text, invocation of witnesses, blessings and curses, and the performance of a rite as ratification. A covenant was both solemn and binding. A man's honor, even his life, was at stake in the making of a covenant. Thus, to Abraham and the people of his day, the concept of covenant was well understood, formalized, solemnly important, and irreversibly binding. A bilateral covenant was binding on both parties; both were obligated to stated pledges. A unilateral covenant was binding only on one party, the one making the pledge. The Abrahamic covenant is a unilateral covenant, a divine covenant in which God alone pledges Himself to a course of action through Abraham and his seed, which cannot be reversed (else God would prove untrue) and cannot be annulled by the failure of either Abraham or his seed, for the existence and continuance of the covenant depends not upon the fidelity of Abraham or his seed, but on God alone.

Importance of the Covenant

From an interpretive standpoint, the Abrahamic covenant is the single most important event in the Old Testament. It governs God's entire program for Israel and the nations and is thus determinative of God's program in history. The Abrahamic covenant is foundational to all of Scripture. It is the key to both the Old and New Testaments and is foundational to the whole program of redemption. All subsequent revelation is the outworking of this covenant. This covenant, and the subsequent covenant framework, is the key to understanding Scripture.

The essence of God's covenant with Abraham consists of three basic aspects: *land, seed,* and *blessing*. Each of the divine covenants that follow are the outworking of the Abrahamic covenant. The Palestinian covenant (Deut. 28–30) amplifies the *land* aspect of the Abrahamic covenant. The Davidic covenant (2 Sam. 7:8–17) amplifies the *seed* aspect, and the new covenant (Jer. 31:27–37; Ezek. 36:22–32) amplifies the *blessings* aspect. Thus, the Abrahamic covenant is the fountainhead from which the others flow. The Abrahamic covenant, then, is determinative for the entire outworking of God's program for both Israel and the nations and is the key to biblical eschatology. The

Abrahamic covenant is in fact the cornerstone of premillennialism. At issue is whether the covenant is to be understood literally.

A literal interpretation requires the perpetuation of national Israel and their restoration to the land in blessing and everlasting possession.

Background to the Covenant

At the time of Abram, wickedness had again spread over the earth. Terah, Abram's father, was an idolator (Josh. 24:2), and presumably Abram too. Divine intervention was again required. Rather than destroying the wicked as before, God chose Abram out of a land of idolatry to build a new nation through whom He would bring blessing to the entire world. In order to deal exclusively with Abram, God had to separate him from his family and environment. Thus, He issued a threefold command to Abram. Abram was to leave (1) his country, (2) his father's house, and (3) his relatives (Gen. 12:1). Obeying the first of these commands, Abram left his country, Ur of the Chaldeans. He came as far as Haran and settled there. He was there until his father died. Why he brought his father and why he stayed in Haran is uncertain. But it is significant that God did not appear to Abram again until Abram had fulfilled the second part of God's instructions, that of leaving his father's house (it should be noted that Genesis 12:1–3 is parenthetical to the narrative). It is not until Abram separates from Lot (his nephew), fulfilling the final part of God's instructions, that God appears to Abram a third time (Gen. 13:14) and reiterates the promises initiated in 12:1–3.

These new promises are to be fulfilled through an entirely new people. God did not adopt a family nor did He deal with an existing tribe. God radically altered the life of one man, Abram, by appearing to him (Acts 7:2) and calling him to be the "father" of a new people, a chosen people, the people of God. God so revealed Himself to Abram that when God gave him a promise, Abram believed God would fulfill it and be faithful to His Word.

While Abram's movements of physical withdrawal, from the general (your country) to the specific (your father's house), are geographically historical, they perhaps bear theological overtones of a spiritual withdrawal beginning at the periphery and ending with the inner core.

God calls Abram to be set apart (physically) from all that he knew (country, relatives, father's house) and to be set apart spiritually (from all prior idolatry) to God alone.

The Initiation and Promise of the Covenant

In Genesis 12:1–3 the covenant is initiated and the promises set forth. The use of the Hebrew nonsequential, or *waw,* disjunctive in 12:1 indicates that this section is an epexegetical parenthesis linking 11:32 with 12:4 (i.e., it explains *why* Abram is making the journey from Ur [11:31] to Canaan). God had appeared to him in Ur (Acts 7:2, see above) and made the promises as stated in Genesis 12:1–3, promises that were antecedent to 11:31. Three important aspects of the promise that should be carefully distinguished are the content, recipients, and beneficiaries of the promise. The content of the promise is threefold: Promises were made concerning the land, seed, and blessing (unspecified at this point). The recipient of the promise was Abram alone (at this point), though he is told the beneficiaries are Abram himself, his seed (descendents), and all the families of the earth (12:1–3; 13:15; 15:18; 17:7–8). Later, the promise is extended to Isaac (17:19; 26:24–25), Jacob (28:13–15), and Jacob's sons (28:14; 35:12; Deut. 4:40; 29:1–9) as the recipients of the covenant promises and through whom the promises would be fulfilled.

Thus the promise of the covenant consists of personal blessings to Abram, national blessings to Abram's descendents, and universal blessings to all nations. This promise is the seedbed of God's entire program for Israel and the nations. In regard to personal blessing, Abram is promised that he shall be the father of a great nation (Gen. 12:2); other nations shall come forth from him, even kings (Gen. 17:6); his name shall be great and he himself shall be a blessing; he will be the recipient of spiritual and material blessing; and he shall have everlasting possession of the land (Gen. 12:1; 13:15; 17:8). Abram's descendents are promised blessing and everlasting possession of the land (12:7; 13:15; 15:18; 17:8). Concerning the nations, Abram is given a general promise that through him they shall be blessed. Though this blessing is here unspecified, later in the progressive development of revelation, the nature of these blessings is made clear.

In tracing the outworking and fulfillment of the Abrahamic covenant, it is imperative to carefully distinguish the different aspects of the promise. If the blessings ascribed to one recipient are applied to another, confusion can only result. The land aspect of the promise is restricted to Abram and his physical seed, and then only through Isaac and Jacob. Since Abram could only have understood *seed* to mean his physical descendents and since the promise of the land was later narrowed to Isaac (disinheriting Ishmael, Gen. 17:15–21) and then to Jacob (disinheriting Esau, Gen. 25:23; 27:29, 33; 28:13–15), the promise of the land is to Israel only, beginning with Abram. This distinction must be held consistently. To say that the promise to Abram is fulfilled in the church ignores the fact that the land is never promised to the church or Gentiles, but Israel alone. It will not do to say that as Abram's spiritual seed (Gal. 3:29) the church fulfills the promise to Abram. Since when has the church been in everlasting possession of Palestine and its surrounding territories? We cannot spiritualize "land" to mean heaven or some other Christian experience. As Abram stood in Canaan (13:14–18), God told him to lift up his eyes from where he stood, in all four directions. All the land that Abram saw, God promised to give him and his descendents forever. The boundaries of this land are outlined in Genesis 15:18–21. A literal, geographic, earthly real estate was promised to Abram and his descendents as an everlasting possession. Only with Israel can the promise be fulfilled and only when they are in everlasting possession of the land whose boundaries are described in Genesis 15:18–21.

Some use Galatians 3 to say that the church as the new Israel fulfills the promise given to Abram. Since Christ is the Seed of Abraham (Gal. 3:16), those who are in Christ are also seed of Abraham (Gal. 3:29). Since the church is clearly seed of Abraham, the promises of the Abrahamic covenant must somehow be seen as fulfilled in the church. Thus, the promises of the land must be spiritualized or seen as abrogated due to Israel's disobedience. It is true that Galatians 3 teaches that believers, who are in Christ (i.e., the church), are seed of Abraham.

It is also true that these same are also heirs of the Abrahamic covenant. But Paul's point in Galatians 3 is that Gentiles who are in Christ inherit the universal blessings aspect only of the Abrahamic covenant *as Gentiles*, without having to become Jews or becoming subject to the Law. This does not mean that they come under all the promises given to Abraham personally or to his seed in a physical or national sense. The Scripture distinguishes the three types of seed of Abraham as (1) physical descendents of Abraham, but without Abraham's faith and who inherit none of the covenant promises, (2) physical descendents of Abraham who also have Abraham's faith and who inherit all of the covenant promises including the land, and (3) spiritual descendents of Abraham who have not Abraham's blood but do have his faith, and who inherit the universal blessings aspect of the Abrahamic covenant. It is this third type to whom Paul refers in Galatians. (There is, of course, a fourth type who is Christ, the ultimate Seed of Abraham).

Nature of the Covenant

The church can only be the new Israel and the inheritor of Israel's promises given in the Abrahamic covenant if either (1) the Abrahamic covenant is shown to be conditional, or (2) the promises of the covenant are spiritualized. Neither alternative is acceptable. A consistently literal interpretation of the Abrahamic covenant necessarily leads to dispensational premillennialism and the unavoidable conclusion that Israel and the church, though both beneficiaries of the Abrahamic covenant, are distinct entities with distinct promises peculiar to each. Only by spiritualizing the land promises of the Abrahamic covenant can one find their fulfillment in the church.

Others, rightly rejecting a nonliteral hermeneutic, argue that the Abrahamic covenant was conditional in nature and that Israel's disobedience annulled the promises, so that God is not bound to fulfill His promises to Israel concerning the land and its attendant material blessings. But the Abrahamic covenant is clearly *not* a conditional covenant. The Abrahamic covenant must be considered unconditional for the following reasons.

1. The covenant postdates the promise. That is, any conditions attached to the covenant making it a bilateral covenant (and there were none) would be invalid because the promise came *before* the ratification of the covenant.

2. The covenant is unilateral in that God alone is bound by the obligations of the covenant. No obligations whatever are placed on Abram in the context of its ratification (Gen. 15:9–21). In fact, Abram is *excluded* from passing through the pieces of animals in formal ratification of this covenant. God alone passed through the pieces of animals (Gen. 15:17), eternally and irrevocably binding Himself to His promise to Abram. God thus confirmed His oath to Abram by a blood covenant. This means God alone could break the covenant because God alone is bound by the covenant. Thus the existence and continuance of this covenant does not depend on pledges by both parties (God and Abram) but on God alone.

3. It is expressly said to be eternal and therefore unconditional (Gen. 13:15; 17:7, 13, 19; 48:4; 1 Chron. 16:17; Ps. 105:10).

4. It is reiterated and confirmed to Abraham, Isaac, Jacob, and the nation Israel after repeated disobedience on the part of each.

5. The Palestinian covenant and Davidic covenant are based on the Abrahamic covenant. If the Abrahamic covenant, which gives title deed to the land, were nullified, these covenants would be superfluous.

6. The entire history of Israel in both OT and NT (and beyond) confirms the unconditional nature of the covenant. The literal historical fulfillment of the outworking of this covenant in part demands literal fulfillment of that which yet remains.

There is nevertheless a conditional element to this covenant. From a divine standpoint, this covenant is unconditional in that God *will* fulfill His promises. Disobedience does not annul the covenant. It does, however, determine whether any individual or generation of individuals is eligible for the blessings of the covenant. Any member of the covenant community could forfeit his share of the covenant blessings but not that which belongs to his seed or successors for eternity. The conditionality attaches not to the divine promise, but to the participants who would benefit. This is evident in the narrative of the early experience of Israel's first two "generations."

Because the first generation of Israel (redeemed from Egypt) would not believe God at Kadesh-Barnea, the Lord refused to let them enter the land. He kept them wandering in the wilderness for forty years until that generation passed away (Num. 14:20). He then took their sons into the land. The sons too were warned of the consequences of disobedience. They also stood to forfeit their blessings in the land if they did not obey. Continued disobedience would result in exile from the land itself and captivity in foreign lands (Lev. 26; Deut. 28–30). Inherent in the covenant however, was the promise that when they repented they would be returned to the land in blessing (Deut. 30:1–10). In other words, God *will* place Israel in the Promised Land forever. He only needs a believing and obedient nation in order to fulfill this promise. How will He get a generation to be forever obedient and eligible to possess the land eternally? Israel will one day repent, be spiritually forgiven, cleansed, and regenerated (Deut. 30:6; Zech. 12:10–14; Jer. 31:31–34; Ezek. 36:22–32).

Ratification of the Covenant (Genesis 15)

Immediately following the recapture of his nephew Lot from Chedorlaomer and the kings who were with him, Abram declines the spoils of victory offered to him by the king of Sodom. Though done with righteous intent (Gen. 14:22–23), Abram apparently begins to question the wisdom of his decision (15:1–3). In response to Abram's wavering faith, God reiterates His threefold promise to Abram concerning the land, seed, and blessing. Reversing the order, God assures Abram that in regard to blessing, his reward shall be very great (15:1); as to the seed, he shall from his own body be the progenitor of innumerable descendents (15:4–5); and concerning the land, Abram shall possess it (15:7).

When Abram asks for reassurance concerning his possession of the land (15:8), God confirms His promise with a blood covenant (15:8–21). Since only one animal was necessary for a blood covenant, the multiplicity of animals here emphasizes the solemn importance of this covenant. Normally, in the ratification of a blood covenant, both parties would pass between the pieces of animal, mutually binding themselves to an unalterable covenant. Here, however, Abram is put into a deep sleep (15:12), and God alone passes through the pieces (15:17). Thus, Abram becomes a recipient and beneficiary of this divine covenant, but not a participant. Therefore the existence and continuance of this covenant does not depend on Abram. Since Abram did not make (cut) the covenant, he cannot break the covenant. God alone participated in the oath and ratification, binding Himself to an unalterable promise and irreversible course of action. This then, is a unilateral covenant and therefore unconditional as to its eventual fulfillment. Abram and his seed (physical descendents through Isaac and Jacob), Israel, shall possess the land forever.

It is important to note in connection with the ratification of this covenant that (1) the geographical boundaries are specifically stated (15:18–21), and (2) the destiny of Abram's seed regarding their bondage in Egypt and deliverance four hundred years later are not only foretold but literally fulfilled. Literal fulfillment of Israel's predicted bondage, deliverance, and entrance into the land argues for the same literal fulfillment of the promise of their everlasting possession of the land.

Sign of the Covenant (Genesis 17:1–27)

Immediately following Abram's lapse of faith (Gen. 16), God again reiterates the covenant promises to Abram (17:1–8). He identifies Himself as "the Strong One," emphasizing His ability to do what He has promised (17:1). Abram's name (high, exalted father) is changed to Abraham (father of many nations). Circumcision is instituted (17:9–14) as a sign of the Abrahamic covenant. Circumcision is not intended as the making of a new and separate covenant, but a sign of the already existing Abrahamic covenant. Compliance on the part of the covenant people indicated the reality of their faith and rendered them eligible for blessing under the terms of the covenant. When a father circumcised his son, he did so out of faith in the covenant promises and desire for his son's covenant eligibility.

Circumcision thus identified a people who were eligible for blessing. Circumcision alone however, did not guarantee blessing. Faith was necessary. But lack of circumcision certainly excluded one from the covenant community (17:14). Ishmael's circumcision was necessary not because he was to be the heir of the covenant through whom the covenant would perpetuate, but simply because he was a member of the covenant community. Circumcision was required even of the foreign servants (17:13). Circumcision however, did not insure Ishmael's continued covenant eligibility. Though circumcised, he is banished because he is faithless and hostile to the covenant people.

Historical Fulfillment of the Covenant

Many of the promises given to Abraham have been fulfilled in history, and literally so. Abraham was abundantly blessed with material and temporal things. He possessed land, servants, flocks of livestock, silver, and gold. In spiritual things he lived a happy life of separation to God, communion with God (said to be the friend of God), he was sustained by God and had peace and confidence that comes from an obedient life and dependence on God. Abraham also had a great name (in his own time) which even today is regarded highly in the three greatest religions of the world (Judaism, Islam, and Christianity). He had an heir by Sarah; bore innumerable seed, and was (and still is) a channel of blessing to others (e.g., his own family and household, his descendents, the entire world). Moreover, history has born out the blessings and curses of the Abrahamic covenant. Nations that have persecuted and cursed Israel, God has cursed. Those that have blessed Israel, God has blessed.

Eschatological Implications of the Covenant

Unconditional as it is, made with Israel as it is, and literally understood, the Abrahamic covenant necessitates certain eschatological implications. The nation Israel as the physical seed of Abraham must be perpetuated. If Israel is to possess the land forever, they must exist forever. This is not only implied in the Abrahamic covenant but is specifically confirmed by Scripture (Ps. 89:29–37; Jer. 31:35–37; 33:19–26; 46:28; Amos 9:8–15). In spite of Israel's disobedience they will be preserved as a nation. Israel will be restored to the land. Israel will undergo severe discipline for disobedience that will turn them to repentance. Israel will experience a national conversion and spiritual regeneration that will qualify them for eternal possession of the land in material and spiritual blessing. Israel will be the channel of blessing for all the nations of the earth. The Abrahamic covenant guarantees Israel everlasting possession of, and blessing in, the land as geographically outlined in Genesis 15. Abraham, Isaac, Jacob, and Jacob's sons who shared their fathers' faith and covenant eligibility will be resurrected and placed in everlasting possession of the land (Matt. 22:23–32; Acts 26:6–8; Heb. 11:13).

Implicit also in the Abrahamic covenant are the universal blessings that come to all the families of the earth (Gen. 12:3). These blessings reach into the present church age and into the Millennium. By the shedding of His blood, Christ ratified the new covenant (Matt. 26:26–29; Mark 14:24; Luke 22:17–20) specifically promised to Israel (Jer. 31:31). The new covenant amplifies the universal blessings aspect of the Abrahamic covenant. And while Israel presently forfeits these blessings due to unbelief, the church, by its association with the Mediator of the new covenant, inherits the spiritual blessings of the new covenant (forgiveness of sin, spiritual regeneration, indwelling Holy Spirit, etc., see Jer. 31:33–34; Ezek. 36:25–27). When Israel repents and accepts Christ (Zech. 12:10–14), the nation shall inherit all these spiritual blessings and restoration to the land with its attendant material blessings (Ezek. 36:22–38).

See also COVENANTS, THE.

Steven L. McAvoy

Willis J. Beecher, *The Prophets and the Promise* (Grand Rapids: Baker, 1975); Paul N. Benware, *Understanding End Times Prophecy: A Comprehensive Approach* (Chicago: Moody Press, 1995); Clarence E. Mason Jr., *Prophetic Problems With Alternate Solutions* (Chicago: Moody Press, 1973); J. Dwight Pentecost, *Things to Come* (Grand Rapids: Zondervan, 1958) and *Thy Kingdom Come* (Wheaton: Victor Books, 1990); Charles C. Ryrie, *The Basis of the Premillennial Faith* (Neptune, N.J.: Loizeaux Brothers, 1953); Bruce K. Waltke, "The Phenomenon of Conditionality within Unconditional Covenants" in *Israel's Apostasy and Restoration*, ed. Abraham Gileadi (Grand Rapids: Baker, 1988); John F. Walvoord, "The Abrahamic Covenant and Premillennialism" in *Vital Prophetic Issues*, ed. Roy B. Zuck (Grand Rapids: Kregel, 1995), and *The Millennial Kingdom* (Grand Rapids: Zondervan, 1959).

ACTS, ESCHATOLOGY OF

The book of Acts records the founding of the church and the spread of Christianity. It is commonly called the Acts of the Holy Spirit, based on the fact that He is referred to more than fifty times in the book. The book begins with the ascension of Christ to the right hand of the Father and the subsequent arrival of God's Holy Spirit. At His coming the Holy Spirit began His ministry of indwelling, filling, and leading believers. Only in Acts is the inspired account of the beginning and expansion of the church given. The book chronicles the spread of the church from Jerusalem to Rome, as well as the Jews' rejection and the Gentiles' acceptance of God's salvation.

The author of the book is Luke. Authorship is primarily supported by the three *we* sections where the narrative is first person plural (16:10–17; 20:5–21:18; 27:1–28:16) and by similarity in literary style to the gospel of Luke. The date of writing is placed at A.D. 60–62.

There are numerous prophecies recorded in the book of Acts. They include those that were fulfilled within the historical narrative of the book and those that are yet future. The coming of the Holy Spirit is promised (1:4–5), and fulfilled (2:1–4). The disciples ask Christ about the future millennial kingdom (1:6) and are told that it would remain a mystery until God chose to reveal that time (1:7). The disciples were aware of this future time based on the Old Testament teaching (Isa. 32:15–20) where a future blessing on the land and on the people is promised. Next the second coming of Jesus Christ is prophesied (1:11) and becomes the prevalent theme from this point forward through the end of the New Testament writings.

The events at Pentecost (2:1) were foretold in the Old Testament (Exod. 23:16; Lev. 23:15–22; Num. 28:26–31; Deut. 16:9–12). Pentecost occurred fifty days after the Feast of Firstfruits which is a type of Christ's resurrection as the firstfruits of the dead. As the Feast of Pentecost signified the wheat harvest, the Day of Pentecost marked the beginning of the church age. Chapter 2 (vv. 17–20) is a quote from the Old Testament (Joel 2:28–32). There are essentially two prophecies given here: 2:17–18 speaks of the events that take place at Pentecost and thus are fulfilled; the rest of the passage (2:19–20) presents the signs that will precede the future Day of the Lord when moral decline and apostasy prevail. The fulfillment of the prophecy concerning Christ's exaltation (Ps. 110:1) is found in 2:34–36; concerning His crucifixion (Isa. 52:13–53:12) is found in 3:13–15.

Acts 15:16–18 is a quotation from the Old Testament (Amos 9:11–12), which speaks of the time when Christ will return. At that time the tabernacle of David will be established in the millennial kingdom. This was an assurance given to the Jews that although God had allowed Gentiles to partake of His salvation, He had not deserted His program for Israel. During Paul's sermon (17:22–34), he prophesied that God would judge the whole world through Jesus Christ, the righteous judge, who has been raised from the dead (v. 31). This will literally be fulfilled at the Great White Throne (Rev. 20:11). Acts records the prophecy given to Paul by Jesus (23:11) that he was going to Rome to witness. The fulfillment of this is recorded in 28:11–16.

Finally, Paul speaks of the hope of Israel (28:20), which looks to the resurrection and the day when Jesus returns and establishes Himself as King of Kings and Lord of Lords.

See also HOLY SPIRIT, BAPTISM OF THE.

Rick Bowman

Charles F. Pfeiffer and Everett F. Harrison, eds., *The Wycliffe Bible Commentary* (Chicago: Moody Press, 1962); John F. Walvoord, ed., *The Prophecy Knowledge Handbook* (Wheaton: Victor Books, 1990); John L. Walvoord and Roy B. Zuck, eds., *The Bible Knowledge Commentary* (Wheaton: Victor Books, 1985).

ACTS 2 AND PENTECOST

The outpouring of the Holy Spirit on the Day of Pentecost in Acts 2 is the antitype of the Old Testament Feast of Pentecost, and it is a fulfillment of several prophecies of our Lord Jesus, notably Acts 1:5, 8, as well as John 14:16–17, 26; 15:26; 16:7–15. But it is not the fulfillment of Joel's prophecy.

The Pentecost of Acts 2 fulfilled many particulars of the Feast of Pentecost in Leviticus 23. The fifty-day interval of the Mosaic feast (Lev 23:16) was the exact time between Christ's resurrection (John 20:17) and the outpouring of the Spirit in Acts 2. The two loaves presented (Lev. 23:17) parallel the Jews and Gentiles being made into one loaf in Christ (1 Cor. 12:13). The loaves were made with leaven (Lev. 23:17), which represents sin or evil among the saints on earth.

The firstfruits were presented (Lev. 23:17), and Christ is the firstfruits (1 Cor. 15:23).

The Lord Jesus prophesied about the Holy Spirit's ministry after His return to the Father's side, making clear that it was a new ministry, distinct from what the apostles had experienced before (John 14:17). On the Day of Pentecost several workings of the Holy Spirit can be identified. In the speaking in tongues (Acts 2:4) is the gifting ministry (1 Cor. 12:11) of the Spirit. The filling ministry of the Spirit is also mentioned (Acts 2:4). Empowerment for witnessing (Acts 1:8) is seen in the boldness of the disciples. The convicting ministry (John 16:7–11) is evident in the response of the listeners (Acts 2:37). The baptizing work of the Spirit is not mentioned as such, but is clearly in evidence. The Lord Jesus had referred to the baptizing work of the Spirit as something yet future in Acts 1:5. Peter points back to Pentecost as the time when the apostles received the fulfillment of that promise (Acts 11:15–17).

The baptizing by the Holy Spirit on Pentecost also began the fulfillment of Christ's words about building His church (Matt. 16:18). The church was inaugurated that day. It is by Holy Spirit baptism that a believer is joined to the body of Christ (1 Cor. 12:13), which is the church (Eph. 1:22–23). This baptism of the Spirit was based on Christ's death and resurrection (Rom. 6:3–4). Until Christ ascended to become the head of the church (Col. 1:18) and from the right hand of the Father poured out the Spirit (Acts 2:33) to bring people into His body, there was no *church* in the New Testament sense of the word. The baptizing of believers into the body of Christ appears to be unique to this dispensation.

With regard to Peter's quotation from the prophet Joel on the Day of Pentecost, interpreters have not agreed in their understanding. What did Peter mean when he declared that the phenomena was that which was spoken of by the prophet Joel? Some have taken Peter as indicating the complete fulfillment of Joel's prophecy. Others have understood him to mean that the spiritual activity of Pentecost was the inauguration of that which was spoken by Joel. Others take Peter to mean that this is the conditional offer of that which was spoken of by the prophet Joel. But it seems best to understand Peter's reference to Joel simply as an illustration the work of the Spirit. Peter was saying, this is that kind of thing spoken of by the prophet Joel.

Peter's introduction to the quotation of Joel in Acts 2:16, "This is that which was spoken of by the prophet Joel [*touto estin to eiremenon*]," does not necessarily indicate a fulfillment, as is clear from a careful look at Peter's style. In 1 Peter 1:23–25, Peter uses the same formula, "This is the word [*touto de estin to rhema*] that was preached to you," in regard to a quotation from Isaiah that is clearly not a literal fulfillment. Peter is indicating a comparison, this is the kind of word (an everlasting word) that was preached to you. On the other hand, contrast his clear introductory formula declaring fulfillment of a prophecy in Acts 1:16.

There are solid reasons for taking Peter to mean that the events of Pentecost are like, but not the fulfillment of, what Joel wrote.

1. Joel speaks of an outpouring of the Spirit on Judah (see Joel 2:28 with the repeated use of the "your" to describe the all flesh that will receive the outpouring of the Spirit; Joel 2:32 speaks of Mount Zion and Jerusalem as the recipients of deliverance; Judah and Jerusalem are mentioned in Joel 3:1).

2. The events spoken of in Joel 2 that precede the outpouring of the Spirit have never been fulfilled. The heavenly wonders of Joel 2:30–31 did not take place on Pentecost. The judgment of the Gentiles and the restoration of the land of Israel that follow the outpouring of the Spirit (Joel 3) have not been fulfilled. The experience of Pentecost does not touch upon all that Joel predicted.

3. The outpouring of the Spirit on Pentecost was for the formation of the church. It is similar to the outpouring of the Spirit upon repentant Judah. The outpouring of the Spirit on Pentecost is viewed as the fulfillment of the baptism of the Spirit and the beginning of the church (Acts 1:5; 11:15–17).

See also HOLY SPIRIT, BAPTISM OF

THE; ISRAEL AND THE CHURCH, THE DIFFERENCES.

Clifford Rapp Jr.

Lewis Sperry Chafer, ed., *Systematic Theology*, vol. 4 (Grand Rapids: Kregel Publications, 1993); Charles C. Ryrie, "The Significance of Pentecost" in *Vital Theological Issues*, ed. Roy B. Zuck (Grand Rapids: Kregel, 1994); Robert L. Saucy, *The Church in God's Program* (Chicago: Moody Press, 1972); Henry C. Thiessen, *Lectures in Systematic Theology* (Grand Rapids, Eerdmans, 1949).

ADVENT, CHRIST'S FIRST AND SECOND

The term *advent* means "the reaching of a destination" or "a coming or arrival." In referring to Jesus Christ's arrivals, or advents, we know that they have a divine origin or purpose.

The First Advent is clearly pictured in the prophecies that speak of Christ coming to earth to redeem all humanity back to God. Dr. David Reagan states in his book *Christ in Prophecy* regarding the prophecies of His first coming that "Most scholars agree that there are about 300 prophecies in the Old Testament that relate to the first coming of the Messiah, but these are not 300 different prophecies. Many, like the prophecy that the Messiah will be born of the seed of Abraham, are repeated several times. When all of the repetitive prophecies are pulled out, there remains slightly more than one hundred distinctively different, specific prophecies about Messiah's First Advent."

Christ's first coming was so ordered and intricately forecast in the Scriptures that it proves beyond a doubt that there is an all-knowing God, for God alone could reveal so many detailed prophecies of one man's life. The prophecies of His first coming vividly prove that Jesus is the Christ. Dr. A. T. Pierson reveals three important canons by which true prophecy can be tested. All three point to the accuracy of these prophecies. They include:

1. It must be such an unveiling of the future that no mere human foresight or wisdom could have guessed it.

2. The prediction must deal in sufficient detail to exclude shrewd guesswork.

3. There must be such lapse of time between prophecy and fulfillment as precludes the agency of the prophet himself in effecting or affecting the result.

All three of these canons are represented in the prophecies of the first advent of Christ. The fulfillment of Scriptures in His first coming should give us full confidence in the prophecies relating to His Second Coming. The First Advent portrays Christ's life as a painting on a canvas, and many of God's holy prophets were moved by the Holy Spirit to contribute portions of His life in their prophecies. The details of Christ's life were predicted with precision. He would be: born of a virgin (Isa. 7:14; cf. Luke 1:33–35), a descendant of Abraham and David (Gen. 12:3, 18:18, 22:18; 2 Sam. 7:12; Ps. 89:3; cf. Acts 3:25; Gal. 3:8; Matt. 21:9, 22:42, etc.), born in Bethlehem (Micah 5:2; cf. Matt. 2:1; Luke 2:4), taken to Egypt as an infant (Hosea 11:1; cf. Matt. 2:13), a prophet (Deut. 18:15; cf. Matt. 21:11; Luke 24:19), a Messiah and Savior (Ps. 2:2; Dan. 9:24–25; Isa. 59:20, 62:11; cf. Mark 8:27–29; Luke 2:11; John 4:42; Acts 2:36, 5:31).

There are many prophecies in Scripture that reveal that Christ would come once as a Savior and again as a King. Christ Himself quoted from Isaiah 61:1–2 in the synagogue, stopping before the phrase, "and the day of vengeance of our God" since that referred to the Second Advent when He comes to judge the nations (Rev. 19:11–21). In Luke 1:31–33 the prophecy is that Jesus will be "great, and will be called the Son of the Most High; and the Lord God will give Him the throne of His father David; and He will reign over the house of Jacob forever; and His kingdom will have no end." Yet, at His first coming He was rejected by Israel's leaders and never inherited His father David's throne. This will be fulfilled at the Second Advent when His rule is established in the millennial kingdom. These prophecies and others like them show that the Lord will come a second time to literally fulfill the remaining details of the prophecies just as He did the first time.

Dr. J. Dwight Pentecost, in his monumental

work *Things to Come,* gives the following body of evidence for a literal second coming. He writes, "The large body of unfulfilled prophecy makes the Second Advent absolutely essential. It has been promised that He shall come Himself (Act 1:11); that the dead will hear His voice (John 5:28); that He will minister unto His watching servants (Luke 12:27); that He will come to earth again (Acts 1:11), to the same Mount Olivet from which He ascended (Zech. 14:4), in flaming fire (2 Thess. 1:8), in the clouds of heaven with power and great glory (Matt. 24:30; 1 Peter 1:7; 4:13), and stand upon the earth (Job 19:25); that His saints (the church) shall come with Him (1 Thess. 3:13; Jude 14); that every eye shall see Him (Rev. 1:7); that He shall destroy the Antichrist (2 Thess. 2:8); that He shall sit on His throne (Matt. 25:31; Rev. 5:13); that all nations will be gathered before Him and He will judge them (Matt. 25:32); that He shall have the throne of David (Isa. 9:6–7; Luke 1:32; Ezek. 21:25–27); that it will be upon the earth (Jer. 23:5–6) that He shall have a kingdom (Dan. 7:13–14); and rule over it with His saints (Dan. 7:18–27; Rev. 5:10); that all kings and nations shall serve Him (Ps. 72:11; Isa. 49:6–7; Rev. 15:4); that the kingdoms of this world shall become His kingdom (Zech. 9:10; Rev. 11:15); that the people shall gather unto Him (Gen. 49:10); that every knee shall bow to Him (Isa. 45:23); that they shall come and worship the king (Zech. 14:16; Ps. 86:9); that He shall build up Zion (Ps. 102:16); that His throne shall be in Jerusalem (Jer. 3:17; Isa. 33:20–21); that the Apostles shall sit upon twelve thrones, judging the twelve tribes of Israel (Matt. 19:28; Luke 22:28–30); that He shall rule all nations (Ps. 2:8–9; Rev. 2:27); that He shall rule with judgment and justice (Ps. 9:7); that the temple in Jerusalem shall be rebuilt (Ezek. 40–48), and the glory of the Lord will come into it (Ezek. 43:2–5; 44:4); that the glory of the Lord will be revealed (Isa. 40:5); that the wilderness shall be a fruitful field (Isa. 35:1–2); and His rest shall be glorious (Isa. 11:10). The entire covenant program with Israel, which has not yet been fulfilled, necessitates the Second Advent of Messiah to the earth. The principle of literal fulfillment makes it essential that Christ return."

As certainly as Christ's first coming was literal and He fulfilled the prophecies very literally, the Second Advent will be literally fulfilled as well.

Donald Perkins and Russell L. Penney

Herbert Lockyer, *All the Messianic Prophecies of The Bible* (Grand Rapids: Zondervan, 1973); Donald Perkins, *The First and Second Advent of Christ* (Lemon Grove: According To Prophecy Ministries, 1996); J. Dwight Pentecost, *Things to Come* (Grand Rapids: Zondervan, 1958); David Reagan, *Christ In Prophecy* (Plano, Tex.: Lamb and Lion Ministries, 1987).

ALBURY CONFERENCES

The Albury Conferences (1826–30) were an annual gathering of British clergy and laymen at the estate of Henry Drummond (Albury House) in Albury, England to study Bible prophecy. The Albury Conference is not to be confused, as sometimes occurs, with the later Powerscourt Conference (1830–33).

The Albury Conferences were convened "for the purpose of examining the Scriptures–and especially the prophetic writings–with a view to interpreting the political and social events of the day, and also of determining the extent to which biblical prophecies had already been fulfilled in the life of Christ and the history of the Christian church, thus making it possible to identify those still awaiting fulfillment in the future." Such an interest appears to have been stirred by concern over the ideas of radical democracy championed by the French Revolution. Many evangelicals saw this interruption of European society as a prelude to a premillennial return of Christ and not contributing to the advancement of a postmillennial kingdom as made popular by Daniel Whitby. Postmillennialism had risen to dominance in Europe during the eighteenth century but declined in the 1800s.

Albury's forty members included participants who were Anglicans, Independents, Presbyterians, Methodists, and Moravians. The majority were Anglican and two-thirds were clergy. The conference was dominated by Chairman Drummond and Edward Irving.

It is not surprising that Albury served as a springboard for establishment of the Catholic Apostolic church (i.e., Irvingites).

The conference did produce the following statement of conclusions which is believed to have been agreed upon by all of the participants.

1. The present Christian dispensation is not to pass insensibly into the millennial state by gradual increase of the preaching of the Gospel, but that it is to be terminated by judgments ending in the destruction of this visible church and polity, in the same manner as the Jewish dispensation had been terminated.

2. During the time that these judgments are falling upon Christendom, the Jews will be restored to their own land.

3. The judgments will fall principally, if not exclusively, upon Christendom and begin with that part of the church of God that has been most highly favored and is therefore most deeply responsible.

4. The termination of these judgments is to be succeeded by that period of universal blessedness to all humankind, and even to the beasts, which is commonly called the Millennium.

5. The Second Advent of Messiah precedes or takes place at the commencement of the Millennium.

6. A great period of 1,260 years commenced in the reign of Justinian and terminated at the French Revolution and that the vials of the Apocalypse began then to be poured out.

7. Our blessed Lord will shortly appear and that therefore it is the duty of all who so believe to press these considerations on the attention of all people.

While Albury was a definite boon for premillennialism, it still largely reflected the older historicist, not futuristic, prophetic approach, as is clear from point six of the statement. Albury has more in common with Adventist premillennialism than with the soon to be asserted dispensational premillennialism. Albury stands as an important event in the history of premillennialism.

Thomas Ice

Henry Drummond, *Dialogues on Prophecy,* 3 vols. (London: Nisbet, 1828–29); Columba Graham Flegg, *Gathered Under Apostles: A Study of the Catholic Apostolic Church* (Oxford: Clarendon Press, 1992); Le Roy E. Froom, *The Prophetic Faith of Our Fathers,* vols. 3 and 4 (Washington, D.C.: Review and Herald, 1948–54).

AMILLENNIALISM

The amillennial view holds that the kingdom promises in the Old Testament are fulfilled spiritualy rather than literally in the New Testament church. Those who hold this view believe that Christ will literally return, but they do not believe in His thousand-year reign on the earth. According to the amillennial view, the kingdom of God is present in the church age, and at the end of the church age the second coming of Christ inaugurates the eternal state. The book of Revelation is interpreted as a description of those events that take place during the church age.

This type of allegorical interpretation can be seen in Plato's time when the blatant hedonism of the deities were interpretated symbolically in order to make them acceptable. Unable to reconcile their views with the literal interpretation of Scripture, early Jewish commentators began to allegorize. The rabbis of Alexandria, Egypt, began to teach allegorically in order to counter Gentile criticism of the Old Testament.

Schaff helps us pinpoint just what happened culturally and historically that destroyed the prevailing literal millennial interpretation of Revelation and opened the way for the amillennial view in the early church. Schaff writes: "In Alexandria, Origen opposed chiliasm as a Jewish dream, and spiritualized the symbolical language of the prophets. . . . But the crushing blow came from the great change in the social condition and prospects of the church in the Nicene age. After Christianity, contrary to all expectations, triumphed in the Roman empire, and was embraced by the Caesars themselves, the millennial reign, instead of being anxiously waited and prayed for, began to be dated either from the first appearance of Christ, or from the conversion of Constantine and the downfall of paganism, and to be regarded as realized in the glory of the dominant imperial state-church."

Origen was a prime mover in making allegory the key method of interpreting the Bible. Origen understood that God's Word was inspired, but in places it appeared to be irrelevant to the human condition, unworthy of God, or simply commonplace. Thus, if no spiritual significance was apparent on the surface it must be concluded this surface meaning is to be taken symbolically. Origen restated the conquest of Canaan as Christ's conquest of the fallen human soul, and concerning the Lord's prayer, the hallowing of God's name and the coming of God's kingdom refer to the believer's gradual sanctification.

Origen's interpretive method paved the way for such misunderstanding of the millennial reign. Trigg, in his analysis of Origen's commentary on Matthew, gives us an example of how this type of interpretation left Origen as the authority and not the text of Scripture. In his *Commentary on Matthew* , Origen tends to psychologize the Gospel's apocalyptic eschatological imagery. Thus, when the Gospel predicts that Christ will come "on the clouds of heaven with power and great glory" (Matt. 24:30), it refers to his appearance to the perfect [or mature] in their reading of the Bible. Likewise, the two comings of Christ, the first in humility and the second in glory, symbolize Christ's coming in the souls of the simple when they receive the rudiments of Christian doctrine and his coming in[to] the perfect [the mature] when they find him in the hidden meaning of the Bible.

In Origen's other works that he displays a similar confusion by saying that the coming of Christ, as viewed from a human perspective, is a phrase that is not always to be held to one meaning; it is in this aspect, analogous to the "kingdom of God." There are many comings of Christ: in the flesh, at the destruction of Jerusalem, as a spiritual presence when the Holy Spirit was given, and He comes now in every single manifestation of redeeming power. Any great reformation of morals and religion is a coming of Christ. A great revolution that violently sweeps away evil to make way for the good is a coming of Christ. Jerusalem stands as the type of the good cause and thus is the church of Christ. The book of Revelation becomes the unfolding of a dream that is from God, and it is a book of living principles, not a manual of tiresome details, in Origen's view.

It was in the church in Alexandria, North Africa, that this new school of interpretation developed along the lines of paganism and liberal Judiasm. Morris explains: "In the Alexandrian church a spiritualizing approach was developing due in part to the influence of Greek thought, the fact that centuries had passed without the establishment of the awaited kingdom, and in reaction to the excessive chiliasm of the Montanist movement. Origen played a major role in the rise of an allegorical method of exegesis. The mysteries of the Apocalypse can be learned only by going beyond the literal and historical to the spiritual. The spiritualizing method was greatly advanced by the work of Tyconius, who interpreted nothing by the historical setting or events of the first century. Augustine followed Tyconius in his capitulation to a totally mystical exegesis. For the next thousand years this allegorical approach was normative for the interpretation of Revelation."

Because of the maze of interpretation possible when one interprets allegorically, there is understandably much confusion over the purpose and contents of Revelation. S. Cox gives us a sampling of the amillennial attempt to prove that the Revelation was penned by John, since the reason taken from a literal interpretation cannot be accepted within its faulty interpretive system.

St. John was not a prophet in the ancient and vulgar sense; he was not a mere seer of coming events, a mere student and interpreter of the shadows they cast before them. And, hence, the Apocalypse of St. John is not a series of forecasts, predicting the political weather of the world through the ages of history; it is rather a series of symbols and visions in which the universal principles of the Divine Rule are set forth in forms dear to the heart of a Hebrew Mystic and poet. What is most valuable to us in this book, therefore, is not the letter, the form; not the vials, the seals, the trumpets, over which interpreters, who play the seer rather that the prophet, have been wrangling and perplexing their brains for centuries; but the large general principles which these mystic symbols of Oriental thought are apt to conceal from a Western mind.

Such interpretation is not unusual, and as a result of the departure from a literal hermeneutic in prophetic sections of Scripture, it is no wonder that the liberal and the amillennial views hold that the apostle John wrote Revelation in order to make martyrdom attractive. It is this kind of allegorical thinking and theory that has resulted in speculative but unsuccessful attempts to fit the events of Revelation into the present church age. It represents a serious neglect of a consistent system of theology and leaves the door open for individual speculation as to the meaning and application of any given passage of Scripture. The only point that unifies amillennialism is the denial of the earthly thousand-year reign of Christ.

Amillennialism displays the great lengths it must go to in denying the literal sense of Scripture when it states that one of the great lessons of the Apocalypse is its unfolding of such a bright view, not of a world beyond the grave, but of this present world—when it is contemplated with the eye of faith. What is set forth in apparent visions of future happiness is rather the present experience of believers.

See also ALEXANDRIAN SCHOOL; ANTIOCHIAN SCHOOL; AUGUSTINE.

Rick Bowman and Russell L. Penney

Lewis Sperry Chafer, *Systematic Theology* (Grand Rapids: Kregel, 1993); Mal Couch, *Introductory Thoughts on Revelation* (Ft. Worth, Tex.: Tyndale Seminary Press, 1995); Paul Enns, *The Moody Handbook of Theology* (Chicago: Moody Press, 1989); Robert H. Mounce, "The Book of Revelation" in *The New International Commentary on the New Testament* (Grand Rapids: Eerdmans, 1977); J. Dwight Pentecost, *Things to Come* (Grand Rapids: Zondervan, 1958); *The Preacher's Complete Homiletic Commentary,* vol. 30 (Grand Rapids: Baker, n.d.); Philip Schaff, *History of the Christian Church* (Grand Rapids: Eerdmans, 1910); Joseph Wilson Trigg, *Origen* (Atlanta: John Knox Press, 1983); John F. Walvoord, *The Millennial Kingdom* (Grand Rapids: Zondervan, 1959).

AMOS, ESCHATOLOGY OF

The meaning of the name *Amos* is probably "burden bearer" (derived from the verb *amas*, "to lift a burden, carry") according to Archer. Amos was a sheepherder and a grower of sycamore figs, from Tekoa (1:1; 7:14), which is located about five miles southeast of Bethlehem in the Judean mountains. Amos did not have the advantage of a formal education or training in the school of the prophets but at the call of God he left his home and traveled to Bethel (7:13), site of one of the two state sanctuaries of the northern kingdom, to proclaim "Thus says the LORD" to a hostile audience. Almost all conservative scholars agree that Amos's ministry can be dated between 760 and 757 B.C., toward the later part of the reign of Jeroboam II (793–753 B.C.). Amos's prophecies were primarily to the northern kingdom but also included warnings to Judah.

Amos lived in a time of significant material prosperity. The reigns of Jeroboam in the northern kingdom and Uzziah in the southern kingdom (790–739 B.C.) had brought gains in stability, prosperity, and expansion to both kingdoms. As had happened so often in a time of God's blessing, rampant sin followed. Both kingdoms were guilty of social and moral failures, and though a form of religious worship was being carried out, their actions betrayed their lack of sincerity. The rich flourished, built expensive homes (3:13; 5:11; 6:4, 11) and exploited the poor (2:6–7; 5:7, 10–13; 6:12; 8:4–6), some of whom were even being enslaved as payment for their debt to the rich (2:6; 8:6). Amidst all this ungodliness the people still traveled to shrines such as Gilgal and Bethel to present their offerings (4:4–5; 5:5, 21–23; 8:3, 10) and to offer sacrifices. As a result of this, they believed that God was with them (5:14; 18–20; 6:1–3; 9:10). Amos spoke to this religious hypocrisy stating that

God's judgment was against Israel and Judah as well as the other nations that had rebelled against His authority (1:3–2:3). Even in the midst of Israel's destruction God would preserve from among the people a repentant remnant that one day would be restored.

The book is outlined by Walvoord as follows: 1:1–2:5, prophecy of judgment against Israel's neighbors; 2:6–16, judgment against the kingdom of Israel; 3:1–6:14, reasons for God's judgment on Israel; 7:1–8:14, the inescapable character of Israel's future judgment; 9:1–10, Israel to be destroyed; and 9:11–15, the restoration of Israel.

The book begins with prophecy of judgment against Israel's neighbors. In 1:3–5, God issues a condemnation of Damascus. Because they threshed Gilead with implements of sharp iron (1:3), God would punish them severely (1:4–5). The judgment was carried out in 732 B.C. when the Assyrians under Tiglath-Pileser III captured Damascus and took the people away to exile in Kir (2 Kings 16:7–9). In 1:6–8, God condemns Gaza, Ashdod, Ashkelon, Ekron, and the entire remnant of the Philistines stating that they will perish. This was fulfilled during the Maccabean period (168–134 B.C.). Tyre is condemned next, in 1:9–10. The prophecy was fulfilled in 332 B.C. when Alexander the Great took the city. Six thousand were slain, two thousand were crucified, and thirty thousand were sold as slaves. Edom was condemned for pursuing his brother with the sword (1:11). Edom became a vassal to the Assyrians in the eighth century B.C. and had by the fifth century turned into a desolate wasteland (Mal. 1:3). The Nabateans overtook the land around 400–300 B.C. In 1:13–15, the Ammonites are condemned because they ripped open the pregnant women of Gilead (1:13). Their judgment would come on Rabbah, Ammon's capital city. The judgment was fulfilled in 734 B.C. during the Assyrian conquest under Tiglath-Pileser III. Moab is accused of burning the bones of the king of Edom to lime (2:1). As a result, Amos says punishment will come and the citadels of Kerioth shall be consumed. Moab also fell in 734 B.C. to the Assyrians under Tiglath-Pileser III. Judgment is also passed on Judah because they rejected the law of the LORD, and have not kept His statues (2:4). The judgment for this was meted out in 586 B.C. when the Babylonians under Nebuchadnezzar destroyed Jerusalem, including the temple, and took almost the entire population to Babylon (2 Kings 25:1–12). Note that each of these judgments had a literal fulfillment in history.

In the rest of chapter 2, Amos deals with the judgment against the kingdom of Israel. They were involved in sins of injustice and oppression of the poor (2:6–8), as well as being involved with temple prostitutes (2:7). Although it was the Lord who had been their strength in the past (2:9–11), they had turned their backs on Him and didn't want to hear from the prophets (2:12). As a result, He would humble even mighty men (2:13–16).

Amos then describes the reasons for God's judgment on Israel (3:1–6:14). Chapter 3 is Amos's first message to Israel. Because Israel is chosen of God, He will punish them for their iniquities (3:1–2). Amos uses a series of rhetorical questions to make the point that the very fact that the prophets have proclaimed that His judgment is coming proves that it is (3:3–8). Samaria had hoarded up violence and devastation, therefore an enemy would pull down its strength and loot its citadels. The luxurious mansions of the rich would perish also (3:15).

In 4:1–13, Amos gives his second message to Israel. He condemns the cows of Bashan who were the upperclass women of Samaria. They were guilty of suppressing the poor and crushing the needy. Because of this the Lord God swears by His holiness that they will be dragged off to captivity with meat hooks and fish hooks. In addition, the sons of Israel will be judged for their religious hypocrisy (4:4–5). God had brought divine chastisement on them in the past through famine, drought, blight and mildew, locusts, plagues, military defeat, and devastation (cf. Deut. 28–29), but they had not repented. Now they are called on to prepare to meet their God (4:12).

Amos's third message covers all of chapter 5. The house of Israel will fall and its cities will be decimated by the Captivity (5:1–3). Although the nation will be judged, there is always mercy extended on an individual basis to those who seek the Lord (5:4). They should seek Him somewhere else beside the shrines in Bethel, Gilgal, and Beersheba since these are all doomed (5:5–7). In 5:8–9 Amos reminds Israel that God is sovereign. He is in control of the physical universe and can surely bring destruction on the strong and on fortresses. Again, in 5:10–13, God lists the numerous injustices of Israel which include a hate for justice and integrity, heavy taxes on the poor, persecuting the righteous, and accepting bribes. Then, in 5:14–15, God calls again for individual repentance and ends this message with the assurance of His judgment (5:17–18).

The fourth judgment (5:18–27) begins with a description of the Day of the Lord. Israel wrongly believed that the Day of the Lord would only be a time of God destroying their enemies, so Israel looked forward to the day. But Amos makes it clear that the day would be darkness and not light (5:18) for them and its judgment would be inescapable (5:19–20). The reason is that God hates their festivals, burnt offerings, and idolatry (5:21–26). The judgment would be to go into exile beyond Damascus (5:27).

The fifth message is given in chapter 6. In 6:1–7, Amos describes their complacent and luxurious living. They recline on beds of ivory and drink wine from sacrificial bowls. They were so complacent they did not grieve over the ruin of Joseph. "The Lord God has sworn by Himself. . . . I will deliver up the city and all it contains" (6:8). The devastation will be complete with massive death (6:10), complete destruction of homes (6:9), and tremendous affliction over all the land from Hamath (a city of the northern frontier) to Arabah (the valley extending from the Sea of Kinnereth to the Dead Sea). Israel would realize then that their strength was from the Lord, not themselves (6:13).

In chapters 7 and 8, Amos speaks of the inescapable character of Israel's future judgment. Amos's first vision involves a locust swarm that denudes the land during the harvest time. Amos pleads with God on behalf of the people and the Lord heeds his prayer and does not send the locusts (7:1–3). Then God shows Amos fire that He will send to consume the farmland. But again Amos pleads on behalf of the people and the Lord changed His mind (7:4–6).

The third vision involves the Lord holding a plumb line, used by builders to check if a wall was straight. If the wall was not straight it would be torn down. Since the people of Israel were not lining up with the law of God, He would spare them no longer (7:8). In 7:10–17, Amos gives a historical account of being confronted by Amaziah, the priest of the sanctuary at Bethel. Amaziah reports to Jeroboam, the king of Israel, that Amos is prophesying against him and claiming that he (Jeroboam) will be killed and Israel will go into exile. Amaziah then confronts Amos and tells him to leave the sanctuary at Bethel. Amos replies to Amaziah that he cannot leave for the Lord has called him to this task, thus Amaziah is going against the Lord by his command. As a result, Amaziah's wife would become a harlot, his sons and daughters would fall by the sword, his land would be parceled up and Amaziah would die on unclean soil. In addition, Israel would go into exile just as Amos has prophesied. Chapter 8 begins with a fourth vision, in which the Lord uses a basket of summer fruit as an object lesson to show Amos that the time was ripe for Israel's judgment. The result will be that corpses will litter the landscape. This will occur because Israel trampled the needy and did away with the humble (8:4). They also cheated with dishonest scales and even forced the needy into slavery (8:5–6). The Lord had sworn that He would not forget their pride (8:7). The Lord's judgment would fall and turn their festivals into mourning and their songs into lamentation (8:10). An even worse judgment would follow. Since Israel had rejected all of the Lord's words, He would send a famine on them, not a normal famine, but a famine "for hearing the words of the Lord" (8:11). The Lord would be silent.

In 9:1–10, Amos deals with the destruction of Israel. As people gather around the altar at Bethel the Lord would be there, but this time His presence would signal destruction for Israel and not blessing (9:1). No matter where they try to flee from His judgment He will find them and destroy them (9:2–4). His eyes will be set against them for evil and not for good. The surety of the judgment is guaranteed because of the sovereignty of the almighty Lord (9:5–6). The Lord promises destruction of the house of Jacob except for a remnant (9:8). He will shake them, like grain, among the nations (9:9). The destruction and captivity was literally fulfilled in the Assyrian and Babylonian captivities.

In 9:10–15, Amos tells of a time in the future when Israel will be restored. After a time of cleansing (9:10), there will come a day when God will restore both the northern and the southern kingdoms under Davidic reign. The cities will be restored and the kingdom will be restored to its former greatness (cf. Jer. 30:3–10; Ezek. 37:15–28; Hos. 3:4–5). This will fulfill the Davidic covenant (2 Sam. 7:11–16, 25–29). The presence of the Davidic kingdom will be the source of blessing for Edom and all Gentile nations (9:12), thus fulfilling the Abrahamic covenant promises to the Gentiles (Gen. 18:18; 22:17–18; 26:3–4; 28:13–14). Amos 9:11–12 is quoted by James at the Jerusalem council, in Acts 15:16–18. James concluded that since the Gentiles will partake of the Millennium as Gentiles and not as Jews (circumcised), there was no need in the church age for them to become Jews by being circumcised. During this time the Lord will restore covenant blessing to the land. Israel will experience incredible fruitfulness (9:13). All their cities will be rebuilt and repopulated (9:14). This will be accomplished by the Lord, who will plant them in the land and they will not again be uprooted (9:15). In fulfillment of the Palestinian covenant, Israel will be given the land that the Lord their God has promised them (cf. Gen. 13:14–15; 17:7–8; Deut. 30:1–5; 2 Sam. 7:10; Jer. 30:10–11; Joel 3:17–18; Mic. 4:4–7).

Walvoord describes how this process of returning to the land is in stages, with the first stage already fulfilled in the twentieth century. A second stage will be fulfilled after the covenant is signed with the Middle East ruler. The third stage will be fulfilled when Israel goes through its period of trouble in the Great Tribulation. The final stage will occur when Israel will be rescued at the Second Coming, and the prophecies of verses 11–15 will be completely fulfilled.

Just as all the previous prophecies were literally fulfilled, this future restoration of Israel to the land and covenant blessing will be literally fulfilled also.

See also JEWS, RETURN OF THE.

Russell Penney

Gleason L. Archer, *A Survey of Old Testament Introduction* (Chicago: Moody Press, 1994); Thomas E. McComiskey, "Amos" in *The Expositor's Bible Commentary*, ed. Frank E. Gaebelein, vol. 7 (Grand Rapids: Zondervan, 1985); Donald R. Sunukjian, "Amos" in *The Bible Knowledge Commentary,* eds. John F. Walvoord and Roy B. Zuck (Wheaton: Victor Books, 1988); John F. Walvoord, *The Prophecy Knowledge Handbook* (Wheaton: Victor Books, 1990).

ANDERSON, SIR ROBERT

Sir Robert Anderson (1841–1918) was born into an influential Dublin family. His father, Matthew, served as Crown Solicitor for the city and was a distinguished elder in the Irish Presbyterian Church. Robert was converted to Christ in his late teens during the great Irish Revival that swept the country. Soon he became a lay preacher and was used of the Lord to win many to Christ.

After graduating Trinity College, Dublin, in 1863, Anderson became a member of the Irish bar and served on a legal circuit preparing legal briefs. He ended up in London, working with the metropolitan police, and serving as Chief of the Criminal Investigation Department. He retired in 1901 after serving with distinction. Using his experience to think logically and succinctly, Anderson wrote some outstanding works on the Scriptures. Charles Spurgeon said of his book *Human Destiny* that it was "the most valuable contribution on the subject" he had ever seen. Other titles were *Forgotten Truths, The Lord from Heaven, Types of Hebrews,* and *The Silence of God.* On Bible prophecy he wrote *Unfulfilled Prophecy and the Hope of the Church* and *The Coming Prince.*

In *The Coming Prince*, Anderson meticulously dissects Daniel's seventy weeks. He also analyzes carefully the date of Christ's birth and deals with the most important issues of prophetic hermeneutics. Though more recent work in Bible chronology may shed new light on Anderson's prophetic calculations, his work stands as a classic in the attempt to understand Daniel's datings. Anderson's books highlight the dependable authority of the Bible, the deity of Jesus, the necessity of the new birth, and the blessed hope in the premillennial return of Christ.

See also DANIEL'S SEVENTY WEEKS, DISPENSATIONAL INTERPRETATION OF.

Mal Couch

Robert Anderson, *The Coming Prince* (Grand Rapids: Kregel Publications, 1983).

ANTICHRIST

In premillennial eschatology the final world ruler who opposes God and His Christ (particularly in relation to His deity), oppresses God's elect (especially the Jewish people), and seeks to usurp the place of divine worship through desecration of the holy (especially Jerusalem and its temple) is known as the Antichrist. According to 1 John 4:3, this antitheocratic, antisemitic spirit is characteristic of the present age, indicating that these are the last days (i.e., "last hour"). The designation *Antichrist*, appearing only in the epistles of John (1 John 2:18, 22; 4:3; 2 John 7), is made up of the Greek words *anti* (against, in place of) and *christos* (Christ), and indicates any agent of the Evil One (Satan) who acts contrary to or as a counterfeit of God's Anointed, who is destined to rule the world (Ps. 2:2, 6–8; 110:1–2; Isa. 9:6–7, et al.). The plural use of this term allows for both a comprehensive and a concentrated expression of the Antichrist, and ultimately the eschatological duo known as the first beast (the Antichrist) and the second beast (the False Prophet), who, with the Dragon (Satan) as the origin of their power (authority), form a sort of counterfeit trinity (Rev. 13:1–2, 11). While the specific term *antichrist* may be rarely used, the Bible is filled with descriptive terminology of his diabolical and desecrating nature. Among the more obvious epithets are: little horn (Dan. 7:8), insolent king (Dan. 8:23), prince who is to come (Dan. 9:26), one who makes desolate (Dan. 9:27), despicable person (Dan. 11:21), strong-willed king (Dan. 11:36), worthless shepherd (Zech. 11:16–17), man of lawlessness, and the son of destruction (2 Thess. 2:3); the lawless one (2 Thess. 2:8), the beast (Rev. 11:7; 13:1; 14:9; 15:2; 16:2; 17:3, 13; 19:20; 20:10). Only the futurist school (which includes premillennialism) has been able to develop a self-consistent interpretation of the Antichrist concept from the witness of the two testaments.

Antichrist in the Old Testament

While the term *antichrist* is not employed until the New Testament, the apostle John's reference (1 John 2:18) that many "antichrists" have arisen in token of the coming Antichrist that will arise during the Tribulation period, encourages an examination of the Old Testament text for proleptic imagery that suggests this eschatological figure. In the Old Testament this ultimate Antichrist is progressively revealed through a series of human antichrists who appear as opponents of the Jewish people, and especially as desecrators of Jerusalem and/or the holy temple. Antichrist allusions usually take the form of a human being (usually a monarch or military commander) set in direct opposition to God. In this position the human personality often takes on superhuman proportions by virtue of the divine/human contest, and as such, serves as a prefigurement or type of the eschatological Antichrist who will seek to usurp divine worship.

Types of the Antichrist revealed during the biblical period are: (1) the serpent in Eden who deceived man and sought to corrupt the divine order (Gen. 3); (2) Nimrod, the blasphemous ruler who sought to usurp divine worship (Gen. 10:8; 11:1–9); (3) Amalek, the son of Esau (Gen. 36: 12, 16) whose descendants opposed Israel in the wilderness (Exod. 17:8–16; Deut. 25:19;

1 Sam. 15:2–3); (4) Balaam, the foreign prophet who opposed Israel (Num. 22–24); (5) the pharaoh of the Exodus who oppressed the Israelites in Egypt (Exod. 1:11, 22; 5:2) and was unnamed in Scripture, perhaps to emphasize his role as a divine adversary; (6) the Assyrian king Sennacherib, who oppressed the northern kingdom and arrogantly sought to capture Jerusalem (2 Kings 18:13–19:37); and (7) the Babylonian king Nebuchadnezzar, who destroyed the temple in Jerusalem, persecuted Israel in exile, and usurped divine sovereignty (2 Kings 24:13–14; Dan. 4:30).

The most developed types appear in Daniel's blasphemous ruler designated as the little horn who makes war with the saints and is destroyed by the "Ancient of Days" (Dan. 7:8, 21); the wicked and tyrannical king (Dan. 8:11–14; 11:31), assumed to be Antiochus IV, Epiphanes, who desecrated the Jewish temple in 186 B.C.; and the prince that shall come (Dan. 9:26), possibly the Roman general Titus who destroyed Jerusalem and the temple in A.D. 70. By comparing the more obvious types (the "antichrists") with the antitype (the Antichrist), we can observe, first, that in every case the type is either a Gentile or one outside the legitimate line of inheritance, and second, there is a progressive development of opposition to God finally centering on the desecration of the temple.

The development of these figures from type to antitype reveals that the movement of the typological antichrist's actions begin with elements of opposition to the divine program, manifested as opposition to God and oppression of God's people, which escalates with each figure toward desecration of the temple as place where the divine Presence is represented on earth. As Daniel's revelation (Dan. 8:9–25; 11:21–45) of the Antichrist imagery is the last and most highly developed of all the types (embodying all the previously revealed types), and focuses on his abominable desolation of the Holy Place (Dan. 8:11–14; 11:31), it casts the mold for the New Testament's portrayal of the future Antichrist (Dan. 11:36–45; cf. 2 Thess. 2:3; Rev. 13:1–10; 17:11–17), and his end-time Abomination of Desolation in the Tribulation temple (Dan. 9:27; 12:11; cf. Matt. 24:15; Mark 13:14; 2 Thess. 2:4).

Antichrist in the New Testament

In the New Testament, the witnesses to the Antichrist are Jesus and the apostles Paul and John. However, this is to be expected since they present the most extensive treatments of eschatology (Olivet Discourse, Thessalonian epistles, and Revelation).

In the Gospels

Jesus assumes Daniel's figure that desecrated the temple through the Abomination of Desolation will be understood by His future Jewish audience as the Antichrist who will set himself against the nation and their God (Matt. 24:15; Mark 13:14). Implied in Jesus' selective description (primarily from Dan. 9:27; cf. 11:36–37) in the Olivet Discourse is the incompatibility of that which is holy with the Antichrist. Whether a holy city, a holy temple, or a holy (chosen) people, the Antichrist by his very nature must seek to destroy them all. For this reason the Jewish people living in Jerusalem in the day of Antichrist's power are warned to flee (Matt. 24:16–21; Mark 13:14–19). Jesus' statement of the Antichrist's "Abomination of Desolation" is the signal event that marks the midpoint of the Tribulation.

Studies in the chiastic structure of Matthew 24 and Mark 13 reveal that the elements corresponding to the first and second half of the Tribulation are arranged with Matthew 24:15 and Mark 13:14 as the pivot. Thus, the prophecy of Antichrist is the chronological determinative for the Tribulation, with Antichrist's covenant with the Jewish leaders marking its beginning (Dan. 9:27), the temple desecration its middle (Dan. 9:27; Matt. 24:15; Mark 13:14; 2 Thess. 2:4), and the Antichrist's destruction its end (Dan. 9:27; cf. 2 Thess. 2:8).

In Paul

Paul also emphasizes the incompatibility of holiness and unholiness by contrasting Christ with the Antichrist (2 Cor. 6:15–16), though he uses the cognomen *Belial* ("wicked" *or* "worthless one"), familiar from the intertestamental Jewish literature (see ANTICHRIST, JEWISH VIEWS OF THE). While some have thought Paul's reference is to Satan, Paul could have easily used the available Greek term *satanas* (Satan). He more than likely chose this obscure expression (used only here in the New Testament) because of its apocalyptic usage of Messiah's quasi-human end-time opponent. Furthermore, the context uses temple imagery (v. 16) and Paul's command for separation in 6:17 and 7:1 is "come out of their midst," an escapist tone analogous to the Antichrist contexts such as Christ's warning to "flee" (Matt. 24:15–16; Mark 13:14). If Paul had these ideas in the background, *Belial* may make a more fitting allusion to the Antichrist than *Satan*.

Paul's more explicit statement concerning the character and activity of the Antichrist is in 2 Thesselonians 2:3–4. The character of the Antichrist is defined in this text as he "who opposes" (v. 4), a word in the Greek that was used by the LXX in 1 Kings 11:25 as a rendering for the Hebrew word *satan* (adversary). This points to Antichrist's link with Satan, which verse 9 says more precisely is "in accord with the activity of Satan." Since Satan's adversary is God, and his original goal was to become like God (cf. Isa. 14:14; Ezek. 28:17), the Antichrist's actions are apparently an attempt to fulfill this by usurping worship as God (v. 4; cf. Rev. 13:4–8).

His counterfeit is apparently of the God of Israel, since in verse 4 he is pictured as one who will exalt himself above every "god or object of worship" (i.e., above all pagan gods) and enthrones himself "in the temple of God displaying himself as being God," the language of theophanic installation (cf. 1 Kings 8:10; 2 Chron. 7:1–3; Ezek. 43:1–7). In this way the Antichrist appears as a rival to Christ, not by an assumption of the messianic role, but as His superior (economically speaking) as God (the Father). Note too, that in this passage, the Antichrist usurps the place of God in a blasphemous act of self-deification. This is why Paul uses the descriptive terms "the man of lawlessness" and "the son of destruction" (v. 3). The word "lawlessness" apparently describes his nature as characterized by his opposition to the temple as the repository of the Law (v. 4), while the word "destruction" refers to his destiny, that is, destined for destruction or perdition (v. 8).

Paul seems to connect the revelation of Christ (vv. 1–2) with the revealing of the Antichrist (vv. 3–4) in such a way as to imply that Christ's return to earth is related to the Antichrist rebellion on earth, a cause/effect relationship clearly drawn in Revelation 19:11–20. Because the Antichrist is here said to be revealed it has been suggested that his revelation is a counterfeit to that of Christ's (2 Thess. 2:9). From Paul's description of the destruction of the Antichrist at the revelation of Christ (v. 8), it appears that he identified the lawless one with Daniel's little horn (Dan. 7:8, 11).

In the Book of Revelation

In the book of Revelation, the term *antichrist* does not appear (although John previously used it in his epistles). The reason for this may be partly explained from the symbolic character of his prophetic vision, for his expression of the Antichrist is *beast*, a term descriptive of his inhuman nature which was often revealed to John in animal form. The Revelation provides the most complete information about the career of the Antichrist, even offering an identification of his person in the cryptogram 666 (13:16–18). Since the text does not give an explanation for this number, other than that it is the number of a man (i.e., Antichrist), no one until the appropriate hour in the Tribulation will be able to discern this meaning. John (with Paul) understands the Antichrist is to be energized by Satan, or in Johannine terminology, "the dragon" (13:2; cf. 12:5). John's picture of the Antichrist is of a world ruler (13:1, 4, 7; 17:12–13, 17) whose political position is so dominating that it encroaches into the religious realm (13:15). This is accomplished for the Antichrist by a diabolical religious figure John presents as a second beast, who is a lesser Antichrist. He is a duplicate of the Antichrist as the first beast (13:12), but inferior to him, having only two horns compared with his ten (13:11).

In contrast to the first beast who arises out of the *sea*, the second beast comes up out of the *earth* (13:11). These contrasting terms are indicative of the origin of the two beasts. The sea may symbolize the Gentiles (17:15; cf. Dan. 7:2–3), and if this is the case here, the opposite term, the earth, symbolizes the Jews. There is precedence for the Gentile origin of the Antichrist in the Old Testament allusions, and the Jewish identification may be strengthened if here "the earth" has technical sense of "the land" [of Israel] as it sometimes may in Revelation (11:18; cf. Dan. 8:9). While most premillennial interpreters have accepted the view that the Antichrist's geographical origin is in Europe as a revived Roman Empire, based on Daniel 9:26 having Rome in the background, a Middle Eastern origin has been proposed, based on Assyria being the "slain" [kingdom] of Revelation 13:3 (cf. Rev. 17:9–11; Dan. 11:40) that is revived as Iraq (Goodman, Hodges).

The second beast acts as a lieutenant of the Antichrist in the religious realm, duplicating the miraculous signs of the biblical prophets (13:13–14). Just as many antichrists appeared during the last days to prepare for the Antichrist (1 John 2:18, 22), so many false prophets and false Christs will appear throughout the Tribulation (cf. Matt. 24:10, 24) to prepare for the greater deception of the second beast (Rev. 13:13–14) as the superlative False Prophet (Rev. 13:14 with Matt. 24:24; cf. Rev. 19:20). He possesses counterfeit, but subordinate, authority like that of the first beast (13:4, 12), which is why he is called a second beast. In this position he promotes the universal worship of the Antichrist (13:16), who will apparently at this time claim the status of deity (Rev. 13:4–8, 12–13). While the False Prophet is said to deceive the earth-dwellers, or Gentiles (Rev. 13:12), he is also shown to perform signs that are peculiar to Israel (Rev. 13:12–15). Because these signs include the ability to restore life (v. 12), call fire down from heaven (v. 13), and to create (vv. 14–15), his actions particularly recall those of the prophet Elijah (cf. 1 Kings 17:14–16; 17:21–23; 18:36–38). This might imply that the False Prophet will, like Elijah (cf. Mal. 3:1–2; 4:5), act as a messianic forerunner proclaiming the Antichrist as Messiah; however, the Antichrist receives worship as a god exalted above all other gods (Rev. 13:4, 8; cf. 2 Thess. 2:4), so it is more probable that the False Prophet is for Israel also a false messiah, who performs expected messianic signs (Isa. 35:5; 42:7; 61:1; cf. Matt. 11:3–5; Luke 4:18–19) to confirm and magnify the supreme status of the Antichrist through their counterfeit god/prophet relationship (John 5:36; 8:54; 10:18; 17:4; cf. Matt, 24:24 with Acts 2:22). This counterfeit messianic status accords with his description as having horns like a lamb (probably a counterfeit of the messianic nature, Rev. 5:6; cf. Isa. 53:7) and speaking as a dragon (satanic empowerment), 13:11.

The two signs performed for/by the Antichrist, resuscitation and presence in the temple, are connected with each other and with messianic expectation. In accordance with messianic expectation of Messiah at the temple as divine judge (Mal. 3:1–2), Jesus came into the temple precincts and, acting judicially, overturned the tables of the money changers (John 2:13–21). After this act He was asked for a sign by the Jewish crowd who had apparently made the messianic connection. Jesus answered with the sign of resurrection. The satanic resuscitation of the Antichrist may be an attempt to counterfeit this sign of resurrection (Rev. 13:3, 12–14) as a means to deification and enthronement as divine judge. The Antichrist's role as universal judge and executor may point to this investiture (Rev. 13:8–10, 15). However, the intention of the Antichrist in his persecution of Israel and invasion of the land (Dan. 11:41; cf. Rev. 8:9–13) may be to reverse the demonstration of divine blessing, evident with the 144,000 and the two witnesses (Rev. 7:1–8; 14:1–5; 11:3–12), by returning the whole nation to an exilic (scattered) state. Daniel 9:27 describes the "desolation" that follows the Antichrist's "abomination." This same term is used to depict the condition of Israel and its land as a result of desecration and exile (cf. Lev. 26:34–35; Ps. 73:19; 2 Chron. 30:7, 36:21; Jer. 4:7).

This may occur with the worldwide Jewish persecution that follows Antichrist's enthronement in the temple (12:13–17; cf. Matt. 24:16–22; Mark 13:14–18).

The defeat of the Antichrist accompanies the Second Advent (19:1, 19–20) and apparently takes place in Jerusalem at the final campaign of Armageddon (cf. Zech. 14:1–4; cf. Dan. 9:27). The eternal destiny of the Antichrist is the lake of fire (19:20), designed especially for the punishment of Satan and the rebel angelic (demonic) order (Matt. 25:41) with whom these have joined ranks. The Beast and False Prophet are consigned to the lake of fire at the conclusion of the Battle of Armageddon (20:20), but Satan is bound until the end of the Millennium (20:1–3, 7), at which time he is defeated and he is reunited to his satanic trinity in eternal condemnation (20:9–10). The sober warning for the unsaved and those who accept the mark of the Antichrist during the Tribulation is that they will share the eternal destiny of the Antichrist in the lake of fire (20:13–15; 21:8).

See also DANIEL'S SEVENTY WEEKS, DISPENSATIONAL INTERPRETATION OF.

J. Randall Price

Nonevangelical View:

W. Bousset, *The Antichrist Legend: A Chapter in Christian and Jewish Folklore*, trans. A. H. Keane (London: Hutchinson and Co., 1896); Bernard McGinn, *Antichrist: Two Thousand Years of the Human Fascination with Evil* (San Francisco: Harper Collins, 1994); Ernst Renan, *Antichrist*, trans. W. G. Hutchinson (London: W. Scott Publishers, 1899); Béda Rigaux, *L'Antéchrist: et l'Oppostion au Royaume Messianique dans l'Ancien et le Nouveau Testament*. Universitas Catholica Lovaniensis Dissertationes Seires II. Tomus 24 (Paris: J. Gabalda et Fils, 1932); Samuel P. Tregelles, *The Man of Sin* (London/Aylesbury: Hunt, Benard & Co., 1930).

Evangelical View:

Arthur W. Pink, *The Antichrist* (Grand Rapids: Kregel, 1988).

Dispensational Premillennial View:

David Hocking, *The Coming World Leader* (Portland: Multnomah, 1988); Tommy Ice and Timothy Demy, *The Truth About the Antichrist and His Kingdom* (Eugene, Oreg.: Harvest House, 1995); J. Dwight Pentecost, *Things to Come* (Chicago: Moody Press, 1961); Walter K. Price, *The Coming Antichrist* (Chicago: Moody Press, 1974); and *In the Final Days* (Chicago: Moody Press, 1977); Robert Thomas, *Revelation 8–22: An Exegetical Commentary* (Chicago: Moody Press, 1995); John F. Walvoord, *The Revelation of Jesus Christ* (Chicago: Moody Press, 1966).

Assyrian View:

Phillip Goodman, *The Assyrian Connection: The Roots of Antichrist and the Emerging Signs of Armageddon* (Lafayette, La.: Prescott Press, 1993); Zane C. Hodges, *Power to Make War: The Career of the Assyrian Who Will Rule the World* (Dallas: Redención Viva, 1995).

ANTICHRIST, JEWISH VIEWS OF THE

The concept of the Antichrist was implicit in much of the Old Testament and explicit in the book of Daniel. The figure of a last-days opponent of the Jewish people and the Messiah is especially prominent in some of the Jewish apocryphal and pseudepigraphical writings before the birth of Christ, including the apocalyptic texts of the Dead Sea Scrolls. Michael Stone, a leading Israeli expert on this literature, has observed that "the background to this figure lies in Jewish eschatology." A much stronger conclusion was drawn by Hebrew University professor David Flusser. As an expert on Second Temple Judaism and the origins of Christianity, he categorically states: "The idea of Antichrist is strictly Jewish and pre-Christian." This is evident from the expression itself, for just as the Greek word *Christos* (Christ) is the translation of the Hebrew word *Mashiach* (Messiah), so "Antichrist" is in fact "Anti-Messiah."

In Jewish apocalyptic literature a final rebellion by the wicked against the righteous in Israel is predicted to occur at the Last Day (cf. Jub. 23:14–23; 4 Ezra 4:26–42; 6:18–28). The earliest references to a specific evil king over the forces of the wicked is of "Beliar" (*worthless one*), a superhuman being who is the embodiment of evil and who is destined to be the end-time opponent of God and His Messiah. In the Testaments of the Twelve Patriarchs, the figure of Beliar serves as a portent of the imminent conclusion of the age and its cataclysmic end (cf. T. Jo. 20:2; T. Sim. 5:3; T. Naph. 2:6; T. Iss. 6:1; 7:7; T. Reub. 2:1; T. Dan 5:10; T. Levi 18:12; T. Judah 25:3). Not only does Beliar lead astray, but whoever sins is said to be doing the works of Beliar (T. Naph. 2:8). He is attended by a contingent of seven evil spirits that comprise his unholy court (cf. T. Reub. 2:1; T. Iss. 7:7), and these spirits will in the last days be joined by a large company of men (cf. T. Iss. 6:1). The eschatological deliverance (redemption) of Israel cannot be obtained without the ultimate defeat and destruction of Beliar, and his defeat comes from the Lord from Levi and from the Messiah (T. Dan 5:10; cf. 5:3-7), who will fight with him and finally cast him into eternal punishment (T. Dan 5:10; T. Iss. 6:1; T. Levi 18:12; T. Judah 25:3).

The Dead Sea (Qumran) literature (c. 196 B.C.–A.D. 68) developed a complex eschatology based on a *pesher* (literalistic) interpretation of the biblical prophets. It has been thought, based on the assumption that Beliar/Belial=Satan, that Beliar was only a cognomen for the Devil. Although Beliar is presented as the seducer and corrupter of Israel, he is a creation of God destined for this purpose (1QM 13:9–11), and appears as a quasi-human adversary. Even if there is an overlapping with Satan, some texts such as 2 Ezekiel (4Q385–89) distinguish a "son of Beliar" and a "blasphemous/boastful king" who will arise and oppress the Jewish people. These titles occur in texts that are within a context alluding to the national regathering and restoration of Israel (from the vision of the valley of dry bones in Ezekiel 37:4–6), which is immediately followed by a prayer concerning the time of this end-time regathering.

In a fragmentary pseudo-Daniel text from Qumran Cave 4, the description of an evil end-time king who oppresses Israel includes the words: "[ ]he shall be great on earth . . . [all] will worship and all will serve [him] . . . great . . . he shall be called and by His name he shall be designated. He shall be named son of God and they shall call him son of the Most High" (4Q246 1:8–10). This might appear to be a reference to the Messiah rather than the Antimessiah if it were not describing an opponent of Israel. This seems confirmed in the words that follow where a contrast is made between the arrogant oppressor of Israel in these lines and the defender of Israel who makes peace and establishes their kingdom: "Like a shooting star that you saw, so shall be their kingdom. They shall reign for [some] years on earth and will trample all. One nation [or people] shall trample on another nation and one province on another province [*vacat*] until the people of God shall arise and all will desist from the sword. His kingdom will be an eternal kingdom and its/his ways will be in righteousness; He will [judge] the earth in righteousness, and all will have/make peace; The sword will cease from the earth and every nation will submit to/worship him" (9–12).

Of importance is the *vacat* (a deliberate space separating ideas) that divides Israel's oppressor from its savior. If this interpretation is correct, we have in this text the earliest Jewish commentary on Daniel's vision of the Antimessiah and a dramatic parallel to Paul's teaching in 2 Thesselonians 2:4. This is similar to what is said concerning Daniel's blasphemous tyrant who usurps the divine prerogative in the Oracles of Hystaspes. They describe a king that "shall arise out of Syria, born from an evil spirit, the overthrower and destroyer of the human race . . . that king will not only be the most disgraceful in himself, but he will also be a prophet of lies, and he will constitute, and call himself God and will order himself to be worshipped as the son of God" (*Lactantius divinae institutiones* 7.17: 2–4). Likewise, the Assumption [or Testament] of Moses in which an end-time king of supreme authority persecutes the Jewish people, blasphemes God, violates the Law, and desecrates the temple by forcing entrance to the Holy of

Holies and offering pagan sacrifices on the altar. Temple pollution is also one of the three "nets of Beliar" according to the Damascus Document (CD 4).

These texts bear great resemblance to Jesus' Olivet Discourse in which is predicted a massive defection from the true faith, deceiving false prophets, and the Abomination of Desolation in the temple (Matt. 24:10–15; Mark 13:14–22).

Jewish apocalypses also developed certain themes concerning the Antimessiah (see ESCHATOLOGY, JEWISH). One example is the Roman origin of the Antimessiah (based apparently on the interpretation in Daniel's prophecy of a Roman connection, Dan. 9:26–27) in the Sibylline Oracles (4:119–39). Here the eschatological Antimessiah is cast in the mold of the worst of the deified Roman emperors, Nero, who was expected to reappear in the end time as *Nero redivivus* (Nero risen [from the dead]). In the Ascension of Isaiah Nero is the epitome of evil into whom Beliar entered to do wonders and much evil (4:3, 13). Early patristic writers were also influenced by the Jewish *Nero redivivus* tradition (e.g., Commodian, A.D. 250). Some, however, such as Hippolytus (*Commentary on the Benedictions of Isaac and Jacob* [Gen. 49:14]), who began the Christian tradition that the Antichrist originates from the Israelite tribe of Dan, apparently made this connection from the Jewish Testaments of the Twelve Patriarchs (T. Dan 1:4–9; 5:6–7), which states that evil spirits would be active in the tribe (5:5), that Satan was their prince (5:6), and that they would be hostile in the future to the tribes of Levi and Judah (5:6–7).

The doom of the Antimessiah was predicted following the pattern presented in Daniel (9, 11). The Psalms of Solomon describes the son of David delivering Israel by destroying the lawless one with the word of his mouth, purging Jerusalem, and restoring the Promised Land to the Jews (17:13, 23–27). This is similar to the New Testament, where the coming of the Messiah ends Jewish persecution and destroys the armies of the Antichrist (Matt. 24:30–31; Mark 13:26–27; Luke 21:27–28; 2 Thess. 2:8; Rev. 19:14–21).

In the Jerusalem Talmud (A), Targum pseudo-Jonathan, and the later Jewish apocalyptic Midrashim (commentaries), the legendary name given to the Antimessiah is Armilus. Works such as *Sefer Zerubbavel* and those by Saadiah Gaon reveal his characteristics in striking detail. According to these Jewish sources, Armilus will deceive the whole world into believing he is God and will reign over the whole world. He will come with ten kings and together they will fight over Jerusalem. Armilus is expected to persecute and banish Israel to the wilderness and it will be a time of unprecedented distress for Israel; there will be increasing famine, and the Gentiles will expel the Jews from their lands, and they will hide in caves and towers. God will war against the host of Armilus, and there will be a great deliverance for Israel, and the kingdom of heaven will spread over all the earth.

Other references further describe Armilus as arising from the Roman Empire, having miraculous powers, and being born to a stone statue of a virgin, because of which he was called "the son of a stone." It is also interesting that he makes this statue the chief of all idolatry with the result that "all the Gentiles will bow down to her, burn incense and pour out libations to her." This resembles Daniel's wicked king and coming prince and his Abomination of Desolation (Dan. 18:1, 31 36–37), and especially the Apocalypse's statue of the Beast which is brought to life and made an object of worship (Rev. 13:4, 15).

The Jewish hermeneutic of a literal, futurist interpretation was followed by the Jewish writers of the New Testament, and Jewish views of the Antimessiah influenced both early Jewish-Christian interpretation and the interpretation of the many of the early (ante-Nicene) church fathers. For example, Irenaeus (c. A.D. 185) wrote: "But when this Antichrist shall have devastated all things in this world, he will reign for three years and six months, and sit in the temple at Jerusalem; and then the Lord will come from heaven in the clouds, in the glory of the Father, sending this man and those who follow him into the lake of fire; but bringing in for the righteous the times of the kingdom." Eusebius also mentions (scornfully) a Jewish-Christian writer named Jude (dated to A.D. 202–203) whose treatise on Daniel's seventy-weeks prophecy held out an imminent expectation of the advent of Antichrist in his generation (*Ecclesiastical History* 6:6).

By contrast, the nonliteral interpretation, also seen in later rabbinic Judaism, does not fully appear until the third century A.D. with Origen and Augustine, who were influenced by the allegorical interpretations of the Hellenistic idealist school of the Jewish philosopher Philo. While in reality both amillennial and premillennial interpretations had been influenced from Jewish sources, during the chiliast controversy the amillennial charge against millenarianism was that it was "Jewish." While apocryphal elements in Jewish eschatology are to be rejected, premillennialists should find support from the Jewish roots of their interpretation which attest to its proper biblical context.

See also DANIEL, ESCHATOLOGY OF.

J. Randall Price

David Flusser, "The Hubris of the Antichrist in a Fragment from Qumran" in *Immanuel* (Spring 1980); Jacob Klatzkin, "Armilus" in *Encyclopedia Judaica,* vol. 3 (Jerusalem: Keter Publishing House Jerusalem, Ltd., 1972); J. Randall Price, "Prophecy and the Dead Sea Scrolls" in *Secrets of the Dead Sea Scrolls* (Eugene, Oreg.: Harvest House, 1996); Michael E. Stone, "Antichrist" in *Encyclopedia Judaica,* vol. 3 (Jerusalem: Keter Publishing House Jerusalem, Ltd., 1972).

ANTICHRIST, OLD TESTAMENT REFERENCES TO THE

Genesis 3:15

This verse not only contains the first prophecy of the coming of the Messiah, at the same time it gives the first prophecy of the Antimessiah, or Antichrist. This verse speaks of enmity in two pairs. First, there is going to be enmity between Satan and the woman. But, second, this verse states that there is going to be enmity between the woman's Seed and Satan's seed. The Seed of the woman is Jesus the Messiah. As God, He was eternally existent; as a man, he was conceived of the Holy Spirit and born of a virgin. He was truly both God and man. The very mention of a seed of a woman goes contrary to the biblical norm, for nationality was always reckoned after the seed of the man. This is why in all the genealogies of Scripture only the male names are given, with some very rare exceptions.

The reason the Messiah must be reckoned after the seed of the woman is explained by Isaiah 7:14: the Messiah will be born of a virgin. Because the Messiah would not have a human father, His national origins would have to be reckoned after the woman, as His humanity comes only from her. The very expression, "her seed," implies a miraculous conception. In reference to Satan's "seed," this term, being in the same verse, implies the same thing: that of a supernatural and miraculous conception. The enmity against the Seed of the woman comes from the seed of Satan. If the Seed of the woman is the Messiah, the seed of Satan can only be the Antichrist.

From this passage, then, it may be deduced that Satan will counterfeit the virgin birth and will someday impregnate a woman who will give birth to Satan's seed, who is going to be the Antichrist. The woman herself may not be a virgin, but the conception of the Antichrist will be through the miraculous power of Satan. By this means, the Antichrist will have a supernatural origin.

Isaiah 14:3–11, 16–21

In 2 Thessalonians 2:8, Paul states that the Antichrist will be killed at the time of the Second Coming. Isaiah 14:3–11 describes what happens to the soul of the Antichrist when it arrives in hell. At the time of the redemption of Israel, the Jews whom the king of Babylon sought to destroy will taunt him with a new parable (vv. 3–4) commemorating the greatest strength of the power of God (v. 5). The Antichrist ruled the nations of the world (v. 6), but then the whole world will rejoice over his demise (vv. 7–8). As the spirit of the Antichrist enters into the gates of hell, the previous great ones of the earth who are already there will suddenly rise up off their thrones (vv. 4–9) in utter shock that he, too, has entered the abode of hell (v. 10). Yet it will be so, and all the pomp of his worldwide reign will suffer the demise of hell (v. 11). Having described the spirit of the Antichrist in hell, Isaiah then goes on to describe the fact of his death on earth (vv. 16–21). Many will be able to view the body of the Antichrist and will stare in utter disbelief that he died so suddenly and easily, considering he had shaken the kingdoms of the world and the earth had trembled in his presence (vv. 16–17). While lesser kings are buried in pompous sepulchres (v. 18), not so the Antichrist, whose body will be trampled by the fleeing feet of his own armies (v. 19). In fact, his body will never be buried at all (v. 20); he will be resurrected sometime later, for he is destined to be thrown alive into the lake of fire. His entire family will be destroyed so that they cannot try to follow in their father's footsteps and attempt to rule the world (v. 21).

Habakkuk 3:13

The third chapter of Habakkuk describes the Second Coming and Messiah's war against the nations of the world. This verse mentions the leader of the confederacy and states: "Thou woundedst the head out of the house of the wicked man, laying bare the foundation even unto the neck" (ASV). This, too, is a reference to his death at the Second Coming, and it is the Old Testament corollary to 2 Thessalonians 2:8.

Daniel 7:7–8, 11, 19–26

Daniel describes the development of the four Gentile empires, with the fourth Gentile empire undergoing five successive stages, the fifth stage being the Antichrist stage. In the first half of the Tribulation, the Antichrist is one ruler having to share his power with ten others. In the middle of the Tribulation, he will be strong enough to uproot three of the ten kings, and the other seven will simply submit to his authority. When the other seven submit their authority to the Antichrist, this will begin the final stage of the fourth Gentile empire, the Antichrist stage, which is the stage of absolute imperialism. In this sense he will, indeed, be diverse from all the others. He will then rule the world for the second three years of the Tribulation.

Daniel 8:23–25

From the backdrop of Antiochus Epiphanes, a type of the Antichrist, this passage describes the character and the rise of the Antichrist to power. Verse 23 provides one of the many names of the Antichrist: the King of Fierce Countenance. He will have the understanding of dark sentences, meaning he will have the same supernatural abilities to solve riddles that Daniel had in 5:12. Daniel's source was God, but the source for the Antichrist will be Satan. The Antichrist will have the power of the occult behind him. This is further spelled out in the following verses where it is clearly stated that his power is going to be mighty, but it will not be his own power. In other words, the Antichrist will have access to a tremendous amount of power, but the power is not his own; it originates from another source, that of his father, Satan. He will seek to destroy the holy people of Israel with supernatural power. He will be characterized by craftiness and deceit and, by these means, he will lull rulers into a sense of false security and take advantage of it for the purpose of uprooting them. For a time, he will prosper, that is, be successful in his goals. He shall magnify himself in his heart and this will lead to a self-declaration of deity. He will stand against the prince of princes, the Messiah, and so truly be the Antichrist.

Daniel 9:26–27

This passage reveals a number of things about the Antichrist. First, it reveals the human nationality of the Antichrist. In verse 27, the Antichrist is spoken of as the one who makes a covenant. By the rules of Hebrew grammar, the pronoun *he* in verse 27 must go back to its nearest antecedent. And the nearest antecedent is the prince that shall come of verse 26. So, then, the he who makes a covenant, in verse 27, and the prince that shall come, of verse 26, are one and the same person, the Antichrist. This prince that shall come is the prince already spoken of earlier in Daniel's book, in chapters 7 and 8. Verse 26 also states that the prince that shall come is of the same nationality as the people who will destroy the city and the temple. The people who destroyed the temple is now a matter of history: the Romans in A.D. 70. The obvious conclusion is that the Antichrist will be a Gentile of Roman origin. The deduction of his Roman origin can be summarized in the following five steps: (1) The one who makes a covenant and the prince that shall come are the same person. (2) They both have reference to the Antichrist. (3) The Antichrist is of the same nationality as the people who destroyed Jerusalem and the temple. (4) The Romans destroyed Jerusalem and the temple in A.D. 70. (5) The Antichrist, therefore, will be of Roman origin. The conclusion is that the Antichrist will not be a Jew, but rather a Gentile of Roman origin.

The second main thing taught in this passage is the Antichrist's role in the start of the Tribulation. The starting point of the Seventieth Week of Daniel is clearly the signing of a seven-year covenant between Israel and the Antichrist. Therefore, it is not the rapture of the church that starts the Tribulation, but rather it is the signing of the seven-year covenant that starts the Tribulation.

The third point the passage makes is that although the covenant was intended to last for seven years, it will not. In the middle of the seven-year period, the Antichrist will break the covenant and make a forced cessation of the sacrificial system. This is followed by two things: (1) the Abomination of Desolation, which is the point of time that the Antichrist declares his own deity from within the temple building; (2) this also signals the worldwide persecution of the Jewish people and the persecution will continue until "the full end," until the very end of the Seventieth Week of Daniel.

Daniel 11:36–45

This passage deals with two main elements about the Antichrist. First, it deals with the character and rise of the Antichrist (vv. 36–39). In this passage, Daniel refers to the Antichrist as the willful king (v. 36) because he is characterized by self-exaltation above all people and self-deification by magnifying himself above even God (vv. 36–37). In his self-exaltation, he will speak against the God of gods (Dan. 7:25), deifying himself and magnifying himself above all humanity. He will not desire the love of women, which is natural to men, and so he will be inhuman in his disregard of women. The enmity of Satan against womanhood continues through Satan's seed. Furthermore, he will be under the total control of Satan (vv. 38–39). The passage states that he will honor a god that his ancestors on his mother's side never honored: the god of fortresses, who is Satan. His policy will be that "might makes right." Furthermore, with the help of this foreign god, Satan, he will be able to take over the strongest defenses in the world, and he will appear totally invincible. Those who submit to his authority and deity will be increased and given positions of status and authority in his kingdom. He will divide territory he has conquered among those who will be loyal to him and confess him to be god. Thus, the Antichrist will be a Satan-controlled and Satan-energized being who will set up a worldwide conquest.

The second part of the passage deals with the antichrist's war against the ten kings in the middle of the Tribulation (vv. 40–45). He is seen as moving out in all directions in conquest, and so he moves against the north (vv. 40, 44), the south (vv. 40, 42–43), and the east (v. 40). The three kings he will succeed in killing (Daniel 7:8–20, 24), will be the king of the north (Syria), the king of the south (Egypt), and the king of the east (Mesopotamia). His conquest of Egypt opens the door for his conquest of Africa (vv. 42–43). He will also invade Israel, the glorious land (v. 41), setting the stage for the Abomination of Desolation. Although the Antichrist will eventually gain political control of the whole world, three countries will escape his domination: Edom, Moab, and Amman (v. 41). These three ancient nations comprise only one nation today: the kingdom of Jordan. This will, in turn, provide a place of refuge for Jews to flee.

The passage concludes, stating where the

Antichrist will set up his headquarters: And he shall plant the tents of his palace between the seas and the glorious holy mountain (v. 45). The word for "tent" refers to a military tent of a general and the word for "palace" to a royal tent. It is a royal tent of a military general (the Antichrist) that is set up. It is set up between the seas, meaning between the Mediterranean Sea and the Dead Sea. Furthermore, it is at the glorious holy mountain, meaning the temple mount, Mount Moriah, or Mount Zion. This, again, sets the stage for the Abomination of Desolation.

See also ANTICHRIST, THE; ANTICHRIST, JEWISH VIEWS.

Arnold Fruchtenbaum

APOCALYPSE

The Greek term *apocalypsis* means to "uncover," "disclose," or "reveal" — hence a "revelation." The verb form *apocalupto* is formed from *kalupto* (to cover up) and *apo* (from). In secular Greek it means to disclose things previously hidden. In the LXX the noun is used only in 1 Samuel 20:30 ("nakedness"). The verb form is used some eighty times in the LXX for "strip, expose, or uncover." In the NT the verb appears twenty-six times and the noun eighteen times, with thirteen of these occurring in Paul's epistles. Significant NT usage is found in Luke 2:32 (a light for the revelation of the nations); Matthew 11:25 (truth revealed to babes); 11:27 (no one knows the Father except the Son and any one to whom the Son chooses to reveal Him).

The term *revelation* in Christian theology refers to the self-disclosure of God to humanity. Thus, all of Scripture is a part of that divine revelation of inspired truth. As the title of the book of Revelation, *apocalupsis* refers to the unveiling or revealing of the future. Its use in Revelation 1:1 with the genitive *of* means that Jesus Christ could be either objective, with Christ as the object, or subjective, referring to Jesus Christ as the one who originates the revelation (cf. Rienecker, vol. 2, 465).

Since the Greek title of the book of Revelation is Apocalypse, the term *apocalyptic* has come to refer to any prophetic literature that speaks of divine judgment in the end times (e.g., Dan. 7–12; Isa. 24–27, 34–35; Amos 7–9; Zech. 1–6; Joel 1–3; and parts of the Apocrypha: Jub., 2 Esd., 1 and 2 Enoch, Bar.).

Scholars have attempted to isolate certain characteristics of apocalyptic literature: determinism, pessimism, imminent expectation of the end; visions of worldwide catastrophe; extensive symbolism; and messianism. While these are certainly characteristic of Daniel and Revelation, they are by no means limited to those books. From a sociological standpoint, *apocalyptic* generally describes literature arising from intense human struggle with persecution and fear of radical change in society. But this is not true of all apocalyptic literature. The article on the Rapture in *NIDNTT* (vol. 3, 602) notes: "In 1 Thess. 4:17, Paul deals with the final rapture into the fellowship of the redeemed at the last day. It was not the sufferings of the church that caused Paul to make that statement, but the concern of some of its members about the fate of Christians who had already died."

See also JUDGMENTS, VARIOUS.

Edward Hindson

D. E. Aune, "Apocalyptic" in *Baker Encyclopedia of the Bible,* ed. W. A. Elwell (Grand Rapids: Baker, 1988); Colin Brown, "Revelation" in *New International Dictionary of New Testament Theology,* vol. 3 (Grand Rapids: Zondervan, 1978); F. Rienecker, *A Linguistic Key to the Greek New Testament,* vol. 2 (Grand Rapids: Zondervan, 1980); D. S. Russell, "The Message and Method of Apocalyptic" in *Between the Testaments* (London: SCM, 1960); R. F. Youngblood, "Apocalyptic Literature" in *Nelson's New Illustrated Bible Dictionary* (Nashville: Thomas Nelson, 1995).

APOCALYPTIC LITERATURE

Apocalypse, from the Greek *apokalupsis,* is literally an "unveiling." As a literary term, it describes a genre that flourished in intertestamental Jewish writings from the third century B.C. through the first century A.D. The main characteristics of apocalyptic literature mark most of these writings. A disclosure of heavenly secrets is made to a biblical character through an angelic mediator by means of highly symbolic language. These visions usually describe a direct divine intervention in wicked human affairs whereby sinners are judged and the righteous are rewarded.

Some canonical OT books utilize, in an anticipatory way, some of these features: Ezekiel, Zechariah 1–6, Daniel 7–12. The animal symbolism, particularly of Daniel, may have even inspired later apocalyptic authors. A group of intertestamental writings known as the *pseudepigrapha* often employed apocalyptic language. Some of the most notable of these are 1 Enoch, 4 Ezra, 2 Baruch, and the Apocalypse of Abraham.

The New Testament book of the Revelation was the first work to utilize the term "apocalypse" to describe itself. The book also exhibits nearly all of the principal characteristics of the genre. The first two verses identify the book as a revelation given by God through an otherworldly mediator to a human seer disclosing future events. The heavenly journey of John in chapter 4 as well as the visions throughout the book are also features of earlier apocalyptic writing.

The Apocalypse, however, stands apart from the noncanonical apocalyptic literature. It is not pseudonymous, but bears the name of its author, who writes as a prophet. Furthermore, John does not share the pessimism of the apocalyptists who despaired of all human history. The book declares that God is working redemptively through the Lamb now as well as in the future. Moreover, NT apocalyptic is Christ-centered. Jesus is the focus of faith both in the past and in the future. Apocalypticism is a means for John and the other NT writers to declare His significance for the whole world. Finally, the author, John, possesses the moral urgency of the OT prophets, rebuking a faithless church and demanding repentance to avoid divine judgment—a note often lacking in the earlier apocalypses.

The uniqueness of John's apocalypse is due to its divine inspiration, whereas the earlier apocalyptic writings were the result of the fevered imaginations of their authors. While the last book of the Bible is the best of the Jewish apocalyptic literature, it follows more in the prophetic tradition of the Old Testament than in the footsteps of the apocalyptists.

See also ANTICHRIST, THE; ANTICHRIST, JEWISH VIEWS.

William Varner

Paul Hanson, *The Dawn of Apocalyptic* (Philadelphia: Fortress Press, 1987); Leon Morris, *Apocalyptic* (Grand Rapids: Eerdmans, 1973); D. S. Russell, *The Method and Message of Apocalyptic* (Philadelphia: Fortress Press, 1964).

APOCRYPHAL LITERATURE: ITS USE IN PROPHECY

The apocryphal literature (200 B.C.–A.D. 100) has many messianic and kingdom references. The problem, however, with this genre is that there is a corruption of the prophetic sections in both how it handles historic accounts and how it often uses outright fiction. Though Roman Catholics have a high regard for the material, it is not inspired or seen as carrying authority. There are five areas of value in this literary collection.

1. The writings fill in the gap between Old and New Testaments. They supply a link of information that covers around four and a half centuries of history.

2. The literature gives valuable insight into the spiritual, philosophical, and intellectual life of Judaism.

3. The books of Maccabees, especially, spell out a careful outline of the fierce struggle the Jews had politically with pagan Greece. They catalog events of one of the most heroic periods of the history of the Jewish nation.

4. Despite inaccuracies, contradictions, and absurdities, the Apocrypha gives to historians a library of priceless secular literature (Unger).

5. It is in the area of prophecy that this body of literature has such importance as well.

Though sometimes embellished with exaggeration and fiction, the Apocrypha still gives us a panorama of the belief of the Jews about the coming of Messiah. And after cutting through certain fictionalizations, one sees the literalness of the Jewish hopes. Because the core of the prophetic hope comes from the Old Testament prophecies, we know how the Jews interpreted their messianic expectations.

In the books of Enoch (first century B.C.), the Old Testament character Enoch (Gen. 5:24) sees messianic visions of a future judgment. In his second vision he sees the world from the Flood down to the establishment of the messianic kingdom. In a similitude or allegory, Enoch's concept of the Messiah is that of the supernatural Son of Man. He is the Elect One seated on the throne of His glory which is also the throne of the "Head of Days," the Almighty. The Messiah will overwhelm wickedness and sit in judgment over angels and human beings.

In the Book of Jubilees (135–105 B.C.), also called the Apocalypse of Moses, the messianic age brings blessedness and roots out wickedness. The Psalter of Solomon (70–45 B.C.) contains strongly developed messianic expectations. These psalms show a strong Pharisaic sentiment, and they picture the Messiah, as the Son of David and king of Israel, cleansing Jerusalem from pagan influence and bringing back the Dispersion. The Gentile world will be subject to Him, and He will rule them as His subjects. In the first-century A.D. Book of the Secrets of Enoch (2 Enoch), the Lord shows Enoch the thousand-year millennial rest. It is for certain the rabbis read parts of the New Testament, and their view of the millennium could have the book of Revelation as its source. The Apocalypse of Baruch, written before A.D. 70, shows the Tribulation in twelve parts, in which the last empire mentioned (the Roman) is crushed by the Messiah. Though written in heavy symbolism, the literalness from the Hebrew prophets of the Old Testament is clear.

The Sibylline Oracles, dating from the fifth century B.C. up to the Christian era, is a wide collection of Jewish and Christian materials that seem to bind together beliefs about the Messiah's return. Toward the close of this book the sibyl predicts the coming of the Messiah-king and gives a full picture of the kingdom prosperity awaiting the righteous. And, the book concludes, the sons of God will dwell around a rebuilt temple.

The apocryphal writers clearly drew their prophecies from Daniel, Ezekiel, Zechariah, and other Old Testament prophets. They possibly borrowed, as well, ideas from New Testament writings. But "their interest centered in the day of the Lord as the day of Israel's redemption" (Fairweather).

Is the Apocrypha quoted in the New Testament? As cited by Unger, C. C. Torrey concludes "in general, the apocryphal scriptures were left unnoticed." On the supposed Jude 14–16 quote of Enoch 1:9, the *New Scofield Reference Bible* makes an interesting observation about the Jude passage, "written by an unknown person who used Enoch's name for the title of the book. Jude's use of this quotation from Enoch does not suggest that he considered the book of Enoch as authoritative. Besides, it is not impossible that Jude is the source from which the quotation eventually found its way into the book of Enoch, since there is no evidence as to the precise contents of this apocryphal book until many centuries after the time in which Jude was written."

Mal Couch

James H. Charlesworth, ed., *The Old Testament Pseudepigrapha,* vols. 1–2 (Garden City, N.Y.: Doubleday & Co., 1985); William Fairweather, *The Background of the Gospels* (Minneapolis: Klock & Klock, 1977); Bentley Layton, trans., *The Gnostic Scriptures* (Garden City, N.Y.: Doubleday & Co., 1987); C. I. Scofield, ed., *New Scofield Study Bible* (New York: Oxford University Press, 1988); Merrill F. Unger, *Introductory Guide to the Old Testament* (Grand Rapids: Zondervan, 1981).

APOSTASY

The Greek word *apostasia* is used twice in the New Testament and is variously translated "forsake," "turn away," "turn the back on," (Acts 21:21), and "falling away," "apostasy," "rebellion," "final rebellion" (2 Thess. 2:3). The word is also found a number of times in the Septuagint (Josh. 22:22; 2 Chron. 29:19; Jer. 2:19; 1 Esd. 2:14,

17; Ezra 4:12, 15; 1 Macc. 2:15). In Attic Greek the word meant "rebellion" or "defection" and is also used in the papyri to refer to political rebels, but most of the biblical and apocryphal references are to religious apostasy. Based on etymology (Gk. *apo* [away from] and *stasis* [standing]) and the meaning of some cognate forms (*aphistemi, apostasios*), some scholars (notably E. Schuyler English, K. Wuest, and more recently H. Wayne House) have postulated a sense of "physical departure from." The most theologically significant passage is 2 Thessalonians 2:3, where the *apostasia* is mentioned as one of two events that must precede the Day of the Lord. In that passage there are at least four views on the meaning of *apostasia*: (1) a designation for the Man of Sin (Chrysostom, Theophylact, Augustine, Alford, Moffatt); (2) the religious apostasy that will precede the second coming of Christ (Calvin, Chafer, Walvoord, Ryrie, Gundry); (3) the religio-political rebellion against Christ that will culminate in the Battle of Armageddon (Hogg and Vine, Moore, Morris, Bruce); and (4) the rapture of the church, in the sense of physical departure from the earth (English, Wuest, House).

A parallel term is the Greek *aphistemi* (to withdraw, depart, or fall away). It is used in 1 Timothy 4:1 where it is translated "some shall depart from the faith." This apostasy is said to occur in the latter times. It results in the apostates giving heed to seducing spirits and doctrines of devils. Parallel expressions include: "go away," "turn away," "lead astray," "miss the mark," "suffer shipwreck." In Hebrews 3:12, *aphistemi* is used of those departing from the living God. It implies a deliberate abandonment of one's beliefs.

Biblical examples of apostates include Judas Iscariot, Demas, Hymenaeus, and Alexander (cf. 2 Cor. 4:10; 1 Tim. 1:20). Church history includes Julian the Apostate (A.D. 361–363), the Roman emperor who renounced Christianity and encouraged the return to pagan worship in the Roman Empire. Whether such denials reveal that one was never truly saved or that one lost thier salvation will depend on one's view of eternal security and the perseverance of the saints.

J. Dwight Pentecost (p. 155) lists the following characteristics of the future apostate Christianity:

1. Denial of God (2 Tim. 3:4–5)
2. Denial of Christ (1 John 2:18; 4:3)
3. Denial of Christ's return (2 Pet. 3:3–34)
4. Denial of the faith (1 Tim. 4:1–2)
5. Denial of sound doctrine (2 Tim. 4:3–4)
6. Denial of morality (2 Tim. 3:1–8);
7. Denial of divine authority (2 Tim. 3:4)

See also RAPTURE, DOCTRINE OF THE.

George Gunn and Edward Hindson

Bauer, Danker, Gingrich, eds., *A Greek-English Lexicon of the New Testament and Other Early Christian Literature* (Chicago: University of Chicago Press, 1979); Colin Brown, ed., *New International Dictionary of New Testament Theology,* vol. 1 (Grand Rapids: Zondervan, 1975); E. Schuyler English, *Re-Thinking the Rapture* (South Carolina: Southern Bible Book House, 1954); H. Wayne House (paper presented to the Pre-Trib. Study Group, 1994); Liddell and Scott, eds., *Greek-English Lexicon* (Oxford: Clarendon, 1940); J. Dwight Pentecost, *Things to Come* (Grand Rapids: Zondervan, 1958); A. T. Robertson, *Word Pictures in the New Testament,* vol. 4 (Grand Rapids: Baker, 1971); L. G. Whitlock, "Apostasy" in *Evangelical Dictionary of Theology,* ed. Walter Elwell (Grand Rapids: Baker, 1984).

ARMAGEDDON, BATTLE OF

The term *armageddon* (Gk., *harmegedon*) appears only once in the entire Bible, in Revelation 16:16. The location, the hill of Megiddo, overlooks the Valley of Jezreel in northern Israel. It was the site of numerous biblical conflicts (cf. Josh. 12:12; Judg. 5:19; 2 Kings 23:29). Megiddo itself served as a military stronghold for several generations (cf. Judg. 1:27; 2 Kings 8:27). It is in this great valley in Israel's breadbasket that the New Testament places the final conflict between Christ and the Antichrist. Old Testament prophecies also point to a final conflict between Israel and the nations of the world in the last days (cf. Joel 3:2–15; Zech. 14:1–5; Zeph. 3:8).

Theologically, Armageddon is a symbolic term for the final apocalyptic conflict between the forces of Christ and Antichrist. It is not limited to the Valley of Jezreel, but its climax is focused there. The entire series of battles instigated by the Antichrist will climax at Armageddon when the kings of the earth and the whole world converge for the battle of that great day of God Almighty (Rev. 16:14). Pentecost notes that this is not an isolated battle but a military campaign that includes several battles and extends throughout the Tribulation period (p. 340).

Biblical references to the final end-times conflict also refer to events in the Valley of Jehoshaphat (Joel 3:2, 13), the Lord's coming from Edom (Isa. 34), and Jerusalem itself being the center of the conflict (cf. Zech. 12:2–11; 14:2). While the troops may be deployed from Armageddon, they apparently spread out to cover the land. The conflict extends from the plains of Esdraelon on the north, down through Jerusalem, out into the Valley of Jehoshaphat and southward to Edom.

The Bible describes the nations of the world, under the leadership of the Antichrist, allied against Israel and the people of God in the last days. Difference of opinion exists among premillennialists regarding the relationship of the Battle of Armageddon to the biblical predictions of the invasion of the king of the north and the king of the south (cf. Dan. 11:4–45). Revelation 16:12 also refers to the drying up of the Euphrates River as a prelude to this great battle. With this miraculous act, the way will be paved for the kings of the east to join the final battle.

Walvoord notes that "the Battle of Armageddon will occur during the final days of the Great Tribulation," (p. 420) after the pouring out of the bowls (KJV, vials) of judgment (cf. Revelation 16). It will be the culmination of the ongoing conflict between the Antichrist and the people of God. Walvoord (p. 422) also notes: "Armies will be fighting in Jerusalem on the very day of the second coming of Christ (Zech. 14:1–3)." At the point of Christ's return the Battle of Armageddon will be won by Jesus and His triumphant church (bride of Christ) which returns with Him (Rev. 19:1–16).

The Battle of Armageddon also culminates in the final collapse of political and ecclesiastical Babylon. The kingdom of the Antichrist and its false religious system will be utterly destroyed at the same time (cf. Rev. 17–18). Again, premillennialists disagree on whether "Babylon" refers to literal Babylon in modern Iraq or whether it is a symbolic term for Rome. In either case, the Scripture makes it clear that Babylon represents the worldwide, global, political, and ecclesiastical world system of the end times.

At the Battle of Armageddon, Christ is victorious by the power of His spoken word. The Antichrist and the False Prophet are defeated and cast into the lake of fire and Satan is bound in the abyss (KJV, bottomless pit) for one thousand years during the millennial reign of Christ on earth (cf. Rev. 19:17–20:3). Thus, Armageddon stands at the end of the Great Tribulation, culminating its worldwide devastations. Sometime after Armageddon, the millennial reign of Christ is inaugurated for one thousand years of peace on earth.

See also TRIBULATION, THE GREAT.

Edward Hindson

Edward Hindson, *Final Signs* (Eugene, Oreg.: Harvest House, 1996); W. S. LaSor, *The Truth About Armageddon* (Grand Rapids: Baker, 1982); *Nelson's New Illustrated Bible Dictionary* (Nashville: Thomas Nelson, 1995); J. Barton Payne, ed., *Encyclopedia of Biblical Prophecy* (Grand Rapids: Baker, 1973); J. Dwight Pentecost, *Things to Come* (Grand Rapids: Zondervan, 1958); Merrill C. Tenney, ed., *Zondervan Pictorial Bible Dictionary* (Grand Rapids: Zondervan, 1963); John F. Walvoord, *Major Bible Prophecies* (New York: Harper Collins, 1991).

ASCENSION OF CHRIST

The ascension of Christ to the right hand of the Father occurred forty days after His resurrection or ten days before He sent the Holy Spirit on the Day of Pentecost. The Ascension is mentioned in Mark 16:19, Luke

24:50–51, and in detail in Acts 1:3–11. "The departure of Jesus was bodily, visibly, gradually, and with a cloud. These same factors enter into His Second Coming as portrayed in other Scriptures, including Revelation 19:11–18" (Walvoord). This event took place on the Bethany side of the Mount of Olives (Luke 24:50; Acts 1:12), in full view of His disciples, and it marked the end of His earthly ministry. The bodily departure of Jesus was necessary in order that the promised Comforter (the Holy Spirit) could come (John 16:7). "The coming of the Holy Spirit would be the main factor in the present church dispensation" (Walvoord). The Holy Spirit would empower the disciples to minister the Gospel and continue the work of Christ on earth.

Just before Jesus ascended to the Father His disciples again asked Him, "Lord, is it at this time You are restoring the kingdom to Israel?" (Acts 1:6). There are some that believe Jesus Christ is sitting on the throne of David while in heaven. However, "the New Testament is totally lacking in positive teaching that the throne of the Father in Heaven is to be identified with the Davidic throne. The inference is plain that Christ is seated on the Father's throne, but that this is not at all the same as being seated on the throne of David" (Walvoord). Jesus Christ fulfills the Davidic covenant on the earth during the Millennium. The disciples still expected a literal fulfillment of the Davidic covenant, which is why they asked the question. Jesus Christ's response was not a rebuke, but rather a simple "It is not for you to know times or epochs which the Father has fixed by His own authority" (Acts 1:7 NASB). If this prophecy was fulfilled through His ascension, certainly Jesus would not have responded with this answer!

Jesus Christ the High Priest entered the Holy Place of God and (1) presented His blood once and for all to the Father, obtaining eternal redemption (Heb. 9:11–14; 10:12); (2) presented Himself as the Son of Man to the Father for humanity (Dan. 7:13–14); (3) sat down at the right hand of the Father indicating that our redemption is complete (Heb. 10:12); (4) became the Head of His body (Eph.1:20–23; Col. 1:18); (5) gave gifts to the body (Eph 4:7–13); (6) empowered the body, it is Christ in you the hope of glory (Col. 1:26–27); (7) intercedes for us (Rom. 8:34; Heb. 7:25); (8) prepares a place for us (John 14:2); and (9) waits for the time when His enemies are made His footstool (Heb. 10:13).

The ascension of Christ is referred to in many passages including Psalm 68:18 (quoted in Eph. 4:8–10); Psalm 110:1 (quoted in Acts 2:33–36); Luke 9:51; 1 Thessalonians 1:10; 1 Timothy 3:16; Hebrews 4:14; 9:24; and 1 Peter 3:22.

It is interesting to note that while the disciples were still gazing up into heaven, God sent two angels to comfort them and let them know that this same Jesus that had just been taken away from them would return in the same way, physically, in full view, gradually, and with the clouds, probably the cloud of the Shekinah glory mentioned in the Old Testament.

Brian K. Richards

Charles C. Ryrie, *Basic Theology* (Wheaton: Victor Books, 1986); J. F. Walvoord, *The Millennial Kingdom* (Grand Rapids: Zondervan, 1959) and *The Prophecy Knowledge Handbook* (Wheaton; Victor Books, 1990).

AUGUSTINE

Augustine (A.D. 354–430), the bishop of Hippo Regius in Numidia, North Africa, was the most gifted of the Latin fathers and the early church's greatest theologian. Noted for his contributions to the doctrines of the church, predestination, sin, and grace, Augustine was also a principal factor in the rise and acceptance of amillennialism and the consequent decline and rejection of the premillennial doctrine that until his time was regarded as a settled point of orthodoxy in early patristic eschatology. Before Augustine, amillennialism was championed by theologians who, well-trained in the Alexandrian school's unrestrained practice of allegorical interpretation of Scripture, often distorted the sacred text to the point of heresy (e.g., Origen).

Early on, Augustine himself held premillennial views, cast in the form of the year-day or sexta-/septamillennial tradition commonly accepted in the early church. This view was based on the Creation account of six days of creative activity followed by a day of rest and the symbolic equation of one day as representative of a thousand years (based on 2 Peter 3:8; Ps. 90:4). It led to the belief that the world would endure for a period of six thousand years—usually divided into thousand-year ages in biblical history—which would be followed by a thousand-year sabbath rest, the millennial kingdom age.

Augustine abandoned the premillennial position for the superficial reason that some millenarians had envisioned a kingdom age of unparalleled fruitfulness featuring banquet tables set with excessive amounts of food and drink (*City of God* 20.7). He favored instead the position of his contemporary, the Donatist and lay theologian Tyconius who offered a spiritualized interpretation of the Apocalypse. Proceeding from this position, Augustine articulated an amillennial view in which no future thousand-year earthly millennium was expected. His modified year-day millennial belief explained the seventh day or "sabbath rest" as symbolically representative of eternity (a common interpretation among anti-premillenarian fathers of the fourth and fifth centuries), while the millennium of Revelation 20 was spiritualized to signify the period of Christ's present reign with the saints in the church age—reckoned from Christ's first to His Second Coming (*City of God* 20.9). Augustine maintained that during this spiritual millennium, Satan is bound, or limited in power, but still free to seduce and deceive the church (*City of God* 20.8).

Augustine envisioned the present age as a struggle between the church and the world, between the "city of Christ" and the coexistent "city of the devil" (*City of God* 20.11). He believed that while God has already gained essential victory over Satan by means of the Cross, and therefore the church can experience degrees of triumph in this age, there will nevertheless be no final victory until Satan's residual power is stripped from him and his final rebellion put down at Christ's Second Coming. In this, Augustine differs markedly from the postmillennial belief in the triumph of righteousness in the present church age.

Augustine outlined God's program in history this way in the *City of God*:

1. Creation to the Incarnation was five thousand years (20.7)
2. Church age—between two advents of Christ—is one thousand years, during which:
   a) Satan is bound, i.e., limited in power (20.8)
   b) Saints reign with Christ, i.e., "the kingdom of Christ" (20.9)
3. Final persecution of the church begins at the end of the millennial kingdom, lasts for three-and-one-half years, and features:
   a) Satan's loosing at the end of the thousand years (20.11)
   b) Satan's incitement of Gog and Magog (nations of the whole earth) to savagely persecute the church (20.11)
   c) Antichrist's centrality in the final persecution (20.13)
4. Christ comes again:
   a) To strike the persecutors of the church (Gog and Magog?) (20.12)
   b) To kill the Antichrist (20.12)
5. Last judgment (of the wicked) follows with:
   a) The second resurrection of the flesh (20.14). The first resurrection was explained as spiritual—revival "from the death of sin" (20.9)
   b) The wicked, the Antichrist, and the Devil are all cast into lake of fire (20.15)
6. New heaven and new earth are created for the righteous (20.16)

While Augustine's view of the millennial kingdom of Christ was spiritualized, he nevertheless believed that the thousand years of Revelation 20 was the literal period of time that would transpire between Christ's first and second comings, the period of the church age. But when the year 1000 came and went without Christ's return, Augustine's chronology was discredited. It then became necessary for amillennialists to spiritualize the duration of the millennial kingdom as well as its meaning. The thousand years came to represent an indefinite period of time between Christ's two advents.

With this and some other modifications, Augustine's allegorical interpretation of Bible prophecy dominated the understanding of eschatology during the medieval period. It found acceptance also with the Roman church and among the leaders of the Reformation. Even today, Augustinian eschatology continues to find ready acceptance in large segments of the Christian church.

See also AMILLENNIALISM.

Larry Crutchfield

P. Brown, *Augustine of Hippo* (Los Angeles: University of California Press, 1967); W. A. Jurgens, *The Faith of the Early Fathers*, 3 vols. (Collegeville, Minn.: The Liturgical Press, 1979); P. Schaff and H. Wace, eds., *Nicene and Post-Nicene Fathers*, vols. 1–8 (Grand Rapids: Eerdmans, n.d.).

B

BABYLON

The city and territory of Babylon plays a key role in the Bible in four important ways: geographically, nationally, spiritually, and prophetically. The name "Babylon" is derived from the Hebrew *babel* meaning "gate of God." A distant related word is the verb *balal,* which means "to confuse, confound." In a family of related words there is the Hebrew negative *bal* (not), *bele* (wearing out), *balay* (to be in trouble).

The larger geographical area of Babylonia encompassed some 8,000 sq. miles between the Tigris and Euphrates Rivers, the traditional site of the Garden of Eden where early humans were also placed (Gen. 2:14). Following the Great Flood, the kingdom of Babel was located here (Gen. 10:10) in what was also called the land of Shinar (Shenar). This word may be related to *shanah* which can mean "shine," "year," or "to repeat" as in the yearly cycle of months. This could have a distant allusion to the fact that astronomy/astrology was first perfected in this area and from here the gods were conceived as the beings who ruled the heavens and the earth. From this general area came Nimrod, the first king of Babylon. His name means "let us revolt" (Gen. 10:8–10). Genesis further tells us that the peoples related to Erech, Accad, and Calneh settled here. Also to the north, ancient Assyria had it roots along with the city of Nineveh (Gen. 10:11). These peoples and locations will played a significant role in the long conflict with God's chosen people, the Israelites.

Abraham migrated from this area, called in his day "Ur of the Chaldeans" (Gen. 11:28). Hammurabi ruled Babylon around 1792–1750 B.C. The kings of Assyria began with Ashurnasirpal II around 883 B.C. The Neo-Babylonian Empire emerged around 626 B.C. with Nebuchadnezzar coming to power in 605 B.C., who would later destroy Jerusalem and its temple in 586 B.C. Dispite its long history, Babylon would fall to the Medes in 539 B.C. In all of these events, Babylon played a major role as a nation and as an instrument in God's hands to judge Israel.

For example, Isaiah prophesied that because of Israel's sins Babylon would come into the land and take the people into captivity, leaving nothing in the country (2 Kings 20:17). Jeremiah predicted the captivity to be seventy years (Jer. 25:11), but for her idolatry Babylon would be punished (Jer. 51:52) and repaid for the evil she had brought on Zion (51:24). The nations would no longer stream into her gates and the walls would fall down (51:44). The period of a dominant empire would cease, and there no longer would there be the great overshadowing power that once dominated the Middle East. Various Babylonian cities did play, however, a part on the world scene for the hundreds of years that followed.

Spiritually, Babylon represents rebellion against God, the seat of satanic evil, and the birthplace of polytheism. In a taunting poem against the sovereign (and system) of Babylon (Isa. 14:1–23), the king is portrayed as the epitome and illustration of Satan himself. The song of Isaiah goes beyond the living ruler of the Babylonian nation to a personification of Lucifer. In view is the fall of Satan, who said in eternity past, "I will ascend above the heights of the clouds; I will make myself like the Most High," and "I will raise my throne above the stars (angels) of God" (14:13–14).

The polytheism of Babylon is nowhere more graphic than in the Babylonian flood account found in the Gilgamesh Epic. There the deities act like selfish and depraved humans. They are self-accusing, disagree and quarrel, crouch "like dogs," and swarm in greed "like flies." The gods are capricious and outrageous in their sins. They childishly disclaim responsibility for the terrible destruction of the flood and attempt to attach guilt to one another (Unger). From Babylon, the worship of such deities spread throughout pagan cultures of the ancient world. The worship of the gods was typically connected with sexual pervesions which further corrupted civilization. Thus, Babylon is culpable as the starting point of the pagan distortion of the true God of creation.

Nonetheless, Babylonians made the pagan religions fashionable. They took the idea of pantheism (that the gods were present in every act or expression of nature and physical matter) and elevated it to an art form. They incorporated art, drama, and music into religion until the pagan ideas were attractively represented as the highest expressions of the their culture. Babylon also took the ancient idea of the city-state and expanded into a system of bureaucracies that established control over the population.

Revelation 17–18 gives the final prophetic chapters about Babylon. Among premillennialists and dispensationalists, there is difference of opinion as to whether Babylon is only an illustration of something diabolical and spiritual or if the chapters foreshadow a restored national Babylon in the Tribulation period. Earlier amillennial scholars have almost always seen these chapters as representing the Roman Catholic Church and its pagan spiritual harlotry. Some dispensationalists see this revived Babylon as the restored global system of the final form of Rome. Others take the chapters as pointing to an actual rebuilt city and nation of Babylon in the Middle East (Dyer). For example, Saddam Hussein fully expects Babylon to become a world city, if not the world capital. Some dispensationalists believe the final Antichrist kingdom cannot be revealed without the ancient city of Babylon.

Some dispensationalists are returning to the view that "mystery" Babylon represents a system that has endured since ancient times. As a deceptive evil, it has become embedded in the religious system of Roman Catholicism. The reference in Revelation, therefore, to "Babylon the great, the mother of harlots and of the abominations of the earth" (Rev. 17:5) may be identified with not just a place, but with a system. This harlot "rides" or controls for awhile the revived Roman Empire, but the powers that constitute the revived empire turn on the harlot and "make her desolate and naked, and will eat her flesh and will burn her up with fire" (17:16). From chapter 18, none can argue that she is also a city with an economic influence. Hunt argues forcefully that this could still be papal Rome that has tremendous economic influence on the world and will have the same in the Tribulation period.

A kind of compromise position says Revelation's Babylon represents the spiritual harlotry through the Catholic Church and its control worldwide, but also the physical place in Iraq that will have a dictator like Saddam Hussein. Whichever, dispensationalists confine the events of these Revelation chapters to the time of the Tribulation, although the dark, evil influences of ancient Babylon have been ongoing throughout history. Some strongly argue that though a long time has passed since the early wickedness of Babylon, it only seems as if God has forgotten her sins. But the Lord will recall them to mind. The last Babylon is but the final outgrowth of the same principles that animated the first. Old offenses will help flame the final vengeance (Seiss).

See also TRIBULATION, THE GREAT.

Mal Couch and Joseph Chambers

Charles H. Dyer, *The Rise of Babylon* (Wheaton: Tyndale, 1991); Dave Hunt, *A Woman Rides the Beast* (Eugene, Oreg.: Harvest House, 1994); Merrill F. Unger, *Archeology and the Old Testament* (Grand Rapids: Zondervan, 1956); John F. Walvoord, ed., *The Prophecy Bible Handbook* (Wheaton: Victor Books, 1990).

BALE, JOHN

John Bale (1495–1563) was educated at Jesus College, Cambridge, England. He renounced his Carmelite vows and became a leading Protestant writer as both a dramatist and theologian. Bale wrote several plays under the patronage of Thomas Cromwell. He was the first English dramatist to combine historical drama with a morality play to illustrate the failure of the papacy and the need for ecclesiastical reform. In *A Comedy Concerning Three Laws* he proposed the view that the three moral laws (nature, bondage, and grace) encompassed seven ages of world history, each ending in divine judgment. Bale's seven ages closely parallel the concept of seven dispensations. He was exiled to Germany from 1541 to 1547, where he wrote his commentary on the Apocalypse, entitled *The Image of Both Churches*, in which he paralleled the seven ages of church history to the seven seals of the Apocalypse. Bale's commentary was very popular with the English exiles who later produced the Geneva Bible using many of Bale's ideas in their annotations.

Edward Hindson

J. S. Farmer, *The Dramatic Writings of John Bale, Bishop of Ossory* (London: Early English Drama Society, 1907); K. R. Firth, *The Apocalyptic Tradition in Reformation Britain, 1530–1645* (Oxford: Oxford University Press, 1979); J. Harris, *John Bale: A Study in the Minor Literature of the Reformation* (Urbana: University of Illinois, 1940).

BARON, DAVID

David Baron (1855–1926) was born in a strict, orthodox Jewish home in Russia. He studied Hebrew under rigorous rabbinical training. After a personal search of the Scriptures on his own, he converted to Christianity. Immediately he set out to accomplish two things: to explain Christianity to the Jews and to help Christians understand prophecy and the future restoration of Israel. To do this, he began an organization called Hebrew Christian Testimony to Israel. Through his publications, he created one of the greatest testimonies of God's working in the lives of the Jewish people.

Baron published premillennial books such as *The Servant of Jehovah* and *Types, Christ, and Israel*. His classic *Commentary on Zechariah* is considered a giant among expositions of this Old Testament book. In this work, Baron alerts readers where many in the Gentile church have spiritualized Scripture when it refers to Jerusalem or Israel. In his preface, Baron writes, "Almost all the existing works on this prophetic book are in one way or another defective, and some of them misleading. The older commentaries are commendable for their reverent spiritual tone . . . but they more or less are vitiated by the allegorizing principle of interpretation, by which all references to a concrete kingdom of God on earth, a literal, national restoration of Israel, and the visible appearing and reign of Messiah, are explained away."

Baron further explains he set out to work only in the Hebrew text and to explain as much as possible the great messianic prophecies. Too, he attempted "to unfold . . . prophetic events which center around the land and the people of Israel—events the rapid fulfillment of which men may now begin to see with their own eyes."

Mal Couch

David Baron, *Commentary on Zechariah* (Grand Rapids: Kregel, 1988).

BIRTH PANGS, THE

Based on a literal interpretation, the ancient rabbis looked for a time of suffering for Israel called the Time of Jacob's Trouble, or the Birth Pangs. Great, awesome cosmic cataclysms would take place—pestilence, famine, conflagrations. "These will be paralleled by evils brought by men upon themselves" (Patai). By calculating Daniel 9:24–27 literally as premillennialists do, the rabbis came up with a seven-year period of Tribulation on earth, and then afterward the Messiah will come. Some Jewish sages divided the seven years: First, rain will be withheld on some cities. Second, arrows of famine will be sent forth. Third, more famine comes with many dying. Fourth, there will be plenty, yet no plenty. Fifth, there will be plenty, and some will return to Torah study. Sixth, there will be sounds of a trumpet. Seventh, the Son of Man will come (Apocalypse of Abraham). "The advent of the Messiah was pictured as being preceded by years of great distress" (Babylonian Talmud).

Birth pangs refer, of course, to the labor pains of a woman about to bring forth a child. Sometimes in Scripture this is translated as "travail," "distress," "sorrows." This is really referring to the Day of the Lord or the coming Tribulation and is mentioned many places in the Bible. Jeremiah speaks of "the time of Jacob's distress" (30:4–7). Faces turn pale, there is a sound of terror—as a woman in childbirth. This happens just before the Lord brings Israel and Judah back "to the land that I gave to their forefathers, and they shall possess it" (v. 3). Isaiah writes of the travailing. He pictures Zion as a woman who gives birth at the first pain of labor. The prophet likens this to the beginning of the restoration of the nation when the Messiah comes. "Can a land be born in one day? Can a nation be brought forth all at once? As soon as Zion travailed, she also brought forth her sons" (66:8). Some premillennialists see this as the birth of the state of Israel in 1948. If God started the building of the new nation even now, will He not complete that task in the future? In other words, what is now happening in Palestine will lead to the restoration of the Jews in the future (v. 9).

Jesus speaks of the "beginning of sorrows," literally "the beginning of birth pangs" (Matt. 24:8). Here, "He introduced the Abomination of Desolation and the Great Tribulation (Matt. 24:15–21), and it appears that He introduced and discussed events in chronological order in this section of Matthew 24. This implies that the beginning of birth pangs will precede the Abomination of Desolation . . . and the Great Tribulation (of the second half of the Seventieth Week [of Daniel]) and therefore will occur during the first half of that seven-year period" (Showers). Paul also refers to the Day of the Lord falling suddenly on those left after the Rapture as "destruction" coming "suddenly like birth pangs upon a woman with child; and they shall not escape" (1 Thess. 5:2–5). That day will come like a thief (v. 2). Paul further equates that day as wrath which is not destined for those who know Christ as Savior (v. 9) and are living in this dispensation of the church. That is why the apostle urges believers to be comforted with these words (4:18).

Showers well concludes: "These consistent associations indicate that the broad Day of the Lord will not be totally separate or distinct from the Time of Jacob's Trouble or the Great Tribulation. Indeed, they indicate that the Day of the Lord will cover or at least include the same time period as the Time of Jacob's Trouble and the Great Tribulation."

See also DAY OF THE LORD; TRIBULATION, THE GREAT.

Mal Couch

Raphael Patai, *The Messiah Texts* (Detroit: Wayne State University Press, 1979); Renald Showers, *Maranatha, Our Lord Come!* (Bellmawr, N.J.: The Friends of Israel Gospel Ministry, 1995).

BROOKES, JAMES HALL

Life and Ministry

From James Brookes's (1837–1897) Presbyterian pulpit in St. Louis, his participation in the annual Niagara Bible Conference, and his prolific pen which produced religious best-sellers, he became an early and nationally recognized proponent of dispensational premillennialism in the United States. He was born in Pulaski, Tennessee, the son of a Presbyterian minister. His father died of cholera when he was still a child, and he was raised by his mother. After attending Stephenson Academy in Ashewood, Tennessee and working as a country schoolmaster, he matriculated as a junior into Miami University in Oxford, Ohio in 1851. Upon graduation in 1853, he entered Princeton Theological Seminary. His studies lasted less than a year due to an unexpected call to serve as pastor of the First Presbyterian Church in Dayton, Ohio. He was ordained by the presbytery in Oxford on April 20, 1854 and twelve days later married Susan Oliver, with whom he had fallen in love during his college years.

An extremely popular preacher and pastor, he received a call in February 1858 to pastor the Second Presbyterian Church in St. Louis and six years later accepted a call to the Sixteenth and Walnut Street Church (later the Washington and Compton Avenue Presbyterian Church). He remained pastor of this church until entering an emeritus status in 1894. Brookes served as commissioner to the General Assembly in 1857, 1880, and 1893, and was stated clerk of the Missouri Synod in 1874.

It was largely through his writings and conference ministry that Brookes gained national recognition. In the early 1870s he published *Maranatha*, a massive volume on eschatology that was to become one of his most popular works. In 1875, he began to edit a monthly periodical called *The Truth or Testimony for Christ*, which became a widely circulated and influential premillennial publication. He was a regular speaker at Bible conferences, YMCA meetings, and prophecy conferences, and in 1875 was one of the founders and president of an annual conference that eventually became known as the Niagara Bible Conference.

Throughout his life Brookes was in influential leader, pastor, and Bible teacher. Through his efforts, premillennialism and dispensationalism were widely disseminated across denominational boundaries within conservative Protestantism. His most visible disciple was C. I. Scofield, later editor of the *Scofield Reference Bible*, to whom Brookes introduced dispensationalism and through whom he had his greatest influence. Brookes died on Easter morning, April 18, 1897, leaving a written and pastoral legacy of compassion, dedication, and proclamation.

Eschatology

Brookes was one of the first prominent ministers in the United States to teach the pretribulational rapture. One of the most significant and fervent students of prophecy of his era, he can rightly be considered the father of American pretribulationism. In an 1896 article in *The Truth*, "How I Became a Premillennialist," Brookes claimed that he came to his premillennial eschatology through his own reading and study of Revelation and Daniel after entering the pastorate and after many years of the neglect of prophecy. This independent study, along with some influence in the years after the Civil War from Plymouth Brethren, provided the historical background for his beliefs. Brookes denied that he was the direct recipient of Plymouth Brethren eschatology, although he did acknowledge an appreciation of their eschatological enthusiasm. As early as 1871, Brookes was publishing and teaching views similar to dispensationalism. By 1874 his system was well developed.

Well versed in the eschatological options within premillennialism, Brookes argued against both a partial rapture theory and posttribulationism. He refused to set dates for the Rapture and held to a strong doctrine of the Lord's return and imminence. He was very much aware of the charge by uninformed critics that dispensationalists taught more than one way of salvation and adamantly rebutted it in writing. "It is needless to remind any ordinary reader of the sacred Scriptures that from the opening verses of Genesis, down to Malachi, the Spirit is brought into view in creation, providence, and redemption, and that all who are saved were quickened into life through His divine power and grace, as they are now" (*Israel and the Church*, 38).

Timothy Demy

James H. Brookes, *Israel and the Church* (New York: Revell, n.d.) and *Maranatha* (New York: Revell, 1889); Larry Dean Pettegrew, "The Historical and Theological Contributions of the Niagara Bible Conference to American Fundamentalism" (Th.D. diss., Dallas Theological Seminary, 1976); Harry S. Stout, *Dictionary of Christianity in America* (Downers Grove, Ill.: InterVarsity Press, 1990); David Riddle Williams, *James H. Brookes: A Memoir* (St. Louis: Presbyterian Board of Publication, 1897).

BULLINGER, E. W.

Ethelbert William Bullinger (1837–1913) was born on December 15 in Canterbury, England. He was a direct descendent of Johann Heinrich Bullinger, a covenant theologian who succeeded Zwingli in Zurich in December of 1531.

Educated at King's College, London, he was a recognized scholar in the field of biblical languages. The Archbishop of Canterbury granted him an honorary Doctor of Divinity degree in 1881 in recognition of his biblical scholarship.

Dr. Bullinger believed in and taught the pretribulation, premillennial rapture. He was also considered an ultradispensationalist because "he taught that the gospels and Acts were under the dispensation of law, with the church actually beginning at Paul's ministry after Acts 28:28" (Enns). He held a heretical view of the extinction of the soul between death and the resurrection. Many of his admirers were annihilationists.

Some of his best known works are his *Commentary on Revelation*, *Word Studies on the Holy Spirit*, *The Witness of the Stars*, *The Book of Job*, *Figures of Speech Used in the Bible*, *Great Cloud of Witnesses*, *The Critical Lexicon and Concordance to the English and Greek New Testaments*, and *The Companion Bible*.

Dr. Bullinger died on June 6, 1913, in London, England.

Brian K. Richards

E. W. Bullinger, *Commentary on Revelation* (Grand Rapids: Kregel, 1984) and *Great Cloud of Witnesses* (Grand Rapids: Kregel, 1979); P. Enns, *The Moody Handbook of Theology* (Chicago: Moody Press, 1989).

BULTEMA, HARRY

Harry Bultema (1884–1952) was born in Holland and was one of six siblings who came to America in the early 1900s. He was raised and nurtured by devout parents. In the U.S. he studied at Calvin College and Calvin Seminary in Grand Rapids, Michigan. After graduation he pastored Christian Reformed churches in Illinois, Iowa, and Michigan. Through his own intense study of the Bible, he concluded that there is a major difference between Christ as coming King over Israel and Jesus as present Head of the church. These newly discovered truths resulted in his becoming a premillennial dispensationalist and leaving the Christian Reformed denomination. His writings in English include *Commentary on Isaiah, Commentary on Daniel,* and *Maranatha!*

All of his works are from his premillennial and pretribulational viewpoint. In his commentary on Isaiah, Bultema writes: "Christ, as the true theocratic King, shall reign over restored Israel and the entire earth. He will rule from Mount Zion and Jerusalem in the presence of His ancients in glory." Elsewhere he writes: "In all of Scripture there is not a semblance or shadow of justification for the identification of Israel as a nation with the church as the body of Christ. In the New Testament the word Israel appears seventy times, but it must always be taken in its literal historical meaning."

Mal Couch

Harry Bultema, *Commentary on Isaiah* (Grand Rapids: Kregel, 1981).

C

CHAFER, LEWIS SPERRY

Lewis Sperry Chafer (1871–1952) was a well-known American premilleniarian, dispensationalist, founder of Dallas Theological Seminary, writer, and conference speaker. Chafer was born in Rock Creek, Ohio, the second of three children born to a graduate of Auburn Theological Seminary, a Presbyterian/Congregational institution in New York. His father, Thomas Franklin Chafer, was a Congregational pastor, and Thomas and his wife, Lomira Sperry Chafer, were devoted, caring parents.

Thomas Chafer's battle with tuberculosis, however, brought a constant strain to the family as pastorates were chosen with the hope that a more beneficial climate would assuage the disease. The battle was lost in 1882. Aside from the pain and loss of his father, which brought severe sadness and uncertainty into an otherwise music-filled, joyful home, two important events occurred that would shape the young man's life. First, though rarely mentioned, he was converted to Christ under the tutelage of his parents at the age of six during his father's first pastoral charge in Rock Creek; and, second, in the context of his father's death he heard an evangelist named Scott, who was suffering with tuberculosis also, who challenged him to a career in Christian service.

Facing financial uncertainty, Lomira, a school teacher in the Rock Creek schools, determined to provide for the family. When the eldest, Rollin Thomas Chafer, finished elementary school, she moved the family to South New Lyme, Ohio, where the children entered the New Lyme Institute, a preparatory school under Jacob Tuckerman, the man who has been instrumental in their father's conversion at Farmer's College in Cincinnati. Then the family moved to Oberlin, Ohio, where Lomira managed a boarding house so that the children could attend college. Initially, Lewis entered the preparatory school attached to the college (1889) and then the Conservatory of Music of Oberlin College. He studied music in the conservatory for three semesters, fall and spring 1889–90 and the spring of 1891. There are no indications that Chafer took religious studies at Oberlin College or elsewhere.

Financial constraints prevented further study. Beginning in the fall of 1889, he associated with A. T. Reed, an evangelist under the auspices of the Congregational Church in Ohio, as a baritone soloist and choir organizer in the meetings. During these years he gained enormous insight into the work of the traveling evangelist. In 1896, he married Ella Lorraine Case, whom he had met at Oberlin College, and the two formed an evangelistic team (Lewis preaching and singing with Lorraine playing the organ). They briefly settled in Painesville, Ohio, where they served as directors of the music program of the Congregational church though they continued to travel, often with other evangelists such as Wilbur Chapman and A. T. Reed.

In 1889 Lewis became the interim pastor of the First Presbyterian Church of Lewiston, New York, although in the fall of the year he began a two-year ministry as an assistant pastor in the First Congregational Church of Buffalo. The initial year appears to have been an apprenticeship with a view to his formal ordination as a minister in the Congregational community, which took place in April 1900.

The circumstances of Chafer's move to Northfield, Massachusetts, in 1901 are not at all clear. It is reasonable to assume that he became increasingly well known within evangelical circles through his ministerial gifts and within the Congregational ranks by his ordination and pastoral associations. Residing at Northfield, where he operated a farm and his wife served as organist at the annual conferences, Chafer continued to travel in evangelistic endeavors, particularly in the winter months. In 1904 the Southland Bible Conference was inaugurated in Florida, a counterpart of the Northfield conferences; Chafer was president of the conference after 1909. Through the Northfield conferences, the Chafers met an array of prominent evangelicals from both sides of the Atlantic, among them G. Campbell Morgan, F. B. Meyer, A. C. Gaebelein, James M. Gray, and W. H. Griffith Thomas.

By far, however, the most important contact was with Cyrus Ingerson Scofield, then pastor of the Trinitarian Congregational Church, Moody's church, in Northfield. Chafer found in Scofield a clear, biblically oriented teacher, and the two were thereafter bound together in ministry for two decades. Scofield lead the younger Chafer into his particular understanding of the Scriptures, as well as into a change of careers. No longer an itinerant evangelist, Chafer progressively joined his mentor as a traveling Bible teacher, increasingly becoming a central participant in the Bible conference movement. Gradually, through enlarged exposure in the major Bible and prophetic conferences, the publication of books and articles, and teaching in short-term Bible institutes, Chafer emerged in the early 1900s as a quiet, energetic leader of one segment of the emerging evangelical movement.

From 1906 to 1910, he taught at the Mount Hermon School for Boys, instructing in Bible and music (his first published book was *Elementary Outline Studies in the Science of Music*, 1907). In 1906, he left the Congregational community to join the Troy Presbytery, Synod of New York, Presbyterian Church (U.S.A.), reflecting his discomfort with liberalizing trends in the denomination and Scofield's ecclesiastical sympathies. In these years, he published two additional books, *Satan* (1909, Scofield wrote the foreword) and *True Evangelism* (1911).

His close identification with Scofield increased in the second decade of the century as Chafer moved to East Orange, New Jersey, to join the staff of the New York School of the Bible, an agency that distributed Scofield's increasingly popular Bible correspondence course, written in 1892, and an office for the coordination of conference activities. As a member of the "oral extension department" of the "school," Chafer began a rather extensive traveling conference ministry throughout the South.

In 1913, he assisted Scofield in founding the Philadelphia School of the Bible, apparently writing the curriculum. Due to his growing southern ministry, Chafer joined the Orange Presbytery of the Presbyterian Church (U.S.A.) in 1912. In 1915, he published *The Kingdom in History and Prophecy*, a work endorsed by Scofield and dedicated to Chafer's father. It was a defense of pretribulational, dispensational premillennialism. Several other works followed: *Salvation* (1917), *He That Is Spiritual* (1918), *Seven Major Biblical Signs of the Times* (1919), and *Must We Dismiss The Millennium?* (1921).

Scofield's declining health, resulting in increasingly limited itinerant ministry, brought another shift in the sphere and nature of Chafer's work. Moving to Dallas, Texas, in 1922, he became pastor of the First Congregational Church, which had been founded in 1882 by Scofield (it was renamed Scofield Memorial Church in his honor during Chafer's pastorate in 1923); Chafer pastored the church from 1922 to 1926 in addition to increased conference speaking. Further, he became general secretary of the Central American Mission, a missionary society founded by Scofield in 1890. He transferred his ministerial credentials to the Dallas Presbytery of the Presbyterian Church (U.S.A.) in 1923.

During this period, Chafer founded the Dallas Theological Seminary (originally, the Evangelical Theological College) in 1924, serving as its president as well as professor of systematic theology from its inception until his death in 1952. Though he resigned from both the church and the mission, he continued a rigorous conference ministry; his publications mushroomed. In addition to regularly contributing to evangelical periodicals, he wrote *Grace* (1922) and *Major Bible Themes* (1926). After the seminary acquired *Bibliotheca Sacra* in 1933, a journal with roots in the early nineteenth century, Chafer wrote numerous articles that, combined with portions of his books, were published as his largest work, *Systematic Theology* (1948). The advanced age, the burden of carrying on a school without secure financing, the growing turmoil over Scofieldian dispensationalism in his own Presbyterian church, and the death of his wife in 1944 were factors that progressively limited his public ministry. After 1945, the operations of the school devolved to his executive assistant, John F. Walvoord. Chafer died due to heart failure while on a conference tour in Seattle, Washington, in August 1952.

Chafer's contribution and lasting legacy to American evangelicalism in the twentieth century was enormous; he stands with his mentor, C. I. Scofield, as well as his successors, John F. Walvoord and Charles Ryrie, as a proponent of the Bible conference movement's distinctives from the late nineteenth century, which emerged as an integral and influential subsegment of twentieth-century evangelicalism, the premillennial dispensational camp. In essence, Chafer's con tribution to the ongoing life of the church can be seen as the broadening and deepening of the Bible conference movement. This can be illustrated through both his institutional and theological contributions.

Institutionally, Chafer's legacy is the creation of Dallas Theological Seminary in 1924; it represented an extension of the Bible-conference emphases at the postgraduate level of education, just as the Bible institutes extended them at the undergraduate level. Chafer's vision for a ministerial school began with his contact with students at the Mount Hermon School for Boys. His travels under Scofield's auspices lead to contact with numerous pastors (whom he consulted about the deficiencies of their formal ministerial training), denominational colleges, and seminaries, particularly throughout the South. He came to believe that the unique emphases of the Bible conference movement—intensive English Bible instruction, dispensational premillennialism, and the victorious Christian life teachings—were the additional ingredients, when added to an otherwise standard seminary curriculum, that could adequately prepare Christian missionaries and pastors—a combination of ingredients he described as "a new departure" in ministerial training. The stress on the English Bible provided the content of the minister's preaching; dispensational premillennialism was the intellectual grid for interpreting the Bible; a mild Keswick holiness emphasis on two works of grace in the believer's life (as well as the distinction between obedient and fleshly Christians as spiritual states) provided the ground for a right relationship to the Holy Spirit, the source of power in ministry.

The goal of the institution—to place men into the mainline churches after training in an independent school—proved illusive, however. Though the school was deeply influenced by Presbyterianism—Chafer and Scofield were both ordained in the Presbyterian Church (U.S.A.) as were most of the early faculty—the distinctive ideas of the Bible conference movement were not accepted by many Presbyterian leaders or by other mainline denominations as useful preparation for the ministry. They increasingly viewed the emphases as antithetical to historic Presbyterianism. In the 1930s and 40s, Presbyterians in the North and South became openly hostile to dispensationalism. As a result, graduates of the seminary found placement in the mainline churches difficult.

At the same time, numerous denominational splinter groups, independent churches, and para-ecclesiastical organizations (Chafer supported many of them) were emerging in the country. The seminary became the major graduate-level source for their leaders. Thus, the distinctives of the Bible conference movement were carried into this emerging evangelical submovement of the American church.

In addition to institutionalizing the Bible conference movement, Chafer systematized its unique theological emphases with the publication of his *Systematic Theology* (8 vols.)

in 1948, the first major attempt to set forth the teaching of dispensational premillennialism within the rubric of traditional systematics. What Scofield's notes delineated in a dispensational approach to the Bible, Chafer's theology book simply enlarged. The work reflects Chafer's attachment to Scofield and the notes of the *Scofield Reference Bible* (1909, 1917). The work became the definitive statement of dispensational theology.

Chafer's theology, and subsequently that of the seminary's, reflects his attachment to three somewhat diverse traditions within historic orthodoxy: Augustinianism, Keswick theology, and (Plymouth) Brethrenism. From the first source, Chafer's systematics is Reformed or Calvinistic in anthropology and soteriology (i.e., the doctrines of election, predestination, humanity's plight, and the origin and cause of Christ's redemptive mercies). It reflects his adherence to Presbyterian confessionalism, although he deviated from the tradition by advocating an unlimited view of the intent of Christ's sacrifice. It is profoundly Princetonian (i.e., Warfieldian inerrancy) in its delineation of the doctrine of the Scriptures.

In the second, Chafer's understanding of the spiritual life, as put forth in *He That Is Spiritual*, reflects a view that Warfield opposed. It was essentially a counteractivist understanding of the relationship of the Spirit and the believer relative to the duty of spiritual progress (i.e., a stress on the believer's duty to be rightly related to the Spirit as the cause of growth), rather than the more traditionally Reformed emphasis on suppressionism by the Holy Spirit (a stress on the activity of God as the cause of the believer's sanctification).

Finally, reflecting the influence of the Brethren movement, which made significant inroads into American evangelicalism in the late nineteenth century through the emerging Bible conference movement, Chafer embraced the teachings of dispensationalism, modern premillennialism, and pretribulational eschatology.

Chafer's third major legacy, and arguably the primary one, was his emphasis on the centrality of Christ and the grace of God; the preeminence of Christ and Calvary was the very heart of Chafer's religious passion. In this Chafer stands without question in the orthodox tradition of the church. Chafer was at heart a heralder of the Gospel, and the motto of the seminary he founded reflects this emphasis: "Preach the Word" (2 Tim. 2:2). To effect this mission, he felt that one had to know the Bible with intensity and affection, which implied a correct understanding of its overall purposes (i.e., dispensational premillennialism), and one must be in a correct relationship to the Holy Spirit (i.e., sanctified). This is clearly seen in his career; he was involved in itinerant evangelism for over a decade, and out of that experience he published a criticism of the errors he found in it (*True Evangelism*), causing quite a stir among his contemporaries in the field. Two works devoted to the theme of the Gospel followed: *Salvation* and *Grace* as well as briefer statements in other works, *Major Bible Themes* and *Systematic Theology*.

It can be argued that the centrality of Christ in Chafer's understanding of the unfolding plan of redemption in the Bible is why he seemed to denigrate the revelation of God in the Old Testament. The superior light of the revelation of God in Christ caused a shadow of insignificance to fall over the less clear revelation of Him in the Old Testament. This created in his mind, as Scofield had seen before him, a discontinuity between the two testaments that became a defining characteristic in his understanding of the Bible.

See also SCOFIELD, C. I.; WALVOORD, JOHN; RYRIE, CHARLES.

John D. Hannah

John D. Hannah, "The Intellectual and Social Origins of the Evangelical Theological College" (Ph.D. diss., University of Texas at Dallas, 1988).

CHRONICLES, 1 & 2, ESCHATOLOGY OF

First and 2 Chronicles were originally one book. The Hebrew title means "The words (events, affairs) of the Days." The books were probably completed between 450 and 425 B.C. The author was most likely Ezra, although the author is not stated by name in the Bible.

> "Chronicles was written to provide a spiritual perspective on the historical events from the time of David to Cyrus' degree in 538 B.C. It traces Israel's lineage back to the dawn of the human race and forward to the end of the Babylonian captivity to reveal God's faithfulness and continuing purpose for His people" (Wilkinson).

The first nine chapters of 1 Chronicles deals with the royal line of David, while chapters 10 thru 29 discuss the reign of David.

> "Pivotal for the book of First Chronicles as well as for the rest of the Scriptures is the Davidic covenant recorded in Second Samuel 7 and First Chronicles 17. God promised David that He will establish him (David's ultimate offspring, Jesus Christ) in My house and in My Kingdom forever; and his throne shall be established forever (1 Chron. 17:14)" (Wilkinson).

This prophecy awaits fulfillment in the future millennial kingdom which will take place after Jesus Christ's second advent.

Second Chronicles continues by recording the reign of King Solomon (chap. 1–9) and the reign of the kings of Judah from Rehoboam through Zedekiah (chap. 10–36). Second Chronicles covers the same time period as 1 and 2 Kings.

See also DAVIDIC COVENANT.

Brian K. Richards

Charles C. Ryrie, *Ryrie Study Bible,* expanded ed. (Chicago: Moody Press, 1995); B. Wilkinson and K. Boa, *Talk Thru The Bible,* (Nashville: Thomas Nelson, 1983).

COLOSSIANS, ESCHATOLOGY OF

In the context of motivating his readers to seek and to set their affections (minds) on things above, Paul's ultimate motivation is the believer's manifestation with Christ at His coming.

The Believer's Manifestation with Christ in Glory (Col. 3:4)

Paul has already explained that here in this life the believer is *hidden* with Christ in God (v. 3). Concerning the perfect tense of the verb, Gromacki states "hidden, [is] the resultant state of safety and secrecy which a believer presently possesses because he trusted Christ as Savior in the past" (v. 3).

However, when Christ shall appear at the Rapture, He who is the believer's very life will be manifested when the Father will "make visible what is invisible" (*phanerothei*). Kent says: "Christ's return will reveal Him and His followers 'in glory' . . . the essence of this glory in which Christians will be displayed is the glory of Christ Himself, which they will reflect without the sinful defilements which now mar that reflection."

The Believer's Inheritance (Col. 3:22–24)

In the context of Christ within the life of the Christian (1:27), relating to the believer's home and workplace, Paul again motivates his readers to obey completely and work heartily day by day, knowing that from the Lord they "shall receive the reward of the inheritance"; for they "serve the Lord Christ" (v. 24).

The believer is promised an inheritance, unlike the slave of that day, not only because he or she is an heir of God and joint heir with Jesus Christ (Rom. 8:17), but also because, as Gromacki so simply states, "faithful service will receive a divine reward."

Work done in the spirit of this context will receive God's "Well done, thou good and faithful servant," at the judgment seat of Christ in heaven.

Alden Gannett

Robert G. Gromacki, *Stand Perfect in Wisdom: An Exposition of Colossians and Philemon* (Grand Rapids: Baker, 1981); Homer A. Kent Jr., *Treasures of Wisdom: Studies in Colossians and Philemon* (Grand Rapids: Baker, 1978).

CORINTHIANS, 1 & 2, ESCHATOLOGY OF

First Corinthians

The first letter to the church at Corinth was written in response to a letter asking about marriage and about the use of foods that had been sacrificed to idols (7:1–8:13). In answering these questions the apostle also dealt with the deepening divisions, contentions, and the sin in the church that had not been dealt with. The letter expresses deep concern over the unspiritual and immoral condition of the church. The overall theme of the letter is that of Christian conduct. Attestation of authorship is made in 1:1, 3:4, 16:21. He wrote from Ephesus about A.D. 56.

The book contains several important prophecies. The believers in Christ are assured that they will be blameless before Him when He comes, a reference to the Rapture (1:8–9). The believer has a future judgment before Christ at the bema seat where Christians' works are tested by fire (3:10–15). Again the judgment seat of Christ is seen as the place where all sin will be revealed and praises bestowed upon the faithful (4:5). The Great White Throne judgment is where the unrighteous will be judged for their immorality (6:9–10). The persevering saints will receive their rewards at the judgment seat of Christ (9:24–27). The resurrection of believers is based upon Christ's resurrection and thus ought to be their motive for faithful service (15:12–20). The end of the millennium and the final judgment of the wicked and the destruction of all rule and power is when Christ returns the kingdom to the Father (15:24). The believers' guarantee of receiving new immortal and imperishable bodies is seen at their resurrection, the Rapture, (15:35–50). Then finally the mystery of the Rapture is explained (15:51–52).

Second Corinthians

Paul wrote his second letter to the Corinthians in A.D. 57, soon after the first letter. This epistle focuses on dispelling the lack of trust that had risen against Paul. Paul's purpose was to authenticate his apostolic authority and to reveal his spiritual burden for the church.

The prophecies in this letter are concerned with the Rapture and the judgment seat of Christ. Paul tells these believers that at the judgment seat of Christ, bema seat, that both they and Paul will commend each other before the Lord (1:14). The promise is given that believers will receive heavenly bodies at the Rapture (5:1–9). Last is the prophecy that the believers will be rewarded at the judgment seat of Christ based on what they have done in service to Him (5:10).

See also JUDGMENTS, VARIOUS; RESURRECTIONS, VARIOUS.

Ervin R. Starwalt

John F. Walvoord, *The Prophecy Knowledge Handbook* (Wheaton: Victor Books, 1990); John F. Walvoord and Roy B. Zuck, eds., *The Bible Knowledge Commentary* (Wheaton: Victor Books, 1985); Charles F. Pfeiffer and Everett F. Harrison, eds.,*Wycliffe Bible Commentary* (Chicago: Moody Press, 1962).

COVENANTS, THE

A covenant is an agreement between two parties and represents relationships formed between God and man, man and man, or nation and nation. Scripture identifies two kinds of covenants, conditional and unconditional. A conditional covenant is binding on both parties for its fulfillment, that is, the response of the one making the covenant is conditioned by the response of the party with whom the covenant was made. Conversely, an unconditional covenant is only binding on the one who makes the covenant, although certain blessings attached to the unconditional covenant may require some response from the party with which the covenant was made in order for that party to receive the blessing. There are four characteristics that must be noticed concerning the nature of the covenants: (1) they are literal, (2) they are eternal, (3) they depend entirely on the integrity of God, and (4) they were made with a covenant people, Israel.

Before identifying the biblical covenants, there are three theological covenants that must be identified. These are held by the covenant theologian, who views the ages of history as the progressive fulfillment of the covenant God made with sinners in which all who would come to Him by faith would be saved. These covenants are:

1. The covenant of redemption (Titus 1:2; Heb. 13:20), into which the members of the Godhead entered before time, and in which each member assumed that part of the plan of redemption that is their present position as set forth in the Word of God. This covenant is supported primarily by the fact that it seems reasonable and inevitable.

2. The covenant of works designates certain blessings from God conditioned upon human merit. It has its origins in amillennial theology.

3. The covenant of grace is understood to indicate all aspects of divine grace toward humankind through all ages. The first of these covenants, redemption, has weak scriptural support, while the remaining two have none. They are based primarily on human reason with little or no regard for scriptural support.

There are six biblical covenants, of which only one, the Mosaic, is conditional. The remaining are unconditional, meaning that God will fulfill them sovereignly at some future point in history.

1. The Noahic Covenant (Gen. 9:1–18). This is a perpetual agreement made with Noah in which God promises to never again destroy the earth by a flood. It is unconditional.

2. The Mosaic Covenant (Exod. 20:1–31:18). The fulfillment of this conditional covenant is based on human obedience and faithfulness to God. This covenant was broken almost immediately after it was made (Exod. 32:15–29).

3. The Abrahamic Covenant (Gen. 12:1–15:17). This unconditional covenant is progressive in its fulfillment and consists of three parts, or subcovenants, the Palestinian, the Davidic, and the new. These three subcovenants contain the prophecies concerning the land, the seed, and the future blessings to Abraham and his seed.

4. The Palestinian Covenant (Deut. 28–30). This covenant guarantees that Israel will possess the Promised Land. It is unconditional.

5. The Davidic Covenant (2 Sam. 7:4–16; 1 Chron. 17:3–15). This unconditional covenant promises that David's throne, lineage, and kingdom will be eternal. It assures the millennial kingdom in which Christ will reign on the earth.

6. The New Covenant (Jer. 31:31–33). Many older dispensationalists taught that there were two new covenants, one for Israel in the kingdom and one for the church. This unconditional covenant has its ultimate fulfillment in the millennial kingdom. The covenant is made first with the nation of Israel (31:31) and would replace the Mosaic covenant which the nation of Israel broke and could not fulfill (31:32). At the Passover meal with His disciples, Jesus tells the reason or His coming sacrifice: "This cup which is poured out for you the new covenant in My blood: (Matt. 22:20). At Pentecost the new covenant was initiated and launched by the coming of the Holy Spirit. The sacrifice of Christ now benefits believers in the present dispensation of the church. Also, the apostle Paul, in 2 Corinthians 3:5–9, compares the new covenant with the covenant of Law and writes, "God, who also made us adequate as servants of a new covenant, not of the letter, but of the Spirit; for the letter kills, but the Spirit gives life. But if the ministry of death, in letters engraved on stones [the Mosaic law], came with glory, . . . how shall the ministry of the Spirit [the new covenant] fail to be even more with glory? For if the ministry of condemnation [the Mosaic law] has glory, much more does the ministry of righteousness [the new covenant] abound in glory."

Because both Israel in the kingdom, and presently the church as well, benefits from the new covenant, this in no way mixes together the church and the kingdom. They constitute two different dispensastins. And in both dispensations people are saved by faith, as was true in all other periods of history.

See also ABRAHAMIC COVENANT; DAVIDIC COVENANT.

Rick Bowman

Lewis Sperry Chafer, *Major Bible Themes* (Grand Rapids: Zondervan, 1974) and *Systematic Theology,* vol. 1 (Grand Rapids: Kregel, 1993); Paul Enns, *The Moody Handbook of Theology* (Chicago: Moody Press, 1989).

CRAVEN, E. R.

Elijah Richardson Craven (1824–1908) was one of the many northern Presbyterian pastors who spearheaded a shift from postmillennialism to premillennialism among evangelicals between the Civil War and World War I.

Craven received his B.A. in 1842 at College of New Jersey (Princeton) and then finished Princeton Seminary in 1848, but not before studying law (1842–44). He served as a math tutor at the College of New Jersey (1847–49). He first pastored the Dutch Reformed church at Somerville, New Jersey (1850–54), before settling in as the longtime pastor of the Third Presbyterian Church in Newark (1854–87). He then served as secretary of the Presbyterian Board of Publication and Sabbath School Word (1887–1904), from which he retired as secretary emeritus.

He served in a number of important denomination positions during his ministry. He was chairman of the committee for the revision of the Book of Discipline of the Presbyterian Church (1879–82) and moderator of the General Assembly of the Presbyterian Church North in 1885.

Craven, as did almost all Presbyterian premillennialists of his era, worked hard to fight the rising tide of liberalism that eventually gained ascendancy in his denomination. He was old school in his theology, which likely contributed to his conversion to premillennialism.

He was a speaker at many of the prophecy conferences that were convened during the last quarter of the nineteenth century. Craven delivered a spirited address at the famous 1878 prophetic conference in New York City, entitled "The Coming of the Lord in its Relations to Christian Doctrine." His greatest work accomplished on behalf of premillennialism was as the American editor who enlarged Lange's commentary on the book of Revelation. In this work, Dr. Craven supplied many helpful comments and excursuses that reflect a strong, uncompromising premillennialism.

"Excursus on the Basilea" is a helpful explanation on the futurity of the kingdom. Craven defends the view that while the messianic kingdom was near at Christ's first coming, it did not actually arrive since Christ returned to heaven without establishing it on earth. Thus, it is future and will be set up at Christ's premillennial advent.

Craven's excursus is also well known for his employment of the term *normal* as he sought to describe and defend literal interpretation as opposed to the spiritual method often used to interpret prophetic literature.

Craven, along with James H. Brookes and Nathaniel West, were late-nineteenth-century premillennial leaders within the Presbyterian Church and evangelicalism at large. It is largely due to their work that premillennialism became synonymous with evangelicalism.

Thomas Ice

E. R. Craven, "The Coming of the Lord in Its Relations to Christian Doctrine" in *Premillennial Essays,* ed. Nathaniel West (Chicago: Revell, 1879) and "The Revelation of John" in *Lange's Commentary on the Holy Scriptures*, vol. 12 (Grand Rapids: Zondervan, 1960); Samuel M. Jackson, ed., *The New Schaff-Herzog Encyclopedia of Religious Knowledge*, vol. 3 (Grand Rapids: Baker, 1952).

D

DANIEL'S SEVENTY WEEKS, AMILLENNIAL INTERPRETATION

The historical and theological developments that produced the amillennial interpretation of Daniel's seventy-weeks prophecy (Dan. 9:24–27) were the result of direct opposition to premillennialism, which was considered Judaistic. The New Testament, early Jewish-Christian, and patristic evidence supports premillennialism as the dominant eschatological view until the third century A.D. In the controversy over chiliasm, the hermeneutic of the Alexandrian school (followed by Augustine and consequently the Roman Catholic Church, the Protestant Reformed churches, and modern amillennialism) was a nonliteral, allegorical hermeneutic. It was applied to the seventy- weeks prophecy to prove the political and spiritual program for the Jewish people had ended with the first advent of Christ and had been replaced by the church. While adopting an historicist approach, the amillennialists' spiritual hermeneutic permits only a subjective application of events, which in turn invites a broad spectrum of interpretation. This is particularly problematic for their interpretation of the Seventieth Week in which the events do not fit any known history.

For the amillennialist, the focus of the seventy-weeks passage is wholly Christological (see TRIBULATION, VARIOUS VIEWS). The six infinitives of Daniel 9:24 that form the purpose of the prophecy and establish its *terminus ad quem* (conclusion), are viewed as completed by Christ. The traditional school of amillennialism sees this completion having taken place in the Seventieth Week, which followed consecutively (and historically) after the sixty-nine weeks. Christological fulfillment occurred in the ministry of Christ or, at the latest, the time of the first preaching of the Gospel to the Gentiles (i.e., Pentecost). The symbolic school, however, extends final fulfillment to an indefinite period, which includes the Second Advent and the eternal state. In this case, the six statements represent the successive stages in the history of Christ's kingdom. In like manner, the last of the six prophetic goals, "to anoint the most holy [one]," is taken either as Christ's own anointing by the Spirit (traditional school), or the eschatological anointing of the new Holy of Holies (Christ) in the New [heavenly] Jerusalem (symbolic school). While some amillennialists follow premillennialists in attempting to determine historical dates for the *terminus a quo* (commencement) and *terminus ad quem* (conclusion) of the 490 years (v. 25), other amillennialists concluded that the figure of 490 is only symbolic (70 x 7).

Amillennialists and premillennialists agree on the messianic interpretation of the anointed prince (v. 25) as Jesus the Messiah; however, the reference to his being cut off and having nothing (v. 26) is variously interpreted to apply to Jesus' death (traditional school) or Jesus' influence and prestige as Messiah (symbolic school). Most in the traditional school support their interpretation that Messiah was cut off in the middle of the Seventieth Week by identifying the prince who is to come (v. 26) with the one whose activity is described (the "he" of v. 27) as occurring in the middle of the week, with Christ. On this basis, the firm covenant that this prince makes with the many is interpreted as the new covenant (Jer. 31:31–37) that Christ made with the church. In this view the city and the sanctuary are interpreted literally as Jerusalem and the temple, while the destruction wrought by the prince is applied nonliterally to Christ's pronouncements of destruction. However, while E. J. Young agrees that the "he" of verse 27 refers to Christ, he identifies the prince that shall come with Titus, the commander of the Roman forces in A.D. 68–70, who destroyed Jerusalem. In a dramatic departure from the traditional school, the symbolic school approximates the view of premillennialism and identifies the prince that shall come with the Antichrist and the firm covenant as one made in imitation of Christ and imposed on the masses (H. C. Leupold) or made to deceive people to follow him as God (C. F. Keil), but in any case it is a covenant of terror and violence.

The difficulty with interpreting Christ's being cut off in the middle of the Seventieth Week is present again in the problem of resolving the statement of cessation of sacrifice and oblation as having occurred at this time. Recognizing that these sacrifices did not immediately stop with the death of Christ, but continued another forty years, amillennialists apply the meaning spiritually to either the rending of the veil in the temple or the beginning of the preaching of the Gospel, both of which (in their view) delegitimized the sacrificial system. Thus, according to Young, at Christ's death Jerusalem "ceased to be a holy city" and its temple was "no longer the house of God, but an abomination," while the actual destruction of both was "but the outward manifestation of what had already been put into effect by our Lord's death." The New Testament, however, depicts a continued reverence for Jerusalem during the apostolic period as the center for the mother church (Acts 1:8; 15; Gal. 1:18–2:2) and the temple as a place for Christian meeting (Acts 2:46; 3:1; 5:12–13), ritual festival observance (Acts 2:1; 20:6), and even worship (Acts 18:18; 21:23–26; 22:17; 24:11, 17–18). Amillennialists generally conclude that while the *terminus ad quem* of the sixty-nine weeks is Christ, the *terminus ad quem* of the seventy weeks is unstated in the text. However, the destruction of the desolator at the conclusion of verse 27 is stated as the event that terminates the desolations of the last half of the Seventieth Week, apparently concluding the week itself. Again, the amillennial interpretation has difficulty reconciling this event with historical events. For this reason, Young (traditional school) advises against an emphasis on dates, while Leupold (symbolic school) abandons any historic fulfillment to the Seventieth Week.

See also AMILLENNIALISM.

J. Randall Price

Oswalt T. Allis, *Prophecy and the Church* (Philadelphia: Presbyterian and Reformed Publishing Co., 1949); Charles L. Feinberg, *Premillennialism or Amillennialism?* (Wheaton: Van Kampen Press, 1954); Michael Kalafian, *The Prophecy of the Seventy Weeks of the Book of Daniel: A Critical Review of the Prophecy as Viewed by Three Major Theological Interpretations and the Impact of the Book of Daniel on Christology* (New York: University of America Press, 1991), 107–36; C. F. Keil, *Biblical Commentary on the Book of Daniel*, trans. M. G. Easton in *A Commentary on the Old Testament,* 10 vols. (Grand Rapids: Eerdmans, 1973), 9:336–402; Abraham Kuyper, *Chiliasm or the Doctrine of Premillennialism* (Grand Rapids: Zondervan, 1934); H. C. Leupold, *Exposition of Daniel* (Grand Rapids: Baker, 1949), 403–40; Philip Mauro, *The Seventy Weeks and the Great Tribulation*, revised ed. (Swengel, Pa.: Reiner Publications, n.d.); J. Barton Payne, *Encyclopedia of Biblical Prophecy* (New York: Harper & Row, 1973), 383–88; John F. Walvoord, *The Millennial Kingdom* (Findlay, Ohio: Dunham, 1959); Edward J. Young, *The Prophecies of Daniel: A Commentary* (Grand Rapids: Eerdmans, 1949), 191–222 and *The Messianic Prophecies of Daniel* (Grand Rapids: Eerdmans, 1954).

DANIEL'S SEVENTY WEEKS, DISPENSATIONAL INTERPRETATION

Daniel's prophecy of the seventy weeks (Dan. 9:24–27) is part of the division of his book (chapters 7–12) that records visions of future earthly kingdoms (both human and divine). In chapter 7, the archangel Gabriel explains to Daniel that seventy weeks are required to fulfill the petition Daniel has made concerning the restoration of Israel (vv. 3–19). Daniel's prayer had been based on his observation (v. 2) of the seventy-years prophecy in Jeremiah 25:11–12; 29:10. Daniel is told of six restoration goals that will be accomplished during the seventy weeks (9:24), which the remainder of chapter 9 outlines in events to unfold in Israel's subsequent history. Dispensationalism joins with most Christian scholarship in holding that the seventy weeks are to be interpreted as seventy weeks of *years*. This resulting period of 490 years (70 x 7) is divided, according to the text (vv. 25–27), as periods of *seven* weeks (49 years), *sixty-two* weeks (434 years), and *one* week (7 years). Dispensationalism is also in agreement with most evangelical scholarship in interpreting the context of this passage as messianic, with the coming of Messiah taking place after the sixty-nine weeks (i.e., after the seven weeks + the sixty-two weeks = 483 years). However, dispensationalism (classical) is distinct in its interpretation of Daniel's Seventieth Week (v. 27) as future. With Israel's rejection of the Messiah and His death taking place after the sixty-ninth week (v. 26), the completion of the six restoration goals for Israel (v. 24) is left for the Seventieth Week. If the Seventieth Week immediately succeeds the sixty-ninth week historically, then the expected restoration must be applied spiritually to the church as a new Israel (see DANIEL'S SEVENTY WEEKS, AMILLENNIAL INTERPRETATION). Because dispensationalism adheres to the principle of literal interpretation and recognizes the scriptural distinction between God's program for Israel and for the church, it understands the historical completion of Israel's restoration must take place in a future week. During this time (as described in v. 27), there is a resumption of the messianic program for Israel with the overthrow of the Antichrist (the apocalyptic prerequisite to the establishment of the messianic kingdom).

This interpretation requires a prophetic postponement (older writers referred to this as a "gap" or "parenthesis") between the events of verses 26 and 27. The revelation of a prophetic postponement in the fulfillment of the eschatological aspect of the messianic program is in harmony with numerous passages in the Old Testament that reveal the two advents of Christ (e.g. Gen. 49:10–12; Deut. 18:16; 2 Sam. 7:13–16; Isa. 9:1–7; 11:1–2, 11; 52:13–59:21; 61:1–11, cf. Luke 4:16–19; 7:22; Joel 2:28, cf. Acts 2:17; Zeph. 2:13–3:20; Zech. 9:9–10; Mic. 5:2–15; Ps. 2:7–8, cf. Acts 13:33; Heb. 1:5; 5:5; Ps. 22:1–32; 34:14, 16; Mal. 3:1–3; 4:5–6; 53:10–11). Daniel's concern is with his people (vv. 20, 24; cf. 12:1) and the restoration that Jeremiah predicted would come after the seventy-year exile (Jer. 25:11–12; cf. 2 Chron. 36:21). Jeremiah's prophecy of restoration (Jer. 30–33), like the prophecies of Isaiah (Isa. 40–66) and Ezekiel (Ezek. 33–48), included predictions of both immediate (postexilic) restoration and future (eschatological) restoration. The postexilic prophets understood this distinction, realizing that though they were enjoying a restoration under Ezra, the complete national spiritual restoration had been delayed for the future. This is seen, for example, in one of the signal events of restoration—the rebuilding of the temple (Hag. 2:3–9).

The six restoration goals of Daniel's seventy-weeks prophecy (v. 24) may have a near fulfillment in the experience of the nation (Messiah's redemptive advent) but must wait for its complete fulfillment in the future (Messiah's restorative advent). The postponement understood between verses 26 and 27 is the consequence of partial and complete fulfillment in the messianic program. The first phase of the messianic program accomplished spiritual redemption for ethnic Israel in the First Advent (Matthew 1:21; cf. Luke 2:11). National rejection of Messiah (Matt. 23:37, cf. Acts 3:13–15, 17; 4:25–27), while fulfilling the promise of Gentile inclusion (Acts 15:14–18; Rom. 11:11, 25, 30), necessitated a second phase of the messianic program to apply spiritual redemption to Israel nationally (Acts 3:18–21; Rom. 11:26–29, 31) and complete the promise of national restoration (Matt. 23:39; Acts 1:6–7; 3:22–26; 15:16), which will be fulfilled at the Second Advent (Zech. 12:10–13:2; 14:3–11).

The dispensational view depends on the

validity of interpreting the Seventieth Week eschatologically. This is justified by the presence of numerous eschatological time markers, such as *qetz* (end), *yash^{e}bitim* (cause to cease), and *kalah* (end), *'ad* (until), and *nech^{e}ratzah tittak* (an appointed end). These terms indicate that this section belongs to the same eschatological period, qualified later in Daniel as the end time (cf. Daniel 12:4, 9, 13). This identification is enhanced by the parallel concepts in chapters 9 and 12 (e.g., prayer for understanding, 9:2/12:8; desolation of Jewish people, 9:27/12:7; three-and-one-half-year period, 9:27/12:7, 11; the abolition of sacrifice, 9:27/12:11; and the Abomination of Desolation, 9:27/12:11). Thus, Daniel's prayer for an end to exile will be fulfilled in the eschatological age when all of the elements of his petition will be realized.

Further confirmation of the postponement of the Seventieth Week and of a parenthetical period of history involving further exile and persecution for the Jewish people is supported by the New Testament's use of the seventy-weeks prophecy. John McLean has demonstrated that the sequence of events of the Olivet Discourse and the judgment section of the book of Revelation (chapters 4–19) reveal a structural dependence on the seventy-weeks prophecy.

See also DANIEL, ESCHATOLOGY OF.

J. Randall Price

Robert D. Culver, *Daniel and the Latter Days,* revised ed. (Chicago: Moody Press, 1977), 144–69; "Daniel" in *The Bible Knowledge Commentary*, John F. Walvoord, Roy B. Zuck, eds. (Wheaton: Victor Books, 1985), 1:1323–75; Paul D. Feinberg, "An Exegetical and Theological Study of Daniel 9:24–27" in *Tradition and Testament: Essays in Honor of Charles Lee Feinberg,* John S. Feinberg and Paul D. Feinberg, eds. (Chicago: Moody Press, 1981), 189–222; Frederick Holtzman, "A Re-examination of the Seventy Weeks of Daniel" (Th.M. thesis, Dallas Theological Seminary, Dallas, 1974); H. A. Ironside, *The Great Parenthesis* (Grand Rapids: Zondervan, 1943); William Kelly, *Daniel's Seventy Weeks* (Colorado: Wilson Foundation, n.d.); Alva J. McClain, "The Parenthesis of Time between the Sixty-Ninth and Seventieth Weeks" in *Daniel's Prophecy of the Seventy Weeks* (Grand Rapids: Zondervan, 1960); John A. McLean, "The Seventieth Week of Daniel 9:27 as a Literary Key for Understanding the Structure of the Apocalypse of John" (Ph.D. diss., University of Michigan, 1990); J. Dwight Pentecost, *Things to Come* (Grand Rapids: Zondervan, 1958); J. Randall Price, "Prophetic Postponement in Daniel 9 and Other Texts" in *Issues in Dispensationalism*, eds. W. R. Willis and John R. Master (Chicago: Moody Press, 1994), 132–65; John F. Walvoord, *Daniel: The Key to Prophetic Revelation* (Chicago: Moody Press, 1971), 403–40.

DANIEL'S SEVENTY WEEKS, RABBINIC INTERPRETATION

The seventy-weeks prophecy of Daniel 9:24–27 was originally regarded by the rabbis as one of the most important predictive texts in the Bible. This significance was testified to by the first-century Jewish historian Flavius Josephus: "He [Daniel] not only predicted the future, like the other prophets, but specified *when* the events would happen" (*Antiquities* 10.268). The belief that Daniel's prophecy provided information as to the precise time of predicted events was no doubt a significant factor in the timing of the war with Rome in A.D. 66, since the seventy years of wrath in Daniel 9:3, which figured prominently in the Qumran War Scroll (1QM), could have been interpreted as the period between the first outbreak of revolutionary activity in 4 B.C. (the time of Herod's death and possibly also of Jesus' birth) and the final uprising in A.D. 66.

However, in the earliest versions of the present Hebrew Bible, the book of Daniel was placed in the division known as the Writings. This placement removed Daniel from the ranks of the prophets and reduced his prophecies to the status of pedagogical stories. Yet, undisputed evidence for Daniel's location in the Hebrew canon appears to be limited to later Hebrew manuscripts and to statements that may be traced no further back than the early rabbinic period. Two of the oldest available manuscripts of the Hebrew Bible which attest to the present canonical order are Codex Leningradensis and the Aleppo Codex which are dated only to the ninth and tenth centuries A.D. Two of the most explicit rabbinic statements are in the Gemara of the Babylonian Talmud: Baba Bathra 14b (where Daniel appears before Esther and Ezra), and Megilla 3a (where Haggai, Zechariah, and Malachi are called prophets but are distinguished from Daniel), are within material composed in the fifth to eighth centuries A.D.

Earlier Jewish tradition reveals a different rabbinic concept of Daniel with prophetic status. The oldest manuscript of the Hebrew Bible, Codex Cairensis (895 A.D.) includes Daniel in its list of the prophets, and a Hebrew-Aramaic-Greek canon list dated tentatively to the second century A.D. also lists Daniel following the three major prophets. Furthermore, in all the Jewish sources of the first century A.D.—the Septuagint, the Dead Sea Scrolls, Josephus, Jesus, and the New Testament writers—Daniel is reckoned among the prophets. Why, then, did the later rabbis exclude Daniel from the prophetic corpus?

The evidence of Daniel's prophetic influence upon the religious and political events of earlier periods indicates that the book could have dangerous effects. The Zealots considered Daniel an important prophetic voice, whose visions held the key to the interpretation of world events, especially concerning the Romans. Josephus referred to one such prediction (probably the seventy-weeks prophecy) in *Jewish War* (6) that the Zealots relied upon to instigate and support the first (and possibly second) revolt(s) against Rome. This trend was also followed by first- and second-century rabbis. The fall of Jerusalem in A.D. 70 and the events subsequent to it had confirmed to these rabbis (as it had to the early Jewish-Christians and church fathers), that the interpretation of the fourth monarchy in Daniel 2 and 7 as the Roman Empire was correct. Therefore, Daniel's prophetic timetable was accurate as his book alone contained the key for the destruction of the second temple and of Israel's future restoration after a further exile (the seventy-weeks prophecy). So influential was Daniel in this regard that Targum Jonathan on the Prophets (c. 50–1 B.C.) reveals that all of the prophets were interpreted along the lines set out in Daniel to calculate the end time.

This use and influence of Daniel as predictive prophecy led the rabbis to regard Daniel as a dangerous book since the application of an apocalyptic timetable to contemporary events had brought both disappointment and decline to the nation. By separating it from classical prophecy and grouping it with other narratives of the Exile (e.g., Esther and Ezra), it was removed from exerting a paradigmatic influence on the prophetic corpus. Once it was incorporated among the heroes of the Exile, the accent of the book was shifted from prophecy to pedagogy. Perhaps fear of Daniel's eschatological influence also led the rabbis to allow an allegorical interpretation of the Prophets and the Writings, an allowance never permitted for the Torah. By permitting the prophecies to be allegorized, the problems of literal interpretation (and application) could be avoided.

With regard to the interpretation of the seventy-weeks prophecy, the rabbis interpreted the weeks as weeks of years and saw it as having prophesied the Roman destruction of Jerusalem. The Seventieth Week is not entirely included in that event. Because it predicts the destruction of the Romans, its final statement is retained as a future event. The Jewish chronological record of Rabbi Jose known as the Seder Olam Rabbah, preserves the oldest rabbinic tradition for interpreting the seventy weeks. In chapter 28 of this work, the first seven weeks are related to the Exile and return, the next sixty-two weeks are in the land, and the final week predicts a period partially spent in the land and partially spent in exile. In this case, the Seventieth Week could include events that occurred after A.D. 70.

According to Abarbanel, the condition of Israelite punishment in exile required the 490 years of this prophecy to complete the sins committed in addition to the violation of the sabbatical law (cf. 2 Chron. 36:21). Other Jewish commentators such as Rashi and Metzudos, held that this referred to a period following the 490 years (which they believed ended with the destruction of the second temple), "the last exile whose purpose it will be to terminate [i.e., *to atone for*] transgression of the Jewish Nation." Rabbi Hersh Goldwurm, summarizing their views, observes: "Thus, seventy weeks have been decreed upon your people and your city [for relative well-being] after which the Jews will receive the remainder of their punishment in the last exile whose purpose will be to terminate [i.e., atone for] transgression." One reason for this interpretation is because these commentators believed that Jewish suffering would atone for their transgression. Abarbanel noted that the return to Jerusalem and even the rebuilding of the second temple did not bring the expected redemption nor atone for past sins, since it was itself a part of the exile and atonement. He held that the real and complete redemption was still far off in history, awaiting fulfillment according to Daniel's prophecy.

The Seventieth Week (v. 27) was not included in the sixty-two weeks of verse 26, according to Ibn Ezra. He thought it was not counted because of the turmoil and unrest preceding the destruction during which an anointed was killed. He arrived at seventy weeks by adding the seven weeks of verse 25 to the sixty-two of verse 26. This may indicate his difficulty in reconciling verse 27 with verse 26. Rashi has no difficulty identifying the the people of the prince that shall come as the Romans (i.e., the legions of Vespasian and Titus). Both Rashi and Rambam are examples of those who ascribe the breaking of the covenant (with the Jewish rulers ["great ones" rather than "many"]) to a broken promise of the Romans. However, none of the sages who hold this opinion provide any historical source in support. The Jerusalem Talmud (Taanis 4:5) apparently attempts to connect this with the Romans substituting pigs for the agreed-upon lambs for the daily sacrifice. It states that at that very hour the sacrifices were stopped and the temple was destroyed immediately after. Some rabbis believed that the abomination that makes desolate (v. 27) referred to Hadrian's erection of a pagan temple on the site of the Jewish temple after the Bar-Kokbha war (Rashi). As regards the temple, some rabbinic interpreters (cf. Malbim) referred the last of the restoration goals of Daniel 9:24, to anoint the Most Holy Place to the third temple, since Tosefta Sotah 13:2 records that the second temple had not been anointed. The sages also considered this anointing of the Holy Place to take place in relation to the restoration of the Shekinah and the temple vessels. Mishnah tractate Yoma 21b recorded that the ark of the covenant with the tablets of the Law, the altars, and the holy vessels were not in the second temple. These were to be revealed through the messianic King at the time He would build and anoint the third temple (cf. Zech. 6:12–13).

Earlier rabbis apparently had understood the term *mashiach* in verse 25 literally as the Messiah. However, later rabbis (Rashi, Yossipon, ch. 47) interpreted the term figuratively as "one who is anointed [with oil]," "an anointed ruler." Thus, no historical figure could be precisely determined, and the rabbis offered various candidates: Cyrus, Zerubbabel, Nehemiah, a high priest (e.g., Yehoshua ben Yehotzadak) or a descendant of Herod (Agrippa II). Nevertheless, it was Rashi's opinion that the destruction of the desolator at the end of the Seventieth Week was expected to be the promised King-Messiah, who would wage the final wars and the war of Gog and Magog. This accords with the futurist perspective of almost all of the rabbinic commentators that the redemption depicted for the seventy weeks was yet to be realized.

See also HERMENEUTICS, ORTHODOX RABBINICAL.

J. Randall Price

Philip Blackman, *Mishnayot,* 6 vols. (New York: The Judaica Press, Inc., 1964); George W. Buchanan, *Revelation and Redemption: Jewish Documents of Deliverance from the Fall of Jerusalem to the Death of Nachmanides* (Hillsborough, N.C.: Western North Carolina Press, 1978); K. J. Cathcart and R. P. Gordom, "The Targum of the Minor Prophets" in *The Aramaic Bible* (Wilmington, Del.: M. Glazier, 1987); Pinkhos Churgin, "Targum Jonathan to the Prophets" in *The Library of Biblical Studies*, ed. Harry M. Orlinsky (New York and Baltimore: KTAV Publishing House, Inc., 1983); Rabbi Hersh Goldwurm, *Daniel: A New Translation with a Commentary Anthologized from Talmudic, Midrashic, and Rabbinic Sources* (New York: Mesorah Publications, Ltd., 1989); *Jerusalem Talmud*, 4 vols. (Hebrew) (Jerusalem: Kol Hazuyot Semurot m^{e}phali Yitzur v^{e}hutzah l'or, n.d.); Flavius Josephus, *Jewish Antiquities*, trans. H. St. J. Thackery and *Jewish Wars*, trans. H. St. J. Thackery, Ralph Marcus, Allen Wilgren, L. H. Feldman in *Loeb Classical Library* (Cambridge, Mass.: Harvard University Press, 1930–65); R' Avraham ben Meir Ibn Ezra, *Perush HaKatzer* (Commentary on Daniel) (London: 1887); R' Solomon ben Yitzchak (Rashi), *Commentary to the Bible* (Hebrew) (Jerusalem: 1956); R' Saadiah ben Nachmani, compiler, R' Saadiah (ben Yosef) Gaon's *Commentary on the Bible* (Hebrew); R' Sh'muel Masnuth, *Midrash Daniel* (Hebrew) (Jerusalem: I. S. Lange & S. Schwartz, 1968); R' Yitzchak Abarbanel, *Mayenei HaYeshuah* (Commentary on Daniel).

DANIEL, ESCHATOLOGY OF

This book outlines the times of the Gentiles. It chronicles the rise and fall of kingdoms in a chronological order. The visions given in the book cover the entire period of Gentile rule to the time of the Tribulation, as well as the establishment of the millennial kingdom. A strong emphasis is placed on the sovereignty of God, His faithfulness to protect and preserve His covenant people, and Israel's future restoration.

The author is Daniel, who as a youth was taken captive and spent the remainder of his life in Babylonian captivity. The book was written about 537 B.C.

The prophecies begin with Nebuchadnezzar's vision that identified the Gentile world empires (Babylon, Medo-Persia, Greece, and Rome), their rise to power (2:37–40), their ultimate destruction by Christ (2:34), and the setting up of His future millennial kingdom on the earth (2:35). Next is seen the deliverance of the three who had been thrown into the furnace for refusing to worship the image of Nebuchadnezzar, which looks forward to the deliverance of the believing remnant from the Tribulation (Chap. 3). The fall of Babylon is predicted (Chap. 5). Daniel is protected from the lions based on his faith in God (6:18–28), and this is a foreshadow of the rescue of the godly remnant of Israel at the Second Coming. The Second Coming of Christ is seen (7:13–14), and the coming Antichrist is foretold (7:24–25) and the Second Coming and the annihilation of the Antichrist (7:26). The destruction of the sanctuary in Jerusalem is foretold (8:13), fulfilled by Antiochus Epiphanes, 171–164 B.C. The prophecy of the latter days is given (10:13). The vision of the seventy weeks (9:20–27) is a prophecy that concerns the nation Israel and the city of Jerusalem. The seventy weeks begin with the command to rebuild the city of Jerusalem and its wall (9:25). After this is the prophecy of the death of Christ, the coming Antichrist (the prince who is to come), and the destruction of the temple at Jerusalem (9:26). The final week of the seventy weeks, which has been put on hold to accommodate the church age, will see the influence and control of the Antichrist as he makes a false covenant with the Jews, breaks it at the three-and-one-half-year point, puts an end to Jewish worship, declares himself the one deserving worship, and is destroyed by Christ at His Second Coming (9:27). The conflicts that the Jews will experience before they experience peace from Christ at the Second Coming are foretold (10:14). The final world ruler, the Antichrist, and his future works are detailed (11:36–45) looking forward to the period of the Tribulation. The Great Tribulation is seen (12:1), as is the resurrection of the righteous dead of the Old Testament, as well as the righteous martyrs of the Tribulation at the Second Coming of Christ (12:2). The completion of the Great Tribulation is foretold (12:7, 11). The beginning of the millennial kingdom is seen (12:12), and the assurance of the resurrection of Daniel in the millennial kingdom is promised.

This book is instrumental in the understanding of Old Testament prophecy as well as being the key to comprehending the book of Revelation.

See also DANIEL'S SEVENTY WEEKS, DISPENSATIONAL INTERPRETATION OF.

Erwin Starwalt

Merrill F. Unger, *Unger's Bible Dictionary* (Chicago: Moody Press, 1966); John F. Walvoord, *The Prophecy Knowledge Handbook* (Wheaton, Ill.: Victor Books, 1990); John F. Walvoord and Roy B. Zuck, eds., *The Bible Knowledge Commentary* (Wheaton: Victor Books, 1985); Everett F. Harrison and Charles F. Pfeiffer, eds., *Wycliffe Bible Commentary* (Chicago: Moody Press, 1962).

DARBY, JOHN NELSON

Life and Writings

Early leader among the Plymouth Brethren and developer of dispensational premillennialism, John Darby (1800–1882) invested his life in strengthening the saints as they gathered simply "to His name" and awaited their Lord's any-moment return. Born in London of wealthy Irish parents, Darby received his middle name from Admiral Lord Nelson. Upon returning to Ireland in 1815, he entered Trinity College, Dublin, graduating in 1819 as a classical gold medalist. Although called to the Irish Chancery Bar in 1822, he gave up a career in law after only one year to enter religious ministry. After a prolonged spiritual struggle leading to his conversion, Darby was ordained as a deacon in 1825 and as a priest in the Church of England in 1826. He had an unusually fruitful evangelistic ministry among Catholics in his parish of County Wicklow, Ireland.

From 1827 to 1833, Darby's ecclesiology and eschatology were formed. Disenchanted with the state-church religion, Darby addressed in his earliest writing the heavenly nature of the church and the need for it to be unencumbered with earthly things. He soon discovered a group of like-minded people meeting in Dublin for Bible study, worship, and breaking of bread without ecclesiastical ritual and hierarchy. By 1831, he had left the church of England and joined others in Plymouth, England, who were opposed to denominationalism, one-man ministry, and church formalism. From this time on, Darby's life would be inextricable from the influential Plymouth Brethren movement. The Powerscourt Conferences from 1831–33 would provide the context in which Darby's eschatology would be aligned consistently with his ecclesiology. Afterward his innovations in both fields of theology would be widely accepted throughout the Brethren movement, yielding a new perspective and interpretation of Scripture that would be known as dispensationalism.

Darby travelled, taught, and wrote extensively from 1832 to 1845. He worked in Switzerland and France from 1838 to 1845, and soon afterward began to write in French what would be called in the English translation his *Synopsis of the Books of the Bible.* He did not finish these five volumes until 1865. His chief aim was to give the reader a guide to clearly apprehend the difference between the church called to heavenly places and the governments of this world with which the Jews play a central role in God's ways. Darby skillfully explained the "argument" of each book by showing how various sections of them relate to the main point. His sense for the historical and developmental dimensions of "biblical theology" stands out in his *Synopsis.*

In 1845, the Great Schism over B. W. Newton's differing views concerning the "secret rapture" and his supposed lapse into clericalism brought tremendous dissension among the Brethren assemblies. Combined with the Bethesda Question (in 1848, George Muller and Darby disagreed as to the interrelationship of assemblies over matters of discipline), the Schism would leave the Brethren from this time forward divided into Exclusive and Open Brethren.

Darby would remain the dominant voice

among the Exclusives for the next 30 years. During this time, both groups would be deeply involved in missions, although the Exclusives seemed to be more occupied with truth for the believer while the Opens were given to evangelizing the lost. Between 1853 and the time of his death, Darby himself would make at least three trips to Germany, spend considerable time in France, visit Italy, New Zealand, and the West Indies. He preached fluently in both French and German. During one span of time (1859–74), he made seven visits to Canada and the U.S.A. Amid his extensive teaching tours, he found time to translate the New Testament into English, French, and German, and he assisted in translating the Old Testament into both French and German.

The *Letters of J. N. Darby* comprise three large volumes addressing a wide range of topics. Most of his papers and articles are gathered in thirty-four volumes of *The Collected Works of J. N. Darby*, edited by his longtime associate and friend William Kelly. In general, *Collected Works* is organized chronologically within a volume, and thematically from volume to volume. Subject headings include "Ecclesiastical" (vols. 1, 4, 14, 20), "Prophetic" (vols. 2, 5, 8, 11), "Doctrinal" (vols. 3, 7, 10, 15, 18, 22, 23, 29, 31), "Apologetic" (vols. 6, 9), "Evangelical" (vols. 12, 21), "Critical" (vol. 13), "Practical" (vols. 16, 17), "Expository" (vols. 19, 24–28, 30), and "Miscellaneous" (vols. 32–34). An excellent general index volume aids in researching topics not only throughout Darby's *Letters* and *Collected Works,* but also throughout the two volumes of *Miscellaneous Writings of J. N. Darby* (actually vols. 4 and 5 of his miscellaneous writings since vols. 1-3 are the last three volumes of the *Collected Works*), seven volumes of *Notes and Comments on Scripture*, and *Notes and Jottings from Various Meetings with J. N. Darby.* The last volume seems to be nuggets preserved by students and listeners. A small volume of poetry, meditations, and hymns entitled *Spiritual Songs* and Darby's *Synopsis of the Books of the Bible* are not included in the index.

Eschatology

Acknowledged father of modern dispensational premillennialism, Darby is remembered especially for his recalling the church to expectancy for its rapture at the return of the Lord before Daniel's Seventieth Week. To a large degree, his eschatology flows out of his ecclesiology, which underwent radical change between 1827 and 1831. To understand this change, Darby's background at Trinity College, Dublin, and the state of the Anglican church at that time must be seen.

While at Trinity College, Darby came under the influence of theologians like Regius Professor Richard Graves who was an advocate for the Jewish people in the British empire. Graves, a postmillennialist, believed that through the conversion of Israel and their return to their ancient homeland, the millennial era would be ushered in. A Gentile "parenthesis" had existed since the rejection of Jesus as Messiah by Israel. Old Testament promises to Abraham and his seed concerning their homeland, however, were unconditional. Prophesied blessings on the Jewish people could be fulfilled soon by zealous missionary activity among them. Darby took into the ministry this respect for the Old Testament vision of a future for national Israel.

As a young parish priest, Darby became disillusioned with the state-church system which took advantage of governmental sanction. His belief that the church as the body of Christ was to be a heavenly people and not court earthly favors was formulated by 1827. During the same year, an accidental fall from his horse forced him into a lengthy convalescence and gave him much time alone with God and His word. Isaiah 32 convinced him that there was to be a future economy in which Israel would enjoy earthly blessings, not at all like the present heavenly blessings he was conscious of because of his union with Christ. Dispensational distinctives were taking shape in his thinking.

The Powerscourt Conferences of 1831 to 1833 most probably moved Darby from his earlier historicist premillennialism to futurist premillennialism. The transition from the present church dispensation to the millennial kingdom in which Israel had center stage under Christ's rule was supplied by seeing Daniel's Seventieth Week as yet future. Before that time the church would be raptured to heavenly glory, while during that time God would bring into existence a remnant of Israel who would experience deliverance from their enemies at the return of Christ to the earth. By his own testimony, Darby's dispensational premillennial eschatology was fully formed by 1833.

For Darby, a dispensation is an economy, any order of things that God has arranged on the earth. The primary characteristics of a dispensation include governmental administration, responsibility, and revelation to fulfill both. Secondary characteristics include testing, failure, and judgment. When a group fails the test to exercise their responsibility given to them by God, judgment falls and ends the dispensation. Given these parameters, Darby saw three "worlds" or ages: from Adam until Noah's flood, from Noah until the renovation of the heavens and earth by fire at the end of the millennium, and the eternal state. Properly speaking, Darby did not think that any dispensations existed in the first world. God just left the race to itself. Also the eternal state is not a dispensation. Thus only from Noah through the millennium could dispensations be distinguished. Darby traced eight dispensations as follows: (1) Noah, (2) Abraham, (3) Israel under law (prophet), (4) Israel under the priesthood, (5) Israel under the kings, (6) Gentiles (from Nebuchadnezzar to the Antichrist), (7) church or Christian (although he hesitates to call the church in its heavenly perspective a dispensation), and (8) Millennium or kingdom.

Darby's order of end-time events may be grouped as follows: (1) the rapture and first resurrection, (2) postrapture events in heaven, (3) postrapture events on earth, (4) the millennial kingdom, (5) postmillennial events, and (6) the eternal state.

1. The Rapture occurs before the final time of trial to come upon the earth. The church must already be with Christ in heaven to be able to appear with Him at His glorious return. Darby hesitated to call the Rapture secret, although he believed the time of its occurrence was unknown, yet possible at any moment. The first resurrection of the just coincides with the Rapture. Thus all those who have died in faith from both the Old Testament and New Testament eras will be raptured with the living church saints. Although all who have a resurrection body will be related in some way to the New Jerusalem, Darby called only the church the bride so as to give it the chief position among those glorified.

2. After the Rapture, several things transpire in heaven. First, Satan is cast out of heaven to the earth. Then the saints will experience the judgment seat of Christ in preparation for the marriage of the Lamb. The latter event will take place after the judgment of Babylon.

3. Events on earth after the Rapture relate to Daniel's Seventieth Week. At times Darby spoke of this seven-year period as entirely future, but at other times as only three and one-half years remaining for the future (the first three and one-half years being the earthly ministry of Christ). Some future time of trial was necessary after the Rapture to prepare a Jewish remnant that would be delivered by Messiah's personal return to the earth. During that time, the Beast would arise as the secular head of evil imperial government, and the False Prophet would arise as the Antichrist, the spiritual head of evil religious energy. The Day of the Lord is at the appearing of Christ at the end of the Tribulation period. Armageddon ends the Beast's and Antichrist's power, and Satan himself will be bound soon after. Next the land of Israel is cleansed. Then the judgment of the living on earth takes place to determine who among them will enter the millennial kingdom. After a short time of peace and security in their land, Israel will be attacked by Gog (= Russia) whom the Lord utterly destroys.

4. In the millennial kingdom, the land promises given to Abraham will be fulfilled for a restored Israel. Messiah delivers the remnant, which becomes the blessed nation by destroying all its enemies. Afterward Israel will occupy the chief place among the nations on earth in Messiah's kingdom, just

as the church as the bride of Christ will occupy the chief place among those resurrected in the New Jerusalem.

5. Events after the Millennium include the final revolt of Satan, the second resurrection, and the Great White Throne judgment of the unbelieving dead. Darby believed in the eternal conscious punishment of the lost in the lake of fire.

6. The eternal state will bring an end to Israel's special position above the nations of the millennial kingdom. But there will eternally be a distinction between the church and the earthly people in its eternal state format. "The tabernacle of God" (for Darby, meaning the church in Rev. 21:2–3) would be "with men" (the earth inhabiters without national distinction). Thus the church will have special distinction in eternity since "to Him be glory in the church throughout all ages" (Eph. 3:21) refers to a relationship that persists forever. Two peoples of God, an earthly and a heavenly, will be eternally distinct simply because saved humans in natural bodies will be distinguished from the saved who have resurrection bodies in the eternal state.

See also DISPENSATIONALISM.

Floyd Elmore

Larry Vance Crutchfield, "The Doctrine of Ages and Dispensations as Found in the Published Works of John Nelson Darby" (Ph.D. diss., Drew University, 1985); John Nelson Darby, *The Collected Writings of J. N. Darby*, vols. 2, 5, 8, 11 (reprint, Sunbury, Pa.: Believers Bookshelf, 1971); Floyd S. Elmore, "A Critical Examination of the Doctrine of the Two Peoples of God in John Nelson Darby" (Th.D. diss., Dallas Theological Seminary, 1990); H. A. Ironside, *A Historical Sketch of the Brethren Movement* (Grand Rapids: Zondervan, 1942); William B. Neatby, *A History of the Plymouth Brethren* (London: Hodder and Stoughton, 1901); W. G. Turner, *John Nelson Darby* (London: C. A. Hammond, 1944).

DAVID'S ROLE IN PROPHECY

David, king of Israel, is usually not viewed as being in prophecy. He was the most important king of ancient Israel and is the one from whom the Messiah, Jesus Christ, descended, but does he have a future historical purpose in God's program?

The reason for this question relates to several instances in the Old Testament in which David is said to have a ruling position in the coming kingdom (Isa. 55:3–4; Jer. 30:9; 33:15, 17, 20–21; Ezek. 34:23–24; 37:24–25; Hos. 3:5; Amos 9:11). Generally, three explanations are offered as to the meaning of David's future role mentioned in these texts: (1) Messiah, as David's heir, fulfills the texts, (2) a literal son of David will arise from the line of David, or (3) the resurrected David will actually occupy some form of governmental role during the millennial reign of his greater son, Jesus.

Some believe the use of David in the aforegoing passages refers to Christ, so that David is used only typically. Since Jesus is David's son, and Christ establishes David's throne, then David, in that sense, will reign. All the references to David are actually to Jesus sitting on David's throne. For example, Isaiah and Jeremiah speak of David's throne being established forever (Isa. 9:7; Jer. 33:15). The future capital of Zion will be the city of David (Isa. 2:1–4). Moreover Christ's name is closely associated with David in the Bible; He is called the son of David. Isaiah refers to the coming ruler as being from the line of Jesse, David's father (Isa. 11:1–10), as do also New Testament authors (Mark 11:10; John 7:42; Rev. 5:5; 22:16).

There are several objections raised to Christ being the fulfillment of these biblical texts. First, Jesus Christ is never called David in the Bible. Rather, He is called the Branch unto David (Jer. 23:5), Son of David (fifteen times), Seed of David (John 7:42), Root of David (Rev. 5:5), and the Root and Offspring of David (Rev. 22:16). Second, the term "my servant, David" is regularly used for the historical David (2 Sam. 3:18; 7:5, 8; 1 Kings 11:3, 32, 34; 2 Kings 20:6). Third, Yahweh (who is Messiah) is clearly distinguished from David (Hos. 3:5; Ezek. 34:24; 37:21–25; Jer. 30:9; Isa. 55:4). Last, there are aspects of the prophecy about David in Ezekiel 45:22 that cannot refer to the Messiah. The prince mentioned offers sacrifice for his own sins, which cannot refer to Jesus. Moreover, the prince of Ezekiel 46:16 has sons and divides an inheritance.

The position is that a son in the line of David will sit on the Davidic throne. Though Christ could fulfill portions of the prophecy, there are portions which He cannot. Another heir of the Davidic throne must be in view. The references to the prince in Jeremiah 33:15, 17, 20–21 would seem to argue that a son of David would fulfill this office.

Three basic objections have been raised against this view. First, after the destruction of Jerusalem, no Jew is able to trace his family lineage. Second, if another son of David is in view besides Christ, then Christ was not the complete fulfillment of the Davidic promises. Third, and last, literal interpretation demands that the word *David* be understood naturally.

The last perspective on David in prophecy is that the passages in question actually refer to the historical personage David, who during the millennium will reign as a regent under the King of Kings, Jesus Christ. He will be resurrected and reign in Jerusalem.

There are three primary arguments for King David ruling during the future kingdom of Messiah. First, this best represents a literal interpretation of the passages. Second, David could be regent in the millennium without this being a violation biblical prophecies about the reign of David. Third, we know that various resurrected saints will have positions of responsibility during the millennium (Matt. 19:28; Luke 19:12–27). David, then, during the millennium would reign over Israel as a prince under the authority of Jesus, David's son. In this capacity, David would lead worship, offer memorial sacrifices, administer the laws, and provide inheritance for his children.

This rulership during the millennium is consistent with other forms of rulership during that period that are presented in the Old Testament (Isa. 32:1; Jer. 30:21; Ezek. 45:8–9), as well as the New Testament teaching regarding the apostles who will rule over the twelve tribes of Israel.

The objections to this position pertain to the fact that Jesus will be king over the earth and Israel in specific and He is the complete fulfillment of the promises to David. If Christ is the greater son of David, there really is no need for the prophecies to be fulfilled in the historical king.

See also DAVIDIC COVENANT; THRONE OF DAVID.

H. Wayne House

Walter A. Elwell, ed., *Baker Encyclopedia of the Bible*, Vol. 1:A-I (Grand Rapids: Baker, 1988), 585–86; J. Dwight Pentecost, *Things to Come* (Grand Rapids: Zondervan, 1958), 498–503.

DAVIDIC COVENANT

Two main passages detail the making of the Davidic covenant: 2 Samuel 7:11–17 and 1 Chronicles 17:10–15. In these passages, a covenant was made between God and David, with David standing as the representative head of the house of David, or the Davidic dynasty.

The Provisions of the Davidic Covenant

There are a total of seven provisions to this covenant. First, David was promised an eternal house, or dynasty (2 Sam. 7:11, 16; 1 Chron. 17:10). Second, one of David's own sons, specifically Solomon, was to be established on the throne after David (2 Sam. 7:12). Third, Solomon would build the temple (2 Sam. 7:13). Fourth, the throne of David's and Solomon's kingdom was to be established forever (2 Sam. 7:13, 16). It was not Solomon himself who was promised to be established forever, but rather the throne upon which he would sit. Fifth, Solomon would be disciplined for disobedience, but God would not remove His lovingkindness from him (2 Sam. 7:14–15). God did remove Saul, but Saul was not under an unconditional covenant, as was Solomon. Sixth, the Messiah will come from the seed of David (1 Chron. 17:11). Seventh, the Messiah's throne, house, and kingdom will be established forever (1 Chron. 17:12–14).

To summarize the seven provisions, the Davidic covenant promised David four eternal things: an eternal house, or dynasty, an eternal throne, an eternal kingdom, and an eternal descendent. The eternality of the house, throne, and kingdom are guaranteed because the seed of David culminated in a person who is Himself eternal: the Messiah, the God-Man.

Its Importance

The importance of the Davidic covenant is that it amplifies the seed aspect of the Abrahamic covenant. According to the Abrahamic covenant, the Messiah was to be of the seed of Abraham. This only meant that He was to be a Jew and could be of any of the twelve tribes. Later, in the time of Jacob, the messianic seed aspect was limited to a member of the tribe of Judah only (Gen. 49:10). Then, the seed aspect was further narrowed to one family within the tribe of Judah, the family of David. It was narrowed further, in Jeremiah 22:24–30, where it is decreed that while the Messiah was to be of the seed of David, he would be apart from Jechoniah.

Its Confirmation

The Davidic covenant is reconfirmed in 2 Samuel 23:15; Psalm 89:1–52; Isaiah 9:6–7, 11:1; Jeremiah 23:5–6, 30:8–9; 33:14–17, 19–26; Ezekiel 37:24–25; Hosea 3:4–5; Amos 9:11; Luke 1:30–35, 68–70; and Acts 15:14–18. The Davidic covenant, being unconditional, is still very much in effect.

Its Outworking in this Age

This covenant promised four eternal things, one of which was the eternal descendent. The fact that the Messiah, the eternal descendent, is now seated at the right hand of God the Father, as David himself prophesied in Psalm 110:1, shows that the covenant is still functioning. In fulfillment of the eternal seed facet of the Davidic covenant, Jesus is called the son of David (Matt. 1:1; Luke 1:32) and the root of David (Rev. 5:5). True, Jesus is not now ruling from the Davidic throne over a kingdom of Israel, but He will do so in the future. Replacement theologians insist that the entire covenant has now been fulfilled and insist that the promise of the throne was fulfilled when Jesus sat on His Father's throne (Rev. 3:21). There is no question that Jesus is now sitting on the throne of God the Father. However, the promise of Luke 1:32 is that He will someday sit upon the throne of His father, David. It is foolish to claim that the throne of David and the throne of God are the same unless replacement theologians wish to insist that David once sat upon the throne of God the Father!

Its Outworking in the Future

A major facet of Israel's final restoration is the reestablishment of the Davidic throne, which is clearly based upon the Davidic covenant. Jesus holds three offices: Prophet, Priest, and King. However, He does not function in all these offices simultaneously, but in chronological sequence. During His First Coming and in His public ministry, He functioned in His first office of Prophet. Since His ascension, He has been functioning in His second office of Priest. With the Second Coming, He will begin to function in His third office, that of King, the King of Israel, and the King of the world. The reestablishment of the Davidic throne also received a tremendous amount of prophetic elaboration, which includes the following: Psalm 89; Isaiah 9:6–7, 16:5; Jeremiah 23:5–6, 33:14–26; Amos 9:11–12; Luke 1:32–35.

See also DAVID'S ROLE IN PROPHECY.

Arnold G. Fruchtenbaum

DAY OF THE LORD

The most common biblical term for the seven years of Tribulation in both testaments is the *Day of Jehovah*, or the *Day of the Lord*. There are many who use the term, the Day of the Lord, to apply to both the Tribulation and the messianic kingdom. This is generally based on the assumption that the phrases, the Day of the Lord and *that day*, are synonymous. While it is true that the expression, that day, has a wide meaning that includes both the Tribulation and the messianic kingdom, in those passages where the actual phrase, the Day of the Lord (Jehovah) is used, they never refer to the Millennium, but always to the Tribulation, and this study will list every passage where the term is used; not once, in any context, is that term ever found in a millennial context.

The Day of the Lord (Jehovah) and the World in General

There are a total of seven passages that deal with the Day of Jehovah and the world in general. (1) Isaiah 2:12–22 emphasizes the terror of Jehovah that will be manifested in that day. (2) Isaiah 13:6–16 elaborates on one major purpose of the Tribulation, to make an end of wickedness and wicked ones. (3) Ezekiel 30:1–9 describes the effects of the Day of Jehovah on the Middle East nations, particularly on Egypt. (4) Joel 1:15–20 stresses how the Day of Jehovah will affect the crops of the earth. (5) Obadiah 10:20 describes the effects of the Day of the Lord on the land of Edom, or present-day southern Jordan. The Day of Lord will be particularly heavy on Edom because of its special mistreatment of Israel. Though other nations are equally guilty, Edom has unique shame due to its blood relationship to Israel. (6) Zephaniah 1:14–18 portrays the Day of Jehovah as a time of darkness and distress and also refers to the major purpose of the Tribulation of making an end of wickedness and wicked ones. (7) First Thessalonians 5:1–3 states that the Day of the Lord will hit the world suddenly, unexpectedly, just at a time they are expecting "peace and safety" and, therefore, living in a period of false security. (8) Second Thessalonians 2:1–4 emphasizes that before the Day of the Lord can actually come, there must be a falling away and the revelation of the Man of Sin. (9) In 2 Peter 3:10–12, the Day of Jehovah is described as a time of the burning of the earth. The process by which the earth will be burned is the fiery judgments contained in the seal, trumpet, and bowl judgments. In summary, then, the Scriptures give some general descriptions of the Great Tribulation, or the Day of the Lord, as a time of darkness, torment, anguish, turmoil, confusion, death, and massive destruction, especially by fire.

The Day of the Lord (Jehovah) and Israel

There are five passages that directly relate the Day of Lord to Israel. (1) Ezekiel 13:1–7 describes the Day of Jehovah in relationship to the false prophets in the Tribulation. (2) Joel 2:1–11 describes the Day of Jehovah as a time of darkness and invasion for the people of Israel. (3) Joel 3:14–17 describes the Day of Jehovah as a time of refuge for Israel. (4) Amos 5:18–20 describes the Day of Jehovah as a time of darkness for the Jewish people. (5) Zephaniah 1:7–13 describes the Day of Jehovah as being especially severe for the city of Jerusalem.

Other References

Two other references describe events that are stated to come before the great and terrible Day of Jehovah. The first passage is Joel 2:31, which mentions there will be a blackout of the sun, moon, and stars before this day occurs. Second, Malachi 4:5-6 prophecies the return of Elijah before this period hits the world.

See also TRIBULATION, THE GREAT.

Arnold G. Fruchtenbaum

DE HAAN, M. R.

M. R. De Haan (1891–1965) was a pioneer in Christian broadcasting with the weekly radio program *Radio Bible Class*. Many listeners did not realize that De Haan trained as a medical doctor, receiving his M.D. from the University of Illinois Medical School. After practicing medicine for several years, De Haan's greater love of teaching the Word of God led him to study Bible and theology at Western Theological Seminary. He carried this ministry forth as a popular public teacher through radio and as an author. He wrote more than twenty-five books and published countless daily devotionals in *Our Daily Bread*. De Haan focused on medical themes with books like *Chemistry of the Blood*, *Dear Doctor: I Have a Problem*, and *Genesis and Evolution*. He also had a love of teaching Bible prophecy as evidenced by *Coming Events in Prophecy, Daniel the Prophet, Revelation, The Second Coming of Jesus,* and *Signs of the Times*.

In the study of prophecy, De Haan was a thoroughgoing premillennialist and dispensationalist. Over and over again in his writings he reminded his readers of the difference between Israel and the church.

Because of the explosive nature of world events following World War II and at the urging of his radio audience, he wrote his well-known commentary on the book of Daniel. He saw the nations, and especially those countries in the Middle East, moving toward the prophesied end times. Daniel, he noted, gave his attention to the times of the Gentiles while in the first of the book of Revelation, John concentrated on the church during this present dispensation. John gave most of his space to the Tribulation period, but both authors "present to us a very graphic description of the chief actor of the end-time . . . the 'man of sin.'"

In lay terms, De Haan often reminded his audiences of basic interpretative principles. He liked to point out that: 1) all Scripture has one primary interpretation; 2) all Scripture has several practical applications; and 3) most Scripture passages have also a prophetic revelation. "To ignore the primary . . . and to be occupied only with its practical applications may result in fanaticism and losing the real purpose for which the revelation was given." Few Bible teachers have sustained their ministry as long and been as popular as De Haan.

Mal Couch

M. R. De Haan, *Daniel the Prophet* (Grand Rapids: Kregel, 1995).

DEAD SEA SCROLLS, ESCHATOLOGY OF THE

The more than eight hundred documents discovered in caves in the vicinity of the Dead Sea have been commonly referred to as the Dead Sea Scrolls. This material is composed of biblical texts, commentaries on biblical texts, apocryphal and pseudepigraphal texts, sectarian and ritualistic documents, and apocalyptic literature. Every book of the Old Testament is represented, except Esther, although there is evidence it too was known. The community that preserved this collection (generally thought to have resided at the site of Qumran in the Judean desert) represented a type of messianic Judaism more closely related to early Jewish Christianity than the Jewish sects encountered in the New Testament.

The eschatology of the sect was consistent with mainstream Judaism (see ESCHATOLOGY, JEWISH), but where more traditional groups played down apocalyptic expectations, they were the sect's characteristic feature. This led Israeli scholar Shemaryahu Talmon to classify them as "the most decidedly millenarian movement in second temple Judaism and possibly in antiquity altogether, Christianity included." Their apocalyptic literature presents not only the eschatological perspective the community, but perhaps that of an earlier postexilic community as well. As such, it offers us an unparalleled glimpse into the eschatological setting of Jesus and the New Testament writers who, while not dependent upon such literature, wrote within a context that was familiar with this worldview.

Their eschatological interpretations are preserved in commentaries they wrote on Old Testament books (e.g., Psalms, Prophets) and in their sectarian documents (e.g., Damascus Document, War Scroll). The form of their interpretation is called *pesher* because this noun is used frequently in the scrolls themselves for the "interpretation" of a *raz*, an Aramaic term for "mystery." The *pesher* developed through the prophetic influence of the book of Daniel as a special means of reconstructing the hidden history revealed to the prophets concerning the end of time, but reserved in mystery form for the generation upon whom the end would come.

The sect's eschatology is derived from its understanding of human history as being built up in stages determined by God and linked together to move toward an inevitable goal, the *eschaton*. This defined order of the ages unfolds progressively and successively in predetermined periods of time. The Ages of Creation (4Q180) consecutively enumerates these periods beginning with the time prior to the creation of man (cf. CD 2:7; 1QS 3:15–18; 1QH 1:8–12). The history of humanity is traced from the Creation (1QS 4:15–17) and leads up to the eschaton or the latter generation, or the end time, finally culminating in the latter days (QpHab 4:1–2, 7–8, 10–14; cf. 2:5–7). This culminating period also looks forward in its description of this age ending the era of wickedness as "the decreed epoch of new things" (1QS 4:25; cf. Dan. 9:26–27; 11:35–36; Isa. 10:23, 28:22, 43:19). The dividing point of this order of the ages is the destruction of the first temple (586 B.C.), with ages preceding it termed the generations of wickedness, and those that follow after (the postdestruction/postexilic period) as the generations of the latter days.

The present age of wickedness will escalate until the final conflict between the sons of darkness and the sons of light. According to the War Scroll the final age was to be preceded by a period of tribulation or "birth pangs [of the Messiah]" (1QH 3:7–10), which "shall be a time of salvation for the People of God . . ." (1QM 1). Central to this coming age of conflict is the image of eschatological evil rulers and deceivers (counterparts to the true Messiah). In Dead Sea texts that depict this period of great spiritual declension of Israel, the apostasy is said to be spearheaded by a figure referred to as "Belial" and a "son of Belial." The term appears also in the New Testament at 2 Corinthians 6:15. In other texts, this figure is called "son/man of sin" (cf. CD 6:15, 13:14, 1QS 9:16, 10:19). This expression is quite similar to an expression found in the Pauline description of the eschatological desecrator, the Antichrist, in 2 Thess. 2:3. It is complemented by another term, son of iniquity" ,n 1QS 3:21, which is comparable to the phrase "the man of lawlessness" paired with "man of sin" in 2 Thessalonians 2:3. Even the phrase "the mystery of lawlessness," found only at 2 Thessalonians 2:7, has an almost identical expression at Qumran: "the mystery of iniquity" (1QH 5:36, 50:5. In addition, Hebrew University professor of Second Temple Judaism David Flusser claims to identify an Antichrist figure (a wicked king who calls himself the "son of God") in the late first-century B.C. Aramaic pseudo-Daniel fragment 4Q24. In his opinion it proves that the idea of Antichrist is pre-Christian and clearly of Jewish origin.

According to the scrolls, the present age was also to see the imminent visitation of Elijah as the precursor of Messiah (4Q521) and the advent of the Messiah. The Messiah of the Dead Sea Scrolls is clearly eschatological. His coming is at the end of days, and is royal (Davidic), priestly (Aaronic), and prophetic (Mosaic) in nature. It may be that the sect envisioned two or three messiahs, and such interpretive confusion is understandable in light of the developing messianism of Second Temple Judaism. Nevertheless, the application of Old Testament messianic texts in the scrolls appears to have predominately combined the messianic offices in one person, and this is the Jewish theology reflected in the Gospels (cf. Matt. 2:4–6; 22:42; Mark 14:61; Luke 2:25–38; 3:15; John 6:14, 7:27, 31, 12:34).

After the Messiah had defeated all of Israel's enemies and slain the wicked (the correct interpretation of 4Q285) in the great forty-year (Gog and Magog) war (cf. 1QM; 4QpIsa[a] 7–10, 22–25; 4QpIsa[b] 2:1; 4Cantena[b] 3:7–8), at the Day of the Lord (4Q558), a time of redemption would come with a universal peace; people would live a thousand generations, evil would be destroyed, and an ideal world will come about. The sect apparently expected to build an interim third temple in Jerusalem at some point and had blueprints preserved in a temple scroll (11QT). Perhaps the means to build this temple was to be funded from a vast treasure (considered temple treasure) that they had hidden throughout the land. The locations for this treasure they preserved with a catalog of items on a copper scroll (3Q15). They also held that a final temple (the New Temple) would be built by Messiah for the age to come (cf. Zech. 6:12–13).

One problematic characteristic of their eschatology was their conviction that the precise dates of prophetic events could be determined. They believed that their "Teacher of Righteousness" was inspired by the Holy Spirit to properly discern the hidden timetable of the last days. Just as Daniel had reinterpreted Jeremiah's prophecy of the seventy-year exile (Jer. 25:1) to encompass the greater seventy weeks of years (Dan. 9:24–27), so the "Teacher of Righteousness" reinterpreted various prophetic passages from the Old Testament and reapplied them to the situation of his day. Based on this method of interpretation, they expected the coming of the Messiah would take place between 3 B.C.E. and A.D. 2. When their predictions failed, the community seems to have not attempted further calculations, but apparently reformulated their earlier expectations to accommodate a divine postponement or delayed judgment, although some may also have adopted a more militaristic posture that saw the urgent need for intervention to bring about the next age.

The Dead Sea Scrolls offer to us a window into the eschatological worldview of Jesus and the New Testament. Their eschatology followed a literal interpretation of prophetic texts and a numerological calculation of temporal indicators in judgment pronouncements, and understood a postponement of the final age, while not abandoning their hope of it. In many ways their eschatology was not dissimilar from modern Christian premillennialism and reveals that as a system of interpretation, premillennialism is more closely aligned to the first-century Jewish context than competing eschatological systems.

See also PREMILLENNIALISM.

J. Randall Price

John Marco Allegro, *The Treasure of the Copper Scroll* (New York: Doubleday, 1960); F. F. Bruce, *Biblical Exegesis in the Qumran Texts* (London: The Tyndale Press, 1959); James H. Charlesworth, *Jesus and the Dead Sea Scrolls* in *The Anchor Bible Reference Library* (New York: Doubleday, 1992); John J. Collins, *The Scepter and the Star: The Messiahs of the Dead Sea Scrolls and Other Ancient Literature* in *The Anchor Bible Reference Library* (New York: Doubleday, 1995); David Flusser, *Judaism and the Origin of Christianity* (Jerusalem: The Magnes Press, 1988) and *The Spiritual History of the Dead Sea Sect* (Tel-Aviv: Mod Books, 1989); Johann Maier, "The Temple Scroll: An Introduction, Translation & Commentary" in *Journal for the Study of the Old Testament,* eds. David J. A. Clines and Philip R. Davies (Sheffield: JSOT Press, 1985); Florentino Garcia Martinez, "Qumran and Apocalyptic: Studies on the Aramaic Texts from Qumran" in *Studies on the Texts of the Desert of Judah,* eds. F. Garcia Martinez and A. S. Van Der Woude (Leiden: E. J. Brill, 1992); J. Randall Price, *Secrets of the Dead Sea Scrolls* (Eugene, Oreg.: Harvest House, 1996); Helmer Ringgren, *The Faith of Qumran: Theology of the Dead Sea Scrolls,* expanded ed. (New York: Crossroad, 1995); Lawrence H. Schiffman, *Reclaiming the Dead Sea Scrolls* (New York: Doubleday, 1995); Hershel Shanks, ed., *Understanding the Dead Sea Scrolls* (New York: Random House, 1992); Shemaryahu Talmon, *The World of Qumran from Within* (Jerusalem: The Magnes Press, 1989); Eugene Ulrich and James VanderKam, eds., "The Community of the Renewed Covenant" in *Christianity and Judaism in Antiquity Series 10* (Indiana: University of Notre Dame Press, 1994).

DEUTERONOMY, ESCHATOLOGY OF

Deuteronomy is a series of sermons given by Moses to Israel concerning the law, in order to impress upon them the seriousness of God's Word. His goal was to exhort the people to recommit their lives to the Lord. Moses understood that it would be this commitment that would carry the people into the land and allow them to overcome its inhabitants. This was a reminder that the land had been promised to them and that it was truly theirs, having been guaranteed to them by God. The emphasis is that only obedience to God's law can bring well being, and disobedience brings disaster. The book contains five main sections concerning the covenant God made with the nation through Moses: (1) covenant mediator (1:1–5), (2) covenant history (1:6–4:49), (3) covenant life (5:1–26:19), (4) covenant ratification (27:1–30:20), (5) covenant continuity (31:1–34:12).

Authorship of the book is asserted within the book where Moses is mentioned more than forty-five times.

The major prophecy found in this book is that of the land that God had promised to Abraham and his posterity, found in chapters 28–30. God announced unconditionally that the land that was promised to Abraham (Gen. 15:18) would be his forever. The deeding of the land to Abraham allows for his future generations to legally claim the land as an inheritance. This land promise is termed the *Palestinian covenant*; the Palestinian, the Davidic, and the new covenant constitute the complete Abrahamic covenant.

The various divisions of the Palestinian covenant are recorded in these three chapters.

1. First is the prophecy concerning Israel's occupancy of the land. There is anticipation for three periods of dispossession (Gen. 15:13–14,16; Jer. 25:11–12; Deut. 28:63–68) and three periods of reparation (Gen. 15:14 with Josh. 1:2–7; Dan. 9:2 with Jer. 25:11–12; Deut. 30:3; Jer. 23:5–8; Ezek. 37:21–25; Acts 15:14–17). All these periods have been accomplished except for the final restoration which is yet future for the nation.

2. Next is the final restoration of Israel (30:1–3). Israel's scattering identifies their suffering which will be remedied when they recognize their true Messiah upon His return. In their place of rejection they neither repented nor received their king.

3. The final possession of the land is relative to the return of the Messiah (Deut. 30:3–6). Israel's sin and rejection of God is such that only a work of grace can return them to fellowship with God. The manner of life (described in 30:4–8; Jer. 31:31–34; Matt. 5:1–7:29) that Israel will live in the kingdom age displays a nationwide change of heart.

4. The prophecy foresees judgments on nations that oppressed Israel from the beginning of its history (Gen. 12:3). The full expression of these judgments will be realized when one day the nations stand before the throne of Jesus Christ. It is there that Christ will declare, "Depart from me, you cursed" (Matt. 25:41).

5. Finally the nation will be blessed in the land (30:15–20). The blessing is based upon Israel's obedience to God and His Word. By holding fast to the Lord and living in obedience the nation will experience a godly life. All of the blessings, both earthly and spiritual, will become Israel's upon its entry into the Promised Land.

See also PALESTINIAN COVENANT.

Rick Bowman

Merrill F. Unger, *Unger's Bible Dictionary* (Chicago: Moody Press, 1966); John F. Walvoord, ed., *The Bible Prophecy Handbook* (Wheaton: Victor Books, 1990); John F. Walvoord and Roy B. Zuck, eds., *The Bible Knowledge Commentary* (Wheaton: Victor Books, 1985).

DIDACHE, ESCHATOLOGY OF THE

The Didache, the shortened title of "The Teaching of the Lord to the Gentiles through the Twelve Apostles," was an instructional handbook for Gentiles dealing with matters of morality, liturgy, and church life. The discovery of this oldest extant handbook of church order and conduct in 1873 prompted a torrent of scholarly debate and discussion. But to the present, the author (or compiler) remains unknown and the setting (Syria, Palestine, or Egypt) can be given with no real confidence. As to the date of composition, reasonable estimates range from A.D. 60–90. Perhaps the oldest noncanonical document extant, it could have been penned before the apostle John ceased writing. It therefore provides evidence of views held and taught in the church's earliest period.

In interpretive approach, the didachist attempted to present the basic precepts and practices of the Christian faith to the uninitiated without exaggerated or fanciful notions. The crass allegorism found in other works, like the Epistle of Barnabas and the Shepherd of Hermas, is conspicuously absent in the Didache. Prophetic passages are interpreted in a straightforward manner, unadorned by spiritualized speculation.

The Didache provides one of the best early examples of extrabiblical teaching on the second coming of Christ and attendant events. One of the chief eschatological concepts in this work is that of imminency. In the shadow of the Lord's any-moment appearance, the Didachist urged watchfulness among believers (Did. 10.6; 16.1–2; comp. 1 Cor. 16:22 and Rev. 22:20), frequent fellowship and mutual upbuilding to counter the proliferation of "false prophets and corrupters" in the last days (Did. 16.2–3).

The Didache presents the fullest outline of

things to come to this point in early patristic writings. The didachist maintained that after the appearance of the many false prophets and corrupters, the "world-deceiver" would come to bring fiery trial upon all humanity so that many will stumble and perish "but they that endure in their faith shall be saved from under the curse itself" (Did. 16.3–5).

The time of the Antichrist will be followed, said the didachist, by the revelation of three signs of the truth, the last of which will be the "resurrection of the dead; yet not of all, but as it is said: The Lord shall come and all His saints with Him [Zech. 14:5]" (Did. 16.8). Though not specifically stated, the company of "all His saints," seems to include the whole of church-age believers, the resurrection and the Rapture both having taken place. Finally, the whole world will witness the coming of the Lord "upon the clouds of heaven" (Did. 16.6–8). The parallel passage in the Constitutions of the Holy Apostles (chap. 32; date of composition early-third to mid-fourth century), the compiler of which seems to have used the Didache as a source, adds references here to the final judgment and the eternal state (chap. 32).

Like many other early patristic writers, the didachist held to an imminent intratribulational position in which contemporary persecution was confused with the events of the final Tribulation. Christ, it was held, would appear suddenly in the midst of Roman persecution, resurrect and rapture the saints. This would introduce the millennial kingdom.

There is no direct statement regarding the millennium in the Didache. It is probable that at the time of its composition, the book of Revelation had not yet been written. Most likely, therefore, the Didache relied upon Pauline rather than Johannine eschatology. Nevertheless, while a number of the early fathers merely spoke of the fact of the resurrection of all humankind from the dead, the didachist's intriguing reference to "the resurrection of the dead; *yet not of all*," suggests an understanding of the multistaged nature of the resurrection program and consequently of an intervening millennial age.

Larry V. Crutchfield

Larry Crutchfield, "The Blessed Hope and the Tribulation in the Apostolic Fathers" in *When the Trumpet Sounds*, eds. Tommy Ice and Timothy Demy (Eugene, Oreg.: Harvest House, 1995), 85–103; J. Quasten and J. C. Plumpe, eds., *Ancient Christian Writers: The Didache, The Epistle of Barnabas, The Epistles and the Martyrdom of St. Polycarp, The Fragments of Papias, The Epistle to Diognetus*, trans. James A. Kleist, vol. 6 (New York: Newman Press, 1946), 2–25; A. Roberts and J. Donaldson, eds., *The Ante-Nicene Fathers*, vol. 7 (Grand Rapids: Eerdmans, n.d.), 369–87.

DISPENSATIONALISM

The English word "dispensation" is an anglicized form of the Latin *dispensatio*, which the Vulgate uses to translate the Greek word *oikonomia*. The Latin verb means "to weigh out or dispense." Three principal ideas are connected to the meaning of the English word: (1) the action of dealing out or distributing; (2) the action of administering, ordering, or managing; the system by which things are administered, and (3) the action of dispensing with some requirement. In further defining the use of the word theologically, the Oxford English Dictionary says that a dispensation is "a stage in a progressive revelation, expressly adapted to the needs of a particular nation or period of time. . . . Also, the age or period during which a system has prevailed."

The Greek word *oikonomia* comes from the verb that means to manage, regulate, administer, and plan. The word itself is a compound whose parts mean literally "to divide, apportion, administer or manage the affairs of an inhabited house." In the papyri the officer (*oikonomos*) who administered a dispensation was referred to as a steward or manager of an estate, or as a treasurer. Thus, the central idea in the word *dispensation* is that of managing or administering the affairs of a household.

The various forms of the word *dispensation* appear in the New Testament twenty times. The verb *oikonomeo* is used once in Luke 16:2 where it is translated "to be a steward." The noun *oikonomos* appears ten times (Luke 12:42; 16:1, 3, 8; Rom. 16:23; 1 Cor. 4:1, 2; Gal. 4:2; Titus 1:7; 1 Peter 4:10) and is usually translated "steward" of "manager" (but "treasurer" in Rom. 16:23). The noun *oikonomia* is used nine times (Luke 16:2, 3, 4; 1 Cor. 9:17; Eph. 1:10, 3:2, 9; Col. 1:25; 1 Tim. 1:4). In these instances it is translated variously, "stewardship," "dispensation," "administration," "job," "commission."

System of Theology

Dispensational theology is a system that embodies two essential concepts: (1) The church is distinct from Israel, and (2) God's overall purpose is to bring glory to Himself (Eph. 1:6, 12, 14).

The church is seen as distinct from Israel for two reasons. The first is its character. In the Old Testament God was dealing primarily with the nation of Israel, which consisted of the descendants of Abraham through Isaac and Jacob. On the other hand the church consists of believing Jews and Gentiles baptized into the body of Christ (1 Cor. 12:13) and indwelt by the Holy Spirit. There is also a distinction between the church and Israel based upon time. The church age began after the resurrection of Jesus Christ (Eph. 1:20–22), and His ascension (Eph. 4:7–12). Therefore, since all believers of this age are baptized into the body of Christ (1 Cor. 12:13), the church age began with the baptizing ministry of the Holy Spirit on the day of Pentecost (Acts 2; 11:15–16).

The church is a mystery that was not revealed to past generations (Eph. 3:3–5, 9; Col. 1:26–27). This mystery, now revealed, includes the uniting of Jewish and Gentile believers in one spiritual body, Christ indwelling believers, and the future rapture of this unified body (1 Cor. 15:50–58).

This distinction between Israel and the church is the result of *historical-grammatical* interpretation. Literal interpretation is not used solely by dispensationalists, but its *consistent* use in all areas of biblical interpretation is.

The second essential concept is that of God's purpose of glorifying Himself. Scripture is not human-centered, as though salvation were the principal point, but God-centered, because His glory is at the center. The glory of God is the primary principle that unifies all the dispensations, the program of salvation being just one of the means by which God glorifies Himself. Each successive revelation of God's plan for the ages, as well as His dealings with the elect, nonelect, angels, and nations all manifest His glory.

Hermeneutics

The fundamental assertion of dispensational hermeneutics is that of literal interpretation which gives to each word the same meaning it would have in its normal usage. This is also called the grammatical-historical method of interpretation. The principle relies on the normal meaning of words as the approach to understanding them. It is also known as *plain interpretation* to keep from ruling out symbols, figures of speech, and types. These are interpreted plainly in order to communicate their intended meaning to the reader. Symbols, figures of speech, and types are normal literary tools that are used to clarify or emphasize thoughts and ideas.

This position is supported in the following ways.

1. Language was given by God for the purpose of communication with humankind. Therefore, God would give His linguistic communication in the most understandable way—literally and normally. It seems unlikely that God would go to all the trouble of revealing Himself to people in a manner that only caused people confusion and uncertainty in their understanding of who God is and how He works.

2. The Old Testament prophecies concerning Christ's birth and rearing, ministry, death, and resurrection were all fulfilled literally.

3. In order to maintain objectivity the literal method of interpretation must be employed. This insures that impartiality is maintained and prevents the interpreter from overlaying biblical truth with personal thoughts.

Thus, normative dispensationalism is the result of the consistent application of the basic hermeneutical principle of literal interpretation. This claim can be made by no other system of theology.

Literal interpretation results in accepting the text of Scripture at its face value, which involves recognizing distinctions in the Bible. The text taken at face value and the recognition of distinctions in the progress of revelation reveals the different economies God uses in the outworking of His program. The consistent hermeneutical principle of plain or literal interpretation is the basis of dispensationalism.

The opponents of dispensationalism say that it gives the view of compartmentalizing the Bible, which has the effect of destroying its unity. Nothing could be further from the truth. C. I. Scofield identified seven evidences that the Bible is one book, (1) from Genesis it bears witness to one God, (2) it forms one continuous story, (3) it sets forth the most unlikely future predictions, (4) it is a progressive unfolding of the truth, (5) from beginning to end the Bible testifies to one redemption, (6) it's great theme throughout is the person and work of the Christ, and (7) the forty-four writers over a period of sixteen centuries have produced a perfect harmony of doctrine in progressive unfolding ("A Panoramic View of the Bible" in the introduction to *The Scofield Reference Bible*).

Instead of clouding biblical unity, dispensationalism serves to clarify it. It brings into sharp focus the progressive unfolding of God's plan throughout the ages. It is this disclosure of God's absolute truth that stands in direct opposition to modern self-centered relativism. Thus, dispensationalism sees the unity, the variety, and the progressive character of God's purposes for the world as no other system of theology does. It is through these progressive stages that God is glorified.

Divisions

The first dispensation is usually called *innocence.* Adam was the key person and his responsibilities involved the upkeep of the garden and not eating of the tree of the knowledge of good and evil. As a result of failing the eating test came far-reaching judgments on him, his wife, all of humanity, the serpent, and the entire creation. The Scripture covering this economy is Genesis 1:28–3:6.

The second dispensation is called *conscience.* The title does not intimate that people did not have consciences before or after this period, but that this is the manner in which God chose to govern them. Human responsibility was to be obedient to the dictates of their consciences. During this period there was murder (Gen. 4:8), unnatural affection (Gen. 6:2), and widespread evil desire and purpose of heart (Gen. 6:5). God closed this period with the universal flood. God spared Noah, his wife, his sons, and their wives by grace (Gen. 6:8). The Scripture covering this period is Genesis 4:1–8:14.

Next was the dispensation of *civil government.* This period began after the Flood and included the animals' fear of people, animals given to people to eat, the promise of no more flood, and the institution of capital punishment. God gave people the right to take human life which established the right to govern others. From the beginning people failed this test when Noah became drunk with wine and thus was incapable of ruling. This period ended with the tower of Babel. The Scripture covering this period is Genesis 8:15–11:9.

The fourth dispensation is that of *promise,* or *patriarchal rule.* During this period God chose one family and one nation which He used as a representative test of all. Until this dispensation all humanity had been directly linked to God's governing principles. The patriarchal obligation was to believe and serve God, and God provided many material and spiritual provisions. A specific land was promised and blessing as long as the Israelites stayed in that land. The nation's failure ended in slavery in Egypt. The Scripture covering this period is Genesis 11:10 through Exodus 18:27.

The fifth dispensation is that of the *Mosaic Law.* The people were responsible to do all the law (James 2:10) but they failed (Rom. 10:1–3). Failure brought judgments: The ten tribes were carried into Assyrian captivity, the two tribes to Babylonian captivity, and they were ultimately scattered throughout the world (Matt. 23:37–39) because of their rejection of Jesus Christ. The Scripture covering this period is Exodus 19:1 through Acts 1:26.

The sixth period is the dispensation of *grace*. The apostle Paul was the principal agent of the revelation of the grace of God for this dispensation. Human responsibility under grace is to accept the gift of righteousness freely offered by God to all (Rom. 5:15–18). The two aspects of the grace of God during this dispensation are: (1) salvation is entirely of grace, and (2) grace is available to all. No longer does God deal with just one nation; now He deals with all humankind. This dispensation will end with the second coming of Christ. The Scripture covering this period is Acts 2:1 through Revelation 19:21.

The seventh and last dispensation is that of the *Millennium*. After the Second Advent the millennial kingdom will be set up in fulfillment of all the promises given in both the Old and New Testaments. The Lord Jesus Christ will personally be in charge and govern the affairs of the world during this period. This period will last for one thousand years, and human responsibility will be obedience to the King and His laws. Satan will be bound, Christ will rule, righteousness will predominate, and obvious disobedience will be dealt with swiftly. This period ends with an unsuccessful rebellion against Christ's government. This results in those rebels being cast into eternal punishment. The Scripture covering this period is Revelation 20:1–15.

Stewardship responsibilities are placed on all who live under a dispensation. This responsibility means active participation for those who respond to the principles of the administration and judgment for those who reject its standards.

Aspects of a dispensation do not necessarily end when another period begins. There are promises given in one dispensation that are not always fulfilled during that period; for example, the promises in the Old Testament about Christ's First Advent were not fulfilled until He came. Too, there are things instituted in one dispensation that continue on through every age, such as the creation of people in the image of God. There are those things that are set out in one period and then presented again in another period, that is, nine of the ten commandments of the Law are restated as part of the dispensation of grace, though restrictions concerning certain foods are done away with.

The requirement for salvation remains the same during all dispensations—it is through faith, though the content of faith differs in different ages.

Progressive Dispensationalism

Progressive dispensationalism began on November 20, 1986 in the Dispensational Study Group in connection with the annual meeting of the Evangelical Theological Society in Atlanta, Georgia. The label "Progressive Dispensationalism" was not actually introduced until the 1991 meeting of this group. It was used to describe the significant revisions that had taken place in dispensationalism by that time. Those at the forefront of this movement include: Darrell L. Bock, Professor of New Testament Studies, Dallas Theological Seminary; Craig A. Blaising, Professor of Systematic Theology, Southern Baptist Theological Seminary; and Robert L. Saucy, Professor of Systematic Theology, Talbot Theological Seminary.

The basic beliefs of progressive dispensationalism include:

1. The kingdom of God is the unifying theme of biblical history. This view is not clearly defined. Those that hold to this belief have imprecisely defined it as God's rule over the whole earth. This inclusive definition blurs important distinctions between various kingdoms.

2. Within biblical history there are four dispensational eras, namely patriarchal, Mosaic, ecclesial, and Zionic. The patriarchal era eliminates the pre- and postfall contracts God made with Adam and Eve, which were different from the stewardship that God made with Abraham. This blends together prefall, postfall, and the Abrahamic covenant under a joint stewardship. The progressives end the Mosaic dispensational era at Christ's

ascension rather than His death (Col. 2:14). The ecclesial dispensation is this present church age and the inaugurated Davidic kingdom. The Zionic dispensation is subdivided into the millennial kingdom and the eternal kingdom. The millennial kingdom is seen as an intermediate time between the inaugurated Davidic rule now in heaven and the fullness of the kingdom of God on the new earth.

3. Christ has already inaugurated the Davidic reign in heaven at the right hand of the Father, which equals the throne of David, though He not yet reigns as Davidic king on earth during the Millennium. This stance ignores the fact that Christ's first act after His ascension was to send the Holy Spirit (Acts 2:33), which is nowhere found in the Davidic covenant. Scripture (Heb. 12:2) clearly states that Christ sat down at the right hand of God's throne, not David's. Also Christ's present activity is as a priest only. He shall not function as Davidic king until the Second Coming (Rev. 1:5; 11:15; 12:10; 17:14; 19:16), when He becomes the absolute ruler of the kingdoms of the earth.

4. Likewise the new covenant has already been inaugurated, though the blessings are not yet fully realized until the Millennium. The new covenant is promised to the house of Israel and the house of Judah in Jeremiah 31:31–34. It is based on the death of Christ, which is the payment for sins of all ages. For Israel in the future, the covenant promises forgiveness of the nation Israel, Israel restored to favor with God, peace, and the sanctuary of God being rebuilt.

5. The concept of the church as completely distinct from Israel and as a mystery unrevealed in the Old Testament must be abandoned along with the idea of two purposes and two peoples of God. Israel is spoken to as a nation in contrast to Gentiles after the establishment of the church at Pentecost (Acts 3:12, 4:8, 10, 5:21, 31, 35, 21:28). Paul prayed for Israel (Rom. 10:1), clearly regarding them as a people distinct and separate from the church. The church enjoys distinct relationships to her living Lord Jesus Christ, (Eph. 1:22–23; Col. 1:18; 1 Cor. 12:27). The union of believing Jews and Gentiles in the body of Christ is a mystery that was not revealed to previous generations (Eph. 3:5–6). The church is indwelt by Christ Himself (Col. 1:27). The church has a distinct time as stated by Paul (Eph. 2:15), which was only possible after Christ's death. Lastly, it was the baptizing work of the Holy Spirit that brought into existence the church (Acts 11:15–16). It was at Pentecost that people were first placed into the body of Christ and since the church is the body of Christ (Col. 1:18) it is quite clear that the church did not exist prior to this event.

6. A complementary hermeneutic means that the New Testament makes complementary changes to Old Testament promises without abandoning those original promises. This view allows for spiritualizing concepts found in the New Testament so as to make complementary additions to promises. For instance, the reference to a temple in Revelation 11:1–2 is a literal building according to literal hermeneutics, but the complementary hermeneutic would permit one to conclude that this is a reference to a body of believers based on the fact that it is used in that manner elsewhere in the New Testament. The danger of this position is where are the limits, and who determines them?

7. The one divine plan of holistic redemption encompasses all peoples and all areas of human life, personal, societal, cultural, and political. The content of holistic redemption can easily lead to faulty priorities. Scripture teaches about social responsibilities, such as the use of money, vocations, and civic duties. Scripture also calls on believers to obey church ethics, not kingdom ethics, and to do good particularly to the believers (Gal. 6:10).

Progressive dispensationalism appears to be a change from rather than a development within normative dispensationalism. Where it will lead or what significance it will have cannot be predicted.

Ultradispensationalism

The prefix *ultra* simply means more extreme than the point of view held by the one who uses the term. The principal difference between ultradispensationalism and normative dispensationalism concerns when the church, the body of Christ, began historically. The ultradispensationalist believes it began with Paul some time after Pentecost, while the normal dispensationalist holds that the church began at Pentecost (Acts 2). This difference affects what ordinances are practiced and what Scripture is directly for the church.

There are two types of ultradispensationalism, the extreme and the moderate. There is agreement between these two types on six points; (1) The great commission in the Gospels is Jewish and not for the church. (2) The ministry of the Twelve was a continuation of Christ's earthly ministry. (3) The church did not begin at Pentecost. (4) Water baptism is not for this church age. (5) There is a difference between Paul's early and later ministries. (6) Israel, not the church, is the bride of Christ.

There are four differences between these two types:

1. When did the church begin?
   Extreme: Acts 28
   Moderate: before Acts 28
2. How long is the transition period in the book of Acts?
   Extreme: until Acts 28
   Moderate: until Acts 9 or 13
3. What is the proper place of the Lord's Supper?
   Extreme: no place
   Moderate: proper to observe in the church
4. What Scripture is actually written to the church primarily?
   Extreme: the Prison Epistles only
   Moderate: the other Pauline epistles also

The weakness of ultradispensationalism is that it fails to recognize that the nature of a dispensation is based on what God does, not on human understanding of His purposes. The error of ultradispensationalism lies in a faulty concept of a dispensation, exegesis of key passages, understanding when the mystery was revealed, and the baptizing ministry of the Holy Spirit. The biblical evidence does not support ultradispensationalism.

Charles C. Ryrie

Charles C. Ryrie, *Dispensationalism* (Chicago: Moody Press, 1995); Wesley R. Willis and John R. Master, gen. eds., *Issues In Dispensationalism,* consulting ed. Charles C. Ryrie (Chicago: Moody Press, 1994).

DISPENSATIONALISM, PROGRESSIVE

Progressive Dispensationalists (PD) consider themselves to be in the lineage of dispensational theology but see the dispensations not as different arrangements between God and the human race, as traditional dispensationalism does, but as successive arrangements in the progressive revelation and accomplishment of redemption. At the same time, their quest is to move toward a mediating position between dispensationalism and nondispensationalism. In incorporating new elements into their theological approach, they have become almost the same as historic premillennialists, who are generally outspoken critics of dispensationalism. The rise of PD is attributable to a change in interpretive approach. Instead of following a traditional grammatical-historical system which results in dispensationalism, they advocate historical-grammatical-literary-theological hermeneutics in explaining Scripture. The new system differs from traditional literal interpretation in the following respects:

1. It replaces the quest for objectivity by focusing on the interpreter's preunderstanding as a starting point in exegesis.

2. Instead of limiting a text's meaning to that dictated by its original context, it allows "complementary" meanings to be added to a text years and even centuries after a biblical writer penned it.

3. Traditionally, interpreters have looked for one meaning intended by the author of each text, but the PD position allows for later added meanings that alter the original sense intended by the author.

4. Historically, Protestant interpreters have denied that a text has a fuller meaning beyond what it meant originally, but the newly proposed methodology allows a fuller meaning beyond that of a text's original sense.

5. Grammatical-historical exegetes have insisted on assigning each text its own meaning based on an in-depth examination, but pve dispensationalists generally make only selective comments on a passage rather than treating it thoroughly, in advocating a presupposed but exegetically insupportable position. In light of these five tendencies, it is obvious that the major difference between PD and Dispensationalism is a hermeneutical one, with PD deviating from the grammatical-historical method advocated by dispensationalism.

See also HERMENEUTICS, CONTEMPORARY BIBLICAL.

R. L. Thomas

C. A. Blaising and D. L. Bock, *Progressive Dispensationalism* (Wheaton: Victor, 1993); Charles C. Ryrie, *Dispensationalism* (Chicago: Moody, 1995), 161–82; R. L. Saucy, *The Case for Progressive Dispensationalism* (Grand Rapids: Zondervan, 1993); R. L. Thomas, "A Critique of Progressive Dispensational Hermeneutics" in *When the Trumpet Sounds*, eds. Tommy Ice and Timothy Demy (Eugene, Oreg.: Harvest House, 1995), 413–25.

E

EDWARDS, JONATHAN

Jonathan Edwards (1703–1758) is generally recognized as America's greatest theologian and philosopher. At the time of Edwards's ministry most of Protestant theology, being heir to the amillennialism of Augustine and Calvin, spiritualized the Scripture's teaching concerning the Millennium. Edwards, on the other hand, was innovative in the development of a postmillennial eschatological vision. Edwards saw the millennium as a literal historical reality which was the *telos* toward which history had been progressing since the fall of Adam. He thought it probable that this latter-day glory would begin in America. His millennial expectation is often considered to have been a major factor in the social movement resulting in the American Revolution.

Edwards interpreted tribulational passages as predictions of the apostasy of the Roman Catholic Church and the suppression of true religion. He believed that the Reformation marked the shortening of days (Matt. 24:22), which is to be identified with the restricting of the powers of spiritual Rome and the papal Antichrist. Applying the year-day theory of interpretation to the twelfth chapter of Revelation, Edwards proposed that the Millennium would arrive approximately 1260 years after A.D. 606, when the bishop of Rome was recognized as having universal authority. Thus, the Millennium was imminent and the revival fires of the Great Awakening could very well be harbingers of the coming age when great progress in technology would free humanity from material concerns to engage more fully in the noble exercises of mind and vital religion. At this time the kingdom of the Antichrist will be utterly overthrown and there will be a national conversion of the Jews. Following the Millennium will come a period of great apostasy and tribulation, which will be superseded by the personal Second Coming of Jesus Christ in infinite majesty. The saints will be gathered to their Head, forever to be in His presence, and the wicked will be summoned before the judgementseat of Christ.

Kevin Stilley

Jonathan Edwards, *The Works of Jonathan Edwards*, eds. Perry Miller and John E. Smith, 10 vols. (New Haven: Yale University Press, 1957–1993) and *The Works of Jonathan Edwards*, reprint 1992, 2 vols. (Edinburgh: Banner of Truth Press, 1834).

EDWARDS, MORGAN

Morgan Edwards (1722–1792) was born May 9 in Trevethin Parish, Wales, and after education at Bristol College, began preaching in 1738. He served several small Baptist congregations in England for seven years before moving to Cork, Ireland, where he pastored for nine years. Edwards emigrated to America and in May, 1761, became pastor of the Baptist church in Philadelphia, having been recommended by Baptist stalwart John Gill. After the Revolutionary War (he was the only known Baptist clergy of Tory persuasion), Edwards became an educator and the premier Baptist historian of his day. His major work, *Materials Toward a History of the Baptists,* is an important seminal work outlining American Baptist history of the era. Edwards founded the first Baptist college in the colonies, Rhode Island College, which we know today as Brown University of the Ivy League.

One historian characterized Edwards as follows: "Scholarly, laborious, warmhearted, eccentric, choleric Morgan Edwards, one of the most interesting of the early Baptist ministers of our country and one of those most deserving of honor. His very faults had a leaning toward virtue's side, and in good works he was exceeded by none of his day, if indeed by any of any day. . . . He was an able preacher and a good man, but not always an easy man to get on with."

During his student days at Bristol Baptist Seminary in England (1742–44), Edwards wrote an essay for eschatology class on his views of Bible prophecy. This essay was later published in Philadelphia (1788) under the following title: *Two Academical Exercises on Subjects Bearing the following Titles; Millennium, Last-Novelties.* Upon reading the fifty-six-page work, it is clear that Edwards published it with only minor updates from his student days. Thus, it represents a view developed by the early 1740s.

Edwards taught some form of pretribulationism, as can be gleaned from the following statement in his book:

> The distance between the first and second resurrection will be somewhat more than a thousand years.
>
> I say, *somewhat more*—, because the dead saints will be raised, and the living changed at Christ's "appearing in the air" (1 Thess. 4:17); and *this will be about three years and a half before the millennium,* as we shall see hereafter: but will he and they abide in the air all that time? No: they will ascend to paradise, or to some one of those many "mansions in the father's house" (John 14:2), and 80 *disappear during the foresaid period of time.* The design of this retreat and disappearing will be to judge the risen and changed saints; for "now the time is come that judgment must begin," and that will be "at the house of God" (1 Peter 4:17) (p. 7).

What has Edwards said? Note the following:

He believes that at least 1,003.5 years will transpire between resurrections.

He associates the first resurrection with the Rapture in 1 Thessalonians 4:17, occurring at least 3.5 years before the start of the Millennium (i.e., at least 3.5 years before the second coming of Christ at the start of the Millennium).

He associates the meeting of believers with Christ in the air and returning to the Father's house with John 14:2, as do modern pretribulationists.

He sees believers disappearing during the time of the Tribulation, which he details in the remainder of the section.

He, like modern pretribulationists, links the time in heaven, during the Tribulation, with the *bema* judgment of believers.

The only difference, at least as far as the above statements go, between current pretribulationism and Edwards is the time interval of 3.5 years instead of 7. This does not mean that he is a midtribulationists, since it appears that he thought the totality of the Tribulation was 3.5, not 7 years.

Taking into account the totality of his essay, it is clear that Edwards was premillennial, a futurist, held to principles of literal interpretation, and held to a prophetic chronology similar at most points to current pretribulationism. However, he did not hold to an any-moment rapture, he does not appear to be influenced in his thinking by the Seventieth Week of Daniel, nor does he appear to see the church and Israel as distinct.

Edwards notes in his introduction that his views are not those normally held in his day and that he was approaching eschatology with a literal hermeneutic. Such an approach is said by modern pretribulationists to be the primary determinative factor leading to pretribulationism. Edwards says to his instructor, "I will do my possible: and in the attempt will work by a rule you have often recommended, viz. 'to take the scriptures in a literal sense, except when that leads to contradiction or absurdity.' . . . Very able men have already handled the subject in a mystical, or allegorical, or spiritual way" (pp. 5–6).

Later in his essay, Edwards speaks again of the rapture: "Another event previous to the *millennium* will be the appearing of the son of man in the clouds, coming to raise the dead saints and change the living, and to catch them up to himself, and then withdraw with them, as observed before. [i.e., p. 7] This event will come to pass when the Antichrist be arrived at Jerusalem in his conquest of the world; and about three years and a half before his killing the witnesses and assumption of godhead (p. 21).

Still later Edwards once again separates the Rapture and the Second Coming in the following statements: "The last event, and the event that will usher in the *millennium,* will be, the coming of Christ from paradise to earth, with all the saints he had taken up thither (about three years and a half before) . . . millions and millions of saints will have been on earth from the days of the first Adam, to the coming of the second Adam. All these will Christ bring with him. The place where they will alight is the 'mount of Olives, which is before Jerusalem on the east' Zech. 14:4" (pp. 24–25).

Of interest is the fact that Edwards wrote forty-two volumes of sermons, about twelve sermons per volume, that were never published. Other than his historical writings and ecclesiastical helps, his essay on Bible prophecy was his only other published work. It is significant that this essay from his youth was published and not something else. This evidences that there was some interest in his views on this subject. Such an interest would have surely risen out of his bringing it to the attention of those to whom he ministered. Yet, on the other hand, the book only went through one printing, showing that it must have had limited interest. It could also reflect the fact that Baptists were not a large denomination at this time in America. Nevertheless, Edwards's work on Bible prophecy did have some circulation and exposed early Americans to many of the ideas that would come to dominate evangelicalism a century later.

Detractors of pretribulationism often want to say or imply that our view cannot be found in the pages of the Bible and must have come from a deviant source. Of course, we strongly object to such a notion and have taken great pains over the years to show that the New Testament not only teaches pretribulationism, but holds it forth as our Blessed Hope—a central focus of faith. The bringing to light of Morgan Edwards's views of the Rapture do demonstrate (again) that a consistently literal approach to Bible interpretation leads many to distinguish between Christ's coming in the air *for* His bride and His return to earth *with* His saints. Edwards, along with others, make it clear that, while Darby may have restored the pretribulational Rapture, he did not originate it. Pretribulationism is found first in the New Testament and at times throughout the history of the church.

See also RAPTURE, DOCTRINE OF THE.

Thomas Ice

Morgan Edwards, *Two Academical Exercises on Subjects Bearing the Following Titles: Millennium, Last-Novelties* (Dobson and Lang: Philadelphia, 1788); Frank Marotta, *Morgan Edwards: An Eighteenth Century Pretribulationist* (Morganville, N.J.: Present Truth Publishers, 1995); Thomas R. McKibbens Jr. and Kenneth L. Smith, *The Life and Works of Morgan Edwards* (New York: Arno Press, 1980); John S. Moore, "Morgan Edwards: Baptist Statesman" in *Baptist History and Heritage* (VI:1; January 1971).

EPHESIANS, ESCHATOLOGY OF

This letter was written to clearly set forth the believer's position in Christ. It has been viewed as a letter that was circulated among several local churches is Asia. Support for this is based on two facts: (1) the words "in Ephesus" (1:1) are not found in three of the early manuscripts, and (2) Paul does not mention anyone by name, which is unusual based on the fact that he lived and worked there for three years (Acts 20:31). The unity of both Jewish and Gentile believers in Christ is stressed and that this unity ought to be demonstrated by expressing Christian love to one another.

The apostle Paul authored this letter from his prison cell in Rome. This is the first of what are called the Prison Epistles. The date of writing is A.D. 60.

The prophecy found in this letter is concerned with the church as it is comprised of believers. The security of believers is promised by the giving of the Holy Spirit as a seal to the redemptive transaction performed by

Christ (1:13–14). The mystery of the church, Jew and Gentile united in one body, is explained (2:14–18; 3:6, 9). The sealing ministry of the Holy Spirit points to the rapture and resurrection of believers (4:30). A future time in heaven is foretold (5:27) when Christ presents His church to Himself as holy and blameless. The promise of rewards, looking forward to heaven, is tendered for those Christians who do good in their service to Christ (6:8).

See also ISRAEL AND THE CHURCH: THE DIFFERENCES.

Ervin R. Starwalt

John F. Walvoord, *The Prophecy Knowledge Handbook* (Wheaton: Victor Books, 1990); John F. Walvoord and Roy B. Zuck, eds., *The Bible Knowledge Commentary* (Wheaton: Victor Books, 1985); Charles F. Pfeiffer and Everett F. Harrison, eds.,*Wycliffe Bible Commentary* (Chicago: Moody Press, 1962).

ESCHATOLOGY, JEWISH

As in Christianity, Judaism is represented by many different traditions, each with its own interpretation of prophetic Scripture. This discussion is limited to orthodox Jewish eschatology which, though differing in many particulars, presents a general outline that approximates premillennial interpretation of end-time events. The comprehensive nature of Jewish eschatology precludes a discussion of only the two principal eschatological periods, however, they are sufficient to provide the comparison with premillennialism.

Eschatological Divisions

The rabbis made a broad distinction between this age (*ha-'olam hazeh*) and the age to come (*ha-'olam habba*), as well as a more specific distinction between the days of the Messiah (*Yemot ha-Mashiach*), the Redemption (*Ge'ulah*), and the resurrection of the dead (*techiyyat ha-metim*). From a premillennial perspective, these distinctions are roughly equivalent to the larger division of the present age (including the Tribulation) and the Millennium, and the smaller division between the Tribulation and Millennium. In rabbinic eschatology, the days of the Messiah was a transitional stage that would last an undetermined number of jubilees or generations. A number of proposals were made for the length of this stage—2,000, 5,000, and 7,000 years, or forty, fifty, seventy, eighty-five jubilees, firty, sixty generations, or 365, 400 years. Chronological reckonings of these days were not discouraged by the rabbis, only the attempt to calculate the precise time of the messianic advent. Several chronological chronicles existed for this purpose. The oldest of these is called the Seder Olam (the order of the world), edited by Jose ben Halafta (c. A.D. 140). It lists the biblical and postbiblical events until the Bar-Kokhba revolt. The Seder Olam Zutta (compiled in the eighth century A.D.), completes the Seder Olam Rabba (great Seder Olam) by adding the number of years to its historical outline and continuing it until Rabbi Hazub (c. A.D. 800). Computations for the latter days are based on biblical texts (e.g., Jer. 30–33; 50–51; Dan. 9–11, Ezek. 34–48) and interpreted both literally and mystically (Kabbalistic method).

Another chronological scheme for eschatological reckoning is preserved in the Babylonian Talmud. The Amoraic sage R. Aha, sought deeper insight as to why the seventh benediction in the Eighteen Benedictions concerned "the redemption of Israel"; R. Rava answered it was to teach that Israel will be redeemed in the seventh year of Messiah's advent (T.B. Megilla 17b; cf. Tosefta Sanh. 13. 1; Rosh Hashana 16b). An eschatological Baraita explains this: "The septennium (seven 1,000-year periods) at the end of which the son of David will come—in the first year the following verse will be fulfilled: 'I will cause it to rain upon one city and cause it not to rain upon another city,' in the second, the arrows of famine will be sent forth; in the third, there will be a great famine and men, women and children, men of piety, and miracle workers will die, and the Torah will be forgotten by its students; in the fourth, there will be plenty; in the fifth, there will be great plenty, and people will eat and drink and rejoice, and the Torah will be restored to its students; in the sixth there will be (heavenly) sounds; in the seventh, wars; and at the end of the septennium the son of David (Messiah) will come" (Sanh. 97a; 'Avoda Zara 9a). The Gemara to this observes that: "war is also the beginning of redemption," indicating that the messianic era would also be throughout the seventh millennium.

Another account is that of a Tannaitic sage of the School of Elijah. In this Baraita we learn: "The world will exist for 6,000 years, for 2,000 there will be desolation, for 2,000, Torah, and for 2,000 the Days of the Messiah" (Sanh. 97a–b; Av. Zar. 9a; cf. Rosh Hashana 31a). After this, the 7,000th year will be a year of renewal (Sanh. 97b). This Great Sabbath Week of 7,000 years is patterned after the six days of creation (6 days = 6,000 years) and the rest on the seventh day (the last day = last 1,000 years). God is said to hide behind the *'olam ha-zeh* (this present world of the 6,000 years), for the three Hebrew root letters that make up the word "world"—*ayin, lamed, mem*—indicate a vanishing; though not of God, but of God from the world. In the last 1,000 years, the *'olam ha-ba* (the world to come), He will not be in the background, but will appear and transform the natural order into one that is spiritual. It is in this context that the prophecy of Isaiah concerning the restored natural order (11:6–9; 65:20–25) will be fulfilled. In Jewish terms this time is referred to as the messianic millennium, a period of peace on earth that precedes the final Day of the Lord.

Tribulation

The Jewish apocalyptic literature presents an eschatological setting for the Tribulation period. The book of 1 Enoch describes an end-time assault by Gentile forces against God's elect in which demonic spirits, or fallen angels, incite the nations to war against Israel (56:5–8). God gives Israel the power to defend itself against its enemies (90:13–15), however, an increase in violence and wickedness must be endured (91:5–7) before the reign of righteousness can begin in the eighth week (91:12–13). Great confusion will also come upon the Gentiles before the final judgment, and they will slaughter one another (100:4). The final eschatological conflict will be between God, Michael, and the angels, and Beliar and his demons, which extends to the earthly realm in the war between the righteous (Israel) and the unrighteous (Gentiles). The Testaments of the Twelve Patriarchs also pictures the general condition of these times as one of unbelief and wickedness (T. Levi 4:1), and especially of the defilement of the priesthood (T. Levi 17:7–11). The Syriac Apocalypse of Baruch begins by answering the question: "Will that tribulation which is to be continue a long time, and will that necessity embrace many years?" After a long discourse detailing twelve divisions that comprise this Tribulation period, it adds, "when all is accomplished that was to come to pass . . . Messiah shall then begin to be revealed" (26–29; cf. 1 Enoch 101:12–17).

The rabbis, though rejecting the nonbiblical literature as uninspired, nevertheless had developed their own views from the same source (the Old Testament). Rashi, the leading Jewish biblical commentator, apparently speaks of an end-time fulfillment for the Tribulation in his commentary on Deuteronomy 4:28–30. Following the Targum's explanation, he places the Tribulation after the period of Gentile domination has ended. While the reading of the Masoretic text has as a consequence of Israelite exile the punishment of serving idols, Targum Onkelos renders this as "you shall serve *peoples* who serve idols," thus, following the Targum, Rashi understands that the deliverance from this Tribulation (v. 30) will be the end of Gentile domination and the restoration of covenantal blessings (v. 31) resulting from Israelite repentance (v. 29).

In like manner, rabbinic commentators interpreted the time of trouble (Dan. 12:1) as a future eschatological time equivalent with the period known as the *ch^{a}valim* (birth pangs), or *chevlo shel mashiach* (birth pangs of the Messiah). This term expresses the idea that Israel, like a mother, was to bring forth the Messiah through the labor pains of childbirth. As such, they would begin at a determined point and increase in intensity until the time of delivery. In Isaiah 66:7–9 the figure of birth pangs is applied to Israel at its national rebirth (v. 8). This may have served as the principal Old Testament reference for the rabbis in their conception of the messianic birth pangs. The term as a technical expression is first seen in rabbinic literature in the Mishnah (Sanh. 98b and Mek. on Exod. 16:25), where it is attributed to Eliezer, who may be the son of Hyrcanus (c. A.D. 90). At any rate, the Jewish concept of the messianic woes was already in place by the first century, as revealed by the Greek term *odinon* (birth pangs) used in the Gospels (Matt. 24:8; Mark 13:8). In a manner similar to the Olivet Discourse, the Mishnah identifies ten signs that are to accompany messianic birth pangs. These are enumerated in Sanh. 97b as: (1) the world is either all righteous or all guilty, (2) truth is in short supply, (3) inflation will soar, (4) Israel will have begun to be repopulated according to Ezekiel 36:8–12, (5) wise people will be scarce, (6) the Jews will have despaired of redemption, (7) the young will be contemptuous of the old, (8) scholarship will be rejected, (9) piety will be in disgust, and (10) a growing number of Jews will turn on their own people. Similar statements are given in Sotah 9:15 concerning the days of messianic advent, called here the footprints of the Messiah.

Typical of those making this interpretation of the birth pangs were the medieval sages Rashi and R' Sh'muel Masnuth. In his commentary on Daniel (c. A.D. 1230) R' Masnuth states that "this generation will see the pangs of the Messiah—the tribulations of the generation described in tractate Sanh. 97b." Rashi, in his commentary on Daniel (c. A.D. 1100), interpolated the signs of religious enmity and civil lawlessness among Jews in "the generation of the Messiah" (from Kethubot 112b) to "the sons of your people" in this verse. So frightening was the prospect of encountering this time of Tribulation preceding the messianic arrival that some of the sages hoped that it would not come in their lifetimes. Among such sages was Rabbi Yochanan who exclaimed: "Let [the Messiah] come, but may I not see it!" (Sanh. 98b; see DANIEL'S SEVENTY WEEKS, RABBINIC INTERPRETATION OF).

Millennium

In the apocalyptic work called Fourth Ezra, a detailed description of the events of the millennial age is preserved. Here, after a preliminary judgment the Jewish kingdom will be set up for 1,000 years (other sources suppose 400 years). This is followed by the final, general judgment in which the earth is destroyed, the Messiah dies, and creation returns to chaos. After this comes the Resurrection, the creation of a new heaven and earth, and a state of eternal bliss. In rabbinic eschatology the term kingdom of heaven (*malkut ha-shamayim*) frequently appears to describe the dominion and order of heaven that is to be imposed on earth. This kingdom is apparently understood as a national and political establishment since it is not considered to be complete until the final redemption, which includes the regathering of Israel in its land, the restoration of national sovereignty, and a new spiritual reality, never before experienced, which is evidenced by Gentile conversion and subservience to God, Messiah, and the Jewish people. In the Midrash Rabba, during this age of redemption, the natures of people are changed (cf. Ezek. 36:26–27) to obedience to Torah by God uprooting or eradicating the evil inclination (*'etzer ha-ra'*) and relacing it with a new heart or heart of flesh (Num. R. 15:16; 17:6; Lev. R. 35:5; cf. Ex. R. 41:7; Cant. R. 1:4).

Eternal State

The eternal state, generally called the world to come, and sometimes compared to the Garden of Eden, follows the Millennium, but is not described in detail. However, it is clearly distinguished from the Millennium for in it is "no eating and drinking, no begetting of children, no bargaining, no jealousy and hatred, and no strife; but the righteous sit with their crowns on their heads enjoying the effulgence of the *Shekinah* ("Presence of God")" (Bab. Berakot 17a).

See also HERMENEUTICS, RABBINICAL.

J. Randall Price

George W. Buchanan, *Revelation and Redemption: Jewish Documents of*

Deliverance from the Fall of Jerusalem to the Death of Nachmanides (Dillsboro, N.C.: Western North Carolina Press, 1978); H. J. de Jonge, ed., *Jewish Eschatology, Early Christian Christology and the Twelve Patriarchs: Collected Essays of Marinus de Jonge. Supplements to Novum Testamentum,* 63 (Leiden: E. J. Brill, 1991), 3–62, 147–313; Pasquale De Santo, "A Study of Jewish Eschatology with Special Reference to the Final Conflict" (Ph.D. diss., Duke University, 1957); *Encyclopedia Judaica* s.v. "Eschatology" (Jerusalem: Keter Publishing House Jerusalem, 1972) 6:872–83; Aaron Judah Klingerman, *Messianic Prophecy in the Old Testament* (Grand Rapids: Zondervan, 1957); Sigmund Mowinckel, *He That Cometh,* trans. G. W. Anderson (New York: Abingdon Press, 1954), 261–79; Elihu A. Schatz, *Proof of the Accuracy of the Bible* (New York: Jonathan David Publishers, 1973), 356–538; Solomon Schechter, *Aspects of Rabbinic Theology* (New York: Schocken Books, 1969), 97–115; Ephraim E. Urbach, *The Sages: Their Concepts and Beliefs,* trans. Israel Abrahams, 2 vols. (Jerusalem: The Magnes Press, 1975), 649–90.

ESCHATOLOGY, SCOPE OF

The scope, blends, and possibilities for many different systems of eschatology is derived from a commingling of many different prophetic factors. For many, trying to understand the differences between premillennialism, postmillennialism, and amillennialism is a significant challenge. However, it becomes even more complex when the four timing approaches of preterism, historicism, futurism, and idealism are added to the prophetic mix. When these are combined with different hermeneutical approaches, Israel and the church, covenant theology verses dispensationalism, interpretative differences within systems, eschatology can become the most complicated of all areas of systematic theology to understand, let alone master.

However, like many complex appearances, things are not as difficult as they first appear if an effort is put forth to learn the basic characteristics of each aspect. When an individual learns the characteristics of each possible element, then they will be able to penetrate the different blends. In terms of the logic of the various aspects, what are some of the possible mixes that can be produced? The following chart summarizes this information.

PROPHETIC TIMING AND MILLENNIAL VIEWS

Timing	Amill	Postmill	Premill
Preterism	YES	YES	NO
Historicism	YES	YES	YES
Futurism	NO	YES	YES
Idealism	YES	YES	NO

Within premillennialism, there are other possibilities, as charted below:

PREMILLENNIAL TIMING VIEWS

Timing	Pretrib	Midtrib	Posttrib
Preterism	NO	NO	NO
Historicism	NO	YES	YES
Futurism	YES	YES	YES
Idealism	NO	NO	NO

The differences can be resolved by following a consistently literal hermeneutic. Such an approach results in a dispensational, premillennial, pretribulational, futurist eschatology that sees a future for national Israel.

See also ESCHATOLOGY, THEOLOGY AND VIEWS OF.

Thomas Ice

ESCHATOLOGY, THEOLOGY AND VIEWS OF

Eschatology is the theological term for the study of the end times. It comes from the Greek word *eschatos,* meaning "last" or "last things." Thus, it is used as a broad designation for biblical prophecy.

One of the unique features of biblical prophecy is that it has been interpreted by different hermeneutical methods. Millard Erickson (p. 1154) distinguishes four general views of eschatology that have been proposed within Christian theology.

Futurist View

The futurist view holds that prophetic events will be fulfilled in the future at the time of the end. Christ is viewed as coming in the future to establish His kingdom.

Preterist View

The preterist view holds that prophetic events were actually fulfilled at the time they were written and are now in the past. Christ is viewed as already having come to destroy Jerusalem (A.D. 70) and establish His kingdom.

Historicist View

The historicist view holds that prophetic events have been continually fulfilled throughout church history. Some may still come to pass in the future. Christ is viewed as continually coming.

Idealist View

The idealist view holds that prophetic events have no specific fulfillment in the past or the future but are being fulfilled in the present experience of the individual. Christ is viewed as coming within the individual's own experience.

Within the Christian church there have been a variety of approaches to the study of eschatology. Some refuse to consider it at all, preferring to dismiss prophecy as hopelessly confusing or generally irrelevant. Liberal schools of thought have included various forms of modernized (Ritschl), realized (Dodd), existentialized (Baltmann) or politicized (Moltmann) eschatology. Each of these views rejects the literal interpretation of prophecy. But among evangelicals, prophecy has always been taken seriously. Jesus Christ Himself predicted His return to earth as well as several significant end-time events (Matt. 24–25).

Within evangelical circles, several schools of thought have developed around the theme of the Millennium or the millennial reign of Christ. The issue at stake among evangelicals has generally involved *how* one interprets prophecy. Three main schools of thought have been proposed. While most evangelicals are premillennialists in their view of eschatology, amillennial and postmillennial options also exist.

Postmillennial

This school of thought believes that the Millennium (the thousand years of Revelation 20:1–13) is to be interpreted symbolically as synonymous with the church age. Satan's power is viewed as being bound by the power of the Gospel. Postmillennialists believe that during this "Millennium" (church age) the church is called upon to conquer unbelief, convert the masses, and govern society by the mandate of biblical law. Only after Christianity succeeds on earth will Christ return and announce that His kingdom has been realized. Postmillennial advocates have included Catholics, Puritans, charismatics, and dominionists, who urge believers to take dominion over the earth and its political governments in order to actualize the kingdom of God on earth.

Amillennial

This approach sees no Millennium of any kind on the earth. Rather, amillennialists tend to view so-called millennial prophecies as being fulfilled in eternity. References to the thousand years are interpreted symbolically. In this scheme the church age ends with the return of Christ to judge the world and usher in eternity. God's promises to Israel are viewed as having been fulfilled in the church (the New Israel of the new covenant); therefore, amillennialists see no specific future for national Israel. They view the church age as the era of conflict between the forces of good and evil which culminates with the return of Christ.

Premillennial

This view holds that Christ will return at the end of the church age in order to set up His kingdom on earth for a literal thousand years. Most also believe there will be a Great Tribulation period on earth prior to the return of Christ. Among premillennialists are those who believe the church will go through the Tribulation (posttribulationists) and those who believe the church will be raptured prior to the Tribulation (pretribulationists) and even a few who believe the church will be raptured in the middle of the Tribulation (midtribulationists). Despite these differences in regard to the rapture of the church, premillennialists generally believe in the future restoration of the state of Israel and the eventual conversion of the Jews to Christianity.

The premillennial view of eschatology looks forward to the Rapture (translation of believers to heaven) as the next major prophetic event. This, they believe, will end the church age and prepare the way for the Tribulation period and the return of Christ. The Rapture is suggested by such biblical passages as Paul's words to the Thessalonians: "For the Lord himself will come down from heaven, with a loud command, with the voice of the archangel and with the trumpet call of God, and the dead in Christ will rise first. After that, we who are still alive and are left will be caught up with them in the clouds to meet the Lord in the air. And so we will be with the Lord forever" (1 Thess. 4:16–17).

Eschatological Terms

Biblical history moves from a starting point with Creation (Gen. 1:1) and progresses toward a final consummation of all things. The Bible itself describes it like this: "Then the end will come, when he [Christ] hands over the kingdom to God the Father after He has destroyed all dominion, authority and power" (1 Cor. 15:24).

Several biblical words describe eschatological events.

Last Days

Last and *latter* are adjectives that describe the times just before the end of the age. Paul said, "There will be terrible times in the last days" (2 Tim. 3:1), and "in the latter times some shall depart from the faith" (1 Tim. 4:1 KJV). Peter said, "In the last days scoffers will come" who deny the promise of Christ's return (2 Peter 3:3).

End of the Age

The end (Gk., *telos)* points to the final outcome of all things. Jesus had this is mind when He said, "But the end is not yet" (Matt. 24:6) and "then the end will come" (Matt. 24:14). Age (Gk., *aion)* is generally translated "world" in the King James Version, as in Matthew 24:3, "the end of the world." Unfortunately, most think of this as the end of the earth, whereas the Greek phrase means only, "the end of the age" (NIV). This points to a time when the present age will conclude, but it will not be the end of the planet.

Consummation of the Age

The consummation of the age (Gk., *sunteleia)* is similar to end of the age and expresses the final unfolding of all things. Jesus promises to be with us "to the very end of the age" (Matt. 28:20).

Second Coming

This term itself does not appear until the writings of the church fathers, but the concept is clearly expressed in the New Testament. It is synonymous with "come back" (John 14:3) and "appear a second time" (Hebrews 9:28). In Greek, the term *parousia* (coming) describes the arrival and presence of a ruler. This term is used frequently to describe the coming of Christ, as in Matthew 24:3, 27, 37, 39.

Unveiling

Apocalupsis (unveil, or uncover) is the Greek title for the book of Revelation, the Apocalypse. It conveys the idea of a glorious revelation or appearing, as in "you eagerly wait for our Lord Jesus Christ to be revealed" (1 Cor. 1:7) or "when Jesus Christ is revealed" (1 Peter 1:7).

Appearing

The term "appearing" (Gk., *epiphaino*) means to bring to light, or glorious, as in "by the splendor of his coming" (2 Thess. 2:8). From this term comes the liturgical season of Epiphany, which refers to the coming of Christ.

Day of the Lord

The Day of the Lord and its corollary, the Day of Christ, refer to the time of final judgment that culminates with Armageddon. It appears in the Old Testament as "that great and dreadful day of the LORD" (Mal. 4:5) and is generally thought to be synonymous with the "time of Jacob's trouble" (Jer. 30:7; Dan. 12:1). In the New Testament it is the "great day of [Christ's] wrath" (Rev. 6:17).

Eschatology is the study of the end times and is generally associated with the study of biblical prophecies of future events. Jesus spoke of the "end of the age" in response to His disciples' questions. There can be no doubt that He viewed human history as moving toward a final climax, not as an endless cycle of repetitious events. The Jews of the intertestamental period distinguished between this age (Heb., *hauolam hazzeh)* and the age to come (Heb., *hauolam habbah).* The expression, the end of the world, comes from Judeo-Christian roots and is understood by both Jews and Christians as referring to this world (or age) coming to an end and being replaced by the age to come.

A similar concept is found in the Old Testament expression, the latter days (Heb., *beaharit hayyamim).* Moses foretold the future apostasy of Israel, its scattering, and its return to the Lord in the latter days (Deut. 4:30; cf. 31:29). The prophet Hosea spoke of the future repentance of Israel in the latter days (Hos. 3:5). The prophet Jeremiah predicted numerous events that would occur in the latter days (Jer. 23:20, 30:14, 48:47, 49:39). Ezekiel predicted the invasion of Israel by a coalition of nations, Gog and Magog, in the latter days (Ezek. 38:16), also using the alternate expression in the latter years (Ezek. 38:8).

How Will It All End?

The question of how this will all come about divides evangelicals according to their eschatological views. Pretribulationists believe that Christ will rapture the church to heaven prior to the Great Tribulation and then return with His bride at the end of the Tribulation to set up His kingdom on earth. Mid- and posttribulationists believe the church will suffer to some extent during the Tribulation period and be caught up at a midpoint or at the very end of the Great Tribulation.

Amillennialists believe that things will get worse at the end of the church age. While most view the entire church age as a time of tribulation for believers, many feel that the persecution of the saints (Christians) will get worse in the last days. At the very end, the Battle of Armageddon will commence and Christ will return to judge the world and to usher in eternity.

Postmillennialists believe that the church is the kingdom of God on earth and that it is our responsibility to bring in the kingdom by the preaching of the Gospel and the enactment of Christian laws, values, and principles in society until the whole world is converted to Christ.

Obviously, there are great differences in each of these views and yet each one contains an element of truth that all Christians need to remember. From the pretribulationist view we are reminded to be ready for the coming of Christ at any moment. From the mid- and posttribulationist viewswe are reminded that many times Christians are called to suffer for their Lord. Certainly, believers in the Third World could teach us much about what it means to suffer for Christ.

The amillennialist view reminds us all that we must be ready to face the judgment of God. While it is exciting to think about our Lord's coming, we must also realize that His judgment is coming as well. While we pre millennialists look forward to Christ's earthly kingdom, we must also remember that even that will come to an end and be merged into eternity into the eternal kingdom of God. The apostle Paul reminds us there is coming a time when Christ "hands over the kingdom to God the Father" (1 Cor. 15:24).

From the postmillennialist view we are reminded of our Christian responsibilities to the world in which we live. Since we do not know the exact time of Christ's return, we dare not sit back and do nothing but wait for the Rapture. Christ has given us very specific orders about our responsibilities to one another and to the world at large. We are called to be the light of the world and the salt of the earth until our Lord returns (Matt. 5:13–16).

See also AMILLENNIALISM; POSTMILLENNIALISM; PREMILLENNIALISM.

Edward Hindson

Paul Benware, *Understanding End Times Prophecy* (Chicago: Moody Press, 1995); John J. Davis, *Christ's Victorious Kingdom* (Grand Rapids: Baker, 1986); Millard Erickson, *Contemporary Options in Eschatology* (Grand Rapids: Baker, 1977); Edward Hindson, *Final Signs: Amazing Prophecies of the End Times* (Eugene, Oreg.: Harvest House, 1996); Anthony Hoekema, *The Bible and the Future* (Grand Rapids: Eerdmans, 1979); Herman Hoyt, *The End Times* (Chicago: Moody Press, 1969); J. Dwight Pentecost, *Things to Come* (Grand Rapids: Zondervan, 1958).

EXODUS, ESCHATOLOGY OF

Exodus deals with the redemption of the Israelites from Egyptian bondage. Although the preeminent theme is redemption the book also deals with God's preparation of these people to be His own. Thus, it is documentation of the birth of the nation Israel. The book typifies redemption and traces the descendants of Jacob as they are made a theocratic nation at Mount Sinai. These are the people from whom the promised Redeemer will come and they are placed under the Mosaic covenant as a sign that they have been set aside for this purpose. The book documents the giving of the law as well as the beginning of ritual worship.

The book itself verifies that Moses is the author (17:14; 24:4, 7, 34:37). There are other references in the Scriptures that also point to Moses as the author (i.e., Deut. 31:9, 31:34; 1 Kings 2:3; Neh. 8:1, 13:1; Mark 7:10, 12:26). Evangelicals view the writing of the book to have taken place during the period 1450–1410 B.C.

The prophecies contained in the book deal primarily with events recorded in the book itself. The calling of Moses to be the deliverer of his people is described in 3:5–12, and the promised sign (3:12) was fulfilled in 17:6. The ten plagues on Egypt were each fulfilled when Pharaoh resisted letting Israel go. Exodus 19:1–3 reveals the preliminary promise of the Mosaic covenant, and 23:20–31 contains the prophetic promise to Israel that as the nation would be guided into the Promised Land. The tabernacle is a foreshadowing of the coming work of the Messiah. The bronze altar (27:1–8) is a type of Christ's offering Himself on the cross; the laver (30:18–20), His cleansing of the believer's sin; the golden candlestick (25:31–40) is the divine light brought to the believer; the table of showbread (25:23–30) is representative of Christ our Bread of Life; the altar of incense (30:1–2) illustrates Christ's work as intercessor; the veil (26:31–35) represents the human body of our Lord which was symbolically torn in two at His death; the ark of the covenant (25:10–22) symbolizes His humanity in the acacia wood, and connects with Isaiah 53:2 where Christ's humanity is spoken of; the gold overlayment of the ark represents His deity.

Rick Bowman

John F. Walvoord, ed., *The Bible Prophecy Handbook* (Wheaton: Victor Books, 1990); John F. Walvoord and Roy B. Zuck, eds., *The Bible Knowledge Commentary* (Wheaton: Victor Books, 1985); Everet F. Harrison and Charle F. Pfeiffer, eds., *Wycliffe Bible Commentary*, (Chicago: Moody Press, 1962).

EZEKIEL 36–37, INTERPRETATION OF

These chapters fall within the larger context of Ezekiel's eschatological discourse. Chapters 33–48 deal extensively with Israel's restoration to the land, blessing, and worship in the millennial kingdom. The transition from the historical to the prophetic is logical. Having warned the nation of Jerusalem's impending destruction at the hands of the Babylonians, Ezekiel describes the destruction of Jerusalem in 586 B.C. (33:21). What, then, is the future of Jerusalem and the Hebrew people? Have God's unconditional covenants been revoked? Has the church replaced Israel as the people of God? Is there no future restoration of the Jewish people and their nation?

In chapters 33–48 Ezekiel relates in precise detail that God has determined a glorious future for Israel of restoration to the land and of blessing in the land. God will fulfill the promises in bringing the Jewish people back into the land and blessing them in the land.

The church remains a distinct entity, a people of God distinct from Israel. A literal [normal] interpretation of these chapters demands a glorious future for Israel in the Promised Land.

Chapters 36–37 describe in elaborate detail the repopulation of the land of Israel. The mountains, valleys, and previously desolate cities are again inhabited by the returning Jews. But this restoration is also related to the people's spiritual conversion: God will give them new hearts and will put His Spirit within them, enabling them to walk in obedience to His Word. This is a prerequisite to the fulfillment of the unconditional Palestinian covenant guaranteeing Israel's return to the land (Deut. 30).

Restoration of the Mountains of Israel (36:1–15)

Ezekiel prophesied about Israel's future restoration, addressing the "mountains of Israel," a reference to both the people and the land in which the mountains were located (36:1). With passionate emphasis Ezekiel declares five times (NASB), "therefore"—Israel will be established in the land (vv. 3–7). Ezekiel's passion is further seen in the phrase "For good cause" (Heb., *ya'an beya'an,* 36:3; lit., because, indeed because). In holy jealousy Ezekiel declares that the land that the enemy sought to appropriate for itself will be inhabited by Israel, but the nations will suffer scorn. It is the law of retribution; since Israel has suffered indignation through captivity, therefore, those nations will now experience indignation and judgment. A normal reading of the text demands both a literal judgment upon those nations and a literal restoration of Israel to the land.

Although Israel would soon return from Babylon, these prophecies were not fulfilled at that time. The restoration from captivity was a harbinger of Israel's return from Gentile nations just before Messiah's Second Advent. When this restoration occurs, Israel will return in a regenerated condition and in obedience to the Lord (36:25–27), which was not the case when Israel returned from Babylon (Ezra 9–10; Neh. 5:1–5; 13:1–31; Hag. 1:1–11; 2:13–14; Mal. 1–4). Moreover, in the final return, Israel will never again be subjugated by a foreign nation (36:12).

Ezekiel predicts the future blessing on the nation. The general statement of 36:8 is expanded in 36:9 and following. The explicit reason for Israel's future restoration and blessing is given in 36:9: "For, behold, I am for you, and I will turn to you." It is an unconditional promise, an extension of the Palestinian covenant (Deut. 30). Israel's future restoration to the land depends on the faithfulness of God. If His Word is reliable, then Israel has a future in the land. The land that had been emptied of its population will be repopulated; moreover, it will involve "all the house of Israel," representatives of all twelve tribes, not merely Judah. At that time Israel will enjoy greater blessings than previously (36:11).

Restoration of the People of Israel (36:16–38)

The promise to restore Israel to the land is related to God's holiness; because Yahweh has concern for the integrity of His name, He will restore Israel to the land as a testimony to the nations. The Lord will act on behalf of His own name, not because of any claim Israel may have on Him (Isa. 48:11; Deut. 9:6). The mighty act of bringing Israel into the land will demonstrate the Lord's power to the nations and thereby reveal His holiness.

Israel's future return to the land is marked by spiritual conversion, described in figurative language (36:25–32). The Lord will sprinkle clean water on the nation, suggesting the nation's conversion and forgiveness (cf. Ps. 51:4, 9). This is also seen in Israel's receiving a new heart. Removal of the heart of stone indicates the rebellion and stubbornness is removed, enabling the person to love God (Deut. 6:5). In that future day Israel will also be the recipient of the Holy Spirit. Whereas the Holy Spirit was given at Pentecost, a nonrepeatable event, the Holy Spirit will be appropriated by Israel on their conversion at the end of the age (cf. 37:14, 39:29; Isa. 44:3, 59:21; Joel 2:28–29). As a result Israel will walk in conformity with God's law, enabling the nation to live in the land (36:28) while enjoying heaven-sent prosperity (36:29–30). The supernatural productivity in the Millennium is a theme in the prophets (Isa. 35:1–2, 65:21–23; Jer. 31:5, 12; Joel 2:21–27; Amos 9:13–14; Mic. 4:4; Zech. 8:12, 9:17).

The prophet compares the land's past desolation with the prosperity of the Millennium (36:33–36). Four times in 36:34–36 the Hebrew text emphasizes "the desolate [Heb. *haneshamah*] land." In the millennial age, however, it will be likened to the Garden of Eden (36:35). The restoration and prosperity of Israel will be a witness to the nations that Yahweh is responsible for Israel's renewal.

In that future day there will be no holocaust; no longer will Israel experience persecution and death because of its enemies; rather, Israel's population will multiply like flocks of sheep. Jerusalem will be teeming with people like the flocks of sheep that filled the city on feast days (Mic. 2:12; cf. 2 Chron. 35:7).

Restoration of the People As One Nation (37:1–28)

In one of the most graphic, glorious pictures in the OT, Ezekiel envisions the restoration of Israel and Judah united as one nation (37:16–19), back in their land of promise (37:12–14, 21), regenerated (37:14), and under Messiah's rule (37:24–25).

In Ezekiel's vision of the valley of dry bones, the prophet sees the restoration of Israel to the land in visionary language. The context of the book of Ezekiel, and particularly the context of chapters 33–39, demands that these verses refer to Israel's return to the land in the messianic age. To relate these verses to anything other than Israel's future restoration reflects a betrayal of proper biblical hermeneutics. The subject of the book of Ezekiel is Israel's judgment and future restoration—a common theme of the prophets. To relate these verses to the church is hermeneutically unwarranted.

In a vision similar to 8:3 and 11:5, 24, Ezekiel was taken up and brought to a valley full of dry bones (37:1–10). The valley looked like an ancient battlefield with bones of the slain scattered across the field. The bones depict death, while the emphasis of their aridity, "very dry" emphasizes a death of long duration. "Can these bones live?" After all these years can the dead be revived? The answer lies with the power of God (Deut. 32:38). God commands Ezekiel to prophesy over the bones announcing that He will cause breath to enter them, giving them life. Through the prophet, the Lord announced that these bones will live. As Ezekiel prophesied, the bones were miraculously joined to precisely the right connecting bones, with tendons, flesh, and skin covering the bones (37:8). Then God breathed into them the breath of life.

But what is the meaning of the bones? Ezekiel clearly identified the meaning of the vision: "these bones are the whole house of Israel. . . . I will bring you into the land of Israel" (37:11–12). The interpretation is clear—it pertains to the nation Israel and their future restoration to the land. This prophecy of Israel's future relates to both Israel's future restoration to the land as well as Israel's future regeneration (37:14; cf. 36:25–27; 39:29; Joel 2:28; Isa. 32:15). Once more, normal language usage referring to "house of Israel," "land of Israel," "My Spirit within you," and "I will place you on your own land" prohibits an amillennial interpretation applying these verses to the church. If language means anything, these verses speak of a future spiritual conversion of the Jewish people and a physical restoration to the land with the attendant millennial blessings.

Israel's restoration as a nation is developed further in 37:15 and following. In the acted parable of the two sticks, one stick was for Judah, representing the southern kingdom; the other stick was for Joseph and Ephraim, representing the northern kingdom. The meaning of this acted parable is clearly explained: "I will take the sons of Israel from among the nations where they have gone, and I will gather them from every side and bring them into their own land" (37:21). Under Messiah the Israelites will be united as one nation (37:22). Again it is reaffirmed that they will return to the land in a converted state, for in that day Israel will be cleansed from idolatry (37:23) and will be God's people (cf. 14:11, 36:28).

When Israel is converted and restored to the land, "My servant David will be king over them" (37:24). This is probably not a reference to resurrected David but rather a title of Messiah. He is also denominated, My servant, and one shepherd, under whose authority all Israel will come.

Messiah will rule as king over Israel in the Millennium, and He will also be their shepherd. At that time they will possess the land promised to the patriarchs in the unconditional Abrahamic covenant (Gen. 12:1–3; 13:14–18; 15:12–21; 28:13–15). The text also stresses the permanence of Israel's habitation. The Israelites will inhabit the land forever (37:25); Messiah will be their king forever (37:26, 28). At that time Israel will enjoy a covenant of peace with Yahweh because the unconditional covenants with Israel will be fulfilled (Abrahamic covenant, Gen. 12:1–3; Palestinian covenant, Deut. 30; Davidic covenant, 2 Sam 7:12–16; new covenant, Jer. 31:31–34).

See also JEWS, RETURN OF THE.

Paul Enns

Charles L. Feinberg, *Millennialism: The Two Major Views* (Winona Lake, Ind.: BMH Books, 1985); J. Dwight Pentecost, *Things to Come* (Grand Rapids: Zondervan, 1958); John F. Walvoord, *The Millennial Kingdom* (Grand Rapids: Zondervan, 1959).

EZEKIEL, ESCHATOLOGY OF

This book was written during Judah's bondage to Babylon. The prophet first predicted the fall of Jerusalem and future restoration after the fall. The book details the efforts of the prophet Ezekiel to justify the captivity as a just response of God in answer to continued sin. Although captive Israel is given assurance that at some future point God's blessing would again be theirs, God's purpose was to instruct the people that He is God and that He is in control. In His time He would restore them and cause judgment to fall on their enemies.

The author is identified as Ezekiel (1:3). The date of writing is placed from 592–570 B.C.

The prophecies concerning Judah and Jerusalem are in chapters 4–24. These prophecies tell of the coming siege of Jerusalem in 587 B.C. (4:1–3), the duration of the exile and the associated discomforts (4:4–17), and the destruction of the people of Jerusalem (5:1–17). Next is foretold the coming judgment by God (7:1–27), the profaning of God in the temple (chap. 8), the foretelling of killing of the people in Jerusalem (chap. 9), and the vision of God's glory departing the temple (10:18). This was all was accomplished during the Babylonian invasion and subsequent captivity.

Next is the judgment upon the wicked leaders of Israel (11:1–13), and the restoration of Israel to the land (11:16–17). The promise of the new covenant (11:19–20) looks forward to the Millennium. The restoration of Israel at the Millennium is again promised (16:53–63). The judgment of the Jews at the end of the Tribulation when Christ returns is foretold (20:32–44). Once again the judgment of Israel is foretold (21:18–24; 22:13–22), and Israel is told that it will have no king until Messiah comes again to rule on the earth from Jerusalem (21:27). Further reference to the pending destruction of Jerusalem is given in the parable of the boiling pot (24:1–14).

Chapters 25–32 are prophecies concerning the Gentile nations and the judgments on them: Ammon (25:1–7), Moab (25:8–11), Edom (25:12–14), Philistia (25:15–17), and Tyre (26:1–28:19). There has been partial fulfillment of these prophecies during the course of history. But a complete fulfillment is yet future, as seen in the reference to the Day of the Lord (30:3).

The final prophecies are concerned with the restoration of Israel. The millennial kingdom is seen in the prophecy of the good shepherd gathering up His sheep who have been scattered (34:11–31). Israel's restoration to the land is foretold (36:1–25, 37:1–10, 15–19), as is the new covenant that God will make with Israel in the Millennium (36:26–38). Looking forward to a time just preceding the second coming, the future invasion of Gog of Palestine and his immediate destruction by God are foretold (chaps. 38–39). The millennial temple is prophesied (40:1–42:20), the return of the glory of the Lord to the temple (43:1–5), and the ministers and functions of the new temple are described (44:1–46:24). The remainder of the book describes the boundaries of the Promised Land in the future and describes the river that flows out of the temple which gives the land its life.

The book of Ezekiel is bursting with descriptions of future events, many of which await fulfillment. To fully understand Israel, its judgments, and its restoration the book must be carefully and diligently studied.

Ervin R. Starwalt

Merrill F. Unger, *Unger's Bible Dictionary* (Chicago: Moody Press, 1966); John F. Walvoord, *The Prophecy Knowledge Handbook* (Wheaton: Victor Books, 1990); John F. Walvoord and Roy B. Zuck, eds., *The Bible Knowledge Commentary* (Wheaton: Victor Books, 1985); Charles F. Pfeiffer and Everett F. Harrison, eds.,*Wycliffe Bible Commentary* (Chicago: Moody Press, 1962).

EZRA, NEHEMIAH, ESTHER, ESCHATOLOGY OF

While Ezra, Nehemiah, and Esther do not contain prophetic matter, strictly speaking, they are nonetheless important in demonstrating the outworking of God's prophetic plan.

Ezra

The book of Ezra carries on with the history of the Israelites from where Chronicles leaves off. It was written to the exiles who had returned from the seventy-year captivity during the time of Zerubbabel and Ezra. The book was written to encourage those people who were wavering in their relationship and response to God. It contains a far more important message then just the narration of historical facts.

The author is Ezra. This is based upon Hebrew tradition and internal evidence where he refers to himself in the first person (7:27–9:15). The two distinct time periods covered in the book are (1) the first six chapters cover the period from the decree of Cyrus to the rebuilding of the temple and (2) the remainder of the book covers the events that took place after Ezra returned from Babylon. The date of the book is placed from 450–444 B.C.

Nehemiah

This booked is closely linked to the book of Ezra. It too is a postexhilic writing that shows God's faithfulness to the restoration of His exiled people to their land. The completion of the history of the restoration is contained in this book. The beginning of Daniel's seventy weeks (Dan. 9:25) began when Artaxerxes commissioned Nehemiah to go and rebuild Jerusalem (Neh. 2:1–10).

Nehemiah is accepted as the author based on his identification (1:1), and the fact that the writing is a first-person account of the events that took place. The book was written about 445–425 B.C.

Esther

Esther obtains its name from the main character of the book. The book is unique in that it contains no references to God. Nonetheless the purpose of the book is to demonstrate God's providential care of His people as they experience trials. It is a proclamation of God's ceaseless preservation of His people. The book is the basis of the feast of Purim, and it explains the origin of that feast.

The author is unknown and there are no clues provided within the book. It is clear that whoever wrote it had an understanding of the Persian culture and was probably an eye-witness to the events. The book was written about 470–465 B.C.

Rick Bowman

Charles F. Pfeiffer and Everett F. Harrison, eds., *Wycliffe Bible Commentary* (Chicago: Moody Press, 1962); John F. Walvoord and Roy B. Zuck, eds., *The Bible Knowledge Commentary* (Wheaton: Victor Books, 1985).

F

FAITH, SAVED BY (DISPENSATIONAL VIEW OF)

Dispensationalists have long been accused of believing in multiple ways of salvation. This criticism is often based upon incorrect perceptions, the misinterpretation of statements, or an inadequate understanding of dispensationalism by nondispensationalists. At times, however, dispensationalists have made statements related to this issue which were poorly framed, easily misconstrued, or even incorrect. Nevertheless, for as long as this criticism of dispensationalism has continued to surface, dispensationalists have continued to affirm and defend their belief in only one basis and means of salvation. people are always saved by grace through faith.

Multiple Dispensations

Dispensationalism does assert that God has employed multiple dispensations in the course of earth history. This assertion does not logically imply, much less affirm, that God designed multiple ways of salvation. A dispensation is not a means of salvation, but an administrative arrangement or stewardship designed by God to direct human living. The purpose of such a stewardship is not to provide salvation, but to establish divine order (that way of living that reflects the nature of God) and to restrain human sin (that way of living that is contrary to God's nature). The system of order and the means of restraint designed by God in each dispensation are not devised to establish human righteousness. Ultimately they expose human unrighteousness, human inability to live according to God's criteria. This exposé of human sinfulness is, ideally, that which drives a man in any dispensation to the one and only means of salvation. People must place their faith in a gracious God who can absolve human sin apart from human merit.

For example, after the human fall in the Garden of Eden, God apparently chose to restrain the sin of humankind and establish divine order on earth by means of the internal governance of the Holy Spirit in each individual (Gen. 6:3). This ministry of the Spirit was undergirded by special revelation from God. That which had been revealed to humans by the time of their expulsion from the garden included truth regarding the person and nature of the Creator-God (Gen. 1–2) and the breach that had developed between people and God due to the altered, sinful human state (Gen. 3:1–10). Also included was truth about the consequences of sin, truth about enmity between God and Satan and between Satan's seed and the woman's seed, and truth about the ultimate triumph of the woman's seed over that of Satan (Gen. 3:14–19). It is likely that they were also instructed in the art of bloody sacrifice (Gen. 3:21; cf. 4:4), which was designed to maintain some level of human joy and fellowship with God (see Gen. 4:7). If there was to be divine order and the restraint of sin, then each person had to obey the internal promptings of the Spirit of God as grounded in God's revelation, while refusing to obey the dictates of his or her own fallen, fleshly nature. People could not be saved by perfectly fulfilling this stewardship, for no one could ever perfectly obey a Spirit-directed conscience and restrain the sin nature. In fact, this divine stewardship ultimately confirmed people's innate inability to live God-ordered and sin-resistant lives (Gen. 6:1–5). Yet even in this dispensation people could receive unmerited favor from God (Gen. 6:8) and be declared righteous (Gen. 6:9) if, in recognition of their own sinfulness, they feared God and evidenced genuine faith by responding positively to God's special revelation (Heb. 11:7).

An identical pattern can be found in each dispensation. God continued to administer various stewardships that would model divine order and restrain people's innate sinfulness: human government, ethnic promise, national law, and so forth. Each of these economic arrangements was grounded in further objective revelation, and all of these dispensations ultimately were designed not to save people but to evidence human sinfulness. Every dispensation demonstrates human inability to comply with God's demands. Even the final dispensation, the millennial kingdom, though it begins with an entirely regenerate human populace and is ruled directly by Christ and His glorified saints, ends in human rebellion against God (Rev. 20:7–9). The administrative strictures of the various dispensations were never intended to save people through their own efforts to comply with God's standards but were intended to demonstrate the lack of human compliance. In any dispensation, including that of Moses with its law-centered stewardship or that of the church with its grace-centered stewardship, people are not saved by conforming themselves to the external forms of the stewardship. People are saved by casting themselves in faith on the mercy of the God who has revealed Himself to fallen hummankind.

Incremental Revelation

Dispensationalism also asserts that the content of the revelation upon which someone bases his or her faith may differ in each dispensation since God has chosen to reveal truth in progressive increments. This assertion, likewise, must not be construed to imply that different ways of salvation existed. Everyone who has ever been or ever will be saved from sin is saved on the basis of God's grace by means of faith. However, the expression of genuine faith in each dispensation may differ. Genuine faith is expressed by an obedient response to that special revelation that God has disclosed up to and during the time of a particular stewardship.

Abraham, before the Law of Moses, expressed his absolute and exclusive faith in Jehovah, the God of biblical revelation, by leaving Ur at God's command and implicitly believing God's promises (Heb. 11:8–19). On the basis of that faith, God graciously imputed righteousness to Abraham (Gen. 15:1–6; Rom. 4:1–22). David, under the Law of Moses, experienced forgiveness apart from animal sacrifice based solely on his faith in God's mercy and grace (Ps. 51:1–2). David believed what God had objectively revealed about divine holiness and human sinfulness (Ps. 51:3–5). In fact, David's recognition of his sinfulness and his need to cast himself wholly upon the mercy of God for forgiveness had, at some point in his life, brought him to the assurance of complete forgiveness above and beyond the continuous rituals of the Law (Ps. 32:1–2, 103:8–12; Rom. 4:5–8). Once the stewardship of Law had convinced David that ultimate forgiveness must come from God and not from law-keeping, then David found great delight in law-keeping as the expression of divine order and the means of restraining sin in that era (Ps. 19:7–11, 51:18–19; 119:97–104). Hebrews 11 provides ample evidence that the expression of genuine faith, under every stewardship, is based upon the objective revelation that God has dispensed until that time. The Scriptures do not support the view that people in every age had a thorough understanding of the atoning death of the incarnate Son of God for the complete forgiveness of their sin.

Singular Salvation

Dispensationalists have always asserted that the Bible teaches only one basis and means of salvation. God, throughout history, has instituted different methods of administering human affairs, different stewardships by which people might acceptably live and by which sin might be effectively restrained. God has also disseminated, in increments, revelation about Himself and about human needs—progressively teaching people more about God's nature, God's plan for humanity, human sinfulness, and God's method of complete release from sin. In each era of history, people were expected to believe God's revelation regarding the divine nature and recognize the complete inability of humankind to live up to the established criteria of God's stewardship. People, acting on the basis of the revelation for which they were responsible in their particular era of history, were expected to acknowledge their insufficiency and cast themselves, by faith, wholly on the mercy of God. God, on his part, would wholly forgive each person's sin and impute divine righteousness to each by grace. Only then could people experience complete forgiveness, eternal acceptance, and an unhindered relationship with God. Such persons, then, could express faith by living in accordance with God's expectations under the stewardship that God had placed over them.

This great transaction, salvation by grace through faith, has never varied as to basis or means. In every age, this transaction is legally enacted by God as grounded in the atoning death of the incarnate Christ, the Lamb slain before the foundation of the world (Rev. 13:8; cf. 1 Peter 1:18–20). However, many who experienced complete forgiveness had an extremely incomplete understanding of its ultimate grounds. They were saved by faith in God as He had willed to reveal Himself up to their time. As we look back on the history of this singular salvation, the distinction must be made between what God always knew regarding the death of the incarnate Christ and how God progressively revealed to people, within the spectrum of time, that truth about a sinless, dying Savior.

Roy E. Beacham

Lewis Sperry Chafer, "Inventing Heretics Through Misunderstanding" in *Bibliotheca Sacra* 102 (1945):1–5; J. S. Feinberg, "Salvation in the Old Testament" in *Tradition and Testament* (Chicago: Moody Press, 1981); A. P. Ross, "The Biblical Method of Salvation" in *Continuity and Discontinuity* (Westchester, Ill.: Crossway Books, 1988); Charles C. Ryrie, *Dispensationalism* (Chicago: Moody Press, 1995).

FIG TREE, PARABLE OF THE

Jesus used a parable that speaks of what a fig tree does in springtime to illustrate what happens before the Second Coming. In Matthew 24:32, Christ says that when the fig tree's branch becomes tender, putting forth leaves, you know that summer is near.

Some say that the budding of the fig tree speaks of the reestablishment of Israel as a nation (in 1948), seeing it as a precursor of Christ's return. Several things work strongly against that interpretation.

Nowhere does Matthew 24–25 speak of Israel's return to Palestine. In fact we do not find Israel's return anywhere in Matthew's gospel. Jesus' Olivet Discourse, in its flow of future historical events, has moved beyond Israel's return, portraying the Jews already in the land.

Furthermore, Luke says in his parallel account, look at the fig tree, and all the trees (21:29). Not just one tree is in view, but many. Thus Christ refers to trees in general and what they do in the spring, not to a particular fig tree that pictures Israel.

In Matthew 24, the budding fig tree, rather than picturing Israel, depicts eleven signs that Jesus reveals in 24:4–24. Nine begin to occur in the first half of the Tribulation and two more appear in the second half.

Thus what we see unfolding is that as new leaves each spring signal the return of summer, so the signs Christ reveals will signal His return.

In Matthew 24:33 Jesus applies the fig tree to His disciples saying, so you also, when you see all these things, know that it is near, at the very doors. His immediate audience did not live to see the fulfillment of all He reveals. That remains for those alive during the Tribulation.

What will this future group of Jewish believers see? To what does "all these things" refer? They denote all the signs of the first and the second half of the Tribulation, including the Abomination of Desolation (24:15–22) and the wonder-working false prophets and christs (24:23–26).

Thus, the budding of the fig tree illustrates signs *in* the Tribulation and we may not say it buds until all the signs are taking place. This not only rules out 1948 as a sign of the Tribulation and Second Coming, but all else before the Tribulation as being the budding of the fig tree. The fig tree has not yet started to bud because "all these things" have not yet started to happen.

Yet when the tree does begin to bud, that is, when all the signs do appear, know that it is near, at the very doors. The third gospel puts it this way, "know that the kingdom of God is near" (Luke 21:31 NIV).

So what does the fig tree teach us about the end of the age? When all the things Christ revealed in Matthew 24:1–23 begin to happen, it is like new leaves putting forth shoots on a fig tree in spring. As the new leaves indicate summer is around the corner, so the signs mean that the Second Coming is indeed near. Matthew 24 neither says nor implies that Israel's reestablishment in the land in 1948, or at any other time, indicates the end of the age. What Matthew does say is that the indicators of Christ's return are eleven signs.

Christ identifies the generation who will experience the signs of Matthew 24:34. One of the important clauses to interpret in the verse is "this generation." What is a *generation*? The term may denote: (1) a family or clan of people descended from a common ancestor, that is, a race of people, yet we do not have a clear use of this notion in the New Testament; (2) a generation of people in the sense of contemporaries born and living about the same time (Matt. 11:16; Acts 2:40); (3) since we naturally associate the idea of an age with a generation of people, we find the term sometimes used of a period of time, the people falling into the background (Eph. 3:21; Col. 1:26).

Because Jesus speaks of Jews who see all the signs of the end times, it is best to understand "generation" as those contemporaries living during the Tribulation. "This" generation, then, is the Jewish contemporaries coexisting during Daniel's Seventieth Week; they see all eleven signs of Matthew 24:4–24. In other words, only those who see all the buds of the fig tree, or the signs, are "this generation."

The tribulational generation will by no means pass away, emphasizing its existence throughout the seven-year period; events do not annihilate them. Jesus does not mean that each and every Jew survives. Over half of them do not, yet that generation as a whole goes through the entire seven years, till all these things are fulfilled.

Christ next guarantees His teaching, saying that "heaven and earth will pass away, but My words will by no means pass away" (24:35). And, finally, He makes a concluding announcement regarding that day and hour for the benefit of His disciples (24:36). The Lord's point is that no one knows when the fig tree will bud, thus no one knows (before the budding) when Christ's coming is at the very doors.

In Matthew's context the word "days" occurs four times (24:19, 22 [twice], 29), each time in the plural to denote the days of the Tribulation. Now for the first time "day" is singular denoting the Second Coming (24:36). It is a day when God turns out the celestial lights on planet Earth (24:29), the Shekinah glory brilliantly appears flashing like lightning to announce Christ's Second Coming (24:30, cp. v. 27), and the angels harvest the earth (24:31).

When does this day happen? No one knows, no, not even the angels is Christ's teaching. We need to remind ourselves, however, that once the tribulational generation is in Daniel's Seventieth Week, we cannot say no one knows. This is because those people will know the exact number of years (Dan. 12:7; Rev. 11:9, 11, 12:14), months (Rev. 11:2; 13:5) and even days (Rev. 11:3; 12:6).

They will know because of divine revelation. Daniel 12:5–13 indicates that though the angels do not know now, they will then; they can count. The countdown begins when the Antichrist signs a treaty with Israel (Dan. 9:27).

Thus when Jesus says no one knows, He refers to people living before the countdown begins. Those who live before the Tribulation cannot know. Accordingly, before the Tribulation it is impossible to set dates for the Tribulation, or the Second Coming. Such attempts are mere conjectures.

To sum up: Jesus teaches that as spring buds on fig trees are signs announcing summer, so the eleven signs experienced by a future, presently unknown, generation of Jews are to them indicators of Christ's nearby (within seven years) Second Coming. All signs occur in, not before, the Tribulation.

See also OLIVET DISCOURSE.

George E. Meisinger

Walter Bauer, F. W. Gingrich, and Frederick Danker, *A Greek-English Lexicon of the New Testament* (Chicago: University of Chicago Press, 1979); Arnold Fruchtenbaum, *Footsteps of the Messiah* (Tustin, Calif.: Ariel Press, 1984); John F. Walvoord, *Matthew–Thy Kingdom Come* (Chicago: Moody Press, 1974).

G

GAEBELEIN, ARNO

Gaebelein (1861–1945) was born in Thuringia, Germany and came to America at the age of eighteen. Ordained in the Methodist Episcopal church, he held pastorates in Baltimore and New York City. In New York he began an important ministry to reach the Jewish population. He began a magazine for Jewish readers entitled *Our Hope*. He supplied a great amount of reading for Jews, especially along the lines of biblical and prophetic publications.

Gaebelein was a remarkable scholar. He knew biblical Hebrew and Greek as well as many Middle Eastern languages. He wrote nearly fifty books and many pamphlets on prophecy. He lectured widely and was active in the Bible conference movement. Gaebelein was popular with audiences because of his vast knowledge of the Jewish people and Hebrew customs. Though avoiding seminary training, he was self-taught in languages, history, systematic theology, apologetics, and prophetic studies.

It was in New York City working with the Jewish community that Gaebelein became a premillennialist (ca. 1887). He wrote: "This attempt to bring the Gospel to the Jews led me deeper into the Old Testament Scriptures. I began to study prophecy. Up to this time I had followed in the interpretation of Old Testament prophecy the so-called 'spiritualization method' (allegorical)." He realized that only with literal interpretation would *Israel* mean Israel and not the church. He realized that a promise of redemption back to the land of Palestine still held for the Jews.

Gaebelein realized that the differences in Bible interpretation were caused by a conflict in hermeneutics. He followed two basic rules for interpreting the Scriptures. He felt a literal-grammatical interpretation led to a national restoration for Israel's future. And secondly, this approach led one to see the church as a new entity unrevealed in the Old Testament but clearly outlined in the book of Ephesians.

Gaebelein also used a dispensational hermeneutic. He saw three major dispensations: law, grace, and kingdom. He also used the analogy of faith and the concept of progressive revelation combined to provide a way of looking at passages that went beyond the grammatical-historical interpretation of an individual text. He also felt strongly about the doctrine of the rapture of the church. No signs were needed to herald Christ's coming. The church clearly would not go through the Great Tribulation. The coming of Christ in the air to receive the church is a separate event from His coming to the earth to set up His kingdom seven years later. Finally, three crucial doctrines were behind Gaebelein's dispensationalism: (1) the inerrancy of Scripture, (2) the premillennial coming of Christ to earth to reign on David's throne, and (3) the pretribulational Rapture.

Gaebelein viewed the Abrahamic covenant as having past, present, and future fulfillment. He wrote, "The nations of the earth, all the families are unconsciously waiting to be blessed by Abraham's seed. Salvation is still of the Jews." And he expected the terms of the covenant to yet be fulfilled literally, physically to the descendants of Abraham and the Jewish nation.

A biblical passage that arrested Gaebelein's attention was Deuteronomy 28. In this he saw "prewritten the sad history" of Israel. Moses predicted the scattering, suffering, tribulation, and ultimate final restoration for the Jews, "the enigma of history." About this Gaebelein wrote, "the Old Testament is practically a sealed book to every person who does not believe in a literal restoration of Israel to their land" (Stallard).

See also PROPHECY, LITERAL; ABRAHAMIC COVENANT.

Mal Couch

J. D. Douglas, ed., *The New international Dictionary of the Christian Church* (Grand Rapids: Zondervan, 1978); Michael D. Stallard, "The Theological Method of Arno C. Gaebelein" (Ph.D. diss., Dallas Theological Seminary, 1992).

GALATIANS, ESCHATOLOGY OF

Galatians teaches the doctrine of justification by faith. It contrasts legalism with true Christian liberty and places dependence on the Holy Spirit's ability to overcome the power and penalty of sin. It is addressed to a group of churches in Galatia. The Galatians were notorious for being impetuous and having a strong desire to seek out new and different activities to become involved in.

The author is the apostle Paul. Attestation of authorship is made in 1:1 and 5:2. Also, chapters 1 and 2 are largely biographical and display consistency with Paul's life as recorded in Acts. The date of writing is placed at A.D. 49 or 52.

The prophecy found in this letter is concerned with the outworking of the Christian life. Specifically, those who follow the sin nature will receive destruction, and those who abide in the Holy Spirit will gain eternal life (6:8). This verse looks forward to the Rapture for the believer, and the Great White Throne judgment for the unbeliever.

See also JUDGMENTS, VARIOUS.

Ervin R. Starwalt

John F. Walvoord, ed., *The Prophecy Knowledge Handbook* (Wheaton: Victor Books, 1990); John F. Walvoord and Roy B. Zuck, eds., *The Bible Knowledge Commentary* (Wheaton: Victor Books, 1985); Charles F. Pfeiffer and Everett F. Harrison, eds.,*Wycliffe Bible Commentary* (Chicago: Moody Press, 1962).

GENESIS, ESCHATOLOGY OF

Moses authored Genesis as part of the Pentateuch more than likely during the wilderness wandering (1445–1440 B.C.). The word *genesis* implies that this is a book of beginnings. Genesis is a most remarkable document in that it begins with a wide sweep into eternity past with the history of Creation. As Genesis progresses, it focuses down to the Abrahamic covenant (chap. 12–17) and finally closes with the next two generations after Abraham sojourning in Egypt. The authenticity and inspiration of the book is well attested in the New Testament by Christ and the apostles. Jesus affirms the historicity of human creation (Matt. 19:4) and the apostle Paul continually shows the theological importance of Abraham in his many quotes of the Abrahamic covenant. Through the covenants and dispensations of Genesis, the pages of world history are written. The prophecies given in this book are awesome, the implications of which we can even see today.

The Covenants

There is a wide gap as to how covenant theologians and dispensationalists understand Genesis. Covenant writers see a covenant of works and a covenant of grace in Genesis. Concerning the covenant of works, the "record of God's transactions with Adam presents definitely all the essential elements of a covenant" (Hodge). The "parties" were God and Adam, and in Adam representatively all his natural posterity. "Although it was a sovereign constitution imposed by God, there is no reason to suppose that Adam did not enter upon it voluntarily" (Hodge). Dispensationalists have no problem seeing God giving Adam a command not to eat the forbidden fruit (Gen. 2:16–17) or the fact that Adam's disobedience caused the human race to be cut off from God, but technically this event is not called a covenant in Scripture.

Many covenant theologians call the covenant made with Abraham the covenant of grace. But theologians like Hodge expand the wording and intention of such a covenant (*berith*). He gives two Calvinistic views of the covenant of grace. "The first view regards the Covenant of Grace as made by God with elect sinners. . . . The second view supposes two covenants, the first, called the Covenant of

Redemption, formed from eternity between the Father and the Son as parties. The Son promising to obey and suffer, the Father promising to give him a people and to grant them in him all spiritual blessings and eternal life." With most Covenant theologians, one big plan emerges, void of significant distinctions of time, plans, and especially, a difference between Israel and the church. Promises and prophecies concerning the children of Abraham fade and disappear. The overwhelming issue becomes spiritual redemption by Christ. Different plans and programs of Scripture fuse together and lose their meanings. "The covenant of grace and redemption are two modes or phases of the one evangelical covenant of mercy" (Berkhof).

There are some points of agreement between dispensationalists and covenant theologians. Both see in the Proevangelium the prophecy of redemption, in the cryptic messianic promise of the seed of the woman crushing the head of the serpent, Satan (Gen. 3:15). Both see the promise to Noah as an eternal covenant. The Lord in the Noahic covenant gives a sovereign assurance that no flesh would again perish by water (Gen. 9:9–13, 11:16).

The Abrahamic Covenant

The Abrahamic covenant is seen by dispensationalists as the driving engine of the Bible. So much of the Word of God unfolds from Genesis 12 all the way to the book of Revelation. The Abrahamic covenant is initiated in verses 1–3 of this chapter. Abraham is told to go forth from his country, relatives, and father's house to a land that God will show him. The Lord then promises to make of him a great nation and to give him a blessing. Finally, "in you all the families of the earth shall be blessed." The covenant clearly speaks of (1) a nation (the Jewish people), (2) a land (Canaan and beyond), (3) a blessing, ultimately to all families of the earth. This agreement is clearly called a covenant (Gen. 17:4). (1) It is a literal agreement in that God instructs Abraham to walk through the land he and his descendants will receive (13:15–18). As well, the Lord speaks of literal children that will be so many they are uncountable (Gen. 16:10). (2) The covenant promises are also eternal. "I will give [the land] to you and to your descendants forever" (Gen. 13:15). (3) The Abrahamic promises also are unconditional in that God put Abraham asleep when He further assured him of the final fulfillment of the agreement. "A deep sleep fell upon Abram" (Gen. 15:12). Though a covenant is between two individuals, God sovereignly finalized the promise Himself.

The Lord confirmed the promises with Abraham's son Isaac. "I will be with you and bless you, for to you and to your descendants I will give all these lands, and I will establish the oath which I swore to your father Abraham" (Gen. 26:3). To Jacob the covenant was also repeated as a future national promise (Gen. 35:10–12). The Abrahamic covenant is affirmed as a literal, eternal agreement. Genesis closes with Joseph referring to it. "I am about to die, but God will surely take care of you [the tribal families], and bring you up from this land [Egypt] to the land which He promised on oath to Abraham, to Isaac and to Jacob" (Gen. 50:24).

Two of the most striking things about the Abrahamic covenant is that it is seen as a *forever* promise and also literal. It was not spiritualized or allegorized. The patriarchs understood the promises in a literal context: a literal land and actual descendants, or children, who would receive the promises. Some say, for sin the nation of Israel was cut off from the promises. Though a specific generation would be scattered from the land (Deut. 28:64), a future generation would be regathered by the Lord to the promised region. "The LORD your God will restore you from captivity . . . and will gather you again from all the peoples where the LORD your God has scattered you. . . . The LORD your God will bring you into the land which your fathers possessed" (Deut. 30:3, 5). This cannot be allegorized to a spiritual Gentile generation or to the church age. This clearly means Jewish descendants of Abraham—literal children returning to a literal land!

The Dispensations

The dispensations are an important part of Genesis. Four of the seven are seen. The early chapters of Genesis represent time and history compressed and the dispensations are readily seen in this setting of the early beginnings of human history.

Dispensation of Innocence, Genesis 1:28–3:6.

God dealt with Adam on the basis of sinlessness. He was commanded not to eat of the tree of good and evil (2:16–17). Adam failed the test and along with Eve, ate of the fruit (3:6).

Dispensation of Conscience, Genesis 3:7–8:14.

With no revelation of law, how would Adam and future generations live? Can man who is now sinful, leave the perfect environment of Eden, and live righteously? The answer comes quickly with the killing of Abel by his brother Cain. Conscience could not stop sin!

Dispensation of Government, Genesis 8:15–11:32.

Can early man live in communities, clans, nations, and tribes in righteousness and peace? The answer is again, no. The early tribes came together at Babel to build a city and tower to reach into heaven. The Lord said "now nothing will be withheld from them, which they have imagined to do" (11:6).

Dispensation of Promise, Genesis 12:1–Exodus 18:27.

The Lord now concentrates on one man and his descendants. Promises are made that should sustain Abraham and his children. But by the end of the book of Genesis, the family failures, the sins of jealousy, hatred, and even a near murder by the brothers of Joseph, bring the entire family out of the Promised Land into sojourning in Egypt.

Dispensationalism does not mean a different way of salvation in each period. Salvation is always the same in Scripture: through faith. Neither do some of the principles within each dispensation have to end abruptly. For example, the promises given to Abraham continue throughout the rest of Bible history. But the dispensations do signal that God is dealing differently with individuals or nations for distinct purposes.

Genesis 49

Genesis 49 is the final great prophetic section of the book. Jacob makes near and far prophecies about his children. There were good words for the firstborn, Reuben, excelling in honor, excelling in power (v. 3). But the praise was cut short by the fact that he had defiled his father's couch. "You no longer excel, for you went up onto your father's bed" (v. 4). Simeon and Levi are seen together in Jacob's prophecy (vv. 8–12). They were characterized as violent, having killed men in their anger (v. 6). Judah is a major subject in prophecy (vv. 8–12). He would be a strong lion (vv. 8–9). The Messiah (the scepter) would come through him (v. 10). This was literally fulfilled in Christ (Rev. 2:27). Of Zebulun, Jacob predicted he would live by the seashore and become a haven for ships (v. 13). Concerning Issachar, he would be a rawboned donkey lying down between two saddlebags (v. 14). Dan does not come up to expectations to be a judge (vv. 16–17). Some believe that idolatry appeared first among the sons of Jacob in the tribe of Dan (Ju. 18:30), and he would therefore be omitted in the description of the 144,000 of Israel in Revelation 7:4–8. Gad will attack and also be considered an attacker. Some feel 1 Chronicles 5:18–19 refers to this. Of Asher, Jacob said his food will be rich (49:20). The tribe lived in an area of rich soil and provided much food. Naphtali is a doe set free that bears beautiful fawns (v. 21). This could refer to the fact that the tribe settled in the northwest of the Sea of Galilee in a mountainous area and is pictured here like a deer that is free. A long prediction was given concerning Joseph who would be a fruitful vine whose branches climb over a wall (49:22). He is pictured as strong and able to defend himself against all attacks because he is under the blessing of God. Jacob concludes with a prophecy concerning Benjamin who is a ravenous wolf (v. 27). Benjamites were warriors and here described as wolves (Walvoord).

The major prophetic programs of Scripture are in seed form in Genesis.

See also ABRAHAMIC COVENANT; DISPENSATIONALISM.

Mal Couch

L. Berkhof, *Systematic Theology* (Grand Rapids: Eerdmans, 1962); Mal Couch, *God's Plan in the Ages* (Dallas: Tyndale Seminary Publications, 1994); A. A. Hodge, *Outlines of Theology* (Carlisle, Pa.: The Banner of Truth Trust, 1991); John F. Walvoord, *The Prophecy Knowledge Handbook* (Wheaton: Victor Books, 1990).

GOG AND MAGOG

A massive future invasion of Israel by the armed forces of six nations is foretold (Ezek. 38–39). Five of those nations are identified in 38:5–6 with the names they bore in Ezekiel's time.

Persia, now the modern state of Iran, is ruled by an Islamic fundamentalist government that is building significant military power, including the development of nuclear weapons. It has openly declared its commitment to the annihilation of the Jewish state of Israel.

Ethiopia, is known today as Sudan and is dominated by an Islamic fundamentalist government that is using brutal means, including crucifixion of Christians, to try to establish a pure Islamic state.

Libya, the western neighbor of Egypt, is also an Islamic nation today. It is strongly anti-West and anti-Israel, and western intelligence has been informed that Libya has hired Soviet and east European military scientists to aid its development of military power.

Gomer was originally located north of the Caucasus Mountains in the southern part of what today is Russia. By Ezekiel's time it had relocated to what is now central Turkey.

Togarmah, was identified by Josephus as the Phrygians (*Antiq.,* I, 6, 1 [126]) who settled in Cappadocia, now eastern Turkey.

It should be noted that the present government of Turkey is being threatened by Islamic fundamentalists. As a result, some leaders fear that Turkey could become another Iran. If that happens, then all the nations named in Ezekiel 38:5–6 will be characterized by a militant Islamic hatred of Israel.

The five nations (Ezek. 38:5–6) will be led by a sixth in the future attack against Israel. God gave three identification marks of that leader. The leader will be Gog, the land of Magog (Ezek. 38:2). Jerome, a prominent church leader (A.D. 345–420), declared that Magog was located north of the Caucasus Mountains, near the Caspian Sea. Josephus (*Antiq.*, I, 6, 1 [123]) and Greek writers associated the name *Magog* with the Scythians. The major group of Scythians lived in the vicinity of the Black Sea from the Caucasus around to the Danube. It appears, then, that the land of Magog was located near the Black and Caspian Seas north of the Caucasus Mountains in the southern part of twentieth-century Russia. Further, the leader is identified as the chief prince or ruler of Meshech and Tubal (Ezek. 38:2, 39:1). Classical Greek writers called the people of Meshech the *Moschoi*, and Assyrian records referred to them as the *Muski*. This group settled in the area of Armenia where the borders of Russia, Iran, and Turkey converge. The people of Tubal were located in the central part of Turkey immediately west of Togarmah. Finally, Gog's location is the north parts (38:15, 39:2). The Hebrew word translated "parts" means "extreme or uttermost parts." Since Ezekiel was a Hebrew prophet, he would refer to geographical locations from the vantage point of his homeland. Thus, his statement in 38:15 indicates that, when Gog will lead the six-nation attack against Israel, he will come from his location in the extreme or uttermost parts directly north of Israel. Russia is the nation situated in the extreme or uttermost parts directly north of Israel.

It appears then that Russia will lead the future invasion against Israel foretold in Ezekiel 38–39. Why would Russia do this? One reason is anti-Semitism. Before Communism, Russia was notorious for severe persecution of Jews. While Communism held an iron grip on the government of that nation, it suppressed the outward expression of hatred for Jews. Now that Communism has lost that grip at least for a while, anti-Semitism has been allowed to raise its ugly head again. Some members of Pamyat, a strongly anti-Semitic organization that wants to get rid of all Jews in Russia, blame all of that nation's problems on Jews. Some have even accused Jews of being the source of AIDS. As a result of these ominous trends, a mass exodus of Jews from the former Soviet Union has been taking place since the early 1990s, with the majority going to Israel.

Another reason for Russia to lead the future invasion is its desire for status. According to an independent intelligence agency, officers of the armed forces of the former Soviet Union believe that Russia can still have superpower status, even without Communism, if it will ally itself with Islamic nations against Israel. In line with this, early in the 1990s an official Russian government representative stated that young people in that nation's schools are being required to learn Arabic as their second language because his government had concluded that the future of their nation lies with the Islamic nations of the world.

God declared (Ezek. 38:8, 16) that this future invasion of Israel would take place in the latter years and latter days. It would be after Israel had been regathered from the nations to its homeland and felt so safe and secure that it would have no defenses of its own (vv. 8, 11–12, 14). There has been an amazing regathering of Israel to the homeland since its reestablishment as a nation in 1948, but certainly Israel does not feel so safe and secure there today that it has no defenses of its own.

Since the Scriptures indicate that there will be no warfare during the future reign of Messiah (Isa. 9:6–7; Ps. 72:7; Mic. 4:3–4), this invasion cannot take place during the Millennium. Is there any time between now and Christ's Second Coming to establish the Millennium when Israel will feel so safe and secure that it will not maintain its own defenses? It appears so.

According to Scripture (Dan. 9:27), at the very beginning of the future seven-year Tribulation, Antichrist will enforce a strong covenant with Israel. It will so strongly bind Israel to the Antichrist that he will regard that nation as an extension of himself and his empire in the Middle East. As a result, through that covenant the Antichrist will guarantee Israel's national security. This guarantee will cause Israel to feel so safe and secure that it will discontinue the costly burden of maintaining its own defenses. This feeling of security will not last long, however. In the middle of the Tribulation Antichrist will begin to desolate Israel (Dan. 9:27; Matt. 24:15–21). Thus, that nation will feel safe and secure only during the first half of the seven-year Tribulation. It appears, then, that the invasion of Israel by Russia and its Islamic allies will take place during the first half of the Tribulation, perhaps shortly before its midpoint.

The invaders will have the attitude that, since Israel has let down its own guard militarily, it will be their opportune time to strike and plunder its resources (Ezek. 38:10–13). As a result, they will launch such a large invasion force that it will seem like a massive cloud that covers the land (38:9, 15–16). God's initial action will be that of pulling these invaders into Israel for His sovereign purpose (38:4, 16; 39:2). When they attack, His attitude toward them will be characterized by fury, jealousy, and fiery wrath (38:18–19). He will then actively intervene to destroy the massive invading force through a fierce earthquake, landslides, self-destructive panic, pestilence, excessive rain, great hailstones, and fire and brimstone (38:19–22). The destruction of the invading army will be so extensive that the mountains and open fields of Israel and a valley near the Dead Sea will be congested with corpses. God will bring fowl and beasts to eat many of them. It will take all the Jews seven months to bury the rest of the dead and seven years to destroy their weapons (39:3–5, 9–20). If this invasion takes place shortly before the middle of the Tribulation, then this destruction of weapons will continue into the early part of the Millennium.

God's purpose for all this will be to glorify Himself before Israel and all the nations, to so impress them with His existence and power that He will have life-changing influence with them (38:16, 23; 39:7, 13, 21–22). Many Jews and Gentiles will get saved during the Tribulation (Rev. 7). No doubt the fulfillment of the Ezekiel 38–39 prophecy will be one of the means through which God will bring people of that time to Himself.

See also DANIEL, ESCHATOLOGY OF; EZEKIEL, ESCHATOLOGY OF.

Renald E. Showers

"Brain Drain" in *U.S. News & World Report*, Nov. 11, 1991; "Call For Elimination of Israel" in *Until,* vol. 1, issue 1, 1992; "Gog and Magog" in *The Jewish Encyclopedia*, (New York: Funk & Wagnalls, 1910); John E. Hartley, *Theological Wordbook of the Old Testament,* vol. 1 (Chicago: Moody Press, 1980); C. F. Keil, *Biblical Commentary on the Book of Daniel* (Grand Rapids: Eerdmans, 1959); W. S. LaSor, "Cush," in *International Standard Bible Encyclopedia Fully Revised* (Grand Rapids: Eerdmans, 1979); Elwood McQuaid, "A Window In Sudan" in *Israel My Glory* (April–May 1994; Special Office Brief, issue no. 384, Jan. 31, 1992.; "Will Turkey Be the Next Iran?" in *U. S. News & World Report*, 1994.

GOSPELS, ESCHATOLOGY OF THE

Matthew

The primary theme of Matthew is that Christ is king. Because of this He is linked to both the Davidic covenant (2 Sam. 7:8–16) and the Abrahamic covenant (Gen. 15:18). The life of Jesus is seen in relation to its affect upon the Jewish believers. Matthew wrote to confirm persecuted believers in their faith and to turn them away from thinking that the Gospel of Jesus Christ was a rejection of the Old Testament prophecies.

The author is Matthew, the Jewish tax collector. The date of writing is placed at A.D. 50–55.

There are many prophecies in this book. The prophecy of the conception and birth of Jesus (1:18–24), of the Magi's visit (2:1–12), and of the return to Nazareth of Joseph and Mary (2:19–23). The coming of John the Baptist is foretold (3:1–12), as is the promise that believers will enter the kingdom of heaven (8:5–13). There's a promise of judgment against those cities that refuse to repent and call upon the Lord (11:20–24) and a warning that there will be no forgiveness for the one who speaks against the Holy Spirit (12:32–37). The betrayal of Christ is foretold (26:21); there is a reference to the future millennial kingdom (26:29) and the falling away of His disciples when Jesus is taken prisoner (26:31–32). The final judgment is referenced, in which the righteous will enter God's kingdom and the unrighteous will enter eternal damnation (13:24–30). Israel is seen as God's hidden treasure (13:44), the church is seen in the parable of the pearl of great price (13:45–46), and the judgment that will take place at the Second Coming is seen in the parable of the dragnet (13:47–50). The death and resurrection of Christ is foretold (16:21–28, 20:17–19, 26:2–5) and fulfilled (27:51–66, 28:1–15). His Second Coming as King is predicted in the Olivet Discourse (chaps. 24–25). The suddenness of His coming is foretold in the parable of the ten virgins (25:1–13) and the parable of the talents (25:14–30). The judgment of the Gentiles is foretold (25:31–46) where the sheep [saved Gentiles] are separated from the goats [unsaved Gentiles]. This special judgment takes place at the second coming of Christ after the Tribulation, and involves all the Gentiles that survive the Tribulation. Finally the millennial kingdom is referenced (26:29) when Christ speaks of the reunion with His disciples there. The fulfillment of the prophecy concerning His death is given (27:45–56) and His resurrection (28:1–10).

Mark

Mark presents Christ as a servant, the one who came to minister, not be ministered to. Thus, the book records the actions of a servant. The purpose of the book is pastoral. The author wrote to give understanding to the nature of discipleship and dealt with what it means to follow Jesus.

The author is Mark, a Christian Jew and cousin of Barnabas. The writing of the book is set between A.D. 50–60.

Mark records the prophecies given at the last Passover feast, which include Jesus' betrayal, the millennial kingdom, and the scattering and falling away at the arrest of Jesus (14:12–72). The prediction of His death is given (8:31–9:1, 10:32–34, 14:1–9), and of His Second Coming (13:1–27) The signs of

His Second Coming are seen in the parable of the fig tree (13:28). The betrayal of Christ is foretold (14:18), as is His departure (14:21). Peter's denial is foretold (14:30). The millennial kingdom is referenced (14:25) when Jesus speaks of His reunion with the disciples to take place there. The fulfillment of prophecy concerning Christ's death is given (15:33–41), and His resurrection (16:1–8).

Luke

In Luke's account Christ is presented as the Son of Man, and it was written for the Gentile reader. The book is a product of meticulous research by the author in the gathering and sifting of information, this work being divinely directed by the Holy Spirit. That the author was not an eyewitness to the events is attested in the opening verses. The sympathy of the Lord for the brokenhearted, the sick, and the poorly treated is stressed to show His humanity.

The author is Luke, the beloved physician (Col. 4:14). He was a companion of and coworker with Paul. The book is dated at A.D. 60.

The prophecies in Luke include the birth of John the Baptist (1:5–25), which was fulfilled (1:57–66), and the birth of the Son of Man (1:36–56), which was fulfilled (2:1–7). Simon prophesies concerning Jesus as the Redeemer of many (2:34) and concerning the crucifixion of Jesus (2:35). The kingdom is seen when Christ states that only through Him can it be entered (13:24). The future destruction of the temple is foretold (13:35). The coming kingdom is again foretold (17:21–24). The rewards of the kingdom are promised for those who faithfully follow Christ (18:29–30). The destruction of Jerusalem is foretold (21:20–24), and the Tribulation is spoken of (21:8–19, 25–28). The signs of Christ's Second Coming are foretold in the parable of the fig tree (21:29–33). Christ's reunion in heaven with His disciples is promised (22:16), and the assurance is given that faith in Christ will gain entrance into heaven with Him (23:43).

John

John's gospel is intended to conduct people to saving faith in Christ. The method used to do this is to display the nature and person of Christ and what it means to have faith in Him. The overall theme of the book is the deity of Jesus Christ. The book contains no parables, but it does record seven miracles and several personal interviews. The reality of physical weakness experienced by Jesus is presented as a rebuttal to the gnostic denial of His human nature. The seven miracles manifest and authenticate that He is the true Messiah.

The author is the disciple whom Jesus loved (21:20), John. He was a Palestinian Jew who was an eyewitness to the events of the life of Christ. The book was written about A.D. 85–90.

The book contains prophecies about the coming Messiah (1:26–27) and His purpose as the Lamb of God to redeem people from their sin (1:29–34). Christ predicted His own death, resurrection (2:19), and crucifixion (3:14). Jesus makes reference to His ascension into heaven (7:33–34), and tells the Jewish authorities that because of unrepentance they cannot go there to be with Him. Jesus speaks of the Holy Spirit that will come (7:38–39) after He, Jesus, is glorified. Christ again spoke of His pending death (10:11). Chapter 11:1–44 details the death and subsequent resurrection of Lazarus. It is given as a type of Christ's own death and resurrection, which becomes security for believers that they will be resurrected to eternal life with Christ. Jesus foretold His betrayal by Judas Iscariot (13:21–26), the denial by Peter (13:38), and His departure (13:36). A place in heaven is promised to those who are in Christ (14:2), and His return to gather them to be with Him, the Rapture (14:3). Jesus promises the Holy Spirit (14:16–17) and speaks again of the Spirit coming (16:7–8). Jesus foretells the persecutions that will come upon those who follow Him (16:1–4); this prediction has been fulfilled throughout history and will continue until the end of human history. Jesus tells the disciples of His coming death, resurrection, and Second Coming (16:16–33). The foretold crucifixion of Christ was fulfilled (19:17–37), and as well the fulfillment of His promised resurrection (20:1–9).

See also OLIVET DISCOURSE.

Ervin R. Starwalt

Paul Enns, *The Moody Handbook of Theology* (Chicago: Moody Press, 1989); John F. Walvoord and Roy B. Zuck, eds., *The Bible Knowledge Commentary* (Wheaton: Victor Books, 1985); John F. Walvoord, *The Prophecy Knowledge Handbook* (Wheaton: Victor Books, 1990); Everett F. Harrison and Charles F. Pfeiffer, eds., *Wycliffe Bible Commentary*, (Chicago: Moody Press, 1962).

GRAVES, JAMES ROBINSON

Graves (1820–93), born in Chester, Vermont, originally was a congregationalist but later became a Baptist. He completed the equivalent of a college degree on his own in four years, learning four languages in the process. He then began a long study of the Scriptures on his own. Before the Civil War, Graves planned and organized the Southwestern Publishing House and the Southern Baptist Sunday School Union. He became an accomplished writer and editor and was also recognized as a popular preacher and skilled debater.

Graves was deeply involved in the landmark movement and became a key spokesman for this group within Southern Baptist circles. Landmarkism argued that Baptist churches had existed in unbroken succession since the apostolic era. He argued this point in almost everything he wrote.

Graves held to a strong premillennial position that he felt was evident in the early church from at least the second century. Many believe he should also be labeled a dispensationalist who had embraced the hermeneutics of Darby. Graves's magnum opus was *The Work of Christ Consummated in Seven Dispensations*. To prove his point as to how important Bible prophecy was, Graves was familiar with, and could quote from, a great number of well-known and unknown premillennial scholars.

In 1859 Graves came out against a postmillennial article in the *Family Baptist Magazine*. He pointed out that postmillennialists could not give a single prophecy to support their belief. He boldly asserted that if his stance on premillennialism placed him in the chiliast camp, then he was proud of it because the Lord and all the prophets were chiliasts!

Graves held two very successful prophecy conferences in 1878 (New York) and 1886 (Chicago). The *New York Tribune* called the lectures at the first even "refreshing and inspirational." The paper noted that the subject of prophecy was gaining interest and pastors should study the issues and share with their people. At these conferences Graves gave a complete dispensational scenario. Literal interpretation was attacked by his many critics. He also argued strongly at these conferences for the restoration of the Jews to Palestine. The magazine *The Baptist* noted the "profound impression made in California and else where with Graves's premillennialism." In 1891 *The Baptist* ran a series of articles pushing for the Jews' return to Palestine. Graves wrote that the Jews' "dispersion is literal, so will their restoration be literal."

Graves has had a profound premillennial influence on Baptists through the decades. He wrote and lectured continually in conferences and churches. He influenced many Southern Baptist teachers and also kept company with many like-minded preachers and pastors. He came along at a time when premillennialism was gaining ground and during the period of great discussion about the Jews returning to the land.

See also DARBY, JOHN.

Mal Couch

Danny Eugene Howe, "Analysis of Dispensationalism and Its Implications for the Theologies of James Robinson Graves, John Franklin Norris, and Wallis Amos Criswell" (Ph.D. diss., Southwestern Baptist Theological Seminary, 1988).

GRAY, JAMES MARTIN

Reformed Episcopal clergyman, author, editor, educator, Bible teacher, first dean and first president of Moody Bible Institute, Gray (1851–1935) played a key role in the fundamentalist movement of the 1920s and in the promotion and establishment of dispensational premillennial theology.

The names of Gray's parents are unknown. It *is* known that his father died shortly after James was born and that James's eldest brother became the protector and provider for the family, a Christian family (at least nominally) in the Protestant Episcopal church. Confirmed in 1865 at age fourteen by a bishop in that denomination, it was not until he was twenty-two years old and in seminary training for a ministerial career in the Protestant Episcopal Church that Gray was converted to Christ. Transferring his denominational ties, Gray apparently completed his education in the Reformed Episcopal Church, by that he was ordained in 1877.

Gray served two successful pastorates, one year each, first at the Church of the Redemption in Greenpoint, New York, and then at Church of the Cornerstone, located outside New York City at Newburgh-on-the-Hudson. He then served from 1877 to 1894 as rector, First Reformed Episcopal Church in Boston, where he also taught Bible synthesis at the Boston Missionary Training School founded by A. J. Gordon, which later became Gordon College. In 1892, Gray moved to Philadelphia where he taught Bible classes in the newly founded Reformed Episcopal Seminary, resigning his third pastorate in 1894.

In 1892 or 1893, Gray became associated with D. L. Moody, through Gordon, who brought Gray to the Northfield Bible Conferences in Northfield, Massachusetts. Gray was also invited to lecture at Moody's Bible Institute for Home and Foreign Missions of the Chicago Evangelistic Society (later Moody Bible Institute). Invitations increased and in 1904 Gray was selected as the first dean of Moody Bible Institute. His title was changed to the president in 1925, the position that he held until his death in 1935. He was listed in *Who's Who in America* from (at least) 1916 to 1935.

During the 1920s he played a key role in the fundamentalist-modernist controversy. Devout student of the Bible and staunch defender of verbal inspiration, he was one of the contributors to *The Fundamentals* (1910–15). As teacher and administrator, Gray was chiefly responsible for the sound doctrinal and conservative solidarity in the foundation that set the future course of Moody Bible Institute. Involved in every aspect of the Institute, Gray was the prime mover in the improvement of the music program (he authored a number of hymns), and in the establishment of the Institute's first radio station. He also edited the Institute's periodical (now *Moody Monthly*) from 1907 until 1935. He was also instrumental in the organization of the Evangelical Teacher Training Association in 1931. One of the seven editors of the *Scofield Reference Bible*, Gray was a popular and much sought after Bible teacher. He introduced and popularized synthetic Bible study, or "Bible synthesis," a means of studying the Bible as an organic whole.

Gray's contributions to Moody Bible Institute, to the Bible institute movement in general, to the growth of the fundamentalist movement, and to the popularization and propagation of dispensational premillennial theology is incalculable. His theological foci were bibliology, Christology, soteriology, pneumatology, and eschatology and were due in part to the demands of the era and in part to his personal interest. Dr. Gray's writings were essentially the product of his evangelistic and teaching ministries and of his defense of fundamentalism against the threat of modernism. At the forefront of the controversy was the doctrine of the Bible (revelation, inspiration, inerrancy, etc.). But the ramifications led, of course, to questions concerning the person and work of Christ, human sinfulness (vs. inherent goodness), the nature of salvation, and the person and work of the Holy Spirit, although Gray's treatment of the Holy Spirit was more pastoral and sprang more from personal interest than polemical concern.

Gray's interest in eschatology is traceable to the first American Prophetic Conference held in the Protestant Episcopal Church of the Holy Trinity, New York City, 1878. The consensus was decidedly premillennial. He was convinced of the truth of it. Through his own study of the Bible, along with intercourse with Moody, Gordon, F. L. Chapell and many other premillennialists at

Northfield, including C. I. Scofield, Gray adopted a premillennial, dispensational, pretribulational interpretation of Scripture.

Gray held that the covenant promises given to Abraham and David concerning everlasting possession of the land would shape future history and one day be fulfilled. Because of the nation's disobedience, Israel was removed from the place of blessing and subjected to Gentile domination. The Times of the Gentiles Gray took to be the empires of Babylon, Medo–Persia, Greece, and Rome as the final form of Gentile world power. Gray understood Daniel's Seventieth Week to begin with a Persian decree to build the walls of Jerusalem and to end at the commencement of the Millennium, when God's promises to Abraham and David would be literally fulfilled. He saw a gap between the end of the sixty-ninth week ("cutting off" of Christ in A.D. 32) and the beginning of the Seventieth Week. During the interim, Christ would build His church. Gray drew a sharp contrast between Israel and the church. Christ's second coming was in two stages. At the end of the church age, Christ would return and catch up the church into the air (pretribulational Rapture), take the church to heaven where the wedding of the bride and Bridegroom is consummated. Daniel's Seventieth Week would follow the rapture of the church and be brought to a conclusion by Christ's return to earth with the church to establish the millennial kingdom.

Gray held a futuristic view of Revelation 4–18 as describing the Tribulation period, that he equated with Daniel's Seventieth Week. For Gray, the Day of the Lord begins with the Rapture, though he was careful not to identify (necessarily) the Rapture of the church as that event that marks the beginning of Daniel's Seventieth Week. At the end of the seven year Tribulation, at Christ's second advent, Israel receives Messiah and is established in the millennial kingdom. Prior to the Millennium Satan is bound and the judgment of the nations occurs. At the end of the Millennium, Satan is loosed, there is a final revolt that Christ quells, and a final judgment pertaining only to the unsaved (Great White Throne). Gray's eschatology, based as it was in a literal hermeneutic, differed little from the premillennial position of other prominent dispensationalists of his day and is representative of the school in that he taught.

See also MOODY, D. L.

Steven L. McAvoy

Henry Warner Bowden, ed., *Dictionary of American Religious Biography* (Westport: Greenwood Press, 1977); James Martin Gray, *Christian Workers' Commentary on the Old and New Testaments* (Chicago: The Bible Institute Colportage Association, 1915), *Prophecy and the Lord's Return* (New York: Revell, 1917), *Synthetic Bible Studies* (New York: Revell, 1906) and *A Text-Book on Prophecy* (New York: Revell, 1918); John David Hannah, "James Martin Gray, 1851–1935: His Life and Work" (Th.D. dissertation, Dallas Theological Seminary, 1974); Daniel G. Reid, Robert D. Linder, Bruce L. Shelley, and Harry S. Stout, eds., *Dictionary of Christianity in America* (Downers Grove, Ill.: InterVarsity Press, 1990); William M. Runyan, *Dr. Gray at Moody Bible Institute* (New York: Oxford University Press, 1935).

GUNDRY, ROBERT H.

Professor of New Testament and Greek, and chairman of the Department of Religious Studies, Westmont College, Santa Barbara, California, Robert Gundry (b. 1932) received his B.A. and B.D. from Los Angeles Baptist Seminary and his Ph.D. from the University of Manchester, England. A capable and erudite scholar, Gundry is the author of a number of scholarly publications that include *The Use of the Old Testament in St. Matthew's Gospel*, NovTSup 18 (1967); *A Survey of the New Testament* (1970, 1981, 1994); "Soma" in *Biblical Theology*, Monograph Series—Society for New Testament Studies, 29 (1976); *Matthew: A Commentary on His Literary and Theological Art* (1982; revised and retitled, *Matthew: A Commentary on His Handbook for a Mixed Church under Persecution*, 1995); *Mark: A Commentary on His Apology for the Cross* (1993). He is also a frequent contributor to journals, periodicals, and *festschriften*. His primary contribution so far to eschatology was *The Church and the Tribulation* (1973). This book is the first serious attempt by a dispensationalist to exegetically articulate posttribulationism. A provocative and innovative book, it has been influential in moving some pretribulationists to posttribulationism.

Though writing within the framework of dispensational premillennialism, Gundry nevertheless holds a number of views at variance with this theological system, views that are at variance both with dispensationalism and premillennialism as they are commonly held. As a premillennialist, Gundry takes a futuristic view of Revelation 4–22. Chapters 4–18 are descriptive of the Tribulation period and are to be identified with Daniel's Seventieth Week. Christ's return to earth at His second advent (Rev. 19) is after the Tribulation and before the Millennium. As a dispensationalist, Gundry draws a distinction between Israel and the church and avows adherence to a literal hermeneutic. The following views held by Gundry, however, are not commonplace to dispensational premillennialism.

Gundry holds that the church will go through, and be raptured after, the Tribulation. For Gundry, the New Testament does *not* teach the imminent return of Christ for the church; the Day of the Lord does not begin until after the Tribulation; the wrath of God is confined to the very end of, or after, the Tribulation (he's not sure which); on the one hand, the church is protected while on earth during the outpouring of God's wrath, on the other hand the church is raptured before this wrath is poured out; Armageddon occurs after the Tribulation (but before the Second Advent); the judgment of the nations (sheep and goats) is to be placed after the Millennium and identified with one general judgment (the Great White Throne); the Olivet Discourse is addressed to a Jewish segment of the church; the millennial kingdom is populated by the 144,000 Jews (Rev. 7) who remain unconverted until after the posttribulational rapture of the church and by some of the wicked Gentiles who survive Christ's second advent; the first resurrection is two–phase: Christ the first phase, all other saints at the end of the Tribulation. Gundry later changed his view on the 144,000. Instead, they represent a Jewish Palestinian segment of the church during the Tribulation period. Ethnic Israel, which constitutes the Jewish population of the Millennium, is not saved until after the rapture of the church, but before or at Christ's second advent. Thus, there is a very brief interval between the rapture of the church and the return of Christ to earth during which Israel is converted.

Though Gundry attempts to reconcile these views with dispensational premillennialism, and the consistent adherence to a literal hermeneutic, his methods and conclusions actually run counter to all three. This is perhaps reflected in his latitudinal move from biblical inspiration and inerrancy as held by the Chicago statements of the International Council on Biblical Inerrancy and the doctrinal statement of the Evangelical Theological Society to his use of such critical methodologies as used in the production of his commentaries on Matthew and Mark. When his views of inerrancy were questioned and challenged by other members in the Evangelical Theological Society, Gundry resigned (1984) his membership in ETS, though he continues to profess evangelical views of inspiration and inerrancy.

See also RAPTURE, POSTTRIBULATIONAL.

Steven L. McAvoy

D. A. Carson, "Gundry on Matthew: A Critical Review" in *Trinity Journal,* 3 (Spring 1982): 71–91; Robert H. Gundry, *The Church and the Tribulation* (Grand Rapids: Zondervan, 1973); *JETS,* 26 (March 1983); Steven L. McAvoy, "A Critique of Robert Gundry's Posttribulationalism" (Th.D. diss., Dallas Theological Seminary, 1986); *An Open Letter to Dr. John F. Walvoord Concerning His Book "The Blessed Hope and the Tribulation"* (Wesmont College, September 1977); John F. Walvoord, *The Blessed Hope and the Tribulation* (Grand Rapids: Zondervan, 1976).

H

HABAKKUK, ESCHATOLOGY OF

Habakkuk is unique in that it records a dialogue with God about people. In this dialogue Habbakuk pleaded with God for divine judgment, in contrast to other Old Testament prophets who proclaimed God's divine judgment. The prophet asks why God has withheld His judgment from the oppression, the injustice, and the prosperity of evildoers. God resolves the prophet's questions by instruction in confidence and faith. The message of this book is summed up in 2:4, "the righteous will live by his faith." The book gives the assurance that God will overcome the wicked and deliver the righteous.

Little is known about Habakkuk; only his name and profession are recorded. He was an ordained prophet and his literary style informs us that he is as much poet as prophet. The book was written about 606–604 B.C. The prophet wrote during a time of international crisis and national decadence. Habakkuk wrote in response to the violence, greed, and injustice that surrounded him.

The book contains both near and far prophecies. The near prophecy is seen in 1:5–11, where God, in response to Habakkuk's question concerning the lack of judgment upon the ungodly (1:2–3), informs him that He will use the Babylonians as instruments of His judgment. Habakkuk asks why God would use such an evil people (1:12–17). Again God responds to the prophet (2:2–3) by assuring him that in His appointed time He will deal with this wicked nation. This was fulfilled in 539 B.C. when the Medes and Persians conquered Babylon. A messianic prophecy is given in 2:14. This declaration that the entire earth will be full of the knowledge of the glory of the Lord will be fulfilled in the millennial kingdom.

See also THEOCRATIC KINGDOM.

Rick Bowman

Everett F. Harrison and Charles F. Pfeiffer, eds., *Wycliffe Bible Commentary* (Chicago: Moody Press, 1962); John F. Walvoord and Roy B. Zuck, eds., *The Bible Knowledge Commentary* (Wheaton: Victor Books, 1985).

HAGGAI, ESCHATOLOGY OF

Haggai was the name of the writer of this book, although little else is known about this prophet (1:1). Archer states, "Of all the books of the Old Testament, this one enjoys the unusual status of being uncontested by all critics of every persuasion." Haggai is the first of the postexilic prophets to speak to the house of Israel. He was a contemporary of Zechariah. At the time Haggai delivered his messages the exiles had returned to Jerusalem and had started to rebuild the temple. There was opposition to the work and those that opposed were successful in getting King Artaxerxes (465–424 B.C.) to stop the rebuilding. Eighteen years had passed since the exiles had returned. Haggai rebukes the people for not rebuilding the temple and encourages them to get started (Ezra 5:1–2).

The book is made up of four messages. Lindsey classifies them as follows:

1. A judgmental call to rebuild the temple (1:1–15)
2. A prophetic promise of the future glory of the temple (2:1–9)
3. A priestly decision to illustrate the present blessings of obedience (2:10–19)
4. A messianic prophecy concerning Zerubbabel (2:20–23)

A Judgmental Call to Rebuild the Temple (1:1-15)

Haggai's first message came on the first day of the sixth month (Aug.–Sept.) in the second year of Darius (520 B.C.). It is directed to Zerubbabel, governor of Judah, and Joshua, the high priest (1:1). God's anger was over the fact that they were living in "paneled houses" but the temple was not finished (1:2–4). Their spiritual neglect was having economic consequences (1:6). The command was to rebuild the temple (1:8). The lack of produce and the drought they were experiencing were a direct result of being concerned about their own houses but not God's (1:9–11). The people's response was to reverence the Lord and so the Lord stirred up the spirit of Zerubbabel, the spirit of Joshua, and the spirit of the remnant of the people, and they commenced the work on the house of the Lord (1:12–15).

A Prophetic Promise of the Future Glory of the Temple (2:1–9)

This second message came on the twenty-first day of the seventh month (Sept.–Oct.) of the same year (2:1). Again the message is directed primarily to Zerubbabel and Joshua (2:2). Although the temple that they were constructing did not compare to Solomon's temple, which some of them had seen in the years before the Exile, the Lord encouraged them to continue with their work. He promised His Spirit was with them (2:3–5). Haggai then prophesies a future time when the heavens, earth, sea, dry land, and all the nations will be shaken (2:6). This will occur when Christ returns to the earth (Joel 3:16; Matt. 24:29–30). As Lindsay points out, "This 'shaking' of the nations may refer to God's gathering the nations for the battle of Armageddon" (see Zech. 14:1–4). The nations will come with great wealth and this will provide the adornment for the future glorious temple (2:7). It is only appropriate since God owns it all anyway (2:8). The future temple's glory will be greater than that of Solomon's, and it will be a place of peace (2:9). This will find its ultimate fulfillment in Christ's Second Coming, when He will judge the nations and rule and reign here on earth. At that time a millennial temple will be built, which is described in Ezekiel chapters 40–43.

A Priestly Decision to Illustrate the Present Blessings of Obedience (2:10–19)

The third message came on the twenty-fourth day of the ninth month (Dec.–Jan.) of the same year. The Lord uses a simple illustration to show them why they were not blessed in the past. Holy meat cannot touch bread, cooked food, wine, oil, or any food and make them holy. In addition, if a person who touched a corpse and becomes ceremonially unclean and touches any of these things, they become unclean. The Lord's point was that since the nation and people were unclean, all that they were doing and offering to God was unclean (2:10–15). The result was that the harvest was limited and God brought blasting winds, mildew, and hail on them (2:16–17). Even this chastening did not push them back to Him. But now that they had turned back to Him and were rebuilding the temple, the Lord said He would bless them (2:18–19).

A Messianic Prophecy Concerning Zerubbabel (2:20–23)

This fourth message came on the same day as the third but is specifically addressed to Zerubbabel, governor of Judah (2:20–21). The message is that the Lord will shake the heavens and the earth, overthrow the thrones and destroy the power of the kingdoms of the nations, and destroy the armies of the nations through fighting against one another (2:21–22; cf. Zech. 12:2–9; 14:1–5). This is the event described in Daniel 2, where the "stone" shatters the nations and the eternal kingdom is set up (Dan. 2:44–45). This will be the battle of Armageddon discussed in Revelation (Rev. 16:16–18) at the Lord's Second Coming (Rev. 19:11–21). Haggai closes this message with the following words: "'On that day,' declares the LORD of hosts, 'I will take you, Zerubbabel, son of Shealtiel, my servant,' declares the LORD, 'and I will make you like a signet ring, for I have chosen you,' declares the LORD of hosts." Walvoord comments on this verse, "The closing verse of Haggai was another confirmation of the restoration of Israel with a background of judgment of Gentile power in the world. God promised to honor Zerubbabel and make him like a signet ring, a token of authority. This was not to be fulfilled in Zerubbabel's lifetime but was symbolic of the coming Messiah at which time Zerubbabel will be raised from the dead and share delegated authority with David in the millennial kingdom. In this revelation God was reassuring his people of His ultimate blessing on her and the ultimate fulfillment of the promises to David concerning his kingdom and his people."

See also THEOCRATIC KINGDOM; EZEKIEL, ESCHATOLOGY OF.

Russell L. Penney

Robert L. Alden, "Haggai" in *The Expositor's Bible Commentary,* vol. 7, ed. Frank E. Gaebelein (Grand Rapids: Zondervan, 1985); Gleason L. Archer, *A Survey of Old Testament Introduction,* rev. ed. (Chicago: Moody Press, 1994); F. Duane Lindsey, "Haggai" in *The Bible Knowledge Commentary,* eds. John F. Walvoord and Roy B. Zuck (Wheaton: Victor Books, 1988); John F. Walvoord, *The Prophecy Knowledge Handbook* (Wheaton: Victor Books, 1990).

HEAVEN, DOCTRINE OF

Old Testament

The most common word in the Old Testament for heaven is *shah-mah-yim.* The word refers to the sky the birds fly in (Ps. 104:12), the atmosphere and source of rain (Gen. 7:11), and the firmament (Gen. 1:8), or outer space, and the abode of the stars and planets (Neh. 9:23). But heaven is also used to describe the seat of God's throne (Ps. 103:19), the direction we pray when beseeching God (Deut. 32:40), and the place where the Lord resides (Josh. 2:11). The heavens are where God keeps the records of human history (Deut. 31:28), where injustice reaches (2 Chron. 28:9), where prayers are heard and recorded (30:20). Elijah went up to heaven alive (2 Kings 2:1) and it was the promised haven for Old Testament saints after death. "With Thy counsel Thou wilt guide me, and afterward receive me to glory. Whom have I in heaven but Thee? And besides Thee, I desire nothing on earth" (Ps. 73:24–25).

Many believe, though not all agree, that Old Testament saints apparently went to a place of waiting until their sins were paid for by Christ's sacrifice. Jesus speaks of this place as a sanctuary of mercy called "Abraham's bosom" (Luke 16:22). The Lord tells the story of the poor man Lazarus, who was carried to this place of waiting by the angels. In contrast, and in the same account, the wealthy unrighteous man was sent to hades. In torment, he lifted up his eyes and pleaded to Abraham for relief from the "agony in this flame" (v. 24).

New Testament

Matthew and John mention heaven (*ouranos*) more than any of the other books. The word is used in its singular and plural form about three hundred times. The most prevalent use is as the abode of God, but it can also refer to the sky, the atmosphere, the stratosphere, and outer space. To begin the dispensation of the kingdom, the Son of Man comes in the clouds of the sky with power and great glory (Matt. 24:30). At the close of the Tribulation, the stars (*asteres*) will fall from outer space (sky, *ouranos*) and the powers of the heavens will be shaken (Matt. 24:29).

Prior to Christ's return, fire and brimstone will rain down from the atmosphere (Luke 17:29–30), along with huge hailstones weighing one hundred pounds (Rev. 16:21). Sometimes the word *heaven* represents the stars, galaxies, and the universe. The stars of heaven are innumerable (Heb. 11:12) and this same outer space is described as being very old, not created by evolution (Heb. 1:10). "By the word of God the heavens [universe] existed long ago" (2 Peter 3:5). And this same universe, and its elements, will someday be destroyed by fire, melting and burning, "The present heavens and earth by His word are being reserved for fire, kept for the day of judgment" (2 Peter 3:7, see v. 12). Sometimes the word *heaven* has a climatological meaning. "The sky [heaven] poured rain, and the earth produced its fruit" (James 5:18).

Heaven is used mainly to describe the abode of God. And since He is the "heavenly" Father (Luke 11:13), to sin against heaven is to sin in His sight (Luke 15:18). It is from heaven that the Lord also providentially cares for His own, the little ones (Matt. 18:10, 14). Representing spiritual pictures, the earthly temple and tabernacle of the Old Testament were but copies of the true that are in heaven where the Lord dwells (Heb. 9:23–24; Rev. 15:5). As well, God's throne of sovereign rule is also said to be in heaven (Rev. 4:2).

Being the Son of God, Christ descended from heaven (John 3:13), and because of this, He who comes from heaven is above all (v. 31) and He now has been given all authority in heaven and on earth (Matt. 28:18). After being with the disciples for forty days, Jesus ascended, "whom heaven must receive until the period of restoration of all things about which God spoke by the mouth of His holy prophets from ancient time" (Acts 3:21), that is, the kingdom that will be restored. Besides Christ, the angels originate from heaven (Luke 22:43) and in heaven they express joy when a sinner repents (15:7).

Until eternity begins, heaven is the place where the redeemed reside (Rev. 19:1) and during this dispensation, it is the ultimate residential goal of believers whose citizenship is heaven (Phil. 3:20), with a hope laid up there when death or the Rapture comes (Col. 1:5). The Lord promised heaven as the destination when He said, I go to prepare a place for you in My Father's house (John 14:2) and, "I will come again, and receive you to Myself; that where I am, there you may be also" (v. 3). The apostle Paul says now we live in the body, an earthly tent, the house which is to be torn down (2 Cor. 5:1), but we will be someday clothed with a new building, a house not made with hands, eternal in the heavens (5:2). The Scriptures tell us that it is in heaven where treasures are stored (Luke 12:33) and the Lord keeps records. "Rejoice that your names are recorded in heaven" (Luke 10:20).

During this dispensation of the church age, the Holy Spirit has been sent from heaven for special tasks with the believers (1 Peter 1:12). This church age will end with the rapture of the dead in Christ caught up to the Lord who descends from heaven. Both those who have fallen asleep in Jesus and those alive will be caught up together in the clouds to meet the Lord in the air (1 Thess. 4:13–18).

Following the Tribulation, the kingdom of heaven will come. This is the reign of the Messiah promised in the Gospels. Most dispensationalists believe this expression refers to the millennial reign. The *kingdom of heaven* expresses the fact that God's rule comes down to earth, the kingdom *from* heaven (Matt. 7:21). Dispensationalists differ on the full meaning of the mysteries of the kingdom of heaven. Some see the parables cited in Matthew 13 as referring to truths about the kingdom in this present day. Others see these parables expressing the hidden spiritual principles that will govern the millennial kingdom when it arrives.

Following the dispensation of the kingdom and the Great White Throne judgment (Rev. 20:11–15), there will be a renovation of the universe in which the first heaven and earth will be burned and will pass away. A new heaven and new earth will come, along with a new Jerusalem, coming down out of heaven from God (Rev. 21:1–2). With this, eternity begins. Though the redeemed may certainly have access to heaven, the saints will actually be abiding here in the holy city, Jerusalem (Rev. 21:10). Peter tells us this is the ultimate hope, "according to His promise we are looking for new heavens and a new earth, in which righteousness dwells" (2 Peter 3:13).

See also KINGDOM OF GOD, OF HEAVEN; NEW HEAVEN AND NEW EARTH.

Mal Couch

HEBREWS, ESCHATOLOGY OF

The Authorship of the Epistle

The authorship of the anonymous epistle to the Hebrews remains an open matter of speculation. The doubts of the Western church fathers in particular and differences in literary style have been compelling evidence to most modern scholars that the writer was not Paul. Of the possible candidates who are known to us from the New Testament, Martin Luther's suggestion that it was Apollos has probably gained the largest following. What we know of Apollos as an eloquent Jew from Alexandria who powerfully refuted the Jews by proving from the Scriptures that Jesus was the Christ (Acts 18:24, 28) accords well with the Alexandrian coloring of the epistle and the polished rhetorical skill of its author. Still we lack positive identification, and scholarship has not advanced much beyond the conclusion of Origen: "who wrote the epistle, God only knows."

The Background of the Readers

The View Associating Them with Qumran

On the basis of similarities between Hebrews and 11Q Melchizedek, some scholars have postulated that Hebrews was written to an Essene community in Palestine, or at least to a community that had been influenced by Qumran's beliefs about Melchizedek. Melchizedek's precise identification in Qumran is not entirely clear, but 11QMelch portrays him as some kind of heavenly being, perhaps even an archangel, who performs an eschatological role in atoning for sin, defeating the enemies of God, and judging the world. He is even called *Elohim.*

There are some apparent similarities between Hebrews and Qumran documents. Upon closer examination, however, these similarities do not concern their respective understandings of Melchizedek; rather they are found between Qumran's view of Melchizedek and Hebrews' view of Jesus (6:20, 7:3, 15). The two sources present very different pictures of Melchizedek. The eschatological, military, and judicial images of 11QMelch are lacking in Hebrews' portrayal of Melchizedek; our writer regards him as a historical prototype of Christ, not an eschatological redeemer of the world.

If the writer of Hebrews had held Qumran's view of Melchizedek, it would have had significant eschatological and theological implications for the epistle. By granting the same status to Melchizedek that Qumran held, Hebrews would have introduced a rival to Christ. But the writer of Hebrews omits any mention of Melchizedek from the discussion of Jesus' superiority to the angels (1:4–2:9). Conversely, the writer finds it necessary to prove that Melchizedek is superior to Abraham, which would not have had to be done if readers believed that Melchizedek was an angelic being. For these reasons, it does not seem likely that the original readers of Hebrews were associated with Qumran.

The View Locating Them at Rome

Hebrews was most likely written to a group of Jewish Christians meeting in a house church at Rome (13:24). In the early days after their conversion to Christianity, they had undergone persecution. They were publicly ridiculed; some of them were imprisoned, and others had their property confiscated. Nevertheless, they cheerfully endured it (10:32–34; 13:3).

This persecution probably refers to the expulsion of the Jews from Rome in A.D. 49. The Roman historian Suetonius tells us that they were expelled by the emperor Claudius because of "riots instigated by one Chrestus." The most common interpretation of this statement is that "Chrestus" is a Latin misspelling of *Christos* and that the riots mentioned refer to the outbreak of hostilities between orthodox Jews who remained loyal to traditional Judaism and other Jews who had converted to Christianity. From Acts 18:2 we know that Claudius's decree had forced Aquila and Priscilla, along with many other Jews, to leave the city, but by the time that Paul wrote his epistle to the Romans around A.D. 57, this couple had returned, and they were hosting a church in their home (Rom. 16:3–5).

At the time Hebrews was written, a fresh persecution was starting to build. In the face of it, many of these Jewish Christians were becoming weary and disheartened (12:3). They were tempted to avoid persecution by reverting to their former Judaism (10:23–29, 35–39), which enjoyed state recognition as a *religio licita*. In its early days Christianity enjoyed the same protection as a legally permitted religion because it was thought to be sect of Judaism; now that its distinct character had emerged, it stood alone as a separate and despised religion, and the attitude of the state was growing increasingly hostile to it. So far none of the first readers of Hebrews had died for their faith (12:4), but some of them would soon be cruelly tortured to death by Nero following the fire of Rome in A.D.

64. It is probably against this background of persecution that the writer of Hebrews exhorts them to consider the future as a means of remaining steadfast in the present.

The Philosophical Orientation of the Writer

In the past it has been popular to associate the hermeneutical methodology of Hebrews with that of Philo, the Alexandrian Jew who tried to accommodate Judaism to Greek philosophy by allegorizing the Pentateuch. As a result, the writer of Hebrews has also been suspected of adopting Philo's Platonic idealism, which viewed the present phenomenal world as a shadowy and inferior reflection of the suprasensible world of eternal ideas.

The Platonic mind-set of the writer of Hebrews supposedly shows through in the book's teaching that the earthly sanctuary and its ministry is an imperfect copy of the true tabernacle set up in heaven by God (8:2, 5). It is also supposedly seen in the doctrine of rest. Hebrews has been characterized as a story about the wandering people of God that was patterned after Philo's allegorization of the wilderness wanderings into the long journey of a virtuous mind trying to escape the limitations of the physical body so that it might reach its heavenly home.

But the philosophical orientation of Hebrews differs markedly from that of Philo in several respects. Because Philo viewed the spiritual world from a Platonic perspective as transcendent and antecedent to the sensory world, he characteristically interpreted all of reality in timeless, metaphysical categories and showed little interest in the future. The writer of Hebrews, however, was greatly interested in eschatology. In Hebrews, eschatology is the decisive factor in determining the shape of its hermeneutical and theological outlook. Unlike Philo, it does not use allegory to speculate about timeless, metaphysical categories; instead, Hebrews employs typology to draw historical correspondences from the past anticipations of the Old Testament to their recent fulfillment in the Christ event and then extends them into the yet-to-be-realized future. The epistle is filled with a sense of messianic expectation that is conspicuously lacking in Philo's writings. Furthermore, there is no denigration of matter in Hebrews; its writer makes the doctrine of the incarnation an integral part of its theology (2:14, 10:5), but the Platonic dualism of Philo would have made the Incarnation unthinkable.

Upon careful reflection, Hebrews is very un-Platonic in its teaching on the heavenly sanctuary. It predicates the commencement of Christ's priestly ministry in heaven upon a physical sacrifice that took place on earth within history (7:27, 9:11–12, 23–28). Philo would never have allowed an eternal, heavenly ideal to depend upon an earthly, time-bound event.

Hebrews' concept of rest also differs significantly from that of Philo. In Hebrews the wandering of the Israelites in the wilderness until the last one died is not a type of the Christian life, but of condemnation for lack of faith and stubborn refusal to enter into rest (3:10–11, 16–19; 4:2, 6). Unlike Philo, who slants his allegory in a Platonic and individualistic direction, Hebrews is eschatological and corporate in its outlook. Its knows nothing of a long journey of the virtuous soul; rather, its repeated allusions to Numbers 14 place the emerging nation of Israel at Kadesh Barnea, at that crucial juncture in history where they stood right on the border to the Promised Land poised to step in. Because that generation failed to enter rest, Hebrews holds out an eschatological promise of rest to its readers (4:1, 6, 9). Typologically, it places them in a similar position to the Israelites in Numbers 14; now that Christ has come, they stand at the end of the present age and on the verge of entering into the blessings of rest in the *eschaton.*

It appears that Hebrews is not Platonic in its philosophical outlook. Its roots are solidly biblical, historical, messianic, and eschatological.

The Eschatology of the Epistle

The Doctrine of the Two Ages

The Jews traditionally divided all of world history into two ages: the present age and the age to come. Their experience of persecution had convinced them that history could not be understood from within the present perspective of suffering and injustice. It could only be understood from the vantage point of the final consummation when God would cataclysmically break in to judge evil and establish His kingdom.

The early Christians adopted the Jewish doctrine of the two ages, but unlike the Jews who constantly looked forward to the climax of history in the coming of the Messiah, they maintained that the consummation had already begun in Jesus Christ, who, by His death and resurrection, once and for all dealt with sin in a way that determines the course of all subsequent history (cf. 1 Cor. 10:11; Heb. 1:2; 2:5, 8, 9; 6:5; 9:11, 26; 1 Peter 1:20). For them the decisive midpoint of time no longer lay in the future but in the past appearing of Christ; consequently, all of history could only be understood in terms of Him (Luke 24:27).

By living shortly after Christ's death and resurrection, the readers of Hebrews were divinely placed at a privileged position in history where they could look back at the former age. The believers who lived during that age anticipated an age to come, in which the subjection of all of creation originally promised to Adam would be realized (Gen. 1:26, 28; Ps. 8:4–6; Heb. 2:5–8), and they sought a city to come, which would last forever (11:10, 16; 13:14). Moses, one of the greatest representatives of that age, witnessed faithfully concerning what would be spoken later (3:5), but no one from the former age realized the blessings anticipated by the Old Testament in the way that was now made possible (11:39–40).

The former age was incomplete and self-confessedly inferior to the coming age, to which it pointed in types and shadows (10:1–4). The religious system imposed under it was only a temporary provision until the coming of a new order (9:10). By prophesying the establishment of a new covenant, the Old Testament, itself, recognized that the system that it sanctioned was inadequate and would be superseded. With the inauguration of the new covenant in Jesus, the old covenant became obsolete; and Hebrews states that it was already rapidly disappearing in its day (8:6–13; Jer 31:31–34).

Now the readers of Hebrews had entered the last days, in that God had spoken directly in His Son (1:2). Although they were still living in the present, the age to come had already come in an inaugurated sense (9:11, 26), and they had tasted its power (6:5). They had come to Mount Zion, the heavenly Jerusalem (12:22).

Although all of creation is not presently subject to humans, as it one day will be through the representative of the race (2:8), the readers of Hebrews stood at a vantage point where they could see the One to whom everything will be subject, Jesus Christ. He is crowned with glory and honor (2:9). The appearing of the new age, which they still anticipated in its fullness, had already dawned. By peering off into the distance, they could see the approach of the final day when the promised hope will be fully realized (10:25). That day is now drawing near, and the readers are promised that their wait for its arrival will only be a little while longer (10:37).

Hebrews sets us between the two ages and allows us to feel the tension between the "already" and the "not yet." In Jesus the future became potentially present. He has already sat down at the right hand of God (Heb 1:3, 8:1, 10:12, 12:2; Ps. 110:1), but there is a time delay in that the first readers of Hebrews, along with the rest of us, must wait until God places all enemies under His feet (Heb. 1:13, 10:13; Ps. 110:1). The world to come has been placed in subjection to Jesus, and in an inaugurated sense, it has already come and His reign begun. But the world to come is not now actually present, and His reign has not yet been fully realized (2:8). Even as Jesus had to be made for a little while lower than the angels, so we too must endure faithfully for a little while (3:6, 14, 6:11, 10:36–37). We now live in this exciting period of tension between the two ages in that the already accomplished fact of redemption reaches forward to lay hold of the not yet fulfilled universal reign of Christ.

The Power of the Future to Transform the Present

The readers of Hebrews are reminded that they have a heavenly calling (3:1); therefore, they can never feel completely at home in this present world. They should follow Abraham's example by making the goal of their earthly pilgrimage the heavenly city that God has designed and built for them upon solid foundations that will endure; conversely, they should not be overly concerned with the present world that will pass away (11:10, 13–16, 13:14).

Hebrews presents hope in the promises of God as a means of drawing near to Him and anchoring the soul (6:19; 7:19). So that hope might achieve these beneficial functions, Hebrews takes pains to show that the promises are secure (10:23). Abraham had solid grounds for his assurance because God, who cannot lie, confirmed the promise to him with an oath (Gen. 22:16–17; Heb. 6:13–16); we may have even greater assurance because Jesus, our High Priest, has entered within the veil of the heavenly tabernacle as a forerunner for us (6:17–20).

Faith is the means of apprehending God's promises in which we confidently hope even though we do not presently see what was promised (Heb. 10:38; 11:1, 6; Hab. 2:4). As examples for our encouragement, the writer of Hebrews offers a long list of Old Testament saints who by their faith, both in the objective sense of belief in God's promises and in the subjective sense of faithfulness in living out the implications of that belief, accomplished many heroic deeds (11:4–38; 12:1), even though they did not receive the ultimate fulfillment of those promises (11:13, 39–40). For all of them faith was the key in subjecting the visible goals of this passing, temporal world to the greater, unseen rewards of the coming age (6:12, 11:13–16, 25–27). The supreme example of faith is Jesus, who endured the suffering and shame of the cross and accomplished the goal of redeeming fallen humanity by looking past the evil of this present, visible world to the glory of the future, unseen one, which He has now attained (12:2–3).

The writer does not hesitate to use the promise of rewards (10:35–36, 12:11) or the threat of accountability to God (Deut. 32:36; Ps. 135:14; Heb. 10:30; 13:17) as incentives for believers to perseverance and responsible living. This present life is a limited period of training to prepare us for seeing the Lord and sharing in His holiness (12:10, 14). With that goal in mind, the readers are urged to help and encourage one another on to steadfastness, health, love, and good deeds (10:24–25, 12:12–13).

In particular, the breaking of the future into the present forms the eschatological framework for Hebrews' exhortations to not give up under persecution but to enter into God's rest by faith and perseverance. Hebrews encourages readers to hold fast their confidence and hope firm until the end (3:6, 14, 6:11) and not be like their fathers, who failed to enter into rest because of disobedience and unbelief (Ps. 95:7–11; Heb. 3:7–11, 16–19; 4:1–2, 11). He urges them to pay attention to the Holy Spirit, who is at that very moment calling out, "Today if you hear [God's] voice, do not harden your hearts" (3:7)! It exhorts them to "encourage one another day after day, as long as it is still called 'today'" (3:13, 15). Even though they were facing persecution, the "today" of the Holy Spirit's speaking was a day of unprecedented opportunity in that the prospect of entering into rest lay within reach (4:11). From the fact that the promise had not been fulfilled in the past, Hebrews argues that it must still remain open for believers to enter into it (4:9). Without denying its geographic aspect, Hebrews reasons that this promised rest must include more than just the physical occupation of Canaan under Joshua, or God would not have spoken of another day of rest in Psalm 95 (4:7–9). By linking together God's designation of rest in Psalm 95:11 as, "*My* rest," with Genesis 2:2, which states that on the seventh day of creation God rested "from all *His* work," Hebrews concludes that the rest that remains for the people of God is similar to God's Sabbath rest in ceasing from the labor of His works (4:3–5, 9–10). Hebrews introduces the new term *sabbatismos* (4:9) to distinguish the sabbatical characteristics of rest from its geographic association with Canaan. This rest includes both present and future aspects; in its fullest sense it remains as a promise to be realized in the future (4:1, 6, 9), but believers are already entering into it now (4:3).

Although there are important differences of interpretation, we also find the doctrine of rest developed along eschatological lines in rabbinic literature and the Epistle of Barnabas. Many of the rabbis identified the six days of creation with the age of the world and the creation Sabbath with a millennium of rest that would pass into the eternal age. Rabbi Eliezer, for example, taught that "God has created seven ages. . . . There are six for the coming and going of men, but . . . the seventh is completely Sabbath and rest in everlasting life" (*Pirke,* 18).

The Epistle of Barnabas, which shares Hebrews' Christian orientation, calculates the dawn of the new world by equating the completion of creation in six days with the duration of the present world, which will last for six thousand years (cf. Ps. 90:4; 2 Peter 3:8). After God judges the wicked, He will truly rest on the seventh day, and on the eighth day, which is the day of Jesus' resurrection, He will begin a new world (Epis. Barnabas, 15:3–9).

While these eschatological interpretations of rest may be interesting, we cannot say if the writer of Hebrews would have endorsed them. The book does not set up a speculative time line and does not specifically identify the future rest with the Millennium.

A Preview of What Is Yet to Come

Not everything that will come has come yet, but the sacrificial death and glorious exaltation of Christ have consummated the former age of promise and ushered in the new age of fulfillment. The rest of time and eternity will be a natural outworking of His finished work.

The death of Christ emancipates us from the Devil's tyranny and will ultimately destroy the one who once held the power of death (2:14–15). Christ's perfect sacrifice has constituted Him the mediator of a new and lasting covenant, which is superior to the former one (8:6–7, 13; cf. 7:22). This new covenant contains provisions for the internalization of the Law, fellowship between God and His people, universal knowledge of God, and complete forgiveness of sin (Heb. 8:10–12; Jer. 31:33–34). Hebrews applies the new covenant to its readers in terms of the indwelling of the Holy Spirit and the finality of Christ's sacrifice for sin (10:15–18). Since this covenant was specifically made with the house of Israel and with the house of Judah (8:8), however, and everyone does not yet know the Lord (8:11), it must still have a greater, future fulfillment.

The salvation that Jesus obtained applies to us eternally (5:9) because, first of all, the sacrifice that He offered, being perfect, never needs to be repeated (7:27, 9:12, 25–26, 28, 10:10, 14); and because secondly, the intercessory ministry of His Melchizedekian high priesthood, being founded upon His eternal life, will never come to an end (5:6, 6:20, 7:3, 8, 16–17, 21, 24–25, 28; cf. Ps. 110:4).

Hebrews assumes as fundamental doctrines that there will be a general resurrection of the dead (6:2, 11:19, 35; cf. 12:23) and a future, eternal judgment of the wicked (6:2, 10:39). It describes this dreadful judgment as a raging fire that consumes God's adversaries (10:27, 31, 12:29). Inasmuch as the sin of despising the Gospel and the God who graciously offers it is graver than rejecting the Law of Moses, those who do so will be punished even more severely without any mercy (10:28–30, 12:25). In contrast Hebrews also holds that God's children will share with the Son in His glory in the subjection of all creation to Him (2:6–10).

In the midst of change throughout the ages, Jesus Christ remains unchangeable; He is the same yesterday, today, and forever (13:8). His years will never end. He existed before the universe, which He created, and will remain after the present heavens and earth have perished (1:10–12; Ps. 102:25–27). In a great cataclysmic event that draws its imagery from the earthquake at the giving of the Law at Mount Sinai, God will violently shake the entire created order so that He may dislodge anything that is not permanent and set up His unshakable kingdom

(12:26–28; cf. Haggai 2:6). In fulfillment of the Davidic covenant the Son will rule this kingdom in righteousness forever (Ps. 2:7; 45: 6; 2 Sam. 7:12-16; Heb. 1:5, 8).

Dale F. Leschert

C. K. Barrett, "The Eschatology of the Epistle to the Hebrews" in *The Background of the N.T. and Its Eschatology*, eds. W. D. Davies and D. Daube (Cambridge: University Press, 1956), 363–93; Oscar Cullmann, *Christ and Time: The Primitive Christian Conception of Time and History*, trans. Floyd V. Filson (Philadelphia: Westminster Press, 1950); Ottfried Hofius, *Katapausis Die Vorstellung vom endzeitlichen Ruheort im Hebräerbrief* (Tübingen: J. C. B. Mohr [Paul Siebeck], 1970); Lincoln D. Hurst, "Eschatology and Platonism in the Epistle to the Hebrews" in *SBL Seminar Papers*, 23:41–71 (1984); Dale F. Leschert, *Hermeneutical Foundations of Hebrews* (Lewiston, N.Y.: Edwin Mellen, 1994); George W. MacRae, "Heavenly Temple and Eschatology in the Letter to the Hebrews" in *Semeia,* 12:179–99 (1978); William Robinson, "The Eschatology of the Epistle to the Hebrews," *Encounter* 22:37–51 (1961); Jeffrey R. Sharp, "Philonism and the Eschatology of Hebrews: Another Look" in *East Asia Journal of Theology* 2:289–98 (1984); Albert Vanhoye, "Longue marche ou accès tout proche? Le contexte biblique de Hébreux 3:7–4:11" in *Biblica* 49:9–26 (1968).

HELL

Hell is the place described in Scripture as the place of the damned. It is the place where all sin will spend eternity. Satan, fallen angels, fallen people, and all who offend will find their places there.

Hell is pictured as a place of torment, sorrow, and loneliness for those who choose to rebel against God. It is a place where the wicked go and endure pain, agony, and endless suffering from burning fire. The punishment of hell is eternal in duration.

Hell was created by God for the express purpose of dealing with the Devil and his angels (Matt. 24:41). God created hell to destroy the rebellion of Satan and sin. It was never created for people, but when they first sinned in the Garden of Eden, God had to accommodate the human fall. The Scripture clearly teaches that hell has been enlarged because of human sins (Isa. 5:14).

The term *hell* is used to translate one Hebrew word in the OT and several different Greek words in the NT. The Authorized Version first uses the word "hell" in Deuteronomy 32:22 where it translates the Hebrew word *sheol.* The corresponding Greek word is *hades,* which is used eleven times in the New Testament. The Septuagint translated the Hebrew, *sheol*, with *hades* sixty-one times. Generally though, neither of these words represent the place of eternal torment but, according to Vine's, simply "the region of departed spirits of the lost (including the blessed dead in periods preceeding the ascension of Christ). . . . It never denotes the grave, nor is it the permanent region of the lost; in point of time it is, for such, intermediate between decease and the doom of Gehenna." Hades is always referred to as down (Matt. 11:23; Luke 10:15) and is referred to as being in the heart of the earth (Matt. 12:40).

According to Vine, sheol or hades was the region of the departed spirits before the ascension of Christ. In Luke 16:19–31 we have the story of Lazarus and the rich man. It tells us that before the Ascension there were at least two separate abodes in hades. One was referred to here as Abraham's bosom, which was apparently the place of paradise of Old Testament believers at the time of death (cf. Luke 23:43; 2 Cor. 12:4). It was the place where all the righteous dead of the Old Testament dispensation were kept before Jesus paid the price of redemption. There was no torment or suffering in Abraham's bosom. Once Jesus paid the eternal price required by God this compartment was emptied and the righteous were allowed into heaven. The other compartment was a place of the unsaved dead. It is clearly a place of conscious torment and agonizing flame (Luke 16:23–25). It is also clear that the rich man still had his memory during the torment (Luke 16:25–31). This is the place where the unsaved dead await their final judgment at the Great White Throne (Rev. 20:11–15). H. Bietenhard points out in the *New International Dictionary of New Testament Theology* that "at the resurrection [of the dead] Hades must give up its dead again (Rev. 20:13). So it is not an eternal but only a temporary place or state."

Another of the Greek words translated "hell" in the Authorized Version is *gehenna.* Paul Enns states of the word, "it occurs twelve times in the New Testament, [and] is a designation for eternal punishment taken from the Hebrew *ge hinnom,* referring to the Valley of Hinnom that runs on the south and east sides of Jerusalem. The worship of Molech in which infants were sacrificed in fire to the god Molech also occurred in the Valley of Hinnom (2 Kings 16:3, 17:7, 21:6). . . . The valley also became the place where refuse and dead bodies of animals and criminals were burned. As a result, gehenna became synonymous with eternal punishment, the fire of hell. It describes the punishment connected with the final judgment, a punishment that has eternal duration, not annihilation (Matt. 23:15, 33, 25:41, 46)." Gehenna is stated in Scripture as having been prepared for the Devil and his angels (Matt. 25:41). It is the place where death and hades are thrown at the final judgment and it is there referred to as the second death, the lake of fire (Rev. 20:13–14). Its punishment is of eternal duration (Matt. 25:41, 46, 23:15, 33). This will be the place of final doom for the demons, the Beast, the False Prophet, and Satan (Matt. 8:29; 25:41; Rev. 19:20; 20:10, 14).

When the unsaved are cast into hades or gehenna they will be cast as a total, complete and physical people. When an unrighteous person dies, the spirit and soul are separated from the body. The body goes back to the dust of the earth, and the spirit and soul go to hades to be tormented there until the Great White Throne judgment of God (Rev. 20:11–15). The body of the unsaved will not always stay in the grave, though; the Bible is clear that there will be a resurrection of the body and some will awake to everlasting life and some to everlasting shame and contempt (Dan. 12:2; John 5:28–29). There is coming a time when the lost will be in their physical, resurrected body to face the pains of eternal punishment.

The last Greek word translated "hell" in the Authorized Version is the word *tartaroo.* Tartaroo is only found once in the New Testament, in 2 Peter 2:4, where it is said to be the place where God cast some of the angels that sinned and committed them to pits of darkness, reserved for judgment. The Greek word *abyssos* is also used in a similar sense to refer to a prison for demons (Luke 8:31; Rev. 9:1). It is apparently ruled by a prince (Rev. 9:11) and during the Tribulation demons are released from it to inflict punishment on those on the earth (Rev. 9:1–3). It is also the place where Satan will be bound for a thousand years during the millennial reign of Christ (Rev. 20:1–4).

See also HEAVEN.

Donald Perkins and Russell L. Penney

H. Bientard, "Hell" in *The New International Dictionary of Theology*, ed. Colin Brown (Grand Rapids: Zondervan Publishing House, 1975); Paul Enns, *The Moody Handbook of Theology* (Chicago: Moody Press, 1989); John A. Martin, "Luke" in *The Bible Knowledge Commentary* (Wheaton: Victor Books, 1983); Donald Perkins, *The Reality of Hell* (Lemon Grove: According To Prophecy Ministries, 1993); W. E. Vine, Merrill F. Unger, and William White Jr., *Vine's Expository Dictionary of Biblical Words* (Nashville: Thomas Nelson, 1984).

HERMENEUTICS, MEDIEVAL

The logical, grammatical principles used to interpret and explain the Bible in the Middle Ages were dominated by allegorical persuasions and the authoritative doctrinal rule of the papacy. As a result, many doctrines that were deduced from Scripture during this period violated and often negated the original intention of the writers inspired by the Holy Spirit. A shift from the literal hermeneutic of the first-century church to an allegorical approach began to take place as early as the third century.

Origen was the first theologian to spiritualize, or explain away, the future kingdom as the present reign of Christ in the human heart. Augustine spiritualized major events of prophecy and his interpretations became the universal eschatology until the Reformation. By the fifth century, the influence of Origen and Augustine had caused the belief in a literal millennial kingdom to disappear. During the Middle Ages, millenarianism was generally regarded as heretical.

A movement that came to be known as scholasticism began around the year 1000 with Anselm and Thomas Aquinas recognized as the most influential leaders. Depending almost exclusively on the allegorical method and giving no recognition to the importance of the original language of biblical texts, this movement further perverted the truth of Scripture. This method of interpretation dominated the Middle Ages and was characterized by unlimited speculation without any objective, consistent standard for correctness. Medieval interpretation was influenced and restrained by three factors: the prevalence of illiteracy among both the clergy and the congregation; the study of Scripture was restricted primarily to monasteries; and the desire to support the dogmas of Rome.

One of the most significant dogmas that developed from medieval hermeneutics was transubstantiation. Declared as dogma by Innocent III in 1215, it decreed that priests had the power to transform the bread and wine into the body, blood, soul, and divinity of Jesus Christ. The figurative language of Christ in the sixth chapter of John's gospel and at the Last Supper was interpreted as literal to support the practice of transubstantiation. Many serious consequences developed from this dogma. If Christ really is substantially present, then the wafer is to be adored and worshiped. Furthermore, those who consume the wafer are receiving Christ not by faith and the will of God, but of human decision. The immolation of Christ in the wafer on church altars was decreed as the continuation Calvary's sacrifice for the propitiation of God's wrath.

From the Middle Ages also emerged the dogma of purgatory that proclaimed the temporal punishment and purging of sins by fire was necessary for entrance into heaven. With no literal support from Scripture, it has been used by Rome to supplant God in His righteous judgment of sin. It was in conjunction with this doctrine that the practice of selling indulgences developed. The church began to give indulgences as a remission before God of the temporal punishment due to sins by means of reducing time spent in purgatory. The church condemned with anathema those who said indulgences are useless or the church does not have the power to grant them.

The fusion of papal ideology with biblical interpretation reached a new low in 1302 when Boniface VIII's bull, *Unam Sanctam*, decreed that submission to the pope "is absolutely necessary to salvation." Papal decrees replaced conciliar canons as the routine form of authoritative interpretation. Since Rome interpreted the kingdom of God as the church, the pope wielded dogmatic control over people's eternal destiny. With the "keys of the kingdom" he exercised the power to open and close the gates of the kingdom based on people's allegiance to him. To be excommunicated by the pope meant there was no hope of salvation and such a person was labeled as an outlaw in society.

In the late fifteenth century, in the midst of great spiritual depression, came a movement to return to a literal hermeneutic and a quest for doctrinal purity. Out of this reexamination of the meaning and explanation of Scripture came a spiritual revival and the Reformation.

See also HERMENEUTICS, REFORMATION.

Michael P. Gendron

Louis Berkhof, *The History of Christian Doctrines* (Grand Rapids: Baker, 1937); Mark S. Burrows and Paul Rorem, *Biblical Hermeneutics in Historical Perspective* (Grand Rapids: Eerdmans, 1991); David S. Dockery, *Biblical Interpretation Then and Now* (Grand Rapids: Baker, 1992); William Webster, *The Church of Rome at the Bar of History* (Carlisle, Pa.: The Banner of Truth Trust, 1995).

HERMENEUTICS, ANTIOCHIAN SCHOOL

It is no exaggeration to say that the development of hermeneutics in the early periods of church history centered around the gradual abandonment of allegorical interpretation, leading to the eventual triumph of normal-literal interpretation. While this development suffered many setbacks throughout history (particularly during the Middle Ages), one of the important groups in the history of the church that aided this progress was the school of Antioch. This catechetical school, founded in Syria in the third and fourth centuries, developed a systematic hermeneutic aimed at debunking the objectionable features of the allegorical approach of Origen and the Alexandrian school.

The School of Alexandria

The school of Alexandria was influenced by the Jewish exegete Philo, who used and popularized the allegorical method to explain away the anthropomorphic portrayals of God in the Hebrew Scriptures so objectionable to Platonic philosophers. Clement of Alexandria, the founder of the school of Alexandria, adopted Philo's allegorical approach as an apologetic device to explain away elements in Scripture that were objectionable to Greek detractors of Christianity (anthropomorphic portrayals of God, earthy Hebrew expressions that offended Greek sensibilities, low level of morality of many Israelites, and the annihilation of the Canaanites) and to demonstrate that Christian theology, the true philosophy, was compatible with Greek philosophy (e.g., Clement allegorized the two fish in the feeding of the five thousand as the merging of Greek philosophy with Christian theology). Clement believed that God intentionally placed stumbling blocks to the reader in the literal meaning to awaken people's minds to find the hidden truths buried beneath the surface of the text. Unfortunately, by using the allegorical method for his apologetical agenda, he distorted the meaning of Scripture.

Origen (d. 254), the most influential teacher of the Alexandrian school, was drawn to the allegorical method of Philo because it allowed him to reconcile Scripture with Platonism, the foundational presupposition behind all of his thinking. Just as Philo used the allegorical method to reconcile the Hebrew Scriptures with Platonic philosophy, Origen used the allegorical method to reconcile the New Testament with Platonic philosophy.

While Origen believed that spiritual truth was self-consistent and accurate, he argued that the historical accounts were sometimes inconsistent and inaccurate (e.g., Genesis describes days before the creation of the sun; Satan showed Jesus all the kingdoms of the earth from atop a mountain; the Gospels disagreed among themselves about the order of the events of the life of Jesus). From a modern hermeneutical perspective, these issues seem rather naive; however, to Origen, they were unresolvable with the literal method. Origen attempted to resolve these alleged inconsistencies and other historical- exegetical dilemmas through the allegorical method: the stories do not mean what they say; their real meaning lay in the allegorical level. According to Origen, the difficulties of Scripture suggest the existence of a deeper meaning: "Wherever in the narrative [of Scripture] the accomplishment of some particular deeds did not correspond with the sequence of the intellectual truths, the Scripture wove into the story something which did not happen, occasionally something which could not happen, and occasionally something which might have happened but in fact did not" (*First Principles* 4.2.9).

Origen was the first to set forth a systematic method of biblical interpretation and hermeneutical theory utilizing the allegorical method (*First Principles* 4). Based on Proverbs 22:20–21 ("Record them three times . . . that you may answer with words of truth"), he argued for a threefold meaning of Scripture: the literal, moral, and allegorical (spiritual) senses. According to Origen, the Bible must be interpreted in a special way because it was divinely inspired. Inspiration did not mean that the words recorded and the events recounted in Scripture were the true message from God; rather, inspiration meant that behind the words and hidden in the details of the text was a deeper meaning that was the true Word of God.

The allegorical method became a popular apologetic tool against Jewish opponents to Christianity to surface hidden prophecies about Jesus in the Old Testament. The basis for the unity of the Old and New Testaments was the allegorical method. For example, the account of Noah and the dove became a prophetic allegory of Christ and the Spirit. The tree planted beside streams of water in Psalm 1 was a prophetic allegory of the cross of Christ and Christian baptism. Rahab's scarlet cord and the two spies were a prophetic allegory of the Trinity and the work of Christ. The Greek numerals for the 318 servants of Abram was a prophetic allegory of Christ's death: the first two numerals were the two letters in the Greek name of Jesus and the third was a graphic representation of the cross.

The School of Antioch

The extremes of Origen and other Alexandrians sparked a reaction among many early church leaders who rejected the allegorical approach as a legitimate, reliable method for interpreting Scripture. As a reaction against the allegorization of the school of Alexandria, church leaders in Antioch of Syria founded a school in the third and fourth centuries whose curriculum emphasized normal-literal interpretation and was self-consciously opposed to the method taught by the school of Alexandria.

The earliest representatives of Antiochian exegesis were Theophilus (ca. 115–188), bishop of Antioch, and Dorotheus (ca. 240–312), who paved the way for the founding of the school. The second and most influential period of the school began in the fourth century under Diodorus of Tarsus (d. 393), the teacher of Theodore of Mopsuestia (ca. 350–428) and John Chrysostom (ca. 347–407). Chrysostom went on to become the bishop of Constantinople and the greatest preacher of the early church; his sermons clearly demonstrate how this method was applied in preaching. Theodore became the greatest exegete of the early church, teaching as an instructor at the school, along with Theodoret (ca. 393–460).

Although they used the same basic method, Wallace-Hadrill has shown that the Antiochians represented a spectrum; Theodore was the most extreme in emphasizing historical exegesis, while Chrysostom was inconsistent in using the literal method when drawing applications in his expositions. The school of Antioch began to develop the historical-grammatical approach: they stressed the importance of Hebrew and Greek exegesis and historical backgrounds and recognition of figures of speech. In contrast to the multiple meanings generated by the allegorical method, the Antiochians argued that every passage has only one plain, simple meaning conveyed by its words and grammar. Just as the Alexandrians were influenced by Philo, the Antiochians were influenced by the prominent Jewish community in Antioch; in general, their exegesis was soberly literal. Instead of forcing Scripture to comply with Platonic preconceptions, they interpreted Scripture from the vantage point of its own Semitic thought.

While the Alexandrians claimed that the literal meaning of a text did not include its metaphorical meaning, the Antiochians insisted that the literal meaning cannot exclude metaphor. While the Alexandrians employed allegory to defend the unity of the Old and New Testaments, the Antiochians based this unity upon directly predictive prophecy and indirectly predictive typology viewed retrospectively through progressive revelation. However, it is ironic that they often practiced an extreme typology that bordered on the allegorical approach they so strongly rejected. For example, some of Theodoret's Christological typologies are virtually indistinguishable from Alexandrian allegory: he claimed that "the dew from heaven and fatness of the earth" (Gen 27:39) was a prophetic typology of the divine and human natures of Christ. Unfortunately, such extremes in typological exegesis would plague the church until this hermeneutical issue of *sensus plenior* versus *sensus unum* would be better addressed in the nineteenth and twentieth centuries.

Although the Antiochians normally practiced sober historical-grammatical exegesis, they occasionally used a less-than-literal approach in their popular expositions. For example, Theodore, relentless in his attack on allegorical interpretation, allowed himself considerable freedom, as in his exposition of Psalm 45. Likewise, Chrysostom, who emphasized historical exegesis, occasionally departed from the historical meaning of the text to draw applications, as in his sermon on the wedding feast at Cana. Chrysostom often made a methodological break when he moved from exegesis to application a difficulty faced by every preacher who roots himself in historical exegesis but desires to draw out relevant applications. Unfortunately, the hermeneutical movement from historical exegesis (what it meant) to contemporary significance (what it means) would not be adequately addressed until the rise of the biblical theology movement in the twentieth century.

Representatives of the School of Antioch

In contrast to the allegorical method of the Alexandrians, Theophilus of Antioch (ca. 115–188), bishop of Antioch, stressed historical-grammatical exegesis.

In contrast to the Alexandrians who denied the historicity of OT narratives, Theophilus, influenced by the prominent Jewish community in the city, stressed that the OT was an authentic historical record of God's dealings with the Jewish nation. To demonstrate his commitment to its historicity, in his treatise, *To Autolychus*, he worked out a chronology from the Creation to his own day. He affirmed the unity of the Old and New Testaments, suggesting that the Logos of John 1 had spoken through Moses and was the source of the light created in Genesis 1 before God created the sun. While the Alexandrians allegorized OT laws, Theophilus interpreted the laws in a historical-grammatical manner, and used many parts of the laws as guidance for the Christian life.

Diodorus of Tarsus (d. 393) made three important contributions: (1) He wrote the first systematic treatment defending and explaining the literal historical-grammatical method. (2) He affirmed the validity of a historical-typological method and refuted Origen's argument that Paul had used an Alexandrian-like allegorical method in Galatians 4:21–31. (3) He was the teacher of Theodore of Mopsuestia and John Chrysostom, who would become the greatest exegetical and expositional exponents of the school of Antioch.

Diodorus's most important publication (*What Is the Difference Between Insight and Allegory* [Greek]) denounced the Alexandrian method and set forth basic principles of the historical-grammatical method. According to Diodorus, the key to interpreting Scripture was not allegory, but *theoria* (insight).

Insight is the ability to perceive both the literal historical facts in a text, as well as the spiritual (theological) reality to which these facts point. Diodorus did not downplay the literal meaning in favor of a hidden spiritual one, like the Alexandrians; rather, he argued that, like an image, the historical sense directly corresponded to the spiritual (theological) sense. In his concept of *theoria*, the prophet's vision and the interpreter's insight encompassed more than what is immediately evident in the bare historical details of the text.

The biblical text leads the reader upward into spiritual (theological) truths that are not immediately obvious and that provide a fuller understanding of God's plan of salvation. Diodorus did not sharply distinguish between the meaning intended by the human author and by the divine author, as the Alexandrians had. The OT did contain spiritual meanings and messianic references; however, these are culled out, not by allegory, but by insight into the integral relationship between the historical and theological meanings of the text.

Diodorus laid the foundation for the later articulation of the illumination of the Spirit that allows the interpreter to perceive the overall theological unity and contemporary relevance of the Scriptures. Origen had argued that Paul's treatment of the Abraham-Hagar story in Galatians 4:21–31 was an example of Alexandrian-like allegorization. He claimed that Paul denied the historical character of the narrative. Diodorus argued that, whatever else Paul intended by his reference to Abraham and Hagar, he was not denying the narrative's historicity. Paul used typology; he affirmed the historicity of the narrative but discerned the theological significance in the events. Diodorus pointed out that the historical issue was the distinguishing characteristic between the typological method of Paul and the allegorical method of Origen.

The historical-theological typological approach was valid; the nonhistorical allegorical approach was not. Each of the Antiochians handled the issue of Old Testament prophecy differently. In his commentary on the Psalms, he interpreted Psalm 2 as directly prophetic of the Jews' handing Jesus over to Herod and Pilate. However, he rejected the popular view that Psalm 22 was a direct prophecy of Christ's passion; the sufferings of the psalmist did not correspond to those of Christ.

Many regard Theodore of Mopsuestia (ca. 350–428) as the greatest interpreter of the school of Antioch. He was the most adamant in rejecting the allegorical method of Origen and the Alexandrians, the most extreme in emphasizing historical-grammatical exegesis, and consequently, the most original in his exegetical conclusions. While he stressed analytical exegesis, synthesis was also important to him: seeing the whole passage in the light of its parts. His commentary on the epistles of Paul is the first and almost the last exegetical work produced in the ancient church that bears any similarity to modern exegetical commentaries.

Like Diodorus, he challenged the nonhistorical aspect of the allegorical method in the last of his five books, *Concerning Allegory and History Against Origen* (Greek) in which he argued that Origen deprived biblical history of its reality, seen most clearly in his denial of the historicity of Adam. Theodore asked, "If Adam was not a real person, how did death enter the world?" Theodore argued that Origen's denial of the reality of the fall of Adam destroyed the reality of redemption. Paul, however, interpreted all these events as historical. Contrary to Origen's claims, Paul was not using an Alexandrian-like allegorical interpretation in Galatians 4:21–31, but was merely using Abraham and Hagar as an example or illustration.

Theodore was the first to clearly and explicitly include the figurative meaning as part of the literal meaning, in contrast to the Alexandrians, who did not include the metaphorical meaning in the literal meaning of a text. For example, according to the Alexandrians, the literal meaning of "the arm of God" was that God really has an arm. Rather than view this as a metaphorical anthropomorphism, the Alexandrians allegorized the text into something completely unrelated. However, Theodore argued that the literal meaning of a passage included the metaphor and its natural meaning. In his view, every passage has a literal meaning, whether normal or figurative.

Reacting to the extreme Alexandrian allegories, he departed from traditional views of messianic prophecy by dramatically minimizing the number of Old Testament texts that were genuinely Christological. In his commentary on the Minor Prophets, he attempted to remain consistent in his commitment to historical-grammatical exegesis and rejection of allegory. His operative principle was that a text was not Christological unless the New Testament actually cited it. Simple allusion was insufficient to establish a text as a messianic prediction. And even when the New Testament did cite an Old Testament text, it was often merely illustrative rather than an indication of a directly prophetic messianic prediction. Even though Matthew 2:15 cited Hosea 11:1, it contained no direct reference to Christ. On the other hand, Theodore accepted that Joel 2:28–32 predicted the outpouring of the Spirit; its eschatological meaning was unveiled in the coming of Christ. Emphasizing historical-grammatical interpretation, he claimed that most Old Testament prophecies were historical and referred to events in Jewish history; very few were genuinely Christological. According to Theodore, only four psalms were directly prophetic of Christ (Pss. 2, 8, 45, 110). The apostolic use of other Old Testament texts in reference to Christ were not examples of directly prophetic predictions, but were either analogical applications or typological illustrations. Many of the psalms cited in the New Testament were not predictive, but merely provided analogous examples of difficulties that the psalmist and Jesus shared. Many Old Testament texts lent themselves to analogical use because their metaphors were hyperbolically true of the psalmist but literally true when applied to Christ. Theodore claimed that the apostolic uses of these passages were accommodations of the wording of the original texts to analogous settings in Christian revelation. He also rejected the allegorical interpretations of the Song of Solomon. It did not symbolize Christ and the church. Instead, it was a love poem written by Solomon to celebrate his marriage to an Egyptian princess. While Theodore consistently rejected the Alexandrian method, some Antiochians felt he went too far. Theodoret, one of his students, even criticized him as being more Jewish than Christian and said that the Jewish community in Antioch had overly influenced him to minimize the number of Christological prophecies in the Old Testament. While Theodore minimized the number of direct Christological prophecies, he developed Iraneus's idea of typology, but limited types as showing a historical correspondence, not making predictive prophecy.

According to Theodore, when Scripture was interpreted literally and historically, it set forth a unified record of God's redemptive work in history. This unity was sometimes indicated by typological elements in the Old Testament whose complete meaning did not become clear until the New Testament. However, the original meaning of a text was its historical meaning. Later in redemptive history, one might notice historical correspondences that stem from patterns in God's plan. Thus, Psalm 22 must be interpreted historically; it only applies to Christ tangentially as it would apply to any sufferer. Its hyperbolic imagery of suffering dramatically applied to Christ, not because it was prophetic, but because He was the ultimate Sufferer. Typological correspondences did not indicate that a prophetic element was present; rather, they merely reflected the continuity of the work of God in His unified program in history. Although Theodore rigidly rejected Alexandrian allegorization in theory, the actual results of his exegesis were not as far from Origen as one might expect. Theodore used typology in a manner similar to allegorization. The major difference was that he affirmed the historicity of the biblical narrative and emphasized that the historical meaning was the primary meaning of the text. For example, in his exposition on Psalm 45 he affirmed the historical meaning of Solomon's historical wedding, but perceived a typological correspondence with Christ and the church. Unfortunately for the church, his hermeneutical gains were minimized because he was somewhat unorthodox in other ways. He was declared heretical, partly because of the views of his pupil Nestorius and partly because he rejected several canonical books as not being inspired (the Wisdom Literature, Chronicles, Ezra, and Nehemiah).

John Chrysostom (ca. 354–407) was archbishop of Constantinople, the center of the Eastern church. The Antiochian method is well illustrated in his commentaries and more than six hundred sermons that combine historical exegesis with practical applications. His writings later exercised a great influence on John Calvin, who sought to emulate him. While Chrysostom emphasized the importance of literal interpretation, he argued that this did not exclude a recognition of figurative language in Scripture. He sought to steer a middle course between the Alexandrians who allegorized everything and the simple literalists who refused to acknowledge the presence of symbolical language in Scripture: "We must not examine the words as bare words, else many absurdities will follow, but we must mark the mind of the writer." Although he rejected the Alexandrian method that turned historical narratives into absurd allegories, he also acknowledged that Scripture sometimes employs allegories that must be interpreted sanely: "We are not irresponsible exponents of the laws of this matter, but may only apply the system of allegorical interpretation when we are following the mind of Scripture . . . and this is the universal law of Scripture when it speaks in allegory, viz., to supply the interpretation of the allegory." Chrysostom affirmed the relative clarity of Scripture as interpreted by the historical-grammatical method. However, he limited perspicuity to the essentials of the faith: *panta ta anankaia dgla* (all the things that are necessary are plain). While he did find Christological predictions in the Old Testament, he usually restricted himself to historical typology. His typological view of the Old Testament was based on the refrain of Psalm 117, "His truth endures forever." Old Testament history has relevance for all ages. The historical meaning of the Old Testament is the outline of God's truth, while the final form is found in the typological meaning that provided a fuller portrait of the significance of the Old.

Impact of the School of Antioch

Unfortunately, the school of Antioch began to lose its hermeneutical influence in the fourth and fifth centuries as a result of theological controversies. When some of its teachers were accused of departing from orthodoxy in the Nestorian controversy (relationship between the human and divine natures of Christ), the school lost some of its credibility. Its loss of hermeneutical influence was further aggravated when the church split into Eastern and Western segments. Without the opposition of Antioch to keep it in check, the school of Alexandria grew in power and influence, and the allegorical method became more prevalent. By the Middle Ages, the allegorical method had become the dominant hermeneutical approach. The church would not begin to be loosened from its grip again until the Reformation. Its deathblow would not be dealt until the post-Reformation and modern periods.

See also ORIGEN; PHILO.

Gordon H. Johnston

Raymond E. Brown, *The Sensus Plenior of Scripture* (Baltimore: St. Mary's University, 1955), 45–51; John Chrysostom, *Commentary on Saint John the Apostle and Evangelist: Homilies 1–47*, trans. T. A. Goggin (Washington, D.C.: Catholic University of America Press, 1957); D. S. Dockery, *Biblical Exegesis Then and Now: Contemporary Hermeneutics in the Light of the Early Church* (Grand Rapids: Baker, 1992); Frederic W. Farrar, *History of Interpretation* (Grand Rapids: Baker, 1961), 182–222; Karlfried Froehlich, *Biblical Interpretation in the Early Church* (Philadelphia: Fortress Press, 1984), 82–94; Daniel P. Fuller, "Interpretation, History of" in *International Standard Bible Encyclopedia*, rev. ed. (Grand Rapids: Eerdmans, 1982), 2:863–74; Robert M. Grant, "History of the Interpretation of the Bible: Ancient Period" in *The Interpreter's Bible* (Nashville: Abingdon Press, 1952), 1:106–14; Robert M. Grant and David Tracy, *A Short History of the Interpretation of the Bible* (Philadelphia: Fortress Press, 1984), 63–74; K. Grobel, "Interpretation, History and Principles of" in *Interpreter's Dictionary of the Bible* (Nashville: Abingdon Press, 1962), 2:718–24; Robert J. Kepple, "An Analysis of the Antiochene Exegesis of Galatians 4:24-26" in *WJT* 39: 239–49 (1976–77); Bertrand de Margerie, *Introduction a l'historie de l'exegese* (Paris: Cerf, 1980–83), 1:188–213; Bernard Ramm, *Protestant Biblical Interpretation* (Grand Rapids: Baker, 1979); A. R. Roberts and J. Donaldson, eds., *The Ante-Nicene Fathers*, 10 vols. (New York: Charles Scribner's Sons, 1913); J. W. Rogerson, "Interpretation, History of" in *The Anchor Bible Dictionary* (New York: Doubleday, 1992), 3:424–33; John R. Walchenbach, "John Calvin as Biblical Commentator: An Investigation into Calvin's Use of John Chrysostom as an Exegetical Source" (Ph.D. diss., University of Pittsburgh, 1974); D. S. Wallace-Hadrill, *Christian Antioch: A Study of Early Christian Thought in the East* (Cambridge: Cambridge University Press, 1982); M. F. Wiles, "Theodore of Mopsuestia as Representative of the Antiochene School" in *The Cambridge History of the Bible* (Cambridge: University Press, 1970), 1:489–510; Dimitri Z. Zaharopoulos, "Theodore of Mopsuestia's Critical Methods in Old Testament Study" (Ph.D. diss., Boston University, 1964).

HERMENEUTICS, CONTEMPORARY BIBLICAL

The Expansion of Scope

The scope of evangelical biblical hermeneutics expanded in the second half of the twentieth century. It began to include the discipline of biblical theology due to a recognition of inner-biblical diachronic development of antecedent theology in the progress of revelation. Grammatical study expanded beyond language and syntax to include literary study due to appreciation of contributions of form, rhetorical, and literary criticism. Historical interpretation included the historical-cultural context and rhetorical situation of the original audience. This has opened new vistas not considered by earlier generations.

These developments are reflected in a shift in the description of biblical hermeneutics from traditional historical-grammatical (Ramm, 1956; Ryrie, 1965) to historical-grammatical-rhetorical (Mickelsen, 1963) to historical-grammatical-literary-theological interpretation (Kaiser, 1981; McKim, 1986; McKnight, 1989; Johnson, 1990; Osborne, 1991; Klein, Blomberg, and Hubbard, 1993; Blaising and Bock, 1993; Kaiser and Silva, 1994). Because this is not a radical paradigm shift, it is not always articulated in recent literature. For example, "The Chicago Statement on Biblical Hermeneutics" (1982) continued to employ the traditional rubric "historical-grammatical" (Article XV), while acknowledging the need for literary sensitivity in exegesis (Article XIII).

Biblical Theology As Analogy of Antecedent Scripture

What method can serve as a vehicle for *analogia scriptura?* Several contemporary scholars propose that "biblical theology" be used as the theological element in exegesis (Childs, 1970; Kaiser, 1978, 1981; Johnson, 1990; Osborne, 1991; Blaising and Bock, 1993). Distinct from systematic and historical theology, biblical theology traces the longitudinal themes as they are progressively revealed throughout the various periods of salvation history from OT into NT. Kaiser proposes that biblical theology be used as an "analogy of antecedent Scripture" (Kaiser, 1978, 1981). This brand of "theological exegesis" differs from the "analogy of faith" because it draws from the diachronic unfolding of the major biblical theological themes in the revelatory progress of salvation history. The "analogy of antecedent Scripture" consists of the "informing theology" drawn from similar (sometimes rudimentary) affirmations in earlier phases in the progress of revelation. Every biblical text contains some facet of theology as part and parcel of the fabric of its contents, which often has roots that were laid down antecedent to that text. For example, Isaiah's promises that God will pour forth blessing through the Spirit upon the offspring of Israel (Isa. 44:23) alludes to the Abrahamic promise of blessing on the offspring of Abraham (Gen. 12:2–3) but expands this earlier generic promise to include the spiritual blessings of the new covenant Spirit (Jer. 31:31–34; Ezek. 36:24–32).

According to Kaiser, the role biblical theology plays in hermeneutics is to provide an "informing theology" for exegesis by gathering the major theological themes, organizing them into the diachronic periods of revelatory progress, and arranging them around the canonical center (1981:138–39). Due to the recent revival and growth of this discipline, this integration and interplay between biblical theology and biblical hermeneutics is now available.

The Development of Biblical Theology in the Twentieth Century

During the nineteenth and early twentieth centuries, interest in OT biblical theology and its impact on biblical hermeneutics was minimized by: (1) the destructive impact of the documentary hypothesis, which denied the unity of Israel's religion and theology, (2) the view that OT and NT theology were independent and separate disciplines, and (3) the rise of classical dispensationalism which viewed the church as a parenthesis in salvation history and suggested a radical discontinuity between God's plan for Israel and His plan for the church, denying the practical relevance of the OT in the life of the NT believer.

During the 1930s–1940s, interest in OT biblical theology and its impact on biblical hermeneutics was revived by several factors: (1) the documentary hypothesis was superseded in critical scholarship by form criticism and redaction criticism that allowed for the unity of the theology of Israel in the final form of the text; (2) the reaffirmation of the overall unity of Scripture; (3) the view that OT biblical theology be integrated with NT biblical theology; (4) return to the Reformation emphasis of the relevance of OT to Christianity; and (5) the rise of revised dispensationalism, which saw more continuity between the dispensations than classical dispensationalism. These factors allowed the continuity within OT biblical theology to surface, as well as its continuity with NT theology. In turn, biblical hermeneutics saw greater continuity between OT and NT themes.

During the 1950s–1970s, OT biblical theology blossomed in the "biblical theology movement," marked by several features: (1) in reaction to von Rad, there was a new emphasis on the reliability of biblical narrative; (2) due to the impact of the biblical archaeology movement led by W. F. Albright, a new appreciation was placed upon the role of history in relation to theology; and (3) new attempts were made to find the integrating center for the whole of OT biblical theology.

Important Issues in Contemporary Hermeneutics

The Role of the Spirit in Interpretation

During the Reformation and post-Reformation, Spirit illumination was generally understood as operating in the cognitive domain (particularly by Luther, Pietists, and Plymouth Brethren): the unregenerate cannot understand the Gospel apart from illumination, nor can the believer properly interpret Scripture apart from illumination. This view is still held by many today. Some go so far as to claim that the work of the Spirit renders hermeneutics irrelevant.

Several contemporary scholars have concluded, from exegesis of 1 Corinthians 2:14–16, that Spirit illumination primarily operates in the volitional rather than cognitive domain. Scripture has a basic clarity that even the unregenerate understand but knowingly reject. The Spirit does not cognitively reveal truth to them but renders a person willing to receive (welcome) the Gospel and perceive (discern) its value, worth, significance, and authority in their own person, situation, and setting. The illumination of the Spirit does not offer the interpreter a shortcut that avoids the perspiration of exegesis (Ramm, 1958, 1959; Fuller, 1978, 1980; Kaiser, 1980–81; Klooster, 1984; Zuck, 1984; Johnson, 1990; Klein, Blomberg, and Hubbard, 1993).

Typological Interpretation

As far back as the school of Antioch (third to fifth centuries A.D.), interpreters using historical-grammatical exegesis viewed typology as the basis of unity between OT and NT, primarily in predictive prophecy. In the early twentieth century, typology was championed by classical dispensationalists who used a dual hermeneutic of spiritual (typological) and literal (historical-grammatical) interpretation. Because each dispensation was self-contained, typology functioned in a vertical (heaven-earth) not horizontal (historical) manner. Earthly objects represented or symbolized heavenly objects, but were not predictive of salvation history.

Foulkes (1958) demonstrated that the typological (theological-eschatological) interpretation of history originated in the OT. Typological interpretation of the OT is based on theological continuity (unchanging character of God, nature of man, and continuity in the basic relationship between God and man). Because of the repetition of the acts of God in the past and the unchanging character of God, the future is predictable in terms of the past. The prophets portrayed God acting in the future as He had in the past (e.g., call of Abraham, Exodus, reign of David) but in an elevated and unprecedented manner (e.g., new exodus, new temple, new covenant, new creation). Messiah is pictured in terms of past great leaders and deliverers (new

Moses, new Gideon, new David, new Cyrus). These typological depictions within the OT itself served as the basis of the NT's typological interpretation of OT history.

Contemporary progressive dispensationalists view typology as an aspect of historical-literary interpretation (Blaising and Bock, Saucy). God acts in similar ways in different times, so that an original event becomes the basis and pattern for a subsequent event. One event comes to picture and thus explains the other. But in the long run this seems to violate the grammatical-historical method of interpretation that has carried the evangelical world so far in strong, solid hermeneutics. And this has been the hallmark of dispensationalism. The progressive dispensationalists (PDs) have really made a major shift that could have adverse effects on clear Bible study and scriptural understanding.

Other factors seem to be added in the PD approach. For example, there are the elements of the historical context of the interpreter, the matter of tradition, the role of the interpreter's preunderstanding and something called the hermeneutical spiral. Blaising and Bock call this the "historical-grammatical-literary-theological" approach which is to them more sophisticated and thus very different from simple grammatical-historical interpretation.

Many believe the PD approach will radically shift dispensationalism from its consistency and strength, which is a uniform approach to opening up Scripture. With PD, a greater area of subjectivity will be added to hermeneutics. Though maybe not intentioned, there comes about a multilayered reading of the biblical text. This results in a "complementary" meaning. Thus, there can be up to three layers of textual reading. As Bock writes, "such a hermeneutic produces layers of sense and specificity for a text, as the interpreter moves from considering the near context to more distant ones." Many feel that PD is too complicated to sustain with serious students of hermeneutics.

See also DISPENSATIONALISM, PROGRESSIVE.

Gordon H. Johnston and Mal Couch

D. L. Baker, "Typology and the Christian Use of the Old Testament" in *SJT,* 29:137–57 (1976); A. Berlin, *Poetics and Interpretation of Biblical Narrative* (Sheffield: The Almond Press, 1983); C. A. Blaising and D. L. Bock, *Progressive Dispensationalism* (Wheaton: Victor Press, 1993); D. A. Carson and J. D. Woodbridge, eds., *Hermeneutics, Authority, and Canon* (Grand Rapids: Zondervan, 1986); D. P. Fuller, "The Holy Spirit's Role in Interpretation," in *Scripture, Tradition, and Interpretation*, eds. W. W. Gasque and W. S. LaSor (Grand Rapids: Eerdmans, 1978), 189–91; E. E. Johnson, *Expository Hermeneutics: An Introduction* (Grand Rapids: Zondervan, 1990); W. C. Kaiser Jr. "Legitimate Hermeneutics" in *Inerrancy*, ed. N. Geisler (Grand Rapids: Zondervan, 1979), 117–47, *Toward an Exegetical Theology* (Grand Rapids: Baker, 1981), and *The Uses of the Old Testament in the New* (Chicago: Moody Press, 1985); W. C. Kaiser Jr. and M. Silva, *An Introduction to Biblical Hermeneutics* (Grand Rapids: Zondervan, 1994); W. W. Klein, C. L. Blomberg, and R. L. Hubbard, *Introduction to Biblical Hermeneutics* (Dallas: Word, 1993); R. Knierim, "Criticism of Literary Features, Form, Tradition, and Redaction," in *The Hebrew Bible and Its Modern Interpreters*, eds. D. A. Knight and G. M. Tucker (Philadelphia: Fortress Press, 1985), 126–27; T. Longman III, "The Literary Approach to the Study of the Old Testament: Promise and Pitfalls" in *JETS,* 28: 385 (1985); D. McCartney and C. Clayton, *Let the Reader Understand* (Wheaton: Victor, 1994); D. K. McKim, ed., *A Guide to Contemporary Hermeneutics* (Grand Rapids: Eerdmans, 1986); G. Osborne, *The Hermeneutical Spiral* (Downers Grove, Ill.: InterVarsity, 1991); B. Ramm, *Protestant Biblical Interpretation* (Grand Rapids: Baker, 1970); E. D. Radmacher and R. D. Preus, eds., *Hermeneutics, Inerrancy, and the Bible* (Grand Rapids: Zondervan, 1984); R. L. Thomas, "The Hermeneutics of Progressive Dispensationalism" in *TMSJ* 6:79–95 (1995); R. B. Zuck, "The Role of the Holy Spirit in Hermeneutics" in *BibSac* 141:120–29 (1984).

HERMENEUTICS, ORTHODOX RABBINICAL

Some scholars believe Jewish biblical interpretation was divided as far back as the time of King Solomon. The Sadducees and Pharisees and their different views of Scripture can be traced to the rivalry of Abiathar and Zadok for the office of the high priesthood. The two sects and their approaches to interpretation flowered during the period of Ezra and Nehemiah. Since the word *Pharisee* means "to separate" (thus, "be more holy") some point to Ezra 6:21, which reads "and all such as had separated themselves unto them [the leaders] from the filthiness of the nations of the land."

During the period of Hellenism, the two groups were divided into political parties. The Sadducees represented the ruling priestly aristocracy, the Pharisees the middle class (Avi-Yonah and Baras). The Pharisees built many fences around the biblical commandments and thus cultivated an entire school of scholarship. In time, the Sadducees were a powerful element. They rejected providence, retained the belief that God rewards and punishes on earth for good and evil, and rejected life after death.

Though the Sadducees were a force to be reckoned with during the time of Christ, Pharisaism was dominate in terms of interpretation. It is interesting to note that Jesus did not chide the Pharisees for their biblical doctrines, but for their hypocrisy and legalism! Though basically holding to a literal hermeneutic, the chief characteristic of the Pharisees was belief in the Oral Law. From this, a huge body of laws on top of laws was accumulated. They argued for this from Nehemiah 10:32: "Also we made ordinances for us."

By the time of the New Testament there were two rival academic schools of interpretation. Rabbi Hillel systematized the chaotic mass of rules that had evolved from the Law. He set up seven rules by which the mass of Jewish traditions could be deduced from Scripture. Though not meant to, this opened the floodgates to excessive allegorization. Rabbi Shammai founded a more narrow school of interpretative thought. He believed Scripture must be interpreted with full legal maxim and extreme rigidity (Tan). A Jewish proverb noted: "Shammai bound and Hillel loosed."

Overall, the Jewish rabbis are to be commended for being scrupulous with the very letters of Scripture. Tan notes, "The Jewish rabbis did not really misuse the literal method. Literalism and letterism are two different things. It was the exclusion of any more than the bare letters of Scripture which set the rabbis on a tangent. . . . The interpreter who is properly conversant with the literal method of interpretation can never be too literal in interpreting God's Word."

Without question, the Egyptian city of Alexandria produced Jewish scholars who were sensitive as to how the Greeks would look upon the Old Testament. They reasoned the pagans would call the Scriptures too bloody with Judah's seduction of Tamar, David's military victories, and other stories. Thus, the rabbis began to accept Greek philosophy and literary forms. Allegory became a binding feature. It was Philo (ca. 20 B.C.–A.D. 50) who said the literal sense was milk and the allegorical sense meat. He believed something unusual is lurking beneath the pages of the Bible when "expressions are doubled . . . when there is a repetition of facts already known . . . when words admit of a slight alteration; when the expression is unusual; when there is anything abnormal in the number or tense" (Farrar).

The Talmud has been described as down-to-earth rationalism. In opposition is the Cabala, or body of mystical literature, the "hidden wisdom" writings collected over a long period. Two most prized books are the Book of Creation and the Zohar, an encyclopedia of occult lore. The Cabala was aimed at superstitious people. The cabalists hoped to achieve a renewed hope of redemption by showing the suffering of the Jewish people. They wanted to explain spiritual truth in such a simple way that the Jews would be even more so seeking God. Though such works had some effect on the common, uneducated person in the Middle Ages, the mainstream of rabbinical interpretation remained basically literal.

Literal interpretation was shored up by the influence of Rashi of Troyes (A.D. 1040–1105) who is called the Prince of Bible Commentators." Maimonides was an ardent rationalist follower of Aristotle who interpreted the Old Testament freely and allegorically. But it was Rashi who laid down an undeviating rule: "Scripture must be interpreted according to its plain natural sense, each word according to the context. Traditional explanations, however, may also be accepted" (Ausubel). Until the Age of Rationalism, a literal hermeneutic dominated most rabbinical commentators. Except for the orthodox segment of Judaism, an allegorical and nonhistoric approach to biblical interpretation dominates. Christian premillennialism is the closest to what the orthodox Jews have always held, in terms of the Millennium and the coming of the Messiah. At issue has always been, "But who is the Messiah?"

See also PHILO JUDAEUS.

Mal Couch

Nathan Ausubel, *Pictorial History of the Jewish People* (New York: Crown Publishers, 1964); Michael Avi-Yonah and Zvi Baras, eds., *Society and Religion in the Second Temple Period* (Jerusalem: Massada Publishing Ltd., 1977); Frederic W. Farrar, *History of Interpretation* (London: Macmillan and Company, 1886); Raphael Patai, *The Messiah Texts* (Detroit: Wayne State University Press, 1979); E. P. Sanders, "Judaism" in *Practice & Belief,* 63 B.C.E.–66 B.C.E. (Philadelphia: Trinity Press International, 1992); Paul Lee Tan, *The Interpretation of Prophecy* (Rockville, Mass.: Assurance Publishers, 1988); C. D. Yonge, trans., *The Works of Philo* (Peabody, Mass.: Hendrickson Publishers, 1993).

HERMENEUTICS POST-REFORMATION (1650–1800)

The post-Reformation period featured a diversity of hermeneutical approaches. The historical development of hermeneutics was affected by eight primary influences: creedalism, pietism, historicism, textual criticism, rationalism, scientific and philosophical empiricism, and higher criticism.

Creedalism created the hermeneutical problem of the relationship between the defense of doctrinal orthodoxy and exegetical freedom. Pietism created the hermeneutical problem of the relationship between private and public understanding of Scripture. Historicism focused on hermeneutical issues of the method of historical-grammatical exegesis in the light of the original historical texts of Scripture (textual criticism) and their original meaning in their original historical contexts. Rationalism created the hermeneutical problem of the relationship between faith and reason in the interpretation of Scripture. Empiricism created the problem of demanding empirical verification for theological truth. Higher criticism forged a hermeneutical method focused solely on determining the authorship and composition of the biblical texts and so evaluating the authenticity of the contents (source and literary criticism).

Hermeneutics of Dogmatic Theology

After the Council of Trent (1545–63), the Protestants began drawing up their own creeds to defend their views. The period became a time of theological dogmatism, heresy-hunting, and rigid creedal Protestantism. Exegesis was exchanged for dogmatism and liberty for tradition. Creedalism parted company with free learning, turned its back on culture, held out no hand to awakening science, and succumbed to in-house theological debates.

Replacement of Exegetical Hermeneutics with Dogmatic Hermeneutics

After the Council of Trent, seeking to overthrow the traditionalism of the Roman Catholic Church, the Reformers returned to the Scriptures and stressed exegesis. However, under the pressure of the Counter Reformation creedal reaffirmations, the post-Reformation church responded by establishing its own dogmatism. Ironically, the very movement that was born by rejecting traditionalism gave birth to a traditionalism and dogmatism of its own. The hermeneutics of the Reformation had stressed the sole authority of Scripture and historical-grammatical exegesis freed from Catholic traditionalism. The results of Reformation exegesis were systematized into creedal statements that became the new orthodoxy of the post-Reformation church. The hermeneutics of the post-Reformation degenerated into little more than a proof-text method of eisegesis, based on the theological presuppositions from the Reformation. Biblical hermeneutics became little more than a subtly disguised presuppositionalism designed to defend the dogmatic assumptions of the creeds. Hermeneutics were reduced to a set of rules that read texts in such a literal way that the dogmatic preunderstandings of the orthodox theologians were confirmed.

In reaction against the Council of Trent, M. Flacius in his *Clavis Scripturæ Sacræ* (1567) implied that the catechisms and creeds of the Reformation were the controlling norm for Protestant interpretation. Following this trend, post-Reformation Protestant interpretation was not based on exegetical historical-grammatical hermeneutics, but on dogmatic hermeneutics designed to support of creeds through presuppositional deductions drawn from disconnected proof texts. The operative hermeneutical principle was dogmatic presuppositional eisegesis. Proof-text theology controlled exegesis, in opposition to the Reformation ideal that exegesis should control theology. The result was an arrest in hermeneutical progress, a loss of originality in exegesis, and the restraint of new theological insight under the deadweight of petrified dogmas.

Growth of Creedalism and Dogmatic Hermeneutics

During the Reformation period, exegetical commentaries were published with fervor, scholars having been freed from the rigid controls of Catholic traditionalism; however, during the post-Reformation period, rigid creedal statements abounded. The growth of creedalism was motivated by two factors. First, in response to the Council of Trent, post-Reformation Protestants began drawing up their creeds in defense of their teachings. Second, the exegetical freedom won by the Reformers encouraged the individual study of Scripture, resulting in a plethora of new interpretations and differing theological conclusions. The motto of the Reformers, The Bible is its own interpreter, worked well as long as everyone arrived at the same interpretations. But rather than allowing exegetical freedom and promoting mutual theological discourse, post-Reformation Protestantism splintered into contentious faction, each drawing its own rigid line of the new orthodoxy.

At one time, almost every important city and Protestant group published its own creed or confession, for example, the Articles of Marburg (1529), the Confession of Augsburg (1530), the Confession of Tetrapolitana (1530), the Wittenberg Concord (1536), the Articles of Schmalkald (1537), the Confession of Helvetica Posterior (1566), the Formula Concordia (1580), the Thirty-Nine Articles (1562), and the Westminster Confession (1643). Each hoped it could secure doctrinal unity by a nominal uniformity and that controversies could be stemmed—instead of created and multiplied—by minute creedal formulas. Instead, the rigid creeds and lack of tolerance among the groups lead to the splintering of Protestantism. Esoteric doctrinal disputes bordering on hairsplitting consumed the energies of the Lutheran and Calvinist churches.

Hermeneutics of the Westminster Confession

The growth of creedalism had a negative effect on exegetical hermeneutics in many ways. The development of the Westminster Confession reaffirmed the exegetical ideals of the Reformers and refined exegetical hermeneutics. Approved by the English Parliament in 1647 and by the Scottish Parliament in 1649, it spelled out the tenets of British Calvinism. Among all the creeds, it addressed the issue of hermeneutics the most directly, reaffirming and refining the hermeneutical tenets of Luther and Calvin. The illumination of the Spirit was necessary to understand the basic message of Scripture: "Nevertheless, we acknowledge the inward illumination of the Spirit of God to be necessary for the saving understanding of such things as are revealed in the Word" (1.6). This illumination resulted in the basic perspicuity of Scripture: "All things in Scripture are not alike plain in themselves, nor alike clear unto all; yet those things which are necessary to be known, believed, and observed for salvation, are so clearly propounded, and opened in some place of Scripture or other, that not only the learned, but the unlearned, in a due use of the ordinary means, may attain unto a sufficient understanding of them" (1.7). This ordinary means of understanding the unclear passages was through the "analogy of the Scriptures" (*analogia scripturae*): "The infallible rule of interpretation of Scripture is the Scripture itself: and therefore, when there is a question about the true and full sense of any Scripture (which is not manifold, but one), it must be searched and known by other places that speak more clearly" (1.9).

The Rise of Pietism

The first critique of the post-Reformation creedalism was the Pietist Movement, which deplored the dogmatic and formalistic way of reading Scripture. The Protestant church had lapsed back into its own form of Scholasticism that placed more importance on intellectual conformity with Protestant dogma than on personal piety and holiness. In reaction to this sterile dogmatism, Pietism emphasized personal piety and inner spirituality. Against the arid intellectual dogmatism of Protestant Scholasticism and the sterile formalism of Protestant worship services, it revived the practice of Christianity as a way of life through group Bible study, prayer, and a cultivation of personal morality. To undergird its agenda, Pietism created a new hermeneutical emphasis on the personal experience of the biblical interpreter. Thus, Pietism created the hermeneutical problem of the relationship between the private and public understanding of Scripture.

Jakob Böhme

Pietism began in Germany in the seventeenth century and later spread to western Europe and America. However, its roots were laid in the mysticism of Jakob Böhme (1575–1624). He taught that people could have direct knowledge of and communion with God by subjective experience apart from Scripture. He emphasized personal experience over creedal conformity. Subjectivity replaced objective exegetical hermeneutics of the Reformers and the rigid dogmatic hermeneutics of the creedalists.

Philip Jacob Spener

Philip Jacob Spener (1635–1705), a German Lutheran pastor, was the founder of Pietism. He deplored the dead formalism and rigid creedalism of Protestant scholasticism which had degenerated into a theology of mere words void of personal piety and subjective communion with God. He stressed the necessity of personal conversion to Christ, an intimate personal relationship with God, the need for holy living, the priesthood of every believer, and a life of Bible study and prayer in *Pious Longings* (1675) and *Spiritual Priesthood* (1677). Reacting against dogmatic hermeneutics concerned only with doctrinal interests, Spener stressed the devotional and practical study of the Bible. He advocated an exegetical historical-grammatical hermeneutic, the ultimate goal of which was the devotional and practical implications of Scripture in the life of the believer.

August H. Francke

August H. Francke (1663–1727) stressed direct personal study of Scripture by the individual. While commentaries were helpful, they should not replace the study of Scripture itself. While the individual had the right to personal interpretations, Francke also emphasized the need for historical grammatical-exegesis, especially philology and word studies. He also emphasized that only the regenerate could understand the Bible and that the illumination of the Spirit was necessary for correct interpretation.

John Wesley

John Wesley (1703–1791) was the leader of the Pietistic Movement in England who sought to encourage vibrant personal piety and holiness through personal Bible study and prayer. Wesley was the strongest advocate of the perspicuity of Scripture yet; not just the basic message of salvation was plain, the entire Bible was plain and could be understood by the common believer, conditioned on the degree of their personal piety. Wesley defended the complete perspicuity of Scripture by teaching that the Bible as a whole directed the reader to Christ. If anything did not appear clear, simply read Christ into the passage.

Jonathan Edwards

Jonathan Edwards (1703–1758), the leader of Pietism in America, achieved a balance lacking in other Pietists. Unlike Spener and Wesley, he approached Scripture not only for practical application, but also for doctrinal teaching. His hermeneutics featured the use of typological exegesis in the OT to draw out Christological prophecies and practical applications. For example, the seven years of hard work that Jacob endured out of love for Rachel (Gen. 29:20) was a type of Christ who endured the cross out of love for the church.

The Rise of Historical Criticism

During earlier periods, Theodore of Mopseustia, Chrysostom, and the Reformers had sought, to some extent, to interpret Scripture historically. However, with the development of the empirical sciences, the understanding of what constituted a precise historical science increased. Scripture was subjected to a more rigorous historical investigation than ever before. The importance of the historical date, historical cultural background, and historical occasion of the biblical books was more fully appreciated. This new emphasis on the historical situation behind the biblical text exposed the inadequacies of using Scripture for nothing more than a source of proof texts taken out of their literary and historical contexts. The rise of historicism led to the breakdown of the dogmatic proof-text hermeneutical method of creedalism and ushered in the period of historical critical research. Historical criticism led to an understanding of progressive revelation (Cocceius) and the development of an historical biblical theology (Gabler).

Representatives of Historical Criticism

Much of the impetus for the new emphasis on historical criticism came from Hugo Grotius (1583–1645) who emphasized an historical interpretation solely in terms of the historical circumstance of the writers. For example, Grotius argued that the servant of Isaiah 53 was not Jesus, but Jeremiah, the prophet of God who suffered unjustly during the Babylonian exile.

Jean-Alphonse Turretin (1648–1737), a Reformed theologian in Geneva, published a systematic hermeneutic in 1728 that aimed at an historical literary interpretation of Scripture. His hermeneutical approach can be summarized thus.

Scripture should be interpreted like any other book. Since the God who gave revelation in Scripture also endowed people with the rational faculty necessary for understanding communication, Scripture can be grasped in the same way as other communication.

Since it is a historical book, Scripture must be understood from the historical cultural viewpoint of the biblical authors, rather than from any modern vantage point—the words and opinions of the sacred writers must be understood in terms of their own historical cultural background.

The goal of interpretation is to determine the original purpose of the author in its historical literary context.

Scripture must be interpreted in light of the law of noncontradiction (a thing cannot be both true and false at the same time)—no interpretation is true that clashes with what is already known to be true.

The interpreter should use the light of natural reason (following Aquinas) to reconcile seeming contradictions.

Since Scripture should be allowed to speak for itself like any other book, the mind, subject to the law of contradiction, must come to the Bible as a tabula rasa (blank slate), emptied of modern presuppositions.

In 1750 Johann Wettstein (1693–1754) emphasized the importance of the historical cultural environment of the biblical authors for correct interpretation. Interpretation should take place in the light of the worldview, thinking habits, and linguistic peculiarities of ancient worlds that were contemporaries of the biblical authors. For example, Wettstein demonstrated that exegesis of the Gospels is helped by the study of rabbinical literature.

Johann Ernesti (1707–1781). Ernesti, one of the most distinguished exegetes in the eighteenth century, published a textbook on hermeneutics that would dominate NT interpretation for more than one hundred years (*Principles of New Testament Interpretation*). He stressed the importance of exegesis in the light of the historical cultural and literary backgrounds of the biblical authors.

Impact of Textual Criticism

Textual Criticism of the Old Testament

When the new study of ancient texts begun during the Renaissance was applied to the Scriptures, it became evident that the biblical text had been affected by the same historical forces that affect other documents. Although Old Testament textual studies were hampered by a lack of textual materials, progress was made when scholars became aware of the lateness of the Masoretic vowel points and that the Masoretic consonants in certain places were not always reliable. Elijah ben Asher (Elias Levita) shocked the scholarly world in 1538 by proving that the vowel points and accents of the Masoretic text were considerably later (no earlier than the sixth century A.D.) than the consonantal text. The view that the MT consonants were sacrosanct eventually gave way to the publications of Louis Cappel (1585–1658), John Morinus (1659), and Richard Simon (1678), who demonstrated variations between LXX and MT. In a series of publications, Louis Cappel, often called the father of OT textual criticism, proved not only that ben Asher's conclusions about the Masoretic vowel points were correct, but also that the Masoretic consonantal text itself was far from reliable. In his epoch-making work *Critica Sacra* (1650), Cappel investigated the Kethiv-Qere readings, Samaritan Pentateuch, Septuagint, and Old Testament quotations in the New.

Textual Criticism of the Greek New Testament

Similar research was taking place in NT textual studies. Previously, the first editions of the Greek text by Erasmus (1516), Ximenes (Computensian, 1522), and Simon de Colines (1534) had revealed that the various Greek manuscripts differed widely among themselves. In his third edition of the Greek text (1551), Robert Estienne collated for the first time variants from the Greek NT of Erasmus's fourth (1527) and fifth (1535) editions, the marginal readings of the Computensian, and the witness of fifteen other manuscripts. In his numerous editions of the Greek NT, Theodore of Beza utilized the witness of several ancient versions. Lucas Brugensis (1580) noted the importance of NT citations in the patristic literature. However, further development of NT textual criticism was hindered by the widespread commitment to the Textus Receptus (in English designating the 1550 edition of Estienne, and in continental Europe the 1663 edition of the Elzevirs).

When Codex Alexandrinus surfaced in England in 1628, a new zeal for textual criticism arose. This prepared the way for scientific attempts to reconstruct the wording of the original text in the seventeenth and eighteenth centuries when great strides were made in determining the original text of the NT. Johann A. Bengel (1687–1752), known as the father of modern NT textual criticism, was the first to recognize the existence of textual families based on common characteristics. Bengel published a critical edition of the Greek New Testament with a critical commentary in 1734. He selected his readings in his Greek NT based on the division of manuscripts into textual families and the principle that the more difficult reading was to be preferred. Johann J. Wettstein (1693–1754) correlated many NT manuscripts and published a two-volume Greek NT with a textual commentary in 1751. Protestantism's virtual canonization of the Greek Textus Receptus in 1633 finally yielded before the more thoroughgoing labors of Bengel and Wettstein. Following their lead, other scholars began to classify and evaluate NT manuscripts, becoming increasingly aware of how much needed to be done in cataloging all the variants in any particular passage and deciding which variant was the best.

Impact of Rationalism

The increasing reliance on human reason that created the Renaissance gave birth to an intellectual movement that dramatically affected biblical hermeneutics in the post-Reformation period, namely, rationalism. Ironically, the roots of Rationalism lay in the Christian humanism of scholars like Erasmus. In the service of the church, they had employed human reason to study the Bible in its original languages. They also believed that the use of reason to investigate the Bible helped Christians to establish their faith. In the seventeenth and eighteenth centuries the tool of reason was applied not only against the authority of the church, but also against Scripture. This set the stage for the complete overthrow of biblical and ecclesiastical authority in the nineteenth century.

The leading rationalists were Thomas Hobbes (1588–1679), René Descartes (1596–1650), John Locke (1632–1704), and Baruch Spinoza (1632–77). They challenged the hermeneutical foundations of traditional orthodoxy when they claimed that human reason becomes the criterion of faith and truth. Human intellect was capable of deciding what is true and false, and what is right and wrong. It does this by reflection on all that the mind encounters in a time-space world, not by revelation from a transcendent God. The Bible is true where it corresponds to the conclusions of independent human reason. However, what does not correspond to reason can be ignored or rejected. Rationalism deemed that the faith of traditional orthodoxy was irreconcilable with reason. In response, John Wesley and other Protestants simply repudiated human reason as corrupt and fallen.

Disenchanted with creedal orthodoxy, the rationalists shucked away what they considered the theological husk of Scripture and sought, by means of historical investigation and human reason, to find the simple kernel of biblical truth. Hobbes argued from internal evidence that Moses lived long before the Pentateuch was completed and, hence, could not be its author. Spinoza drew attention to alleged literary inconsistencies, historical contradictions, and chronological difficulties in Genesis. He concluded that Ezra, not Moses, was the author of the Pentateuch, as well as Joshua, Judges, Samuel, and Kings. Later editors revised Genesis thru Kings, and Chronicles was written after 164 B.C.

Thomas Hobbes's (1588–1679) rationalistic view of revelation produced a subjective hermeneutic with a purely political agenda. He did not deny that God could reveal Himself directly or indirectly through the mediation of a human instrument. However, people cannot know whether or not God has revealed Himself, therefore, no one can know whether or not to accept the theological authority of Scripture. Thus, Hobbes embraced only those portions of Scripture with practical, pragmatic value, for example, the civil laws could benefit political institutions.

Baruch Spinoza (1632–1677), the Jewish philosopher from Holland, attempted to liberate the field of philosophy from the claims of theologians by arguing that theology (revelation) and philosophy (reason) had separate spheres. Scripture should be subject to the authority of human reason rather than the other way around. In his originally anonymous *Tractatus Theologico-Politicus* (1670), Spinoza argued for the primacy of reason in interpreting Scripture. Scripture should be studied like any other book—by using the rules of historical investigation. Reason understands scriptural claims to God's direct intervention in history to be simply a common Jewish way of speaking, not actual revelation. Miracle stories were nothing more than a powerful way to move ignorant people to obedience. Thus, the Bible is to be studied only for its historical interests. Spinoza set forth several hermeneutical rules for historical interpretation, including the importance of Hebrew and Greek, historical backgrounds, Hebrew figures of speech, and the ancient worldviews. Correct interpretation was impossible without a criticism of the text through reason. To understand the Bible, the interpreter must look at it just as a naturalist observes the phenomena of nature. People must listen to Scripture through human reason, rather than appeal like the orthodox creedalists.

The English Deists

The impact of rationalism on hermeneutics is reflected in the exegetical treatises produced by the deists, who accepted the primacy of reason in matters of truth and faith. They found parts of the OT to be barbaric and needing to be rejected. The life and teaching of Jesus could be explained on the basis of natural religion, not revealed religion. Thomas Woolston (1670–1733) dismissed the miracle narratives as merely "romantic tales."

Impact of Scientific Empiricism

During the seventeenth and eighteenth centuries, new scientific discoveries were made that clashed with the orthodox worldview and challenged its hermeneutical foundations. The Western discovery of China and its ancient culture challenged the traditional view of the age of humankind from Adam, conflicting with Bishop's chronology of the world and his hermeneutical approach to the chronologies of Genesis. The astronomical observations of Copernicus (1473–1543), Bruno (1550–1600), Kepler (1571–1630), and Galileo (1564–1642) turned natural scientists away from biblical teaching. Many biblical interpreters did not feel that they could claim that the Bible provided a scientifically accurate picture of the cosmos. Under the sway of scientific empiricism, many were critical of any theological proposition that could not be demonstrated by sense experience or empirical verification.

Unfortunately, the Protestant and Catholic creedal orthodoxies refused to engage in scientific discussions, instead attacking scientists for challenging their creedal statements about the cosmos. Instead of modifying their naive hermeneutics of the object of special revelation to accommodate the new scientific discoveries offered by general revelation, they simply turned their backs on the scientific revolution. For example, when Calovius was confronted with the scientific evidence that the earth revolved around the sun rather than the earth being the center of the universe, Calovius simply declared that it was "contrary to Scripture." Thinking that the new scientific discoveries were challenging the authority of Scripture rather than the inadequacies of their narrow hermeneutical methods, the creedalists created an unnecessary antagonism between faith and science that would last for centuries. They polarized faith and science, creating an unnecessary dichotomy that would severely undermine the authority of Scripture in the eyes of the scientific world.

Ironically, the Lutheran, Reformed, and Catholic traditionalists found common cause in defending an orthodox worldview. Only a few Protestants accepted the challenge of reconciling a biblical worldview and the new reason, such as Balthasar Bekker (1643–98) and Christoph Wittich (1625–87). Instead, they adopted a defensive posture; the orthodoxies simply retrenched and hardened their traditional creeds even further. The simplistic post-Reformation hermeneutic of creedalism was inadequate to engage the rationalists and to deal with its questions. Biblical hermeneutics was reduced to a set of rules that read texts in such a literal way that the dogmatic preunderstandings of the orthodox theologians were confirmed. The failure of orthodoxy to address the issues eventually led to the devastating attacks of higher criticism.

Impact of Philosophical Empiricism

David Hume (1711–76) argued that facts cannot be proven by a priori reason, but are discovered or inferred from experience. All knowledge comes through the senses and by reflecting on the ideas that come through the senses to the mind. Nothing is in the mind that was not first in the senses. To test the validity of an idea, one must ask what sensory impressions brought it about. There is no light of reason to pierce through this sense-delivered impression that will lead to an essential understanding of the things that exist. The human being is reduced to a physical object to be studied, just as other physical objects are studied. The human being is all matter and substance; the idea of an immaterial soul is banished. God's existence, the origin of the world, and other subjects that transcend finite human experience are unverifiable and meaningless.

Hume was antagonist to revelation and the miraculous. Since a miracle is a violation or exception to a law of nature, by definition it is based on the lower degree of probability. The wise will always base their belief on the highest degree of probability; therefore, a wise person will disbelieve in miracles. Hume's skepticism challenged the very foundations of biblical hermeneutics as the study of objective, understandable, propositional truth.

Immanuel Kant (1724–1804) was a watershed, a turning point from all preceding him. His effect was so broad and fundamental that no intellectual discipline escaped his impact—not even hermeneutics, though few exegetes were conscious of it.

Kant arose in the midst of the struggle between the Continental allegiance to rationalism and the British devotion to empiricism as the methods for arriving at truth. He attempted a synthesis between empiricism and rationalism to determine whether it was possible to have metaphysical knowledge about God.

While Kant accepted the role of empiricism, he rejected its skeptical conclusion that those beliefs that fell outside of experience could not be justified. However, Kant rejected the rationalist claim that factual truths about what does and does not exist can be established by the use of reason alone. In the end, Kant was agnostic. No one can have any true knowledge about ultimate reality. One cannot cross the lines of appearances. It is not possible to know the difference between the appearance and reality which is unknowable. It has often been remarked that Hume gave Kant the problem of knowledge and Kant gave it back as if it were the solution. In many ways, Kant is the single progenitor of human confidence in the power of reason to grapple with material things and its incompetence to deal with anything beyond the material. All that is manifestly real is rationally justifiable, and all that is ultimate is rationally indefensible.

Kant was concerned with the tension that the Enlightenment and Rationalism had created between science/reason and faith. His solution to the problem was to divorce the two, circumscribing the roles performed by both. Religion must recognize its limitations: the basic tenets of faith cannot be proven by theoretical reason. Science is also restricted: observers never see things as they really are, since the mind is no mere receptacle molded by physical sensations but rather is an active organ that brings order to the chaotic stream of the data it confronts. The world that is known to us is a world created by our own ordering of sensations. Thus, the interpreter should interpret Scripture accordingly. Kant's hermeneutical approach has been characterized as nothing more than a revival of the allegorical method.

The Impact of Higher Criticism

Numerous cultural and hermeneutical developments contributed to ushering in the birth of higher criticism.

1. The development of new hermeneutical approaches (the mysticism of Böhme, the Pietism of Spener, and the progressive nature of revelation emphasized by Cocceius) unshackeld the minds of Protestant theologians from the straitjacket of creedalism, allowing them to study Scripture free from dogmatic concerns.

2. The development of textual criticism (lower criticism) naturally opened the door to the empirical investigation into the authorship, date, composition, and meaning of each of the biblical books (higher criticism). Since historical criticism had provided a more accurate knowledge of the original texts, it was only natural to seek for a more precise understanding of biblical content through historical investigation.

3. Between 1640 and 1750 the bond between the OT and the NT was loosened to the point where the OT was no longer

interpreted according to hermeneutical schemes derived from the NT.

4. The rise of scientific empiricism and the failure of orthodox theology and hermeneutics to accommodate the new insights into general revelation led many biblical interpreters to feel that they could not view the Bible as scientifically accurate.

5. The dawn of rationalism and the impact of deism influenced the minds of many biblical interpreters, making them more open to the idea that the OT could contain inconsistencies and even that Scripture itself was not inspired.

6. Scholars began to investigate the composition and authorship of ancient documents, initiated by Lorenzo Valla's devastating work on the so-called Donation of Constantine (1440), opening the door for the source-critical investigation of the authorship and composition of the biblical books.

These factors all eventually led to the development of the "historical critical method." Traditional beliefs about the authorship and composition of the books of the OT were challenged, leading to the rise and domination of source criticism.

Representatives of Higher Criticism

An unexpected source of critical scholarship came from Catholic France in the form of Richard Simon's *Histoire critique du Vieux Testament* (1678). Simon, a French Catholic, became the father of biblical criticism. Simon rejected many traditional views of the authorship of OT books. They had not been written by Moses, Joshua, Samuel, or David, but had been compiled by scribal schools. Simon argued that the study of the additions or corrections that may have been made in the original writings is legitimate. He insisted that these additions and alterations were of as great authority as the original form of the text. Parts of the OT reflect a confusion in chronology and errors.

Simon believed that a scholar should have freedom to investigate such matters critically so long as he accepted the teaching authority of the Catholic church. Theologically conservative, Simon did not attack the traditional views of revelation, but in a series of scholarly treatises he applied the hermeneutical principles of Spinoza to Scripture. He claimed the right to investigate the Bible as one looks at any other literary piece of the ancient world. Simon's purpose was to study the Bible with objectivity in contrast to the prejudice and presuppositions of the Catholics and Protestants.

The alternation of the names YHWH and Elohim was one of the clues that led the physician Jean Astruc in 1753 to distinguish in Genesis two main sources, two secondary sources, and the traces of about twelve other documents. Although many of Astruc's hypotheses were later abandoned, he must receive credit for initiating the documentary theory of Pentateuchal composition.

See also EDWARDS, JONATHAN.

Gordon H. Johnston

Frederic W. Farrar, *History of Interpretation* (Grand Rapids: Baker, 1961); Daniel P. Fuller, "Interpretation, History of" in *International Standard Bible Encyclopedia*, rev. ed. (Grand Rapids: Eerdmans, 1982), 2:863–74; R. M. Grant and D. Tracy, *A Short History of the Interpretation of the Bible* (Philadelphia: Fortress Press, 1984), 100–109; K. Grobel, "Interpretation, History and Principles of" in *Interpreter's Dictionary of the Bible* (Nashville: Abingdon Press, 1962), 2:718–24; Werner G. Jeanroud, "History of Hermeneutics" in *Anchor Bible Dictionary* (New York: Doubleday, 1992), 3:433–43; Willam W. Klein, Craig L. Blomberg, and Robert L. Hubbard Jr., *Introduction to Biblical Interpretation* (Dallas: Word Publishing, 1993), 21–51; W. Neil, "The Criticism and Theological Use of the Bible, 1700–1950" in *The Cambridge History of the Bible* (Cambridge: University Press, 1970), 3:128–65; Bernard Ramm, *Protestant Biblical Interpretation* (Grand Rapids: Baker, 1979); J. W. Rogerson, "History of Interpretation" in *Anchor Bible Dictionary* (New York: Doubleday, 1992), 3:425–33; Samuel Terrien, "History of the Interpretation of the Bible: The Rise of Biblical Criticism (ca. 1650–1800)" in *The Interpreter's Bible* (Nashville: Abingdon Press, 1952), 1:127–32.

HERMENEUTICS, REFORMATION

The historical sparks that ignited the sixteenth-century Protestant Reformation were many, but the hermeneutical debate was at the center. The Reformation was a time of social and ecclesiastical upheaval, but it was primarily a hermeneutical revolution. It introduced a revolution in the interpretation of Scripture the effects of which continue to the present.

More than anything, this hermeneutical revolution was the product of the cultural climate in Europe coming out of the Middle Ages and the Renaissance. During the late Middle Ages, the frozen traditionalism of the Scholastics began to be questioned by the fresh new learning of Christian humanists like Erasmus. The humanists derided the esoteric, hairsplitting, convoluted logic of Scholastic theology, which offered no spiritual food for hungry Christian souls. Many openly yearned for the simple faith and devotion of the early church. Since Scholastic systematic theology provided traditional orthodoxy with its rational buttress, the humanists viewed traditional Scholasticism as a fortress that needed to fall.

Growing dissatisfaction with the allegorical method fueled a desire for a better interpretative approach. Already in the fifteenth century, Geiler of Kaiserberg lamented that the allegorical method made Scripture a "nose of wax" to be turned interpretively any way the reader wanted. Many rued the arbitrary speculative nature of allegory. Thus, the stage was set for the Reformers' rejection of allegory and adoption of the literal historical-grammatical method.

The Renaissance, beginning in the fourteenth century in Italy and extending into the seventeenth century across Europe, had a direct impact on the Reformers, particularly Erasmus, Luther, and Calvin. There was a revival of interest in classical writings and particularly in their historical character, including the Bible and its historical background. The Renaissance also witnessed a renewed interest in the study of ancient languages, including Hebrew and Greek, providing scholars with a fresh glimpse into Scripture.

In 1506 the philologist Johann Reuchlin began to publish several books on Hebrew grammar, founding the modern study of Hebrew. In 1516 Desiderius Erasmus, the leading humanist of the Renaissance, edited and published the first modern edition of the Greek New Testament with a fresh Latin translation appended to it. Erasmus also published annotations on his Greek text, as well as paraphrases on the entire NT except Revelation. The publications of Erasmus, in particular, introduced a new era in biblical learning and went far toward supplanting the Scholasticism of the previous ages by better methods of exegetical and theological study.

The increasing interest in the early Greek and Hebrew manuscripts exposed many translation errors in the Latin Vulgate, undermining the absolute authority it had enjoyed in supporting church doctrine. The Roman Catholic Church had staked its own authority in part on the Vulgate. Now, doubts about the accuracy of the Vulgate cast shadows of doubt on the authority of the teachings of the church. Although Erasmus did not initiate the Reformation, his publications paved the way for the exegetical and hermeneutical revolution of Luther. According to a popular sixteenth century saying, Erasmus laid the egg and Luther hatched it.

Martin Luther

Luther's Rejection of the Traditional Allegorical Method

As a monk, Luther (1483–1546) had been schooled on the allegorical method that had held a stranglehold on the church during the Middle Ages and medieval period. However, while lecturing on Romans and the Psalms, he became disenchanted with the traditional allegorical method of the Roman Catholic Church. His attempt to wrestle with the exegesis of the text led him to confront the inadequacies of his hermeneutical heritage. The fourfold interpretation of the allegorical method created only a confusion of multiple meanings, none of which adequately dealt with what he confronted in the biblical text. Looking back, he later wrote, "When I was a monk, I was an expert in allegories. I allegorized everything. But after lecturing on the epistle of Romans I came to have knowledge of Christ. For therein I saw that Christ is no allegory and I learned to know what Christ is" (*Luther's Works,* 42.173). He rejected the allegorical method and had strong words for it: "Allegories are empty speculations and as it were the scum of Holy Scripture." "Origen's allegories are not worth so much dirt." "To allegorize is to juggle the Scripture." "Allegorizing may degenerate into a mere monkeygame." "Allegories are awkward, absurd, inventive, obsolete, loose rags."

Luther abandoned the fourfold allegorical meaning and affirmed that Scripture had only a single meaning (*sensus unum*). The single sense was the historical-grammatical meaning: "Only the historical sense gives the true and sound doctrine" (*Luther's Works,* 42.173). This is discerned by applying the ordinary rules of grammar in light of the original historical context.

He also stressed the literal sense (*sensus literalis*). The Scriptures "are to be retained in their simplest meaning ever possible, and to be understood in their grammatical and literal sense unless the context plainly forbids" (*Luther's Works,* 6:509). Luther said, "When I was a monk, I was an expert at allegorizing Scripture, but now my best skill is only to give the literal, simple sense of Scripture, from which comes power, life, comfort, and instruction" (*Table Talks,* 5285). His rejection of traditional allegorization was revolutionary; its implications quickly snowballed.

The Basic Clarity of Scripture. By rejecting the esoterism of allegorical interpretation, Scripture became accessible to ordinary thought; the basic meaning of Scripture became clear and simple to Luther. While the fourfold allegorical approach led only to confusion, the single historical meaning revealed the clarity of Scripture.

Although Luther was not the first to affirm the clarity of Scripture, he was the most forceful: "There is not on earth a book more lucidly written than the Holy Scripture" (*Exposition on Psalm 37*). Previously, the basic perspicuity of Scripture was affirmed by Chrysostom ("all the things that are necessary are plain") and Origen ("All Christians understand the fundamentals"). Likewise, Luther defined Scripture perspicuity in terms of its foundational truths, defined as "the supreme mystery brought to light, namely, that Christ the Son of God has been made man, that God is three and one, that Christ has suffered for us and is to reign eternally" (*On the Bondage of the Will,* 110).

While defending the doctrine of perspicuity, he did not deny Scripture's inexhaustible profundity, but rather asserted that it was understandable insofar as it was interpreted historically and grammatically. Thus, the study of the original languages should be stressed: "We shall not long preserve the Gospel without the languages. The languages are the sheath in which the sword of the Spirit is contained" (*Luther's Works,* 4:114–15). It would be a misunderstanding of Luther's emphasis on perspicuity to mean that scholarship was unnecessary or unimportant. The basic clarity of Scripture does not preclude the need for specialists to bridge the historical-grammatical gaps separating the common people from the languages and culture of the biblical writers. Luther recognized the indispensable service of humanism to interpretation: "As for me, I am persuaded that without skills in literature, genuine theology cannot stand. . . . Indeed, I see that the remarkable disclosure of the Word of God would never have taken place had He not first prepared the way by the rediscovery of languages and sciences, as by Baptist forerunners" (*Works of Martin Luther,* 3:50).

Luther recognized that there were some obscurities in Scripture requiring scholarly research: "I admit, of course, that there are many texts in the Scriptures that are obscure and abstruse, not because of the majesty of their subject matter, but because of our ignorance of their vocabulary and grammar; but these texts in no way hinder a knowledge of the basic subject matter of Scripture. . . . The basic matter of the Scriptures is all quite accessible, even though some texts are still obscure owing to our ignorance of their terms. Truly it is stupid and impious, when we know that the subject matter of Scripture has all been placed in the clearest light, to call it obscure on account of a few obscure words" (*On the Bondage of the Will,* 110–11).

Nor did he deny the limitations of one's knowledge or receptivity. Christians differ in their levels of maturity, and extensive study is often prerequisite for correct interpretation. The obscurity of Scripture is often found in the minds of the readers: "It is true that for many people much remains abstruse; but this is not due to the obscurity of Scripture, but to the blindness or indolence of those who will not take the trouble to look at the very clearest truth. . . . Let miserable men, therefore, stop imputing with blasphemous perversity the darkness and obscurity of their hearts to the wholly clear Scriptures of God" (*On the Bondage of the Will,* 113).

As a corollary to basic perspicuity of Scripture, he affirmed the "analogy of faith" (*analogia scripturae*) by which obscure passages are to be understood in the light of clear passages: "If the words are obscure in one place, yet they are plain in another; and it is one and the same theme, published quite openly to the whole world, which in the Scriptures is sometimes expressed in plain words, and sometimes lies as yet hidden in obscure words" (*On the Bondage of the Will,* 111). He emphasized that Scripture is its own best interpreter: "This is the true method of interpretation which puts Scripture alongside of Scripture in a right and proper way" (*Luther's Works,* 3:334). His view echoed Augustine: "Accordingly the Holy Spirit has, with admirable wisdom and care for our welfare, so arranged the Holy Scriptures as by the plainer passages to satisfy our hunger, and by the more obscure to stimulate our appetite. For almost nothing is dug out of those obscure passages which may not be found set forth in the plainest language elsewhere" (*On Christian Doctrine,* 2.6).

The Illumination of the Spirit. Luther saw an indispensable link between interpretation and illumination of the Spirit: "The inseparable companion of Holy Scripture is the Holy Spirit" (*Luther's Works,* 5:397). He stressed Spirit illumination. Training in linguistics, history, and theological reasoning alone was not enough. Apart from the quickening of the Spirit, the interpreter would only have words and phrases. Only through the Spirit can one enter into a meaning of the biblical writers and express that meaning as a vital reality. Bible students must be more than philologists—they must be illumined by the Holy Spirit.

According to Luther, illumination had both objective and subjective aspects. Objectively, the Spirit revealed the basic message of Scripture. Luther wrote: "If God does not open and explain Holy Writ, no one can understand it; it will remain a closed book, enveloped in darkness." Subjectively, the illumination of the Spirit guides Christians to apply the content of Scripture to their lives, resulting in "spiritual interpretation" [*sic* "application"].

Although Luther stressed the historical-grammatical meaning of the text, his view of the objective illumination of the Spirit led to seeing a *sensus plenior*. This Spirit-given sense produced a "new interpretation" that then became the new literal sense. Although he rejected Origen's multiple levels of allegorical meanings, he was perhaps nearer to Origen than he knew.

The Christocentric Nature of Scripture. According to Luther, the key to the analogy of faith was the doctrine of justification by faith—the basic message of Scripture that was clear to all who were illumined by the Spirit. The importance of Christ was God's imputation of His righteousness to believers, so the Christocentric focus of the Bible also meant that the hermeneutical key was the imputed righteousness of God that was given to the believer through faith alone.

Luther's biblical interpretation is centered in Christ. He stressed that the grammatical-historical meaning of the text was not an end in itself; the historical meaning of any passage was to lead us to Christ. The entire Bible has meaning by virtue of, and in proportion to, its emphasis upon the Gospel of Christ. Luther argued for a Christological meaning of the whole Bible based on Luke 24:44–46.

Following Lefevre, who advocated a twofold literal sense (a literal historical and a literal prophetic sense), Luther held to a twofold historical sense: of what God had done in the past and of what God would do in the future. While a Christological reading of the Old Testament was not new, Luther suggested that Christ, the center of Scripture, was also communicated in the historical meaning in Old Testament narratives. He pointed to Romans 10:6–8 where Paul used Deuteronomy 30:12 in a different sense than the historical sense: "Paul is teaching us that the entire Scripture deals only with Christ everywhere, if it is looked at inwardly, even though on the face of it, it may sound differently, by the use of shadows and figures" (*Luther's Works,* 8.236; 10.576).

While rejecting allegory, Luther adopted a typological approach to the Old Testament that allowed him to see numerous prophecies and foreshadowings of Christ and the church. For example, he viewed Psalm 2 typologically: the kings of the earth were Herod and Pilate; Zion, my holy hill was the church; and the rod of iron was the Gospel (*Luther's Works*, 5:47–49). He saw Christ frequently in the Old Testament, often beyond what seems legitimate. For example, he viewed Noah's ark as a typological prophecy of the church.

His Christocentric hermeneutic produced a new, dramatic presentation of Scripture in which the OT was made to support the teaching of the NT. The whole Bible became a testimony to the central doctrines of Christianity. This also led him to develop a strong Law-Gospel antithesis because the Law only convicts of sin, while the Gospel offers forgiveness. In his doctrine of salvation the Law stands in dramatic antithesis to the Gospel and therefore, has no relevance whatsoever in the life of the Christian.

His Christocentric hermeneutic also affected his evaluation of biblical books. In the parts of Scripture where he could find no direct prophetic or indirect typological testimony to Christ, he spent little time. He held some in higher esteem than others. He had little use for James and Revelation—James, because it failed to supply corroboration of Paul's doctrine of justification by faith, and Revelation, because it exhibited so much Jewish imagery.

The Authority of Scripture. Due to the *analogia scripturae* and the historical-grammatical method, readers no longer needed to depend on patristic commentary to understand the Bible. While Luther acknowledged the benefit of tradition, he rejected its authority: "The teaching of the Fathers are useful only to lead us to the Scriptures as they were led, and then we must hold to the Scriptures alone" (*Luther's Works,* 18.1588). As a corollary to this, Luther laid down the foundational principle of the Reformation: *sola scriptura* (Scripture alone). He broke with the long-entrenched principle that church tradition and ordained leaders held the same doctrinal authority as the Bible. Only Scripture, not church tradition nor the pope, held divine authority for Christians.

Hermeneutics played a crucial role in Luther's break with Rome and the inauguration of the Protestant Reformation. When Luther met with Cardinal Cajetan at Augsburg in 1581 over the controversy created by Tetzel's sale of indulgences, the discussion quickly developed into a discussion of *Unigenitus* (a papal bull published in 1343), which asserted the notion of a treasury of merits. Cajetan affirmed the bull, but Luther refused as he wrote, "to discard so many important clear proofs of Scripture on account of a single ambiguous and obscure decretal of a pope who is a mere human being." In response, Cajetan objected that someone has to interpret the Bible and that the pope is supreme in this area. Interpretation, however, had been a crucial element in Luther's "individual struggle for spiritual existence." He unambiguously denied the pope's supreme authority and proceeded to make his hermeneutical concerns a key element in the conflict that erupted.

In his *Address to the German Nobility* (1520), he vehemently denounced the view that the interpretation of Scripture belonged to the pope alone. It belonged to pious and competent Christians. Luther said, "The church is a daughter born of the Word, [it is] not the mother of the Word." Moreover, Luther emphasized that the task of interpretation is never completed. It is in a degree of fluidity and must not be held static by ecclesiastical authority.

Until the time of the Reformation, the Bible was perceived by most people as a fundamentally obscure book. The common folk could not be expected to understand it, and they were discouraged from reading it. Indeed the Bible was not even available in a language they could understand. They were almost completely dependent on the authoritative interpretation of the church. The genius of Luther was that he argued that the Bible was not to be allegorized. Each passage had not several meanings, but one simple, literal meaning. In that case, all Christians may be encouraged to read the Bible. The Scriptures should be translated into the common tongue. Every believer has a right to private interpretation. Thus, Luther expended tremendous energy on his most enduring work, the translation of the Bible into German.

Rome considered the Bible so abstruse that it could be properly interpreted only by the clergy, who with the help of allegory kept the Scriptures submissive to church tradition. Likewise, Erasmus distrusted the ability of the common believer to understand the Bible. However, Luther emphasized that the common believer could understand because the basic meaning of Scripture was plain and accessible to all; every devout Christian can understand the Bible. Thus, Luther advocated translating it into the language of the people and he advocated the right of each believer to interpret the Scriptures personally.

Luther's View of Tradition

Luther's actions are usually characterized as a massive break with tradition. While this is true in general, it is often overstated. He opposed the authority of tradition and of the church, but only insofar as this authority usurped the authority of Scripture. Luther never rejected the value of the church's exegetical tradition when used in submission to the Scriptures. He was under no illusion that he could somehow skip a millennium and a half of exegetical tradition and approach the Bible free from the influence of the past. He could not have been the exegete that he was without the heritage of the church. It gave him a footing on which he could and did move and shift but which he never lost. Luther knew the difference between gratitude and idolatry in his reception of the church's heritage. Thus, he marked a break with the abuse of tradition but not completely with tradition itself.

Luther's Surprising Use of Allegory

Although one might think otherwise, Luther did not resolve the basic tension of literal versus allegorical interpretation. While he advocated the historical-grammatical method of interpretation and rejected the authority of traditional allegory, it is a misrepresentation to suggest that he never indulged in allegorical interpretations. There are sections in his commentaries that are surprisingly medieval in this respect. He often drew on the stock allegories of the fathers and displayed a fertile mind in inventing his own. On the basis of Galatians 4:21–31, Luther acknowledged that allegories may be used as "illustrations" and "pretty adornments" (*Luther's Works,* 42). But unlike Origen and traditional allegorists, he affirmed the historicity of narratives and the historical-grammatical meaning as primary.

In the midst of his commentary on Genesis 9 in his *Lectures on Genesis* (1535–45) he inserts an excursus on allegories and his use of them. He says that as a monk, he had been led into allegorical interpretations by the fathers (Origen, Jerome, and Augustine), but when he found that they were a "vain shadow," he began to detest them. He asserts that Munster and the Anabaptists were wrong to turn everything into allegory. But allegories are permitted if one observes the analogy of faith, so the allegory points to Christ. Some of the fathers leave out faith and their allegories do not point to Christ. For example, claiming that the sun and moon in Genesis 1 asserted papal supremacy was nothing but rash impudence and ambition. However, he approves of those who allegorize the ark of Noah as Christ, as well as their observation that the ark, like the human body of Christ, is six times as long as it is wide.

Elsewhere, he clarifies that the literal historical-grammatical meaning is primary, but the allegorical can be used as an illustration if it is based on his Christocentric analogy of faith: "I have often said what theology was when I entered upon this kind of study. They used to say 'the letter kills.' Therefore I disliked Lyra most of all interpreters because he followed so diligently the literal meaning. But now, in commendation of this very thing, I prefer him to almost all interpreters of Scripture. And I admonish you with the utmost earnestness, seek to be diligent in appraising historical matters. But if ever you wish to use allegory, do so observing the analogy of faith; that is, accommodate it to Christ, the church, faith, and the ministry of the Word" (*Luther's Works,* 42:377).

John Calvin

Along with Luther, the other figure who led the hermeneutical revolution was Calvin. While many people know of Calvin (1509–64) only from his *Institutes*, he was first and foremost an interpreter and exegete and only secondly a theologian. He was a diligent exegete and a prolific writer, producing commentaries on nearly every book of the NT (except 2 John, 3 John, and Revelation) and many of the OT.

Like Luther, Calvin affirmed Scripture as the church's only ultimate authority (*sola scriptura*) and that Scripture interprets Scripture (*analogia scripturae*). He stressed the literal historical-grammatical method of interpretation, the Christological nature of Scripture, the illuminating ministry of the Holy Spirit, and a balanced approach to typology. He also emphasized that an interpreter should not allow personal theological presuppositions to color the interpretation. In the preface to his commentary on Romans, Calvin wrote, "It is the first business of an interpreter to let his author say what he does say, instead of attributing to him what he thinks he ought to say."

Calvin stressed the plain meaning of Scripture, that is, "the true meaning of Scripture is the natural and obvious meaning." The aim of interpretation was to determine the meaning intended by the human author, plainly determined by the literary and historical context. Calvin's exegetical principles also focused on lucid brevity and simplicity (*brevitas et facilitas*). According to Calvin, the Scriptures were inherently clear: "Scripture exhibits fully as clear evidence of its own truth as white and black things do of their color."

Like Luther, he argued passionately for the *sensus literalis*. And he was more successful in translating this concern into practice. His commentaries are an extraordinary testimony to sober, historical exegesis at a time when the dominant approach was motivated by other concerns.

Like Luther, Calvin rejected allegorical interpretations and stressed literal historical-grammatical exegesis. He said allegories are "frivolous games" and that Origen and many others were guilty of "torturing the Scripture, in every possible sense, from the true sense." Calvin argued that Paul's use of Abraham and Hagar in Galatians 4:21–31 did not imply that Moses wrote with the purpose that biblical history should be turned into allegory.

Calvin was more consistent in his rejection of allegory than Luther, who continued to indulge in allegorizing from time to time. Calvin, almost in the spirit of Theodore of Mopsuestia, was very slow to find direct references to Christ (even typologically) in the Old Testament unless the New Testament gave specific warrant or it was clearly implied in the context of the passage. Calvin avoided even the illustrative or adornment use of allegorical interpretation in which Luther enjoyed indulging. However, at one point, he remarks that God's promise to Abraham, according to Paul, "is to be fulfilled, not only allegorically but literally, for Abraham's physical offspring" (*Institutes,* 4.15–16).

While Calvin emphasized objective exegesis, he also allowed for a subjective element in interpretation—"the internal witness of the Holy Spirit." Unlike Luther who believed the Spirit played an important role in interpretation, Calvin taught that the Spirit's witness served not to illuminate the process of interpretation but to confirm in the Christian's heart that an interpretation was correct. He wrote: "The testimony of the Spirit is more excellent than all reason. For as God alone is a fit witness of himself in his Word, so also the Word will not find acceptance in men's hearts before it is sealed by the inward testimony of the Spirit. The same Spirit, therefore, who has spoken through the mouths of the prophets must penetrate into our hearts to persuade us that they faithfully proclaimed what had been divinely commissioned" (*Institutes,* 1.7.4). Again he states: "Even if it wins reverence for itself by its own majesty, it seriously affects us only when it is sealed upon our hearts through the Spirit. Therefore, illumined by his power, we believe neither by our own nor by anyone else's judgment that Scripture is from God; but above human judgment we affirm with utter certainty . . . that it has flowed to us from the very mouth of God by the ministry of men" (*Institutes,* 1.7.5). Similarly, Calvin emphasized that the ability to understand the basic message of Scripture was a gift given by the Spirit to the elect: "Whenever we are disturbed by the paucity of believers, let us . . . remember that none but those to whom it was given have any apprehension of the mysteries of God" (*Institutes,* 1.7.5).

Calvin's doctrine of the analogy of faith centered on the sovereignty of God and predestination, and salvation by faith in Christ. Unlike Luther who too often forced Christological meanings into texts whose historical-grammatical exegesis belied it, Calvin argued that the analogy of faith should not eclipse the objective of a clear understanding of the author's original intended meaning.

An example of Calvin's used of the analogy of faith can be seen in his attempt to resolve his preconception of a conflict between salvation by grace and inheritance by works in Matthew 25:41–46. Calvin relies on Ephesians 1:18 and Galatians 4:7 to interpret the promise that those who perform good deeds would inherit eternal life: "Even in these passages where the Holy Spirit promises everlasting glory as a reward for works, yet by expressly terming it an 'inheritance' he is showing that it comes to us from another source than works" (*Institutes,* 3.18.2).

Calvin emphasized the progressive nature of biblical revelation throughout the course of salvation history. God employed an order and economy in dispensing His covenant of mercy, making additional revelations "from day to day." The promise to Adam was a feeble spark; the light enlarged in course of time until the coming of Christ, who illumined the whole world (*Institutes,* 2.10, 20).

According to Calvin, the unity between the OT and NT was revealed by typological interpretation of the OT. For example, the land of Canaan was a type of the eternal inheritance (*Institutes,* 2.1–4). Apart from his Christological typology of the OT narratives and cultic rituals, Calvin avoided nonliteral meanings.

Like Theodore of Mopsuestia, Calvin treated many messianic references in the Psalms as typological rather than direct predictions that, he felt, ignored the obvious historical context. For example, while church tradition interpreted Psalm 2:7 ("You are my son, today I have begotten you") as a direct prophecy of Christ, Calvin interpreted it historically as the coronation of David and his adoption as the royal political "son" of God.

While Calvin had no peer in the sixteenth century as an expositor of Scripture, he was not under the illusion that he could not benefit from sixteen centuries of past scholarship, nor that he was free from the influence of the past. Calvin actually spent considerable time studying the major theologians of the church, and there are numerous references in the *Institutes* to the fathers (e.g., Augustine, Ambrose, Cyprian, and Theodoret). Calvin believed that, as far as possible, that he should hold to the work of earlier exegetes. He saw himself as bound by and indebted to the exegetical tradition of the church, above all the early church and especially Augustine. He was unwilling to give up the consensus of interpretation, but he was willing to part company when the Roman Catholic Church abused tradition and refused to acknowledge the plain meaning of Scripture.

Other Reformation Scholars

Philip Melanchthon (1497–1560), Luther's associate, was thoroughly acquainted with Hebrew and Greek, which qualified him for a leading role in biblical exegesis. Although he veered into allegory at times, he generally followed the historical-grammatical method.

While Calvin was the leader of the Reformation in Geneva, Ulrich Zwingli (1484–1531) was the leader of the Reformation in Zurich. Zwingli broke from the Roman Catholic Church over the issue of its authority and wrote that "all who say that the gospel is nothing without the approval of the church err and cast reproach upon God." Zwingli emphasized contextual interpretation. Pulling a passage from its context "is like breaking off a flower from its roots." Zwingli's view of the illumination of the Spirit was similar to Calvin's: "Certainty comes from the power and clarity of the created activity of God and the Holy Spirit."

William Tyndale (1494–1536) is best known for his 1525 translation of the New Testament into English. Like the other Reformers, Tyndale stressed the literal meaning of Scripture: "Scripture has one sense, which is the literal sense." Tyndale stated that the interpretation of figures of speech fell within literal interpretation.

During the sixteenth century many scholars adopted the historical-grammatical method and published numerous commentaries. Calvin heaped approval on those written by Melanchthon, Bucer, Zwingli, Oecolampadius, and Bullinger.

The Anabaptist Movement began in 1525 in Zurich. Followers of Zwingli felt that he was not making a complete break with Catholicism on the issues of state control of the church and infant baptism. They believed that if a person had been baptized as a baby by the Reformed (Zwinglian) church and then professed Christ as an adult, he should be rebaptized. The Anabaptists stressed the ability of the individual to interpret Scripture aided by the Spirit. However, they indulged in considerable allegories, which Luther denounced. The founders of the Anabaptists were Conrad Grebel, Felix Manz, and Georg Blaurock. Other leaders included Balthasar Hubmaier, Michael Sattler, Pilgram Marpeck, and Menno Simons.

The Counter Reformation: The Council of Trent

In response to the Protestant Reformation, the Roman Catholic Church convened the Council of Trent (1545–63), which met several times. It rejected the Greek translation of Erasmus and upheld the authenticity of the Vulgate. It reaffirmed the Roman Catholic position that the Bible was not the supreme authority; rather the truth was "in written books and in unwritten traditions" taught by previous church fathers and contemporary leaders. The Council also reaffirmed the Roman Catholic tradition of interpretation and forbade anyone to interpret Scripture out of harmony with church doctrine. Accurate interpretation was possible only through the Roman Catholic Church, the giver and protector of the Bible, not through individuals. The Council wrote: "No one—relying on his own skills shall 'in matters of faith and words pertaining to the edification of Christian doctrine—wresting the sacred Scriptures to his own sense, presume to interpret as according to that sense which the Holy Mother church . . . hath held and doth hold; or even contrary to the unanimous consent of the Fathers." Reacting against the Reformation, the Roman Catholic Church became more adamant about the primacy of church tradition. At the fourth session of the Council of Trent (April 8, 1546), it decreed, "No one shall presume to interpret the said sacred Scripture contrary to that sense which the holy mother church hath held and doth hold."

When the Protestants began to reply, a wealth of literature was published in the seventeenth and eighteenth centuries and the two sides were polarized even farther. Thus, from the momentous events of the sixteenth century flowed two distinct streams of biblical interpretation, one Protestant and the other Catholic. Although four centuries have passed, the two approaches still largely remain at odds.

See also HERMENEUTICS, POST-REFORMATION.

Gordon H. Johnston

Roland H. Bainton, "The Bible in the Reformation" in *The Cambridge History of the Bible* (Cambridge: University Press, 1970), 3:1–37; O. Chadwick, *The Reformation* (Baltimore: Penguin Books,

1972); Frederic W. Farrar, *History of Interpretation* (Grand Rapids: Baker, 1961); Daniel P. Fuller, "Interpretation, History of" in *International Standard Bible Encyclopedia*, rev. ed. (Grand Rapids: Eerdmans, 1982), 2:863–74; Richard C. Gamble, "Brevitas et facilitas: Toward an Understanding of Calvin's Hermeneutic" in *WJT,* 47:1–17 (1985); R. M. Grant and D. Tracy, *A Short History of the Interpretation of the Bible* (Philadelphia: Fortress Press, 1984), 93–104; K. Grobel, "Interpretation, History and Principles of" in *Interpreter's Dictionary of the Bible* (Nashville: Abingdon Press, 1962), 2:718–24; C. M. Jacobs, trans., *Works of Martin Luther* (Philadelphia: Muhlenberg Press, 1932); Hans-Joachim Kraus, "Calvin's Exegetical Principles" in *Interpretation,* 31:8–18 (1977); K. S. Latourette, *A History of Christianity* (New York: Harper & Row, 1953); John T. McNeill, "History of the Interpretation of the Bible: The Reformation Period" in *The Interpreter's Bible* (Nashville: Abingdon Press, 1952), 1:123–26; Jaroslav Pelikan, *Luther the Expositor: Introduction to the Reformer's Exegetical Writings* (St Louis: Concordia, 1959), *Reformation of Church and Dogma (1300–1700), The Christian Tradition* (Chicago: University of Chicago Press, 1984), and *Luther's Works* (St Louis: Concordia, 1958–86); Bernard Ramm, *Protestant Biblical Interpretation* (Grand Rapids: Baker, 1979); N. Sykes, "The Religion of the Protestants" in *The Cambridge History of the Bible* (Cambridge: University Press, 1970), 3:175–76; John R. Walchenbach, "John Calvin as Biblical Commentator" (Ph.D. diss., University of Pittsburgh, 1974); A. Skevington Wood, *Luther's Principles of Biblical Interpretation* (London: Tyndale, 1960).

HIPPOLYTUS

Hippolytus (d. ca. A.D. 236), polemicist and bishop of Rome, held firmly to the year-day (or sexta-/septamillennial) tradition in its basic form. With allusion to Psalm 90:4 and 2 Peter 3:8, he cited the six days of Creation and the seventh day of rest as representative of the time of man and the kingdom age to come (*On Daniel* 2.4). And without specifically mentioning it, Hippolytus hinted at an eighth day signifying eternity (*On the Psalms* 1.4).

Hippolytus's method of working out the chronological timetable (based on the Septuagint) for the 6,000 years of man was unique. He maintained that Christ was born in the year 5500. He arrived at that figure by taking the total measurements of the ark of the covenant (2 1/2 cubits by 1 1/2 cubits by 1 1/2 cubits equals 5 1/2 cubits or 5500 years) as signifying the length of time to elapse before the Savior would appear. This computation, coupled with John's reference to the sixth hour (i.e., a half day; one day equals 1,000 years thus half a day equals 500 years) mentioned in John 19:14, according to Hippolytus, tells us that 500 years "remain to make up the 6000." Christ came in the middle of day six, explained Hippolytus, to allow time for the Gospel to be preached to the whole world. But when the sixth day is completed, Christ will "end the present life" (*On Daniel,* 2.4–6). and the seventh day of rest or Millennium will begin.

Hippolytus carried forth the teachings of his mentor, Irenaeus. The most remarkable advance made by Hippolytus over his predecessors, however, was his exposition of the prophecies of Daniel. These are contained primarily in his *Treatise on Christ and Antichrist*, and in the Fragments from Commentaries, *On Daniel.*

One of the most striking elements of Hippolytus's exposition of Daniel is the placement of a chronological gap between the first sixty-nine weeks of Daniel's prophecy, in chapter 9, and the Seventieth Week (see Daniel 9:24–27). That final week he reserved for the "end of the whole world" (*Christ and Antichrist* 43) and "the last times" (*Appendix to Works of Hippolytus,* 21; cf. 36). In this, Hippolytus appears to have been the first to reach the conclusion that the first sixty-nine weeks of Daniel's seventy weeks extended from Darius the Mede to Christ's First Advent, and that only after a gap of approximately fifty years, would the final week of years take place, just prior to Christ's Second Advent. Hippolytus's calculations for the chronology of the world led him to the erroneous conclusion that the end of the world, and thus the time of the Seventieth Week, must be some 500 years from the First Advent, or roughly 250 years from his own day (*On Daniel* 2.4–6).

Holding to the literal interpretation of prophecy, Hippolytus affirmed that the truth of prophetic utterances would be revealed in all details (*Appendix to Works,* 2–6; *Christ and Antichrist,* 2, 5). Later, however, under mounting pressure from the third-century Roman presbyter Caius (or Gaius), an apparent amillenarian who ascribed authorship of the Apocalypse to the heretic Cerinthus, Hippolytus wavered in at least one aspect of his premillennial belief. He came to regard the thousand years in Revelation 20:2–5 as symbolic of the splendor of the kingdom rather than a literal signification of its duration.

Hippolytus believed that the Antichrist would appear to "cause tribulation and persecution to the saints" (*On Dan.*, 2.2). After the Antichrist's three-and-a-half-year reign of terror (*On Dan.*, 2.43), Christ will appear suddenly (*Christ and Antichrist,* 5) to destroy Antichrist and deliver the saints (*Appendix to Works*, 32, 35). Then follows the kingdom in which the saints will reign with Christ (*On Daniel,* 40), general resurrection of the righteous and the wicked, the judgment seat of Christ, and the creation of a new heaven and earth (*Appendix to Works,* 36–39).

See also PROPHECY, LITERAL INTERPRETATION OF.

Larry V. Crutchfield

L. Crutchfield, "The Blessed Hope and the Tribulation in the Apostolic Fathers" in *When the Trumpet Sounds*, eds. Tommy Ice and Timothy Demy (Eugene, Oreg.: Harvest House Publishers, 1995), 85–103 and "Israel and the Church in the Ante-Nicene Fathers" in *Bibliotheca Sacra* 144:254–76 (July-September 1987); A. Roberts and J. Donaldson, eds., *The Ante-Nicene Fathers*, vol. 5 (Grand Rapids: Eerdmans, n.d.).

HOLY SPIRIT, BAPTISM OF THE

After His resurrection and before His ascension, Christ promised the baptism of the Spirit as a future ministry of the Spirit (Acts 1:5). John, Christ's forerunner, predicted it earlier (Matt. 3:11). That promise came true on the Day of Pentecost. It had already taken place by the time Peter went and ministered at the house of Cornelius, according to Peter's own testimony in Acts 11:15–17.

When the baptism of the Spirit took place, it resulted in the formation of the body of Christ (1 Cor. 12:12–13). The body of Christ is the church (Eph. 1:22–23).

There is no reference in the Old Testament to Spirit baptism, though the Spirit was certainly active before the coming of Christ. This then is a totally new and unique work of the Holy Spirit. Spirit baptism was a mystery not made known until John the Baptist predicted it.

The baptism of the Spirit must be distinguished from all His other ministries—conviction, sealing, indwelling, filling, anointing. It is that work of the Spirit whereby He unites into one body Jews and Gentiles who trust Christ alone as their Savior, creating a new entity totally distinct in its nature and program from Israel.

Not only does Spirit baptism unite believers with each other, making one new man, it also unites each believer with Christ who is the Head of that body (Rom. 6:1–3; Col. 3:1). There is therefore both a vertical union and a horizontal union formed at the same time by Spirit baptism.

Spirit baptism began on the Day of Pentecost and will be concluded at the time of the rapture of the church. The Holy Spirit is the primary Agent who baptizes or identifies the believing sinner with all other members of Christ's body at the time of salvation. Christ is also involved as an Agent since He sent the Spirit to do this work.

See also HOLY SPIRIT IN THE CHURCH AGE, THE.

Robert Lightner

Merrill F. Unger, *The Baptizing Work of the Holy Spirit* (Findlay, Ohio: Dunham Publishing Co., 1962); John F. Walvoord, *The Holy Spirit* (Findlay, Ohio: Dunham Publishing Co., 1954).

HOLY SPIRIT IN THE CHURCH AGE, THE

Through Jeremiah the prophet, the Lord prophesied a new covenant for Israel to replace the old covenant, the Mosaic Law. "I will make a new covenant with the house of Israel and with the house of Judah" (31:31). This new testament would be spiritual and in the future give to the Jews a new heart that would respond to God's dealings with the people (31:32–33). Ezekiel adds the fact that there would also be a "sloshing" (*zāracq*) of water that would cleanse from idolatry (36:25). Dispensationalists hold that the water is symbolic of the Spirit's work (John 3:5) and is not to be taken literally. In the Ezekiel passage, the Lord promises a new heart, a personal relationship, and adds, "I will put My Spirit within you and cause you to walk in My statutes" (36:27). For Israel this promise has its fulfillment ultimately in the promised messianic kingdom.

This new covenant is clearly ratified by the death of Christ as He explained prior to His death: "This cup which is poured out for you is the new covenant in My blood" (Luke 22:20). Paul confirms this and contrasts the new covenant with the old and points out that the letter (the Law) kills but the new covenant with the Spirit's work gives life (2 Cor. 3:6). Jesus predicted all of this coming when He speaks of the necessity of being "born of water even the Spirit" (John 3:5). In this passage He connects the Spirit's work with entering into the kingdom of God.

Because of the Spirit's work in reference to the kingdom, many older dispensational writers argued that there were two new covenants and two distinct workings of the Holy Spirit alluded to in Scripture, one outflowing of the Spirit for Israel and one for the church. But generally dispensationalists today would argue for one new covenant, made first for Israel. That new covenant will be the spiritual dynamic for the millennial kingdom. It has already been ratified by Jesus' death and was launched at Pentecost. However, the church receives the spillover benefits of that new covenant. This in no way makes Israel and the church the same body! Paul ties all this together when he writes: "He saved us, not on the basis of deeds which we have done in righteousness, but according to His mercy, by the washing of regeneration and renewing by the Holy Spirit, whom He poured out upon us richly through Jesus Christ our Savior, that being justified by His grace we might be made heirs according to the hope of eternal life" (Titus 3:5–7).

To say that the church benefits from the new covenant is not the same as saying this covenant is fulfilled in the church. The church does indeed enjoy the blessings of regeneration, the present work of the Spirit, and forgiveness, but the actual covenant completion awaits Jesus' Second Coming. The church is mainly made up of Gentiles who experience this overflow of blessing. Yet the church is not the nation of Israel, the people with whom God made the covenant (Benware).

What are the new and different works of the Spirit in the church age? The Spirit of God baptizes believers into the spiritual body of Christ (1 Cor. 12); He sovereignly gives gifts (1 Cor. 14). By indwelling the child of God (Rom. 8:9) He acts as a Counselor or Helper (John 15:26), bears witness of Christ (John 15:27), glorifies the Lord (John 16:14), convicts the world (John 16:8), guides believers into truth (John 16:13). The Holy Spirit seals believers in Christ (Eph. 1:13), becomes a guarantee or pledge until the saints are taken home (Eph. 1:14). He makes access for the child of God with the Father (Eph. 2:18), fills or "controls" believers (Eph. 5:18), sanctifies (2 Thess. 2:13), illumines (1 Cor. 2:10–14). God's Spirit in this age of grace gives hope (Rom. 15:13), grants an anointing of knowledge (1 John 2:20), touches believers' hearts whereby they can cry "Abba! Father!" (Gal. 4:6), produce spiritual, moral, and character fruit (Gal. 5:22–25).

Upon the rapture of the church, the Holy Spirit is taken out of the way or moves aside in order that the Antichrist, or Man of Sin, may come forth (2 Thess. 2:6–9). The Spirit will still be on earth working in the salvation process during the Tribulation. But since the body of Christ is no longer in the world, His work will not be the same.

Though many other benefits could be listed about the Spirit's work during this church age, His indwelling is one of the most precious gifts. Chafer notes: "The realization of the Spirit's presence, power, and guidance constitutes a wholly new method of daily living. . . . The present age is distinguished as a period of the indwelling Spirit, whose presence provides every resource for the realization of a God-honoring daily life."

See also HOLY SPIRIT, BAPTISM OF THE; ISRAEL AND THE CHURCH: THE DIFFERENCES.

Mal Couch

Paul Benware, *Understanding End Times Prophecy* (Chicago: Moody Press, 1995); Lewis S. Chafer, *Systematic Theology*, vol. VI (Grand Rapids: Kregel, 1993); Mal Couch, *The Biblical Doctrine of the Holy Spirit* (Ft. Worth, Tex.: Tyndale Seminary Press, 1995); John F. Walvoord, *The Holy Spirit* (Wheaton: Van Kampen Press, 1954).

HOLY SPIRIT: THE RESTRAINER

Numerous contradictory views have been given as to the identity of this restraining power mentioned in 2 Thessalonians 2:6–7, emphasizing how little is really known about this subject. Some hold to the belief that the restrainer is the Roman Empire or another form of government or law. Others hold the view that the church is this restraining power. There are even a few that believe Satan himself is the restrainer. From a dispensational viewpoint it has been suggested that it is best to identify the restrainer with the Antichrist.

The Roman Empire would hardly qualify as the restrainer because it ceased to exist hundreds of years ago, and the coming of Jesus Christ or the appearance of the Antichrist has yet to take place. Furthermore, "the Tribulation period is revealed as an era of absolute government in which everything social, religious, and economic is regimented" (Walvoord).

Concerning the church Stanton writes: "The church is at best an imperfect organism, perfect in standing before God, to be sure, but experimentally before men, not always blameless, not always beyond reproach. Similar to human government, the church is being used of God to hinder the full manifestation of the Evil One in this present age, but he who effectively restrains is certainly not the believer himself, but the One who empowers the believer, the indwelling Holy Spirit (John 16:7; 1 Cor. 6:19). Apart from his presence, neither church nor government would have the ability to hinder the program and power of Satan."

An examination of the text will help in further understanding this subject. Second Thessalonians 2:6: "and the thing now holding (him) down (or restraining him) you know, so that he (is) to be revealed in his own time." Verse 7: "for the mystery of this lawlessness is already working only until the one now holding (him) down (or restraining him) shall get out of the way." The Greek verb *katecho* is a compound word coming from *kata* (down) and *echo* (to have or to hold). Thus we get the meaning "to hold down or to restrain." The *Theological Dictionary of the N.T.* defines *katecho* as follows: "to prevent an evil person or power from breaking out" (as one imprisons criminals to protect society against them). The English word *restrain* (according to *Webster's New World Dictionary*) means "to hold back from action, to keep under control, to deprive of physical liberty, as by shackling, arresting, etc." This restraining power is preventing the Antichrist from "breaking out" until his appointed time has come.

It is interesting to note that in verse 6 the neuter present participle is used *to katechon,* being translated "the thing now holding (him) down (or restraining him)," while in verse 7 the masculine present participle is used, *ho katechon,* being translated "the one now holding (him) down (or restraining him)." This fact alone would almost certainly eliminate the church as the restrainer because the church is the bride of Christ and would be referred to using a feminine gender, not a neuter or a masculine gender. Some believe that the neuter in verse 6 refers to the Roman Empire while the masculine in verse 7 refers to the Roman emperor, but as pointed out earlier the Roman Empire ended long ago and there will be some form of government in place even during the reign of the Antichrist.

The question that must be answered is: Who or what has the power to restrain sin so that the Man of Sin cannot be revealed until this restraining force "shall get out of the way"? "The doctrine of divine providence, the evidence of Scripture that the Spirit characteristically restrains and strives against sin (Gen. 6:3), and the teaching of Scripture that the Spirit is resident in the world and indwelling the church in a special sense in this age combine to point to the Spirit of God as the only adequate answer to the problem of identification of the restrainer. The failure to identify the restrainer as the Holy Spirit is another indication of the inadequate understanding of the doctrine of the Holy Spirit in general and his work in relation to the larger providential movements of God in human history" (Walvoord).

One of the primary objections pertaining to the Holy Spirit as this restraining power is the change in gender from the neuter participle *to katechon,* "the thing now holding (him) down" in verse 6 to the masculine participle *ho katechon*, "the one now holding (him) down" in verse 7. There is a simple solution to this problem. The Greek word for Spirit is *pneuma,* which is a neuter noun. Verse 6 is referring to the Spirit whereas verse 7 (being masculine) is referring to the person of the Holy Spirit. This construction occurs in other verses in the New Testament.

John 14:26: "and the Paraclete, the Holy Spirit, whom the Father will send in my name, he will teach you all things and will remind you of all things that I myself said to you." The word *ho parakletos* (Paraclete) is a masculine noun and is followed by the name of the Person being referred to, "the Holy Spirit," which is a neuter noun. The word *ekeinos* being translated "he" is a masculine pronoun referring back to the "Holy Spirit," He (the Holy Spirit) will teach you all things. "The purposeful change in grammar emphasizes the personality of the Holy Spirit. There would have been no reason to change from the neuter to the masculine unless the Spirit was understood to be a person" (Enns).

Another objection to the Holy Spirit as this restraining power is the phrase at the end of verse 7 that states: "until he is taken out of the way." Many find it difficult to see in what sense the Holy Spirit would be taken out of the way or removed. But is this what the text is saying? The Greek word being translated "taken" is *genetai. Genetai* is an aorist middle subjunctive from *ginomai,* a deponent verb. Deponent verbs appear in the middle or passive form but are translated active, meaning that the subject (which in this case is the restrainer) is doing the acting. "The deponent verb does not denote removal by an outside force but rather a voluntary act on the part of the restrainer" (Hiebert). *Ek mesou genetai* does not mean "be taken out of the way" (passive, our versions) but "get out the way" (Lenski). Ellicott states: "until he that now withholdeth disappear from the midst." The Holy Spirit is going to move out of the way, He is not going to be taken out of the way. It is the Holy Spirit working through the church that restrains the Antichrist. It is the church that is removed, not the Holy Spirit.

At the Rapture the work of the Holy Spirit as it pertains to the church will be complete. "The special presence of the Spirit as the indweller of saints will terminate abruptly at the *parousia* as it began abruptly at Pentecost" (*The Expositor's Bible Commentary*). Once the church has been raptured, then the lawless one will be revealed and the Holy Spirit will sustain the multitude of martyrs who die under the Tribulation persecution. Until the gathering of the church saints occurs, the Holy Spirit will continue His restraining work.

See also RAPTURE, DOCTRINE OF.

Brian K. Richards

P. Enns, *The Moody Handbook of Theology,* (Chicago: Moody Press, 1989); F. E. Gaebelein, gen. ed., *The Expositor's Bible Commentary* (Grand Rapids: Zondervan, 1978); D. E. Hiebert, *1 & 2 Thessalonians* (Chicago: Moody Press, 1992); R. C. H. Lenski, *The Interpretation of St. Paul's Epistle to the Thessalonians* (Minneapolis: Augburg Publishing House, 1966); G. B.

Stanton, *Kept from the Hour* (Miami Springs, Fla.: Schoettle Publishing, 1991); J. F. Walvoord, *The Rapture Question* (Grand Rapids: Zondervan, 1979).

HOLY SPIRIT'S WORK IN THE OLD TESTAMENT

Since the Holy Spirit is God, many things about His work are the same in the Old Testament as in the New. There are however, a number of God the Spirit's works unique to the New Testament. The doctrine of progressive revelation must be kept in mind as these comparisons and relationships are considered.

There are types, representations, or illustrations of the Holy Spirit that often speak of His work in the Old and New Testaments. God the Spirit enabled His servants to serve Him, often by endowing them with special abilities in the Old Testament (i.e., Num. 27:18; Exod. 28:3; Judg. 13:25). Likewise, the New Testament describes the gifts of the Spirit enabling God's people to serve (Rom. 12; 1 Cor. 12; Eph. 4). In both testaments the Holy Spirit restrains sin (cf. Gen. 6:3; Isa. 63:10–11). Both the revelation and inspiration of Scripture are works of the Spirit in Old and New Testaments. The Holy Spirit of God is said to guide God's people in both testaments. Common grace as well as efficacious grace are not confined to either the Old or New Testament. Though regeneration by the Spirit is a New Testament term the Spirit's impartation of divine life to believing sinners was doubtless true in the Old Testament period.

There are five ministries of the Spirit that are peculiar to the New Testament, thus indicating how different the Spirit's work was in the Old Testament. These ministries are the Holy Spirit's sealing work, His work as the believer's earnest, His filling, permanent indwelling, and baptism.

Three times in the New Testament the Spirit's work of sealing is mentioned (2 Cor. 1:22; Eph. 1:13, 4:30). It is clear from Ephesians 1:13 that the Spirit Himself is the seal. God the Father is the agent who does the sealing by means of the Holy Spirit (1 Cor. 1:22). This sealing stresses the security of the believer because of God's ownership. It is true of all believers, even carnal ones (cf. 2 Cor. 1:22). The sealing is God's work at the time of salvation and is not something the believer is exhorted to be (Eph. 1:13).

The Feast of Firstfruits in Old Testament times was a pledge or earnest of the harvest to come. But the Holy Spirit is not described there as the believing Jew's earnest. The apostle Paul reminded the Corinthian Christians, however, that the Holy Spirit's presence in them was the personal promise that God would not fail to do for the believer all He had promised (2 Cor. 1:22, 5:5). The Ephesian Christians were also told the Holy Spirit of promise was given them as a pledge or token payment of their inheritance (Eph. 1:14).

To be filled with the Spirit is to be controlled by the Spirit. Only in the New Testament are believers told to be controlled by the Spirit (Eph. 5:18). One who is drunk from alcohol is under its control. Paul commanded the Ephesian Christians to constantly be under the control of the Holy Spirit. Unlike the baptism and indwelling of the Spirit, His filling is a repeated experience requiring obedience from the believer. When the commands to quench not the Spirit (1 Thess. 5:19), grieve not the Holy Spirit (Eph. 4:30), and walk in the Spirit (Gal. 5:16) are obeyed the believer is under the Spirit's control.

The most important works of the Holy Spirit not mentioned in the Old Testament are His baptism of the believer and His permanent indwelling of the believer.

Only in the present dispensation is the Spirit active in baptizing believing sinners into the body of Christ. This work of the Spirit is not mentioned at all in the Old Testament. Neither is it referred to in any prophecy of the coming Great Tribulation or Millennium.

The baptizing work of the Spirit forms the church, which is Christ's body (1 Cor. 12:13). All believers regardless of race, color, or creed are joined to Christ the living Head of the body (Rom. 6:1–5) and to all other believers (1 Cor. 12:13) at the time of salvation. Since the body of Christ did not exist before the day of Pentecost and since the body will be completed at the time of the Rapture, we may conclude that there was no Spirit baptism before the church was born and there will not be any after the church is raptured. This is not to say no one was saved before Pentecost or will be saved after the church is raptured. What it does mean is simply that the baptizing work of the Spirit is limited to this present church age.

The Spirit's indwelling of believers is different in the New Testament from what it was during Old Testament times. The Spirit's indwelling means He takes up residence in the believer's body. The child of God's body becomes the temple in which the Spirit dwells (1 Cor. 3:16, 6:19). If the Spirit does not indwell the person, they are not a child of God (Rom. 8:9).

In this age the Holy Spirit indwells each believer permanently. Jesus promised this in His Upper Room Discourse (John 14:16). Sin in the believer certainly affects the Spirit. It grieves Him (Eph. 4:30) but does not cause Him to leave.

There are three specific passages of Scripture that demonstrate that during Old Testament times the Spirit did not indwell believers permanently. The Spirit of the Lord departed from Saul (1 Sam. 16:14). David was afraid the Spirit would depart from him and prayed that it would not be true (Ps. 51:11). Christ distinguished between the Spirit's presence with His disciples before Christ was with them and the Spirit's presence in them after His ascension (John 14:16–17).

See also HOLY SPIRIT, BAPTISM OF THE.

Robert P. Lightner

Abraham Kuyper, *The Work of the Holy Spirit*, trans. Henri de Vries (Dutch) (New York: Funk and Wagnalls Co., 1900); Charles C. Ryrie, *The Holy Spirit* (Chicago: Moody Press, 1965); George Smeaton, *The Doctrine of the Holy Spirit* (Edinburgh: T & T Clark, 1889); John F. Walvoord, *The Holy Spirit* (Findlay, Ohio: Dunham Publishing Co., 1954).

HOSEA, ESCHATOLOGY OF

The book states that these are the prophecies of Hosea (1:1). The Hebrew name *Hôshēa'* means "salvation." Hosea is accepted as being the author even by most liberal critics. All we know about him we learn from the book itself. Hosea 1:1 tells us that he was the son of Beeri. He was apparently a citizen of the northern kingdom since he refers to the ruler in Samaria as "our king" (7:5) and Archer states his "diction betrays traces of dialect not found in Judah but suggestive of North Israel near the Aramaic-speaking territory of Syria." Hosea's prophecies span the reigns of seven kings in Israel (Jeroboam II, Zechariah, Shallum, Menahem, Pekaniah, Pekah, and Hoshea) and four in Judah (Uzziah, Jotham, Ahaz, and Hezekiah). The prophecies span a period of about twenty-five years and were probably compiled into a book around 725 B.C., though the messages were delivered sometime between 754 and 725 B.C. Hosea is the last of the writing prophets in Israel and was ministering during the time the Assyrians invaded and conquered the northern kingdom in 722 B.C. His prophetic ministry was primarily to the northern kingdom although some of the charges are also directed toward Judah.

Many attempts have been made to make the biographical story of Hosea's marriage to Gomer a parable or to allegorize or spiritualize it away as figurative language, but there is nothing in the text to indicate that it is anything other than straightforward narrative. Many object to the literal interpretation since in the text God explicitly tells Hosea to marry "a wife of harlotry." And since this is expressly forbidden for priests it would mean God was telling this holy prophet to do something He had forbidden for those in the priesthood. This is probably explained by the fact that Hosea's wife is called a *zĕnûn^{a}m* in Hebrew, which indicates not a practicing prostitute, but a "wife of harlotry." Thus, she was not a prostitute when they married, but later led a life of harlotry. This would fit with the analogy of Israel being a faithful wife in regard to her covenant with God (Jer. 2:2–3) and then turning to harlotry. As Archer states, "A basic hermeneutical principle involved here is that the statements of Scripture are to be taken in their plain and obvious sense, unless other Scripture bearing upon the same subject shows that these statements are to be interpreted in some other fashion." Only this principle allows the text to be it's own authority!

The general themes of the book are neatly categorized by Walvoord as: the sins of Israel and Judah, the punishment from God because of sins, and their ultimate spiritual and political restoration. There are five judgment-restoration "cycles" seen in the book (1:2–9 and 1:10–2:1; 2:2–13 and 2:14–3:5; 4:1–5:14 and 5:15–6:3; 6:4–11:7; and 11:8–11; 11:12–13:16 and 14:1–9). Hosea's marriage relation to his adulterous wife Gomer (1:1–3:5) is illustrative of God's relationship with the Jews. As Gomer was Hosea's adulterous wife so also the twelve tribes are God's adulterous wife.

In 1:1–10 we see Hosea's marriage to Gomer, "a woman of harlotry," illustrative of God's marriage to Israel and her subsequent spiritual adultery. The name of the first child, Jezreel, is symbolic of the place where God would put an end to the kingdom of the house of Israel (1:4–5), their daughter's name, Lo-ruhamah (not loved) is symbolic of God's loss of compassion for adulterous Israel (1:6), and Lo-ammi (not my people) the name of their second son is symbolic of God's rejection of Israel (1:9). He does point out that Judah will be delivered as a result of His compassion from the judgment [the Assyrian Army (1:7)]. Then in 1:10–2:1 he prophecies of a future time of restoration when Israel's numbers will "be like the sand of the sea" (v. 10). During this time, instead of being rejected as they are now ["you are not My people"], they will be "sons of the living God" (1:10). Thus, a time of restoration, blessing, and unity under one leader is prophesied. As promised under the everlasting Abrahamic covenant, Abraham's descendants will be as the sand of the seas (Gen. 22:17; 32:12). The two kingdoms, which have been divided since Rehoboam (1 Kings 12:16), will be reunited under one leader (Jer. 30:21; 37:15–28). The Davidic monarchy will be recognized again at the return of Christ by both tribes as Christ returns to occupy the throne of David (cf. Isa. 3:5; 9:6–7; Amos 9:11; Micah 5:2). The Davidic covenant will then be fulfilled (2 Sam. 7:12–14). The prophecy of judgment on Jehu's line (Hosea 1:4) was literally fulfilled in 752 B.C. when Shallum assassinated Zechariah, Jehu's descendent, which cut off Jehu's line from the throne forever. The prophecy of the end of the kingdom of the house of Israel was literally fulfilled in 722 B.C. when the Assyrians took Israel away into captivity. Thus, it is only natural to expect a literal fulfillment of the reuniting of Israel and Judah under one ruler in the future. In fact that is what the Jews expect. Matthew Henry states of this passage, "The Jewish doctors look upon this promise as not having had its accomplishment yet."

The second cycle of judgment and restoration tells about Gomer's unfaithfulness to Hosea. She had played the harlot and acted shamefully going after her lovers who she believed gave her bread and water, wool and flax, oil and drink (her sustenance). This again is used as an illustration of Israel's behavior as God's unfaithful wife. As a result, she would be stripped naked, made like a wilderness, and slain with thirst (2:3). She will pursue her lovers, but she would not overtake them (2:7), because God would build a wall against her so that she cannot find her paths. But following God's judgment and punishment (2:7–13), there will follow a time of restoration, when she will be restored to her husband (2:14–23). She will also then be "sown" back in her land and the bow, the sword, and war will be abolished from the land and there will be safety [no more war (2:18)]. God's act of compassion will include a restoration of the marriage relationship so that he will say, "You are My people" and they will say, "Thou art my God!"

God commands Hosea to, "Go again, love a woman who is loved by her husband, yet an adulteress." He will do this by buying her back and telling her to stay at home and be faithful as he would be faithful to her (3:2–3). This again is illustrative of Israel's future restoration. Israel will be without king or prince (national sovereignty), sacrifice and sacred pillar (formal religious activity), and ephod or household idols (3:4). As a result of this period of isolation, she will repent and "afterward the sons of Israel will return and seek the LORD their God and David their King; and they will come trembling to the LORD and to His goodness in the last days" (3:5). The term "in the last days" was used by eighth-century prophets as a technical expression for the times of Israel's restoration. Hosea's prophecy recognizes that the throne of David would be vacant for many years but affirms its ultimate occupancy in the future in fulfillment of the Davidic covenant (Ps. 89:3–4, 28–29, 30–37; Ezek. 37: 21–28). The prophecy will have its literal fulfillment at Christ's Second Coming.

The last three cycles continue and expand the message of the first two cycles illustrated by Hosea and Gomer's marriage relationship. The third cycle starts with the Lord's case against Israel's unfaithfulness to Him. Instead of faithfulness and kindness there is swearing, deception, murder, stealing, and adultery (4:1–2). One of the reasons for the unfaithfulness of the people was the corruption of the priests. The priests had not communicated the Law of God to the people and as a result the Lord said, "My people are destroyed for lack of knowledge" (4:6). Although the priests increased in numbers, the ungodliness continued to increase (4:7). In fact, the priests only fed on the sins of the people (4:8). The people were involved in gross spiritual harlotry with idols and divination (4:11–14). The Lord's response is to chastise them (5:2) and withdraw from them (5:6). In addition, the Lord says that Ephraim (Israel) will be a desolation in the day of rebuke and oppressed and crushed in judgment as He pours out His wrath like water on them. This was accomplished when He led them into Assyrian captivity (5:14; cf. 2 Kings 17). But Hosea prophesied a time when, "In their affliction they will earnestly seek Me" (5:15). They will in this time remember the Lord's goodness and press on to know Him (6:3) and as the spring rain revives and brings new life, so the restoration by the Lord will be to Israel. The Assyrian captivity was unable to push Israel to repentance, but the Lord's dealing with Israel in the Tribulation will accomplish this and at His Second Coming this prophecy will be literally fulfilled.

The fourth cycle of judgment and restoration again begins with His charges against them for their sins. Their loyalty to Him was like a morning cloud, and the dew which goes away early (6:4). And although they still sacrifice to Him, He makes it very clear His desire is loyalty rather than sacrifice, and the knowledge of God rather than burnt offerings (6:6). Instead of seeking the Lord, they seek Egypt and Assyria like a silly dove (7:11). They had worshipped a calf and rejected the Lord, thus His anger burned against them (8:5–7). They had played the harlot and forsaken their God (9:1), thus they would not remain in the land He had given them (9:3). As a result of Israel's sin, the Lord declares that the days of punishment have come (9:7). The calf idol will be taken away to Assyria as a war trophy (10:5–6). The people too will eventually be chastised (10:10), and they will be taken captive into Assyria (11:5–7). But again the Lord speaks of their ultimate restoration. In 11:8 He asks, "How can I give you up, O Ephraim? How can I surrender you O Israel? . . . . My heart is turned over within Me, all My compassions are kindled." Hosea prophesied a time when no longer will the Lord's wrath be turned against Ephraim (Israel). In fact, in that time "they will walk after the LORD" (11:10). They will return from where they were in captivity (Egypt and Assyria), and the Lord will again settle them in their houses (11:11). This future national restoration is also mentioned in Zechariah 10:10–11. It will occur at the second coming of Christ.

The fifth and final cycle of judgment and restoration presented by Hosea again points out the sin of Israel and Judah. The Lord charges that Ephraim multiplies lies and violence and makes a covenant with Assyria (12:1). Instead of dependence on the Lord for its livelihood and protection, Israel had made covenants with Assyria and Egypt (12:1). The Lord was provoked "to bitter anger" toward Ephraim and so He will not forgive him his guilt and will bring back their reproach to them (12:14). Ephraim is again condemned for involvement in idolatry (13:1–3). And the Lord informs them that He is their only Savior (13:4) and it is He who had taken care of them. But when they were satisfied, their hearts became proud, and they forgot Him (13:6). Their judgment is that "They will fall by the sword, their little ones will be dashed in pieces, and their pregnant women will be ripped open" (13:16). All of these things were literally fulfilled in the Assyrian invasion.

Hosea turns now to a time of future restoration. He appeals to Israel to return to the Lord their God (14:1–3) by repenting of their trust in Assyria and their idolatry and by seeking His mercy. The Lord's response will be to heal their apostasy, love them freely, and turn His anger away from them (14:4). Israel's beauty in that day will be like the olive tree (14:6). They will then be reminded that God is the one who answers them and looks after them and it is He who provides all their needs (14:8). And Hosea closes with a reminder that those who are wise will understand these things (probably the content of v. 8) and will walk in them (14:9). Again, we need to state that just as God's judgment literally came on Israel for their sin and the captivity to Assyria literally took place, there will be a literal restoration of God's covenant people to the land and a return of God's favor in their lives. Just as Hosea still loved Gomer even after her harlotry and restored her as his wife, so God will restore the nation of Israel some day as His wife because of His committed love. As Walvoord puts it, "Though God's judgment was clearly pronounced on Israel and her sins had already been judged in history by such things as the Assyrian Captivity and later the Babylonian Captivity, the prophets were clear that there will come a time for ultimate restoration of Israel. Though some of this will be partially accomplished when they come back from the Babylonian Captivity, the ultimate fulfillment will be when the Lord returns and David is resurrected and she will be regathered to her own land permanently."

Russell L. Penney

Gleason L. Archer, *A Survey Of Old Testament Introduction* (Chicago: Moody Press, 1994); Robert B. Chisholm Jr., "Hosea" in *The Bible Knowledge Commentary,* eds. John F. Walvoord and Roy B. Zuck (Wheaton: Victor Books, 1988); Everett F. Harrison and Charles F. Pfeiffer, eds., *The Prophecy Knowledge Handbook* (Wheaton: Victor Books, 1978); Matthew Henry, *Matthew Henry's Commentary,* vol. IV (Mclean, MacDonald Publishing Company, 1706); Irving L. Jensen, *Jensen's Survey of the Old Testament* (Chicago: Moody Press, 1978); John F. Walvoord, *Major Bible Prophecies* (Grand Rapids: Zondervan, 1991); Leon J. Wood, "Hosea" in *The Expositor's Bible Commentary,* ed. Frank E. Gaebelein (Grand Rapids: Zondervan, 1985).

I

IRENAEUS

The polemicist Irenaeus (ca. A.D. 120–ca. A.D. 202) was apparently a native of Smyrna where Polycarp was bishop. Following his education in Asia Minor under Polycarp, and most likely, Papias as well, both of whom were disciples of the apostle John, Irenaeus set up residence in the Gallican city of Lyons where he first served as presbyter then succeeded Pothinus as bishop. Of the several works ascribed to Irenaeus, only two, *Against Heresies* (in five books), and *Proof of the Apostolic Preaching*, have survived. The former, while refuting Gnosticism, states and defends what was considered to be the true catholic and orthodox faith of the church. The latter work is essentially apologetic in nature and presents the basics of the Christian faith. Irenaeus was a champion of the orthodox faith of the early church, including the doctrine of premillennialism, and the leading representative of the Christian church in the last quarter of the second century.

Irenaeus was a staunch supporter of the literal, plain method of biblical interpretation—especially with respect to eschatological matters. He pointedly warned against trying to allegorize prophecies regarding the kingdom (*Ag. Her.* 5.35.1–2). Furthermore, he espoused principles that today are regarded as essential to any sound hermeneutical method. For example, he stressed the importance of context and the necessity of interpreting that which is ambiguous in Scripture by that which is clear.

The centerpiece of Irenaeus's teaching on the time of the Tribulation and the relationship of the church to it seems to be the prophecies of Daniel 7:7–8, 23–25 (cf. Dan. 2) and Revelation 17:12 (see *Ag. Her.* 5.25.3–4, 5.26.1, 5.30.2–4). He believed that in the last days of the sixth millennium (based on the year-day tradition), the Roman Empire would be partitioned into ten separate kingdoms. Into the midst of that arrangement, Antichrist would suddenly appear out of the tribe of Dan. He would kill three of the ten kings and subjugate the rest, after which he would rule for three and a half years.

Irenaeus believed the Antichrist's persecution of the saints, the purpose of which would be to purify them (*Ag. Her.* 5:28.2), would be the final stage in the persecution by Rome occurring in his day. He seems to have believed that there would be an interval between the rapture of the saints and the final venting of the Antichrist's wrath upon earth. His reference to the church being "suddenly caught up" and to the Antichrist's "sudden coming" provide at least some (i.e., after ten kingdoms established and appearance of Antichrist) sense of imminency (*Ag. Her.* 5.29.1–2). While the evidence is not conclusive, it suggests at least the possibility that Irenaeus held to a remote/imminent, intratribulational rapture of the church. At the conclusion of that final stage of persecution, taught Irenaeus, Christ will come to destroy the Antichrist, raise the righteous, and establish His kingdom on earth (*Ag. Her.* 4.7.2; 5.25.3; 5.26.1-2; 5.30.4; 5.35.1).

Irenaeus was emphatic and thorough in his support of premillennialism as he gave the doctrine its fullest expression to that time. In addition, he stated in the strongest possible terms that premillennialism was traditional orthodoxy (*Ag. Her.* 5.32.1). With regard to his views, Irenaeus maintained that at the conclusion of the six thousand years (reference to the year-day or sexta-/septamillennial tradition), Christ will come to raise the righteous dead (first resurrection) and then reign with the saints of all ages for a thousand years. Only at the conclusion of the thousand years on earth will the wicked dead be raised (second resurrection) to face judgment. In his millennial expectation, Irenaeus stated that he was following in the footsteps of "the elders who saw John, the disciple of the Lord," and he especially cited Papias and Polycarp (*Ag. Her.* 5.33.3–4). While Irenaeus followed tradition in expressing his premillennial hope, Scripture itself was the foundation upon which he established his belief in and understanding of the kingdom.

Irenaeus believed the millennial kingdom would serve a threefold purpose.

1. It would be the venue for the literal fulfillment of covenant promise. In five consecutive chapters, Irenaeus expressed the belief no fewer than seven times (see *Ag. Her.* 5.32.1; 5.32.2; 5.33.1–4; 5.34.1–3; 5.35.1; 5.36.3) that the resurrection of the just will be for the purpose of receiving the inheritance promised to Abraham and the fathers in the millennial kingdom. Irenaeus envisioned a joint participation between Israel and the church in the promised inheritance (*Ag. Her*. 5.34.3).

2. Irenaeus believed the Millennium would provide the saints with a prep school of sorts for eternity, where they might become "accustomed gradually to partake of the divine nature" (*Ag. Her*. 5.32.1; 5.35.1).

3. Irenaeus believed that it would be only fitting that a renewed earth, the place of the saints' toils and affliction, should also be the place where they reign and receive their reward (*Ag. Her.* 5:32.1).

Irenaeus clearly believed that the resurrection program would be carried out in two phases. In book five of *Against Heresies*, between chapters 26 and 36, there are some nine references to the "resurrection of the just," and one mention of the "first resurrection" (see 5.26.2; 5.32.1–2; 5.33.4; 5.34.1–2; 5.35.1; 5.36.3). All of these references place the resurrection of the righteous dead before the millennial kingdom. In chapter 35 of the same book, Irenaeus asserted that John placed "after the times of the kingdom," the "general resurrection" and judgment associated with the Great White Throne. Irenaeus seemed to limit the subjects of this judgment to those whose names are not found in the book of life (5.35.2).

In Irenaeus, the outline of things to come is substantial. To summarize, following the "last kingdom," the tenfold division of the Roman empire at the close of the sixth millennium of mankind's history, Antichrist will suddenly appear our of the tribe of Dan. The three and a half years of his reign will include the devastation of the world and persecution of the saints. At the end of that time, the wicked one will be ejected from his seat in the temple in Jerusalem by the One who is legal heir to the throne of David in that city.

After Christ destroys the Antichrist and his regime, the first resurrection and rapture of the saints will take place in preparation for the millennial sabbath rest. During the millennium, the inheritance promised to Abraham "and to his seed," will be received as the righteous embark upon their thousand-year joint reign with Christ. At the conclusion of the sabbatical, the wicked dead will be raised (second resurrection) to face judgment before the great white throne. Following that event, the eternal state will begin.

See also DANIEL, ESCHATOLOGY OF; TRIBULATION, THE GREAT.

Larry V. Crutchfield

L. Crutchfield, "Ages and Dispensations in the Ante-Nicene Fathers" in *Vital Prophetic Issues* (Grand Rapids: Kregel Publications, 1995), 44–60, "The Apostle John and Asia Minor as a Source of Premillennialism in the Early church Fathers" in *JETS,* 31:411–27 (December 1988), and "Israel and the Church in the Ante-Nicene Fathers" in *Bibliotheca Sacra,* 144:254–76 (July–September 1987); J. Quasten and J. C. Plumpe, eds., *Ancient Christian Writers: St. Irenaeus, Proof of the Apostolic Preaching*, trans. Joseph P. Smith (New York: Newman Press, 1946); A. Roberts and J. Donaldson, eds., *The Ante-Nicene Fathers*, vol. 1 (Grand Rapids: Eerdmans, n.d.), 309–578.

IRONSIDE, HENRY ALLAN, CONTROVERSY OF

Canadian born "Harry" Ironside (1876–1951) was one of the most prolific Bible teachers of the past century. Though never ordained, he traveled for well over fifty years as a home missionary, evangelist, and Bible teacher. Self-taught and brilliant of mind, he published over sixty books and pamphlets. For some time he was with the Salvation Army but later joined the Plymouth Brethren. After 1924 he held meetings continually, under the auspices of Moody Bible Institute, going often as visiting faculty to Dallas Theological Seminary. He also pastored for eighteen years (1930–1948) at the Moody Memorial Church in Chicago. He died while on a preaching tour in New Zealand.

Ironside was an avid dispensationalist and premillennialist. These positions came through clearly in his writings and in his teaching ministry. Around 1943, however, rumors began to arise that Ironside claimed dispensationalism and the pretribulational rapture position was "full of holes." The alleged quote supposedly came from a Stanley Payne who was a staff member with the Moody Bible Institute radio station. Payne added that Ironside also said "I know that the system I teach [the pretrib secret rapture and related subjects] is full of holes, but I am too old and have written too many books to make any changes." This statement is quoted by Robert Summers in his publication the *Biblical Evangelist*, May 13, 1983. This accusation had been spread by Dave MacPherson and John L. Bray, both opponents of dispensational teaching.

Great efforts were made to try to find the truth of this charge. Associates at the Moody radio station vehemently denied that Ironside would have ever made such statements. As a senior student at Dallas Seminary, Ray Stedman spent the summer of 1950 as chauffeur, secretary, and personal companion to Ironside, who was almost blind from cataracts and needed personal help. Stedman strongly denies that any such prophetic recanting on the part of Ironside could have ever been uttered.

If he had changed his mind after 1943, it would seem as if some of his books, such as his commentaries on 1 and 2 Thessalonians, would have reflected his honesty and a shift in prophetic teaching, but they do not. Furthermore, Ironside's daughter, Lillian Ironside Koppin, and his daughter-in-law, Sally Gentry Ironside, both strongly denied ever sensing any theological change. Mrs. Koppin wrote, "I do believe that my father was honest enough that, if he felt strongly concerning this teaching, he would have published something to reveal his stand."

See also DISPENSATIONALISM.

Tim F. LaHaye

J. D. Douglas, gen. ed., *The New International Dictionary of the Christian Church* (Grand Rapids: Zondervan, 1978); Tim LaHaye, *No Fear of the Storm* (Sisters, Oreg.: Multnomah, 1992).

IRONSIDE, HENRY ALLAN, ESCHATOLOGY OF

Producing some of the warmest and most cherished devotional commentaries in the history of dispensationalism, the evangelist, teacher, and pastor, H. A. Ironside (1876–1951) encouraged thousands of people across the English-speaking world to understand dispensational truth. Raised in a Christian home and converted to faith in Christ as a young man, Ironside joined the ranks of the Salvation Army. However, after a few years, he abandoned the group due to the frustration of attempting to maintain the "victory" status of the group's view of sanctification. He found peace and security in the more biblical view of God's matchless grace. His testimony to his conversion and his later views on holiness teaching are found in *Holiness: The True and the False* (1912).

Ironside did not receive much of a formal education but was a self-taught student. He received an honorary doctorate (Litt.D.) from Wheaton College in 1930. Ironside became a nationally known Bible teacher with an itinerant teaching ministry, much like other leading dispensationalists of the first half of the twentieth century such as Arno C. Gaebelein. Ironside's traveling ministry included Bible conferences and seriatim teaching at institutions across the United States such as Moody Bible Institute and the Evangelical College (now Dallas Theological Seminary). Ironside pastored the well-known Moody Memorial Church in

Chicago from 1930 to 1948, from which he spoke on radio for several years. He resigned the pulpit of that well-known church to engage in a full-time writing and conference ministry. That ministry continued until his death in 1951.

The greatest legacy of H. A. Ironside is the voluminous collection of writings that he left. He wrote over sixty books, along with numerous pamphlets and articles. His style is characterized by (1) devotional exposition, (2) the simple outline of complicated issues, (3) a creative ability to provide fresh wording and illustrations aimed at warming the heart and changing the life, and (4) a continuation of the heritage of simple Bible readings that were emphasized in the Niagara Bible Conferences of the late nineteenth century.

Ironside's writings dealt with a wide range of topics. His biblical commentaries covered the entire range of New Testament books, as well as every prophetic book in the Old Testament. In addition, he addressed topical issues such as water baptism, the Second Coming, the rapture of the church, the Holy Spirit, issues of sanctification, and prayer. He showed the skills of a historian in *A Historical Sketch of the Brethren Movement* (1942), which highlighted the development of the movement largely responsible for spreading the dispensationalism of John Nelson Darby which Ironside himself believed. Ironside also provided anecdotal insights into his own life and ministry in *Random Reminiscences from Fifty Years of Ministry* (1939). The heart of a pastor can be seen in *Full Assurance,* the goal of which was to increase the confidence of believers. Ironside also possessed the zeal of an evangelist, as seen in his publication *The Only Two Religions and Other Gospel Papers*. Many of the publications and commentaries were derived from messages he gave, often in series of expository sermons. His ministry lasted around sixty years in fruitful service. In the end he was known as a beloved teacher dedicated to the literal interpretation of prophecy and the resultant belief and hope in the pretribulational premillennial coming of Jesus Christ.

See also DARBY, JOHN; DISPENSATIONALISM; IRONSIDE, HENRY ALLAN, CONTROVERSY OF.

Michael D. Stallard

E. Schuyler English, *Ordained of the Lord: H. A. Ironside: A Biography* (Neptune, N.J.: Loixeaux Brothers, 1976); H. A. Ironside, *Four Golden Hours with Dr. Harry Ironside* (London: Marhsall, Morgan & Scott Ltd., 1939), *Holiness: The False and the True* (Neptune, N.J.: Loizeaux Brothers, 1912), *In the Heavenlies: Practical Expository Addresses on the Epistle to the Ephesians* (Neptune, N.J.: Loizeaux Brothers, 1937), and *Notes on the Minor Prophets* (Neptune, N.J.: Loizeaux Brothers, 1909); L. I. Koppin, ed., *The Best of H. A. Ironside* (Grand Rapids: Baker, 1981); George M. Marsden, *Fundamentalism and American Culture* (New York: Oxford University Press, 1980).

ISAIAH, ESCHATOLOGY OF

Theology of Isaiah

The overall theology of Isaiah may be summarized as follows: Although God called Israel at Sinai to be the model of righteousness and the channel of God's universal blessing to the nations, Israel has broken the Mosaic covenant, failing to be the example of obedience and light to the Gentiles. Despite their history of rebellion and failure, God's ideal for His covenant people and the nations ultimately will be realized. God will discipline Israel and Judah with the Assyrian and Babylonian exiles to purge their rebellion. As foreshadowed by the historical return of the remnant from Babylon under Cyrus, God's ideal Servant (the Messiah) will lead national Israel out of bondage once more and will mediate the new covenant blessings on Israel's behalf. Through the new covenant, Israel will receive forgiveness and Spirit-empowerment obedience to fulfill the covenant requirement of repentant obedience. Succeeding where Israel failed, the Servant will also provide saving light to the Gentiles, extending new covenant spiritual blessings to them as well and bringing them to the place of repentant submission to the Lord.

Structure of Isaiah

The book of Isaiah, an original literary unity written from around 740–681 B.C., contains two major prophetic sections (chaps. 1–35 and 40–66) revolving around two transitional historical narratives that provide the background for the prophecies (chaps. 36–37 and 38–39). Chapters 1–37 revolve around the Assyrian period, while chapters 38–66 center on the Babylonian period. The prophecies in 1–35 focus on the deliverance of Jerusalem from Israel-Aram in 735–734 through Assyria in 732–722, Assyria's destruction of the western nations in 711–710 in retaliation for their revolt in 715, and the deliverance of Jerusalem from Sennacherib's invasion in 701. The prophecies in chapters 40–66 focus on the Babylonian exile in 605–586, the call to the exiles to repent; and the historical return to rebuild Jerusalem and the temple in 539–538. Chapters 36–37 describe the historical fulfillment of many of the prophecies dealing with the Assyrian crisis that permeate chapters 1–35. Chapters 38–39 explain the reason for the Babylonian exile and point toward the return from exile as prophesied in chapters 40–66.

The Davidic King Will Rise

When the ultimate Davidic King will arise (11:1), the Lord will anoint Him with the Spirit, as Samuel anointed David, enabling Him to rule wisely and to judge righteously (11:2). Unlike the wicked kings of Isaiah's day, His reign will be marked by justice: He will intervene for the weak and eliminate their evil oppressors (11:3–4). While Assyria was God's rod of judgment on Judah (10:5, 24), the Messiah will rule all nations with the rod of His mouth (11:4), seen elsewhere as an iron scepter (Ps. 2:9; Rev. 19:15). The cessation of injustice and oppression in human society will be paralleled by a radical change within the animal kingdom and in human relationships with once-hostile animals: predators will lie down in peace with the animals they once devoured, while children will play with creatures that once endangered their lives (11:6–8). The cessation of hostility in the animal kingdom will parallel the removal of hostility in the worldwide kingdom of Messiah (11:9). This universal peace will be caused by the universal saving knowledge of the Lord (11:9).

As a mighty warrior, the Davidic King will raise a banner to rally all nations, not to war, but to regather all the exiles of His people from the nations (11:10–12), reversing the Assyrian and Babylonian exiles. Judah and Israel will be reunited (11:13), reversing their historical hostility (7:2; 9:21). As in the days of David, the united kingdom will conquer the surrounding nations (11:13–14). As a reversal of the Assyrian exile, the remnant will return in a glorious second exodus, as when Israel came up from Egypt (11:15–16). Just as Israel sang the Song of Moses following God's saving miracle at the Red Sea (Exod. 15:2), redeemed Israel will praise Him in the future for this eschatological salvation (12:1–2). Just as God provided Israel with water during the desert wanderings (Exod. 15:25–27), God will provide Israel with life-giving water from the wells of salvation (12:3). In fulfillment of God's calling of Israel to herald His word to the nations (Exod. 19:5–6), the future redeemed community will proclaim His mighty saving deeds to all nations (12:4–6). This worldwide proclamation by Israel will be one vehicle through which the knowledge and Word of God will fill the whole earth (2:3; 9:9).

Obviously, this was not fulfilled in the historical return of the remnant from Assyria under Hezekiah (10:21; 37:4, 31–32). Rather, that historical event foreshadowed the future return of the remnant under the Davidic King who will conquer all nations, which are represented typologically by Assyria (11:11, 16).

Historical/Eschatological Program of the Judgment/Redemption of the Nations

Isaiah 13–23 contains twelve oracles against the nations depicting historical judgments, followed by the mini-apocalypse of chapters 24–27 that pictures an eschatological judgment of all nations. The oracles against these ancient nations culminate in a description of worldwide judgment that ushers in God's eternal earthly kingdom. Judgment would start with ancient enemies hostile to Judah and culminate with the final defeat of all nations hostile to God. The magnitude of this final judgment is so great that even the powers in the heaven above (Satan and the demons) are included in the final judgment with the kings of the earth below (2:21). Despite their historical opposition, God's purposes will be realized in the *eschaton* when He establishes His eternal, universal, earthly rule from Mount Zion.

In some cases, the description of judgment on a nation is immediately followed by a description of the eschatological deliverance of Judah and Israel in the future Davidic kingdom (14:1–2; 19:19–25; 23:17–18). The eschatological enthronement of the ideal Davidic King (16:5) occurs in conjunction with God's judgment on Moab (15:1–16:14) and Assyria (16:4), suggesting that Isaiah is again blending history with eschatology.

Isaiah 24–27, the so-called mini-apocalypse, focuses on the final universal judgment that will devastate the whole earth (24:1–13). God will hold all guilty for shedding innocent blood and polluting the land with sin (24:5, 21) in violation of the Noahic covenant to which all nations are accountable (9:1–17). Fittingly, the final judgment is a reenactment of the Noahic flood (24:18) and a reversal of Creation (24:19–20). Judgment on the wicked will be inescapable (24:17–20)—only the remnant will survive (24:14–16).

In the climactic judgment, God will punish wicked people, as well as Satan and fallen angels: "the LORD will punish the powers in the heavens above and the kings on the earth below" (24:21). Both will be punished eternally: They will be herded together, bound like prisoners in a dungeon, shut up in prison, and punished for many days (24:22). This imagery is the background of Revelation 19:19–20:3. Because none of the eschatological events of Isaiah's mini-apocalypse have occurred, neither has the binding of Satan and the demons.

The Lord will also destroy the final enemy of humanity, death (25:7–8). Isaiah depicts the death of death as the destruction of the burial shroud and the veil worn in mourning (25:7). Ironically, the Lord will swallow death, the great swallower (25:8). Death is often personified as having an insatiable appetite and swallowing its victims whole as they go into the grave (Ps. 49:1; 69:15; 141:7; Prov. 1:12; 27:20; 30:15–16; Isa. 5:14; Hab. 2:5).

During the messianic age, Israel will finally realize all that God had originally called it to be but that it had failed to be throughout history. Although called to be a light for the Gentiles (42:6, 49:6), Israel had failed to bring salvation to the earth (26:18). This will be reversed in the messianic age: Israel will fill the world with spiritual fruit (27:6). In a reversal of the imagery of the unfruitful vineyard that God destroyed (5:1–7), future Jerusalem will be a fruitful vineyard protected by God and flourishing under His care (27:2–6). Although the nations once attacked and plundered Israel, during the kingdom Israel will receive honor and wealth from the converted nations (23:18). The redeemed will enthusiastically praise the Lord (24:14–16; 25:9; 26:1–6) and worship Him in Zion (27:13).

The ideal Davidic King will inaugurate a rule of righteousness, providing protection for all, giving spiritual insight to the wise but vanquishing the wicked oppressors of the poor and needy (32:1–8). The new covenant Spirit will be poured out on the nation as a whole, producing the righteousness and justice required by the Mosaic covenant, resulting in the promised covenant blessings of national peace, security, and abundant agricultural and familial blessings (32:15–20). The repentant, purified nation will experience His rich covenantal blessings (29:17, 23; 30:23–25; 32:20; 35:1–2, 5–7). The repentant will return from exile to Zion in a glorious second exodus that will dwarf the historical return from Babylon (35:1–10).

Unlike the days of Moses, when the wilderness symbolized rebellion and postponed blessing, this wilderness experience will be marked by redemption and holiness (35:3–4, 8–10). Along their journey to Zion, a fundamental change will occur in the physical creation: the desert will blossom (35:1–3) and the physically disabled will be healed (35:5–7). The wicked will be removed and only the holy will enter Zion to worship God and celebrate His eschatological salvation (35:8–10). Purified of injustice, Zion will become a center of justice (29:19–21; 32:1–2, 17–18; 33:5), protected from its enemies (25:1–5; 27:2–6; 33:17–24), and its people will be marked by spiritual enlightenment and wisdom (29:18, 24; 30:20–21; 32:3–8; 33:6; 35:8).

The Historical Background of Isaiah 38–66

Around the time of the siege of Jerusalem in 701 B.C., Hezekiah (729–686 B.C.) fell mortally ill, but YHWH granted him an extension of fifteen years (Isa. 38:1–8; 2 Kings 20:1–11; 2 Chron. 32:24–26). After his recovery, Hezekiah received Merodach-Baladan, the former ruler of Babylonia whom Sennacherib deposed in 703 (Isa. 39:1–2; 2 Kings 20:12–13; 2 Chron. 32:31). Merodach-baladan was attempting to reclaim his former position and draw Hezekiah into an alliance against Assyria. Isaiah denounced Hezekiah and announced the Babylonian exile (Isa. 39:3–7; 2 Kings 20:14–18). Isaiah also prophesied that the Lord would deliver the exiles from Babylon and inaugurate the glorious messianic kingdom—if Judah and Israel would repent (Isaiah 40–66).

The Ideal Servant

At Sinai God called Israel to become an exemplary pattern of holiness and to mediate His salvation to the Gentiles (Exod. 19:5–6; Deut. 4:5–8). Having been chosen and called to be His servant (43:10; 44:21; 45:4; 48:20; 49:3), national Israel was to be a light to the Gentiles (2:6; 49:6), leading them to faith and repentance and promoting obedience to God's law and to social justice (42:3–4). Unfortunately, Israel failed as the servant due to rebellion (42:18–20). However, the Messiah would become the ideal Servant who would succeed where Israel failed (42:1–9; 49:1–7). As a result, all the Gentiles will hear and see the glory of God, many responding in repentant faith and praise (42:10–12; 49:8–23). The eruption of Gentile salvation began during the ministry of Jesus, the ideal Servant of the Lord.

His career is outlined in the Servant Songs of Isaiah: He would first suffer death, then be exalted as universal King to usher in the messianic kingdom and lead the second exodus (42:1–9; 49:1–13; 50:4–11; 52:13–53:12; 61:1–11). Luke 4:16–21 depicts an "already/not yet" fulfillment of the Servant's ministry of Isaiah 61:1–11. The first half of His ministry—preaching good news and proclaiming the year of the Lord's favor (61:1–2)—was fulfilled in the ministry of Jesus (Luke 4:21). The second half of His ministry—proclaiming God's day of vengeance and the second exodus (61:2–11)—is yet to be fulfilled at His return.

The New Covenant

Although Jerusalem had been temporarily abandoned by the Lord in discipline—like a deserted or widowed wife (54:4–6)—He will return her to Himself and renew His covenant (54:7–8). This new covenant will be implemented when national Israel repents (55:1–3; 59:20–21; 61:8). Like pouring water on the thirsty land, the Lord will pour out the new covenant Spirit on Israel's offspring (44:3), in ultimate fulfillment of His promise to bless the offspring of Abraham (Gen. 12:2–3). Just as Jeremiah predicted that the Spirit will write God's law on their hearts (Jer. 31:33), the Spirit will permanently place the Word of God in the mouths of His people, causing permanent obedience (59:20–21). God will rain down His provision of salvation to Israel like showers in the desert (44:4–5; 45:8). National Israel will experience eternal salvation, never again to be disgraced in judgment (45:17). Just as Jeremiah announced that the new covenant would regenerate and redeem national Israel so that all will know the Lord and obey His laws (Jer 31:31–34), Isaiah announced that all eschatological Israel will be taught by the Lord (55:13) and will become righteous (60:21).

Repentant Israel will experience joy, prosperity and salvation, and an intimate relationship with the Lord (58:8–9). The new covenant will be an eternal covenant of peace, patterned after the Noahic covenant, so that Israel will never be judged again (54:9–10). Just as God promised that the ideal Davidic King will rule over the nations, the new covenant promises that national Israel will exercise authority over the Gentiles (55:3). The new covenant promises to Israel will be fulfilled through the universal rule of the Davidic King (9:1–7; 11:1–16; 32:1–8; 33:17). The Davidic covenant promises are intimately connected with the promises to Israel (e.g., 2 Sam. 7:10–11; 1 Kings 6:12–13; 9:4–9; Ps. 72:1–17; 132:11–18; 144:2).

The Renewed Jerusalem

Renewed Zion will be the focal point of the kingdom (65:17–18). This is renewed Jerusalem of the Millennium (Rev. 20:9) is not the New Jerusalem of the eternal state (Rev. 21–22). Renewed Jerusalem is a restored, rebuilt city (58:12; 61:4), part of the renewed and restored earth of the first creation. The New Jerusalem belongs to the second creation following the destruction of the first creation (2 Peter 3:10–13). The millennial renewed Jerusalem inaugurates the eternal kingdom culminating in the New Jerusalem of eternity.

All roads in the second exodus will lead the people of God to Jerusalem (40:3–10; 49:9–23; 51:3, 11; 52:7–12; 58:11–12; 62:10–11; 66:20). Personified alternately as a once-barren woman and as a bereaved mother (49:21; 54:1), Jerusalem will witness the miraculous return of her children (49:19–21; 54:2–3). The number returning will exceed the city's capacity, necessitating the expansion of the city (49:19; 54:1–3) and of national boundaries (33:17).

The redeemed will rebuild the ancient ruins of Jerusalem (58:12; 61:4), assisted by the Gentiles (60:10). Personified Jerusalem will put on ornaments like a bride for her wedding (49:18) and garments of splendor like the high priest (52:1). The wealth of nations will be brought into Zion (54:11–17; 60:4–22; 61:4–6; 62:1–2). The rebuilding of eschatological Jerusalem was prefigured in the historical return of the exiles under Cyrus to rebuild the city (44:26–28; 45:13). The wealth of the nations flowing into eschatological Zion was foreshadowed by the gifts of Cyrus and the Persians to Sheshbazzar (Ezra 1:4–11).

Restored Jerusalem is figuratively described with elaborate imagery: its streets will be paved with stones of turquoise, its foundations built with sapphires, its battlements with rubies, its gates with sparkling jewels, and its walls with precious stones (54:11–12). The entire city will resemble the glorious temple of Solomon built with turquoise (1 Chron. 29:2), the heavenly throne room paved with sapphires (Ezek. 1:26; 10:1), and the ground on Sinai transformed into a pavement of sapphire by the Lord's glory (Exod. 24:10). As the new temple and throne room of God, Mount Zion will be transformed by the glory of God. This radiant glory will emanate from it; the light of the sun and moon will be needed no longer (60:19–20). This imagery is echoed in depictions of the New Jerusalem (Rev. 21:10–25) which also will be the temple of the Lord and the Lamb (Rev. 21:22).

The city will never be conquered again (52:1; 54:11–17; 55:15–17; 60:4–22; 61:4–6; 62:1–2). The Lord will never again bring an enemy against Jerusalem (55:15) and He will protect the city from its enemies (60:11). If an enemy were to attack, it would be forced to surrender (55:16–17). (Note: The final assault on Jerusalem is seen in Ezekiel 38–39 and Revelation 20:7–10.)

The Restored Land

The Abrahamic covenant promises, passed down to Jacob, will be fulfilled in eschatological Israel: Repentant Israel will feast on the inheritance of its father Jacob; that is, all the covenant promises to Jacob will be fulfilled and Israel will enter into the enjoyment of this inheritance (58:14). In a poetic sense, Israel will marry the land just as a young man marries a maiden (62:4–5). In fulfillment of the Abrahamic land promises of an eternal possession of Canaan (Gen. 12:1, 7; 13:14–17; 15:18–21; 17:8), Israel will possess the land forever (60:21).

In a sense, life in the messianic age will be similar to the present age, but the curse will be removed and God's blessing restored. For example, the redeemed will build houses and dwell in them, they will plant vineyards and eat their fruit—without fear of losing either from oppression or exile (65:21–22). Isaiah even pictures the birth of children (65:23), an event that will not occur in the eternal state following the Millennium. It is not clear whether the picture of a "youth" dying at one hundred years (65:20) is intended to suggest that death will be possible, or whether it is a hyperbolic description of the long lifespans and eternal life that the redeemed will enjoy. Their long lifespans will harken back to the original creation before the judgment of the Flood (Gen. 5:3–32).

The Redeemed Gentile Nations

Just as God established His rule over Israel through the Exodus and the conquest of the land, so His return to Zion will cause all nations to recognize His right to rule when He assumes the throne of Israel (52:7). As pictured in 2:2–4, the nations will come to Jerusalem, the source of light (60:3), and escort the redeemed of Israel back to Mount Zion (49:22; 60:4, 9). The redeemed Gentile nations will bring their wealth as tribute to honor Israel and rebuild Jerusalem and will bow down before Israel in acknowledgment of Israel's God and subjugate themselves to Israel as servants (45:14; 49:23; 60:5–17; 61:5, 9; 62:1–2). Even the Gentile kings will subjugate themselves to Israel, hyperbolically licking the dust of their feet and subordinating themselves as menial household servants (49:23; 60:10–14).

Having been reconciled to God and Israel, the redeemed nations will never again invade or defile Jerusalem (52:1; 60:10–11, 18). The nation that will not serve Israel will perish and be destroyed (60:12). Should any Gentile nation try to attack Jerusalem, the Lord will cause it to surrender (54:14–17). (Note: Subsequent revelation elaborates on the peace in the messianic kingdom, followed by a climactic revolt by the nations and attack of Jerusalem that will be vanquished by the Lord. Rev. 20:7–10 and perhaps Ezek. 38:1–39:24.)

The Final Judgment of the Wicked

Following His initial judgment on the nations when He delivers Zion, the Lord will offer reconciliation to the Gentile nations (45:22). While some will heed the exhortation and repent, most will refuse and be destroyed in the final judgment of eternal punishment (45:22–24; 66:15–18, 24). The wicked will be purged by judgment, symbolized by sword and fire (65:12; 66:15–16). Their smoldering corpses will lie exposed in the sight of all as an eternal reminder of the consequences of rebellion against YHWH (66:24).

See also NEW COVENANT; PALESTINIAN COVENANT.

Gordon H. Johnston

B. W. Anderson, "Exodus Typology in Second Isaiah" in *Israel's Prophetic Heritage*, eds. B. W. Anderson, et al. (New York: Harper and Brothers, 1962) and "Exodus and Covenant in Second Isaiah and Prophetic Tradition" in *Magnalia Dei: The Mighty Acts of God*, eds. F. M. Cross, et al. (Garden City: Doubleday & Company, 1976); M. P. V. Barrett, "The Theology of Isaiah" in *BV,* 12 (1978); J. Blenkinsopp, "Second Isaiah: Prophet of Universalism" in *JSOT,* 41 (1988); J. Bright, *Covenant and Promise: The Prophetic Understanding of the Future in Pre-Exilic Israel* (Philadelphia: Westminster Press, 1976); W. Brueggemann, "Unity and Dynamic in the Isaiah Tradition" in *JSOT,* 29 (1984); B. S. Childs, *Isaiah and the Asyrian Crisis* (London: SCM Press, 1967); R. B. Chisholm Jr., "A Theology of Isaiah" in *A Biblical Theology of the Old Testament*, eds. R. B. Zuck, et al. (Chicago: Moody Press, 1991); R. E. Clements, *Isaiah and the Deliverance of Jerusalem* (Sheffield: JSOT Press, 1980), "The Prophecies of Isaiah and the Fall of Jerusalem in 587 B.C." in *VT,* 30 (1980), "Beyond Tradition-History: Deutero-Isaianic Development of First Isaiah's Themes" in *JSOT,* 31 (1985), and "The Unity of the Book of Isaiah" in *Interpretation,* 36 (1982); W. Dumbrell, "The Purpose of the Book of Isaiah" in *TB,* 36 (1985); H. S. Gehman, "The Ruler of the Universe: The Theology of First Isaiah" in *Interpretation,* 11:269–81 (1957);

D. Gowan, *Eschatology in the Old Testament* (Philadelphia: Fortress Press, 1986); G. F. Hasel, *The Remnant: The History and Theology of the Remnant Idea from Genesis to Isaiah* (Berrein Springs: Andrews University, 1980) and "An Appeal to Ancient Tradition as a Literary Form" in *ZAW,* 88 (1976); Y. Hoffman, "The Day of the Lord as a Concept and a Term in the Prophetic Literature" in *ZAW,* 93 (1981); A. S. Kapelrud, "The Main Concern of Second Isaiah" in *VT,* 32 (1982); R. W. Klein, "Going Home: A Theology of Second Isaiah" in *CTM,* 5 (1979); E. H. Merrill, "Isaiah 40–55 as Anti-Babylonian Polemic" in *GTJ,* 8:3–18 (1987), "Survey of a Century of Studies on Isaiah 40–55" in *BibSac,* 573 (1987), and "Literary Genres of Isaiah 4–55" in *BibSac,* 574 (1987); J. Morgenstern, "The Message of Deutero-Isaiah in its Sequential Unfolding" in *HUCA,* 29 (1958), *HUCA,* 30 (1959); J. Muilenburg, "Introduction to Isaiah 40–55" in *The Interpreter's Bible*, 5:381–414, ed. G. A. Buttrick (Nashville: Thomas Nelson, 1952–57); C. R. North, *The Suffering Servant in Deutero-Isaiah* (London: Oxford University Press, 1956); J. Barton Payne, "Eighth Century Israelitish Background of Isaiah 40–66" in *WJT,* 29 (1966–67) and 30 (1967–68) ; J. J. M. Roberts, "Isaiah in Old Testament Theology" in *Interpretation,* 36 (1982); H. van Rooy, "The Nations in Isaiah: A Synchronic Study" in *OTWSA,* 22–23 (1979–80); E. C. Rust, "The Theology of the Prophets" in *RE,* 74 (1977); D. Stuart, "The Sovereign's Day of Conquest" in *BASOR,* 221 (1976); C. Stuhlmeller, "Deutero-Isaiah: Major Transitions in the Prophet's Theology and in Contemporary Scholarship" in *CBQ,* 42 (1980); M. E. Tate, "King and Messiah in Isaiah of Jerusalem" in *RExp,* 65 (1968); T. C. Vriezen, "Essentials of the Theology of Isaiah" in *Israel's Prophetic Heritage*, ed. B. W. Anderson, et al. (New York: Harper and Brothers, 1962); H. E. von Waldow, "The Message of Deutero-Isaiah" in *Interpretation,* 22 (1968); J. C. Whitcomb, "Cyrus in the Prophecies of Isaiah" in *The Law and the Prophets*, ed. J. H. Skilton (Nutley, N.J.: Presbyterian and Reformed Publishing Co., 1974).

ISAIAH 11, ESCHATOLOGY OF

Written between 740–680 B.C., Isaiah is saturated with prophecies about the first and second comings of the Messiah. Some have placed the title, "The Suffering Servant" over the book, but in reality, this is insufficient. A better title might be: "Prophecies of the Coming King Who Will Substitute for the Sins of His People"!

Though sometimes framed in poetic language, all the prophecies in Isaiah are taken literally by the orthodox Jews and by premillennial dispensational theologians. Isaiah 11 is no exception. Antiquity quotes R. Shim'on Laquish: "and the spirit of God hovered over the face of the water (Gen. 1:2)—this is the spirit of King Messiah, as it is written, And the spirit of the Lord will rest upon him (Isa. 11:2)" (Gen. Rab. 2:4). R. Alexandri said of Isaiah 11:3: "This teaches us that they burdened him with commandments and sufferings like millstones." Rava said: "[This teaches us] that he [the Messiah] will scent [the truth] and will adjudicate, as it is written, 'And he shall not judge after the sight of his eyes . . . but with righteousness shall he judge the poor'" (Gen Rab. 2:3–4, *Messiah Texts*). Jewish commentaries refer to this passage as "The Messianic Age" (Slotki). The King will bring in universal peace and harmony among people and will also include the animal world. "In the days of the Messiah of Israel, peace shall be multiplied in the earth" (Targum).

Isaiah 11 speaks of a twig (*hōter*) coming forth from the stem (*gāza'*) of Jesse, who was David's father (v. 1). This One would be the Branch (*nēṣer*) who would grow up out of Jesse's roots. The Spirit of the Lord would rest on (guide over) Him (v. 2). The verses continue to tell of perfect righteousness and judgment coming forth from this One (vv. 4–5) with even the animal kingdom controlled by His power and presence (vv. 6–7). Someday, this root from Jesse would be a signal (flag) for the nations (v. 10). And when that takes place, "the Lord will again recover the second time with His hand the remnant of His people" (v. 11). It is impossible to take these verses in an allegorical way. It is a drama of an actual King having absolute authority over His realm.

This poem predicts the Jewish restoration by a king, sprung from the father of David, who will be equipped by Yahweh's Spirit (Gray). When this King comes, the conditions of Paradise will return and the animals will no longer be at enmity. "The wolf will dwell with the lamb" (v. 6). When this takes place it will be universal, not limited to Palestine, and the King's reign will be worldwide. Isaiah 11 is quoted in reference to Jesus being born in Nazareth, "city of the Branch" (Matt. 2:23), and it is quoted extensively in other New Testament passages (Acts 13:23; Rev. 5:5; 22:16) (Unger).

The promise that the Lord's Spirit would rest on the Messiah is also fulfilled in the New Testament (John 1:33). The Spirit is mentioned in Isaiah 11 in seven references that probably bespeak the sevenfold nature of the Spirit. "There are seven spirits, which are enumerated in order from the highest downwards; since the spirit of the fear of Jehovah is the basis of the whole . . . and the Spirit of Jehovah is the heart of all. . . . In these seven forms the Holy Spirit descended upon the second David [Christ] for a permanent possession" (Keil and Delitzsch). Dispensationally, the Holy Spirit fell on Jesus, as here prophesied, for His kingly work. His First Coming established His person and completed His sacrifice for sins (Isa. 53), and His Second Coming, as promised in chapter 11, will establish His reign over all the earth.

See also DAVIDIC COVENANT; THEOCRATIC KINGDOM.

Mal Couch

Charles John Ellicott, ed., *Commentary on the Whole Bible*, vol. IV (Grand Rapids: Zondervan, 1959); G. Buchanan Gray, *The International Critical Commentary* (New York: Charles Scribner's Sons, 1912); C. F. Keil and F. Delitzsch, *Commentary on the Old Testament*, vol. 7 (Peabody, Mass.: Hendrickson, 1989); Raphael Patai, *The Messiah Texts* (Detroit: Wayne State University Press, 1979); I. W. Slotki, *Isaiah* (London: The Soncino Press, 1972); Merrill F. Unger, *Commentary on the Old Testament*, vol. II (Chicago: Moody Press, 1981).

ISAIAH 52:13–53:12

This is the classic Old Testament passage that clearly predicts both the death of the Messiah and the purpose of His death: atonement.

The Wider Context

The Servant of Jehovah

Isaiah's favorite term for the Messiah is "the Servant of Jehovah," and there are several such Servant passages that run through his book previous to this classic passage. The first is 42:1–6, which emphasizes the mission of the Servant. His mission benefits two groups of people. First, He is to be the covenant of the people, meaning, He will fulfill the covenantal promises to Israel. Second, He is to be the light of the Gentiles.

The second passage is 49:1–13, which emphasizes that the mission of the Servant will be accompanied with difficulties. He will be rejected by Israel (vv. 1–4), but as a result He will become the light of the Gentiles (vv. 5–7). However, eventually Israel will accept Him and be restored (vv. 8–13), at which time He will finally fulfill the covenantal promises to Israel.

The third passage is 50:4–9, which describes the physical sufferings of the Servant, short of death, and no reason is given for those sufferings.

Now, in 52:13–53:12, it is revealed that these physical sufferings will lead to His death, and the reason for that death is given.

The Arm of Jehovah

Another concept in the wider context is that of "the arm of Jehovah." Isaiah declared that the arm will rule for God (40:10), and that the Gentiles will trust in the arm (51:5). This arm will redeem (51:9), and this arm will provide salvation (52:10). Until now, the Servant of Jehovah and the arm of Jehovah have been parallel developments, but in this passage, Isaiah reveals that the Servant of Jehovah (52:13) and the arm of Jehovah (53:1) are one and the same. One more point from the context worth noting is that, in 52:3, Isaiah declared that Israel would be redeemed without money. This passage now details the means of this redemption.

The Prophetic Setting

This passage is a prophecy of the death and resurrection of the Messiah. However, 53:1–9 is put in the form of a confession by Israel, and so the actual prophetic setting is that these other words of Israel's national confession will take place just prior to the Second Coming and, in turn, will be the actual cause of the Second Coming. Israel's confession of its national sin of rejecting the Messiah is the prerequisite to the Second Coming, and this passage provides the words of that confession.

Messiah or Israel?

In all rabbinic literature prior to A.D. 1050, this passage was understood as individual and messianic. Rashi was the first rabbi to innovate the interpretation, suggesting that this passage speaks of Israel as a nation and not Messiah as an individual. It was an obvious attempt to avoid the Christological implications of the passage. While that view was rejected by the majority of the rabbis in his day and in succeeding centuries, by the 1800s, this became the dominant rabbinic view and remains so to this day. There are a number of reasons why such an interpretation is impossible.

1. Isaiah uses distinctive pronouns distinguishing between the *we, us,* and *our* as over against *he, him,* and *his*. It is obvious that the *we, us,* and *our* refer to Isaiah and his listeners, the Jewish people and, therefore, the *he, him,* and *his* is someone other than Israel as a nation, and that would be the Messiah.

2. The Servant dies for "my people" (53:8), a frequent usage in Isaiah referring to the Jewish people. The people are wholly distinguished from the Servant, and the people cannot be anyone other than Israel.

3. Throughout the passage, the Servant is portrayed as a singular, human personality.

4. The Servant is suffering voluntarily, willingly, and silently (v. 7) and this has not been the case with Israel.

5. The Servant suffers a vicarious and substitutionary death (vv. 4–6, 8, 10, 12), yet Israel never suffered on behalf of the Gentiles but only because of the Gentiles.

6. The sufferings of the Servant bring justification and spiritual healing to those who accept it (vv. 5, 11), and Israel has not done this for the Gentiles.

7. The Servant dies (vv. 8, 12), while Israel has always survived.

8. The Servant is resurrected, but Israel has never died and so never needed to be resurrected.

The Structure of the Passage

The passage consists of five strophes, with each strophe containing three verses. The first line of each strophe is the theme of that strophe. The passage begins with God's introduction of the Servant (52:13–15) and, in the Hebrew text, the tenses are mixed. This is followed by Israel's confession (53:1–9); here, the tenses are consistently all perfect. The passage concludes with the theology of the Suffering Servant (53:10–12); here, again, the tenses are mixed.

A Survey of the Passage

The first strophe is entitled: Behold My Servant Shall Prosper (52:13–15). It opens with the exaltation of the Servant (v. 13), pointing out that during His ministry He will deal wisely, or prudently, and will act with intelligence. He will prosper and succeed. He will rise (a reference to the Resurrection), He will be lifted up (a reference to the Ascension), and He is to be exceedingly high (a reference to the present session in heaven). This is followed by a summary of the humiliation of the Servant (v. 14), summarizing His physical sufferings to the point that His visage was so disfigured that He no longer resembled a man. However, the humiliation of the Servant is followed by the victory of the Servant (v. 15), the day will come when kings and nations will be astonished at Him, when they finally understand what they had not understood heretofore, and they will shut their mouths at Him, a sign of respect.

The second strophe is entitled: Who Has Believed Our Message (53:1–3)? It opens with the statement of Israel's unbelief (v. 1), confessing that Israel had heard the report about Him for a long time but did not believe the report they had heard. The humanity of the Servant is summarized next (v. 2), comparing Him to a tender twig that grows on a trunk or branch and draws its life from it. Normally, people cut off sucklings because they draw life from the tree and kill it, and that was their view of Him in the past. Furthermore, He was like a root out of dry ground, emphasizing the lowly condition in which the Servant would appear. Finally, He had no outward physical beauty, and there was nothing about His outward features that would attract people to Him. On the contrary, the opposite occurred (v. 3). The Servant was despised and rejected of *men*, a Hebrew word meaning "men of rank, or the leaders." He was a man knowledgeable of pain; not only were people not attracted to Him, they were repulsed by Him and would hide from Him. He was indeed despised and not esteemed.

The third strophe is: Surely He Has Borne Our Griefs and Carried Our Sorrows (53:4–6). This segment opens emphasizing the substitutionary sufferings of the Servant (v. 4). The confession here is that Israel had considered Him to be suffering for His own sins, that His suffering was a punishment from God. Only now do they finally realize that His sufferings were ritually substitutionary. Not only were His physical sufferings substitutionary, but so was His death (v. 5). His substitutionary suffering and death was necessary because of Israel's condition (v. 6); they have gone their own way like sheep and so God laid their iniquity on the Servant.

The fourth strophe is: He Was Oppressed and Afflicted, yet He Opened Not His Mouth (53:7–9). The previous sufferings mentioned are not revealed to have been sufferings in silence (v. 7). The manner and means of His death are then further expounded upon (v. 8). The Servant underwent a legal trial and suffered a legal execution. But for the most part, His own generation of Israel did not accept the fact that He was dying a penal, substitutionary atonement for their transgression. It was upon them that judgment was due, but it fell upon the Servant. The fact that a real death had taken place is further affirmed by the fact that the Servant was also buried (v. 9). Normally, if one dies a criminal's death, one is buried in a criminal's grave, and such a grave had been assigned for Him. But because of intervention, He was buried in a rich man's tomb, God's way of showing that He did not die for any outward or inward sin.

The fifth strophe states: Yet It Pleased Jehovah to Bruise Him; He Has Put Him to Grief (53:10–12). This passage declares the theology of the sufferings of the Servant and that His death was clearly an offering for sin (v. 10). Though the actual means of the Servant's death was at human hands yet it was God who bruised Him, because the death of the Messiah fulfilled the very program He put into effect from before the foundation of the world. The divine purpose is that His life should become an offering for sin. The verse goes on to say that, after His death, He will both see His seed and prolong His days, a clear implication of a resurrection of the dead; to be able to see after death requires living again. That very resurrection leads to the justification of the Servant (v. 11). God declares that He will be satisfied by the death of the Servant, meaning that the sin offering will be accepted. As a result, justification will come to those who have a saving knowledge of the Servant, for He will bear their iniquities. Finally, the sufferings, death, and resurrection of the Servant leads to the Servant's rewards (v. 12). In the messianic kingdom, both He and the seed He has justified in this dispensation will share in the kingdom rewards. The passage concludes with four basic statements that summarize well the entire passage: He poured out His soul to death, He was numbered with the transgressors, yet He bore the sin of many, and He made intercession for transgressors.

See also ADVENT, CHRIST'S FIRST AND SECOND.

Arnold G. Fruchtenbaum

ISRAEL AND THE CHURCH: THE DIFFERENCES

One of the great theological battlegrounds of orthodox Christianity throughout the centuries has been the nature and character of the church especially in relation to its biblical predecessor, Israel. The two major views are that (1) the church is a continuation of Israel and that (2) the church is completely different from Israel.

First View: The Church Is Israel

The predominant view has been that the church is the "new" Israel, a continuation of the concept of Israel that began in the Old Testament. In this view, the church is the refinement and higher development of the concept of Israel. All of the promises made to Israel in the Scriptures find their fulfillment in the church. Thus, the prophecies relating to the blessing and restoration of Israel to the Promised Land are spiritualized into promises of blessing to the church. The prophecies of condemnation and judgment, though, are retained literally by the Jewish nation of Israel.

This view is sometimes called replacement theology because the church is seen to replace Israel in God's economy. One of the problems with the view, among others, is the continuing existence of the Jewish people, especially with regard to the revival of the new modern state of Israel. If Israel has been condemned to extinction and there is no divinely ordained future for the Jewish nation, how does one account for the supernatural survival of the Jewish people since the establishment of the church for almost two thousand years, against all odds? Furthermore, how does one account for Israel's resurgence among the family of nations as an independent nation, victorious in several wars, and flourishing economically?

Second View: Israel and the Church Are Different

The other view, we believe, is clearly taught in the New Testament, but it has been suppressed throughout most of church history. This view is that the church is completely different and distinct from Israel, and the two should not be confused. In fact, the church is an entirely new creation that came into being on the Day of Pentecost after Christ's resurrection from the dead and will continue until it is taken to heaven at the Rapture return of the Lord (Eph. 1:9–11). None of the curses or blessings pronounced upon Israel refer directly to the church. The church enters into the Abrahamic and new covenants, for instance, only by divine application, not by original interpretation (Matt. 26:28).

This leaves all the covenants, promises, and warnings to Israel intact. Israel, the natural Jewish nation, is still Israel. To be sure, Israel has been sidelined during these past nineteen hundred years of the Diaspora. The church has taken center stage in the Lord's affairs as the Gospel has spread throughout the world. Nevertheless, God has carefully preserved the Jewish people, even in unbelief, through every kind of distress and persecution. Sometimes, the professing church itself (I speak to our shame) has been a cause of these persecutions of the Jews.

Not only has God preserved the Jewish nation, but He has also kept His promise to save a remnant of Israel in every generation. The remnant of Israel in this age are the Jewish believers in Christ who have joined the Gentile believers and form the church, the body of Christ (Rom. 11:5). In this respect, then, a part of Israel (the believing remnant) intersects with the church during the church age. But this does not make Israel the church, or vice versa.

In the future, both God's warnings and promises to Israel will come to pass. After the Lord is finished with the church age and has taken the church to heaven in the Rapture (1 Thess. 4:16–18), God will restore Israel to center stage on the world's divine theater. First comes the devastating Time of Jacob's Trouble (Jer. 30:7), also known as the Great Tribulation. This is a dreadful period of seven years, which begins relatively lightly during the first half but intensifies into full focus during the latter half. During this time the world is judged for rejecting Christ, but, more specifically, Israel is judged, purged, and prepared through the fiery trials for of the Great Tribulation for the second coming of the Messiah. This is the bad news.

The good news is that, when Christ does return to the earth at the end of the Tribulation, Israel will be ready, willing, and eager to receive Him and will proclaim, "Blessed is He who comes in the name of the Lord" (Matt. 23:39). As the stumbling of Israel brought blessing to the world at Christ's First Coming, the reception of Israel to Christ at His Second Advent will be like life from the dead (Rom. 11:15). The remnant of Israel that survives the Tribulation (some one-third of the Jewish people who enter the Tribulation) will be saved, and the Lord will establish His kingdom on the same earth and in the same capital city, Jerusalem, that rejected Him centuries before. Israel will be the head of the nations and no longer the tail, and all nations will send representatives to Jerusalem to honor and worship the King of Kings and Lord of Lords (Isa. 2:2–3; Micah 4:1). The church will return with Christ and will rule with Him for a thousand years (Rev. 20:1–5). He Himself told His disciples that they would rule over the twelve tribes of Israel in the restoration (Matt. 19:28). Thus, Israel has not been forgotten in God's plan. While the Jewish nation still has a dark period facing it, there is a glorious finale to Israel's long history.

How Did the Church Decide the Demise of Israel?

The New Testament church was very much involved with the vicissitudes of Israel. Jesus is an Israeli, as were all the apostles, and the concerns of Israel, spiritually and politically, were very much a part of their lives. The greatest struggles the early church had were over the relationship between Israel and the church, law and grace, and the fellowship between Jewish and Gentile believers in Christ (Galatians). Many of the Jewish believers were not comfortable with the Gentile believers, at first, and, as time went on and Gentiles began to predominate numerically, the attitudes were reversed. Galatians shows how the Jewish party tried to impose the Mosaic Law on Gentile Christians, and Romans shows how the Gentile party began to boast against the branches (Rom. 11:18), resenting the place of Israel in history and theology.

It took some time, perhaps a couple of centuries, but eventually the vast Gentile majority in the church began to view Israel as a vestigial organ that had outlived its usefulness. In fact, the predominant Christian view was that the destruction of Jerusalem and the temple by the Romans in A.D. 70 signaled the official and divinely ordained end of the Jewish nation, never more to be reinstituted as a national entity. The fact that Jerusalem lay in ruins and the Jewish people were scattered over the world was seen as conclusive evidence that God was forever finished with national Israel. If there were any purpose for the existence of the Jewish people, it was to remind the world of the severe judgment of God upon a disobedient people.

Birth: Physical	Birth: Spiritual
Circumcision of Flesh	Circumcision of Heart
Promise: Inheritance of Land	Promise: Inheritance of Heaven
Government:	Government:
Davidic Monarchy	Apostles
Priests	Pastors
National Entity	Body of Christ
Temple Worship	Decentralized Worship
Animal Sacrifice	Lord's Supper
Destiny—Millennial Kingdom	Destiny—Rapture/Reign
Messianic King	Messianic Savior
Wife of God, married in desert	Bride of Christ, espoused
Levitical Priesthood	Melchizedek Priesthood
Jerusalem Centered	Missions Centered
Believing Remnant	Spiritual Minority
Keeps the Sabbath	Celebrates the Lord's Day
Keeps the Feasts	Has Fulfillment of Feasts
Eternity: Gates/New Jerusalem	Eternity: Foundations of New Jerusalem

If this harsh view of Israel were true, though, what of the promises of God to Israel in the Old Testament? For those who claimed to believe in the entire Bible as the Word of God, this was a great problem. How could a faithful God not keep His promises to His ancient people? To deal with this took extraordinary theological dexterity and alchemy. The theologians had to propose that Israel in the Scriptures did not really mean Israel, especially when it came to the promises of eternal blessing. Instead, Israel meant something else, something that came to be known in the New Testament as the church. The church became the new Israel, and, through this remarkable transformation, wherever blessing is promised to Israel in the Old Testament, it was interpreted to mean the church. This is replacement theology, in which the church has become Israel.

Replacement theology was already around before the end of the first century but did not become the official position of professing Christian leadership until Augustine popularized the concept, primarily in *The City of God*, in the latter part of the fourth century. Augustine actually states that he was previously a chiliast, meaning that he was a believer in the thousand-year reign of Christ on the earth after His return. This is the same as our current description of premillennialism. However, Augustine had come to the conclusion that this view was carnal, and had adopted the view that the reign of Christ would be something more spiritual, and would actually occur during the church age. Such a view necessitated the extinction of Israel and the cancellation of all promises God made to the Jewish nation. These promises of blessing would now be fulfilled within the framework of the church.

This view, which had been latent in Christendom, now flourished throughout the Byzantine world. From this point on, the theological legs were cut out from under Israel, and the predominant Christian theology was that there was no future for Israel. Replacement theology has been the rule that has survived the Middle Ages, the Crusades, and the Reformation in church history. Only during the last century or so has the premillennial concept of the future of Israel come to the forefront in evangelical Christianity. Even so, it is a minority view.

Does Israel's Future Demean the Church's Glory?

Some suggest that if Israel has not ceased to exist in its covenant relationship to God and if Israel still has a future in the divine plan, this somehow diminishes the position of the church. Is such a concern valid? It is almost as though the church has been jealous of Israel and afraid that if it recognized Israel's future promises, it would somehow demean Christ and the church. Nothing could be further from the truth.

It is when the church recognizes Israel that the true distinctiveness and glory of the body of Christ becomes evident. This called-out body, composed of believing Jews and Gentiles during the church age, is the highest entity the Lord has created, superior to the universe, all the angels, the nations, and Israel. Our Head, our Husband, our Friend is the Son of God Himself. We shall reign with Him when He rules the earth, and our twelve founding apostles will rule over the twelve tribes of Israel. The angels themselves will study us forever as the greatest exhibit of God's grace, and we will actually judge the angels. This is our destiny. Why, then, be disturbed over what God has promised the Jewish people? Why be jealous over the future destiny of Israel? How shortsighted of us! Indeed, the church's finest and most distinctive hour will be when Israel is restored nationally and spiritually to the Lord at the second coming of Christ. We will return from heaven with Him as His glorious bride to rule Israel and the world. What more could we ask?

So, if we are not to suffer from spiritual myopia, we must recognize what the Lord is doing with Israel, not shrink from it as though our own interests will be overshadowed. Rather, we rejoice in these developments, with full assurance that our own redemption draws ever closer.

This table shows some of the many ways in which Israel and the church differ. While both have a covenant relationship with the

Lord, the characteristics of these covenants are so different that they must not be confused.

See also AUGUSTINE; ISRAELOLOGY, DOCTRINE OF.

Thomas S. McCall

ISRAELOLOGY, DOCTRINE OF

Israelology refers to a subdivision of systematic theology (unique to dispensational systematic theology) incorporating all theological doctrines concerning the people of Israel—past, present, and future.

Israel Past

The Election of Israel

The fact of Israel's election is clearly stated in Scripture (Deut. 4:37; 7:6–8; 14:2; 26:18). The basis of Israel's national election is God's covenant relationship with the fathers (Deut. 10:15–16). The purposes for Israel's election include the call to become a kingdom of priests (Exod. 19:6); to be the recipient of God's revelation (Deut. 4:5–8; 6:6–9; Rom. 3:1–2); to propagate the doctrine of the One God (Isa. 43:10–12); and to produce the Messiah (Rom. 9:5; Heb. 2:16–17; 7:13–14).

The Unconditional Covenants

The second concern is the four unconditional covenants God made with Israel, known as the Abrahamic covenant, the Palestinian covenant, the Davidic covenant, and the new covenant (for details, see discussions under these headings).

The Mosaic Covenant and the Law of Moses

The third concern is the Mosaic covenant and the Law of Moses. The key element of the Mosaic Law was the blood sacrifice (Lev. 17:11); however, the blood of the animal merely covered the sin of the Old Testament saints and did not remove it. The content of the Mosaic Covenant was the Law of Moses, uniquely given to Israel and not to either the Gentiles or to the church (Exod. 19:3–8; Deut. 4:7–8; Ps. 147:19–20; Mal. 4:4). The Law never included a means of salvation since salvation was always by grace through faith. But it was revealed that the Law had at least nine purposes.

1. The Law was to reveal the holiness of God and the standard of righteousness which God demanded (Lev. 19:1–2, 37; 11:44; 1 Peter 1:15–16). For this reason, the Law itself was holy, and righteous, and good (Rom. 7:12).

2. The Law was to provide the rule of life for the Old Testament saints (Lev. 11:44–45; 19:2; 20:7–8, 26). For the Old Testament believer, the Law was the center of the believer's spiritual life and their delight (Ps. 119).

3. The Law was to provide for Israel occasions for individual and corporate worship, for one example, the seven holy seasons of Leviticus 23.

4. The Law was to keep the Jews a distinct people (Lev. 11:44–45; Deut. 7:6; 14:1–2). This was the reason for many specific laws regarding diet, clothing, ad other areas of their daily life.

5. The Law was to serve as a wall of partition to keep Gentiles as Gentiles away from enjoying the spiritual blessings of the Jewish covenants (Eph. 2:11–16).

6. The Law was to reveal sin (Rom. 3:19–20; 5:20; 7:7).

7. The Law was actually to cause them to sin more and place them under even greater condemnation (Rom. 4:15; 5:20; 7:7–13; 1 Cor. 15:56).

8. The Law was to show that the sinner could do nothing on their own to please God and had no ability to keep the Law perfectly to attain the righteousness of the Law (Rom. 7:14–25).

9. The Law was to drive the sinner to faith—ultimately, faith in the Messiah (Rom. 8:1–4; Gal. 3:24–25).

The token of the Mosaic covenant was the Sabbath (Exod. 31:12–17). It was a sign that God had brought Israel out of the land of Egypt, a sign of the Exodus (Deut. 5:12–15; Ezek. 20:12, 20).

The Remnant of Israel

The fourth concern is the remnant of Israel, which means that within the Jewish nation, there are always some who believe, and all those who believe among Israel comprise the remnant of Israel. The remnant at any point of history may be large or small, but there was never a time when it was nonexistent. Only believers comprise the remnant, Jewish believers. Furthermore, the remnant is always part of the nation and is not detached from the nation as a separate entity. The remnant is distinct, but distinct within the nation. While the concept of the remnant was true from the beginning of Israel's history as they began to multiply, as a doctrine, the theology of the remnant began with Elijah the prophet (1 Kings 17–19) and was then developed by the prophets.

Israel Present

The Kingdom of God Program

The kingdom of God concept is essentially defined as "God's rule," which includes God as King and the realm over which He rules. While terms such as "kingdom of God" and "kingdom of heaven" are synonymous terms, there are five facets to God's kingdom program: the universal kingdom or the eternal kingdom; the spiritual kingdom; the theocratic kingdom; the messianic, or millennial, kingdom; and the mystery kingdom. (See also KINGDOM OF GOD, OF HEAVEN; KINGDOM, UNIVERSAL AND MEDIATORIAL; KINGDOM PARABLES OF THE; and THEOCRATIC KINGDOM.)

The Rejection of the Messiahship of Jesus and Its Results and Consequences

In Matthew 12–13 Israel officially rejects the messiahship of Jesus, accusing Him of demon possession and at that point, the messianic kingdom offer is withdrawn; in place of it, the mystery kingdom program is instituted. The consequence for Israel is the coming destruction of Jerusalem and the temple, fulfilled in A.D. 70. The unpardonable sin, or the blasphemy of the Holy Spirit, is defined, therefore, as the national rejection by Israel of the messiahship of Jesus was while He was present and claiming He was demon-possessed.

The Unconditional Covenants

The third concern involves how the unconditional covenants of Israel are relevant to Israel at the present time, between its rejection and its acceptance of the messiahship of Jesus. Another key issue is how the church relates to the unconditional covenants, especially the new covenant. (See also NEW COVENANT.) Issues are involved such as the Gentile obligation to Jewish believers (Rom. 15:25–27); the purpose of Gentile salvation, which includes the gathering from among the Gentiles a people for God's name (Acts 15:13–18); and that of the provoking of individual Jews to jealousy so that they become believers and become members of the present-day remnant of Israel (Rom. 11:11–14).

The Mosaic Covenant and the Law of Moses

What is the place of the Mosaic covenant and the Law of Moses? Israelology rejects any attempt to divide the Law, either in two divisions (the 10 and the 603 commandments) or three divisions (ceremonial, moral, and civil), all for the purpose of trying to retain part of the Law as still in effect and doing away with other parts. Israelology insists that the Law of Moses is a grand unity and, therefore, breaking even one commandment means the breaking of the whole Law (James 2:10). The fact of the New Testament is that with the death of the Messiah, the entire Law of Moses has been rendered inoperative (Rom. 10:4; Gal. 3:19; 3:23–4:7; Heb. 7:11–18; Eph. 2:14–15; 2 Cor. 3:2–11). Although there is no obligation to keep the Mosaic Law any longer, this does not mean that dispensational Israelology is antinomian, for it does teach that there is a new law, called the Law of Christ (Rom. 8:2; Gal. 6:2). Like the Law of Moses, the Law of Christ has many individual commandments, some of which are the same as those of the Mosaic Law, but some are different and even contradictory to those of the Mosaic Law. Furthermore, since the Sabbath was the token of the Mosaic covenant, the mandatory observance of the Sabbath as a day of rest has also been terminated. Thus, in the age of grace, while the church is obligated to meet corporately and on a regular basis (Heb. 10:26), the day of the week is not specified, and there is nothing particularly sacred about Sunday, which is never referred to either as a Sabbath or as the Lord's Day, but only as "the first day of the week."

Israel and the Church

The fifth concern is the distinctions between Israel and the church. (See ISRAEL AND THE CHURCH: THE DIFFERENCES.)

The Modern State of Israel

The sixth concern focuses on the modern state of Israel that came into existence in 1948. Israelology sees this as a definite fulfillment of prophecy, though not the fulfillment of the final restoration predicted by the Scriptures. It is recognized that the Bible speaks of two worldwide regatherings of the Jewish people. First, there is to be a regathering in unbelief in preparation for the judgment of the Tribulation.

Second, there will be a worldwide regathering in faith in preparation for the blessing of the messianic kingdom. While Israel is not a fulfillment of the second-regathering prophecies, it is certainly a fulfillment of the first type (Ezek. 20:33–38; 22:17–22; Zeph. 2:1–2; for corollary evidence see Ezek. 36:22–24 and Isa. 11:11–12).

Romans 9:1–11:24: The Remnant of Israel and the Olive Tree

Paul's Israelology in Romans 9–11, which deals with the remnant of Israel and the olive tree. Discussion here would be interrelated with 1 Peter 2:1–10, which teaches that although Israel the whole failed in its calling of Exodus 19, the remnant of Israel has not failed and, therefore, it is the remnant (and not the church) that is the elect race, the holy nation, the kingdom of priests, and the people for God's own possession. The point of Romans 9–11 is that Israel's rejection of the messiahship of Jesus did not catch God by surprise but is very much a part of God's plan (9:1–29). In this day and age, God is not working nationally, but individually, so that any individual, Jew or Gentile, who calls upon the name of the Lord shall be saved (9:30–10:21). Paul then points out that Israel's rejection is not total, because there is still a remnant coming to faith (11:1–11). Therefore, the concept of the remnant of Israel, already found in the Old Testament, has continued into the New Testament. The remnant today is comprised of Jewish believers in the messiahship of Jesus. The purpose of Israel's stumbling was so that salvation could go out to the Gentiles (11:11–15), yet Gentile salvation is subservient to Jewish salvation in that the purpose of this salvation is to provoke Jews to jealousy and, therefore, the major means by which God brings Jews to become members of the remnant today is through being provoked to jealousy by Gentile believers.

In the illustration of the olive tree (11:16–24), the olive tree is not Israel, as Israel is represented by the natural branches; nor is the olive tree the church or the Gentiles in the church, who are represented by the wild olive branches. Rather, the olive tree represents the place of spiritual blessings that come out of the unconditional Jewish covenants, and now Jewish and Gentile believers are partaking of them. However, the tree itself is still owned by the Jewish people. Because they own the olive tree, it is to be anticipated that there will eventually be a national restoration.

Hebrew Christianity or Messianic Jews

The eighth concern focuses on Hebrew Christianity or messianic Jews today and their role, played as both members of the remnant of Israel and members of the church, the body of the Messiah. Jews who believe in Jesus remain Jews; likewise, Gentiles who believe in Jesus remain Gentiles and do not undergo some kind of spiritual ethnic identity change into spiritual Jews or spiritual Israel. Jewish believers today not only share in the Body of the Messiah and therefore share in its obligations, they also have a Jewish identity, which puts them under other obligations such as the circumcision of the Abrahamic covenant. Messianic Jews are free from the obligation of the Law of Moses, but freedom also means liberty to observe those things that they choose to observe as a matter of free choice.

The Hebrew Christian or Messianic Jewish New Testament Writings

The final concern has to do with the Hebrew Christian or messianic Jewish writings, meaning those parts of the New Testament that are especially relevant for and/or addressed to Jewish believers. This includes the gospel of Matthew, written to Jews and addressing Jewish issues, especially God's kingdom program and how it was affected by the rejection of the Messiah. Furthermore, the first fifteen chapters of the book of Acts are especially relevant to Israelology, as they focus on the early Jewish church and, ultimately, how it relates to Gentile Christianity. Of the twenty-one epistles, five were specifically written to Jewish believers: Hebrews, James, 1 and 2 Peter, and Jude. Finally, the book of Revelation touches on Israelology primarily in chapters 7 and 12.

Israel Future

Israel and the Church Age

The Scriptures clearly demanded a restoration of Israel prior to the start of the Tribulation, which was fulfilled in 1948. Israel's capture of Jerusalem in 1967 was another milestone in biblical prophecy in the church age.

Israel and the Tribulation

Israel is related to the Tribulation in a number of ways. Among the various purposes for the Tribulation, at least two are directly related to Israelology. There is the bringing about of a great worldwide revival by means of the 144,000 Jews (Matt. 24:14; Rev. 7:1–17). Furthermore, a key purpose of the Tribulation is to break the will of the holy people (Dan. 12:5–7) in order to bring them to believe on the Messiah (Ezek. 20:33–38). Thus, a major purpose of the Tribulation is to bring about Israel's national salvation and the Tribulation can only start when there is a signing of a seven-year covenant between Israel and the Antichrist (Dan. 9:24–27; Isa. 28:14–22). A great part of the prophetic Word emphasizes Israel's role in the Tribulation and, therefore, calls it uniquely, the "Time of Jacob's Trouble" (Jer. 30:4–7). A general description of Israel in the Tribulation can be found in Isaiah 3:1–4:1. A number of the "Day of Jehovah" passages uniquely apply to Israel (Ezek. 13:1–7; Joel 2:1–11; 3:14–17; Amos 5:18–20; Zeph. 1:7–13). It is pictured as a time of worldwide anti-Semitism and a worldwide persecution of the Jews (Matt. 24:15–28; Rev. 12:1–17). The latter passage indicates that Satan will have a special war against the Jews and will attempt to annihilate all Jewish people once and for all. On the other hand, Daniel 12:1 points out that the archangel Michael will fight on Israel's behalf to make sure that Israel as a people survives. The final result for the Jews in the Tribulation is that two-thirds of the Jewish population will perish in the second half of the Tribulation, but one-third will survive to become part of Israel's national salvation (Zech. 13:8–9). Furthermore, it is revealed that during the Tribulation, the surviving Jews will have a place to flee for a city of refuge (Isa. 33:13–16; Matt. 24:16; Rev. 12:6). It is also stated that the place where the remnant of Israel will be put into hiding is in the city of Bozrah (Mic. 2:12) located in the land of Edom, or modern-day southern Jordan (Dan. 11:40–45). It is held by many that Bozrah is the modern city of Petra.

Finally, in dealing with the Jews in the Tribulation, one must again focus on the concept of the remnant. Then, too, there will be a segment of the Jewish people who will be believers. Among these will be the 144,000 Jews (Rev. 7:1–8) and the two witnesses (Rev. 11:13). The fact of the remnant is stated in Isaiah 10:20–23, and they are able to survive the Tribulation because they receive divine protection (Isa. 41:8–16) and divine provision (Isa. 41:17–20; 65:8–16).

Israel and the Second Coming

Israelology strongly affirms that while the rapture of the church has no preconditions whatsoever and is imminent, the Second Coming has a specific precondition, Israel's national salvation; until all Israel is saved, there is no Second Coming or messianic kingdom (Lev. 26:40–42; Jer. 3:11–18; Hosea 5:15–6:3; Zech. 12:10–13:1; Matt. 23:37–39; et al.) Eventually, through the Tribulation judgments, there will be a national regeneration of Israel that will occur preceding the Second Coming (Hos. 6:1–3). At this point, the remainder of Paul's Israelology (Rom. 11:25–36) comes into the picture in which he clearly predicts that following the fullness of the Gentiles, God again deals with Israel until all Israel is saved. When Israel is saved by turning to the Messiah, they will then plead for the Messiah to return (Ps. 79, 80; Isa. 64:1–12; Joel 2:28–32; Zech. 12:10–13:1, 7–9). Because the remnant of Israel consists of those Jews who believe and because just prior to the Second Coming all Israel is saved, eventually "all Israel" and "the remnant of Israel" become synonymous terms, a fact indicated in Micah 2:12–13.

One more point Israelology emphasizes is that with the Second Coming there will be the judgment of the Gentiles. These Gentiles will be judged on the basis of anti-Semitism or pro-Semitism, which becomes the evidence of their faith or lack of it, and it further determines who among the Gentiles will enter the messianic kingdom and who among them will be excluded (Joel 3:1–3; Matt. 25:31–46).

Finally, this will also mean the resurrection of the Old Testament saints for the purpose of enjoying—with surviving Israel—the messianic kingdom (Isa. 26:19; Dan. 12:2).

Israel and the Messianic Kingdom

In Israelology, belief in the messianic kingdom is based on two matters: the unfulfilled promises of the unconditional covenant; and the unfulfilled prophecies of the Jewish prophets. It denies that the basis for believing in the messianic kingdom lies solely in Revelation 20. Furthermore, there are four facets of Israel's final restoration, and each facet is based upon a specific covenant: the regeneration of Israel is based upon the new covenant. The regathering of Israel is based on the Palestinian covenant. The possession of the land is based on the Abrahamic covenant. The reestablishment of the Davidic throne is based on the Davidic covenant. Each of these unfulfilled promises of the covenants is further developed by the prophets.

Other characteristics of Israel's final restoration are that they will be reunited as a nation (Jer. 3:18; Ezek. 37:1–23); they will be the center of Gentile attention (Isa. 14:1–2; 49:22–23; 60:1–3; 61:4–9; Mic. 7:14–17; Zeph. 3:20; Zech. 8:23). Furthermore, Israel as a nation will rule over the Gentiles (Deut. 15:6; 28:13; Isa. 49:22–23; 61:6–7). They will be characterized by righteousness, holiness, peace, security, joy, and gladness (Isa. 32:16–20; 35:5–10; 51:3; 55:12–13; 61:10–11). There will also be a new mountain in the center of the country known as "the mountain of Jehovah's house" (Isa. 2:2–4; 27:13; 56:6–8; 66:20; Mic. 4:1–2; Ezek. 17:22–24; 20:40–41; 41:1–4; 45:1–8; 48:8–22). There will be a millennial temple (Ezek. 40:5–43:27) with a millennial system of priesthood and sacrifice (Ezek. 44:1–46:24). This will serve as a visible sign for Israel of what Christ has done on the cross in the same way that the bread and the cup are for the church in this age. Furthermore, it can also serve as a means of restoring the millennial saint who has sinned into the fellowship. There will also be a millennial river (Ezek. 47:1–12) that will begin to flow from the temple area (Joel 3:18), south to Jerusalem (Zech. 14:8). There it will divide in two, half flowing out to the Mediterranean Sea and half flowing out to the Dead Sea. The Jewish people will regather and resettle the land in tribal divisions (Ezek. 47:13–48:29). The description of the millennial Jerusalem is a major theme of Old Testament prophecy.

Finally, since all Israel throughout the messianic kingdom will remain a saved nation, it also means that all Israel will remain the remnant of Israel throughout the kingdom period.

Israel and the Eternal Order

Even in the eternal New Jerusalem, there will be a distinction between Israel (the Old Testament saints) and the church (Heb.

12:22–24). Furthermore, the twelve gates of the eternal New Jerusalem will be named after the twelve tribes of Israel (Rev. 21:12–13), and so for all eternity these Jewish names will be remembered. Through these gates the righteous of the Gentiles will bring their glory (Rev. 21:25–26). The mention of Gentiles (also in v. 24) shows that the Jewish and Gentile distinction will be maintained through all eternity.

Other Relevant Topics

Israelology also concerns issues about Israel that cannot be placed into the three time zones.

The Symbolic Illustrations of Israel

The symbolic illustrations of Israel include the following symbols: the Son of God (Exod. 4:22–23; Isa. 63:16; 64:8; Hos. 11:1); God's treasure (Exod. 19:5; Deut. 14:2; Ps. 135:4); the kingdom of priests (Exod. 19:6; 1 Peter 2:5, 9); the vineyard of Jehovah (Ps. 80:8–16; Isa. 3:14–15; 5:1–7; 27:2–6; Jer. 2:21; Hos. 10:1–3; Matt. 21:33–46; Mark 11:1–12; Luke 20:9–19); the clay and the potter (Isa. 29:16; 45:9; 18:1–12; 19:1–15; Rom. 9:19–24); the Servant of Jehovah (Isa. 42:18–43:13; 44:21–23; 45:4; 48:20); the flock of God (Ps. 28:9; 78:52; 80:1; Jer. 23:1–4; Ezek. 34:1–31; Zech. 11:4–14; 13:7; John 10:1–18); the inheritance of God (Deut. 9:29; 32:9; 1 Sam. 10:2; 1 Kings. 8:51; Ps. 28:9; 33:12; 78:62; 78:71; 94:14; 106:40; Isa. 63:17); and the wife of Jehovah (Isa. 54:1–8; 62:4–5; Jer. 3:1–5; Ezek. 16:1–63; Hos. 2:2–23).

Anti-Semitism

Anti-Semitism is defined as hatred toward the Jew only because the person is a Jew. The cause of anti-Semitism is Satan (Rev. 12:1–17), and those guilty of anti-Semitism will fall under the cursing aspect of the Abrahamic covenant (Gen. 12:3).

How Israelology Relates to Systematic Theology

How does Israelology overlap other divisions of systematic theology?

In the realm of bibliology, Israelology points out that God used the Jewish people to author the Scriptures (Deut. 4:8; 29:29; Ps. 147:19; Rom. 3:1–2; 9:4). Furthermore, Israelology is here concerned with the way the New Testament quotes the Old Testament. Rather than teaching that the New Testament changes the meaning of the Old Testament or reinterprets it, the New Testament merely quotes the Old Testament, in four different ways, without ever changing the original meaning or reinterpreting it as no longer what the original text intended.

In the realm of theology proper, especially as focused on the first person, God the Father, Israelology points out that the Fatherhood of God includes fatherhood to Israel, as well as to individual believers. Furthermore, election belongs to the realm of theology proper, and Israelology emphasizes the fact of national election.

In the realm of Christology, Israelology emphasizes the Jewishness of the Messiah. Two of His many titles emphasize His Jewishness: the Son of Abraham and the Son of David (Matt. 1:1). Concerning the temptation of Jesus, He not only represented all people, but He also represented Israel. Where Israel failed, the ideal Israelite did not fail. Israelology further stresses the nature of the kingdom that Jesus offered. It was not merely a spiritual kingdom, but a literal earthly kingdom. Furthermore, the earthly ministry of Jesus was primarily to Israel (Matt. 15:24), and He was sent to Israel as Savior (Acts 13:23). For that reason, during His public ministry He forbade disciples to go to the Samaritans and Gentiles but limited their ministry to the lost sheep of the house of Israel (Matt. 10:6).

In the realm of pneumatology, the primary element of Israelology emphasizes that in the future there will be an outpouring of the Holy Spirit upon the whole nation of Israel, leading to Israel's national salvation just preceding the Second Coming (Isa. 32:15; 44:3; Ezek. 39:29; Joel 2:28; Zech. 12:10).

In the realm of angelology proper, Israelology points out that Michael, as the archangel, also happens to be the chief prince of Israel and, therefore, the guardian prince over the people of Israel (Dan. 10:13, 21; 12:1).

In Satanology, Israelology emphasizes that Satan has a special antagonistic war against the Jews, and his goal is to try to destroy the Jews in order to prevent the Second Coming from taking place. That is why, during the Tribulation, his primary activity will be to try to destroy Israel once and for all (Rev. 12:6–17). He will be the one to gather the Gentile armies against the Jews in the campaign of Armageddon (Rev. 16:12–16). Furthermore, Satan is continually before the throne of God accusing the Jewish people (Zech. 3:1–2).

Israelology makes no particular contribution in the realm of anthropology, but in the realm of hamartiology, Israelology primarily focuses on the unpardonable sin and the blasphemy of the Holy Spirit, pointing out that, in context, it is the national rejection by Israel of the messiahship of Jesus while He was present, on the basis of accusing Him of being demon possessed. This led to the rescinding of the messianic kingdom offer and the introduction of the mystery kingdom. It led to radical changes in Jesus' ministry for the remainder of His time on earth. It led to the judgment of A.D. 70.

In the realm of soteriology, Israelology points to John 4:22 where it is declared that salvation is from the Jews. In regard to the content of faith, Israelology insists that one not read the New Testament back into the Old. While salvation was always by grace through faith, the content of faith changed based upon what God had revealed up to that point. Israelology also concerns itself here with Israel's national salvation that will precede the Second Coming. Furthermore, it emphasizes the fact that when Messiah died, the Law was rendered inoperative. In contradiction to those who hold limited atonement and base their argument on Matthew 1:21 ("His people"), Israelology points out that these are terms that are used of Israel, both elect and nonelect.

In the realm of ecclesiology, Israelology insists on the distinction between Israel and the church and denies that the church is Israel or spiritual Israel or that the church is the Israel of God. While the church is partaking of the spiritual blessings of the Jewish covenants, it is not replacing Israel in those covenants. A major purpose of the church is to provoke Jews to jealousy (Rom. 11:11–14) and to carry out the Great Commission (Matt. 28:18–20), but it must be carried out in the procedure of "to the Jew first" (Rom. 1:16). Furthermore, Gentile believers in the body have a special responsibility in supporting Jewish ministries in a financial way (Rom. 15:25–27).

Finally, in the realm of eschatology, this is a place where Israelology plays a major role.

See also ABRAHAMIC COVENANT; ISRAEL AND THE CHURCH: THE DIFFERENCES; THEOCRATIC KINGDOM.

Arnold G. Fruchtenbaum

Arnold G. Fruchtenbaum, *Israelology* (Tustin, Calif.: Ariel Ministries, 1989).

J

JAMES, ESCHATOLOGY OF

The epistle of James focuses on the practical model of Christian conduct. The author's purpose was to rally Christians around the pragmatic privileges of their faith and turn them from worldliness. The epistle is both an interpretation of the Old Testament law (references or allusions to twenty-two Old Testament books) and the Sermon on the Mount (fifteen indirect references to the teachings of Christ in the Sermon on the Mount). The book was written primarily to Christian Jews (1:1) who were dispersed throughout the Roman Empire. The overall purpose is to implore the early believers to pursue Christian maturity and holy lives. The epistle presents moral and ethical teachings that are timeless for the church.

The author is traditionally identified with James the Lord's brother. The language used in the epistle is similar to the speech of James recorded in Acts 15. The book of James was written A.D. 45–50.

There are two prophetic references to the coming of the Lord in this epistle. The first speaks of a crown of life that is promised as a reward to those who are faithful to the Lord (1:12). The crown is eternal life, a gift to all those who love God. Although neither human love nor faith gains eternal life, it is an axiom of the Bible that God has abundant blessings in store for those who persevere in their love for Him in spite of the cost.

The second prophecy concerns the believers as they wait for the coming of the Lord (5:7–9). The focus is placed on the end of the race the believer is running. James exhorts believers to be patient and persevere in their cultural situation until Christ comes. The nature of patience is seen in the example of the farmer who must wait for the rain to water the crop and for the crop to complete it's growing process to maturity for the harvest. It is a strong call to the believer to be faithful in service for the Lord and in the endurance of suffering. There is anticipation of the Rapture found in verse 9. Feelings of impatience, complaining, and grumbling invite judgment from the Lord. The bema seat, where each believer will give an account to Christ the righteous judge, is clearly in view here. Patience and perseverance ought to replace dissatisfaction as the believer's eternal condition has been secured by Christ.

See also JUDGMENTS, VARIOUS.

Rick Bowman

John F. Walvoord, *The Prophecy Knowledge Handbook* (Wheaton: Victor Books, 1990); John F. Walvoord and Roy B. Zuck, eds., *The Bible Knowledge Commentary* (Wheaton: Victor Books, 1985).

JEREMIAH, ESCHATOLOGY OF

Summary of the Theology of Jeremiah

Jeremiah announced that, after purifying the nation by means of the "time of Jacob's trouble," the Lord would again have compassion on His people after His anger cooled. He would implement the new covenant, regenerating the entire nation and giving them a new heart to repent and genuinely obey Him forever. The Lord will bring the redeemed of Judah and Israel back to the land in a second exodus when they have met the conditions of national repentance.

National Israel yet awaits the fulfillment of the eschatological expectations of Jeremiah, which will not be fulfilled until the Second Coming. A new time of Jacob's trouble (Dan 12:1; Matt 24:21) will drive Judah and Israel to repentance during the future Tribulation (Joel 2:28–32; Zech. 12:10–13:1; Rom. 11:25–26; Rev. 7:1–8; 14:1–5). When Christ returns, He will gather

Judah and Israel from the four corners of the earth (Matt. 24:31) in the glorious second exodus and then inaugurate the eternal messianic kingdom (Rev. 20:1–22:17).

Historical Background of Jeremiah

Jeremiah had predicted that the Babylonian exile would last seventy years, to be terminated with the destruction of Babylon (Jer. 25:11–12; 29:10). In fulfillment of this, Cyrus II (559–530 B.C.) conquered Babylon and inherited its provinces in 539 B.C. As recorded in the Cyrus Cylinder, he issued a decree in 539 B.C. allowing the exiled peoples of all nations to return to their homelands to rebuild their temples and worship their gods, so their gods might show him favor (2 Chron. 36:22–23; Ezra 1:1–4).

God's Judgment of Judah and Jerusalem

The Time of Jacob's Trouble: History and Eschatology

Jeremiah described the Babylonian exile as the time of Jacob's trouble, out of which the exiles eventually will be saved (30:7).

Note: The destruction of Jerusalem in A.D. 70 foreshadowed the future destruction of Jerusalem, as indicated when Jesus merged these two events in the Olivet Discourse (Matt. 24:4–31) in response to the question: "When will this happen [destruction of Herod's temple], what will be the sign of Your coming and of the end of the age?" (Matt. 24:3). This typological scheme is consistent with the frequent depiction in the prophets of the repetition of the acts of God: Because God does not change, His mighty deeds done in the past will be repeated in the future. Likewise, the abomination of Antiochus Epiphanes in 168 B.C. (Dan 11:31) foreshadowed the abomination of Titus in A.D. 70 (Matt. 24:15), which, in turn, foreshadowed the ultimate future abomination of the Antichrist (Dan. 12:11; Matt. 24:15; 2 Thess. 2:4; Rev. 13:14–15).

The Future Restoration of Israel and Judah

Jeremiah's portrait of Judah and Jerusalem's future was not entirely doom and gloom. Days were coming when God would have compassion on His people and restore their fortunes. When they met the covenant condition of national repentance, He would implement a new covenant that would purify them from stubbornness and enable them to obey Him fully. As the sovereign Creator, He would remove the yoke of Babylon and judge hostile nations surrounding Israel. The Lord would restore His people to the land in a second exodus, rebuild Jerusalem beyond its former glory, and reunite Judah and Israel. He would then fulfill His covenant promises to David and Phineas through an ideal Davidic king and a purified Levitical priesthood.

Restoration of the Land: Fulfillment of the Abrahamic Land Promises

Although the Lord would uproot the people from the land by the Babylonian exile (1:10; 12:14–17;18:7–10), He promised to plant them back in the land after seventy years (24:6). He would restore the land promised to Abraham, Isaac, and Jacob (30:4) and possessed during the united monarchy (16:15). The exiles would be returned to "this land" (24:6; 32:41, 43) and "their own land" (23:8). He would plant them back in the very land from which they were exiled (31:27; 32:41).

God will restore the land of Judah (31:2; 32:44; 33:12–13) and Israel (31:5, 17). The Israelites will again plant vineyards on the hills of Samaria and enjoy its fruit (31:5). Like sheep they will graze on the fertile lands of Carmel and Bashan, and their appetite will be satisfied on the lush mountainsides of Ephraim and Gilead (50:19). The Judahites will again pasture their flocks in the hill country of Judah, the territory of Benjamin, Shephelah, Negev, and the villages around Jerusalem (33:12–13).

The Lord will fulfill the land promises in the Abrahamic and Davidic covenants. He will give them the land promised to Abraham, Isaac, and Jacob (30:4) and plant them in the land (24:6; 31:27; 32:41) as promised to David (2 Sam. 7:10). The land promises will be fulfilled when the new covenant is fulfilled for Judah and Israel (32:41).

Restoration of Davidic Rule

In a reversal of judgment, Jeremiah announced that after the second exodus (23:3–4), the Lord will raise up a righteous Branch from David whom He will place on David's throne (23:5-6) in fulfillment of the Davidic covenant (2 Sam. 7:12). In contrast to the unjust Davidic kings of Jeremiah's day, He will fulfill the covenant requirement (22:1–4) by ruling in wisdom, justice, and righteousness (23:5). While the sin of the last preexilic kings led to the destruction of Jerusalem and exile of Judah (22:5–30), His righteousness and obedience will lead to the restoration and deliverance of Judah/Israel (23:6). His royal name will be "The Lord our Righteousness/Deliverance" (23:6). The deliverance of Judah and Israel provided by the ideal Davidic king (23:6) is associated with the deliverance of the Israelites during the glorious second exodus (23:7–8).

Renewed Covenant Relationship with God: The New Covenant

The highlight of the eschatology of Jeremiah is the new covenant (31:31–34; 32:40; 50:4–5). In contrast to the Mosaic covenant, which Judah and Israel violated throughout their history, YHWH will inaugurate a new covenant (also called an "everlasting covenant") with Judah and Israel at the time of the second exodus (31:31–34; 32:37–41; 50:4–5). This will happen in conjunction with the future national repentance when Judah and Israel will bind themselves to YHWH in a new covenant relationship that will last forever (50:5).

The new covenant will provide forgiveness superior to the Levitical system (31:34). The Lord will cleanse and forgive Judah and Israel from all their sin and rebellion (33:8). A. search will be made for their guilt, but none will be found for God will completely forgive them (50:20). The Mosaic covenant wrote God's Law on stones; the new covenant will write it on the heart (31:33).

In the new covenant God will give Judah and Israel singleness of heart and action to fear Him always and never turn away from Him (32:39–40). Through it the Lord will give His people a heart to know Him, that He is YHWH (24:7). Subsequent revelation explains that this work of the new covenant will occur through the Spirit (Ezek. 36:24–28).

The new covenant will cause the regeneration of the entire nation (31:34). YHWH will provide forensic salvation for the entire nation and bring them into perfect covenant fellowship with Him (31:33). Unlike the Mosaic covenant that the nation repeatedly violated, the new covenant relationship will be kept intact forever, and will realize the goal of the covenant relationship: "They will be my people, and I will be their God for they will return to Me with all their heart" (24:7). Just as YHWH, the covenant-keeping God, promised Moses that He would be with him (Exod. 3:12), YHWH will be with Judah and Israel (30:11; 46:28).

In contrast to the Mosaic covenant in which God's blessings were parceled out based on the condition of Israel's wavering obedience, the new covenant will provide that the Lord will never stop doing good and blessing Israel (31:40) because it will provide consistent obedience for Israel. The new covenant will guarantee that the existence of Israel and Judah before God will be as permanent as His covenant with creation (31:35–37). God will never subject Israel and Judah to exile again (31:37)

The new covenant differs from and superses the Mosaic covenant (31:32). The difference will not be in a change of the basic demands of the covenant, but in the people's ability to obey those commands (31:33; 32:39–40). Under the Mosaic covenant, Israel continually rebelled and violated the covenant demands. In the new covenant God will not only forgive their former sins, but give them the ability and desire to obey Him fully. Under the old covenant, the Israelites needed to exhort one another to obey the Lord because they were prone to wander away from Him. However, the new covenant will render this unnecessary because every Israelite will know and fear the Lord and have the desire and ability to obey Him eternally (31:34; 32:40).

It is true that the new covenant was originally promised to Israel (Jer. 31:31–34) and that the church is presently participating in new covenant blessings (2 Cor. 3:4–6). However, amillennialists and covenant theologians erroneously conclude from this that the church has become Israel or replaced Israel. Rather, Gentile believers have merely become co-heirs with Jewish believers in the new covenant (Eph. 3:2–6).

The Old Testament itself promised that believing Gentiles would participate in new covenant blessings while remaining distinct from Israel (e.g., Isa. 56:3–8). The relationship of the new covenant to the Abrahamic covenant implicitly guarantees that believing Gentiles will receive new covenant blessings, while remaining distinct from Israel. The new covenant blessings are the ultimate fulfillment of the Abrahamic covenant promise of blessing (Isa. 44:3). The Abrahamic covenant promise of blessing for the Gentile nations (Gen. 12:3) finds its ultimate fulfillment in the new covenant blessings for believing Gentiles (Gal. 3:6–9). Paul did not relate new covenant blessings to Gentiles to the Abrahamic blessings for the physical seed of Abraham (Gen. 12:2), but to the universal blessings for the nations (Gen. 12:3).

See also ABRAHAMIC COVENANT; DAVIDIC COVENANT; NEW COVENANT.

Gordon H. Johnston

P. R. Ackroyd, "The Book of Jeremiah: Some Recent Studies" in *JSOT,* 28 (1984); A. Auld, "Prophets and Prophecy in Jeremiah and Kings" in *ZAW,* 96 (1984); J. R. Bright, "An Exercise in Hermeneutics: Jeremiah 31:31–34" in *Interpretation,* 20 (1966); W. Brueggemann, "Jeremiah: Intense Criticism/Thin Interpretation" in *Interpretation,* 42: 268–80 (1988); R. P. Carroll, *From Chaos to Covenant: Uses of Prophecy in the Book of Jeremiah* (London: SCM Press, 1981) and *Jeremiah: A Commentary* (Philadelphia: Westminster, 1986); R. B. Chisholm Jr., "A Theology of Jeremiah and Lamentations" in *A Biblical Theology of the Old Testament*, ed. R. B. Zuck, et al. (Chicago: Moody Press, 1991), 341–63; R. E. Clements, *Jeremiah* (Atlanta: John Knox Press, 1989); J. L. Crenshaw, "A Living Tradition: The Book of Jeremiah in Current Research" in *Interpretation,* 37 (1983); W. L. Holladay, *The Architecture of Jeremiah 1–20* (Lewisburg: Bucknell University Press, 1976) and *A Commentary on the Book of the Prophet Jeremiah* (Philadelphia: Fortress Press, 1986); J. G. Janzen, *Studies in the Text of Jeremiah* (Cambridge: Harvard University Press, 1973); W. C. Kaiser Jr., "The Old and the New Covenant: Jeremiah 31:31–34" in *JETS,* 15 (1972); J. R. Lundblom, *Jeremiah: A Study in Ancient Hebrew Rhetoric* (Missoula: Scholars Press, 1975); J. Lust, "'Gathering and Return' in Jeremiah and Ezekiel" in *BETL,* 5 (1981); W. McKane, *A Critical and Exegetical Commentary on Jeremiah* (Edinburgh: T&T Clark, 1986); R. Paterson, "Reinterpretation in the Book of Jeremiah" in *JSOT,* 28 (1984); L. Perdue, "Jeremiah in Modern Research: Approach and Issues" in *A Prophet of the Nations: Essays in Jeremiah Studies*, eds. L. Perdue and B. Kovacs (Winona Lake: Eisenbrauns, 1984), 1–32; J. A. Thompson, *The Book of Jeremiah* (Eerdmans: Grand Rapids, 1980); E. Tov, "The Literary History of the Book of Jeremiah in the Light of its Textual History" in *Empirical Models for Biblical Criticism*, ed. J. Tigay (Philadelphia: University of Pennsylvania Press, 1985).

JERUSALEM IN BIBLICAL PROPHECY

Jerusalem is the preeminent city of all cities, both prophetically and historically. Though for the most part serious study concerning Jerusalem has concentrated on its historical/political significance, the place that the city of Jerusalem holds in the prophetic Scripture is much larger than is commonly conceived. Jerusalem, by that name alone, is expressly named over eight hundred times in the biblical record, besides its many occurrences under various other names. Under one name or another Jerusalem appears in about two-thirds of the books of the Old and almost one-half of the books of the New Testament. Researchers have found 465 verses in the Old Testament and 24 in the New Testament that speak of the future of Jerusalem subsequent to the time of the utterances. This, of course, does not include the literally thousands of verses narrating the events that have occurred there or yet will. When the city is studied with regard to its prophetic significance what is discovered is not a conglomerate of disassociated events or notations but rather a connected and progressively unfolding theme, a theme inseparably related to God's purposes for the nation of Israel. As such it presents a strong case for the premillennial, pretribulational, dispensational system and offers a marvelous exhibition of the literal fulfillment of prophecy to its smallest details.

Drawing upon the earliest notations and prophecies concerning Jerusalem (Melchizedek and Salem, Abraham at Moriah, the future place of the sanctuary as prophesied in Deuteronomy 12, and the siege of Sennacherib) certain prophetic themes concerning Jerusalem are brought forth that occur again. Among the more significant of these are the city's relationship to God, its associations with righteousness, peace, worship, sacrifice, and joy and its sad acquaintance with military siege. From its earliest mention as Salem (Gen. 14), the city is seen to possess a distinct relationship to Jehovah, through Melchizedek. The city is signified as the city of righteousness, peace, and worship and as the possessor of the king-priest. These characteristic themes of Jerusalem are seen to be constantly associated with the city to lesser or greater degrees throughout its entire history and on into the future. It is significant to note, and it was not without purpose, that with this first recorded mention of the city it is associated with Abraham, the recipient of God's covenant and the father of the Israelites, whose eternal capital Jerusalem was to become. Likewise the second mention of Jerusalem, as Moriah, involved Abraham (Gen. 22). With this event another major theme, only implied on the first occasion, is here clearly presented, the theme of sacrifice. This theme, central to the whole purpose of Jerusalem, is further amplified in the third reference to the city in Scripture, concerning the law of the central sanctuary. Deuteronomy 12 specifies that there was one place where sacrifices were to be offered. It would be that place that Jehovah would choose, that would become His habitation and the place of His name. The earliest theme of worship is here repeated with the added aspect of joy. This line of prophecy finds fulfillment at the completion of the temple in Jerusalem when the visible sign of God's presence descended there. Jerusalem as the capital of the nation became the recognized abode of God's presence, the one place where sacrifices were to be offered, the center of worship, and the city of righteousness experiencing wonderful peace and joy. Later, when the boastful Sennacherib besieged the city (2 Kings 18, 19; 2 Chron. 32; Isa. 36–37) Jerusalem was delivered by supernatural intervention, a foreshadowing of the greater deliverance from the future destroyer who purposes to withstand the holy God and crush His chosen city.

The city might have continued to experience the blessings and protection of Jehovah had it not played the harlot and continued in the progress of its sin. Its love of idolatry and wickedness and refusal to return despite long and repeated warnings and invitations left no alternative but that judgment should fall upon the city as God raised up the Chaldeans. In exact fulfillment of a multitude of detailed prophecies, the city was destroyed and the people were deported (2 Kings 25). This event marked the beginning of an extended time period designated by Christ as the Times of the Gentiles (Luke 21:24). This period has now covered well over two thousand years and will continue so long as Jerusalem remains under the heel of Gentile domination. Its beginning was marked by the fall of Jerusalem to the first great Gentile world powers; its end will be marked by the deliverance of the city from the last Gentile world power by the greater power of the returning Christ at His Second Advent.

With the restoration of Israel to the land after the Babylonian captivity and, more particularly, with the rebuilding and restoration of the city, the beginning of another significant prophetic time period is marked. This is connected with the prophecy of the seventy weeks of Daniel 9, which provides a prophetic chronology of Israel's history during the Times of the Gentiles. The fact that Jerusalem marks the various breaks of this period is unmistakable and again highly significant as a marker of prophetic fulfillment. In the first sixty-nine weeks the two prophecies concerning the deliverance of Jerusalem from Alexander the Great (Zech. 9:1–8) and the suffering of Jerusalem under Antiochus Epiphanes (Dan. 11:21–31) find their fulfillment, again in exact detail. These occur in the period between the Testaments. During the period of our Lord's life upon the earth two more prophecies find their fulfillment. The first (Zech. 9:9), what is usually called the "triumphal entry," marks to the exact day the completion of the first sixty-nine weeks. The second of these, that concerning His death in Jerusalem, actually occurs after the end of the first sixty-nine weeks (Dan. 9:26).

The interval between the sixty-ninth and seventieth weeks is marked by only two prophecies involving Jerusalem. The first (Dan. 9:26), the cutting off of Messiah, His crucifixion, was the action on the part of the nation as a result of their rejection of the Messiah. This was also in fulfillment of the often repeated prophecies of Jesus Himself. The second (Dan. 9:26), the destruction of Jerusalem by the Romans in A.D. 70, was the action on the part of God as a result of the nation's rejection of the Messiah. This too occurred in fulfillment of Christ's declarations. The remainder of this still continuing interval is marked by prophetic silence so far as any specific prophecies concerning Jerusalem. Since God is not dealing directly with His chosen covenant people there is no necessity of prophetic declaration concerning that city which is inseparably related to the fulfillment of His promises to that people. However, the renewed prominence of Jerusalem in this present age is apparently setting the stage for future fulfillments of prophecies concerning this city.

When the Seventieth Week of Daniel 9 begins, it will be marked by the prominence of Jerusalem. In consequence of Israel's covenant with the Antichrist the city will not only be in the possession of the Jews, but will be at peace, with a rebuilt temple and the reinstitution of sacrificial worship (Dan. 9:27; 12:11; Matt. 24:15; Mark 13:14; 2 Thess. 2:4; Rev. 11:1–2). But the time of peace will be brief, for after three and one-half years the Antichrist will break the covenant, move against the land, situate himself in the temple, and make Jerusalem his world capital. The martyrdom of the two witnesses at Jerusalem near or at the end of the Tribulation (Rev. 11:3–12) clearly reveals that the city will not have yet become what God had promised it will be. Rather than being the city of righteousness, the holy city, it will reveal itself as still the wicked city that continues to reject God's messengers as it has always done. The conclusion of the Seventieth Week is marked by events at Jerusalem when the forces of the Antichrist in conjunction with the armies of the East will put the city under siege (Zech. 12, 14). It is then, when the nations are gathered against the city to crush it once and for all, that Messiah returns, delivers the remnant, destroys the enemy, and brings the Gentile domination of Jerusalem to an end. The Times of the Gentiles, as well as the seventy weeks, will have been brought to completion.

Earthly Jerusalem (as distinct from the heavenly New Jerusalem, Rev. 21:9–22:7) will continue into the Millennium. It will be then that the long-awaited promises connected with that city will find their fullest realization (e.g., Isa. 2:2–4; 60:1–20; 62:1–7; Micah 4:1–8; Zech. 14:10).

Spiritually, the city will be the holy city, the city of righteousness. It will be the city of Jehovah, for there once again the visible manifestation of His presence will be seen as Christ rules. It will be the city of worship, not only for Israel, but for all the nations.

Politically, it will be the center of the whole earth, for the Messiah King-Priest will reign from Jerusalem over all the nations. With no fear of an invader, Jerusalem will be the city of unconditional peace and joy, and with no lack of wealth, the glorious city will be the world's most prominent.

Physically, Jerusalem will be exalted above the surrounding area, enlarged greatly, beautified by the waters from the temple, and illuminated by the effulgent glory of the triune God. Interrupted only by Satan's final and futile attempt to destroy the city of God's choice and affection (Rev. 20:7–10), Jerusalem will continue on into all eternity (2 Chron. 33:4; Ps. 48:8; Joel 3:20; Micah 4:7) as the glorious holy city, the city of the Great King (Ps. 48:2; Matt. 5:35).

See also DANIEL, ESCHATOLOGY OF; MICAH, ESCHATOLOGY OF.

Harold D. Foos

Harold D. Foos, *Jerusalem in Prophecy* (doctoral diss., Dallas Theological Seminary, 1965); Lewis Bayles Paton, *Jerusalem in Bible Times* (Chicago: The University of Chicago Press, 1908); J. Simons, *Jerusalem in the Old Testament* (Leiden: E. J. Brill, 1952); George Adam Smith, *Jerusalem* (London: Hodder and Stoughton, 1907).

"JESUS," THE NAME

"Jesus" was the given name of the Lord Jesus Christ. The angel Gabriel commanded His mother Mary, "you shall call His name Jesus." It is the name used most commonly throughout the Gospels, nearly six hundred times, while "Jesus Christ" is used just four times and "Lord Jesus," two times; thus it is the name most natural to the gospel writers.

The name is a transcription from the Greek term, which itself is taken from the Hebrew for "Yehôshua'" (Exod. 17:10), also rendered "Yehôšsua'" (Zech. 3:1) and "Yēshûa'" (Neh. 7:7). One of Jesus' forefathers bore the name (Luke 3:29), as did a coworker of Paul (Col. 4:11) and the sorcerer at Paphos called "Bar-Jesus" (Acts 13:6), who some think was Jesus Bar Abbas, and so did five of the high priests.

Use of the name vanished in the Western world due to the hatred of the Jews and the reverence of the Christians. Interestingly, the Spanish-speaking people continue to use it today.

Since it was the name given to Him at His birth it relates especially to His human nature more than to His deity. It was given on the eighth day and by the command of God through the angel (Luke 1:31; Matt. 1:20–21; Luke 2:21). The occasional use of the name with place names, such as "Jesus of Nazareth" and "Jesus the Galilean" (Mark 1:24; 10:27; Matt. 26:69) also supports the human emphasis.

After the command to name the child Jesus, the angel Gabriel promised that Jesus would receive the throne promised to David (see THRONE OF DAVID) and would reign over the house of Jacob forever (Luke 1:32–33). He was the promised son of David destined to reign over the future millennial kingdom as well as over a future eternal kingdom. His kingly majesty was seen during His incarnation as the soldiers fell back when they came to arrest Him (Mark 14:50) and most of all in His majestic entrance into the city Jerusalem during the last week of His human life before His death and resurrection (Matt. 21:1–9; Mark 11:1–10; Luke 19:29–38). At His cross, the soldiers mocked Him as king of the Jews (Matt. 27:27–31; Mark 15:16–20; Luke 22:63–65); for that He was crucified (Matt. 27:11–12; Mark 15:1–5; Luke 22: 66–23:2); and a sign was attached to the cross saying that He was the King of the Jews (Matt. 27:11; Mark 15:26–32). The apostle, looking for His coming as King of Kings says, "even so, come Lord Jesus" (Rev. 22:20).

The word *Jesus* also means "deliverer." When the angel came to Joseph, the husband of Mary, he said, "You shall call His name Jesus, for it is He who will save His people from their sins" (Matt. 1:21). The name has particular significance because it represents the person of Jesus and what He can do. As the seventy disciples came back from their evangelistic tour of Galilee, they reported, "Lord, even the demons are subject to us in Your name." Peter told the cripple by the temple gate, "In the name of Jesus Christ the Nazarene—walk!" (Acts 3:6). Not only physical healing, but also spiritual salvation came through the name of Jesus; Peter told the Jews, "Repent, and let each of you be baptized in the name of Jesus Christ for the forgiveness of your sins." So the name Jesus is associated with great power both in physical and in spiritual deliverance.

So great was the power to be associated with the name Jesus that the angel Gabriel told Mary that the child "will be called the Son of the Most High" (Luke 1:32). Most directly the meaning of the Hebrew term translated Jesus is "Jehovah is my help" or "the help of Jehovah." So Gabriel further explained, "The Holy Spirit will come upon you, and the power of the Most High will overshadow you; and for that reason the holy offspring shall be called the Son of God" (Luke 1:35).

Because He was born by the Spirit of God and because the name Jesus is associated with the power of God, the name Jesus is used for the whole person, His deity as well as His humanity, in accomplishing the very works of God. Believers have come "to Jesus, the mediator of a new covenant, and to the sprinkled blood" (Heb. 12:24). "Jesus also, that He might sanctify the people through His own blood, suffered outside the gate" (Heb. 13:12). On this basis, as believers confess their sins to Jesus, "He is faithful and righteous to forgive us our sins and to cleanse us from all unrighteousness." Jesus not only provides salvation but He is the object of faith for salvation, for God is the "justifier of the one who has faith in Jesus" (Rom. 3:26). Progressive sanctification is provided by Jesus: "Always carrying about in the body the dying of Jesus, that the life of Jesus also may be manifested in our body" (2 Cor. 4:10); all believers have been enlisted in the service of Jesus: "For we do not preach ourselves but Christ Jesus as Lord, and ourselves as your bond-servants for Jesus' sake" (2 Cor. 4:5). The ultimate and final salvation will be provided by Jesus as well: "knowing that He who raised the Lord Jesus will raise us also with Jesus" (2 Cor. 4:14); all of which will be climaxed at the return of Jesus at the rapture of the saints in Christ: "For if we believe that Jesus died and rose again, even so God will bring with Him those who have fallen asleep in Jesus."

See also THRONE OF DAVID.

John H. Mulholland

O. Cullmann, *The Christology of the New Testament* (London: SCM Press, 1959); R. P. Martin, "Jesus Christ" in *ISBE* (Grand Rapids: Eerdmans, 1982).

JEWS, RETURN OF THE

The past and future history of Israel is one of the two great themes in the Bible, occupying over 80 percent of the text. (The other primary theme is the Messiah). The return of the Jews to their homeland is one of the most dramatic fulfillments of prophecy and the continuing operation of two of God's unconditional covenants, the Abrahamic and the Palestinian.

The Abrahamic Covenant

Six passages pertain to the Abrahamic covenant: Genesis 12:1–3; 12:7; 13:4–7; 15:1–21; 17:1–21; 22:15–18. Of particular significance is Genesis 15, which emphasizes the unconditional nature of the covenant and also lays out the boundaries of the Promised Land committed to Abraham's descendants.

The Abrahamic covenant is subsequently confirmed to Isaac (Genesis 26:2–5, 24) and then to Jacob (Genesis 28:13–15). Because this covenant is unconditional, it is still in effect, although largely unfulfilled. It was the basis of the Exodus from Egypt (Exod. 2:23–25; 6:2–8; Neh. 9:7–8; 1 Chron. 16:15–19; 2 Chron. 20:7–8; Ps. 105:7–12). Paul emphasizes its permanence (Gal. 3:15–18) and the author of Hebrews derived assurance of salvation on the basis of this covenant (Heb. 6:13–20). It is also the basis of the final restoration of Israel (Lev. 26:40–42).

The Palestinian Covenant

"Palestine" is an unfortunate term since it was the name given to the land by the Roman Emperor Hadrian after the second Jewish revolt under Bar-Kochba [A.D. 132–135] for the purpose of erasing any Jewish remembrance of the land as part of his policy to "de-judaize" the land. However, this is the common label for this critical covenant.

The Palestinian covenant is given in Deuteronomy 29:1–30:20. (It's distinctiveness from the conditional Mosaic covenant is highlighted in 29:1). It contains eight provisions: (1) Moses spoke prophetically of Israel's forthcoming disobedience to the Mosaic Law and the subsequent scattering (*diaspora*) over the entire world (29:2–30:1); (2) Israel will repent (30:2); (3) The Messiah will return (30:3); (4) Israel will be regathered (30:3–4); (5) Israel will possess the Promised Land (30:5); (6) Israel will be regenerated (30:6); (7) The enemies of Israel will be judged (30:7); and (8) Israel will receive the full blessings of the messianic kingdom (30:8–10).

Of special importance is that it affirmed Israel's title deed to the land. While enjoyment of the land is conditioned upon obedience, Israel's entitlement to the land is unconditional. This covenant was confirmed centuries later in Ezekiel 16:1–63, which also predicts the dispersion (16:35–52).

The dispersion and persecution of the Jews have been conspicuous facts of history since A.D. 70. The desolation of the land during this period is also a fulfillment of prophecy (Deut. 29:22–28). The miracle of the preservation of the Jew through the centuries has been a convincing testimony to the provision of God. Long before dreams of a Jewish homeland were possible, Leo Tolstoy wrote: "The Jew is the emblem of eternity. He whom neither slaughter nor torture could destroy; he whom neither fire nor sword, nor inquisition was able to wipe off the face of the earth; he who was the first to produce the oracles of God; he who has been for so long a time guardian of prophecy, and who has transmitted it to the rest of the world—his nation cannot be destroyed. The Jew is as everlasting as eternity itself."

As result of efforts of Theodore Herzl, William Hechler, and others before the turn of the century—and, strangely, the Holocaust—the reemergence of the state of Israel on May 14, 1948, is clearly a modern miracle, predicted five hundred years earlier by the prophet Ezekiel (Ezek. 37).

Regathered in Unbelief

A careful examination of Ezekiel 37 reveals that the Jews will be initially regathered in unbelief (v. 14). Other passages yield the same view: Ezekiel 20:33–38 draws a simile between the Exodus from Egypt and the future return; Ezekiel 22:17–22 speaks of regathering in preparation for judgment; and Ezekiel 36:22–24.

The regathering of Jews from lands all over the world is one of the dramatic trends of our time. The return of Ethiopians (Zeph. 3:10) and the Russian Jews (Jer. 23:7–8) have received particular attention in the news broadcasts.

Even the reemergence of the Hebrew language, resulting from the undertakings of Eliezer Ben Yehuda in the latter part of the nineteenth century, is a fulfillment of prophecy (Isa. 29:1–4; Jer. 31:23; Zeph. 3:9).

This regathering in unbelief occurs before the Great Tribulation (Zeph. 2:1–2; Dan. 9:27, et al.). One of the purposes of this period is to bring them to repentance and to prepare them for the kingdom.

One of the key prophetic milestones on the horizon is the rebuilding of the temple. Jesus, Paul, and John all refer to it precedent to the Second Coming (Matt. 24:15; 2 Thess. 2:4; Rev. 11:1–2). The preparations have already begun in anticipation of a literal rebuilding as the opportunity presents itself. This temple is assumed to be the one desecrated by the prince that shall come, the coming world leader commonly known as the Antichrist (Dan. 9:27; 2 Thess. 2:4, et al.).

Most authoritiees view the first regathering to be the return from the Babylonian exile, the final regathering being the second one (Isa. 11:11–12). This would make the current regathering extremely significant.

Others view the final regathering to be a second (international) regathering after regeneration (Isa. 11:11–12:6; Jer. 23:3–8; 31:7–10; Ezek. 11:14–18; Amos 9:14–15; Zeph. 3:18–20; Zech. 10:8–12).

New Testament Perspective

Israel is mentioned seventy-three times in the New Testament, each time referring to national Israel. (Galatians 6:16 is subject to some controversy; however, see Fruchtenbaum, 690–99.)

The future role of Israel, its regeneration, and the vindication of God's righteousness in His relationship to Israel are the subject of three chapters in Paul's definitive statement of Christian doctrine, the book of Romans (chaps. 9–11).

See also EZEKIEL, ESCHATOLOGY OF; ROMANS, ESCHATOLOGY OF.

Chuck Missler

Arnold G. Fuchtenbaum, *Israelology: The Missing Link in Systematic Theology* (Ariel Ministries Press, Tustin: Calif., 1989); Dave Hunt, *A Cup of Trembling* (Eugene, Oreg.: Harvest House, 1995); David Allen Lewis, *Can Israel Survive in a Hostile World?* (Green Forrest, Ariz.: New Leaf Press, 1993); Chuck Missler, *Expositional Commentaries*, various (Coeur d'Alene, Idaho: Koinonia House, 1992); Chuck Missler and Don Stewart, *The Coming Temple* (Orange, Calif.: Dart Press, 1992).

JOB, ESCHATOLOGY OF

Job lived in the patriarchal age, hence his book may well be the oldest in the Old Testament. The author of Job is unknown, although many have been suggested, ranging from Job, himself, to Elihu, Moses, Solomon, Isaiah, Hezekiah, Jeremiah, Baruch, and Ezra.

Job is the first in a series of five books known as the Poetic Books (Job, Psalms, Proverbs, Ecclesiastes, and the Song of Solomon). They link the past of the Historical Books to the future of the Prophetic Books. The Poetic Books emphasize a lifestyle of godliness. Unlike the Pentateuch and the twelve historical books, the Poetic Books do not enhance the story of the nation of Israel. Instead, they delve deeply into the crucial questions about pain, God, wisdom, life, and love, all in the present tense (*Talk Thru the Bible*).

The outstanding prophetic text in Job, to many, is that familiar place in chapter 19, where Job cries out, "For I know that my redeemer liveth" (v. 25), inferring the death and resurrection of the Messiah. However the immediate context of verses 23 and 24, along with the continuing stress in his discourses, emphasizes vindication rather than redemption. The Hebrew noun *go'al*, therefore, should be translated here: "I know that my vindicator liveth." And this translation is in keeping with the following context as well.

Continuing this thought, though seemingly forsaken, Job is unwavering in his faith in his living Vindicator, who will stand up as one does who undertakes the cause of another. Barnes further explains, "There is no necessary reference in this word (stand) to the resurrection." The simple meaning is, "he shall appear or manifest himself as the vindicator of my cause" (Hebrew).

Verse 26, according to Zuck, underscores the meaning, "after my skin (better) has been flayed, that is, after he has died . . . Job would see God. . . . But how could he say he would see the Lord in his flesh after he has just said he would die?" The answer is found in the Hebrew *min*. Zuck explains, "he meant he would see God 'apart from' any physical flesh at all (*min* normally means, without; cf. 11:15b), that is, in his conscious existence after death but before resurrection."

This point is reemphasized by Job in verse 27: "When I shall see for myself," "literally, 'I, even I, know,' and 'I, even I, will see' Him." Thus he will gaze on God for all eternity with his own eyes (either the eyes of his resurrected body, or figuratively the eyes of his soul).

Alden Gannett

Albert Barnes, "Job 19:25–29" and Roy B. Zuck, "The Certainty of Seeing God: A Brief Exposition of Job 19:23–29" in *Sitting with Job: Selected Studies on the Book of Job,* ed. Roy B. Zuck (Grand Rapids: Baker, 1992); Bruce Wilkinson and Kenneth Boa, eds., *Talk Thru the Bible* (Nashville: Thomas Nelson, 1983).

JOEL, ESCHATOLOGY OF

The name *Joel* means "Yahweh (the Lord) is God" and this prophetic book of the Hebrew Bible claims to have been received by Joel, the son of Pethuel (1:1). All that we know about the prophet we find in this book. The precise time of Joel's prophecies are unknown since there is no internal data that helps in definitely confirming the date. Conservative scholars seem split on the dating of the book. Some prefer an early date of approximately 835–796 B.C. during the reign of Joash (and regency of Jehoida, the high priest), based on internal evidence (the type of government implied, Amos's probable quoting from Joel and the enemies that are mentioned as threatening Judah), while others lean toward a late preexilic date (ca. 597–587 B.C.) or postexilic date of sometime after 516 B.C. Joel was a prophet to Judah and if one excepts the early date he would probably follow on the heels of Obadiah [(ca. 848–841 B.C.) although even these dates are debated among conservative scholars], Judah's previous prophet.

The theme of the book of Joel is the Day of the Lord. As Walvoord states, "The Day of the Lord refers to any period of time in which God deals directly with the human situation either in judgment or in mercy. The expression may refer to a specific day or to an extended period of time as in the Day of the Lord eschatologically which stretches from the Rapture of the church to the end of the millennial kingdom (1 Thess. 5:1–9; 2 Peter 3:10–13)." The purposes of the book are set forth by Jensen as follows: (1) to foretell coming judgments upon Judah for their sin; (2) to exhort Judah to turn their hearts to the Lord; and (3) to impress upon all people that this world's history will culminate in the events of the Day of the Lord [the eschatological Day of the Lord], when the scales of justice will finally rest. The book of Joel can be roughly divided in two sections: (1) Near-Future Prophecies (1:1–2:27) and (2) Far-Future Prophecies (2:28–3:21).

Near-Future Prophecies (1:1–2:27)

Chapter 1 starts with an appeal to the elders and all the inhabitants of the land (1:1). Joel asks them a series of rhetorical questions to force them to contemplate the devastation of the land (1:1). Then he follows with a description of an invasion of locusts (1:4). The locusts denude the land (1:4, 6–7). In 1:5–13 four different groups are called on to mourn the destruction: the drunkards (1:5–7), the land (1:8–10), the farmers (1:11–12) and the priests (1:13). Then, in verse 14, Joel calls on the priests to consecrate a fast and to cry out to the Lord in repentance. The tone of the chapter to this point and especially verse 14 reveals that the locusts had been used by God as chastisement for spiritual unfaithfulness (Deut. 28:38, 42). Drastic measures needed to be taken to prevent further chastisement from God (i.e., a holy fast, a sacred assembly, and crying out to the Lord). Joel warned of the impending Day of the Lord that may soon follow such destruction. This would have been logical since the Lord threatened such locust plagues along with exile and death as a result of disobedience (Deut. 28:15, 38, 42, 48–57, 64–68). Joel then returns to describe the aftermath of the locust army. Drought had also set in and Joel uses fire to symbolize the denuding effects on the land of the locusts and the drought conditions (1:16–20). The devastation of the locust plague is included here, no doubt, to foreshadow the coming destruction of the Assyrian invasion (Joel 2:1–11) and, in the context of the entire book, the apocalyptic period of the eschatological Day of the Lord (Isa. 2:12–22; 4:1–6; Ezek. 30:3; Rev. 6:1–19:21, etc.).

In Joel 2:1–11 more detail is given of the coming Day of the Lord mentioned in 1:15. The day will be characterized by darkness and gloom and clouds and thick darkness. As Chisholm states, "Darkness and clouds often associated with the Lord in His role as the mighty victorious Warrior (cf. Deut. 4:11; 5:22–23; Ps. 18:19, 11; 97:2) here symbolize both judgment and destruction (cf. Jer. 13:16; Ezek. 30:3, 18; 32:7–8; 34:12; Amos 5:18–20; Zeph. 1:15)." The army is described in verse 2 as a great and mighty people, and Joel uses the same symbol, a fire, as he used in chapter 1 to describe the utter destruction that is before them and behind them (v. 3). Joel goes on to describe their appearance in 2:4–6, as like war horses and like a flame of fire consuming the stubble. The people are in anguish and pale before them. The attack of the army is then described, setting forth its incredible discipline (vv. 7–8) and the strength and agility of the soldiers (vv. 7, 9). Joel closes by describing the cosmic occurrences that would accompany this Day of the Lord. As Chisholm states, "This cosmic response is a typical poetic description of the Lord's theophany as Warrior [cf. Jude 5:4; Ps. 18:7; 77:18; Isa. 13:13; Joel 3:16]. This invading army is referred to as "The Lord's army in verse 11, as He used the Assyrian army to discipline His people. Thus, the rhetorical question was appropriate, that is, "Who can endure it?" As Patterson points out, "Although Sennacherib failed to take Jerusalem in his third campaign. . . . is beside the point. Sennacherib reported that he had thoroughly devastated the land, though admitting he had failed to take Jerusalem." The passage was thus literally fulfilled in the Assyrian army's devastation of the land.

In 2:12–17 Joel calls for the one thing that can turn away the Day of the Lord: repentance. The people are called on to return to the Lord with fasting, weeping and mourning. Since the Lord is gracious and compassionate and slow to anger, abounding in loving-kindness, He relents of evil (the calamity He had determined for them) when repentance occurs. The elders, children and nursing infants, and bridegroom and bride are called on to come to the Lord, fasting, and to enter into a solemn assembly. Then the priests were to weep and cry out, "Spare Thy people, O Lord" (vv. 16–17. Joel's appeal is so that the nations will not erroneously conclude that the Lord was not powerful enough to save them.

Joel 2:18–27 records the response of the Lord to their repentance. It is difficult to tell whether this section refers to the historical fulfillment of Judah's return from Babylon or the yet future eschatological restoration of Israel. Statements that He would "never again make [them] a reproach among the nations" (v. 19) and "My people will never be put to shame" (vv. 26, 27) seem to refer to the eschatological fulfillment. It is possible, as some conservative scholars have suggested, that there is a merging of near future and far future prophecies as is seen in other places in Scripture (e.g., Isa. 9:6–7; 61:1–2; Zech. 9:9–10). The Lord will at that time destroy the northern army (v. 20) and it will be a time of incredible fruitfulness in the land (vv. 18–19, 21–27). There will be restoration from the devastation of the locusts, the great army (v. 25), and spiritual restoration since it will be very evident that the Lord "is in their midst" (v. 27). This was partially fulfilled in their return to the land from Babylon but ultimately will be fulfilled in their return to the land in the millennial kingdom.

Far-Future Prophecies (2:28–3:21)

In the last section of chapter 2 Joel turns to far-future prophecies. The first section of these prophecies deals with the promise of the Holy Spirit (2:28–32). In addition to the material fruitfulness from their repentance (2:18–27), the Lord will pour out His Spirit on all mankind (2:28). During this period there will be spiritual revival (prophesying, dreams, and visions). This will occur in the eschatological Day of the Lord and will also be accompanied by cataclysmic signs of judgment such as blood, fire, and columns of smoke. This refers to the great warfare that will take place at that time (Rev. 16:6; 19:17–21; cf. Ezek. 38–39). As well the sun will be turned into darkness and the moon into blood (2:31). It is uncertain what will cause this phenomenon. An eclipse has been suggested (cf. 3:15) or maybe an earthquake (cf. Jer. 4:23–24; Rev. 6:12–13). During this time in Jerusalem there will be some who escape. Those who call on the name of the Lord will be saved (2:32). Notice the context is the nation Israel. Paul uses this passage in Romans 10:13 to refer to the salvation of Jews and Gentiles as an analogy, not stating that the strict fulfillment of the passage was occurring. The salvation in this passage refers to those that physically survive because of God's protection of Jerusalem during this time, although the same will be saved spiritually also on the basis of their receiving their Messiah. In addition, Peter quotes Joel 2:28–29 on the Day of Pentecost as explaining the phenomena that was then manifested. Peter was only alluding to the similarity of the situation to Joel's prophecy, that being an outpouring of the Holy Spirit. This outpouring of the Holy Spirit is the only point of similarity with what Joel's prophecy described. Peter's quoting of Joel's prophecy proved to the audience that such an outpouring was possible since one had been prophesied by Joel. This will occur when the Holy Spirit will be poured out on all of Israel toward the end of the Great Tribulation.

In chapter 3:1–8, Joel's prophecy deals with accusation and judgment against the nations. In those days when the fortunes of Judah and Jerusalem are restored, the Lord will gather all the nations and enter into judgment with them there (3:1–2) because they have scattered His people among the nations and divided up His land (3:2). They had also turned God's people into slaves (3:3, 6). The Lord's judgment will occur in the valley of "Jehoshaphat" (the Lord judges) and at that time He will recompense the nations for their treatment of His people by selling the nations into slavery (3:8). There seems to have been a partial fulfillment historically when Antiochus III sold the people of Sidon into slavery in 345 B.C. and again when Alexander the Great enslaved the people of Tyre and Gaza in 332 B.C. The passage will ultimately be fulfilled when the Lord judges the nations at His Second Coming (Matt. 25:31–46).

In 3:9–17 Joel describes the eschatological Day of the Lord when the soldiers of the nations will be aroused and wil prepare for war (v. 9). Even the weak will feel mighty and all the surrounding nations will come to the valley of Jehoshaphat arrayed for battle (vv. 10–12). There the Lord will sit to judge the nations (v. 12). Joel, using the analogy of an agricultural harvest, describes the severity of the judgment. The overflowing of the vats probably symbolizes the blood of the wicked that are slaughtered at the judgment of the Lord (v. 13). This judgment will reveal that it is the Day of the Lord when the Lord will roar from Zion and utter His voice from Jerusalem (v. 16). The Lord's judgment will be preceded by the darkening of the sun and moon and the blotting out of the stars (v. 15). But during this time, the Lord will be a refuge and a stronghold for the Jews in Jerusalem (v. 16). At the Lord's Second Coming He will war against the enemies of Israel who have come against them (Zech. 12:9; Rev. 14:14–20; 16:16; 19:11–21) and they will be destroyed (Rev. 19:21).

Joel 3:17–21 speaks of a time when the Lord's people will know that He is the Lord their God (v. 17). The Lord will again dwell in Zion, His holy mountain, and so Jerusalem will be holy (v. 17; Zech. 8:1–8). The time will also involve unparalleled productivity in the land and a spring will flow from the house of God (v. 18; cf. Ezek. 47:1–12; Zech. 14:8). In contrast with the fertility of Judah, the lands of Egypt and Edom (historic enemies of Judah) will be desolate as payment for their harsh treatment of Israel (v. 19). Judah and Jerusalem will then be eternally inhabited by God's people (cf. Ezek. 37:25; Amos 9:15; Zech. 14:11) and the Lord will avenge the blood of those slaughtered by their enemies (vv. 20–21). In response to the Lord's destroying the enemies of Israel (vv. 9–16) Judah will recognize that He is the Lord their God (cf. 2:27). These events will occur at the second coming of Christ and His millennial reign.

See also ARMAGEDDON, BATTLE OF; DAY OF THE LORD.

Russell L. Penney

Gleason L. Archer, *A Survey of Old Testament Introduction* (Chicago: Moody Press, 1994); Robert B. Chisholm Jr., "Joel" in *The Bible Knowledge Commentary,* eds. John F. Walvoord and Roy B. Zuck (Wheaton: Victor Books, 1988); Irving L. Jensen, *Jensen's Survey of The Old Testament* (Chicago: Moody Press, 1978); Richard D. Patteron, "Joel" in *The Expositor's Bible Commentary,* vol. 7, ed. Frank E. Gaebelein (Grand Rapids: Zondervan, 1985); Merrill F. Unger, *Unger's Survey of the Bible* (Eugene, Oreg.: Harvest House, 1981); John F. Walvoord, *The Prophecy Knowledge Handbook* (Wheaton: Victor Books, 1990).

JOEL 2, ESCHATOLOGY OF

Although Joel's prophecies are undated, they arise out of the historical experience of the prophet. Joel chapter 1 describes a plague of locusts that has decimated the region. Throughout his description of this devastation, Joel calls his people to respond with sorrow (1:5, 8, 11) and with petitions to God (1:14). The plague is not accidental. God had vowed to bring such curses on Israel when they forsook the demands of the covenant (Deut. 28:15–20, 38–42). The goal of these judgments was to drive God's people to repent so that the covenant blessings might be restored (Deut. 30:1–10).

Bisecting Joel's description of this historic locust plague is a warning about a coming

"Day of the Lord" (1:15). In chapter 2 the prophet expands this theme. The locust plague of history (1:1–20) is used as the backdrop for announcing an eschatological day, a future time, when God will severely judge and then abundantly bless Israel. References to the Day of the Lord in chapter 2 most likely signify a time yet future—the consummate *eschaton*—for two reasons.

1. Joel's mention of the defeat of the northerner (2:20) seems to correspond with the battle recorded in Ezekiel 38–39 and Daniel 11:40–12:1. These texts describe an eschatological northern king, attended by a southern coalition, who will challenge the end-time Roman ruler (Dan. 11:40) by invading Israel (Ezek. 38:18; Dan. 11:41), one of Rome's allies (Dan. 9:27). After initial success (Dan. 11:42–43), the northern king and his army will be miraculously defeated by God in the coastal plains and the hills between Jerusalem and the Mediterranean Sea (Ezek. 39:4–11; Dan. 11:45; Joel 2:20). The destruction of the northern king occurs just before the middle of Daniel's Seventieth Week (Dan. 12:1; cf. Rev. 12:7–14) and allows the Roman ruler to initiate his atrocities unopposed (Dan. 12:1).

2. It appears that the prophecies of Joel 2 are still future since the blessings described in verses 18–27 have never been realized historically in Israel, particularly in connection with the promise of never-repeated national shame (Joel 2:19, 26–27). The blessings that are portrayed in Joel 2:18–27 are precisely the same as those blessings that Ezekiel connects with the ratification of the new covenant (Ezek. 34:25–31). These prophesied events are yet future.

Following the versification of the English Bible, Joel chapter 2 is comprised of four sections. First, Joel describes some of the terrors of the future "Day of the Lord" (2:1–11). Then the prophet calls the nation to repentance (2:12–17). Next, Joel announces some of the blessings that could result from Israel's repentance (2:18–27). Finally, the prophet summarizes, in reverse chronological order, two major features of the Day of the Lord: (1) the outpouring of the Holy Spirit and the miraculous signs that would follow the great judgments of that day ("after . . ." 2:28–29) and (2) the miraculous signs which would introduce the great and terrible Day of the Lord (before, 2:30–32).

Important to the last section of the chapter (2:28–32) is the chronology that is found in Joel's prophecy. The term "before" in verse 31 is clearly a chronological reference to the great and terrible Day of the Lord. However, the time to which the term "after" refers in verse 28 is more difficult to determine. Do the events in verse 28 chronologically follow the events in verses 18–27 simply on the basis of their literary arrangement? Some commentators suggest that the term "after" is a general, introductory or transitional word that is not intended to define a specific chronology in this passage. Others, who assert that the prophecy in Joel 2:1–27 is historically fulfilled in close proximity to the prophet's lifetime, believe that the outpouring of the Spirit in verse 28 could occur at any time "after" that historical fulfillment. However, if the prophecies of Joel 2:1–27 relate to a time yet future, as argued above, then a direct chronological connection between verses 18–27 and verse 28 seems unlikely. The outpouring of the Spirit and the revelatory signs mentioned in verse 28 cannot chronologically follow all of the promised blessings in verses 18–27 because those blessings are framed in terms of unending time, particularly the promise of uninterrupted national prosperity (vv. 19, 26–27). Among those who view the prophecies of Joel 2:1–27 as yet future, some assert that the referent "after" is meant to assume the content of verses 12–27 in general. This view suggests that as soon as Israel repents (vv. 12–17) and God begins to bless them (vv. 18–27), then God will pour out His Spirit upon them (v. 28). In a technical sense, this view must link the referent "after" to verse 17, for the outpouring of the Spirit will certainly come after Israel's repentance (vv. 12–17) but it cannot come after Israel prospers (vv. 18–25) to the extent of never being put to shame (vv. 26–27).

It seems most likely that the term "after" in Joel 2:28 refers back to the great and very terrible Day of the Lord in Joel 2:11. The verses between Joel 2:11 and 2:28 constitute a digression that bisects the first and last sections of the chapter (2:1–11; 2:28–32). In this digression (2:12–27), the prophet interrupts his description of the great and very terrible Day of the Lord with his call to repentance (2:12–17) and a forecast of blessings (2:18–27). Then, in verse 28, the prophet returns to his discussion of the great and terrible Day of the Lord, the theme that he was addressing in 2:11. A comparison of Joel 2:10–11 with Joel 2:30–31 strongly suggests that these two sections actually comprise a unit. The terms "earth," "heavens," "sun," "moon," "darkness" and the "Day of the LORD" which is "great and terrible" all serve as structural connectors between verses 10–11 and 30–31. Verses 28–29 are bound to verses 30–31 by the temporal referents "after" (v. 28) and "before" (v. 31). In his return to the theme of the great and terrible Day of the Lord, Joel informs his audience of events that would come "after" that day (vv. 28–29) and events that would come "before" that day (vv. 30–31). The section concludes with another call to repentance (v. 32).

The great and terrible Day of the Lord around which the events of Joel 2:28–32 center ("after . . . before"), is a specific segment of time within the broader Day of the Lord. This distinction corresponds precisely with the biblical referents *wrath* and *great wrath* or *tribulation* and *great tribulation*. The Scriptures support these distinctions. First, it is clear that the Seventieth Week of Daniel, the seven years of judgment that precede the coming of Messiah to establish His kingdom (Dan. 9:24–27), is divided into two equal periods (Dan. 9:27). Second, the major event that marks the midpoint of this "week" is the establishment of an "abomination" by one who "desolates" (Dan. 9:27). Finally, some very specific chronological referents, *time, times, and half a time, forty-two months,* and *one thousand two hundred and sixty days*, set apart the last half of Daniel's Seventieth Week as unique. During this period the final Roman ruler will persecute Israel "for a time, times, and half a time" (Dan. 7:23–25), which corresponds precisely with the "forty-two months" of the Beast's oppression of the saints (Rev. 13:5–8) and the fleeing of the woman (Israel) into the wilderness for 1,260 days or "time, times, and half a time" (Rev. 12:6–14; see Matt. 24:16). Rev. 12:6-14 identifies the midpoint of the Seventieth Week as that time when Michael casts Satan to the earth, a parallel to Daniel 12:1 where Michael, the protector of Israel, arises and the time of unprecedented trouble begins (see Dan. 12:7, "time, times, and a half"). Other events of this period include the forty-two months of Gentile dominion in Jerusalem (Rev. 11:1–2) and the 1,260-day ministry of the two witnesses (Rev. 11:3; cf. Mal. 4:5).

This final three and one-half year segment of Daniel's Seventieth Week, which is inaugurated by the setting up of the abomination, is specifically called the "great tribulation" (cf. Matt. 24:15 with 24:21), a time of "great wrath" (Rev. 12:12–14) and an "unprecedented time of trouble" (Dan. 12:1, cf. 7, 11). This period precisely mirrors Joel 2:11 and 31, the "great and terrible day of the LORD." Joel 2:30–31 indicates that specific signs, a darkened sun and bloodlike moon, will mark the inception of (*lip̄nê*, "before," lit. "at the turning of" or "face of") this great and terrible Day of the Lord (2:31). These are signs that immediately precede the last half of Daniel's Seventieth Week. These same signs are associated with the opening of the sixth seal (Rev. 6:12), which specifically indicates the coming of the great day of wrath (Rev. 6:17)—the same period during which a remnant of Jews is sealed (Rev. 7:1–8) while multitudes of other saints are persecuted and martyred under the duress of great tribulation (Rev. 7:9–14; cf 13:5–17).

The last three and one-half years of Daniel's Seventieth Week, then, equally are called "the great and terrible Day of the LORD," an "unprecedented time of trouble," "the great tribulation," "the great day of his wrath," and a time of "great wrath." Like Joel, other prophets frequently speak of this unbearable time of judgment in close proximity to the glorious advent of Messiah (Joel 2:31–32; Jer. 30:7–9; Dan. 7:25–27; 12:1; Amos 9:8–12; Obad. 15–17). The signs that mark this final, unprecedented judgment are also signs of Messiah's soon return, for God has specifically limited these incomparable judgments to a short (three and one-half year) period of time (Rev. 12:12; see Matt. 24:22; Rev. 6:11; 17:10).

After the great and terrible Day of the Lord (Joel 2:28), God will pour out His Holy Spirit on national Israel (Isa. 32:14–18; 44:1–3; 59:20–21; Ezek. 39:25–29). This supernatural event will be accredited by revelatory signs among Israel's youths and old men (2:28). This Spirit outpouring accompanies the ratification of the new covenant with those Jews in natural bodies who survive the Tribulation and the expulsion of unbelievers after Israel's regathering (Ezek. 20:33–38; 34:17–25; 36:24–27). Some suggest that Gentiles are included in this outpouring as the male and female servants of Joel 2:29. Others suggest that the outpouring is expanded to include Gentiles only in the New Testament. It is clear in both testaments that regenerated Gentiles who survive the Tribulation will also enter the restored kingdom in natural bodies (Matt. 25:31–34) and will be included as God's people under the patronage of Israel (Isa. 14:1–3; 19:16–25; 56:1-8; 60:1–16; Jer. 12:14–17; Amos 9:11–12; Micah 4:1–3; Zech. 2:11–13; 8:20–23).

Peter's quotation of Joel 2:28–32 on the Day of Pentecost has been variously interpreted. Some premillennialists suggest that Joel's prophecy was partially fulfilled or began to be fulfilled on the Day of Pentecost, though final, complete fulfillment awaits the Millennium. Other premillennialists suggest that none of Joel's prophecy was fulfilled on the day of Pentecost. It seems likely that Peter was fully aware of the chronology that is specified in Joel chapter 2, a chronology consistent with other Old Testament prophets. These prophets invariably taught that the outpouring of God's Spirit would follow unprecedented national judgment and the ensuing repentance of Israel (Isa. 32:9–18; 43:26–44:3; 59:1–21; Ezek. 39:25–29; Zech. 12:1–14). Knowing that none of these qualifying events had yet occurred, it seems most likely that Peter was citing Joel's prophecy as analogous to the events that the Jews had witnessed on the day of Pentecost. By this means, Peter was arguing that extraordinary revelatory activity (Joel 2:28; Acts 2:4–11) was objective evidence of the work of God's Spirit (Joel 2:28; Acts 2:4), not evidence of drunkenness (Acts 2:13–15). The quotation from Joel also gave Peter the opportunity to call his audience to a decision, for if the signs that the Jews had witnessed were indeed from God, then they should call upon the name of the Lord (Joel 2:32; Acts 2:21). Building on this thesis, Peter further asserted that God had confirmed the credentials of Jesus Himself by means of such supernatural miracles, wonders, and signs (Acts 2:22). The Jews had rejected that evidence as well (Acts 2:23). The final sign that they were given as miraculous confirmation of Jesus' messianic claims was His resurrection from the dead (Acts 2:24–36). That miraculous sign from God should certainly lead them to repent (Acts 2:37–39; cf. Joel 2:32).

See also DANIEL, ESCHATOLOGY OF; DAY OF THE LORD; JOEL, ESCHATOLOGY OF.

Roy E. Beacham

P. N. Benware, *Understanding End Times Prophecy* (Chicago: Moody Press, 1995); R. B. Chisholm Jr., "Joel" in *The Bible Knowledge Commentary* (Wheaton: Victor Books, 1985); R. B. Dillard, "Joel" in *The Minor Prophets*, vol. 1 (Grand Rapids: Baker, 1992); T. J. Finley, "Joel, Amos, Obadiah" in *The Wycliffe Exegetical Commentary* (Chicago: Moody Press, 1990); R. D. Patterson, "Joel" in *The Expositor's Bible Commentary*, vol. 7 (Grand Rapids: Zondervan, 1985); Charles C. Ryrie, "Joel" in *The Ryrie Study Bible* (Chicago: Moody Press, 1978); D. Stuart, "Hosea-Jonah" in *Word Biblical Commentary*, vol. 31 (Waco, Tex.: Word Books, n.d.).

JOHN, 1, 2 & 3, ESCHATOLOGY OF

John's first epistle was written to Christian readers. It warns against false teaching and encourages the believers to live obedient lives. John wrote this letter in answer to a growing philosophy that was the early beginnings of Gnosticism. This philosophy teaches that salvation is based upon knowledge alone. This heretical teaching had begun to make inroads into the church at Asia Minor. John's answer to this heresy was to emphasize the Incarnation and the example of Christ's physical life. This humanistic philosophy resulted in docetism (Christ only appeared to have a human body), asceticism (one can reach a higher spiritual state by rigorous self-discipline and self-denial), and antinomianism (the belief that because faith alone is necessary to salvation, the moral law has no use to or obligation on believers). The second epistle gives prominence to the commandment of love. It warns against false teachers (v. 7) and says that the heretics were to be treated sternly and without hospitality. The key phrase in this epistle is "the truth." The third epistle is an open indictment against the church for allowing Diotrephes, who had rejected apostolic authority, to exercise authority in the church. This letter stresses personal responsibility in a day of decline.

The authorship of all three epistles is traditionally assigned to John the apostle. The tone of these letters reveals that the author possessed spiritual authority as well as being an eyewitness of the incarnate life of Jesus Christ. Too, early Christian writers, including Irenaeus, Tertullian, and Clement of Alexandria, cite the apostle John as the author. All three letters were written in Ephesus about A.D. 90.

Of these three epistles, 1 John is the only one that contains any prophecy. The writer is primarily concerned with the Christian walking in fellowship with God the Father. First is seen the eternal character of the will of God set over against the temporary character of the things of the world (2:17). This is a warning against apostasy. Next a specific warning is given against the manifestations of the Antichrist (2:18). John warned against the appearance of many who would display hostility towards Jesus Christ. This warning is real and valid for today as the church anticipates the Rapture of the church and the second coming of Jesus Christ. In light of this, believers are encouraged to be diligent in serving the Lord so they will not be ashamed before Him at His coming (2:28). Believers are required to give an account of their lives to the Lord at the bema seat, where they will be judged concerning their works as believers. This judgment takes place in heaven after the Rapture and before the second coming. The judgment is necessary for the appointment of believers to positions of rule and authority that will be exercised with Christ in His role as King of Kings and Lord of Lords in His literal physical reign on the earth. This warning emphasizes the importance of living sanctified lives so that judgment will be favorable. Finally John gives the promise that the believer will be like Christ (3:2–3). When Christ appears the believer will see Him and will experience the transformation into a resurrected, glorified body in the same manner as Christ. The promise will be fulfilled at the rapture of the church to meet the Lord in the air (1 Cor. 15:51–58). This is where the believer will see Christ as He is in His glorified body. The world will not see the King until the glorious Second Coming.

These prophecies serve to connect the present Christian life with the hope (anticipation) of Christ's return when He will call the church out of the world to forever be with Him. The epistles of 2 and 3 John do not contain any prophecy.

See also ANTICHRIST; JUDGMENTS, VARIOUS.

Rick Bowman

Everett F. Harrison and Charles F. Pfeiffer, eds., *Wycliffe Bible Commentary* (Chicago: Moody Press, 1962); John F. Walvoord, *The Prophecy Knowledge Handbook* (Wheaton: Victor Books, 1990); John F. Walvoord and Roy B. Zuck, eds., *The Bible Knowledge Commentary* (Wheaton: Victor Books, 1985).

JONAH

When considering the message of this brief preexilic book, it is easy to focus on Jonah as the main character in the story; however, doing this causes the reader to miss the true protagonist, the Lord, Himself. It is the Lord who calls Jonah (1:2; 3:1), brings the wind (1:4), supernaturally identifies Jonah as the cause for the storm (1:7), rescues Jonah from certain death and transports him to dry land through the instrumentation of a huge fish (1:17; 2:10), is the object of Jonah's prayer for mercy (2:1–9); sends Jonah with a message to Nineveh (1:2; 3:1–4), relents of judgment against Nineveh because of their repentance (3:5–10), provides immediate shelter to protect Jonah from the torrid east wind (4:6), assigns a worm to destroy the vine that sheltered Jonah (4:7), and shows compassion on His creation (4:11). It is the Lord who initiates the events of this entire book with the purpose of teaching Jonah, and all subsequent readers, about His sovereignty over all creation and His distinctive right to love anyone and anything that He creates or chooses; after all, it is certain in Scripture that love is God's preferable or common association with humankind, while judgment could be described as His unwanted and uncommon association (Exod. 34:6–7).

Until the Lord returns, critical scholars will be striving with perpetual tenacity to reject the historicity of the book of Jonah: three days in the belly of a "great fish" is just too much for some to swallow (1:17). The size of Nineveh (inner city was two miles in diameter), a reference to the "king of Nineveh," the swift response of the Ninevites to Jonah's message, and the prompt growth of the vine to help cool Jonah appear to be insurmountable for many commentators. Each of these items can be easily explained by supernatural intervention (certainly not alien to the Old Testament), understanding the enormous population that existed in and around Nineveh proper and the time it would take to move about delivering a message to them (three days ministering throughout the "great city" could easily involve cities in close proximity to Nineveh, Gen. 10:11–12), and knowing that national kings sometimes identified themselves with their city of residence (Ahab is call the "king of Samaria," 1 Kings 21:1). With regard to this debate, premillennialists consistently maintain the historicity of the book without apology. The fact that Jonah is mentioned in 2 Kings 14:25 as a prophet to Israel during the reign of Jeroboam II gives us adequate reason to suggest that the events of the book of Jonah occurred between 794 B.C. and 753 B.C. Adding to this the fact that Jesus recognizes the historicity of Jonah (Matt. 12:39–41), there is little left to do than accept the story as actual and search for its gems. To understand Jonah's actions and emotions, it is important to appreciate the barbaric history of the Assyrian Empire and its dominance of the ancient world during the eighth century. Assyria was also the Lord's instrument of vengeance that Hosea and Amos (Jonah's contemporaries) predicted would destroy Samaria, a prophecy eventually realized in 722 B.C. The book clearly reveals that Jonah has little interest in seeing the Ninevites repent from their wicked ways and avoid the wrath of God (4:1–11). He would much rather they continue in their wickedness and reap the destruction he prophesied (3:4).

A brief warning concerning the tendency to see typology in Jonah revolves around the subjective nature that often accompanies typology. Though it may be intriguing to see correlation between Jonah's actions and that of the nation of Israel, extreme caution needs to be taken to ensure that the integrity and message of the text developed from sound and thorough exegesis is not sacrificed for theological possibilities.

Finding Jonah's obedience in the book absent or, at least, suspect, it seems wise to avoid dividing the book over the theme of his disobedience (Jon. 1–2) and his obedience (Jon. 3–4). A proposed outline that supports the concept of divine sovereignty in the realm of human affairs is: God's Call—Jonah's Rebellion (Jon. 1); God's Control—Jonah's Resolve (Jon. 2); God's Condemnation—Jonah's Response (Jon. 3); and God's Compassion—Jonah's Rejection (Jon. 4). In His own sovereignty, the Lord determines that He is going to send a prophet to warn Nineveh of its impending doom. The prophet He chooses is Jonah, a man committed to ministry in Israel (2 Kings 14:25) but not to her dreaded enemy, the Assyrians. Jonah rebels against God's plan and promptly flees east to Tarshish. The rebellion against an opportunity to preach judgment to an enemy seems strange and suggests that Jonah believed that Nineveh would respond to his preaching and avoid judgment, a possibility he was not prepared to accept. His reaction to their repentance in chapter 4 supports this conclusion. This rebellion cannot interrupt the plan of God, who creates a storm that convinces the Phoenician sailors that the gods are angry and need to be appeased. Through the casting of lots, the Lord directs the sailors' attention to Jonah, whose rebellion is responsible for the storm. Recognizing his inability to flee from the Lord, Jonah advises the sailors to cast him into the sea to his death; this is their only alternative if they hope to survive. Eventually they are forced to accept Jonah's counsel and he is thrown into the sea, an act that brings calm and some form of acceptance of Jonah's God. Jonah finds himself the victim of an object lesson for himself, and eventually the nation, that describes the Lord's commitment to share His grace with a Gentile nation; Jonah is in the stomach of a great fish for the purpose of reflection and transportation.

Chapter 2 describes the reaction of Jonah to God's determination to use him in sharing His message with Nineveh. No longer wanting to die (2:3–5), Jonah resigns himself to the fact that life is ultimately in the hands of the Lord, so he calls out to God for his rescue (2:6–9). Jonah's anger in chapter 4 is an indication that Jonah's prayer is not an act of full repentance, but rather a resolve or acceptance on his part of the sovereignty of God over his life. Mercy for Nineveh is not what Jonah desired for the Assyrian people. In spite of Jonah's attitude, the Lord continues to use him in His plan to show mercy to Nineveh and Jonah is conveniently deposited onto dry land (2:10). Chapter 3 announces God's initial intention of impending condemnation on the city of Nineveh: "Yet forty days [LXX reads three days] and Nineveh will be overthrown" (3:4). This time Jonah faithfully responded to God's call by proclaiming this message for one day throughout the city and its surroundings, but with an unexpected miraculous effect (3:5–10). The entire city, including the king, repented without hesitation. Chapter 4 describes Jonah's total rejection of the compassion the Lord conferred upon repentant Nineveh; he became so despondent that he reverted to his prefish experience, once again desiring to die rather than accept the sovereign initiatives of God (4:1–3). Graciously the Lord creates an environment within which He can explain to Jonah His love and compassion for not only the people of the world, but even animals. Jonah longed to see the plant restored to its healthy condition even though he had nothing to do with its life. How much more would the creator of the vine long for it's restoration? Every people is a creation of the Lord; it is not God's desire to single out one nation for spiritual restoration and to ignore the rest. Rather, He "is patient toward you, not wishing for any to perish but for all to come to repentance" (2 Peter 3:9). God's intentions are driven by love while Jonah's were driven by selfish concern. John D. Hannah describes Jonah as being more concerned for "personal comfort than for the spiritual destiny of thousands of people." Israel, as well as one of her prophets, had forgotten that a major purpose for the nation was to present the claims of the Lord faithfully throughout the world (Ps. 22:27–28; Isa. 49:6; 52:10). That Jonah ultimately understood his need to parallel his outlook of the world with God's is not found in the words of the text, but rather in the fact that he eventually recorded his experience.

The book does not describe prophetical events beyond it's own period; in fact, at the time of its writing the two prophecies were complete. Jonah's request that the sailors cast him into the sea immediately precedes the prophecy regarding the calming effect this action would take (1:12). This storm subsided, fulfilling the prophecy, when Jonah was thrown overboard. The second prophecy was conditional in nature; the Lord told Jonah to inform the Ninevites that their city would be destroyed in forty days. The prophecy was unfulfilled because the Ninevites repented of their wickedness.

Some scholars state that a third prophecy is recorded in Jonah 1:17 that looks to the supernatural character of the death and resurrection of Jesus (Matt. 12:39–41). However, this should not be considered prophetical as if it was written to predict the death of Messiah; rather, it is a portrayal or a type that Jesus alludes to that describes the interim between His death and resurrection. Luke's statement that "Jonah became a sign to the Ninevites" (Luke 11:30) implies that the Ninevites knew about his experience in the belly of the fish. It is not unreasonable to suggest that Jonah related the story of his rebellion and subsequent judgment to the people of Nineveh in order to legitimate the destruction they would soon receive for their rebellion. Their legend espouses the belief that Nineveh was founded by a fish-god; it is no wonder that the people took Jonah's message of judgment as a divine warning and responded so quickly. He was a sign of divine judgment against Nineveh in the same way that Jesus was a sign of judgment in His time. The people of Nineveh were able to see the sign of Jonah and repent; with the kingdom of God at their fingertips, the people of first-century Israel remained blind. Therefore, judgment is inevitable; first on Jesus, who will suffer death and the interim before the Resurrection to pay for the sin of humankind, and secondly, on anyone who continues to resist the sign of Jonah as declared in the person of Jesus Christ.

Gary P. Stewart

H. L. Ellison, "Jonah" in *The Expositor's Bible Commentary*, ed. Frank E. Gaebelein, vol. 7 (Grand Rapids: Zondervan, 1985); John D. Hannah, "Jonah" in *The Bible Knowledge Commentary*, eds. John F. Walvoord and Roy B. Zuck (Wheaton: Victor Books, 1985); A. Helmbold, "Jonah" in *The Zondervan Pictorial Encyclopedia of the Bible,* eds. Merrill C. Tenny and Steven Barabas (Grand Rapids: Zondervan, 1975); Eugene H. Merrill, "The Sign of Jonah" in *JETS,* 23/1, March 1980, 23–30; D. F. Payne, "Jonah" in *The Illustrated Bible Dictionary,* ed. J. D. Douglas, vol. 2 (Wheaton: Tyndale, 1980); John F. Walvoord, *Prophecy Knowledge Handbook* (Wheaton: Victor Books, 1990).

JOSHUA, JUDGES, RUTH, ESCHATOLOGY OF

These three historical books are from approximately the same time period. The books of Joshua and Judges record the conquest of the Promised Land and the repetitive pattern of apostasy, divine judgment, repentance, and restoration. The little book of Ruth presents a contrast to this period of strife and bloodshed.

Joshua

The name *Joshua* means "Jehovah saves," and it adequately describes the career of its author. The book demonstrates the faithfulness of God in keeping His promise to lead Israel into the Promised Land. Joshua is seen as a type of Christ, who is the vanquishing leader. The moral character of the Canaanites during this period had degenerated to the point where their religious practices were licentious and brutal. These rites included serpent worship, infant sacrifices, and prostitution of both males and females. It was this base conduct that caused God to command Israel to exterminate the Canaanites. Their destruction would prevent Israel's religious life from becoming defiled by coming in social and religious contact with these idolatrous people.

Authorship is ascribed to Joshua as the primary writer, with additions made by Eleazar the high priest and Phineas his son. Joshua did not write the entire book as his death is recorded in 24:29–30. In support of Joshua as the main writer it should be noted that (1) an eyewitness authored many parts of the book; (2) Rahab was still living (6:25), the Jebusites were still living in Jerusalem (15:63), archaic names were still being used, such as Baalah for Kiriath Jearim and Kiriath Arba for Hebron (15:9, 13); (3) there is reference that Joshua had written part of the book (8:32; 24:26). Too, there were events that did not take place until after his death. These include the conquest of Hebron by Caleb (15:13–14) and of Leshem by the Danites (19:47).

The date of the book is closely related to the events in the book because of the eyewitness accounts. The date is generally set at 1400–1370 B.C. The intent of the book is to set forth the authentic account of the fulfillment of the Lord's promise to give Israel the land of Canaan.

The prophecies contained in the book are directly connected with the historical narrative. The land promise was given to Joshua (1:1–9), the conquest of Jericho was prophesied (6:1–5) and fulfilled (6:6–27), and the conquest of Ai was promised and fulfilled (7:1–8:29). When Israel was deceived into a covenant with Gibeon they were forced to march against Gibeon's enemies (10:1–28). In verse 8, God gave those enemies into the hands of the Israelites. Joshua was given a message from God concerning the destruction of the northern kings (11:1–15) that was fulfilled the following day. The Lord did not fail in any of the promises that He gave concerning Israel's possession of the land.

Judges

This Old Testament book carries the history of God's chosen people from the death of Joshua to the time of Samuel, a period that covers about three hundred years. In general, the land had been conquered and occupied under Joshua, though there remained many Canaanite strongholds to be subjugated by individual tribes of Israel. Thus, the book sets forth the details of these conflicts as Israel completes the conquest of the land.

The judges were civil and military leaders who governed during this period. The intent of this book is to demonstrate that defection from Jehovah brings severe punishment. The judges ruled over the people and administered the government under guidance from God. The book reports on seven apostasies, seven periods of bondage, and seven occurrences of liberation.

There is no clear indication of who the author of Judges is. The date given for writing is after the coronation of Saul (1051 B.C.) but before the conquest of Jerusalem by David (1004 B.C.). The approximate date has been set at 1040–1020 B.C.

The prophecies in this book are concerned with this people and period. They are (1) victory over the Canaanites (1:1–8), Israel's chastening for disobedience (2:1–3; 20:20–23), victory over Sisera by Deborah and Barak (4:1–11), the selection of Gideon as a judge over Israel (6:11–24), the victory over Midian (7:1–25), and delivery from the Ammonites and Philistines (10:13–14; 11:1–40). The books of Joshua and Judges set the stage for Samuel, the first of the prophets. Judges contains the record of the moral and physical deterioration of the Israelites. Even though the hand of God is seen throughout this book, it is the story of human failure that is most notable.

Ruth

This book details the joys and sorrows of a godly family from Bethlehem. It stands in sharp contrast to the moral decay that prevailed during the period of the judges. Ruth, a Moabite, occupies an important place in the history of the Israelites by becoming an ancestor of King David (4:18–22) and of Jesus (Matt. 1:1, 5). The book is read annually by orthodox Jews on the Feast of Pentecost.

The date of the book is not known, though it is believed the book was written some time after the period of the judges, most probably during the reign of David. This is based on Ruth 4:6–8, where customs that were no longer practiced needed explanation, and upon the genealogy in 4:18–22. The author of the book is also not known although Jewish tradition attributes it to Samuel.

Rick Bowman

Everett F. Harrison and Charles F. Pfeiffer, eds., *Wycliffe Bible Commentary* (Chicago: Moody Press, 1962), John F. Walvoord, *The Bible Prophecy Handbook* (Wheaton: Victor Books, 1990); John F. Walvoord and Roy B. Zuck, eds., *The Bible Knowledge Commentary* (Wheaton: Victor Books, 1985).

JUDE, ESCHATOLOGY OF

Jude is one of the general epistles that deals with false teachers. Christians are urged to contend for the faith that was once for all delivered to the saints (v. 3). Jude uses harsh language to describe the destructive effects of false teaching. Although dealing with the conditions of that time, the book also comprehends conditions at the end of the church age, at which time false teachers prevail and apostasy is the path for many.

The author, Jude,was the brother of James and of Jesus. He was not an apostle and very little is known about him or his life. His authentication is found in the fact that he was a younger brother of Jesus Christ. The date for this book is commonly held to be between A.D. 67–80.

The prophecy is found in verses 14–15 in which a quote from Enoch is given that regards God's judgment upon the wicked. Enoch is an apocryphal book that also contains the prophecy found in Jude. The prophecy concerns the Lord's return to the earth with ten-thousands of His holy ones to judge and convict all the ungodly and their acts against God. A further prophecy is found in verses 24–25. Here believers are given full assurance that they can be kept from the deceitfulness and doctrinal error of the apostate teachers by the awesome power of God.

Rick Bowman

John F. Walvoord, *The Bible Prophecy Handbook* (Wheaton: Victor Books, 1990); John F. Walvoord and Roy B. Zuck, eds., *The Bible Knowledge Commentary* (Wheaton: Victor Books, 1985).

JUDGMENTS, VARIOUS

Although one general judgment, (into which several other judgments are merged), is often assumed by Christian theologians whose biblical interpretation is influenced by amillennial presuppositions, a thoughtful, inductive study of Scripture reveals a minimum of seven major divine judgments and as many as twelve well-defined judgments, depending on where one begins.

Postmillennialism, for example, holds to a general judgment of all people while Historic Premillennialism (nondispensational premillennialism) generally splits the general judgment into two phases, the Second Coming judgment and the judgment at the end of the Tribulation. Two passages of Scripture have been cited to support this position (Matt. 25:31–46; Rev. 20:11–15), and it is often concluded that the judgment of the nations, for example, is synonymous with the Great White Throne judgment.

The task of identifying and hermeneutically supporting the validity of these well-defined judgments has fallen to dispensational premillennialists. Walvoord, for example, lists seven major divine judgments. Hoyt lists twelve categories of final judgment. Chafer holds that there are eight "well-defined judgments presented by the Word of God." And Ryrie lists seven future judgments. However one chooses to describe or enumerate the various judgments, God has revealed in His Word, a responsible, literal interpretation of Scripture unequivocally teaching multiple judgment events that take place at different times in God's eschatological program. The following is a breakdown of various judgments generally acknowledged by dispensational premillennialists.

The Judgment at the Cross

According to John 12:31–33, the judgment at the cross qualifies as a final judgment. It resolved the matter of sin (John 19:30); it took place at the end of the ages (Heb. 9:26–28); and it sealed the doom of both Satan and the world. As Chafer puts it, "the believer has been in court, condemned, sentenced, and executed in the Person of his Substitute, the Lord Jesus Christ" (John 5:24; Rom. 5:9; 8:1; 2 Cor. 5:21; Gal. 3:13; Heb. 10:10, 14–17; 1 Peter 2:24). The cross, therefore, stands as the supreme foreshadowing of all final judgment, for it reveals the righteous judgment of God (Rom. 3:25) and sorts humanity into two categories (John 3:14–18).

The Judgment at the Rapture

Immediately following the Rapture (the snatching of the saints from the earth), the church (composed of all true believers) will stand in heaven before what is described in Romans 14:10 and 2 Corinthians 5:10 as the "judgment seat of Christ." The fact that Revelation 19:8 pictures Christ's bride, the church, as already rewarded when He returns to earth at His Second Coming indicates that this event will be subsequent to the Rapture but before the Second Coming. The Greek term *bema,* used to describe this judgment, portrays a seat or raised platform where a judge sits to adjudicate a case (e.g., Matt. 27:19; John 19:13; Acts 18:12). The Greeks employed the same term to describe the platform on which a judge or referee sat during the Isthmian or Olympic games at Corinth. Here the winners of the various athletic events received their rewards. No doubt the apostle Paul had such a scene in mind when he used the phrase, "judgment seat of Christ." Thus, the contexts and the historical background of the term imply that the bema is for believers a place and time of rewarding rather than punishing. Both Romans 14:10–12 and 1 Corinthians 3:10–4:5 support this view. It is those who have built upon the foundation of Jesus Christ (the church-age believers) who will participate in the judgment seat. No unsaved people or Old Testament saints will be present.

The Judgments at the Second Coming

The Judgment of Israel (Jewish people)

This judgment at the end of the Tribulation, described in Ezekiel 20:34–38 and illustrated in Matthew 25:1–30, concerns Jewish survivors who have been regathered from all over the earth to the land of Israel following Christ's victory over His enemies at Armageddon. The parables of the ten virgins and the talents (Matt. 25:1–13; 14–30) illustrate this event. This judgment will determine who is eligible to enter the messianic kingdom. The righteous of Israel (those evidencing faith in Christ) will enter the kingdom to experience God's covenant commitments to the nation. Those who are proven unfaithful to Christ (rebels) will be purged and cast into outer darkness (Matt. 25:30). Because Israel failed in its appointed role as God's light to the Gentile world, God promised that another Light would light the Gentiles (Isa. 60:1–3). While Christ came as the true light (John 1:9; 8:12) in fulfillment of Isaiah's prophecy, God will set Israel apart once again during the Tribulation as His light to the world (Rev. 7:1–8). Thus, at Christ's Second Coming, individual faithfulness to that appointment will be judged. These Jewish believers will enter the kingdom in their earthly bodies and will be among the first to repopulate the earth during the millennial reign of Christ.

The Judgment of the Gentiles

This judgment will also take place at the end of the Tribulation (Joel 3:1–2; Matt. 25:31–46) at a place near Jerusalem, the Valley of Jehoshaphat. These are the Gentile survivors of the Tribulation who will be judged for their treatment of Israel (probably the 144,000 of Rev. 7) during that terrible period. These may be the "brothers" referenced in Matthew 25:40. The Gentile righteous will be revealed because anyone treating a Jew with kindness, especially during the final three and one-half years of the Tribulation will do so only out of a redeemed heart. Since Messiah's kingdom rule will be over both Israel and the Gentile nations, and since none who are unsaved will enter the kingdom, there will be a separating of the saved (sheep) from the unsaved Gentiles (goats), who will be assigned to everlasting punishment. This judgment will be subsequent to Israel's judgment and will be a judgment of individuals from the nations (Matt. 25:32) not a judgment of national entities.

The Judgment of Old Testament and Tribulation Saints

This judgment (Dan. 12:2–3; Matt. 16:27; Rev. 20:4–6) will take place, as well, at the conclusion of the Tribulation period. Both Old Testament and Tribulation saints will be raised from the dead and rewarded. Revelation 20:4–6 describes this as the first resurrection. Some have found this confusing since many believers will have been resurrected at the time of the Rapture seven years previous. However, "first resurrection" is a reference to a category of resurrected believers rather than to a chronological order. Wood notes that "the idea makes the resurrection of the wicked, which does not occur until after the millennium, the second resurrection, corresponding in name to the 'second death,' as noted in Revelation 20:6, 14." Here again, the numerical term is a reference to kind rather than sequence. The first resurrection, includes those who are raised to life eternal (cf. John 5:29). As

Benware observes, "there are several points in time when believers are raised to life eternal, but all would be considered the 'first resurrection.'"

The Judgments Following the Millennial Kingdom

The Judgment of Satan

Satan's judgment was sealed eternally at the Cross. However, it is not until after he is loosed for a season at the end of the Christ's millennial reign, for a final fling at deception and rebellion, that he will be cast into the lake of fire with the Beast and the False Prophet to suffer eternal torment (Rev. 20:7–10). Although this is Satan's last judgment, other stages of judgment precede his final fate. Midway through the Tribulation he is cast out of heaven and confined to earth (Rev. 12:7–12). Then, at the outset of Christ's millennial reign he is to be bound and thrown into the Abyss (Rev. 20:1–3).

The Judgment of Fallen Angels.

The judgment of fallen angels will be finalized when they, along with Satan, are judged by both believers (1 Cor. 6:3) and Christ (Matt. 25:41; Rev. 20:10) and cast into the lake of fire.

Jude 6–7 and 2 Peter 2:4 reveal that prior to this time many of the angels who initially joined Satan in his insurrection (Rev. 12:3, 4) were cast into the Abyss (Tartarus) for confinement until their final judgment. Others have been at large under the direction of Satan serving as his evil emissaries or demons who war against Christ and His servants (Matt. 12:24–27; Eph. 2:2–3; 6:11–12).

The Judgment of the Unsaved Dead

This judgment will take place at the conclusion of Christ's millennial reign but before the eternal state begins. At this time the unbelievers of every age will be resurrected to face what is called the Great White Throne judgment (Rev. 20:11–15), when they will stand before the Lord Jesus Christ (John 5:22, 26–29). In contrast to believers who are called the "dead in Christ," these individuals are referred to as "the dead." There will be no need to separate believers from unbelievers because all who stand in judgment here will have chosen during their lifetimes to reject God and His Christ. While the Book of Life will be opened at the Great White Throne judgment, it will not list the names of those being judged. Those judged at this time will be judged from the books of works containing incontrovertible evidence that they justly deserve eternal condemnation because of their inability to meet God's standard of holiness. These books may also be used to establish degrees of punishment. The ultimate fate of the unsaved is to be thrown into the lake of fire. This is referred to as the "second death."

The Judgment of the Present Heavens and Earth

This judgment is anticipated in several Scripture passages (e.g., Matt. 24:35; Rev. 20:11), while it is specifically described in 2 Peter 3:10. This destruction is necessary for two reasons: the presence of sin in the universe and the residual effects of the curse placed on creation. While some theologians hold to a renovation of the heavens and earth and others to a re-creation, it is clear that the new heaven and new earth will be in glorious contrast to the first heaven and earth that are passing away (Rev. 21:1–4).

See also RAPTURE, DOCTRINE OF THE.

David R. Nicholas

Paul N. Benware, *Understanding End Times Prophecy* (Chicago: Moody Press, 1995); Lewis Sperry Chafer, *Systematic Theology,* vol. VII (Grand Rapids: Kregel, 1993); Paul Enns, *The Moody Handbook of Theology* (Chicago: Moody Press, 1989); Herman A. Hoyt, *The End Times* (Chicago: Moody Press, 1969); J. Dwight Pentecost, *Thy Kingdom Come* (Wheaton: Victor Books, 1990); Charles C. Ryrie, *Basic Theology* (Wheaton: Victor Books, 1986); John F. Walvoord, *Prophecy Knowledge Handbook* (Wheaton: Victor Books, 1990); Leon Wood, *The Bible and Future Events* (Grand Rapids: Zondervan, 1973).

K

KELLOGG, SAMUEL H.

Samuel Kellogg (1839–1899) is indicative of those who helped turn the tide among evangelicals from postmillennialism to premillennialism between the Civil War and World War I. Kellogg was a Presbyterian scholar, linguist, professor, missionary, and pastor. "But the greatest thing about him was his wonderful knowledge of and love for his Bible," said a friend. "He was a man of the Book."

This "man of the Book" was born on Long Island, New York. He was home-schooled and briefly attended Williams College in 1856, but graduated from Princeton College in 1861. He graduated from Princeton Seminary in 1864 and was ordained a missionary to India.

Kellogg taught at the theological school in Allahabad and completed a monumental grammar of the Hindi language in 1875, which stood for many years as the leading authority. Upon the death of his wife in 1876, he returned to the United States and pastored a Presbyterian church in Pittsburgh. He was then called to the chair of Systematic Theology at Allegheny (Western) Presbyterian Seminary in Pittsburgh. Before returning to India where he died, for the final five years of his life, he pastored St. James Square Presbyterian Church, Toronto. Kellogg's final task in India was to head a triad of translators of the Old Testament into Hindi. "So highly did his colleagues regard his knowledge of the Bible and Indic philology that after his death they asked for no successor, but this is what they say of their custom: 'When we differ between ourselves, and we recall what would have been Dr. Kellogg's view, the one whose opinion differs from this gives way at once.'"

Perhaps Kellogg's greatest gift to Christendom lies in his contribution to the Hindi language. His most well-known English contributions are his commentaries on Leviticus and Samuel, still widely respected and used today. However, he also made an impact in an area that he greatly loved as an Old Testament scholar—eschatology.

Kellogg penned two outstanding works on Bible prophecy. They are *The Jews or Prediction and Fulfillment: An Argument for the Times* (1883) and *Are Premillennialists Right?* (ca. 1890). Kellogg's premillennialism was not developed as an appendage from Revelation 20; rather Revelation 20 serves as the climax to a drama begun in the earliest books of the Old Testament. His understanding of a future for the Jews and a yet-future, literal fulfillment to them as a nationally distinct people drove him to the only possible eschatology to which such an understanding leads. Dr. Wilbur Smith said, "Dr. Kellogg was . . . one of the great Bible scholars of his day. Probably this is the greatest single volume on prophecy in relation to the Jews to be written in our country during the nineteenth century." Kellogg believed that the Jews had a bright future under their eventual Messiah and King—Jesus.

Kellogg's scholarly statement and defense of premillennialism in *Are Premillennialists Right?* involves a survey of church history and Scripture. Convinced that the Bible teaches premillennialism, he interacts with many of the arguments raised against it by postmillennialism. Postmillennialism was dominant during Kellogg's seminary days. A common argument in his day raised against premillennialism by postmillennialists was that it discourages efforts at world evangelization. Kellogg was living proof to the opposite. Toward the end of the nineteenth century, missions were dominated by premillennialists. Kellogg shared the following anecdote about his graduating class at

Princeton Seminary: "Among the fifty graduates were just seven Premillennialists. These all volunteered for the foreign field, while none of the others did. Four were permitted to go, and the three who were found physically unfit engaged in home missions work."

Kellogg was said to have been motivated to enter the mission field in the first place by anticipation of his Lord's return. It was the blessed hope that drove him to excellence in his work. Thus, at his death his friends placed on his gravestone at Landour these precious words, "Till He Come."

See also PREMILLENNIALISM.

Thomas D. Ice

Samuel H. Kellogg, *Are Premillennialists Right?* (New York: Revell, 1923); Daniel G. Reid, ed., *Dictionary of Christianity in America* (Downers Grove, Ill.: InterVarsity Press, 1990), 609.

KINGDOM, KEYS OF THE

The phrase "the keys of the kingdom" is found in only one passage: Matthew 16:19. It comes immediately after Jesus announced for the first time that He would build His *church* and is the first use of that term in the New Testament. This introduces a new facet of God's kingdom program. While the church cannot be equated with the kingdom of God as replacement theology often attempts to do, the church is certainly a facet of God's kingdom program and part of the spiritual kingdom (see PARABLES OF THE KINGDOM for further detail.)

The interpretation of this verse along with the preceding verse 18 has been the subject of debate for hundreds of years. Within the Roman Catholic tradition, doctrines have developed identifying Peter as the rock, with the authority to delegate the power to forgive or retain sins through a sacramental system of penance and absolution. The *Catholic Encyclopedia* states, "The power to confer or withhold forgiveness might well be viewed as the opening and shutting of the gates of heaven." It was used both as admission to as well as excommunication from the kingdom.

The power to bind and loose also gives the pope authority to pronounce doctrinal judgments and to make disciplinary decisions in the church. This gives the pope the supreme authority and power to prescribe what and who Catholics must believe and how and when they must worship, including the liturgy, the canonization of saints and associated festivals. The transmittal of Peter's keys to his successors has given credence for the primacy and power of the papacy to govern the kingdom of God, which, they believe, is the Roman Catholic Church. As a result, Peter and his successors have been rewarded with a special position and spiritual powers as Christ's representatives on earth. Since the fourth century, Catholic theologians have argued the church is the kingdom on earth and have taught an amillennial view of the kingdom promises.

Proponents of the Roman Catholic tradition point to history as supporting evidence for their interpretation of the keys of the kingdom. However, most of their historical support comes from tradition dating back only to the fourth century. An accurate historical and grammatical interpretation must consider the use of terms at the time of the writing of the original text. The concept of *kingdom* and the *keys* must be understood from their usage in the first century.

In the context of Matthew 16:18, whatever the meaning of "the keys of the kingdom," it must somehow refer to the church facet of God's overall kingdom program. The church is the body of Christ (Col. 1:18), and the means of entering the body is by means of Spirit baptism (1 Cor. 12:13). Understanding this will help to understand the exact nature of the keys of the kingdom and especially Peter's role, since the keys of the kingdom are specifically given to Peter and not to any of the other apostles.

In the Old Testament, humanity was divided into only two groups, Jews and Gentiles; but by New Testament times, humanity was consistently divided into three groups: Jews, Samaritans, and Gentiles (Matt. 10:5–6). A knowledge of this will also help in understanding the meaning of the keys of the kingdom and Peter's special role in connection with them.

Having the keys, already known from the Old Testament, carried two concepts: first, authority (Isa. 22:20–24) and, second, the right to unlock the door.

Therefore, the basic point of Matthew 16:19 is that Jesus gives the authority to Peter to open the door of the church, or the body of Christ, to all three segments of humanity. Once he opens the door for a segment of humanity, it will remain open for them. This helps explain Peter's special role in the book of Acts and the sometime delay of the baptism of the Spirit to believers.

In Acts 2, Peter opens the door for the Jews and, from then on, the door stayed open for the Jews. From that point on, the moment a Jew believed, they were baptized by the Spirit into the body of Christ.

In Acts 8, it is Philip the evangelist who goes into Samaria and preaches the Gospel to the Samaritans. The text clearly states that the Samaritans believed and, therefore, did experience the regenerating work of the Holy Spirit. However, none were baptized by the Spirit into the body. The reason is that while Philip had the Gospel, he did not have the keys of the kingdom. Only with the arrival of Peter and the laying on of hands by Peter were the Samaritans finally baptized by the Spirit into the body. In this chapter, Peter opens the door for the Samaritans and, from then on, it stays open for them. From then on, every Samaritan who believed was baptized by the Spirit into the body.

In Acts 9, God saves Paul and Paul is actually the one appointed to be the apostle to the Gentiles. Although Paul is the one to evangelize the Gentiles, he does not have the keys of the kingdom, either. In Acts 10, Peter is sent by divine revelation to the Gentile home of Cornelius and, through the preaching of Peter, these Gentiles believe and are baptized by the Spirit into the body. Here, Peter opens the door for the Gentiles and, from then on, it stays open for the Gentiles. From then on, every Gentile who believed was baptized by the Spirit into the body. Only after this is the way open for Paul to fulfill his calling of being the apostle to the Gentiles (Acts 13–28).

It is Peter's important role as the one with the keys of the kingdom that helps to explain the seeming delay of the coming of the Spirit in certain situations. By the time Paul begins his work of evangelism, all doors have been opened, which terminated Peter's function in using the keys of the kingdom. There would no longer be a delay in receiving the baptism of the Spirit upon salvation. Therefore, by the time Paul wrote 1 Corinthians 12:13, the truth was that by one Spirit were we all baptized into one body.

The modern teaching that makes the baptism of the Spirit a postsalvation experience is based upon historical events while ignoring the propositional statements of Scripture to the contrary.

See also ISRAEL AND THE CHURCH: THE DIFFERENCES.

Arnold G. Fruchtenbaum and
Mike P. Gendron

Catechism of the Catholic Church (San Francisco: Ignatius Press, 1994); *The Catholic Encyclopedia,* ed. Klemens Loffler (New York: The Encyclopedia Press, 1911).

KINGDOM OF GOD, OF HEAVEN

Though Bible teachers of many persuasions recognize a universal kingdom of God's reign and rule, the expressions *kingdom of God* and *kingdom of heaven* for the most part refer to the coming millennial reign of Christ on earth. That this kingdom then goes on into eternity following the one-thousand-year reign of the Messiah is agreed upon by most dispensationalists. The main focus of the kingdom of God issue is found in the Gospels. But there are some surprises when examining them. John, Mark, and Luke used the expression *kingdom of God* exclusively. They do not refer to the kingdom of heaven at all. But in reverse, Matthew uses the phrase *kingdom of heaven* some thirty times and *kingdom of God* only three times!

Though some dispensationalists may disagree, it appears by all the evidence that the two expressions are used synonymously, but with a certain emphasis. The expressions kingdom of God and kingdom of heaven are interchangeable in many parallel Gospel readings (Matt. 4:17 and Luke 6:21 with

Mark 1:14; Matt. 13:11 and Luke 8:10 with Mark 4:11; Matt. 13:3 and Mark 4:30). "Most expositors regard the kingdom of heaven as the equivalent of the kingdom of God, and explain it on the grounds that Matthew, like many Jews, did not like to use the word *God* and used heaven instead. . . . In Matthew's gospel there seems to be a difference in the usage of 'kingdom of heaven,' justifying the conclusion that it refers to the sphere of profession in contrast to 'kingdom of God'" (Walvoord). Interestingly, Jewish historians believe the two expressions point to the same kingdom (Avi-Yonah).

As normally written, kingdom of God (or heaven) is classified in Greek in a genitive form: "The kingdom of (belonging to) God." But it may be better to translate it in an ablative form: "The kingdom of (from) God," or, "The kingdom coming down from heaven." There is much disagreement upon this point. Yet most admit the genitive and ablative meanings are actually not far apart. For whatever reasons, Matthew preferred kingdom of Heaven and the other writers chose kingdom of God. Matthew may have been focusing on Daniel 2:44, which declares the "God of heaven will set up a kingdom which will never be destroyed. . . . It will itself endure forever."

To most premillennialists and dispensationalists, the two expressions are clearly referencing first the Davidic covenant and the millennial reign of David's Son, the Messiah. David tells us "[The LORD] has chosen my son Solomon to sit on the throne of the kingdom of the Lord over Israel" (1 Chron. 28:6). It is the Lord's kingdom (29:11), but it is bequeathed to David's sons and established forever (28:7–8). But there is a second phase to the Lord's kingdom. First Corinthians 15:23–28 shows both phases. Paul teaches that following the millennial rule, Jesus delivers up the kingdom to the God and Father (v. 24). He does this when He has made inoperative every enemy, including death (vv. 25–26). "The dominion over the earth that Adam lost in the Fall will be fully recovered by Christ. When this occurs Christ will turn over the kingdom rule to the Father for the eternal reign over a new heaven and new earth" (Benware). The kingdom of God will continue right on into eternity because Jesus' reign is forever (Rev. 11:15).

The present dispensation of the church is not the kingdom of God. Following His resurrection, Jesus set aside the disciples' question: Are You at this time going to restore the kingdom to Israel? (Acts 1:6). In time, the Lord's followers would understand that the kingdom was postponed and the dispensation of the church is now temporarily in place. But the church saints have an anticipation of the coming kingdom of God. Paul writes of the inheritance of the saints in the kingdom (Col. 1:12). Believers are called into His future kingdom and glory (1 Thess. 2:12) and are to be looking for His appearing and His kingdom (2 Tim. 4:1). The writer of Hebrews refers to the fact that righteousness will be the scepter of the Lord's kingdom (Heb. 1:8). Finally, Peter writes that "the entrance into the eternal kingdom of our Lord and Savior Jesus Christ will be abundantly supplied" to the believers in the Lord (2 Peter 1:11).

See also THEOCRATIC KINGDOM.

Mal Couch

Michael Avi-Yonah, *Society and Religion in the Second Temple Period* (Jerusalem: Massada, 1977); Paul N. Benware, *Understanding End Times Prophecy* (Chicago: Moody Press, 1995); John F. Walvoord, *Major Bible Prophecies* (Grand Rapids: Zondervan, 1991).

KINGDOM, PARABLES OF THE

The kingdom parables, like all parables in Scripture, are stories that illustrate truths by means of comparison. The phrase, "the kingdom of heaven is like" means that elements in the story run tangent to truths about the kingdom. These kingdom parables, recorded chiefly in Matthew 13 (see also Matt. 20, 22, 25; Mark 4; Luke 8, 13–14), have been the focus of much discussion and debate among Bible interpreters. A variety of contrasting views attend these parables even among premillennialists and dispensationalists. Some believe, for example, that the kingdom parables relate to Jewish interests only or describe the future millennial age exclusively. Others believe that these stories redefine the kingdom and correct mistaken Jewish views about God's rule. Some contend that the parables describe the growth of the professing church and introduce an entirely new form of kingdom that precedes the millennial rule.

Perhaps the best approach to the kingdom parables is that which espouses a single, unified, mediatorial kingdom concept throughout the text of Scripture. In this view, the mediatorial kingdom that existed historically under the Mosaic covenant and was predicted by the Old Testament prophets to be restored in its former glory is the same kingdom that John preached and Jesus offered to Israel; it is the same kingdom that the Jews spurned in their rejection of Jesus. This singular, mediatorial kingdom—the historic, prophetic, offered, and rejected kingdom—is the kingdom of which Jesus spoke in these parables (see KINGDOM, UNIVERSAL AND MEDIATORIAL).

The timing of Jesus' parabolic teaching regarding the kingdom is crucial to a correct understanding of these stories (Matt. 13; Mark 4). These parables were not spoken by Christ at the inception of His ministry in order to redefine the prophesied kingdom or to correct Jewish misconceptions about Messiah's rule. Rather, the kingdom parables were spoken by Christ later in His ministry, at a point of crisis in the offer of the restored kingdom to Israel. The religious leaders had determined to destroy Jesus (Matt. 12:14). These scribes and Pharisees openly disavowed Jesus' messianic claims evidenced by His miracles and accused Him of consort with the powers of Satan (Matt. 12:22–32; Mark 3:22–29). That same day (Matt. 13:1), Jesus introduced the kingdom parables. Christ's message abruptly turned from the nearness of the kingdom (Matt. 3:2; 10:7) to His impending death (Matt. 16:21). Rejection of the King was rejection of the kingdom. The kingdom parables, then, were not intended to define the kingdom in its offer but to explain the effects of its rejection. The contextual setting that envelopes the kingdom parables (Matt. 10:1–16:21) must not be ignored in their interpretation.

The audience and the purpose of the kingdom parables are also important to proper exposition. In light of His certain rejection, Jesus addressed the kingdom parables both to the multitudes publicly (Matt. 13:2) and to the disciples privately (Matt. 13:36). Jesus Himself explained to the disciples the dual purpose of the parables (Matt. 13:10–17). On one hand, these stories were designed to hide truth in judgment against determined Jewish unbelievers (Matt. 13:13–15; cf. Isa. 6:9–10). On the other hand, the parables were revelatory to those who believed, opening their eyes to new truths related to the kingdom (Matt. 13:16–17). Those who had insight into kingdom truths, formerly revealed through God's prophets, would now receive more kingdom-related revelation. Those who had shut their eyes to prior revelation regarding the kingdom would not only be deprived of more, but also would suffer loss (Matt. 13:12). This multiplication and deprivation of kingdom insight was, in fact, the point of the introductory parable in Matthew 13 (vv. 1–23). Jesus' initial parable was not about the kingdom itself but about the message of the kingdom (v. 19). Only a few would actually receive and understand God's revelation about Messiah's rule, but these few would bear fruit (v. 23).

The nature of the kingdom parables was also clearly described by Jesus to His disciples. These parables were told in order that the disciples might know the mysteries of the kingdom of heaven (Matt. 13:11). A mystery, in this context, is a newly revealed truth. Jesus himself defined these mysteries as truths that had never before been revealed by God from the beginning of time until that day (Matt. 13:34–35; cf. Ps. 78:2). The nature of the parables, then, was revelatory; they made known previously unknown data related to the kingdom. The kingdom to which Christ referred in Matthew 13 must certainly be the same kingdom of which He spoke earlier that day, the kingdom that had come upon that generation in the person of the King (Matt. 12:28). This must be the same kingdom of Matthew 11, of which John was the potential forerunner in fulfillment of Old Testament prophecy (vv. 10–14), and the same kingdom of Matthew 10, which the disciples were to announce exclusively to Israel (vv. 5–7). This was the same kingdom which Jesus was born to rule (Matt. 2:2)—that kingdom defined and forecasted by the Old Testament prophets. There is nothing in the text that forces the conclusion, much less clearly indicates, that Jesus used the term *kingdom* in multiple or altered senses. The divine kingdom of which Jesus spoke, by any name (kingdom of heaven, of God, of the Son, of the Father, etc.), was the kingdom prophesied in the Old Testament (see KINGDOM OF GOD, OF HEAVEN).

The subject matter of these kingdom parables, then, was new revelation with regard to the prophesied kingdom. The mysteries of the kingdom, therefore, were not intended to describe some new kind of kingdom that was coming in a mystery form. Nor was this a new revelation that confuted, overruled, or redefined previous kingdom prophecies. These were not truths that were found in the Old Testament but not yet fully realized or understood. In these kingdom parables, Jesus was relating truths about the prophesied kingdom that had never before been revealed, truths related to the rejection of the kingdom as personified in the King. In this revelation was something new and something old (Matt. 13:52). That which was old in these parables was their perfect accord with the voluminous kingdom revelation of the Old Testament. That which was new in these parables, as will be demonstrated, was information concerning an era which would follow the departure of the King and precede His later return to restore the kingdom to Israel. Such information regarding the prophesied kingdom had never before been made known. It is notable that the era that Jesus here announced as a mystery in relation to the kingdom corresponds closely to an era that the apostle Paul associates with revelation in the form of a mystery, the era of the church (Eph. 2:11–3:12).

The kingdom parables focused on a new time frame that would attend the establishment of the prophesied kingdom. Jesus was relating to His disciples the fact that the establishment of the prophesied kingdom would be delayed. The intervening time before the kingdom's restoration would be unlike any era previously known. These parables do not portray the kingdom as present on earth during the time of the King's absence. The kingdom's establishment is entirely future in the parables. The stories focus on a harvest (Matt. 13:30), a grown tree (Matt. 13:32), a whole leavening (Matt. 13:33), and a full net (Matt. 13:48). The details of the harvest and the culling out of bad fish make explicit the time of the kingdom's establishment in these parables. The future harvest is explicitly said by Jesus to occur at the end of the age (Matt. 13:39), as is the time of the culling out of the bad fish from the full net (Matt. 13:48–49). At that time, Jesus Himself will call out reapers (Matt. 13:30). These reapers are God's angelic host (Matt. 13:39, 41, 49). The task of the reapers is to gather together all of the good and the bad, segregate them one from the other, and cast out the bad into a place of fire, wailing, gnashing of teeth while preserving the good (Matt. 13:30, 40–42, 49–50). The bad are said to be offenders that the angels will gather out of His kingdom (Matt. 13:41–42) while the good will shine as the sun in the kingdom of their Father (Matt. 13:43). Parallel passages further clarify this chronology.

Jesus reiterates and clarifies the precise time of these events in Matthew 25:31–46. The context, again, is a recounting of kingdom parables (Matt. 25:1). These illustrative stories likewise distinguish between those persons who will be received (Matt. 25:10, 21, 23) and those persons who will be refused (Matt. 25:12). The accepted constituents will be given ruling authority (Matt. 25:21, 23), while the unacceptable persons will be cast into the place of weeping and gnashing of teeth (Matt. 25:30). This segregation clearly occurs at the advent of the Son of Man (Matt. 25:13, cf. v. 19). The Son of Man's coming is explicitly stated to be His arrival in resurrected glory to sit upon the throne of His glory (Matt. 25:31), a reference to Christ's Second Advent and the establishment of the kingdom (see 24:30;

26:64; cf. Dan. 7:13–14). Arriving with Him are the angels (Matt. 25:31), the reapers of Matthew 13:39 who gather those to be judged. This judgment is conducted by Christ, who is seated on his newly occupied throne (Matt. 25:32–46; cf. 24:30–31). A process of segregation ensues, where the accepted, those blessed of the Father, are retained to inherit the kingdom prepared for them from the foundation of the world (Matt. 25:34). The rejected are cast out of this newly inaugurated kingdom (Matt. 25:41). These events immediately follow the judgments of Daniel's Seventieth Week (cf. Matt. 24:27–31).

A comparison of Matthew 25:31–46 with Matthew 13:38–43 clarifies many issues regarding the kingdom parables. It is clear, for example, that the kingdom out of which the offenders are gathered in Matthew 13:41 is not some kingdom that exists during the absence of the King or during the era of the church. Rather, the offenders are cast out of the prophesied kingdom that Christ establishes at His coming (Matt. 25:31–32, cf. 24:30–31). These are discriminatory judgments, one for Jews (Ezek. 20:33–38; 34:17–22) and one for Gentiles (Matt. 25:32–46), which probably take place in the transitional days following Daniel's Seventieth Week as alluded to in Daniel 12:11–12. The comparison of Matthew 25 with Matthew 13 also makes it clear that the kingdom parables cannot refer exclusively to the Jews and the millennial period, as some assert. The sowing of the good seed and the bad (Matt. 13:38) cannot take place during the Millennium, for the discriminatory judgment at the end of the age is clearly tied to the Second Advent, which begins the millennial reign (Matt. 24:30–31; 25:31–32). The parallel contexts, terminology, and descriptions in these passages (Matt. 13:38–43; 24:27–31; 25:31–46) present a unified account. The kingdom parables must be descriptive of a period prior to the Second Advent, yet the actual establishment of the kingdom in these parables is entirely future, immediately following the Second Advent.

The kingdom parables, then, are spoken by Christ in the context of the kingdom's rejection. They are addressed both to the multitudes and to the disciples—to some who will not understand and to others who will. The parables communicate new truth about the old kingdom, the kingdom that was prophesied to come. The new truth describes an era when the King and His kingdom, having been rejected, would be absent from earth. The restoration of the theocratic kingdom must await the future acceptance of the King. During the time of the King's absence, before the harvest and the end of the age, two groups of people develop in proximity. Those who believe God's revelation, the children of the kingdom, will inherit their place in the restored theocracy at Christ's coming. In the meantime, they will dwell among the children of the wicked one, those who will be cast out of the restored kingdom at its inception (Matt. 13:38). During the era that precedes the King's return, those who are kingdom citizens by position (see Col. 1:12–13; Heb. 12:28; cf. Eph. 2:5–7) are to preach the Gospel of the kingdom (Matt. 24:14; cf. Acts 28:31). The kingdom Gospel is preached in anticipation of the future establishment of the kingdom and the discriminating judgments that immediately ensue, for believers of all ages will take their rightful place in this kingdom, but no unbelievers will be allowed to enter (John 3:3). Not only should kingdom citizens preach the Gospel of God's coming kingdom, they also should model kingdom life in this nonkingdom age (Matt. 18:31–35; cf. Rom. 14:17; 1 Cor. 4:20), for they are chosen representatives of their God and coming King in this foreign land (1 Peter 2:9–12).

See also OLIVET DISCOURSE; THEOCRATIC KINGDOM.

Roy E. Beacham

A. J. McClain, *The Greatness of the Kingdom* (Winona Lake, Ind.: BMH Books, 1974); G. N. H. Peters, *The Theocratic Kingdom* (Grand Rapids: Kregel, 1972); R. L. Saucy, *The Case for Progressive Dispensationalism* (Grand Rapids: Zondervan, 1993); S. D. Toussaint, *Behold the King* (Portland: Multnomah Press, 1980), "The Kingdom in Matthew's Gospel" in *Essays in Honor of J. Dwight Pentecost* (Chicago: Moody Press, 1986).

KINGDOMS, UNIVERSAL AND MEDIATORIAL

The concept of God as King is found extensively in the Scriptures. Divine kingship in the Bible is expressed by various explicit terms as well as by metaphors and other word pictures. Most explicit, however, are references to the rule of God in terms of a kingdom (*malkûṯ* [Heb.], *basileia* [Gk.]). Elements that comprise a kingdom in Scripture are (1) a personage with ruling authority and power, (2) an objective realm of constituents over which to rule, and (3) the actual exercise of that regal authority over that constituency.

In examining references to the kingdom of God in Scripture, some distinctions must be made. Specifically, God's kingdom appears to be portrayed in two overlapping yet distinguishable realms. In the broadest sense, the Scriptures teach that God rules at all times over every aspect and entity of the created order. On the other hand, the Bible speaks of a limited rule of God, a rule that is localized on earth, framed within time, and centered on a select human constituency.

The broadest sense of God's rule, His dominion over all of creation at all times, is commonly called the universal kingdom of God. It might be best to speak of God's universal kingdom as His kingdom in *macrocosm*. This macrocosmic kingdom of God is grounded in His sovereignty as the Creator, Sustainer, and Director of all that exists (Ps. 103:19–22). God's universal rule extends through all eras (Lam. 5:19). It encompasses every facet of creation (1 Chron. 29:11–12), and it exists without end (Ps. 10:16). The universal kingdom is directly administered by God through the divine Son, without human intermediary (2 Kings 19:15; Isa. 14:26–27). God rules this macrocosm primarily through providential, secondary causation (Dan. 4:17, 34–35). Occasionally His providential, secondary control (Ps. 135:6–7) is punctuated by primary, supernatural intervention (Ps. 135:8–9). The universal kingdom of God, then, is God's macrocosmic rule through his exclusive, sovereign dominion over all of creation, a rule without pause or end.

In distinction from the universal or macrocosmic kingdom of God, there is found in Scripture a more limited divine kingdom. This earth-oriented, time-related, ethnic-centered kingdom is called, by some, the mediatorial kingdom of God. Other names are assigned to this limited kingdom, such as the kingdom of Israel and Judah, the kingdom of David, or the messianic/millennial kingdom. It might be best to speak of this more limited expression of God's kingdom as His kingdom in *microcosm*. Although some dispensationalists further distinguish between the kingdom of Israel, the kingdom of God, the kingdom of heaven, the spiritual kingdom, the mystery-form kingdom, the messianic kingdom, and others (Chafer, Pentecost, Ryrie, Walvoord), there is no clear evidence that Jesus or the authors of Scripture used the term *kingdom* in these multiple senses. It is better to conclude that the Scriptures refer only to two divine kingdoms: the macrocosmic, universal kingdom of God and the microcosmic, mediatorial kingdom of God (see KINGDOM OF GOD, OF HEAVEN; KINGDOM, PARABLES OF THE).

The universal and mediatorial kingdoms were indistinguishable when God brought the universe into existence (Gen. 1:1). During the period before the human fall (Gen. 1–2), God's universal rule was unopposed on earth and, therefore, was His exclusive method of dominion over humankind. However, when the first human, Adam, sinned against the Creator (Gen. 3), humans exerted an apparent autonomy from God and his universal rule. Although God's sovereign, macrocosmic dominion continued, its immediacy was lost to fallen man. Human sin had veiled God's kingship. God seems to have purposed, then, to establish an objective rule on earth, a theocratic government mediated by a human representative and comprised of a specified human constituency. This microcosmic, mediatorial kingdom on earth would serve to model God-rule and God-life to fallen humanity.

The mediatorial kingdom of God was first established in history with the nation of Israel after the exodus from Egypt. With the call of Abraham, God had segregated a people ethnically as part of His purpose on earth (Gen. 12:1–3). However, it was not until the bilateral ratification of the Mosaic covenant at Sinai that this ethnic group became a theocratic body politic among whom God visibly dwelt and ruled (Exod. 19:3–8; 24:3–8). This theocratic kingdom of God in microcosm continued through the eras of Joshua, the elders, the judges, Saul, and the rulers of David's line (2 Sam. 7:4–17). The curses of the Mosaic covenant, however, eventually issued in the Babylonian captivity (Lev. 26:27–39; Deut. 28:36–68). This dispersion was accompanied by the stunning departure of God's theocratic presence from the temple, His place of rule (Ezek. 8–11, esp. 11:22–25). Although the nation of Israel eventually regained its political identity, the microcosmic, mediatorial kingdom of God on earth had come to an end historically (Hos. 1:9). However, God was not finished with this kingdom. The OT prophets who had forecasted its demise also consistently foretold its consummate restoration (Lev. 26:40–46; Ezek. 11:14–20, Hos. 1:10–11).

God offered to Israel the restoration of this historic, mediatorial kingdom in the person of the ultimate Davidic king, Jesus, at His First Advent (Matt. 3:1–2; 4:17; 21:1–9). Jesus spoke of this kingdom in the Sermon on the Mount (Matt. 5–7). He preached the Gospel of this kingdom (Matt. 9:35) and sent the disciples to proclaim it to the Jews (Matt. 10:5–7). This is the "kingdom of heaven, " the "kingdom of God," the "kingdom of the Father" to which Christ referred in the parables (Matt. 13, 20, 22), in His discourse on the Mount of Olives (Matt. 24–25), and in the Upper Room (Matt. 26:29). With the rejection of the King (Matt. 27:22–25; John 19:13–15), the restoration of the theocratic kingdom on earth was deferred until the return of its ruler and His acceptance by national Israel (Zech. 12:10–13:9; Rev. 1:7). With the second advent of Christ, the former, historic, mediatorial kingdom will be reestablished on earth (Amos 9:11; Micah 4:8). As with the theocracy begun under Moses, this renewed mediatorial kingdom will be governed under the strictures of a covenant. The legal instrument that administers the restored kingdom will be the new covenant, a bilateral, suzerainty treaty (Ezek. 20:35–44; Hos. 2:14–23 [Eng.]; Zech. 13:9) that is ratified with the regathered house of Israel and Judah at the inception of the kingdom (Ezek. 34:1--25; 37:21–28). The Jews with whom this covenant is enacted will be those believing Israelites who survive Daniel's Seventieth Week and enter the renewed kingdom in natural bodies (Ezek. 20:33–38; Rev. 7:1–8; 12:1–17). An innumerable host of surviving Gentile believers will also enjoy the benefits of this kingdom under Israel (Isa. 60:1–16; Zech. 8:20–23). Entrance into this kingdom is restricted to those who have been saved by faith (John 3:3). No unregenerate Jew or Gentile will enter the restored kingdom of God (Ezek. 20:33–38; Matt. 25:31–46).

At the conclusion of the judgments of the seven-year tribulation, in preparation for the Second Advent and the destruction of the end-time Beast of Rome, Christ will be invested as King of the mediatorial kingdom by God the Father (Dan. 7:9–14; cf. Rev. 1:7; 19:11–21). Then Christ Himself will rule the mediatorial kingdom for one thousand years, assisted by the glorified saints of the first resurrection (Rev. 20:1–6), which includes resurrected church saints (1 Cor. 6:2; 2 Tim. 2:12), as well as resurrected believers from Old Testament eras (Dan. 12:2, 13). Near the end of the millennial reign, a host of unbelievers, born to those who entered this kingdom in natural bodies, will rebel against their Sovereign (20:7–8). After Christ destroys these rebels, judges Satan and the unbelievers of all ages, and brings the created order back under total submission to God (Rev. 20:9–15), He will deliver this mediatorial kingdom over to the governance of His Father (1 Cor. 15:24–28). At that time, the microcosmic, mediatorial kingdom will once again merge with the macrocosmic, universal kingdom, ushering in the new created order, the eternal heavens and earth (Rev. 21–22).

See also THEOCRATIC KINGDOM.

Roy E. Beacham

L. S. Chafer, *Systematic Theology*, vol. 4 (Grand Rapids: Kregel, 1993); A. J. McClain,

The Greatness of the Kingdom (Winona Lake, Ind.: BMH Books, 1974); J. Dwight Pentecost, *Thy Kingdom Come* (Grand Rapids: Kregel, 1995) and *Things to Come* (Grand Rapids: Zondervan, 1958); G. N. H. Peters, *The Theocratic Kingdom* (Grand Rapids: Kregel, 1972); Charles C. Ryrie, *Dispensationalism* (Chicago: Moody Press, 1995); J. F. Walvoord, "Biblical Kingdoms Compared and Contrasted" in *Issues in Dispensationalism* (Chicago: Moody Press, 1994).

KINGS, 1 & 2, ESCHATOLOGY OF

The books of 1 and 2 Kings were originally one book in the Hebrew Bible. They recorded the events under the kings of Israel and Judah from Solomon to Zedekiah. The books were most likely written between 562 and 536 B.C. by the prophet Jeremiah, although many believe the author to be unknown. The purpose of the book was not only to record the history of these kings, but to show that the success of any king (and of the nation as a whole) depended on the measure of allegiance to God's Law. Failure resulted in decline and captivity (*Ryrie Study Bible*). The books also clearly show that God is faithful to His promises regarding Israel.

In 2 Samuel 7, God made a covenant with David, known as the Davidic covenant. In this covenant God promised (1) that David would have a son who would succeed him on his throne (2 Sam. 7:12). God literally fulfilled this promise in 1 Kings 1:45. (2) This same son would build the temple (2 Sam. 7:13). Again, God literally fulfilled His promise in 1 Kings 6:1–38. (3) God also promised that the throne of Solomon's kingdom would continue forever (2 Sam. 7:13). If Solomon disobeyed, God would correct him, but He would not take away his kingdom as He took it away from Saul (2 Sam. 7:10–15; 1 Kings 11:34). Solomon's throne continued; however, his descendants were deposed (Jer. 22:28–30). Jesus Christ is the ultimate fulfillment of this prophecy (Luke 1:32–33). Jesus Christ's genealogy has been traced back to David through David's sons Nathan and Solomon (Luke 3:23–38; Matt. 1:2–16). (4) God also promised David that his descendants and his kingdom would endure forever (2 Sam. 7:16).

> "The language of the covenant in 2 Samuel 7 and 1 Chronicles 17, as it was certainly understood by David, referred to his physical lineage and to his political kingdom, not to an entity such as . . . the church. Premillenarians generally interpret the prophecy literally and find it fulfilled in the future millennial kingdom which will occur after the Second Coming of Christ" (Walvoord).

The books of 1 and 2 Kings reveal that God is sovereign over all and that He is faithful to His promises.

See also DAVIDIC COVENANT.

Brian K. Richards

Charles C. Ryrie, *Ryrie Study Bible,* expanded ed. (Chicago: Moody Press, 1995); John F. Walvoord, *The Prophecy Knowledge Handbook* (Wheaton: Victor Books, 1990); John F. Walvoord and Roy B. Zuck, eds., *The Bible Knowledge Commentary* (Wheaton: Victor Books, 1995); B. Wilkinson and K. Boa, *Talk Thru The Bible* (Nashville: Thomas Nelson, 1983).

L

LACTANTIUS

Lactantius (ca. 240–ca. 320), Latin rhetorician, Christian apologist, and historian, was apparently the last of the early fathers to hold to the doctrine of the twofold resurrection found in Revelation 20:4–6. Before him, a double resurrection had been taught by the Didache, Justin Martyr, Irenaeus, Tertullian, and Commodian. But after Lactantius, this belief fell into disfavor, suffering the same fate as its parent doctrine, premillennialism.

Lactantius was also the last father of the ante-Nicene age of the church (the period prior to the Council of Nicea in A.D. 325) to expound the year-day doctrine, and he did so in traditional terms using familiar biblical texts. After remarking that God completed the world in six days and then consecrated the seventh day, upon which He rested, and pointing out the significance of the number seven among the Hebrews, Lactantius asserted that God's "religion and truth must labour during these six thousand years, while wickedness prevails and bears rule." But at the conclusion of that six thousand years, said Lactantius, "all wickedness must be abolished from the earth, and righteousness reign for a thousand years; and there must be tranquillity and rest from the labours which the world now has long endured" (*Div. Instit.* 7.14, cf. *Epit. of Div. Instit.* 70).

Lactantius believed that the conclusion of the six thousand years was drawing near. He explained that those who had written respecting the number of years from the beginning of the world differed in their calculations, yet none differed more than two hundred years (*Div. Instit.* 7.25). Since *The Divine Institutes* was written between 304 and 313, the addition of two hundred years would have placed the end of human history and thus Christ's return around A.D. 500. It was a conclusion supported by Theophilus, Hippolytus, and Julius Africanus.

Lactantius's program for the end times is specific (*Div. Instit.* 7.17–26, cf. *Epit. of Div. Instit.* 72). He taught that the end will be preceded by signs. For example, the prevalence of wickedness will worsen. The Antichrist will then appear to persecute the saints for forty-two months. His persecution will end when Christ returns suddenly to deliver the righteous. At His return, Christ will destroy unrighteousness, execute judgment, and raise the righteous (first resurrection) to reign with Him for a thousand years. Satan will be bound at the beginning of the Millennium but released at the end to assemble the nations for one last contest with God. For three days Satan will rage, during which time the sun will not set and God's people will be "concealed under caves of the earth, until the anger of God against the nations and the last judgment shall be ended" (*Div. Instit.* 7.26). Following the utter destruction of Satan and his allies, the earth will be changed, the wicked raised (second resurrection) and judged, and eternity will begin.

See also THEOCRATIC KINGDOM.

Larry V. Crutchfield

L. Crutchfield, "The Blessed Hope and the Tribulation in the Apostolic Fathers" in *When the Trumpet Sounds*, eds. Tommy Ice and Timothy Demy (Eugene, Oreg.: Harvest House, 1995), 85–103 and "Israel and the Church in the Ante-Nicene Fathers," *Bibliotheca Sacra,* 144:254–76 (July–September 1987); A. Roberts and J. Donaldson, eds., *The Ante-Nicene Fathers*, vol. 5 (Grand Rapids: Eerdmans, n.d.), 1–259.

LADD, GEORGE ELDON

To discuss the eschatology of George Eldon Ladd (1911–1982) is to discuss the entirety of his New Testament theology. Ladd was convinced that eschatology is the basic unifying structure for New Testament theology. Central to his New Testament theology is the kingdom of God, which Ladd identified as God's kingly rule. This rule is dynamic in that it was inaugurated at the first coming of Christ, yet consummation awaits the Parousia of the Son of Man in glory.

Ladd contended that the kingdom of God invaded the present evil age in the person of Christ. Christ's coming established a new era of salvation in which the sovereign rule of God is made manifest and that in some real sense inaugurated the age to come. God, who will accomplish His redemptive plan at the end of the age, is working redemptively in the present through His Son who has come. Thus, the kingdom of God is both a future eschatological victory over Satan and also a present reality. Further, in 1 Corinthians 15, Ladd identified three distinct stages of redemptive activity that accompany the transition. Christ's rule in the present will be superseded by His reign in glory (the Millennium). His reign in glory will give way to the third stage which is the fullest manifestation of the kingdom of God, the Father's reign in glory.

Like many of the early church fathers, Ladd held to a posttribulational premillennialism, generally referred to as historic premillennialism. However, unlike many adherents to this position, Ladd does not identify the difficulties encountered by the church throughout history as the time of Tribulation. Ladd holds to a future scenario in which the church will go through the Great Tribulation. Hence, the Blessed Hope refers to union with the Lord at His Coming. The Second Coming of Christ will conclude the time of Tribulation as He gathers His people to Himself and judges the wicked. His second coming will usher in the thousand-year reign of Christ during which Satan is incarcerated in the bottomless pit. At the end of the thousand years, Satan will be unbound and there will be a final eschatological war in which Christ will subdue all hostile powers.

Ladd identified the church as the spiritual Israel to whom the promises of the Old Testament are to be applied. When Israel rejected Jesus, Israel rejected the kingdom and is now the object of judgment rather than blessing. However, sometime during the Millennium those of the literal Israel will be saved through faith in Christ. Thus, they will become a part of the church but will retain their identity as a distinct people.

Ladd's eschatological dualism has been extremely influential during the last half of the twentieth century. In a survey conducted in 1984 of members of the Evangelical Theological Society, respondents indicated that John Calvin was the only theologian who had been more influential than Ladd in their theological formation.

See also RAPTURE, POSTTRIBULATIONAL.

Kevin Stilley

George Eldon Ladd, *The Blessed Hope* (Grand Rapids: Eerdmans, 1956), *Crucial Questions About the Kingdom of God* (Grand Rapids: Eerdmans, 1954), *The Gospel of the Kingdom* (Grand Rapids: Eerdmans, 1959), *Jesus and the Kingdom; The Eschatology of Biblical Realism* (New York: Harper & Row, 1964), *The Presence of the Future* (Grand Rapids: Eerdmans, 1974), and *A Theology of the New Testament* (Grand Rapids: Eerdmans, 1974); Mark Noll, *Between Faith and Criticism* (Grand Rapids: Baker, 1986).

LARKIN, CLARENCE

A Baptist pastor and author, Clarence Larkin (1850–1924) was born October 28 in Chester, Pennsylvania. As a young man, he worked briefly in his father's feed store before taking a position as a bank clerk. At the age of nineteen he was involved with the YMCA and was converted and confirmed in the Episcopal church. In 1873 he graduated from the Polytechnic College of Philadelphia with a degree in mechanical engineering. After brief employment at a shipyard, he became a supervisor and instructor at the Pennsylvania Institution for the Blind where he served three years before entering private business. During this time he felt led into the ministry.

At age thirty-two, Larkin joined the Baptist church and two years later, he was ordained. He pastored first in Kennett Square, Pennsylvania and later in Fox Chase, Pennsylvania, where he remained for twenty years. It was not until after his ordination that he became a premillennialist. He began making large charts on prophetic truth for use in his pulpit ministry. The popularity of his charts led him to begin printing and distributing them and they received wide distribution. At the beginning of World War I in 1914, Larkin gave an address, War and Prophecy, and soon after began working on a number of charts accompanied with descriptive texts. In the summer of 1918 he first published *Dispensational Truth or God's Plan and Purpose in the Ages*. In 1920, it was revised and enlarged. Utilizing his background as a mechanical engineer, Larkin produced commentaries on Revelation and Daniel as well as other prophetic titles, all of which contained charts and detailed drawings. Though frequently ridiculed by critics today as too intricate or sensational (and also for his presentations on Egypt's Great Pyramid and on the Gap Theory), his charts were especially popular in the years between the First and Second World Wars prior to the advent of contemporary audio-visual and tools technology.

Eschatology

Larkin's eschatology is decidedly premillennial and dispensational, and his published books and charts did much to stimulate dispensationalism and the study of prophecy in the United States in the first half of the twentieth century. He taught and popularized the phrase "the mountain peaks of prophecy," by which he taught that, "the Old Testament prophet saw the future as separate peaks of one mountain. He did not see that these peaks assembled themselves in groups, with a valley, the 'valley of the church,' between" (*Dispensational Truth*, 7). Larkin's understanding of the history of the doctrine of eschatology is flawed in that he misinterprets the views of historical figures such as the Reformers, identifying too many major figures with premillennialism. Also, he acknowledges only premillennialism and postmillennialism. Larkin rejected date-setting schemes but held firmly to the doctrine of imminency. He did, however, argue that there were ten signs of the times that showed that "while we cannot name the exact date of the Lord's Return its nearness may be known by the character of the Times" (*Dispensational Truth*, 173). The signs were: postmillennialism, apostasy, false teachers, spiritualism, heaping up treasure, a Laodicean church (representing present times, the last segment of church history), the fig-tree sign (including Zionism), the distress of nations, and "Noah days" (spiritual apathy).

See also DISPENSATIONALISM.

Timothy J. Demy

Clarence Larkin, *Dispensational Truth or God's Plan and Purpose in the Ages* (Philadelphia: self-published, 1920), *The Book of Revelation* (Philadelphia: self-published, 1919) and "Prospectus of the Publications of the Late Rev. Clarence Larkin" (Glenside, Penn.: Rev. Clarence Larkin Estate, n.d.); Harry S. Stout, *Dictionary of Christianity in America* (Downers Grove, Ill.: InterVarsity Press, 1990).

LAW AND GRACE

It is evident that law and grace have been principles of God's administration during both the Old and New Testament periods. A major question to be answered is: What obligation does the Christian have to the old covenant and/or Mosaic Law? The position that is argued in this article is that the Christian is under no obligation to the old covenant or Mosaic Law. The Christian has been set free from the bondage of the Old Testament law and is under obligation to the new covenant and the teachings of Jesus Christ as stated in the New Testament.

The Christian is not antinomian (opposed to the law): "For whatever was written in earlier times was written for our instruction, that through perseverance and the encouragement of the Scriptures we might have hope" (Rom. 15:4). The law, a reflection of God's spiritual standard, demonstrates to humankind the sinfulness of sin and convict humankind of personal sin (Rom. 4:15; 5:19–21; 7:7–14; Gal. 3:19). The law "has become our tutor to lead us to Christ, that we may be justified by faith" (Gal. 3:24). This does not mean that we are under obligation to it but affirms an important ministry of the law in salvation and sanctification. Unbelievers are under obligation to obey the whole law, which is impossible, therefore they are forced upon the mercy of God to trust God to save them from their sin (2 Cor. 3:4–18).

I do not believe that the Bible teaches that we can divide the old covenant and law into various segments (moral, civil, ceremonial, cultic, cultural, etc.) which must or must not be obeyed today on the basis of classification. The New Testament presents the law as a single and indivisible unit. There is little exegetical justification to divide the old covenant and law into categories in order to suggest that certain moral ones must be obeyed and other ceremonial or cultic motifs are abrogated. We are either obligated to the whole law or set free from its absolute and complete covenant mandate (Gal. 3:10; 5:13; James 2:10).

Christians are not under the old covenant and law but under the new covenant and the teachings of Jesus Christ. Although some Old Testament commands and principles are reiterated in the New Testament, these repetitions do not argue that the Christian is under the old covenant. In fact, some Old Testament principles are given a higher standard by which the Christian is to live in the New Testament period. An example of this is found in Matthew 5:27–28: "You have heard that it was said, 'Do not commit adultery.' But I tell you that anyone who looks at a woman lustfully has already committed adultery with her in his heart."

The New Testament argues that the Christian is not under obligation or bondage to the old covenant. "For sin shall not be your master, because you are not under law, but under grace. What then? Shall we sin because we are not under law but under grace? By no means!" (Rom. 6:14–15). The Christian is able to fulfill the law through the work of the Holy Spirit in their life (Rom. 8:1–4). Paul argues for this dispensational change in Galatians 3:23–25: "Before this faith came, we were held prisoners by the law, locked up until faith should be revealed. So the law was put in charge to lead us to Christ that we might be justified by faith. Now that faith has come, we are no longer under the supervision of the law (see also Gal. 3:19–22; 4:1–11; 5:16–18; Eph. 2:15–16; Heb. 7:11–22).

The old covenant and Mosaic Law have been superseded by the new covenant and teachings of Jesus Christ (Heb. 8:8–13). There is much continuity between the old covenant and new covenant, but this continuity is not the basis for obedient obligation to the Christian today. The old covenant and law have been fulfilled through the life of Christ. The Christian can fulfill the law by the indwelling presence of the Holy Spirit and the outworking of the life of Christ in their life (Matt. 5:17–20; Rom. 8:1–4).

See also NEW COVENANT, THEOLOGY OF THE.

John A. McLean

George Knight, *Law and Grace: Must a Christian Keep the Law of Moses?* (Philadelphia: Westminster, 1962); Daniel Fuller, *Gospel and Law: Contrast or Continuum?* (Grand Rapids: Eerdmans, 1980).

LEVITICUS, ESCHATOLOGY OF

Leviticus deals with the law of the priests, the sons of Levi. It presents God's plan for teaching His chosen people how to approach Him in a holy manner. The book emphasizes the purpose of priest in making this approach to God reverent and holy. Leviticus sets forth the holiness of God, human sinfulness, and atonement whereby the sinful person is able to approach God.

The book continually (fifty-seven times in twenty-seven chapters) stresses the role of Moses in recording the regulations given to him by God concerning correct worship in the rites of the tabernacle. Too, Ezra the scribe (Ezra 6:8) refers to the scroll of Moses as the source used in his day to determine correct procedure in the dedication of the rebuilt temple. Jesus also confirmed the

Mosaic authorship of the book (Mark 1:44). The date of the writing is 1450–1410 B.C.

There are no major prophecies contained in the book, although chapter 23 outlines the feasts of the Lord, which are prophetic of future events. The Passover (23:4–5) points to the sacrifices of Christ. The Lord's feast of unleavened bread (23:6–8) represents holy communion with Christ. Christ's resurrection as the firstfruits from the dead is represented by the Feast of Firstfruits (23:9–14). The Holy Spirit's coming at Pentecost is seen in the Feast of Weeks (23:15–22). The Feast of Trumpets represents Israel's future regathering (23:23–25). The Day of Atonement represents the repentance of Israel at the second coming of Christ (23:26–32). Lastly, the Feast of Tabernacles, the final feast, is prophetic of Israel's regathering and restoration at the Second Coming (23:33–44).

See also HOLY SPIRIT IN THE CHURCH AGE; JEWS, RETURN OF THE.

Rick Bowman

Merrill F. Unger, *Unger's Bible Dictionary* (Chicago: Moody Press, 1966); John F. Walvoord, *The Bible Prophecy Handbook* (Wheaton: Victor Books, 1990); John F. Walvoord and Roy B. Zuck, eds., *The Bible Knowledge Commentary* (Wheaton: Victor Books, 1985).

LINDSEY, HAROLD L.

Harold L. (Hal) Lindsey (b. 1929) authored in 1970 *The Late Great Planet Earth*, which became the greatest selling book in the history of Christendom next to the Bible itself, surpassing combined sales of *Pilgrim's Progress* around 1990. It was declared by the *New York Times* the top selling nonfiction book of the 1970s. *Late Great Planet* became the introduction to dispensational premillennialism for a whole generation of Vietnam-era evangelicals. For tens of thousands of its readers, it played a key role in their conversion to Christ.

Born and raised in Houston, Texas, Lindsey was reared in a nominal church-going family. After what Lindsey called a few "false starts" during his youth, he came to faith in Christ at age twenty-six, while a tugboat captain in New Orleans through reading a Gideon Bible that was given to him at school. Shortly after his conversion he returned to Houston and found his way to Berachah church where he heard his first message on Bible prophecy from the pastor, Robert Thieme.

Within a couple of years of his conversion, Lindsey believed that God was leading him into the ministry. Lindsey, with no college, was admitted to Dallas Seminary through the influence of Pastor Thieme and other circumstances and graduated in 1962. Lindsey went on staff with Campus Crusade as a campus minister and worked on college campuses on the West Coast. He was greatly involved in many of the activities of the Jesus Movement of the late '60s and early '70s. This lead him to develop messages on Bible prophecy, which he often gave to college audiences. Many would ask for more information about prophecy after hearing the messages. Lindsey would direct them to the writings of his professors from Dallas Seminary. Many would ask for a more simple treatment of the subject, which lead him to write *Late Great Planet* in 1969. Lindsey had no idea that his book would sell as it did and he was cast into the limelight, the most visible spokesman for dispensational premillennialism.

Lindsey appears to have developed his views of eschatology from various influences that include Thieme, his Dallas professors, and his own study. Lindsey's system of eschatology is typical of mainstream dispensationalism except in a couple of areas.

1. Lindsey taught that within a generation (a generation equals forty years) of Israel's becoming a nation again, the Lord would return (*Late Great Planet*, p. 43). This was based upon his interpretation that the fig tree in Matthew 24:32 is a symbol for the reconstitution of Israel as a nation. Thus, the generation (Matt. 24:34) that saw Israel become a nation would also see the Second Coming. Since Israel became a nation in 1948, many believe that Lindsey implied Christ's return would occur by 1988. While a few dispensationalists have held a similar

interpretation in the past, none of Lindsey's mentors agreed with his view. This teaching became a point of controversy within dispensational circles and focus for anti-dispensational critique. Most dispensationalists believed that Lindsey's view contradicted an imminent pretribulational rapture, held by Lindsey and fellow dispensationalists. However, through Lindsey's popularity in general, his view gained a considerable following.

2. Lindsey tended to depart from traditional dispensational exposition in some of his understanding of Revelation. He often saw modern human technology as a means that God would use to fulfill the judgments of the seven-year Tribulation rather than direct, divine causality. Such an approach has tended to bring in an element of historicism into his otherwise futurist understanding of prophecy.

Hal Lindsey continues to be a popular and influential force in the area of Bible prophecy in our day. While his speculation about end-time events beginning by 1988 did not materialize, his modified position is that they will within the general lifetime of those living today. Lindsey has done a great deal to expose the modern American public to his version of dispensational premillennialism.

See also PREMILLENNIALISM.

Thomas D. Ice

Hal Lindsey, *The Late Great Planet Earth* (Grand Rapids: Zondervan, 1970), *There's A New World Coming* (Grand Rapids: Zondervan, 1973), *The Liberation of Planet Earth* (Grand Rapids: Zondervan, 1974), *The Terminal Generation* (Old Tappan, N.J.: Revell, 1976), *The 1980s: Countdown to Armageddon* (New York: Bantam Books, 1980), *The Rapture: Truth or Consequences* (New York: Bantam Books, 1983), and *Planet Earth–2000* A.D.*: Will Mankind Survive?* (Palos Verdes, Calif.: Western Front, 1994).

LORD'S PRAYER, THE

The Lord's Prayer, following Matthew's account, is actually a model prayer that Jesus taught His disciples rather than a prayer to be recited (though Luke may permit its recitation). Christ did not teach *what* to pray, but *how* to pray. The prayer is divided into two basic sections, namely, petitions regarding the glorification of God and the physical and spiritual needs of believers. The first prayer sets forth attitude needed toward God when we pray, addressing Him as "Our Father." God is personal and kindly toward His children. His character is magnified in the second petition, "hallowed be Your name." Holding God's name sacred is more than simply not blaspheming the word *God*; we are to honor His person and works among us. The third petition of glorifying God—"Your kingdom come, Your will be done, as in heaven, so on the earth"—recognizes the coming of His future kingdom in which He will rule throughout the earth. Because of the rebellion of humankind, the dominion of God is not universally accepted in the present age, but the petition anticipates the time when it will truly happen at the end of this age when Christ reigns on the earth.

The second portion of the prayer begins, "Give us today our daily bread," referring to the believer's expectation of God's physical provisions. Bread symbolizes food to eat and also other physical needs of life and health. The second petition— "forgive us our debts" (*sins* in Luke)—addresses the spiritual side of life. Even as we need physical help from our heavenly Father, we also need spiritual healing. Not only, however, do we personally need forgiveness from spiritual failure, we need to forgive others their failures too. The last petition may be puzzling—"bring us not into temptation"—since God tempts no person (James 1:13). Since God does, however, control the circumstances of life, the prayer is that He will help us not enter situations in which we might fall into sin, indicating a call for His protection from evil and from the Evil One. The final words, the doxology—"for yours is the kingdom and the power and the glory forever. Amen"—do not occur in the earliest and most reliable manuscripts but have been used by the church from the earliest period (cf. the Didache and the Western Text).

H. Wayne House

M

MACDONALD, MARGARET

Margaret Macdonald (1815–ca. 1840) is alleged by Dave MacPherson, a posttribulational polemicist, to be the originator of pretribulationism as a result of a prophetic revelation in the spring of 1830. Even though there is no actual evidence to support his claim, MacPherson is correct that his spurious charge has served to make the fifteen-year-old Scottish lass "a household name in Christian circles."

Margaret Macdonald was born and lived in Port Glasgow, Scotland, with twin brothers who ran the family shipping business. The Macdonald family had gravitated toward the charismatic influences of the Irvingite Movement by 1830. The Macdonalds were a sickly family and MacPherson says that little Margaret was slowly dying of a terminal disease. In her bedroom she became the recipient of a series of prophetic revelations. MacPherson claims that one of her revelations predicted that the true church would be raptured to heaven before the arrival of the Antichrist. This prophecy was recorded by Robert Norton and later published in a book from which MacPherson claims his discovery of the supposed cover-up of pretribulational origins.

Even though MacPherson's writings are filled with historical quotes and allusions to nineteenth-century sources, he has yet to establish *any* documented basis for his claims. First, J. N. Darby, and others (i.e., Pseudo-Ephraem, Morgan Edwards, probably others) had already developed various forms of pretribulationism. Darby, as early as January 1827 held such a view. Second, a study of Macdonald's prophecy does not reveal *any* aspects of pretribulationism. Instead, Macdonald is a posttribulational historicist who wanted her hearers to wake up to the enlightenment that Christ's coming was near. She believed that only spiritually sensitive Christians would be aware of this. Third, even if Macdonald's prophecy contained pretribulational elements, which it does not, MacPherson has yet to produce one piece of hard evidence that Darby, who had already developed his rapture view, was influenced in any way by Macdonald.

MacPherson's theory of rapture origins has been persuasive only for rabid anti-pretribulationists who, like himself, seem convinced that such a view must have a defective source. MacPherson has found only what he believed he would find before he set out on his quest. This may explain why no other researcher who is familiar with original sources has sided with MacPherson's biased revisionism. Those who propagate the Macdonald myth only reference MacPherson as a source and never contribute original research to advance the view. On the other hand, scholars with expertise in matters relating to MacPherson's claim reject his notion. Flegg, in a comment that directly refers to MacPherson's charge declares, "Several writers have attempted to trace Darby's secret rapture theory to prophetic statement associated with Irving, but their arguments do not stand up to serious criticism." F. F. Bruce concludes, "Direct dependence by Darby on Margaret Macdonald is unlikely."

Margaret Macdonald, in spite of MacPherson's claims, is not a factor in the history of premillennialism. Nevertheless, her alleged role must be dealt with. It is certainly true that the veracity of any viewpoint must be established or disqualified in light of Scripture, not on the basis of historical pedigree.

Thomas D. Ice

Columba Graham Flegg, *"Gathered Under Apostles:" A Study of the Catholic Apostolic*

Church (Oxford: Clarendon Press, 1992); Roy A. Huebner, *The Truth of the Pre-Tribulation Rapture Recovered* (Millington, N.J.: Present Truth Publishers, 1976) and *Precious Truths Revived and Defended Through J.N. Darby*, vol. 1 (Morganville, N.J.: Present Truth Publishers, 1991); Thomas D. Ice, "Why the Doctrine of the Pretribulational Rapture Did Not Begin with Margaret Macdonald," *Bibliotheca Sacra* (April–June 1990), 155–68; Dave MacPherson, *The Incredible Cover-Up* (Medford, Oreg.: Omega Publications, 1975) and *The Rapture Plot* (Simpsonville, S.C.: Millennium III Publishers, 1995).

MALACHI

Dating the book of Malachi is complicated due to the lack of historically detailed events mentioned within its pages. Tradition has always placed Malachi subsequent to Haggai and Zechariah. With Malachi giving clear evidence of an operational temple (1:6–2:7), it appears more than reasonable to date Malachi after the completion of the temple in 515 B.C., especially when we consider that the life and ministry of Zechariah lasted into the fifth century; the writing of Zechariah 9–14 is thought to be around 480 B.C. Certainly the effects of Zachariah's ministry (Ezek. 6:16–22) prevented Judah from deteriorating to the state we find it in throughout Malachi's prophecy. When Ezra arrives in Jerusalem in 458 B.C., he is horrified to discover that God's remnant has forsaken the Law by marrying foreign women which led to other detestable practices (Ezek. 9:1–2). Could the immediate response of repentance to Ezra's shame and disgrace over Judah's sin (Ezek. 9:6; 10:1–16) be the result of having heard the prophecies of Malachi in the recent past? Ezra's impact on Judah apparently lasted the twelve years that transpired until the third return to Judah under Nehemiah. Upon Nehemiah's arrival in 445 B.C., he is not overwhelmed, as was Ezra, with the moral decay of the people. Instead he immediately inspects the walls, claims that his mission is from God, and gains the unhesitating support of the people (Neh. 2:11–18). Even in the midst of opposition, the people prayed to God for strength and trusted Him to provide assistance (Neh. 4:4–15); the wall was completed in fifty-two days (Neh. 6:15). Nehemiah and Ezra had worked together to ensure that the people were taught the Law and that the nation's covenant with God was reinstituted (Neh. 8:1–10:39). The wealthy were also open to the correction of Nehemiah with regard to the way they abused the less fortunate (Neh. 5), and the people praised the Lord for the blessing of sustenance that they enjoyed from 445–433 B.C. (Neh. 5:13–14). This evidence forces a dating of Malachi to just prior to Ezra's return (ca. 470 B.C.) or closer to the end of the fifth century when the influence of Ezra and Nehemiah was diminishing (ca. 433–400 B.C.; cf. Neh. 13, which describes the cultic and relational difficulties Nehemiah was beginning to face with the children of Israel after his return to Jerusalem from Babylon).

Through a series of challenging questions, Malachi confronts Judah with their lack of commitment to the covenant and their detestable attitudes toward YHWH. The questions they ask in reply display the blatant disregard they possess for God's will. They question God's love for them (1:2–5); they dishonor God by bringing to Him the worst of their flocks for sacrifice while the priests turn a blind eye (1:6–2:9); they fail to protect the integrity of their covenant community by marrying foreign women who worship pagan gods; they divorce the wives of their youth and then stand amazed wondering why the Lord does not accept their token offerings (2:10–16); they become complacent and hopeless, believing that the unrighteous prosper and dominate because God is no longer interested in exacting justice (2:17–3:6); they refuse to admit any wrongdoing in relationship to their covenant with God even though their quality of life has diminished in proportion to the quantity of their offerings (3:7–12); because they fail to make the connection between their quality of life and their disobedience, they choose to reject the authority of God in their lives, seeing no value in giving God His due respect through faithful service and again questioning His justice (3:13–4:3). The prophecy ends challenging the people to remember their covenant relationship with God and promising to bring restoration to Israel through the prophet Elijah prior to the great and terrible day of the Lord (4:4–6).

To Judah's belief that the Lord will not differentiate between the righteous and the wicked or that He is uninterested in justice (2:17; 3:13–15), the prophet responds in eschatological proportions. To take such a stand is to accuse God of duplicity and disloyalty to His covenant with Abraham and with every promise He has made to His children since then. An accusation of this magnitude reeks of insolence and demands a counterresponse of equal magnitude, a response that will reach into the future and reveal God's ultimate solution to the sin problem: the great and terrible Day of the Lord (4:5). But what is the path that gets us to this day of judgment? The answer is disclosed in the relationship between the two responses Malachi offers to counter the Judean accusation in 3:1–5 and 3:16–4:6.

In these passages, Malachi reveals the eventual coming of three distinct personalities: the Lord's messenger (3:1), Elijah the prophet (4:5), and the Lord Himself (3:1–5; 4:5). Scholars are unanimous on the identification of the messenger as John the Baptist, the forerunner of the first coming of Jesus Christ. Isaiah spoke of one who would prepare the world for the coming of the Lord (40:3). Jesus clearly links John the Baptist to Isaiah's prophecy (Matt. 3:1–6; see John 1:23 where John clearly identifies himself as "the voice of one crying in the wilderness, 'Make straight the way of the LORD.'") and also identifies John as the fulfillment of Malachi's prophecy (Matt. 11:7–10). With the identification of the messenger certain, it becomes clear that Malachi 3:1 speaks of John the Baptist preparing the way for the Lord, the messenger, or "angel of the covenant" (Jesus Christ), to make His initial appearance into the world of humankind (Eugene H. Merrill identifies the messenger of the covenant as John the Baptist and applies verses 2–4 to his ministry; verse 5 is eschatological). Verses 2–5 then describe events that are connected with the Lord's second return when He purifies worship that is connected with the temple. The questions "Who can endure the day of His coming? And who can stand when He appears?" are asked to make it clear to Malachi's audience that the wicked have no chance in that day and that God is just and will render justice in His time. Verse 5 makes it abundantly clear that wickedness, whether connected with worship in the temple or in the life of the nation as a whole, has no place in God's future kingdom. The God of Abraham, Isaac, and Jacob has not changed His position with regard to the eradication of evil (3:6). With this message being addressed to a Jewish audience, one should not be surprised to see the first and second comings of the Lord viewed as a single event. Malachi's major concern is to respond to the negative accusationby his audience with a statement that describes the ultimate intention of the Lord to purge wickedness from Judean worship. The vantage point of additional progressive revelation allows us to see the full extent of the passage.

To further rebut the ridiculous accusations of the people who saw the immediate prosperity of the wicked as a reason to ignore faithful living, Malachi describes the ultimate fate of those who fear the Lord against those who choose to forsake Him (3:16–4:3). God makes it clear that He does not forget the efforts of those who live faithfully, who fear the Lord (3:16–17). The Lord declares that a day is coming (4:1) when He will place His protection on His own possession (3:17) while letting the arrogant experience the devastation of His wrath (4:1–3) and thus be excluded from the kingdom.

The forerunner of this great and terrible day yet to come is identified as Elijah the prophet (4:5). It must be understood at this point that there is no connection between John the Baptist and Elijah. They are two separate individuals, one being the forerunner to the first coming of Christ, the latter being the forerunner of the second coming of Christ who arrives in the last days prior to the great and terrible Day of the Lord. The priests and Levites who understood the eschatological ramifications of the message of John were not considering the possibility of two comings; a Messiah who would come and die was unacceptable to them even though they should have had some expectation of it (Isa. 53). This fact would cause them to link Malachi 3:1 with 4:5 and ask the inevitable question, "Are you Elijah?" to which John responded, "No" (John 1:19–23). The confusion among scholars is introduced by a remark Jesus made to His disciples who wondered why the scribes adamantly claimed that Elijah must precede the coming of Messiah (Matt. 17:10). Though Jesus confirmed the scribes claim, saying that "Elijah indeed comes, and *will* restore all things" (Matt. 17:11; cf. Mal. 4:5–6), He states that in fact, "Elijah is come already, and they knew him not, but did unto him whatsoever they would" (Matt. 17:12). In what sense is Jesus comparing John to Elijah? Because He makes it clear that the actual Elijah is yet to come, it appears that the comparison Jesus makes between John and Elijah is designed more to draw attention to Himself as the Person, the Lord, the Messiah whom both the messenger (Mal. 3:1) and Elijah (Mal. 4:5) precede, than it is to make John an antitype of Elijah who came in the spirit and power of Elijah (Luke 1:13–17). Certainly John's ministry was similar to Elijah's in that it was powerful and conducted with the same energy and impact on the people being prepared to receive the Messiah, but John was not Elijah. Even Jesus' statement that John's ministry could have brought about the kingdom and accomplished the restorative work of Elijah *if* Israel was willing to receive the message of the kingdom (Matt. 11:14), is philosophical in nature, for Jesus knew that rejection of both John and Himself was inevitable (Matt. 17:12; cf. Matt. 11:15–19; John 2:19–21). From the perspective of the omniscient God and complete revelation, it is obvious that the messenger of Malachi 3:1 is John the Baptist, who prepares the way of the Lord at His first coming, and Elijah of Malachi 4:5 is the prophet who will preface the second coming of the Lord before that great and terrible day. Scholars differ over whether Elijah is the actual prophet or another person who will come in the power and spirit of Elijah. However, only John is said to have come in the power and spirit of Elijah; it is not necessary to make this statement of a character who is identified as the person himself. One author attempted to place John the Baptist in both Malachi 3:1 and 4:5, but this is an unlikely interpretation.

With these eschatological predictions, Malachi successfully responds to the untenable position of the Judeans by assuring them that God will have His day when wickedness will be judged and righteousness will prevail. It is wise for any people to heed the final exhortation of Malachi: "Remember the law of Moses My servant, even the statutes and ordinances which I commanded" (Mal. 4:4). It is only through a knowledge of God's Word that people can understand the love of God, can honor and fear Him, and can hope for the coming day when righteousness will be vindicated once and for all.

See also ABRAHAMIC COVENANT.

Gary P. Stewart

Robert L. Alden, "Malachi" in *The Expositor's Bible Commentary*, ed. Frank E. Gaebelein (Grand Rapids: Zondervan, 1985); Craig A. Blaising, "Malachi" in *The Bible Knowledge Commentary*, eds. John F. Walvoord and Roy B. Zuck (Wheaton: Victor Books, 1985); D. A. Carson, "Matthew" in *The Expositor's Bible Commentary,* ed. Frank E. Gaebelein (Grand Rapids: Zondervan, 1985); Arnold G. Fruchtenbaum, *The Footsteps of the Messiah, A Study of the Sequence of Prophetic Events* (Tustin, Calif.: Ariel Ministries Press, 1983); Walter C. Kaiser Jr., *Malachi: God's Unchanging Love* (Grand Rapids: Baker, 1984); J. Randall Price, *The Desecration and Restoration of the Temple as an Eschatological Motif in the Old Testament, Jewish Apocalyptic Literature, and the New Testament* (Ann Arbor, Mich.: UMI Publications, 1994); Eugene H. Merrill, *Haggai, Zechariah, Malachi: An Exegetical Commentary* (Chicago: Moody Press, 1994); John F. Walvoord, *Prophecy Knowledge Handbook* (Wheaton: Victor Books, 1990).

MARRIAGE SUPPER OF THE LAMB

Revelation 19:9 refers to the marriage supper of the Lamb, an event closely associated with the marriage of the Lamb in Revelation 19:7. Various identifications of the wife of the Lamb described in 19:7–8 have included the redeemed of national Israel, the church, and Israel and the church. Portrayal of Israel as a faithless wife of the Lord in the OT is an obstacle to the first and third possibilities, as is the chronology of Israel's resurrection. The redeemed of Israel will not rise until after the Seventieth Week of Daniel (Dan. 12:1–2), so they will not be part of the bride at the time depicted in Revelation 19:7–8, a time before the Second Advent (Rev. 19:11–16). On the other hand, NT evidence for the church as the bride of Christ is abundant (e.g., 2 Cor. 11:2; Eph. 5:31–32). Description of the new Jerusalem that follows the millennial kingdom implies inclusion of Israel in the bride along with the church, however (Rev. 21:12, 14). The bride represents, then, a growing body of the people of God because the new Jerusalem is also Christ's bride (21:2, 9–10). The marriage supper of the Lamb is an integral part of the marriage. Following the initial presentation of the bride to the Lamb will ensue a long celebration, which in NT times was a component of the marital occasion. This wedding feast will transpire during the earthly kingdom of God, the bride being the church and the invited guests (Rev. 19:9) the saints of other ages. The Gospels several times picture the future kingdom on earth as a wedding feast (Matt. 8:11; 22:1–14; 26:29; Luke 14:15–24). The Lord Jesus promised the Laodicean overcomers the privilege of participation in this feast (Rev. 3:20).

R. L. Thomas

A. J. McClain, *The Greatness of the Kingdom* (Grand Rapids: Zondervan, 1959), 466; J. D. Pentecost, *Things to Come* (Findlay, Ohio: Dunham, 1958), 226–28; R. L. Thomas, *Revelation 8–22* (Chicago: Moody, 1995), 364–71; J. F. Walvoord, *The Prophecy Knowledge Handbook* (Wheaton: Victor, 1990), 617–19.

MARTYR, JUSTIN

The most important figure among the class of second-century defenders of the faith collectively known as "apologists" was the professional philosopher Justin Martyr (A.D. 100–165). Although born in Flavia Neapolis in Samaria, Justin was evidently converted in Ephesus in Asia Minor, where he no doubt met the venerable bishops Papias and Polycarp. Ephesus, too, was the setting for his famous dialogue with the Jew Trypho. Though a prolific writer, only three of Justin's works—two *Apologies* and the *Dialogue with Trypho*—have survived. The latter is the oldest extant apology directed toward the Jews.

Justin was one of the earliest fathers to present the case for a literal interpretation of prophecy. He regarded fulfilled prophecy as the authenticator of Christ's ministry (*First Apol.* 30), an aid to faith (*First Apol.* 33), and the guarantee that future events will be fulfilled (*First Apol.* 52). Justin expected the coming millennial age to be the time during which covenant promises to Abraham and David would be literally fulfilled.

Teaching on the imminency of Christ's return is absent in Justin's writing. His aim, however, was to prove to Trypho, a Jew—and to a lesser extent, the Romans—the fact that two advents of Christ had been predicted, not to proclaim the time (the imminence) of His future return. Had Justin been discoursing with Christians, his focus would no doubt have included this element.

It is evident that Justin expected the church to suffer at the hands of the Antichrist before Christ comes at the end of the age. He viewed this tribulation under the Antichrist as but an extension of persecution already being suffered by believers of his day and of no greater intensity than the current trials (*Dial.* 110). In sum, the Antichrist's persecution would simply take place within the context of Roman persecution.

As to when the Antichrist's persecution would occur and how long it would last, in his discussion of Daniel's reference to a time, and times, and an half (Daniel 7:25; 12:7), Justin concluded that "he whom Daniel foretells would have dominion" for this length of time, "is even already at the door, about to speak blasphemous and daring things against the Most High" (*Dial.* 32). Justin apparently believed that the Antichrist would soon appear, speak blasphemous things against God, and continue the persecution of the saints begun by the Roman state. It was into this context of ongoing persecution that Christ was expected to come at any moment to rescue those who trust in Him (imminent intratribulationism).

The explicit declarations of Justin's premillennialism are numerous. He argued that just as surely as the prophecies concerning Christ's first coming were fulfilled, just so we may expect precise fulfillment of those surrounding His Second Advent (*First Apol.* 52). In his discourse with Trypho, he insisted that "completely orthodox Christians feel certain that there will be a resurrection of the flesh, followed by a thousand years in the rebuilt, embellished, and enlarged city of Jerusalem, as was announced by the Prophets Ezechiel, Isaias and the others" (*Dial.* 80). Justin supported his position on the Millennium from a collective understanding of Isaiah 65:17–25, Genesis 2:17, 2 Peter 3:8 (cf. Ps. 90:4), and John's explicit statements in Revelation 20:4–6 (*Dial.* 81).

One facet of Justin's "orthodox faith" was a belief in the twofold nature of the resurrection. His order of millennial events was (1) the second coming of Christ; (2) the first resurrection—of the righteous dead; (3) the millennial kingdom; and then (4) the general resurrection—of the wicked dead (*Dial.* 80–81, 113). The context suggests that Justin's belief in the twofold resurrection was based upon Revelation 20. The essentials of Justin's overall outline of end-time events are the: (1) appearance of the man of apostasy; (2) Second Advent; (3) Battle of Armageddon; (4) first resurrection; (5) Millennium; (6) second resurrection; (7) general judgment of all; and (8) the eternal state, preceded by conflagration, then renewal.

Larry V. Crutchfield

L. Crutchfield, "Ages and Dispensations in the Ante-Nicene Fathers" in *Vital Prophetic Issues* (Grand Rapids: Kregel, 1995), 44–60, "The Apostle John and Asia Minor as a Source of Premillennialism in the Early Church Fathers" in *JETS,* 31:411–27 (December 1988), and "Israel and the Church in the Ante-Nicene Fathers" in *Bibliotheca Sacra* 144:254–76 (July–September 1987); H. Dressler, et al., eds., *The Fathers of the Church: A New Translation,* vol. 6 (Washington, D.C.: Catholic University of America Press, 1948); R. M. Grant, *Greek Apologists of the Second Century* (Philadelphia: Westminster Press, 1988); A. Roberts and J. Donaldson, eds., *The Ante-Nicene Fathers*, vol. 1 (Grand Rapids: Eerdmans, n.d.), 159–306.

MATHERS, RICHARD, INCREASE, AND COTTON

The Mathers are likely the most significant family in seventeenth-century Puritan New England. Richard (1596–1669) produced a dynasty of sons and descendants who were outstanding Congregational ministers. They held a premillennial viewpoint and had a great interest in eschatology.

Richard was born in England, educated at Oxford, and immigrated to Massachusetts in 1635. He gathered to him a church at Dorchester, Massachusetts, and pastored there from 1636 to 1669. He was an advocate of the Half-Way Covenant, which loosened the strict requirements on church membership and thus broadened participation in Puritan society. He wrote a number of books and helped in the framing of the Cambridge Platform in 1648 that served to codify the practices and government of New England Congregationalsim.

Richard's son Increase (1639–1723) was born in Dorchester and was educated at Harvard College and Trinity College, Dublin, Ireland. Early in his ministry he pastored churches in England and America. In 1664 he became pastor of North Church in Boston and served there until his death. He lead an active and varied life and was involved in many significant activities in addition to the pastorate. Increase was the leading developer of the Half-Way Covenant, president of Harvard (1648–1701), a special agent to England to secure a new charter for the colony of Massachusetts, and published about one hundred books. He is credited with ending executions for witchcraft.

The most famous Mather is Increase's son Cotton (1663–1728). Born in Boston and educated at Harvard, he became joint pastor with his father in Boston and served as sole pastor upon Increase's death until his own death in 1728. Cotton was actively involved in the life of Boston community. He was widely celebrated as a historian and theologian. Cotton was a prolific writer who produced about 385 works, many multivolumed. His *Great Works of Christ in America*, an ecclesiastical history of New England, is still in print today. He became involved in the Salem witch trials of 1692 and advocated execution of witches.

Historicist, premillennial eschatology was woven throughout the thinking, sermons, and writings of the Mathers. It was the lens through which they interpreted events of their day. The premillennialism of the Mathers is also significant because of the perception that Puritan New England of the Mathers' era was awash in postmillennialism. This does not appear to be the case. Furthermore, it appears that premillennialism was more dominant than some have thought. Timothy Weber notes: "The Puritans, for example, had been overwhelmingly premillennial, but since the middle of the eighteenth century their original eschatological vision had been steadily giving way to postmillennialism."

Increase Mather says of New World Puritan premillennialism in 1710: "The first and famous pastors in the New England churches did, in their public ministry, frequently insist on the doctrine of Christ's glorious kingdom on earth, which shall take place after the conversion of the Jews and when the fullness of the Gentiles shall come in. It is a pity that this doctrine is no more inculcated by the present ministry.

Joshua Spalding writes, "Millenarian doctrines were, beyond all dispute, favorite doctrines with the Fathers of New England." James Davidson says, "Historians are probably most familiar with the eschatological opinions of Increase and Cotton Mather, who have generally been cast in the roles of archetypical premillennialists of the period before the Great Awakening.

The Mathers span the first century of Puritan America and are typical of their age. They were premillennial, although historicists, and establish the important role that premillennialism has played in the religious landscape of the New World from the earliest times.

Thomas D. Ice

James West Davidson, *The Logic of Millennial Thought: Eighteenth-Century New England* (New Haven: Yale University Press, 1977); Robert Middlekauff, *The Mathers* (London: Oxford, 1971); Elgin S. Moyer and Earle Cairns, *The Wycliffe Biographical Dictionary of the Church* (Chicago: Moody, 1982), 268.

MEDE, JOSEPH

Joseph Mede (1586–1638) was the father of English premillennialism. Born in Essex, England and educated at Christ's College, Cambridge (M.A., 1610; B.D., 1618), he was one of the leading intellectuals of his time. He served as professor of Greek at Cambridge, but was also fluent in Hebrew. An outstanding linguist, mathematician, and logician, Mede applied his skills to the field of eschatology. His original works were in Latin and were later translated into English. These included: *Clavis Apocalypticae* (*Key to the Revelation),* 1627, translated into English, 1643; *Exposition Concerning the Day of Christ's Second Coming,* 1642; and *The Apostasy of the Latter Times,* 1642.

One of Mede's unique interpretations focused on the "synchronism of prophecies" by which he determined the 1260 days, forty-two months and three and one-half years of Revelation all referred to the same time period. He reconstructed an outline of Revelation based solely upon internal considerations. He clearly believed in the literal return of Christ and the reign of the bride of Christ on earth during a thousand-year millennial kingdom. He also believed in two judgments, separated by the thousand years. The publication of *Key to the Revelation* in English in 1643 took England by storm and became the most popular book of its time. Christianson states: "Upon Mede's shoulders must rest the primary responsibility for the revival of millennial thought in England" (127). Mede strongly influenced Thomas Goodwin, Jeremiah Burroughs, John Milton, Isaac Newton, and Nathaniel Holmes.

Edward Hindson

Paul Christianson, *Reformers and Babylon* (Toronto: University of Toronto Press, 1978); R. Clouse, "The Apocalyptic Interpretation of Thomas Brightman and Joseph Mede" in *BETS,* XI:181–93 (1968); Peter Toon, ed., *Puritans, the Millennium, and the Future of Israel* (London: James Clarke, 1970).

MESSIAH, DEFINITION OF THE

The term *messiah* is a translation of the Hebrew word *māshîaḥ*, a verbal noun meaning "anointed one." The Greek translation of the word, utilized in both the LXX and the NT, is *christos*, from which comes the English word *Christ*. The Hebrew verb and noun are primarily applied to three types of individuals in the OT period—priests (Exod. 28:41; Lev. 4:3), kings (1 Sam. 12:3; 16:13), and prophets (1 Kings 19:16; Ps. 105:15). The idea is one of consecrating persons for sacred tasks, that is, to perform special functions in the theocratic program.

Some critical scholars deny that *mashiach* is ever used in the OT of a personal messiah. Of its thirty-nine occurrences, however, there are at least nine times where it could describe some future anointed one in the line of David who would be Yahweh's king: 1 Samuel 2:10, 35; Psalms 2:2; 20:6; 28:8; 84:9; Habakkuk 3:13; Daniel 9:25–26.

The doctrine of a promised messiah, however, is not limited simply to the term itself. The OT hope of a deliverer who would crush Satan's head (Gen. 3:15) and be the means of blessing to all humankind (Gen. 12:3) is described by a variety of terms. Some of these are "son" (Psalm 2:7), "branch" (Zech. 6:12–13), and "servant" (Isa. 41–53).

Regarding the specific number of promises about the Messiah, there is a wide divergence of opinion. Rabbinical writings refer to 456 separate OT passages used to refer to the Messiah and messianic times (Edersheim, 710–41). One Christian scholar lists 127 personal messianic prophecies (Payne, 667–68). The differences are due to the way in which the NT refers to the OT promises. There are direct messianic prophecies (e.g., Micah 5:2; Zech. 9:9); typical messianic prophecies, utilizing an immediate referent in the prophet's day that pointed to the ultimate referent (e.g., the sacrificial levitical system); and applications of OT concepts to the Messiah (e.g., the reference Matthew 2:23 makes to the prophets saying: "He will be called a Nazarene.") If we limit ourselves to the direct messianic prophecies just mentioned, a conservative number would be around 65. The key to understanding the role of the promised Messiah, and also the main difference between traditional Jewish and Christian messianic views, is His dual role of suffering and reigning. While there are many passages that describe a glorious reign for the Messiah (Jer. 23:5–6; 30:1–10; Zech. 14:3ff), there are others that describe His rejection and suffering (Ps. 22, Isa. 53, Zech. 9:9; 12:10; 13:5–7). The NT views the suffering and glory passages as fulfilled in Jesus' first and second comings. (Luke 24:25–27; 1 Peter 1:10–11).

From a theological perspective, the unique role of the Messiah is that He combines in His person and work the roles of the three different messiahs of the OT theocracy—the prophet, the priest, and the king. In this regard, it is interesting to note that there were individual Israelite examples of a priest and prophet (Ezekiel, Jeremiah), and a king and prophet (David), but no examples of a priest and king (apart from non-Israelite Melchizedek). This was because only the Messiah could combine these two functions (Zech. 6:12–13). Furthermore, the OT expectation of an eschatological prophet (Deut. 18:15–19) found its fulfillment in the messianic priest-king (see John 1:21 and Acts 3:22–26).

Therefore, the final Messiah would be the ideal prophet-priest-king. The relevance of the messianic idea to premillennialism lies in Jesus' fulfillment of these three offices. As the anointed one of the Lord, Jesus was, is, and shall be the Prophet, the Priest, and the King. Each of these roles, however, was emphasized at different times in His redemptive role. During His earthly ministry of teaching and preaching, His role as prophet was in the forefront (see John 6:14; 7:40). His sacrificial death, resurrection, ascension, and current session at His Father's right hand brings His role as priest in view (Ps. 110:1–2; Heb. 4:14; 10:11–12). Following His return to earth, during His millennial reign, His role as king will be stressed (Rev. 19:16). The point is that He is always the anointed king, but He enters into His public office as king during the Millennium. An OT example of this was the period of time between David's anointing as king (Isa. 16:13) and his eventual enthronement as Saul's successor (2 Sam. 5:3).

Only a premillennial framework of theology, therefore, can enable one to fully appreciate the role of Him who is the "Hope of Israel."

See also THEOCRATIC KINGDOM.

William Varner

David Baron, *Rays of Messiah Glory* (Grand Rapids: Zondervan, n.d.); Alfred Edersheim, *Life and Times of Jesus the Messiah* (Grand Rapids: Eerdmans, 1953); E. W. Hengstenberg, *Christology of the Old Testament* (Grand Rapids: Kregel Publications, 1970); Walter Kaiser, *The Messiah in the Old Testament* (Grand Rapids: Zondervan, 1995); J. Barton Payne, *Encyclopedia of Biblical Prophecy* (New York: Harper and Row, 1973).

MICAH, ESCHATOLOGY OF

Micah is a shortened form of the Hebrew name Mal'ākî (*Who is like Yahweh*). He was from Moresheth, a town about twenty-five miles southwest of Jerusalem, very near the Philistine city of Gath. Since his father's name is not mentioned many scholars believe this is an indication that he was from humble beginnings. His ministry was carried out in the days of Jotham (750–731 B.C.), Ahaz (735–715 B.C.), and Hezekiah (728–686 B.C.), kings of Judah (1:1; cf. Jer. 26:18). He is quoted in Jeremiah 26:18 by those who were defending the predictions of Jeremiah. He was a contemporary of Isaiah and Hosea.

The book is a collection of three messages all beginning with "hear." We find the beginning at 1:2: "Hear, O, peoples . . ."; 3:1: "Hear now . . ."; and 6:1: "Hear now what the LORD is saying." Martin outlines the messages as follows: Judgment Will Come (1:1–2:13), Blessing Will Follow Judgment (3:1–5:15), and An Indictment Of Sin and a Promise of Blessing (6:1–7:20). Hosea predicted the Assyrian destruction of Israel, the later defeat of Judah at the hands of the Babylonians, and also a future time of restoration and glory. Also notable are the prophecies about the Messiah's birthplace, lineage, and origin (5:2). He also referred to Him as Israel's King and Ruler (2:23; 5:2).

Judgment Will Come (1:2–2:13)

Micah calls all the peoples of the earth to be attentive to the Sovereign Lord (1:2), for the Lord was coming to tread on the high places of the earth (1:3). The result is that the mountains will melt under Him and the valleys will be split. The place of the Lord's coming forth will be like wax before a fire and like water poured down a steep place (1:4). The Lord's wrath is revealed to be coming on the rebellion of Jacob, which he states is "Samaria." He will make them a heap of ruins (1:6). This was literally fulfilled in 722 B.C. when the Assyrian army laid siege to Samaria and after three years conquered the city, taking most of the population captive (2 Kings 17:1–5). The main reason given for the Lord's judgment was their idolatrous worship, their spiritual adultery (1:7). Micah lamented the destruction coming on Samaria (1:8), and he says that it would also come on Judah and even reach Jerusalem (1:8–9). In 701 B.C., Sennacherib, king of Assyria, came with his army and destroyed forty-six cities (of which some are named here by Micah, 1:8–16), even reaching Jerusalem. This is literal fulfillment of Micah's prophecies.

In 2:1–11, Micah tells why this destruction was coming on Judah. Their first crime was to covet their neighbors' fields, houses, and inheritances and then to seize, take, and rob them of these possessions. The result would be that the Lord will bring calamity on them (2:3), and they will lose the land they had taken (2:4–5). The next problem was that the false prophets were telling the Lord's prophets, "Do not speak out." Micah, however, points out that if the true prophets "do not speak out concerning these things, reproaches will not be turned back." The people were apparently listening to the false prophets that told them what they wanted to hear (2:10–11), thus becoming the Lord's enemy (2:8). Micah closes this section with a message of promise. In the future the Lord will regather the remnant of Israel and will shepherd them (2:12) and be their leader (2:13). This will occur in the Millennium.

Blessing Will Follow Judgment (3:1–5:15)

Micah begins this section with an indictment against the leaders of Jacob and Israel. They of all people should be the ones to know what is just but, instead, they hate good and love evil (3:1). They feed on the people. They are compared to someone preparing an animal for the pot and then eating the stew (3:2–3). As a result, there would come a time when they will cry out for the Lord, but the Lord will not answer them (3:4). Micah then condemns the false prophets who lead the people astray. They were prophets for hire. If they were fed well (paid well) they would cry "Peace" for that individual, but if they were not paid well (nothing in their mouths) they would declare holy war (3:5). In contrast, Micah states, "I am filled with power—with the Spirit of the LORD—and with justice and courage, to make known to Jacob his rebellious act" (3:8). In 3:9–11, Micah lists the indictments the Lord has against them. Then, he reveals God's judgment, which will be Zion plowed as a field and Jerusalem becoming a heap of ruins (3:12). These prophecies were literally fulfilled in the Assyrian and Babylonian captivities.

In light of the prophecy of Jerusalem's destruction Micah prophesies a time yet future, the last days, in Israel's program when "the mountain of the house of the LORD will be established as the chief of the mountains" (4:1). This will occur when the millennial temple is built (Ezek. 40–44). During that time the nations of the earth will take their pilgrimage to the mountain of the Lord to learn His ways (4:2). The Lord will be the judge of those nations, war will not occur during this time between nations, and there will be world peace (4:3–4). In Micah's day each nation walked in the name of its god. In contrast, in the last days Israel will walk in the name of the Lord their God forever (4:5). Even the lame and the outcast will become a strong nation with the Lord ruling over them in Mount Zion which will result in the restoration of Israel's dominion (4:6–8). Then Micah predicts the Babylonian captivity, when agony will grip them "like a woman in childbirth" and they will go to Babylon (4:9–10). But in the same verse he speaks a word of hope. The Lord will redeem them from the hand of their enemies (4:10). The nations will gloat over Zion but like sheaves gathered to the threshing floor they will be threshed by Israel (4:11–13). The Babylonian captivity was literally fulfilled in 586 B.C. Micah 4:11–13 will be literally fulfilled in the great Battle of Armageddon (Rev. 16:16). As Martin points out, "The things Israel will capture in battle will be devoted to the Lord, whom Micah rightly calls the Lord of all the earth" (cf. Ps. 97:5; Zech. 4:14; 6:5).

Micah pictures the Babylonian destruction as a rod that will smite the judge of Israel on the cheek (5:1). Micah then prophesies of a future ruler in Israel that will come from Bethlehem Ephrathah (5:2; cf. Ruth 4:11). This ruler is unique in that he is said to be "from the days of eternity." Only Jesus Christ could fulfill these requirements and did very literally at His first coming (Matt. 2:6). In 5:3, we see that God will give Israel up until they are regathered to the land (cf. 2:12; 4:6–7). At that time, the ruler will arise and shepherd his flock in the strength of the Lord. He will be great to the ends of the earth and in that time He will be Israel's peace (5:4–5). Though Assyria would invade and conquer Israel for a time, ultimately Israel will prevail like a lion among the beasts of the forest and all their enemies will be cut off (5:5–9). This will occur at the Second Coming and in the Millennium. This same Ruler will destroy Israel's military armament and fortifications so they are not dependent on them and also cut off all false worship (5:10–14). He will also rule the nations and pour out His vengeance on them as He rules with an iron scepter (Ps. 2:9; Rev. 12:5; 19:15). This will occur during the millennial kingdom.

An Indictment of Sin and a Promise of Blessing (6:1–7:20)

The Lord now lists the many disputes He has against Israel. He lead them out of Egypt, ransomed them from slavery, gave them leaders (Moses, Aaron, and Miriam), and had done all of this so they would know the righteous acts of the Lord (6:1–5), but in return they did not even understand His righteousness. They questioned with what they should approach the Lord. All that they suggested has to deal with outward things (6:6–7), but the Lord sought the outward manifestations of an inward change, such as doing justice, loving kindness, and walking humbly before the Lord (6:8). Micah tells the people to "Hear" in reverence what the Lord is saying (6:9). The people of the wicked house had treasures of wickedness. They had gained these by wicked scales and deceptive weights (6:11). The rich men of the city had gained their wealth through violence and speaking lies and deceit (6:12). The Lord's judgment will come on Israel as a result of these indictments. The Lord says, "I will make you sick, striking you down, desolating you because of your sins." He also states, "And what you do preserve I will give to the sword" (6:13–15). His judgment is that He will give them up for destruction (6:16). Micah lamented over the situation of the nation.

Micah felt like someone that goes into the vineyard for grapes or a fig but there aren't any to be picked (7:1). In the same way, those who seek a godly person in Israel would not find what they sought. The godly person had perished from the land and the land was full of evil and bribery (7:2–3). The people left in Israel were like briars and even the most upright were like a thorn hedge (7:4). No one could be trusted (7:5) and even family relationships had broken down (7:6). In the midst of such evil Micah did find hope in watching expectantly for the Lord (7:7). Micah then proclaims a message of hope. It was true that Israel's sins would be punished but there will also be a time when Israel will be restored and the Lord will be her light (7:9). Israel's enemies will then be trampled (7:10) and Israel will rebuild her walls (7:11). In that day all of her enemies will come to her to learn of and to worship the Lord (7:12; cf. 4:2). But just previous to that, at His return, the Lord will judge the nations and leave them desolate (7:13; cf. Matt. 25:32–33, 46).

In Micah's closing section he reveals the glorious future the Lord has for His people. A future Shepherd will shepherd Israel with His scepter as Israel dwells in a fruitful land (7:14). Again the Lord will do miracles, and the nations will be ashamed as they see His overwhelming power (7:15–16). They will come out of their fortresses that are obviously useless against His power and they will approach Him trembling (7:17). In that day the rebellious acts of the remnant will be pardoned and He will again have compassion on them (7:18–19). The things Micah described he was confident would occur because of the Lord's truth and unchanging love to Jacob and Abraham. As Martin states, "Therefore Micah was trusting in God's promises to Abraham (Gen. 12:1–3; 15:18–21), which were confirmed to Jacob (Gen. 28:13–14), that He will bless their descendents." Thus, in the future God will fulfill the promises He made to Abraham that He pledged to fulfill regardless of the sinfulness of Israel (Gen.15:15; esp. v. 17). These prophecies will be fulfilled when God brings Israel back into the land and Christ rules over them in the millennial kingdom.

See also ABRAHAMIC COVENANT; THEOCRATIC KINGDOM.

Russell L. Penney

Gleason L. Archer, *A Survey of Old Testament Introduction* (Chicago: Moody Press, 1994); John A. Martin, "Micah" in *The Bible Knowledge Commentary,* eds. John F. Walvoord and Roy B. Zuck (Wheaton: Victor

Books, 1988); Thomas E. McComiskey, "Micah" in *The Expositor's Bible Commentary,* ed. Frank E. Gaebelein, vol. 7 (Grand Rapids: Zondervan, 1985); John F. Walvoord, *The Prophecy Knowledge Handbook* (Wheaton: Victor Books, 1990).

MILLENNIAL VIEWS OF THE CHURCH FATHERS

The word *millennium*, derived from a combination of two Latin words (*mille* and *annus*) meaning "thousand years" (known in the patristic period by its Greek equivalent, *chiliasm*), signifies the thousand-year period of the earthly reign of Christ spoken of six times in Revelation 20:2–7. The belief in a literal earthly kingdom presided over by Christ Himself implies that Christ will return *before* the millennium begins and thus is termed *pre*millennialism. This is in contrast to the *post*millennial view that Christ will return *after* a thousand years of unparalleled peace and righteousness on earth, and the *a*millennial position which holds that Christ will come after a spiritual or heavenly "millennium" of an unspecified period of time.

Character of Early Premillennialism

In the ante-Nicene age (until the Council of Nicea in A.D. 325), premillennialism was considered an article of orthodox faith handed down by the apostles (e.g., Justin M. *Dial.* 80; Irenaeus *Ag. Her.* 5.32.1). It constituted the central feature of ante-Nicene eschatology. The early fathers believed they were living in the last days and looked for the imminent return of Christ to establish the kingdom. Only under the combined impact of the allegorizing tendencies of the Alexandrian theologians (notably Origen, ca. 185–ca. 254), the union of church and state under Constantine (Roman emperor, 306–337), and the influence of the great African bishop and theologian Augustine (354–430), did the doctrine eventually fall into disrepute.

While the outline of end-time events varied in certain respects among the premillennial fathers, they typically held to the visible, imminent return of Christ, the bodily resurrection of the saints to rule with Christ in a literal thousand-year kingdom age, the resurrection and judgment of the wicked dead, followed by the eternal state. A more specific, composite outline of patristic eschatological expectation reveals that the fathers looked for:

1. Tribulation under the Antichrist within the context of Roman persecution
2. Christ's personal, visible return in the midst of persecution to:
   a. raise the righteous dead (first resurrection)
   b. rapture the saints
   c. fight the Battle of Armageddon
   d. destroy the Antichrist and all of his followers
   e. bind Satan
   f. reign on the throne of David with the saints from a restored Jerusalem
3. Establishment of the millennial age, of a thousand-years duration, brought in as the promised sabbath rest for the saints (year-day or sexta-/septamillennial tradition), in which there would be:
   a. literal fulfillment of covenant promises (including those concerning the land)
   b. a time of uncommon fertility and peace
4. Resurrection (second or general resurrection) and judgment of the wicked dead at the conclusion of the Millennium
5. Creation of a new heaven and earth, transformation of the righteous, and inauguration of the eternal state

With regard to the important premillennial issue of the relationship between Israel and the church, the early fathers maintained distinctions among the people of God throughout the ages. While they held that people in every age are justified by faith through the blood of Christ (and in that sense there is a type of soteriological unity among all the faithful who have ever lived), they nevertheless maintained a working concept of *peoples* of God, not *a people* of God. In the *Epistle of Barnabas* and especially in Justin Martyr and Irenaeus, as well as others who followed, there was the understanding that the peoples of God include: (1) the righteous who lived before Abraham (*a* spiritual seed of Abraham?), (2) the righteous physical descendants of Abraham (*a* spiritual seed of Abraham), and (3) those of the church age who are justified by faith after the fashion of Abraham (*the* spiritual seed of Abraham). To these three divisions of the faithful was added (4) the physical, unbelieving descendants of Abraham who comprise disinherited national Israel.

In this, the fathers are in disagreement with covenant amillennialists and covenant (or historic) premillennialists. The church was never confused with national Israel nor was it assumed to have existed in the Old Testament. The church, according to the fathers, began after the First Advent of Christ, not with Adam or Abraham (e.g., Irenaeus *Ag. Her.* 3.3.2–3; Cyprian *Epist.* 69.3).

Proponents of Early Premillennialism

First Century

The premillennial fathers of the ante-Nicene age included church leaders who were contemporary with and in some cases instructed by the apostles and those who were in turn their disciples and pedagogical benefactors. Collectively they are known as the "apostolic fathers." In this group are: Clement (fl. ca. 90–100), bishop of Rome; Papias (ca. 60–ca. 130/155), bishop of Hierapolis; Polycarp (ca. 70–155/160), bishop of Smyrna; and Ignatius (d. ca. 98/117), bishop of Antioch. Works from this period include the *Didache* (composed before the end of the first century); *Epistle of Barnabas* (composed ca. 70/117–138); and *Shepherd of Hermas* (composed apparently in two parts, ca. 96/140–150).

Second Century

The influential Christian leaders and premillennialists of the second century included the apologist Justin Martyr (ca. 100–165); the polemicists Irenaeus (ca. 120–ca. 202), bishop of Lyons, and his disciple Hippolytus (d. ca. 236), presbyter and teacher in Rome; and from the African school, Tertullian (150–225), apologist, moralist, and theologian. Though the evidence is not conclusive, usually listed also as second-century premillennialists are: Pothinus (ca. 87–177), Irenaeus's predecessor as bishop of Lyons; Melito (d. ca. 190), apologist and bishop of Sardis; Hegesippus (second century), church historian; Tatian (ca. 110–172), apologist and disciple of Justin Martyr; and Apollinaris (ca. 175), apologist and bishop of Hierapolis.

Third Century

In the third century, African fathers carried the torch of premillennialism and included Cyprian (ca. 200–258), master of rhetoric and bishop of Carthage; Commodian (ca. 200–ca. 275), Christian Latin poet in North Africa and possibly a bishop; and Lactantius (ca. 240–ca. 320), Latin rhetorician, Christian apologist, and historian. Other important premillennialists included Victorinus of Petau (d. ca. 304), Latin exegete and bishop of Petau near Vienne (in modern Austria); Methodius (d. 311), ecclesiastical writer and bishop of Olympus; and Julius Africanus (d. ca. 240), Christian writer and chronographer. Of secondary value because only sketchy historical accounts of their positions have survived are Nepos (ca. 230–250), bishop of Arsinoe (in Egypt), and his successor, Coracion (ca. 230–280).

Origin of Early Premillennialism

Although the early church's staunch adherence to premillennialism is generally acknowledged, the origin of the doctrine and the reason for its prevalence are disputed. In truth, the early fathers considered premillennialism to be the settled, orthodox belief of the church because they believed Scripture taught it, the apostle John validated it, and a literal hermeneutic required it.

Textual Sources

The early fathers quoted Scripture copiously to support their premillennial views. There was especially heavy reliance upon the Major Prophets and the Apocalypse. While tradition and the teaching of earlier church leaders were important, Scripture was paramount. It was Irenaeus's practice, for example, to draw doctrine from the inspired text first and only then to reference church leaders of the past who were in agreement with the sacred text (e.g., *Ag. Her.* 5.30.1).

In addition to texts from the canonical Scriptures usually cited by the fathers in support of their premillennial beliefs, certain noncanonical apocalyptic sources are frequently suggested by modern writers as possible contributors as well (e.g., 1 Enoch 10:19; 2 Apoc. Bar. 29:5; Jub. 4:29–30; 23:27; et al.). While the fathers did make use of this material, without question the most important single source was the Johannine book of Revelation. The earliest fathers—those closest to the apostles and their teaching—undeniably considered their belief in the premillennial return of Christ to be built first upon Old Testament precedent and then upon the teachings of Christ. But it was the apostle John to whom they turned for both written and oral validation of the premillennial doctrine set forth by Christ.

Apostolic Authority

Since the most direct teaching in Scripture on the millennial reign of Christ is found in the Apocalypse of John, it is instructive to note that most of the early adherents of premillennialism had direct contact either with John, the longest living apostle, or with his most famous disciple, Polycarp. According to tradition, John spent the latter portion of his life at Ephesus in Asia Minor (e.g., Irenaeus *Ag. Her.* 3.1.1; Eusebius *Ch. Hist.* 5.24.3–4). The origin of the views of perhaps seven early fathers usually identified as premillennialists may be traced in some way to the Asia Minor geographical context and the apostle who reportedly survived until the time of Trajan (A.D. 98–117).

Asia Minor was home to the apostolic fathers Polycarp (Smyrna) and Papias (Hierapolis), and the apologists Melito of Sardis and Apollinaris of Hierapolis. On his way to a martyr's death in Rome, Ignatius paused in Smyrna long enough to become acquainted with Polycarp and to write more than half of his extant epistles. And though not Justin Martyr's home, with Ephesus as the probable place of his conversion and scene of the famed dialogue with the Jew, Trypho, Asia Minor had a marked influence upon Justin's life and doctrine. For Irenaeus, the last and greatest of the Asiatic fathers, Smyrna was the probable birthplace of both the man and his theology. As resident apostle-teacher in Ephesus in his declining years, John must be reckoned a major cause of Asia Minor's uncommon ability to produce church leaders possessed of premillennial belief.

Literal Interpretation

As in modern dispensational premillennialism, literalism in prophetic interpretation was a key ingredient in the millenarian belief of the early fathers. The principle was affirmed and practiced by a majority of the church leaders who championed this doctrine. It was not until the allegorism of Alexandria began to take its toll that premillennialism entered a protracted period of decline.

During the first centuries of the church, its leaders were faced with a myriad of problems. With neither an established canon of either Testament nor principles of interpretation other than those of the rabbinical schools and with the three-pronged challenge of heresy from within and Judaism and paganism from without, the practice of biblical exegesis was anything but uniform. In varying degrees, the early fathers combined the allegorical method of interpretation—which had come down through pagan Greeks and subsequently Alexandrian Jews like Philo—with the literal method.

Even though the millenarian fathers of the early church tended to allegorize either relatively little (e.g., Irenaeus, Tertullian) or a lot (e.g., *Epistle of Barnabas*, Justin Martyr), there was nevertheless a marked tendency to argue for the principle of literal interpretation, especially in the understanding of prophecy. Those fathers who upheld the hermeneutical principle of literal interpretation, at least in theory if not always in practice, tended to be premillennialists.

In their hermeneutical approach, the apostolic fathers usually pursued one of two lines: (1) either they followed a moderate, straightforward path between literalism and allegorism (e.g., Clement of Rome, Ignatius, Polycarp, *Didache*), or (2) they leaned heavily upon the allegorical method (e.g., *Epistle of Barnabas, Shepherd of Hermas*). In Barnabas's case, the practice was in opposition to the strict literalism of the Jews. On the whole, these earliest fathers simply interpreted the biblical text without any clear expression of interpretive method.

A new trend began early in the first century, however, and continued for the next one hundred and fifty years. Even though a fair amount of artificial exegesis was produced by Justin Martyr's practice of plundering the Old Testament for what he perceived to be its teachings concerning Christ, he nevertheless became one of the first to argue forcefully for a literal interpretation of prophecy. For Justin, the literal fulfillment of prophecy was the authenticator of Christ's ministry, an aid to faith, and the guarantee that things yet future will be fulfilled (*First Apol.* 30, 33, 52). He expected a literal fulfillment of covenant promises to Abraham and David in the coming millennial period.

The trend in literalism became even more pronounced in Irenaeus and Tertullian. Irenaeus carried Justin's principle even further by insisting that in the understanding of all of Scripture, not only prophecy, there is that which is clear, and plain, and natural. But nowhere was Irenaeus's emphasis upon a clear, plain, natural interpretation of Scripture more evident than in his approach to prophetic texts. With reference to end-time events (e.g., resurrection, Millennium, New Jerusalem, etc.), he insisted on a nonallegorical interpretation (*Ag. Her.* 5.35.2). Irenaeus's position was carried on by his disciple Hippolytus, who insisted that the truth of prophetic utterances will be revealed in all details (*Treat. on Christ and Antichrist* 2, 5).

Tertullian, too, argued for the principle of literal interpretation of Scripture in general and for a literal fulfillment of prophecy specifically. He wrote in his work *Against Praxeas* (chap. 13) that "words ought to be taken and understood in the sense in which they are written, especially when they are not expressed in allegories and parables, but in determinate and simple declarations." With regard to prophetic Scriptures, Tertullian believed that in the wake of a literal fulfillment of past prophecies, a literal fulfillment of future events is naturally to be expected (*Apol.* 20). For this reason, Cyprian concluded that the certainty of the fulfillment of prophetic pronouncements is cause for faith and hope (*Treatises* 1.16–17; 7.2).

Decline of Early Premillennialism

Running concurrently with the trend toward literalism in some fathers was the rise of the distinctly Christian allegorism of the school of Alexandria. Begun by Pantaenus (d. ca. 190), it was carried forward by Clement of Alexandria (ca. 155–ca. 220), Origen (ca. 185–ca. 254), and Dionysus of Alexandria (d. ca. 264). Its aim was to unite philosophy and revelation.

With the rising popularity of the allegorical method, belief in a literal millennial reign of Christ reached a crossroads in the middle of the third century. The Egyptian bishop Coracion, Nepos's successor, buckled under pressure from Alexandria and abandoned the premillennialism of his mentor (Eusebius *Ch. Hist.* 7.24). And Hippolytus, the pupil of Irenaeus, wavered in his stance as well. Among the millenarians to follow, some (e.g., Lactantius and Apollinarus of Laodicea) held to the old ways and continued to stress the literal fulfillment of prophecy, while others (e.g., Methodius and Victorinus of Petau) began to lace their views with allegorical interpretations.

By the time the literal method of interpretation reached its apex in the school at Antioch, premillennialism was virtually dead. Even though literalism naturally leads to a belief in premillennialism and the Antiochene school emphasized that interpretive approach to Scripture, the doctrine was not resurrected or advanced by Theodore of Mopsuestia (ca. 350–428), Chrysostom (354–407), or Theodoret (386–458), the school's three most prominent teachers. Perhaps with the legalization of Christianity by Constantine and the cessation of persecution brought by his Edict of Milan (313), coupled with a continuing anti-Jewish sentiment, it was easy to dismiss the future *Jewish* Millennium as fable, while embracing the

Christian empire of Constantine as the eschatological ideal. It is instructive to note that the Apocalypse as the subject of homily or commentary was uniformly ignored by the three chief representatives of the Antiochene school. The book had in fact already been excluded from the canon of Scripture at the Council of Laodicea (ca. 360).

At least some elements of premillennial doctrine survived in the post-Nicene age, as a reference to the Rapture in *Pseudo-Ephraem* (ca. 374–627) suggests. But as the orthodox position of the church, premillennialism had essentially gone to the grave. The practice of allegorical interpretation with its antimillennialism, however, combined with ecclesiasticism by Augustine (354–430), held sway for more than a millennium.

See also IRENAEUS; HIPPOLYTUS.

Larry V. Crutchfield

L. Crutchfield, "Ages and Dispensations in the Ante-Nicene Fathers" in *Vital Prophetic Issues* (Grand Rapids: Kregel, 1995), 44–60, "The Apostle John and Asia Minor as a Source of Premillennialism in the Early Church Fathers" in *JETS,* 31:411–27 (December 1988), "Israel and the Church in the Ante-Nicene Fathers" in *Bibliotheca Sacra,* 144:254–76 (July–September 1987), and "The Blessed Hope and the Tribulation in the Apostolic Fathers" in *When the Trumpet Sounds*, eds. Tommy Ice and Timothy Demy (Eugene, Oreg.: Harvest House, 1995), 85–103; A. Roberts and J. Donaldson, eds., *The Ante-Nicene Fathers*, 10 vols. (Grand Rapids: Eerdmans, n.d); P. Schaff and H. Wace, eds., *Nicene and Post-Nicene Fathers*, second series, 14 vols. (Grand Rapids: Eerdmans, n.d.).

MILLENNIUM, DOCTRINE OF THE

The millennial kingdom of our Lord Jesus Christ is a biblical theme filled with spiritual blessings and glorious expectation. It forms a highway of prophecy commencing deep within the Old Testament, amplified throughout the New Testament and culminating with a note of triumph in the final book of Revelation.

While there are three primary and often debated views of the Millennium, this is far more than a religious dispute of the twentieth century. It presupposes that the prophetic portions of Scripture share the same inspiration and authority as the sections given over to history and theology and that all of these must share a consistent method of Bible interpretation. The premillennial view of the messianic kingdom rests squarely upon a literal hermeneutic, which is an interpretation based upon the normal use of words, understood within their context and the standard rules of grammar. That this is the cardinal issue is freely admitted by two strong Amillennial authors.

"Literal interpretation has always been a marked feature of Premillennialism" (Oswald T. Allis). "Now we must frankly admit that a literal interpretation of the Old Testament prophecies gives us just such a picture of an earthly reign of the Messiah as the premillennialist pictures" (Floyd E. Hamilton).

Speaking of the millennial issue, theologian John F. Walvoord declares: "It involves a system of interpretation of the entire Scripture from Genesis to Revelation." Even the purpose of God for the present age and our philosophy of Christian life and service are largely determined by our view of the millennial kingdom.

Three Primary Millennial Views

Postmillennialism

Postmillennialism found its principal origin in the writings of Daniel Whitby (1628–1725), a British Unitarian who held that a kingdom of righteousness and peace would finally be brought to earth by our brotherhood and sisterhood, the triumphant progress of Christianity, and the power of the church in world affairs. Bolstered by the industrial revolution and the emerging evolutionary view of humankind, it came to its greatest strength in the late nineteenth and early years of the twentieth century. It taught the triumph of good over evil and a coming thousand years of peace and prosperity prior to the return of Christ to earth. His coming would then be postmillennial. This opinion was well stated by theologian A. H. Strong as "a period in the latter days of the church militant when, under special influence of the Holy Ghost, the spirit of the martyrs shall appear again, true religion be greatly quickened and revived, and the members of Christ's churches become so conscious of their strength in Christ that they shall, to an extent not known before, triumph over the powers of evil both within and without."

Such an overly optimistic view fell into disfavor before the angry violence of two world wars and the evil reality of a new age characterized by crime, immorality, and an abundance of other social evils.

Amillennialism

Amillennialism denies a literal future kingdom of Christ upon earth, holding that the kingdom is spiritual rather than literal and a present rather than a future reality. It affirms that the return of Christ, if literal, must be a single event accompanied by one general resurrection and one general judgment, all of which will take place at the end of time. This popular modern view is frequently traced back to the teaching of Augustine (354–430), who taught that Satan was bound at the first advent of Christ, and that the Millennium is spiritual rather than literal, associated with the Roman church, and to end about A.D. 650. When this date failed, his followers extended the date to A.D. 1000; when Christ still did not return the period was spiritualized and extended indefinitely. For Augustine, Israel and the church are simply one people: "The church now on earth is both the kingdom of Christ and the kingdom of heaven. . . . Christ's kingdom is the church." Therefore the kingdom promises no longer apply to Israel but are transferred to the Christian church.

There are many grave weaknesses attached to the amillennial view. Its earliest roots were in the Alexandrian school of interpretation, whose teachers such as Origen and Clement allegorized the Scriptures to make them conform to the views of Plato. While declaring that the kingdom is a spiritual rather than a literal reality, it is a heavily divided eschatology. It became the standard view of all liberals, the view of the Roman Catholic Church, and also the doctrine of many evangelicals who are attracted to its utter simplicity and the avoidance of considerable prophetic detail.

Premillennialism

Premillennialism is supported by much convincing evidence, the telling of which has filled many a massive volume. Once the literal interpretation of prophetic Scripture is accepted, we are almost overwhelmed by the amount of revelation available. In this brief article it is only possible to suggest that evidence by certain brief declarations, and all the supporting Scriptures should be read and closely considered.

1. Premillennialism is the historic faith of the early Christian church. Early Christians were called chiliasts, derived from the Greek *chiliad* (thousand) rather than from the Latin *mille*, which means the same thing. It was the view of Clement of Rome, Justin Martyr, Tertullian, and a host of other church fathers, causing historian Adolph Harnack to say that chiliasm was "inseparably associated with the Gospel itself."

2. Premillennialism is the product of normal, conservative Bible interpretation, which is literal interpretation. Walvoord declares: "Amillennialism in the first three centuries rests for the most part on silence, on one disputed representative [Barnabas] in the first century, none in the second, and a fallacious and destructive principle of interpretation in the third century."

3. Premilleniallism is confirmed by the clear Old Testament prophecy of a literal earthly kingdom. This kingdom, when established, shall be eternal (2 Sam. 7:16; Dan. 2:44). It will be on earth, not in heaven (Ps. 2:8; Isa. 11:9). The Lord shall reign as King over all the earth (Zech 14:4, 9, 16; Ps. 2:6; Ezek. 37:24–25; Hos. 3:4–5; Zeph. 3:14–17). His kingdom shall be absolute (Dan. 7:27) and He shall judge the world in righteousness (Isa. 11:4–5). Then peace shall finally come to this war-scarred planet (Isa. 2:3–4; Micah 4:3–4).

Israel shall have a final, permanent return

to its homeland (Amos 9:15; Isa. 43:5–6; Jer. 30:3; Ezek. 37:21–22; 38:8). Messiah's government shall center in Jerusalem (Mic. 4:1–2; Zech. 2:10–12; 8:4–5) and no longer will violence be heard in the land (Isa. 60:18). Israel shall rebuild its temple (Dan. 9:27; 12:11; Ezek. 40–48) and be a redeemed people (Jer. 31:33–34; Zech. 12:10; 13:1, 6, 9). Redeemed Israel shall then become a messenger of salvation to the Gentiles (Zech. 2:11; 8:23; Mal. 3:12), who shall believe and become part of the family of God (Isa. 11:9–10; 42:6; 60:3). However, there will be certain geographical changes (Zech. 14:4; Isa. 11:15; Hag. 2:6–7), with fertility restored to the land (Amos 9:13–14) and great changes in the animal kingdom (Isa. 11:6–9).

4. This kingdom hope of the prophets is carried over unchanged into the New Testament.

Matthew, standing at the head of the NT canon, emphasizes the messianic hope of Israel and is the gospel of Christ the King. It proclaims His kingly genealogy that relates Him to the promises of the Abrahamic and Davidic covenants. It gives priority to His virgin birth (1:18–23) and records the coming of the Magi from the east asking, "Where is he that is born king of the Jews?" (2:1–2). There is also emphasis upon John the Baptist, predicted by the prophets as the forerunner of the King (Isa. 40:3; Mal. 3:1; 4:5).

Luke gives the genealogy of Jesus from the viewpoint of His virgin mother, Mary (3:23–38), and records the astonishing declaration of the archangel Michael: "The Lord God will give Him the throne of His father David. And He will reign over the house of Jacob forever, and of His kingdom there will be no end" (1:30–33). Even the multitude recognized Him as King, crying "Blessed is the King who comes in the name of the Lord!" (19:38; Matt. 21:9).

A coming kingdom is fully supported by the personal testimony of Christ, who taught us to pray. "Thy kingdom come. Thy will be done in earth, as it is in heaven" (Matt. 6:10). He and His disciples continually preached the Gospel of the kingdom (Matt. 4:23) and the kingdom of heaven, which is the rule of heaven come down to earth (Matt. 3:2; 5:3). When His disciples argued who would be greatest in the coming kingdom, the promise of Christ included eating and drinking with Him in the kingdom, sitting on thrones, and judging the twelve tribes of Israel (Luke 22:28–30). Such activity hardly fits the amillennial concept that the kingdom is entirely spiritual and within you. A similar response was given to the mother of James and John, who asked for a special privilege for her sons in His kingdom (Matt. 20:20–23). He also declared that this kingdom was still future following His death and resurrection (Acts 1:6).

While granting that there is a spiritual kingdom called the kingdom of God, which includes all under divine sovereignty, whether unfallen angels or the host of redeemed since the beginning of time, a significant number of other Scriptures clearly point to a kingdom that is material and yet future, frequently called the millennial kingdom. During the coming Tribulation, a remnant of Israel shall again proclaim the coming of the King (Rev. 7:4–8), and when He returns in power and glory as King of Kings all Israel shall be saved (Rom. 11:26). This is not now being fulfilled, for it shall be after the tribulation of those days (Matt. 24:29–30). And many other predicted events must come to pass before the coming of the King. These will include the rapture of the church, the judgment seat of Christ, the marriage supper of the Lamb, the destruction of Babylon, the rebuilding of the temple, the Antichrist, Armageddon, and the other events recorded by John in the great prophetic book of Revelation.

5. Central to the millennial debate is the reference to a thousand years recorded in Revelation 20. Amillennialists like to declare that premillennialism rests upon a single Scripture. But we have demonstrated that the fact of the kingdom is a major theme of the entire Word of God. The contribution of Revelation 20 relates to the length of the kingdom and not to the fact of the kingdom. It is to follow the glorious appearing of the messianic king (Rev. 19:11–16), and the thousand years is mentioned not once, but six times in six successive verses (Rev. 20:2–7).

How do amillennialists respond to this passage? William Cox is an ardent amillennialist who calls it "a symbolic picture of the interadvent period . . . a poetic way of referring to this present age." He also allegorizes the binding of Satan, who "though bound, still goes about like a roaring lion . . . The chain with which he is bound is a long one, allowing him much freedom of movement." Yet others present alternate opinions, but it is especially in the matter of a thousand years that Amils show no united front. It is simply "an exalted symbol of the glory of the redeemed" (Milligan); "only the idea that the Lord's victory is absolute" (Kliefoth); "a poetic picture" of what actually happens on one day of the coming of the Lord (Duesterdieck); "a symbolic number denoting the aeon of transition" (Lange); a symbol "that the world is perfectly leavened and pervaded by the Divine" (Fausset). These are radical departures from the simple, unadorned revelation that the saints will live and reign with Christ a thousand years (Rev. 20:4, 6).

A premillennialist believes therefore that Christ will literally return to bind Satan, put down all unrighteousness, and raise the saints from the dead to rule with Him. The time allotted to restore peace and order to a rebellious planet is one thousand years. This is the biblical, conservative and evangelical view, and its opponents have no coherent or biblical doctrine with which to replace it.

See also AMILLENNIALISM; POSTMILLENNIALISM; PREMILLENNIALISM.

Gerald B. Stanton

Oswald T. Allis, *Prophecy and the Church* (Philadelphia: Presbyterian and Reformed Publishing Co., 1945); William E. Biederwolf, *The Second Coming Bible* (Grand Rapids: Baker, 1924); William Cox, *Amillennialism Today* (Philadelphia: Presbyterian and Reformed, 1966); Floyd E. Hamilton, *The Basis of Millennial Faith* (Grand Rapids: Eerdmans, 1942); Gerald B. Stanton, *Prophetic Highways* (Palm Beach Gardens, Fla.: Ambassador Publications, 1993); A. H. Strong, *Systematic Theology* (Philadelphia: Griffith & Rowland Press, 1907); John F. Walvoord, *The Millennial Kingdom* (Findlay, Ohio: Dunham, 1959).

MILLENNIALISM, THE HISTORY OF

Through the inspiration of Scripture and the principle of progressive revelation, the Holy Spirit has revealed the fact that there will be a one-thousand-year kingdom reign of the Son of God on earth. Two words directly reflect the idea of a future kingdom reign, the word *millennialism* itself and the word *chiliasm*. *Mille* in Latin means a thousand. The Greek word is *Xilia*. *Xilia* is only used in Revelation 20:2–4, 6 in the Greek text. However, seen throughout Scripture is this idea of a time when God will bring about an earthly period of peace and righteousness. It is very difficult to deny the fact of a promised messianic era. Generally speaking, only amillennialism allegorizes such promises, given in hundreds, if not thousands, of verses! Though it is impossible to cite all the passages, there are some distinct highlights in Scripture where the promise of an earthly blessing is so clearly made. History confirms that the biblical doctrine of a millennium has been well understood and accepted.

Abraham

As the patriarch pondered the promises God made to him, he clearly had an understanding of an earthly place of future blessing. Hebrews tells us, "he was looking for the city which has foundations, whose architect and builder is God" (11:10). In some limited way, Abraham took the Lord's land promises literally and expected someday to view a place of righteousness and peace on the earth.

Davidic Covenant

Berkhof mistakenly says: "The only scriptural basis for this theory [of a millennium] is Rev. 20:1–6, after an Old Testament content has been poured into it." He expressly denies that 2 Samuel 7:12–16 spells out that David will have seed after him whereby God establishes an eternal house, throne, and kingdom. In fact the Lord says this will be "made sure for ever before thee."

The provisions are: "that (1) David is to have a child, yet to be born, who shall succeed him and establish his kingdom. (2) This son (Solomon) shall build the temple. (3) The throne of his kingdom . . . shall be established forever. (4) The throne will not be taken away from him (Solomon). (5) David's house, throne, and kingdom shall be established forever" (Walvoord). From David forward, the idea of the kingdom is progressively unfolded in the Old Testament prophets. Berkhof fails to connect the word *millennium* with all the kingdom promises that saturate almost all the prophets' predictions.

David

David understood at least in a limited way what God was doing with him when he wrote Psalm 2. He knew (v. 2) that a future son would be called God's Anointed (*māshîaḥ* [Messiah], Greek, *christos*). He knew this Anointed One would be the Lord's King and Son who would be installed on Mount Zion (v. 6). David realized this One would inherit the nations and possess the very ends of the earth (v. 8) and shatter all resistance (v. 9). As well, the rulers and judges of earth must pay Him homage before wrath falls (vv. 10–12). This awesome promise is repeated in striking detail in Psalm 89 and here clearly called a covenant (89:34).

Daniel

In a most profound chapter in his prophecy (chap. 7), the prophet Daniel sees this Anointed One as the Son of Man coming before the Lord in heaven and receiving an earthly kingdom. Here, the Messiah receives glory and a kingdom over all peoples, nations, and people of every language (v. 14). This kingdom follows after four other great earthly dynasties. Though spiritual in nature, it is also historic. "Then the sovereignty, the dominion, and the greatness of all the kingdoms under the whole heaven will be given to the people of the saints of the Highest One" (v. 27).

Apocryphal Writings

The pre-Christian Jewish apocryphal writers picked up from the Old Testament the idea of the coming kingdom. Emil Schuerer gives a systematic survey in his *Geschichte des Juedischen Volkes Im Zeitlter Jesu Christi, II* (cited by Kromminga, p. 25). The Fourth Book of Esdras teaches: (1) A final period of tribulation; (2) the appearance of Elijah as a forerunner of the Messiah; (3) appearance of the Messiah to overthrow evil; (4) a final world attack against the Messiah. (5) the destruction of wicked world powers; (6) the restoration of Jerusalem; (7) the return of the dispersed Jews; (8) the kingdom glory in Palestine shared by Jews resurrected; (9) the renewal of the world; (10) the general resurrection; (11) a final judgment.

Dead Sea Scrolls

One of the most astonishing finds about a promised literal kingdom has been the Dead Sea Scrolls. In these can be discovered how a portion of the Jews around one hundred years before Christ viewed the concept of a messianic reign. The Scrolls refer to a world ruler or star and scepter as mentioned in Numbers 24:17. This one is Shiloh (Gen. 49:10), the Righteous One, the Root of Planting. He is the Son of Man coming on the clouds of heaven (Dan. 7), the Root of Jesse and Branch of David, the Son of God, Son of the Most High, and His kingdom will be an eternal kingdom. The Messiah is a Righteous Branch of David who "comes [forth], because to him and his seed was given the covenant of the kingdom of His people in perpetuity" (Eisenman and Wise).

New Testament

Besides the word *millennium* (Rev. 20:1–6), the New Testament uses many phrases and words to describe the promised kingdom. To the Jews the expressions "kingdom of God" and "kingdom of heaven" were messianic terms. Jesus' disciples spoke with Him about His coming (Matt. 24:3). Christ responded that indeed the Son of Man would be coming (24:27), i.e., the Lord would be coming (24:42). He would be appearing in the sky, all tribes would see Him "coming on the clouds of the sky with power and great glory" (24:30), at which time He would gather His elect (24:31).

He will sit on His glorious throne, and all the nations will be gathered before Him (25:31–32). The literalness of the kingdom is further illustrated by the fact that the King will say to the blessed on His right hand, "inherit the kingdom" (25:34).

In Acts, the disciples refer to the restoring the kingdom to Israel (1:6). Peter says for now, heaven has received Jesus "until the period of restoration of all things about which God spoke by the mouth of His holy prophets" (3:20–21). The epistles speak of church saints as heirs of the kingdom (James 2:5) and the fact that believers have an entrance way into the eternal kingdom (2 Peter 1:11). But there are very few significant references to the kingdom in the other books. Hebrews seems to say that providentially all things have been already subjected to Jesus but all things have not been "placed" (*aphiami*) in His authority. "For in subjecting all things to him, He left nothing that is not subject to him. But now we do not yet see all things subjected to him" (Heb. 2:8). Revelation 3:21 teaches that Christ is now on His Father's heavenly throne but that He is yet to sit on His own earthly throne. "He who overcomes, I will grant to him to sit down with Me on My throne, as I also overcame and sat down with My Father on His throne." The coming of the Messiah for the Millennium reign is graphically pictured in Revelation 19:11–16. These verses tie together all the Old Testament promises of the Lord's literal reign on earth.

The Early Church

It is sufficient to say here that the early church fathers were basically premillennial and looked for the promised Millennium. It is admitted by all that their systemization of prophecy was primitive and incomplete. And yet enough is known to substantiate their affirmation about a one-thousand-year earthly reign of Christ.

George Peters has done the most work on this subject. Citing many scholars, his findings are compiled in *The Theocratic Kingdom*, Vol. 1:482–98. Here he quotes Whitby, who wrote that the Millennium "passed among the best Christians for two hundred and fifty years, for a tradition apostolical . . ."

"The most striking point in the eschatology of the ante-Nicene age is the prominent chiliasm, or millenarianism, that is the belief of a visible reign of Christ in glory on earth with the risen saints for a thousand years" (Shaff).

"This doctrine of Christ's Second Advent, and the kingdom, appears so early that it might be questioned whether it ought not to be regarded as an essential part of the Christian religion" (Harnack).

"A certain man with us, named John, one of the Apostles of Christ, predicted . . . that those who believed in our Christ would spend a thousand years in Jerusalem" (Martyr).

"When the Antichrist shall have devastated all things in this world, he will reign for three years and six months, and sit in the temple at Jerusalem; and then the Lord will come from heaven in the clouds . . . bringing in for the righteous the times of the kingdom" (Irenaeus).

"But we do confess that a kingdom is promised to us upon the earth . . . for a thousand years in the divinely-built city of Jerusalem" (Tertullian). All the quotes and many more are cited in Peters' work.

It was not until around A.D. 200 that opposition began to rise against the idea of a coming Millennium. This was coming about because of the influence of the Alexandrian school and Origen. (See ORIGEN).

Orthodox Judaism

"One of the fundamental tenets of Judaism is the belief in the Messiah, the Savior who is to come, redeem the people of Israel from their sufferings in exile, lead them back to Jerusalem, and establish the rule of peace over all the nations of the world. . . . the basic belief in him who must come remained the same and sustained the Jewish people for two millennia" (Patai).

A flood of testimony to a coming millennial rule of the Messiah has been the hallmark of Israel's faith. The voluminous amount of literature produced by the Jewish sages confirms two things: (1) Basically they studied the Old Testament prophecies with a literal hermeneutic. (2) In some instances they must have borrowed some concepts from the New Testament. Though calling the coming world dictator Armilus, the Midrash also refers to him as the Antichrist (1 John 4:3). Too, the Zohar refers to the kingdom as the "millennium" which word is found only in Revelation 20. Premillennial kingdom and millennial references are so overwhelming in the literature of orthodox Judaism that to quote even a part of them is impossible. But a few from the Zohar are important: "Happy will be all those who will remain in the world at the end of the sixth millennium to enter into [the millennium of] the Sabbath" (Zohar 1:119a). After a period of tribulation "Then will be revealed King Messiah in the whole world, and to him will kingship be given" (Zohar 3:212b).

Jewish scholarship often throws light on the New Testament books. For example, the expressions kingdom of God and kingdom of heaven mean the same in orthodox thinking. Avi-Yonah notes that the kingdom teaching in Daniel portrays "the world dominion of God, an everlasting kingdom—'to perfect the world under the kingdom of God'—a kingdom of heaven upon earth. This renewed messianic idea, envisioned by the author of the book of Daniel, was to be echoed in its essential thrust in the literature that took its clue from it. Its influence on Christianity is unmistakable. Once Christianity, however, introduced a Greek element into Jewish monotheism it changed the basic concept of the kingdom of heaven which it had borrowed from Judaism."

This statement is profound because the "Greek element" is allegorical interpretation that made the kingdom the church. The idea of the one-thousand-year Millennium slowly died after Origen and Augustine and their spiritualizing of kingdom passages to make them read church.

See also DAVIDIC COVENANT.

Mal Couch

Michael Avi-Yonah and Zvi Baras, eds., *The World History of the Jewish People* (Jerusalem: Massada, 1977); Louis Berkhof, *Systematic Theology* (Grand Rapids: Eerdmans, 1941); Moses de Leon, ed., *Zohar* (Vilna, Poland: Rom, 1894); D. H. Kromminga, *Millennium in the Church* (Grand Rapids: Eerdmans, 1945); Raphael Patai, *The Messiah Texts* (Detroit: Wayne State University Press, 1979); J. Dwight Pentecost, *Things to Come* (Findlay, Ohio: Dunham Pub. Co., 1961); George N. H. Peters, *The Theocratic Kingdom*, vol. 1 (Grand Rapids: Kregel, 1988); John F. Walvoord, *The Millennial Kingdom* (Grand Rapids: Zondervan, 1959).

MILLENNIAL YEAR-DAY TRADITION

One of the earliest prototypical expressions of dispensationalism found in the early church fathers was the year-day (or sex-/septa-) millennial tradition. It provided the framework for some of the fathers' first attempts at developing a dispensational understanding of God's redemptive activity throughout the ages. The tradition was based on: (1) the six days of creation followed by a seventh day of rest (Gen. 2); (2) the Sabbath-rest concept found in Hebrews (see Heb. 3:11; 4:1, 3, 5, 8–9, 11); and (3) the belief that in biblical chronology a day could represent a thousand years (2 Peter 3:8; Ps. 90:4).

Many of the fathers understood these passages to teach by analogy and in prophetic symbolism that the world would endure for a period of six thousand years (represented by six days of Creation) and would then experience a thousand-year Sabbath rest (represented by seventh day of rest following Creation). Some fathers added an eighth day to represent eternity. Almost every ante-Nicene father who held to the year-day tradition was also a defender of premillennialism. Proponents of the year-day theory who were not also premillennialists (e.g., Augustine) did not appear until the post-Nicene period after the spiritualizing influence of the Alexandrian school became a dominant force in biblical interpretation.

While the year-day tradition was held by Jews and others before the church age, the Epistle of Barnabas (composed ca. A.D. 70/117–138) marked the beginning of the year-day tradition in Christian literature.

Barnabas's outline of human history (see Epist. of Barn. 15) was as follows:

- Days 1–5 (5,000 years) = the *past* history of man
- Day 6 (1,000 years) = the *present* (on the basis of his belief in the imminent return of Christ, Barnabas placed himself and the church at the close of the sixth day)
- Day 7 (1,000 years) = the *millennium*
- Day 8 (endless time) = the *eternal state*

Barnabas merely divided the history of the world into seven equal thousand-year ages, with reference to God's special dealings with humanity only in the seventh—events to occur during the day of rest. However, his presentation of the year-day tradition set the stage for a more sophisticated understanding of the dealings of God with humanity in writers who followed.

Larry V. Crutchfield

A. D. Ehlert, *A Bibliographic History of Dispensationalism* (Grand Rapids: Baker, 1965); L. Crutchfield, "Ages and Dispensations in the Ante-Nicene Fathers" in *Vital Prophetic Issues* (Grand Rapids: Kregel, 1995), 44–60; J. Quasten and J. C. Plumpe, *Ancient Christian Writers: The Didache, The Epistle of Barnabas, The Epistles and The Martyrdom of St. Polycarp, The Fragments of Papias, The Epistle to Diognetus*, trans. James A. Kleist (New York; Ramsey, N.J.: Newman Press, 1946), 27–65.

MILLENNIUM, NEW TESTAMENT DESCRIPTIONS OF

One of the objections critics have to the idea of an earthly kingdom is that the word *millennium* is only mentioned in Revelation 20. This is a very limited and narrow argument, as well the reasoning is that very little is said about an earthly reign in the New Testament itself. Again, this is overlooking many passages and parallel expressions that clearly indicate a physical, literal messianic kingdom on earth.

Dispensationalists argue that the Old Testament, if understood through a literal hermeneutic, clearly teaches an earthly messianic, Davidic kingdom to come. This does not have to be repeated in the New Testament in detail to be true. There are no indications that those promises have been replaced by spiritualizing as church promises. The New Testament does not have to repeat such promises if they are still in place for the nation of Israel and are yet future, waiting to be fulfilled. The New Testament abounds with important words, contextual phrases, and expressions that indicate a coming earthly kingdom, apart from the word *millennium*. Below are some of the most important ones.

Along with the Greek word *eta* (year), *Xilia* (a thousand) is used six times in Revelation 20. Though the Old Testament does not specify the length of the kingdom on earth, this chapter gives this time frame. Many rabbinical writings agree. "Happy will be all those who will remain in the world at the end of the sixth millennium to enter into [the millennium of] the Sabbath" (Zohar 1:119a).

The rabbis as well taught that these two expressions, the kingdom of God and the kingdom of heaven, refer not to some spiritualized kingdom but to the literal earthly reign of David's Son. In fact it may be argued that, in light of how the Jews understood these two phrases, they only mean in the Gospels the messianic rule on earth. The earlier Dead Sea Scrolls, too, continually refer to the coming messianic kingdom in which the Messiah's rule encompasses both heaven and earth. "The Heavens and the earth will obey His [God's] Messiah, . . . and all that is in them" (Frag. 4Q521). And, Israel leads "until the Messiah of Righteousness, the Branch of David comes, because to him and his seed was given the covenant of the kingdom of His people in perpetuity" (Frag. 4Q252).

Further examining the New Testament (beyond the Gospels), many expressions and passages speak of the coming kingdom reign of the Messiah. Forecasting past the dispensation of the church, Jesus speaks of His throne as separate from His Father's heavenly throne (Rev. 3:21). The word *kingdom* is used many times in Acts and the Epistles, but clearly the expression is not in reference to the church. Paul writes of it as still future, "Christ Jesus, who is to judge the living and the dead, and by His appearing and His kingdom" (2 Tim. 4:1). The apostle is even more specific when he writes in 1 Corinthians: at Christ's coming, "then comes the end, when He delivers up the kingdom to the God and Father" (15:23–24). Paul adds that believers are being called beyond this church administration into His own kingdom and glory (1 Thess. 2:12).

Other expressions can refer to the kingdom and the Millennium. Quoting Amos 9:11, Peter refers to the future rebuilding of the tabernacle of David which has fallen" (Acts 15:16). The kingdom of course includes "the Christ appointed for you" (Acts 3:20). It is also termed "times of refreshing" (3:19) and "period of restoration of all things about which God spoke by the mouth of His holy prophets from ancient time" (3:21). Before the Lord's ascension, the disciples called it "the kingdom of Israel" (1:6) and Christ answered back and referred to this kingdom as the times and epochs fixed by the Father (1:7). The angel spoke to Mary of the coming Son who would reign on the throne of His father David (Luke 1:32), and over the house of Jacob with His kingdom having no end (1:33).

Only by spiritualization can all the references to the kingdom be set aside or reinterpreted. Seen through a consistent and literal hermeneutic, the New Testament clearly projects a future reign of the Messiah Jesus. The doctrine of the coming Millennium is one of the greatest truths of revelation. The Millennium is the reign of Christ for one thousand years on earth after His Second Coming. As such it is the consummating dispensation of history on this globe. Though kingdom truth is basically eschatological, it is integral to all of the Bible and understanding it is important to doctrine as a whole (Walvoord).

See also KINGDOM OF GOD, OF HEAVEN.

Mal Couch

Michael Avi-Yonah and Zvi Baras, eds., *Society and Religion in the Second Temple Period* (Jerusalem: Massada, 1977); Robert H. Eisenman and Michael Wise, *The Dead Sea Scrolls Uncovered* (New York: Barnes & Noble, 1994); Raphael Patai, *The Messiah Texts* (Detroit: Wayne State University Press, 1979); John F. Walvoord, *The Millennial Kingdom* (Grand Rapids: Zondervan, 1959).

MILLENNIUM, OLD TESTAMENT DESCRIPTIONS OF

National Repentance of Israel

The condition for inauguration of the eschatological millennial kingdom is the national repentance of Israel (Isa. 2:5; 6:11–13). God will bring about the conversion of Israel through end-time judgment (Tribulation) on the nation (Isa. 2:6–4:6), as Moses prophesied (Lev. 26:40–45; Deut. 4:30–31). Just as the historical judgments on Israel purified a remnant, the eschatological judgment will purify the nation and lead to national salvation (Isa. 1:21–31; 28:5–6, 23–29).

Seventieth Week of Daniel

At the end of Daniel's Seventieth Week, God will destroy hostile Gentile powers and inaugurate His eschatological kingdom (Dan. 2:31–45; 7:2–27; 9:24–27). During this seven-year period, the "little horn" will war against Israel (Dan. 7:7–8, 19–27), the ruler who will come will commit the Abomination of Desolation (Dan. 9:27), and the king of the north will invade the land of Israel (Ezek. 38:1–16; Dan. 11:36–45). Portrayed typologically as a second Time of Jacob's Trouble (Jer. 30:7), Israel will experience unprecedented affliction (Ezek. 20:37; Dan. 12:1), as Moses had prophesied (Deut. 4:30; 32:23–35). Foreshadowed by the Babylonian exile, Israel will experience worldwide exile (Isa. 42:7; 43:5–6), as Moses predicted (Deut. 30:1). Two-thirds of the nation will be killed (Zech. 13:8–9) and one-half of the inhabitants of Jerusalem will be taken into exile (Joel 3:1–3; Zech 12:1–3; 14:1–2). However, the remnant will be protected through angelic intervention (Dan. 12:1) and supernaturally strengthened (Zech 12:4–9).

Divine Deliverance of Repentant Israel

In response to the penitent pleas of the remnant (Isa. 63:15–64:12; Jer. 29:12–14), the Lord will pour out His wrath on the hostile Gentile nations, miraculously delivering His people (Isa. 59:20; 63:1–6). As foreshadowed by His miraculous deliverance of Jerusalem from Sennacherib in 701 B.C., God will deliver Jerusalem once and for all from all hostile Gentile armies (Isa. 17:12–14; 29:5–8). The Lord will descend to the Mount of Olives to fight for Israel (Joel 3:16; Zech. 14:3–8). The Son of Man will come out of the clouds to destroy the little horn and the hostile Gentile nations (Dan. 2:35, 44–45). The Davidic King will appear on the scene as a mighty warrior, rallying the tribes of Israel from around the world as a mighty army and leading Israel to spectacular victory over its foes (Isa. 9:2–5; 11:12–14) as He subjugates all Gentile nations under Himself and Israel (Ps. 110:1–7; 132:18).

Universal Judgment

YHWH will gather all the Gentile nations to the Valley of "Jehoshaphat" (Judgment of YHWH) in judgment for afflicting His people (Isa. 24:1–23; 63:1–6). As anticipated by God's historical judgment of the traditional enemies of Israel (Isa. 8:6–9:7; 10:5–11:16), He will devastate the whole earth in judgment (Isa. 24:1–23; 25:2). God will imprison all the wicked along with the demons in hell during the messianic kingdom: "The LORD will punish the powers in the heavens above and the kings on the earth below. They will be herded together like prisoners bound in a dungeon," shut up in prison, and punished for many days (Isa. 24:21–22). He will also destroy His ultimate enemy, chaos, depicted as Leviathan, the monster of the sea (Isa. 27:1).

Resurrection of Believers

At the inauguration of the kingdom, God will destroy the final enemy of humanity, death (Isa. 25:7–8). This will allow for the resurrection of His people (Isa. 26:19; Ezek. 37:1–14, 21–22; Dan. 12:2). At the resurrection, God will reward those who demonstrated exceptional wisdom and righteousness (Dan. 12:3). There are two resurrections; the righteous will be resurrected to eternal life and the wicked to eternal condemnation (Dan. 12:2). The resurrection of the righteous will precede the resurrection of the wicked; only the righteous will participate in the earthly messianic kingdom. The wicked will remain in the grave (26:14) and spiritual imprisonment "for many days" (Isa. 24:21–22) until the resurrection to judgment (Dan. 12:2). This suggests two phases of the kingdom: the inaugural messianic kingdom marked by the first resurrection and the eternal kingdom to follow, marked by the second resurrection.

The Regathering of Israel

After destroying the hostile Gentile nations and delivering Israel and Jerusalem, the Lord will regather all Israel from among the nations and bring them into the land in the glorious second exodus and return, which will dwarf the first exodus under Moses and the first return from exile under Cyrus (Isa. 11:12, 15–16). The second exodus will occur after the judgment on the nations (Isa. 42:10–17), in conjunction with the pouring out of the new covenant Spirit on national Israel (Ezek. 36:24–28), the resurrection of Israel (Ezek. 37:14), and the inauguration of the everlasting covenant (Ezek. 37:26). The Lord Himself and His co-regent, the Davidic King, will personally escort the exiles back to the land of Israel and the city of Jerusalem (Isa. 11:10–16; Isa. 40:3–11). The return will be accompanied by fundamental changes in creation: the curse will be reversed, the desert will become a second Eden, and the mountains will be leveled into a roadway (Isa. 35:1–3,7; 40:3–4). During the return, God will provide eschatological salvation and physical bodily healing (Isa. 12:3; 35:4–5). The wicked will be removed; only the holy will take part in the second exodus (Isa. 35:8–10).

Fulfillment of the New Covenant

During the Tribulation, God will refine Israel by eliminating the unrepentant and purifying the believing remnant (Isa. 1:21–31; Ezek. 20:33–38). Only those who submit to His rule in obedience will enter the bond of the covenant and inherit the kingdom; the unrepentant will be destroyed in judgment

(Isa. 65:9–16; Jer. 25:30–33). The repentant will bind themselves to God in the everlasting covenant (Isa. 54:7–8; 55:1–3; 59:20–21; 61:8; Jer. 50:4–5; Ezek. 20:37–38) through the Servant (Isa. 42:6; 49:8). Israel, the once-divorced and deserted wife, will be married to the Lord in an eternal covenant (Isa. 54:1–17; Hos 2:14–23).

The major new covenant texts enumerate numerous spiritual blessings (Isa 42:6; 44:3): (1) the regeneration of national Israel, (2) complete forgiveness, (3) the law written on the heart, (4) the Spirit placed within the heart, (5) inner cleansing, (6) creation of the new nature, (7) removal of the sin nature, (8) complete and perfect obedience for all eternity, (9) intimate relationship with God, and (10) assurance of eternal security from future judgment.

There are numerous physical blessings: (1) the nation will return from exile in the second exodus, (2) deceased believing Israelites will be resurrected, (3) the land will be restored, (4) Israel will enjoy agricultural fertility, (5) Jerusalem and the temple will be rebuilt, (6) Judah and Israel will be reunited, (7) the kingdom will begin, (8) Israel will be protected from its enemies, (9) Israel will never again be exiled or rejected by God, and (10) Israel will exist before God eternally.

Inauguration of the Kingdom and Eschatological Feast

After vanquishing His enemies, the Lord will formally inaugurate the earthly eschatological kingdom (Dan. 2:35, 44–45). God will establish His divine throne on Mount Zion (Isa. 24:23; 25:5–6) and enthrone the Davidic King as co-regent (Ps. 100:1; Jer. 30:9). Following the ancient Near Eastern pattern of victory-kingship-banquet, the Lord will celebrate an eschatological feast on Mount Zion with His people, including both redeemed Jews and Gentiles (Isa. 25:6–8).

Enthronement of the Davidic King

God will fulfill His promises in the Davidic covenant (2 Sam. 7:8–16) to establish the eternal Davidic dynasty over Israel through a single ideal Davidic King who will reign eternally (Ps. 89:20–37; Isa. 9:6–7). He will enthrone the Davidic heir as King over the earth (Ps. 2:7–9; 18:50). God will bless Israel through the Davidic King (Jer. 33:14–22) and plant Israel in the land forever (Jer. 24:6; 31:27). The new covenant promises to Israel will be fulfilled through the rule of the Davidic King (Isa. 9:1–7; 11:1–16).

As the ideal Davidic King, the Messiah is described as the second coming of David (Mic. 5:2) and typologically designated "David" (Jer. 23:5; 30:9; 33:15–17, 26); (Targum often reads "the Messiah"). He will embody all the virtues of his illustrious ancestor and fulfill the conditions of the Davidic covenant (2 Chron. 7:17–22; 1 Kings 2:4; 9:4–9).

The Davidic King will rule as the co-regent, Prince (Ezek. 34:24), under the divine kingship of YHWH (Ps. 72:19; Isa. 40:4–5). The Davidic King is so closely associated with YHWH that His name will be "YHWH our Deliverance" (Jer. 23:6) and He will perform the same tasks as the Lord (Isa. 11:11,16; 40:4–5). Just as God will be enthroned on Mount Zion (Isa. 24:21; 25:6–8), the Davidic King will be enthroned in Jerusalem (Isa. 9:7; Jer. 30:18). As the ideal King-Priest in the order of Melchizedek (Ps. 110:4), He will have unlimited and direct access to God's presence (Jer. 30:21).

As the servant of God (2 Sam. 3:18; 7:5, 8, 26), the Davidic King is also designated the "Servant of the LORD" (Isa. 42:1–6; 49:1–11). He will be enthroned and exalted over all kings of earth (Isa. 49:7; 52:13)—a startling development because of His previous humiliation (Isa. 49:7; 52:14–15) —and will lead the exiles back to Israel in the second exodus (Isa. 49:8–12).

The Davidic King will rule over the entire earth and will wield absolute power and authority over all nations (Ps. 2:6–9; 72:8–11). He will rule over the world with a rod of iron, exacting justice and demanding obedience (Isa. 11:3–5). Judah and Israel will serve the Davidic King (Jer. 30:9). His reign will be characterized by righteousness and justice (Ps. 2:8–9; 72:19). Under Him, righteous judges and counselors will help administer the kingdom (Isa. 1:26). Israel will serve and obey the Davidic King (Isa. 9:6–7; 33:17, 22; 44:6).

Character of the Messianic Kingdom

The messianic kingdom will be characterized by removal of oppression in human society and universal peace in international relations (Ps. 46:8–9; 72:7), paralleled by harmony in the animal kingdom (Isa. 11:6–9; 65:25). There will be universal knowledge of God and perfect obedience (Isa. 2:3; 11:9; 44:4–5; 45:8,17; 55:13; 59:20–21; 60:21; 65:13–16; Jer. 24:7; 30:9,22; 31:1,31–34; 32:38; Ezek. 36:24–32). Any who rebels against the Lord will be put to death or plagued (Isa. 65:20; Zech. 14:16–19).

The Renewed Jerusalem

Jerusalem will be redeemed, renewed, purified, sanctified, restored, rebuilt, adorned, honored, repopulated, expanded, transformed, and glorified (Isa. 1:26; 4:2–6). It will be given new names to emphasize its righteous character and relationship with God (Isa. 1:26; Jer. 33:16). God's radiant glory will emanate from the city (Isa. 60:19–20; Ezek. 43:1–9). Jerusalem will become the political capital and spiritual center of the world (Isa. 2:2–4; 35:8–9). God will protect Zion; it will never again be conquered or destroyed (Isa. 4:5–6). If an enemy were to attack, it would be destroyed (Isa. 54:14–17; 60:12).

The Renewed Temple, Priesthood, and Worship

The Davidic King will serve as King-Priest in the order of Melchizedek (Ps. 110:4). The once-defiled temple precincts will be sanctified (Jer. 31:23; Zech. 14:20–21). The new temple will be built, dwarfing Solomon's temple (Ezek. 40:1–42:20; 43:10–27). The glory of God will return through the east gate and fill the new temple, never to again depart (Ezek. 43:1–9). The Levites will be forgiven and restored to ministry (Jer. 33:17–26); however, as a consequence of their sin, they will no longer serve as priests (Ezek. 44:10–15) but will be replaced by the Zadokites who will minister before the Lord forever and offer sacrificial worship (Jer. 33:18, 22; Ezek. 40:46; 44:15–16). The remnant of Israel will be exalted to priesthood (Isa. 61:6) as will some Gentiles (Isa. 66:21). The Prince (the Davidic King in Ezek. 34:24?) will function as High Priest with duties and privileges (Ezek. 44:3; 45:7). The Prince and the Zadokites will offer sacrifices to YHWH to make atonement for sins and to express worship: sin, guilt, burnt, grain, drink, freewill, and fellowship offerings (Ezek. 40:38–43; 43:18–44:31). The redeemed will render exclusive worship to YHWH, bringing voluntary firstfruit offerings and praise offerings to YHWH (Isa. 19:21). The Sabbath will be reinstituted (Isa. 66:20–23; Jer. 33:18), as will the annual festivals—Israelites and Gentiles will make annual pilgrimages to worship YHWH in Jerusalem (Jer. 31:6, 12–14, 23).

The Restored Land of Israel

Eclipsing the inheritance under Joshua, the redeemed will enjoy a glorious eternal eschatological inheritance (Isa. 14:1–2; Jer. 50:34). The land of Canaan will be the inheritance of Israel (Ezek. 36:8,12). The boundaries of the land of Israel will be enlarged (Isa. 26:15; 33:17) and tribal inheritances reassigned (Isa. 49:8; Ezek. 47:13–48:29). The defiled land will be cleansed and refurbished (Isa. 32:16–18) and the topography of the land will be altered (Isa. 33:10–11). The Mount of Olives will split to form a valley from Jerusalem to the Mediterranean, irrigating the land of Israel (Zech. 14:4). A river will flow out of the new temple into the Arabah, transforming it into a fertile plain (Ezek. 47:1–12). The land will have unprecedented fertility (Isa. 4:2; 29:17) and abundant rainfall (Isa. 30:23–30).

The Renewed Heavens and Earth

The curse on the earth will be removed and God's original Creation blessing will be restored. Having cleansed the world and the heavens of sin, God will fashion a renewed heavens and renewed earth (Isa. 65:17–18). The curse on the ground will be removed and replaced with fertility of Edenlike proportions (Isa. 30:23–24; 35:1–2, 7, 15–20). The curse that rendered human labor a toilsome, vain drudgery will be lifted; work will be fulfilling (Isa. 65:21–25). The curse on childbearing will be removed; families will bear children and raise them with joy, not sorrow (Isa. 65:20–23; Jer. 31:15–16; Ezek. 47:20–22). The curse of death will be removed; the redeemed will live forever (Isa. 65:20; Dan. 12:2). The resurrection will reverse the curse of sickness and physical deformities and disabilities (Isa. 29:18; 33:24; 35:5–6). The curse of hostility between humans and animals (Gen. 9:2) will be removed (Isa. 11:6–9; 65:25). In a reversal of Genesis 3:15, the serpent will be unable to harm those on Mount Zion (Isa. 65:25). The structure of life will be much the same—except the curse will be removed and God's blessing will be restored: people will build houses, plant vineyards, and have families under the blessing of God (Isa. 65:20–23; Ezek. 28:26).

Fulfillment of the Abrahamic Covenant

YHWH will fulfill His promises in the Abrahamic covenant to give Israel eternal possession of the land (Isa. 26:15; 33:17; 58:14); to bless the offspring of Abraham (Isa. 32:15–20; 44:3; Jer. 23:5–6); to multiply the seed of Abraham (Jer. 30:19); and to bless believing Gentiles (Isa. 19:19–25).

The Redeemed Israel

Israel will be forgiven, cleansed, purified, and made righteous (Isa. 1:25; 2:4; 33:20–24; 44:22–24; 45:17–25). Judah and Israel will be reunited as one nation under one King (Isa. 11:13; Jer 3:18). The Lord will remove His covenant discipline from Israel (Jer. 24:6) and bestow His covenant blessings (Isa. 29:17, 23; 30:23–25). Israel will fulfill its commission to be a kingdom of priests (Exod. 19:5–6) by praising YHWH and promoting the Word of God during the kingdom (Isa. 2:2–3; 9:9; 12:4–6). Israel will bring glory to YHWH (Isa. 62:3). Israel will be exalted to rule over all nations (Isa. 11:13–14; 14:1–2; 49:22–23). Israel will never again be removed from the land or exiled (Jer. 24:6).

The Redeemed Gentiles

Through God's judgment on the nations and deliverance of Israel, Gentiles will see God's glory and holiness (Isa. 40:5; 44:23), leading many to repentance and saving faith (Isa. 19:18–23; 45:12–24; 56:8). They will be spared from final judgment (Isa. 54:15–19; 65:15–19) and enter the kingdom (Isa. 2:4; 11:12). God will restore the fortunes of the Gentile nations which will repent (Jer. 46:26; 48:47; 49:7, 39). Redeemed Gentiles will share in salvific blessings with Israel (Isa. 19:24–25; 42:10–12; 56:3–8; Ps. 72:17; 110:1–2, 5–6). Although promised to Israel and Judah (Jer. 31:31–34), God will extend new covenant blessings to believing Gentiles (Isa. 56:3–8). Gentiles will join with Israel in unified worship of YHWH (Isa. 2:2–4).

Surprisingly, redeemed Gentiles will be called "the people of God" along with Israel (Isa. 19:19–25). Some redeemed Gentiles will even become priests like the Levites (Isa. 66:21) and will share in the inheritance with Israel (Ezek. 48:21–23). Although redeemed Gentiles will share in salvation blessings with Israel, they will be subordinate to Israel in political/national position (Isa. 14:1–2). Gentiles will escort the redeemed of Israel back to Zion in the second exodus (Isa. 49:22; 60:4, 9) and will come to Jerusalem for spiritual instruction (Isa. 2:2–4). Redeemed Gentile nations will bring tribute to Jerusalem to worship YHWH and honor Israel and will bow down in voluntary subjugation to Israel (Isa. 18:7). The Babel of languages that kept the nations divided will be reversed in one unified language (Zeph. 3:9). There will be international peace among the Gentile nations (Isa. 2:4; Mic. 4:4). The Gentile nations will never again attack Israel and Jerusalem (Isa. 52:1; 60:10–11, 18); if a nation were to attack, it would be forced to surrender and then would be destroyed by the Lord (Isa. 54:14–17).

The Characteristics of the Redeemed

All the redeemed—Jews and Gentiles—will be characterized by repentance, holiness, righteousness, humility, wisdom, and spiritual enlightenment (Ps. 72:7; Isa. 4:4; 29:18, 24; 30:20–21). God will pour out the Spirit on all flesh to bring about eternal obedience (Isa. 32:15–20; 44:3; 59:21; Ezek. 36:27) and to gift all the people of God (Joel 2:28–32). Sorrow and pain will be removed; the redeemed will experience only joy and gladness (Isa. 12:1–4).

The Presence of Sin and Possibility of Rebellion

The prophets present two different portrayals of the issue of sin and righteousness in the kingdom. Ezekiel, for example, states that the sin nature will not be removed (Ezek. 36:24–27) but also indicates that a person may sin unintentionally or through ignorance (Ezek. 45:20). Some prophets picture sin as removed, cleansed, forgiven, and fully atoned (Dan. 9:24). However, others picture the repentant atoning for sin through sacrificial offerings (Ezek. 43:20, 26; 45:15, 17, 20) and the unrepentant plagued or executed (Isa. 65:20; Zech. 14:17–19). On the one hand, Gentile nations will journey to Jerusalem to worship the Lord (Isa. 19:19–25); on the other hand, Egypt will refuse one year and will be disciplined by God (Zech. 14:17–19). On the one hand, Jerusalem will be protected by God and never again attacked or conquered (Isa. 4:5–6; 14:23). On the other hand, hostile Gentile nations will attack eschatological Jerusalem, only to be destroyed by God (Isa. 54:14–17; Ezek. 38:1–39:8). This dual image probably is due to the distinction between the inaugural millennial kingdom and the eternal new heavens and new earth that is clarified in NT (Rev 20–22). The loosing of Satan at the end of the Millennium (Rev. 20:7–10) may be implicit in a limited imprisonment of the demons before they are finally punished (Isa. 24:21–22).

Final Judgment of the Wicked

The two resurrections (Dan. 12:2) are separated temporally. The righteous will be resurrected to enjoy the messianic kingdom (Isa. 26:19); however, the bodies of the wicked will remain in the grave (Isa. 26:14) and their souls will be imprisoned for "many days" (Isa. 24:21–22). After an unspecified period (Rev. 20 states a thousand years), the wicked will be resurrected to judgment (Dan. 12:2). Their smoldering corpses will be an eternal reminder of the consequences of rebellion against God (Isa. 66:24).

See also DANIEL; ESCHATOLOGY OF; DAVIDIC COVENANT.

Gordon H. Johnston

J. Bright, *Covenant and Promise: The Prophetic Understanding of the Future in Pre-Exilic Israel* (Philadelphia: Westminster Press, 1976); D. K. Campbell and J. L. Townsend, eds., *A Case for Premillennialism: A New Consensus* (Chicago: Moody, 1992); W. J. Dumbrell, *Covenant and Creation* (Nashville: Thomas Nelson, 1984), *The End of the Beginning* (Nashville: Thomas Nelson, 1988); D. Gowan, *Eschatology in the Old Testament* (Philadelphia: Fortress Press, 1986); G. F. Hasel, *The Remnant* (Berrien Springs: Andrews University, 1980); W. C. Kaiser Jr, *Toward an Old Testament Theology* (Grand Rapids: Zondervan, 1978); T. E. McComiskey, *The Covenants of Promise* (Grand Rapids: Baker, 1985); J. D. Pentecost, *Things to Come* (Grand Rapids: Zondervan, 1958); Charles C. Ryrie, *The Basis of the Premillennial Faith* (Neptune, N.J.: Loizeaux Brothers, 1953); J. F. Walvoord, *The Millennial Kingdom* (Grand Rapids: Zondervan, 1959), *The Prophecy Knowledge Handbook* (Wheaton: Victor Books, 1990); R.B. Zuck, ed., *A Biblical Theology of the Old Testament* (Chicago: Moody Press, 1991).

MOODY, DWIGHT LYMAN

Dwight L. Moody (1837–1899) died on the eve of the new century, December 22, 1899. The import of his life is clearly evidenced by the fact that within a year of his death fourteen biographies were written. The details of his personal life and accomplishments are easily researched and recorded. To identify his theology offers a larger challenge, not the least of which pertains to his eschatology.

As early as the 1870s Moody was clearly espousing premillennialism, most likely as a result of his associations with the Plymouth Brethren (Findlay, 250). Moody's premillennialism and dispensationalism was not articulated systematically but rather was a motif running through his sermons, "simple affirmations of premillennial faith without any careful argumentation" (Gundry, 87). These themes were so clear that it has been noted that in the last twenty years of the nineteenth century it is through Moody that one learns much of premillennialism and dispensationalism (Findlay, 21). "Both scriptural inerrancy and premillennialism became central tenets of Moody's mature religious faith" (Findlay, 126). Though some question whether Moody ever became a thoroughgoing dispensationalist (e.g., Findlay, 250–51) "it is sufficient to say that dispensationalists, both English and American, had helped considerably to confirm Moody in his decision to adopt the position of premillennialism" (Findlay, 251).

Moody "did not identify himself as a futurist nor did he speak of the church age as a parenthesis. Not once did Moody mention a seven-year interval between Christ's coming for His church and His return to inaugurate the millennial kingdom. In many references to Christ's return it sounds as if he made no distinction between a secret coming and a coming in power and glory. He never described a period known as the Tribulation, seven years in length" (Gundry, 188). Interestingly, however, in his exposition of Daniel 2 he declared his belief in the "literal fulfillment" of this prophecy, "reflecting both a premillennial and dispensational orientation, with the emphasis on a literal hermeneutic" (Gundry, 186).

Moody may be difficult to pin down with regard to the Rapture as clearly as other dispensationalists of his day. "In dispensational fashion, he at least maintained enough of a distinction between Israel and the church that he insisted upon the regathering of the Jewish people, the restoration of the nation of Israel, and the literal fulfillment of prophecies with reference to Israel . . . he clearly insisted that the believer should expect Christ to return suddenly, unexpectedly, and secretly" (Gundry, 187). Moody said he could find nothing in the Bible that instructed believers to look for signs but rather that the believer "was simply to be ready, watching, and waiting for the Lord who would come as a thief in the night" (Gundry, 188).

This last statement perhaps expresses a major reason for Moody's commitment to premillennialism. To Moody's mind "premillennialism seemed to strike a proper note of urgency about the need for winning souls to Christ, and to him this was crucial," and as the years passed "premillennialism increasingly grasped the mind of the evangelist and shaped it" (Findlay, 254). There was a message there for both saint and sinner, and it became his frequent theme. The practical effect of premillennial teaching was that it should wake up the church to its task and that the world would lose its hold on the believer. The "doctrine of Christ's return in judgment, followed by His kingdom, was to impart a sense of urgency to the evangelistic task. But the doctrine also should impress upon the unbeliever a sense of urgency because of the imminent danger" (Gundry, 185).

Premillennial varieties of interpretation were gaining popularity, and by the 1890s the premillennialists were finding their own house filled with controversy. Moody cautioned against excessive division, urging, "Don't criticize if our watches don't agree about the time that we know he is coming." His eschatological emphasis was "Watch and pray, for you know not when the time is. It was clearly premillennial, vaguely dispensational, and held with such tolerance as to not create a barrier between himself and those who might differ" (Gundry, 192–93).

James M. Gray, a former president of Moody Bible Institute, wrote that "there was one great incentive to Mr. Moody's ministry, the pervading life of his theology . . . namely the hope of the coming of the Lord —His personal and visible appearing. He set no dates for His appearing. He never speculated about it. He did not undertake to teach prophecy, but he was looking for His coming every day" (Gray, 21). His eschatology was above all else Christ-centered—a model for us all.

See also GRAY, JAMES.

Harold D. Foos

James F. Findlay Jr., *Dwight L. Moody: American Evangelist* (Chicago: The University of Chicago Press, 1969); James

M. Gray, *D. L. Moody's Theology* (Chicago: The Bible Institute Colportage Association, ca. 1912); Stanley N. Gundry, *Love Them In: The Proclamation Theology of D. L. Moody* (Chicago: Moody Press, 1976).

MYSTERY

Definition

The New Testament word *mystery* comes from the root *mureo,* which means "one who shuts his eyes" which in turn had a derived meaning of "one who is initiated in the mysteries." In classical Greek, the word had the basic meanings of a hidden thing, a secret, a secret ceremony, a secret teaching. In the New Testament it has the basic sense of something unrevealed in the past (in the Old Testament) that has now or is now being revealed.

Usage and Scripture

The word *mystery* is found twenty-eight times in the New Testament (Matt. 13:11; Mark 4:11; Luke 8:10; Rom. 11:25; 16:25–27; 1 Cor. 2:1, 7; 4:1; 13:2; 14:2; 15:51; Eph. 1:9–10; 3:1–13; 5:32; 6:19–20; Col. 1:26–27; 2:2–3; 4:3; 2 Thess. 2:7; 1 Tim. 3:9, 16; Rev. 1:20; 10:7; 17:5, 7).

The New Testament Meaning

The meaning, as used in the New Testament, refers to something totally unrevealed in the Old Testament revealed for the first time in the New Testament. Matthew 13:11 introduces the mysteries of the kingdom, and in verse 35 Jesus states that the mystery of the kingdom has been hidden from the foundation of the world. Romans 16:25–26 tells us the mystery has been kept in silence through all eternity past, but it is now being revealed. First Corinthians 2:7 declares that the mystery has been hidden, and God has predestined this mystery to our glory. Ephesians 3:4–5 declares that the mystery was not made known to previous generations and is only now being revealed to His New Testament apostles and prophets. Ephesians 3:9 states that the mystery has been hid in God, but now all may know it. Colossians 1:26 declares that the mystery has been hid for ages and generations, but it is now being revealed to the saints. To summarize the meaning of mystery, it refers to the secret thoughts, plans, and dispensations of God that are hidden from humanity and must be revealed by divine revelation. The term is not used the same in Greek as in the English, meaning of something inexplicable or impossible to understand, but rather it is something unrevealed until now, something that is explicable and understandable. By the time Paul was writing, the mystery had been well revealed to the apostles and New Testament prophets and, for that reason, they were to lay down the foundations of the church (Eph. 2:19–22), and they were to record New Testament revelation (Eph. 3:1–10). It can now be understood by the saints with the help of the Holy Spirit (1 Cor. 2:14).

The Origin of Paul's Concept

It has often been taught that Paul's concept of the mystery comes from the pagan mystery religions that were rooted in the Babylonian story of Tammuz and Ishtar. While there were various mystery religions, they shared a number of things in common: there were secret ceremonies performed by a circle of followers to portray the death and resurrection of the god; only the initiated were allowed knowledge of these secret ceremonies; the adherents were promised salvation through these ceremonies by their dispensing of the god's life; and there was a vow of silence, in that the adherents were not allowed to share any information on the secret ceremonies with those outside. However, it is difficult to believe that this was the true source of Paul's concept of the mystery. Raised in Tarsus, Paul certainly would have known about these religions, but as a strict Pharisee, he would not have participated in them. Furthermore, the mystery of these mystery religions was something already known by a few to be revealed to a few, while the biblical mystery was something totally unknown to anyone until God revealed it, and it was not available to all; and, finally, those in the mystery religions who knew the mystery could not share it with others, while the biblical mystery was available to all. It is better to find Paul's source in the Jewish context rather than the pagan context. In the Septuagint translation of Daniel 2, the Greek word for mystery is the translation of the Aramaic word rāzāh (2:18–19, 27– 30, 47). This was translated as "secret"; it is God who reveals the mysteries. A corollary word in the Hebrew sôḏ, a word found twenty-two times in the Hebrew Bible and usually translated as "secret counsel." It usually refers to a divine secret that can be known and understood only if God reveals it to His people through the prophets. The usage of the Aramaic and Hebrew words is really the closest to Paul's usage and is the true source of Paul's concept of the mystery, in addition to the fact that there was a divine revelation given to him from God.

The Mystery of the Kingdom

The first time the word appears is in relationship to a new facet of God's kingdom program, introduced by Jesus in Matthew 13, the mystery kingdom. Keeping in mind the definition that the mystery refers to something unrevealed in the Old Testament, the mystery kingdom must be a facet of God's kingdom program totally unknown in the Old Testament. Therefore, it must be distinguished from the other four facets of God's kingdom program, which are the universal or eternal kingdom, the spiritual kingdom, the theocratic kingdom, and the messianic or millennial kingdom. The mystery kingdom is the outworking of God's rule from the rejection of the messiahship of Jesus by Israel (Matt. 12) until the acceptance of the messiahship of Jesus by Israel just before His second coming (Matt. 23:37–39). The parables of Matthew 13 describe the outworking of the mystery kingdom (see KINGDOM, PARABLES OF THE).

To summarize the teaching about the mystery kingdom through these parables: Positively, there will be the sowing of the Gospel seed throughout the mystery-kingdom age, and the seed sown will spring to life inexplicably by its own power. However, negatively, the true sowing will be imitated by a false countersowing, and the mystery kingdom will assume huge outer proportions, marked by inward doctrinal corruption. But, positively, God will gain a believing remnant from Israel and also from among the Gentiles. Finally, the judgment of the Gentiles at the end of the mystery-kingdom age will bring the righteous Gentiles into the messianic kingdom, while the unrighteous will be excluded.

The Five Mysteries of the Church

The first mystery relevant to the church is the mystery of the seven stars and seven golden lampstands (Rev. 1:20). The seven stars are the seven angels of the seven churches, while the seven lampstands are the seven churches. While in the Old Testament, Israel was represented as the seven-branched lampstand, the mystery here is the fact that seven individual lampstands symbolize seven local churches. Also, part of the mystery is that each local church has a guardian angel assigned to it.

The second mystery is the mystery of the body (Eph. 3:1–12). The content of the mystery specifically (v. 6) is that Jewish and Gentile believers are united in one body, and this one body is distinct from both Israel and the Gentiles.

The third mystery is the mystery of the indwelling Christ (Col. 1:24–29). The actual content of this mystery is "Christ in you, the hope of glory" (v. 27). The fact that the Messiah now indwells every believer is the mystery unrevealed in the Old Testament. The fact of the Spirit's indwelling was not a mystery, because it was known in the Old Testament. While the Old Testament did reveal many things about the Messiah, it did not reveal that He would indwell every believer.

The fourth mystery is the mystery of the church as the bride of Christ (Eph. 5:22–33). The actual content of the mystery (v. 32) is the fact that the church is the bride of the Messiah. In the Old Testament, it was revealed that Israel was the wife of Jehovah, so this could not be the mystery. What was unrevealed in the Old Testament is the fact that the second person will have His own bride, which is the church.

The fifth mystery is the mystery of the

translation (1 Cor. 15:50–58). The specific content of this mystery (vv. 51–52) is that someday there will be a generation of believers who will enter into eternity without first passing through the gates of death. This implies that the Rapture is part of the mystery and would, therefore, have to be distinct from the Second Coming, which was not a mystery.

The fact that these five mysteries are all directly relevant to the church clearly implies that the church, itself, is a mystery; it was totally unknown in the Old Testament and, therefore, another argument against replacement theology, which tends to find the church throughout the Old Testament.

The Mystery of Israel's Hardening

In Romans 9:1–11:36, Paul spells out his own Israelology. The actual content of the mystery is spoken of late in his discussion (11:25). The fact of Israel's rejection of the messiahship of Jesus is not the mystery, because this was well known from the Old Testament. It is not the fact of Israel's future national salvation that is the mystery, because that, too, is well prophesied in the Old Testament. The actual content of the mystery is that of a partial, temporary hardening of Israel until a full number of Gentiles is reached. This fact was unrevealed in the Old Testament. The Greek word sometimes translated "fullness" means "a set number." God has a set number of Gentiles whom He intends to bring into this body (the mystery of Ephesians), and when this number is reached, that facet of the mystery is complete. This, in turn, completes the purpose of Gentile salvation (Acts 15:14), which is to call out from among the Gentiles a people for His name. The fact of Gentile salvation is not a mystery, as that was revealed in the Old Testament. What was not revealed is that God has a set number of Gentiles whom He intends to bring into the body, and when that set number is reached at the end of the mystery-kingdom age, He will bring the righteous Gentiles into the mystery kingdom while the unrighteous will be excluded.

The mystery kingdom has both similarities and dissimilarities with other facets of God's kingdom program.

See also ISRAEL AND THE CHURCH: THE DIFFERENCES; ROMANS, ESCHATOLOGY OF.

Arnold Fruchtenbaum

N

NAHUM, ESCHATOLOGY OF

The only thing we know about the writer is that his name was Nahum, meaning "consolation," and he was from Elkosh (1:1). The exact location of this city is unknown. Walvoord suggests it was probably somewhere in southern Galilee, though others locate it in southern Judah. Since Nahum mentions the fall of Thebes, a city of Egypt, which occurred in 663 B.C., and also predicts the fall of Nineveh which occurred in 612 B.C., the book had to have been penned by Nahum sometime in the seventh century between these two dates.

The subject of Nahum's prophecy is the fall of Nineveh (1:1). As Archer states, "His theme deals with the holiness of God, a holiness which involves both retribution toward rebellious unbelievers and compassion toward His own people, especially those who sincerely believe and trust in Him alone. The believer is represented as rejoicing at the sight of God's righteous vindication of His holiness in the destruction of the God-defying power of Assyria."

In chapter 1 Nahum reminds his hearers of the character of God. Although the Lord is slow to anger and great in power, His holiness prevents Him from leaving the guilty unpunished (1:3). He is a jealous and avenging God (1:2). The awesomeness of the Lord is presented in 1:2–6 as a reminder to the people. At the same time the people are reminded that the Lord is good and a stronghold for those who take refuge in Him (1:7). Nineveh's judgment means that the Lord will bring about a complete end of the city (1:8). Nineveh's sins caused God's wrath to fall (1:9–11). Because of Nineveh's destruction, the yoke that was on Judah as a result of its vassal status would be broken (1:12–13). Nineveh's fame would end and in the destruction its temple and idols would be cut off (1:14). This was literally fulfilled in 612 B.C. In contrast to Nineveh's destruction, there is coming a time when God will bless Judah. Judah will be at peace and again be able to celebrate its feasts and pay her vows to God. She would no longer have to worry about the wicked one (the Assyrian king) since he is cut off completely (1:15). Again we see in history a very literal fulfillment when Nineveh was destroyed and, as Amerding points out, the "renewal of worship was accomplished in the reign of Josiah, after about 631" (see 2 Kings 22:3–23:27; 2 Chron. 34–35).

In 2:1–6, Nahum starts to give a more specific description of the destruction that will take place. He calls on the Ninevites to defend their city although their defense will be futile (2:1). In contrast to the destruction coming on Nineveh there will be future restoration for Jacob (2:2). As Johnson states, "This will not be fully realized till Israel is in the land in the millennial kingdom which the Messiah will establish. This will contrast with her having been laid . . . waste by Assyria (the defeat of the northern kingdom in 722 B.C.)." The siege is descriptively portrayed, showing the battle occurring in the streets and the squares, on the wall, and ending in the taking of the palace (2:3–6). The city will then be stripped and plundered and all its riches will be carried away (2:7–10). Even its armies will be destroyed (2:11–13). "According to the Babylonian Chronicle, 'Great quantities of spoil from the city, beyond counting, they carried off. The city [they turned] into a mound and ruin heap'" (Luckenbill, *Ancient Records of Assyria and Babylonia*, 2:420). These verses were very literally fulfilled in the destruction of Nineveh in 612 B.C.

Chapter 3 predicts Nineveh's complete destruction. It was a bloody city completely full of lies and pillage (3:1). It is a spiritual harlot involved in enslaving the nations and selling them (3:2–4). Because of this the Lord is against Nineveh and will expose its nakedness to the nations and the devastation will be so severe that the nations will shrink back (3:5–7). Just as *No-amon* (Greek name for Thebes) was destroyed earlier, so too Nineveh will become drunk, be hidden, and search for refuge from the enemy (3:8–11). Nahum said that its fortifications were like a fig tree with ripe fruit; when shaken, its fruit will fall into the eater's mouth (3:12). Its troops will be defenseless and its gates would be open wide to its enemies (3:13). Nineveh is encouraged to strengthen their fortifications (3:14), although even this will be in vain, since they are destined to be cut down by the sword and consumed (3:15). Though they were multiplied like grasshoppers, like grasshoppers flee from the walls when the sun rises so the Assyrian armies will flee from the enemies (3:16–17). The people of Nineveh will be scattered on the mountains and there will be no one to regather them; their wound will be incurable (3:18–19). The reason for the destruction is the evil that Assyria had dispensed on all the nations (3:19). As Walvoord states, "In 612 B.C. Nineveh was so thoroughly destroyed that it was never rebuilt and soon became a pile of sand."

Russell L. Penney

Gleason L. Archer, *A Survey of Old Testament Introduction* (Chicago: Moody Press, 1994); Carl E. Armerding, "Nahum" in *The Expositor's Bible Commentary,* ed. Frank E. Gaebelein, vol. 7 (Grand Rapids: Zondervan, 1985); Elliot E. Johnson, "Nahum" in *The Bible Knowledge Commentary,* eds. John F. Walvoord and Roy B. Zuck (Wheaton: Victor Books, 1988); John F. Walvoord, *The Prophecy Knowledge Handbook* (Wheaton: Victor Books, 1990).

NEW COVENANT, THEOLOGY OF THE

The new covenant is an administrative covenant promised to Israel by God, during the late preexilic and exilic periods, as the instrument that would govern the nation's spiritual and political life during the future messianic kingdom. By God's grace the church has become a participant in some aspects of this covenant following its ratification on the cross, although the full realization of the covenant remains future. This covenant administers the provisions of the Abrahamic covenant, replacing the previous administrative covenant (the Mosaic) in the progressive outworking of God's kingdom purposes. It is presently the basis on which anyone maintains a right relationship with God, and it governs the life of all believers. The church, though not one of the original parties to the covenant, falls under the jurisdiction of the covenant both as a subject of its rule of life and as recipient of promised Abrahamic covenant blessings for Gentiles that have come through the Seed of Abraham, Jesus Christ. Individual covenant promises described in the OT are being implemented during the present stage of God's program despite the fact that the entire covenant is not presently being fulfilled.

The new covenant is not a minor concept in the OT but spans a number of major passages in the Prophets. Although only Jeremiah 31:31 makes reference to the new covenant by name, the concept is much more common, being found also in Isaiah 49:8; 54:10; 55:3; 59:21; 61:8; Jeremiah 32:39–40; 50:5; Ezekiel 11:19; 16:60–63; 18:31; 34:25; 36:26; 37:26; and Hosea 2:18–20. In these texts the parties of the new covenant are God and Israel. Jeremiah 31:31 speaks of one covenant and one people, even though the nation was divided and half was exiled at the time of this prophecy. The covenant anticipates a reunited and restored Israel as a national entity. The covenant is not promised to any other group or nation. The OT is unanimous in stating that the new covenant is made with Israel. This does not mean that others are excluded, however. That conclusion could only be drawn logically if the text specified that Israel's status under the new covenant was exclusive. All that can be said is that the OT speaks only of Israel's inclusion.

Drawing from the two major passages

(Jer. 31, Ezek. 36), the new covenant's provisions include: the internalization of the Word of God (Jer. 31:33); a personal relationship with God (v. 33); a comprehensive knowledge of God (v. 34); final forgiveness of sin (v. 34); the continued national existence of Israel (vv. 35–37); Jerusalem to be rebuilt, never again to be demolished (vv. 38–40); restoration to the land (Ezek. 36:24, 28, 33); cleansing from sin (v. 25); a responsive heart guaranteed (v. 26); indwelling of the Spirit (v. 27); motivation and ability for obedience (v. 27); personal relationship with God (v. 28); material prosperity and fruitfulness of the land (vv. 29–30, 34–35); and a large population in the restored land (vv. 37–38).

The new covenant is only promised in the OT; it was not ratified or inaugurated at the time of Jeremiah or any subsequent OT prophet. Ratification is the ceremony at which the provisions and stipulations of the covenant become legally binding. Covenants (both biblical and ancient Near Eastern) were enacted on the basis of a formal oath, often accompanied by a blood ceremony, indicating that the sworn relationship is a bond in blood. Israel looked forward to the new covenant but did not enjoy its provisions—Israel still lived under the old covenant. Although some have argued for a future ratification at the time of the millennial kingdom's inauguration, it is best to view the covenant as having been ratified at the time of Jesus' death. OT data is inconclusive in this regard. Some OT texts refer to making a covenant (Isa. 55:3; 61:8; Jer. 31:31; 32:40; Ezek. 34:25; 37:26), but these usually provide only general, indefinite references to the future. Ezekiel 34:25 does specify that the covenant will be made prior to the millennial reign. Presumably Isaiah 61:8 refers to the millennial era. The preceding context does refer to that period, but Jesus cited 61:1–2 as fulfilled in His day. In light of the lack of clear distinction between the two advents in many OT texts, it would be precarious to assume that verse 8 must be millennial.

The NT provides more specific information as to the time of the new covenant's ratification. Hebrews 7 refers directly to the covenant ratification oath by which Jesus became the Melchizedekian high priest (7:17–22). On the basis of this oath, He has become the guarantee of a better covenant—the new covenant (v. 22). Jesus' mediatorship and high priesthood is based on the new covenant (Heb. 8:6). Since both of these ministries are currently in force, it would seem to require that the covenant on which they are based is also in force. Hebrews 9:12–28 draws explicit contrasts with the old covenant, showing that Jesus' present ministry is superior because it is based on the new covenant. Note the explicit mention of Jesus' death, the shedding of blood, and particularly the phrase "the blood of the covenant" (esp. 9:18–20). This key phrase (also found in Matt. 26:28 and parallels) argues strongly for ratification at the Cross due to the parallel with the ratification of the old covenant in Exodus 24:8. The parallel is clearly implied in the synoptic accounts; it is explicitly stated in Hebrews.

Other NT passages corroborate this conclusion. The references in the Gospels specifically connect the new covenant with Jesus' cross work (Matt. 26:28; Luke 22:20; Mark 14:24). The cup, representing the new covenant, was made on the basis of the blood of Christ. Jesus' words require the covenant's ratification at the Cross. It is not that the Cross simply enabled a future ratification. The blood ceremony of the Cross institutes the covenant just as Jesus' inaugural words instituted the ceremony that would commemorate it. This is most evident in Matthew's record since he explains that the pouring out is for the purpose of forgiveness of sins—a present reality (for both Israel and the church). The cup is what is poured out, and this cup represents the new covenant. Blood, cup, covenant, and forgiveness are inseparably linked by Jesus' words. Paul's account of the Lord's Supper records the words of institution, not as a historical note that is irrelevant to church practice but as significant words that in themselves communicate truth directly relevant to the church. The references to the cup as representative of the new covenant and the forgiveness provided for sin are directly related to those who participate in the memorial.

The most extensive passage in the Pauline corpus regarding the new covenant is 2 Corinthians 3. Here the apostle draws a very evident contrast between the old, Mosaic covenant, and the new covenant. On the one hand there are the tablets of stone, the letter, a ministry of death, and fading glory. On the other there are tablets of flesh (human hearts), the Spirit, a ministry of life, and surpassing glory. The first has passed away. The second is now reigning. Paul claims the status of new covenant minister (3:6) and contrasts the fading glory of the old covenant with the present glory of the ministry that brings righteousness (vv. 7–11). To argue that Paul refers to a new covenant-like ministry misses the point. Even though the construction is *anarthrous* (without an article), this does not demand a qualitative emphasis since the entire construction is anarthrous (Apollonius' Canon). At most it would suggest translating "new covenant ministers." But what is implied by that statement? In light of the emphatic contrast between the two covenants in the context, it means that, in contrast to some people (3:1) who apparently were attempting to promulgate an old-covenant-based ministry, Paul serves under a new covenant. This can be none other than the new covenant with which the old is contrasted. This necessitates the conclusion that the new covenant is in force in the present age and that the church is in some way related to it.

The new covenant was ratified at the Cross—Jesus' death being the blood that sealed the bond of the covenant and brought the provisions of the covenant into effect. Such a conclusion need not require that all aspects of the covenant be presently in force—for Israel, the Gentiles, or the church. It would suggest that God's administrative covenant for the old era—the old, or Mosaic, covenant—has been superseded by a new arrangement. The data would also appear to require that national promises of the covenant will not be fulfilled for Israel until a future reign of Messiah. If God were not to do what He promised to do, He would violate His character and His oath-bound covenant. If God does not fulfill the promises of the new covenant with Israel exactly as He promised and as the prophet understood His promise, then He has failed. But God can enlarge the promise and do more than He has promised. If God has seen fit to apply some aspects of the covenant to the church, it does not change the covenant promises to Israel—they will still be fulfilled. It simply says that He is doing more than He told the OT prophets that he would do.

See also COVENANTS, THE.

Rodney Decker

C. Blaising and D. Bock, *Progressive Dispensationalism* (Wheaton: Victor, 1993); L. Chafer, *Systematic Theology* (Grand Rapids: Kregel, 1993); R. Compton, "An Examination of the New Covenant in the Old and New Testaments" (Th.D. diss., Grace Theological Seminary, 1986); R. Decker, "The Church's Relationship to the New Covenant" in *Bib Sac* 152:290–305, 431–56; C. Hoch, *All Things New* (Grand Rapids: Baker, 1995); W. Kaiser Jr., "The Old Promise and the New Covenant: Jeremiah 31:31–34," *JETS* 15:11–23; H. Kent, "The New Covenant and the Church" in *GTJ* 6:289–98 (1986); J. Master, "The New Covenant" in *Contemporary Issues in Dispensationalism* (Chicago: Moody Press, 1994); L. Pettegrew, *The New Covenant Ministry of the Holy Spirit* (Lanham, Md.: University Press of America, 1993); R. Saucy, *The Case for Progressive Dispensationalism* (Grand Rapids: Zondervan, 1993); T. Schreiner, *The Law and Its Fulfillment* (Grand Rapids: Baker, 1993); B. Ware, "The New Covenant and the People(s) of God" in *Dispensationalism, Israel, and the Church* (Grand Rapids: Zondervan, 1992).

NEW COVENANT, DISPENSATIONAL VIEWS OF THE

There are four major dispensational views of the new covenant: the church has a different new covenant than Israel, the church has no relationship to the new covenant, the church participates in some aspects of the new covenant, and the church fulfills some aspects of the new covenant in a preliminary way.

The Church Has a Different Covenant

The classic form of the two new covenants view is found in Lewis Sperry Chafer's *Systematic Theology* (7:98–99). There are three similarities between these two covenants: their name, their basis (the death of Christ), and some of their provisions. The first new covenant is made with Israel and will govern Israel's life in the kingdom, replacing the old covenant yet including the Mosaic commandments in heightened form. The second new covenant is made with the church by the blood of Christ and is presently in force (in contrast to Israel's new covenant that is yet future). The basis for this view is the presupposition that there can be no common interest between God's purposes for Israel and for the church. This position suffers two fatal flaws: Scripture never explicitly says that there are two new covenants nor does it ever juxtapose them in the same context, and second, it is built on a theological presupposition rather than on an exegesis of the text. Chafer's determination to maintain a complete separation between Israel and the church has forced him to an exegetically indefensible conclusion.

The Church Has No Part in the Covenant

A less common view is that the church has no relationship to the new covenant. This is usually identified as Darby's position. His view is that the new covenant of Jeremiah 31 is made strictly with Israel and will be fulfilled by Israel in the future millennial kingdom. Because of Israel's unbelief, the covenant is not now in effect with that nation. Instead, the church participates in the new covenant ("he brought us into it"), not as a legal party to the covenant, but as recipients of the blessings of the covenant. It does not apply to the church directly as a legal covenant relationship, but as a gracious, spiritual benefit. These benefits come by virtue of a union with Christ, the mediator of the covenant, and are placed into effect at the time of His death. This means that all the references in the NT are to the same new covenant spoken of in Jeremiah 31. True, the church has no direct relationship to that covenant. It is not one of the legal parties of the new covenant. Yet Darby does not hesitate to relate the church to that covenant. He does not suggest that it shares only new covenant-like blessings, but that we share the actual covenant blessings. This covenant is now in effect, having been instituted with the death of Christ. There will be a future implemen-tation with Israel that will result in the fulfillment of the new covenant. Darby nowhere speaks of the church's participation in the covenant in terms of fulfillment.

John Master is a contemporary advocate of a position similar to Darby's. The new covenant is strictly for Israel in the future messianic kingdom. This covenant will guarantee the obedience of God's people Israel in order that the provisions of the Abrahamic, Palestinian, and Davidic covenants might be fulfilled. The church enjoys similar spiritual blessings and promises as those that are specified for Israel but not on the basis of the new covenant. The only relationship between the church and the new covenant is that members of the church are united to the mediator of the new covenant—Jesus Christ.

Master argues, based on Paul's defense of his Spirit-dependent apostolic ministry (2 Cor. 1:12–3:3), that the reference of 2 Corinthians 3:6 is to the character of Paul's ministry in contrast to others who advocated a ministry based on works and self-effort. In this connection, he suggests that the anarthrous construction of *diakonous kaines diathekes* (minister of a new covenant) does not necessitate a present function of the new covenant. *Gramma* (the letter) refers, not to the OT law, but to the misuse of the Mosaic Law. Both of these arguments have difficulties. To argue that the reference is to qualitative factors may be legitimate, but simply the fact of an anarthrous construction does not require a qualitative force. Additionally, to argue that *the letter* does not refer to the Mosaic covenant must ignore numerous contextual indications to the contrary (see Schreiner's discussion). Likewise it must be asked, is the misuse of the law that which was glorious prior to the coming of the new covenant (vv. 7–11)? This position comes closest to the traditional title given to such views: the church has no relationship to the new covenant. It is a more consistent designation for Master's view than for Darby's.

The Church Has Some Part in the Covenant

Many in contemporary dispensational circles would say that the church participates in some way in the new covenant. Two key studies of the new covenant in recent years are Homer Kent's 1985 article in *Grace Theological Journal* and Bruce Compton's dissertation at Grace Seminary in 1986. They view the essence of the new covenant as the spiritual regeneration that is the present reality of the church and the future expectation for Israel at the Second Coming of Christ. The new covenant will be fulfilled with Israel eschatologically but is enjoyed soteriologically by the church now.

The Church Has a Preliminary Part in the Covenant

The fourth view is represented by Bruce Ware, who argues that the new covenant focuses on two key areas: the cross (and the forgiveness it provided) and the indwelling ministry of the Holy Spirit. These new covenant blessings are applied by the NT in a preliminary form to the church as the spiritual seed of Abraham. This provision *began* to be realized with Jesus' ministry, is death for sin providing the basis of the covenant's enactment. Not until the coming of the Spirit at Pentecost, however, was the covenant actually inaugurated. The benefit of this new covenant ministry of the Spirit is to enable the covenant participants to live increasingly righteous lives. The Spirit's role is characterized by a qualitative newness. Israel and the church thus share a number of theological elements in common, including participation in the same new covenant, while at the same time maintaining their distinct identities. In other words, there is both continuity and relationship on the one hand and discontinuity and distinction on the other. The discontinuity comes most sharply into focus when considering the territorial and political promises of the new covenant. The principle of authorial intent necessitates the fulfillment of what God promised to Israel—a future fulfillment of the new covenant (including its territorial and political aspects) for the nation. Continuity comes into play when it is recognized that the church experiences a preliminary and partial fulfillment of some aspects of the new covenant. These include forgiveness and the indwelling of the Spirit viewed in an already/not yet framework. The partial nature of the fulfillment may be seen in the reality of incomplete obedience on the part of God's people. Although obedience may be incomplete, the new covenant believer still has far greater resources in their struggle with sin than were available under the old covenant. The new covenant promises assure that perfect and complete obedience will be a reality when Christ returns and fulfills the new covenant (now inaugurated in a preliminary way). Similar explanations have been proposed by Darrell Bock, Craig Blaising, Larry Pettegrew, and Robert Saucy.

Analysis

The last three positions stand united in rejecting two new covenants although they vary somewhat in how they explain the details or in the divergent emphases. The end result is not, however, a great deal different. There is agreement among the last two positions as to the necessity of relating the new covenant to the church in some way. The arguments that are repeated in one form or another by every writer in these categories include Jesus' words of institution in the Upper Room, Paul's repetition of those words as he explains the church's observance of the Lord's Table, the reference to a new covenant ministry in 2 Corinthians 3, and the several references to the new covenant in Hebrews. Likewise, they agree that the territorial and political aspects of the covenant are not being fulfilled today but will be fulfilled in the future messianic kingdom.

Kent and Saucy place a greater emphasis on soteriology in the covenant, speaking frequently of regeneration and salvation as being the essence of the covenant. Bock and Blaising, Pettegrew, and Ware speak of the new covenant primarily in terms of a believer's relationship to God: sanctification rather than regeneration. "The church participates in the new covenant pneumatologically," as Pettegrew puts it.

Bock and Blaising, Pettegrew, and Ware use inaugurated, already-not yet, and/or partial fulfillment terminology to explain the present aspects of the new covenant. Kent and Compton speak only of the church's *participation* in the covenant. Compton, in particular, argues against using fulfillment terminology because, as he defines *fulfill,* it implies that the church is the *complete fulfillment* of the covenant, replacing Israel as covenant partner. The other writers do not associate fulfillment language with replacement. They often speak of *partial fulfillment* and distinguish various aspects of the covenant that are presently being fulfilled from the complete, future fulfillment, including the national and geographical elements for ethnic Israel that await the earthly reign of Messiah.

If people-of-God status (see PEOPLE OF GOD) is based on a covenant relationship, and if the church is part of the people of God, it seems difficult to avoid some sense of new covenant fulfillment at the present time. In addition, the pneumatological aspects of the covenant (see esp. 2 Cor. 3:6–11) would also appear to necessitate some form of new covenant implementation if the church's relationship to the Spirit is based on the new covenant. Fulfillment language at this point, however, should not be understood to imply any abrogation or substitution of the new covenant promises of the OT. They will be fulfilled with Israel as promised in the future kingdom regency. God may do more than He promised, but He may not do less. Although this position has been discussed extensively in recent literature by "progressive dispensationalists," it does not require that approach to dispensational hermeneutics; it coheres equally well with a more traditional form of dispensationalism.

See NEW COVENANT, THEOLOGY OF.

Rodney Decker

NEW HEAVEN AND NEW EARTH

Revelation 21:1–22:5 furnishes detailed information about a new heaven and a new earth, but Isaiah 65:17; 66:22; 2 Peter 3:13 also mention the two. Another name for them is the New Jerusalem (Rev. 21:2, 10). The title "new heaven and new earth" names a physical reality, and it also speaks of a new order of creation that will replace the present created heaven and earth (Rev. 21:1, 5), an order in which will exist only a people of God with whom He will dwell in the closest of relationships (Rev. 21:3; 22:3–4). The "eternal state" is a name often applied to this new order because time limitations as they exist among human beings will be unknown. It will be unending (Isa. 66:22; Rev. 22:5). Those who have not chosen a personal relationship with God in this creation will have no part in that future creation (Rev. 21:8, 27) because it will be a creation pervaded with righteousness (2 Peter 3:13). It will differ from the millennial kingdom in that the curse placed upon the old creation (Gen. 3:17–19) will no longer exist (Rev. 22:3). Another difference between the two will be the presence of a temple during the Millennium (Ezekiel 40–48) and the absence of the same in the eternal state (Rev. 21:22). Revelation 21:11–21 gives physical features of the New Jerusalem that constitutes the new creation. The dimensions and layout designs are an accommodation to finite minds, because the new heaven and the new earth, as the handiwork of an infinite God (21:5), will exceed present human comprehension. The details of the description show, however, that the bride-city (21:2, 9) will be a real city with a material existence. The materialistic nature of the city has spiritual significance. The city's illumination will come from the immediate presence of the glory of God and of the Lamb (Rev. 21:23–25). The inner life of the city will amount to Paradise restored (Rev. 22:1–5; cf. Rev. 2:7), a reversing of the conditions imposed at the human fall (Genesis 3). But the presence of the Lamb and the effect of His redemptive work promise an even richer fellowship with God than people enjoyed before the fall.

Robert L. Thomas

J. Dwight Pentecost, *Things to Come* (Findlay, Ohio: Dunham, 1958), 561–62; R. L. Thomas, *Revelation 8–22* (Chicago: Moody, 1995), 437–92; John F. Walvoord, *The Prophecy Knowledge Handbook* (Wheaton: Victor, 1990), 632–43.

NUMBERS, ESCHATOLOGY OF

This book is a continuation of the redemptive history of Israel. It focuses on the service and walk of faith of that nation. The book warns of the dangers of unbelief and disobedience and records the thirty-eight years of wanderings in the desert. It clearly identifies the rebellious nature, repeated defeats, and finally the death of those who persisted in rebelling. The name "Numbers" comes from the taking of a census and the resultant numbering of the population.

The author is universally accepted as Moses. The date of writing is believed to be 1450–1410 B.C.

The prophecy found in the book is directed toward the events that took place during the period described or in near the history of that period. The death, before entering the Promised Land, of all the adult men twenty years old and older who left Egypt is foretold (14:20–30); excepted from this are Caleb and Joshua. This judgment is the result of the continued unbelief of that generation. This was fulfilled (26:63–65). The vicarious death of Christ is foreshadowed by the bronze serpent (21:8), and this verse also places emphasis on salvation being an individual responsibility. The cleansing power of the blood of Christ is seen in the sacrifice of the red heifer (19:16–19). The future Assyrian and Babylonian captivities are foretold (33:55) because of Israel's failure to follow God's instructions concerning its enemies.

Ervin R. Starwalt

Everett F. Harrison and Charles F. Harrison, eds., *Wycliffe Bible Commentary* (Chicago: Moody Press, 1962); John F. Walvoord, *The Prophecy Knowledge Handbook* (Wheaton: Victor Books, 1990); John F. Walvoord and Roy B. Zuck, eds., *The Bible Knowledge Commentary* (Wheaton: Victor Books, 1985).

O

OBADIAH, ESCHATOLOGY OF

Obadiah is the shortest book of the Old Testament, consisting of only twenty-two verses. Conservative scholars disagree on its time of writing, with dates ranging from the time of the reign of Jehoram (848–841 B.C.) to 585 B.C., shortly after the destruction of Jerusalem by the Babylonians in 586. There is nothing known about Obadiah, whose name means "Worshiper of Yahweh."

The book of Obadiah predominately deals with the nation of Edom. Armerding states this about the unity of the book, "The book of Obadiah is structured around two interrelated themes: the destruction of 'Edom' (vv. 1, 8), referred to also as 'Esau' (vv. 6, 8–9, 18, 19, 21) and 'Teman' (v. 9), and the vindication of 'Judah' (v. 12), referred to by the names 'Jacob' (vv. 10, 17–18), 'Jerusalem' (vv. 11, 20)." Baker neatly outlines the book this way: (1) Edom's destruction (vv. 1–9), (2) Edom's crimes (vv. 10–14), (3) God's judgment on Israel's enemies (vv. 15–16), and (4) God's blessing on Israel's people (vv. 17–21).

Obadiah's vision started with a call to the nations to come to battle against Edom (v. 1). Edom had become arrogant and believed that its geographical position on Mount Seir was impregnable by its enemies (v. 3). Its pride had caused Edom to be so greatly despised by God that He would make it small among the nations (v. 2). Edom's main cities were located in a narrow ridge of mountainous land southeast of the Dead Sea. From here the Edomites believed they were safe from any attack, but they were wrong. The answer to the question, "Who will bring me down to earth?" that Edom had asked was, "I [the LORD] will bring you down" (vv. 3–4). Thieves come and take much but because of their haste in escaping they leave some things behind. The same thing happens to gleaners who always leave a small portion on the vine. But the Lord, when He comes on Edom, will totally ransack it, even its hidden treasures will not escape (vv. 5–6). God will use Edom's allies to carry out His judgment. They would deceive and overpower by ambush. Baker points out that this occurred, "in the sixth or early fifth century B.C. when the Nabateans went to the Edomites who took them in for a banquet. Once welcomed inside Edomite territory, the Nabateans turned against their ally and killed the guards." The Lord proclaims on that day (God's day of judgment) He will destroy their wise men and slaughter the residents of the mountain of Esau (vv. 8–9). Teman was Edom's capital, here representing the nation as a whole. When the Lord brings His judgment on them neither their geographical location, their wealth, nor their wisdom will be able to deliver them from His hand.

Edom's judgment is a result of its treatment of its brother Jacob (v. 10). Because of this treatment, the Edomites will be covered with shame and cut off forever. Edom's crimes against Jacob include: taking part in the looting of Jerusalem (v. 11), gloating and boasting over Judah's misfortune (vv. 12–13), and cutting down and imprisoning their fugitives (v. 14). If the early date (848–841 B.C.) is accurate, this probably took place at the time of the Philistine and Arabian attack of Jerusalem while Jehoram was king (2 Kings 8:20–22; 2 Chron. 21:16–17).

In verses 15–16, Obadiah turns to a broader judgment that will take place in a time yet future on all the nations, of which the judgment on Edom was illustrative. The day of the Lord here is used in its broader sense of God's judgments in the Great Tribulation and in conjunction with His return to earth to set up His millennial reign. Just as the Lord returned judgment on Edom for their evil treatment of Israel so God will do to all the nations. The principle will be, as you have done, it will be done to you. The nations that come against Israel will be desolated (v. 16). "They will drink and swallow" God's wrath (v. 16; cf. Isa. 51:17, 31:23; Jer. 25:15–33; Hab. 2:16; Rev. 14:9–10; 16:19).

A future day of restoration and blessing for Jacob is foretold in verses 17–21. During this future time, Esau will again be destroyed as one of Israel's enemies in God's judgment on the nations (v. 18) but on Mount Zion (a synonym for Jerusalem) the house of Jacob will be delivered and possess its inheritance (v. 17). At that time the land of the Edomites will be possessed by the Jews who have returned from exile (vv. 19–20). This will take place in the Millennium when the kingdom will belong to the Lord (Zech. 14:9). Baker states, "Israel will be restored as a nation (Obad. 17), she will occupy the land (vv. 18–20), and she will be ruled by her King, the Lord Himself (v. 21)."

See also THEOCRATIC KINGDOM.

Russell L. Penney

Gleason L. Archer, *A Survey of Old Testament Introduction* (Chicago: Moody Press, 1994); Carl E. Armerding, "Obadiah" in *The Expositor's Bible Commentary*, ed. Frank E. Gaebelein, vol. 7 (Grand Rapids: Zondervan, 1985); Walter L. Baker, "Obadiah" in *The Bible Knowledge Commentary,* eds. John G. Walvoord and Roy B. Zuck (Wheaton: Victor Books, 1988); John F. Walvoord, *The Prophecy Knowledge Handbook* (Wheaton: Victor Books, 1990).

OLIVET DISCOURSE

In order to arrive at a proper interpretation of Matthew 24–25, the Olivet Discourse, several questions must be answered concerning it. One critical question is whether the church is in view in this passage. Some hold that Matthew 24 discusses the rapture of the church. However, Matthew does not discuss the church; in fact, the word *ekklesia* (church) occurs only three times in Matthew: once in 16:18 and twice in 18:17. Only the 16:18 reference should be understood in the sense of church; 18:17 refers simply to an "assembly" or "congregation." Matthew 16:18 points to the future when Christ will build the church. It is apparent that the church is not in view in Matthew's gospel which explains to a Jewish audience who Jesus is and what is the future of the Jewish nation. Hence, Matthew does not deal with the Rapture, which is an event related to the church and is discussed by Paul in 1 Thessalonians 4:13–18.

If Matthew 24 deals with the church, then the church must go through the Tribulation; the fact that the church will not go through the Tribulation can be defended both exegetically and theologically. Exegetically, verses like Romans 5:9 and 1 Thessalonians 5:9 state rather forcefully that the church will be spared the wrath of God—which is the Tribulation. Theologically, the matter is resolved by asking the question, what is the purpose of the Tribulation? The answer is that the Tribulation is a time of the outpouring of the wrath of God on unbelievers (Rev. 6:16–17; 11:18; 14:19; 15:1, 7; 16:1, 19; cf. Isa. 24:5–6, 21; Rev. 3:10). How does the church relate to the wrath of God? It doesn't. Christ bore God's wrath for believers. If the church must go through the Tribulation then God is extracting punishment twice—and that is unthinkable (Rom. 5:1; 8:1). Further, God's purpose in the Tribulation relates to Israel, to discipline the nation and bring it to repentance (Dan. 9:24; Jer. 30:7).

The Transition (Matt. 23:37–39)

Following Jesus' denunciation of the Jewish leaders (23:13–36), He announced the future suffering of Jerusalem and the Jewish people. The cause of Israel's future suffering was their rejection of the Messiah (23:37). As a result, Jesus announced, "your house is being left to you desolate." This probably refers to the temple, although it could refer to the nation or city. Matthew 23:38 should be linked with 24:1–2, in which Jesus explains that the magnificent temple of Herod with its massive building stones will be torn apart—every stone of it. These words found their fulfillment in A.D. 70 when Titus destroyed Jerusalem. However, it is clear from 23:39 and the Olivet Discourse itself that chapters 24–25 cannot find their fulfillment in past history. In 23:39 Jesus pointed to the eschatological fulfillment of the Olivet Discourse when He announced, "For I say to you, from now on you shall not see Me until you say, 'Blessed is He who comes in the name of the Lord.'" With these words, Jesus was pointing to His Second Advent for the fulfillment of the events of Matthew 24–25. Micah 4:1 also points to an eschatological event, as the desolation of the temple must precede the restoration of the temple when the people will stream to it in the millennial kingdom.

The Question Concerning the Future (24:1–3)

Jesus' announcement that "not one stone here shall be left upon another, which will not be torn down" awed the disciples, leading them to pose two questions: (1) when will these things be, and (2) what will be the sign of Your coming and of the end of the age?

The Tribulation Period (24:4–26)

In 24:4–8 Jesus describes the signs in the first half of the Tribulation. These are not signs for the church, since the church will be raptured prior to the Tribulation. These signs parallel Revelation 6. Christ prophesies the false messiahs (v. 5; cf. Rev. 6:2), culminating in the Antichrist (2 Thess. 2:4, 9; Rev. 13:4, 11–12). There will be unprecedented wars (cf. Rev. 6:4). Undoubtedly included is the northern invasion of Israel (Ezek. 38:8; Dan. 9:27), climaxing with the campaign of Armageddon (Dan. 11:40–45). Famines and earthquakes will occur (cf. Rev. 6:5–6; 16:18–19) and as a result many will die (Rev. 6:7–8). But this is only the beginning, the first half of the Tribulation.

In the second half of the Tribulation (vv. 9–14) the suffering will intensify. "Then" (v. 9) marks a transition, referring to the occasion when the Antichrist breaks the covenant with Israel and persecutes the nation (Dan. 9:27). The Jews flee from the land of Israel to the nations (Rev. 12:13ff.) as persecution of Israel intensifies. The deception by the false prophets is related to the "power and signs and false wonders of the Antichrist (2 Thess. 2:9). Only those believers who endure, i.e., live through the horrors of this age (Rev. 6–19) will "be saved"—preserved to enter the millennial kingdom. Nonetheless, there will be unprecedented conversions during the Tribulation (v. 14) through the ministry of the 144,000 (Rev. 7:1–8) and the two witnesses (Rev. 11:3).

Matthew 24:15–26 amplifies the period discussed in 24:9–14. In 24:9–14 Jesus foretold many signs; now He singles out one sign—the Abomination of Desolation (v. 15). Historically, this refers to Antiochus Epiphanes, who entered the temple precincts and offered a swine on the altar in 171 B.C. But Antiochus prefigured the greater Abomination of Desolation—the Antichrist who will exalt himself as God as set up an image to himself (Dan. 11:36; 2 Thess. 2:3–4; Rev. 13:8) and will severely persecute the Jewish people (vv. 16–20).

"Then" (v. 21) marks a further transition. What follows relates to the last half of the Tribulation when persecution will be particularly fierce. "And unless those days had been cut short," that is, concluded, "no life would have been saved" (v. 22). The shortening of the days does not suggest the days will be less than twenty-four hours; rather, it means the days will terminate. The length of this intense persecution and suffering is restricted to three and one-half years (Dan. 7:25; 12:7; Rev. 11:2; 12:6, 14; 13:5).

The Second Advent (24:27–51)

The Tribulation concludes with the triumphant return of Christ, portrayed by lightning, as the glorified Christ appears in the brilliance of the Shekinah glory shining from east to west (v. 27; cf. Ezek. 10:19; 11:23). The Shekinah is the sign appearing in the sky (v. 30), reminding the Jewish people of Messiah's return and leading them to repentance (v. 30; Zech. 12:10–14). But Christ's return is a time of judgment (v. 28; 25:1–46).

The unanticipated return of Christ is portrayed by three illustrations (24:32–41). In the parable of the fig tree (vv. 32–36) Jesus explains that when the fig tree puts forth leaves (in April), the summer is near. Similarly, the generation that will see the signs of

Matthew 24:9–26 that His coming is near, this generation, the generation living during the Tribulation that sees these signs, will also be the generation that witnesses the return of Christ. The second illustration (vv. 37–39) portrays the indifference of that generation; they will carry on with mundane things: eating, drinking, and marrying—and they will be swept away in judgment at the return of Christ. The third illustration is in concert with the second; it also illustrates Christ's Second Coming in judgment. This is not a reference to the Rapture. The one who is taken (vv. 40–41) is taken away in judgment (cf. v. 39); the one who will be left is left to enter the millennial kingdom.

Matthew 24:42–51 concludes: be on the alert (v. 42). This section is an admonition to that generation to be alert to the signs they will see reminding them of the impending return of Christ and to be prepared for His return.

Judgment on Israel (25:1–30)

The parables that follow in chapter 25 follow chronologically and logically the events of chapter 24. The emphasis on "be on the alert" (25:13) reinforces the emphasis of 24:42–44, warning that generation to prepare because of the judgments at the return of Christ. The parables of 25:1–30 are usually understood as applying to Israel, since the church was raptured prior to the events of chapter 24. The Rapture is not in view in chapter 25.

In the parable of the ten virgins (vv. 1–13), the five foolish virgins represent unbelieving Israel that fails to prepare for Messiah's return. The oil the foolish virgins failed to take may represent either the Holy Spirit in regeneration (Ezek. 36:26–27; Titus 3:5) or it may refer to the knowledge and preparedness for Messiah's coming. Those of Israel who fail to prepare for Messiah's coming will be excluded from the millennial kingdom, illustrated by the wedding feast (v. 10).

The parable of the talents represents Christ's judgment on Israel concerning watchfulness (vv. 14–30). It teaches Israel's responsibility concerning the knowledge of God that they possess (cf. Rom. 9:4–5). Israel was chosen by God to be a mediator of truth and light to the Gentile nations (Exod. 19:5; Isa. 42:6; 43:10). The nations of the world were to be blessed through Israel as God's chosen people spread God's truth to the nations. In this parable those having the five and the two talents are those who properly interpret the signs during the Tribulation, prepare themselves, and warn others. The one-talent person lives during the Tribulation ignoring the signs and, like the five foolish virgins, is unsaved and therefore excluded from the millennial kingdom.

Judgment on the Gentiles (25:31–46)

Following the judgment of Israel, the judgment of the Gentiles will take place; the term *ethne* (v. 32) identifies this as the judgment of individual Gentiles. It occurs as Christ is sitting on His glorious throne (v. 31), indicative that Christ is ruling in the millennial kingdom. In the parable the sheep, representing believers, are separated from the goats, who represent unbelievers. The basis of the judgment is the good deeds done "to one of these brothers of Mine" (v. 40). The brothers of Christ must be Jewish people; in this context they are the 144,000 who evangelize the nations (Rev. 7). But the 144,000 are dependent on those who respond to their proclamation of the Gospel for hospitality, hence, those who minister to the 144,000 in the Tribulation are also those who respond in faith to their message. They will inherit the kingdom (v. 34) not on the basis of works, but because of their response to the Gospel of the kingdom proclaimed by the 144,000. Their hospitality to the 144,000 is indicative of their faith. Those who refuse to respond to the gospel of the kingdom are also those who fail to show hospitality to those proclaiming the message. They "will go away into eternal punishment" (v. 46), not because they failed to do good works but because they rejected the Gospel of the kingdom.

See also JUDGMENTS, VARIOUS; TRIBULATION, THE GREAT.

Paul P. Enns

Louis A. Barbieri Jr., "Matthew" in *The Bible Knowledge Commentary* (Wheaton: Victor,

1983); Homer A. Kent Jr., "Matthew" in *The Wycliffe Bible Commentary* (Chicago: Moody Press, 1962); J. Dwight Pentecost, *The Words and Works of Jesus Christ* (Grand Rapids: Zondervan, 1981) and *The Parables of Jesus* (Grand Rapids: Zondervan, 1982); Arthur Robertson, *Matthew* (Chicago: Moody Press, 1983); Stanley D. Toussaint, *Behold The King: A Study of Matthew* (Portland: Multnomah Press, 1980); Howard F. Vos, *Matthew: A Study Guide Commentary* (Grand Rapids: Zondervan, 1979); John F. Walvoord, *Matthew: Thy Kingdom Come* (Chicago: Moody Press, 1974).

ORIGEN

Alexandrian theologian Origen (ca. 185–ca. 254) was the first church leader of stature to challenge the premillennial orthodoxy of the early church. Completely dedicated to the allegorical method of interpretation like his mentor, Clement of Alexandria, Origen spiritualized virtually every Christian doctrine. Under Origen's influence, the blessed hope of the Christian apologists—belief in Christ's imminent return to establish His kingdom—began to yield to the spiritual hermeneutics of Alexandria.

Origen maintained a theoretical three-level understanding of the meaning of Scripture: the literal, typological, and spiritual that supposedly corresponded to the threefold human nature—body, soul, and spirit. In practice, however, he most frequently made a distinction between the literal and the spiritual method of interpretation of Scripture (e.g., *De princ.* 1.3.3). The literal method, which Origen considered crude and unreliable, was allowed to the weak of intellect, the mass of Christians in general. The spiritual method, extolled by Origen, was reserved for a few like himself "on whom the grace of the Holy Spirit is bestowed in the word of wisdom and knowledge" (*De princ.* Preface, para. 8).

Origen's method of exegesis was so subjective that it allowed for an almost infinite number of symbolic meanings and interpretations of the biblical text, most of which bore little resemblance to the plain meaning of the words. Mystical theological speculation was typical of Origen's eschatology. For example, according to his doctrine of the *apokatastasis* (restoration of everything in the universe to its original, spiritual, primeval state), there will be no hell or eternal punishment. Rather, the Logos will purify every living being, presumably even demons and Satan himself. Then Christ can return and raise all people, but in spiritual bodies only (*De princ.* 1.6.1–3; 3.4–6).

As for the meaning of the Second Coming, Origen explained away the gospel references to a literal, visible return of Christ and substituted a completely spiritualized interpretation (*De princ.* 2.11.2). In essence, Origen taught that Christ's return signifies His disclosure of Himself and His deity to all humanity in such a way that all might partake of His glory to the degree that each individual's actions warrant (Comm. *On Matt.* 12.30). In effect, Origen took the catalytic event of the prophetic calendar and reduced it to a kind of general, mystical encounter with Christ.

Origen's allegorical interpretations, including his views on Bible prophecy, gained wide acceptance in the church of his day. His influence, followed by Constantine's acceptance of Christianity and Augustine's teaching in the fourth century, are usually cited as the principal causes of premillennialism's eventual replacement by amillennial eschatology. Though he was broken by the persecution under Decius in 250 and died a few years later at the age of sixty-nine, Origen's exegesis still colors prophetic expectations in modern times.

Larry V. Crutchfield

H. Chadwick, *Alexandrian Christianity* (Philadelphia: The Westminster Press, n.d.); W. A. Jurgens, *The Faith of the Early Fathers*, 3 vols. (Collegeville, Minn.: The Liturgical Press, 1979); A. Roberts and J. Donaldson, eds., *The Ante-Nicene Fathers*, vols. 4 and 10 (Grand Rapids: Eerdmans, n.d.).

P

PACHE, RENÉ

Author, educator, Bible teacher, student evangelist, and organizer, René Pache (1904–1979) served as vice-chairman of the International Fellowship of Evangelical Students (IFES) from 1947 to 1963, director of Emmaus Bible and Missionary Institute in Lausanne, Switzerland from 1947 to his retirement in 1971, and as a frequent lecturer at Aix-en-Provence Theological Seminary (France).

Pache (pronounced *posh*) was raised in a Christian home by a godly mother. His father died when he was ten. Pache received a doctorate in law at Lausanne. As a lawyer, he joined the business staff of CIBA (a large chemical works) at Basle, Switzerland. It was there he was converted at the age of twenty-four through reading a Bible that he had purchased. With only one year of Bible school (at age twenty-seven), Pache was largely self-taught. He was significantly influenced by the *Scofield Reference Bible* and instrumental in its publication in French.

His Christian ministry began with pioneer evangelistic work in the suburbs of Paris while he attended Nogent Bible School in France. He organized student evangelistic training camps during the early 1930s, which took on international character in 1936 when IFES was established in Switzerland and in France due largely to Pache. His work with IFES took him to western and central Europe, the Balkan States, and North Africa. He was closely associated with a number of missions, and he sometimes fellowshipped with the Plymouth Brethren. After his retirement, he served as chairman of the Emmaus Publications Committee. He was instrumental in the French publication of the *New Bible Dictionary* and *New Bible Commentary*. He had close associations with Scripture Union in London. Pache is said to have possessed a brilliant mind and phenomenal memory. The story is told that Charles E. Fuller was once visiting the Institute, speaking to the student–body. He remarked, "Do you know, I've traveled all over the world and I can always find someone who can quote Galatians 2:20, but I've never found anyone who can quote Galatians 2:19." Whereupon, Dr. Pache promptly brought the house down by quoting 2:19 from memory.

Pache authored fourteen books that appeared in at least ten languages. Four of his works were translated and published in English by Moody Press: *The Person and Work of the Holy Spirit*, translated by J. D. Emerson, 1954; *The Return of Christ*, translated by William Sanford LaSor, 1955; *The Future Life*, translated by Helen I. Needham, 1962; *The Inspiration and Authority of Scripture*, translated by Helen I. Needham, 1969, which is still used as a text in many Bible schools and seminaries.

In his theological views, Pache was conservative, dispensational, premillennial, and pretribulational. But Pache's pretribulational view of the rapture of the church differed somewhat from that of mainstream pretribulationism as held by Scofield, Gaebelein, Gray, Moody Bible Institute, Chafer, Walvoord, Dallas Theological Seminary, and others. Though uncertain whether Pache would have accepted the label, his view of the *time* of the Rapture could be labeled mid-week, pretribulationism. Pache understood the Tribulation period to be three and one-half years in length. What relationship he saw between Daniel's Seventieth Week and the Tribulation period is not disclosed. In his writings, he neither refers to nor discusses Daniel's prophecy of seventy weeks (Dan. 9:24–27). Apparently, Pache understood only the last half of Daniel's Seventieth Week, as consisting of the Tribulation period. For

Pache, the event that marks the beginning of the Great Tribulation is the rapture of the church. Also distinct from mainstream dispensational, premillennial, pretribulationism was Pache's view that the woman of Revelation 12 refers to the people of God, consisting of both Jew and Gentile.

On most other eschatological issues, Pache was typical of mainstream dispensational, premillennial, pretribulationism. He adopted and used what he called a literal and symbolic method of interpretation that called first for the literal, simplest, plain sense of Scripture.

He distinguished between Israel and the church, saw a future for national Israel, and took a futurist view of Revelation 4–22.

Pache taught that the Day of the Lord begins with the rapture of the church and the Great Tribulation. After the Rapture, the church is judged (at the bema seat) in heaven, where the wedding feast also occurs. Three and one-half years after the Rapture, during which time God's wrath is poured out on earth, Christ returns *with* the church saints to earth, judges the nations, and establishes the millennial kingdom. At that time Satan is bound. At the end of the thousand years, Satan is loosed, creating a rebellion. This rebellion is quashed and Satan is judged. There is a postmillennial resurrection and judgment of the unsaved only. For Pache, hell is a literal place of eternal punishment for the lost. He rejected annihilation of the wicked.

See also PREMILLENNIALISM; TRIBULATION, THE GREAT.

Steven L. McAvoy

Frank Horton, interviewed by the author (Lausanne, Switzerland: November 1995); Douglas Johnson, ed., *A Brief History of the International Fellowship of Evangelical Students* (Lausanne: The International Fellowship of Evangelical Students, 1964); Pete Lowman, *The Day of His Power: A History of the International Fellowship of Evangelical Students* (Leicester, England: InterVarsity Press, 1983); René Pache, *The Future Life,* trans. Helen I. Needham (Chicago: Moody Press, 1962), *The Inspiration and Authority of Scripture*, trans. Helen I. Needham (Chicago: Moody Press, 1969), and *The Return of Christ*, trans. William Sanford LaSor (Chicago: Moody Press, 1955).

PALESTINIAN COVENANT

The Name

The traditional name for this covenant is the Palestinian covenant, a legitimate name at the time it was coined, because this covenant largely concerns the land known for centuries as Palestine. However, this is now an unfortunate term for two reasons. First, it was a name given to the land by the Roman emperor Hadrian after the second Jewish revolt under Bar-Kochba (A.D. 132–135), for the purpose of erasing any Jewish remembrance of the land. Second, due to the historical events in the Middle East in the twentieth century, the name is associated more with Arabs than with Jews. Perhaps a better title would be Land covenant.

Scripture

The main Scripture on the Palestinian covenant is Deuteronomy 29:1–30:20.

The Provisions of the Covenant

There are eight specific provisions in this "Land covenant." First, Moses prophetically spoke of Israel's coming disobedience to the Mosaic Law and subsequent scattering over all the world (29:2–30:1). Second, Israel will repent (30:2). Third, Messiah will return (30:3). Fourth, Israel will be regathered (30:3–4). Fifth, Israel will possess the Promised Land (30:5). Sixth, Israel will be regenerated (30:6). Seventh, the enemies of Israel will be judged (30:7). Eighth, Israel will receive its full blessing, specifically the blessings of the messianic kingdom (30:8–10).

Importance of the Land Covenant

The special importance of this covenant is that it reaffirmed Israel's title deed to the land. Although Israel would prove unfaithful and disobedient, the right to the land would never be taken from Israel. While her enjoyment of the land is conditioned on obedience, ownership of the land is unconditional. Furthermore, it shows that the conditional Mosaic covenant did not lay aside the unconditional Abrahamic covenant. It might be taken by some that the conditional Mosaic covenant displaced the unconditional Abrahamic covenant, but the Palestinian covenant shows that this is not true. It is an enlargement of the original Abrahamic covenant. It amplifies the land aspect and emphasizes the promise of the land to God's people in spite of unbelief.

The Confirmation of the Covenant

The Land covenant received its confirmation centuries later in Ezekiel 16:1–63. This passage describes God's relationship to Israel as husband to wife, and God recounts His love of Israel in its infancy (vv. 1–7). Israel was chosen by God and became related to Jehovah by marriage and, hence, became known as the wife of Jehovah (vv. 8–14). Israel, however, played the harlot (vv. 15–34); therefore, it was necessary to punish Israel by means of dispersion (vv. 35–52). Yet, this dispersion is not final, for there will be future restoration on the basis of the Palestinian covenant (vv. 53–63).

The Outworking of the Land Covenant in this Age

The Palestinian covenant promised a final worldwide regathering following a worldwide dispersion. While the final regathering is still future, the worldwide scattering is a present reality and has been so since the year A.D. 70. Furthermore, the covenant promised that the Jewish people would suffer persecution in the dispersion and the land would become desolate over the centuries. The fact that all these promises have been and are being fulfilled shows that this covenant is still working itself out. A key point of the Palestinian covenant is to teach that while Israel's enjoyment of the land is based on obedience, its ownership or title deed to the land was not. The failure of all other occupiers of the land to set up an independent government again shows that this covenant continues to operate. Many replacement theologians insist that God's promises to Israel concerning the land have already been fulfilled, based on passages such as Joshua 11:23. However, this verse, like all verses of Scripture, must be kept in context and must be viewed within the book of Joshua as a whole. Keeping in mind that originally the book of Joshua did not have chapter divisions, the verse simply states a fact that is then followed by exceptions to the fact. Joshua 11:23 is followed immediately in chapter 12 by a list of the Canaanite kings killed by Israel. Joshua 13:1–6 shows that a great deal of territory did not fall into the hands of the Israelites and that is a sizeable exception to the statement of 11:23. Nor did much of this territory fall into Jewish hands in the immediate future following Joshua. Jerusalem remained under Jebusite control (Josh. 15:63) until David's day (2 Sam. 5:6–9). The city of Gezer was held by the Canaanites (Josh. 16:10) until Solomon's day (1 Kings 9:16). The tribe of Dan had to move because they could not take their territory from the Philistines. Even in the time of the Davidic and Solomonic empire, much of the land was under military control and not actually settled by the Jewish population (1 Kings 4:21). The first chapter of Judges records events that took place after the death of Joshua and records how various tribes failed to take the land allotted to them. Never in Old Testament history did Israel possess, dwell in, and settle all of the Promised Land. Nor did it ever happen in Jewish history since. However, the covenant guarantees that someday it will.

The Outworking of the Land Covenant in the Future

A major facet of Israel's final restoration is the regathering of Israel, and this is based on the Palestinian or Land covenant. What was promised in this covenant was affirmed by the Prophets, as seen in the following passages: Isaiah 11:11–12:6; 43:5–7; Jeremiah 16:14–15; 23:3–4, 7–8; 31:7–10; Ezekiel 11:14–18; 36:24; Amos 9:14–15; Zephaniah 3:18–20; Zechariah 10:8–12; Matthew 24:31; Mark 13:27.

See also COVENANTS, THE.

Arnold Fruchtenbaum

PAPIAS

Papias (ca. A.D. 60–ca. 130), bishop of Hierapolis in Asia Minor, was contemporary with Clement, Ignatius, and Polycarp. Irenaeus affirmed that Papias was "the hearer of John, and a companion of Polycarp" (*Ag. Her.* 5.33.4). Some have called him the father of millenarianism. Papias furnished the earliest extrabiblical witness to the millennial doctrine taught by the Apocalypse and came from the same Asiatic background as its author. He is often credited with influencing many of the early fathers who came after him to accept the premillennial doctrine.

Papias is known to have written a work entitled *Exposition of the Oracles of the Lord*, in five books. Jerome also mentions (in *Lives of Illustrious Men* 18) a volume entitled, *Second Coming of Our Lord or Millennium*, as coming from the hand of Papias. However, only fragments of and notices about Papias's works remain, the most important of which are found in Irenaeus (*Against Heresies*) and Eusebius (*Church History*).

According to Eusebius, Papias taught "that there will be a period of some thousand years after the resurrection of the dead, and that the kingdom of Christ will be set up in material form on this very earth" (*Ch. Hist.* 3.39.12). As to Papias's views on the nature of this kingdom, Irenaeus quoted him as teaching that "the elders who saw John, the disciple of the Lord, related that they had heard from him how the Lord used to teach in regard to these times, and say: The days will come, in which vines shall grow, each having ten thousand branches, and in each branch ten thousand twigs, and in each true twig ten thousand shoots, and in each one of the shoots ten thousand clusters, and on every one of the clusters ten thousand grapes, and every grape when pressed will give five and twenty metretes of wine" (*Ag. Her.* 5.33.3).

In a similar way, the remarkable productivity of grain in the kingdom is described, as well as the harmony that will exist among all animals who will be under peaceful human control. While Irenaeus believed that this teaching came from the apostle John through Papias (*Ag. Her.* 5.32.3–4), others like Eusebius cited the "grape story" as proof of Papias's weak intellect and as sufficient grounds for discrediting premillenarian ideas (*Ch. Hist.* 3.39.12).

In Papias there is but a brief outline of things to come. Eusebius himself revealed Papias's belief in the resurrection followed by the thousand-year millennial reign of Christ (*Ch. Hist.* 3.39.12). This would of course have to be preceded by Christ's Second Coming. While nothing is said about judgment, belief in the eternal state may be taken for granted.

Larry V. Crutchfield

L. Crutchfield, "The Apostle John and Asia Minor as a Source of Premillennialism in the Early Church Fathers" in *JETS* 31:411–27 (December 1988); J. Danielou, *The Development of Christian Doctrine Before the Council of Nicaea*, vol. 1 of *The Theology of Jewish Christianity* (London: Darton, Longman, and Todd, 1964); J. Quasten and J. C. Plumpe, eds., *Ancient Christian Writers: The Didache, The Epistle of Barnabas, The Epistles and the Martyrdom of St. Polycarp, The Fragments of Papias, The Epistle to Diognetus*, trans. James A. Kleist, vol. 6 (New York; Ramsey, N.J.: Newman Press, 1946), 103–24; A. Roberts and J. Donaldson, eds., *The Ante-Nicene Fathers*, vol. 1 (Grand Rapids: Eerdmans, n.d.), 151–55.

PENTECOST, J. DWIGHT,

J. Dwight Pentecost (b. 1915), Distinguished Professor emeritus of Bible exposition at Dallas Theological Seminary, has the distinction of teaching the Bible for nearly half a century (Philadelphia College of Bible, 1948–55; Dallas Theological Seminary, 1955–present). His lucid classroom expositions of Scripture and his writing on biblical themes have educated believers in a premillennial understanding of Scripture. Dr. Pentecost has the distinction of being only one of two professors honored as Distinguished Professor in the history of Dallas Theological Seminary. In addition to his classroom teaching and his writing, Pentecost has had a Bible conference ministry that has covered the globe from the British Isles and Europe to the Middle East and Far East, Australia, New Zealand, and South America. These ministries have given believers new insight in consistent, literal, grammatical, historical interpretation of the Scriptures.

Perhaps the magnum opus of Pentecost's writings is *Things to Come,* a definitive work of dispensational premillennial eschatology, published in 1958. In developing a biblical eschatology, Pentecost exposes the weakness of allegorical interpretation and demonstrates the need for consistent literal interpretation. Literal interpretation is the normal, ordinary, customary usage of words. It is the grammatical-historical method of interpretation. Interpretive principles involve interpreting words in their normal meaning, interpreting according to context and historical setting, considering the grammar of the text in the original languages, as well as recognizing figurative language. This interpretation provides consistency and leads to premillennialism.

The foundation of premillennial eschatology lies in the unconditional covenants of the OT. These covenants are to be understood as literal, eternal, unconditional, and as made with a covenant people (*Things to Come,* 69). The Abrahamic covenant (Gen. 12:1–3) contains the promise of a national land, elaborated in the Palestinian covenant (Deut. 30:1–10); the promise of redemption, elaborated in the new covenant (Jer. 31:31–34); and the promise of numerous descendents to form a great nation, elaborated in the Davidic covenant (2 Sam. 7:12–16). The Abrahamic covenant guarantees Israel a permanent national existence, perpetual title to the land of promise, and the certainty of material and spiritual blessing through Christ.

The unconditional Palestinian covenant (Deut. 30:1–10) enlarges the Abrahamic covenant and is Israel's title deed to the land. It awaits future, literal fulfillment by the physical descendants of Abraham. The Davidic covenant (2 Sam. 7:12–16) enlarges the seed promises of the Abrahamic covenant. The essential features are implicit in three words: *house, kingdom,* and *throne* (2 Sam. 7:16). *House* refers to David's physical descendants; *throne* implies the dignity and right to rule by David's seed; *kingdom* has reference to David's political kingdom. The new covenant (Jer. 31:31–34) guarantees salvation to the nation Israel and is ultimately fulfilled with Israel when there is a national conversion at the second advent of Christ. The church does not fulfill the new covenant.

Things to Come provides a definitive, biblical treatment of the dispensational premillennial scheme of eschatology. Pentecost provides a strong defence for the pretribulation rapture of the church, the basis resting on literal interpretation, which recognizes Israel and the church as two distinct groups. Having been in print for nearly half a century, *Things to Come* must be recognized as the definitive, biblical explanation of premillennial eschatology. *Prophecy for Today* and *Will Man Survive?* develop the same prophetic exposition on a popular, nontechnical level.

The Words and Works of Jesus Christ marks the publication of a subject that Dr. Pentecost has taught for over forty years. He developed a new approach to understanding the life of Christ by noting, not the geographical movements of Christ, but recognizing that the gospel writers wrote the life of Christ from thematic viewpoints. Literal interpretation results in the thematic understanding of the life of Christ. Pentecost explains, "Jesus Christ was introduced to the nation Israel as her Messiah. By His words and His works He authenticated this introduction and offered Israel her promised and covenanted kingdom. The nation considered the offer and, because of the opposition of the leaders, rejected it. Christ announced judgment on that nation and turned from a public ministry to that of preparing chosen men to continue His ministry following His death and resurrection. The rejection by the nation led to His death, by which salvation was provided for sinful men; but the genuineness of His offer was authenticated by the Resurrection" (*Things to Come,* 9). This approach to understanding the life of Christ recognizes the uniqueness of Israel as a people of God, distinct from the church.

Pentecost develops the kingdom theme in *The Parables of the Kingdom.* Concisely written, the format ("The Setting," "The Problem," "The Solution") enables the reader to readily interpret the parables. Pentecost particularly deals with the parables concerning the kingdom of heaven. These present the new form of the theocracy unforeseen in the OT but revealed through Christ's teaching (*Parables,* 18). The parables of the kingdom anticipate the Messiah—the final theocratic Administrator who is a descendant of David and who will rule on David's throne. Unlike many other books on the parables of Jesus, Pentecost's volume properly interprets the parables within the dispensational scheme, anticipating Messiah's earthly rule.

But the apex of Pentecost's discussion concerning the kingdom is committed to *Thy Kingdom Come*, a monumental work in its treatment of God's mediatorial rule on earth from prehistory to the future millennial kingdom and the eternal kingdom of God. The term kingdom is perhaps one of the most misunderstood words in Scripture, and yet, without a knowledge of the term, proper interpretation falters. This volume will help students of the Scriptures to understand the mediatorial kingdom of God as the unifying structure binding the Bible together. In *Thy Kingdom Come*, Pentecost traces the mediatorial kingdom of God as administered through God's appointed representatives from Genesis to Revelation, beginning with Adam and culminating with Christ. Pentecost defines the word *kingdom* as incorporating three interrelated concepts: (1) the right to rule—the authority vested in a king; (2) the realm in which the ruling authority is exercised over people; (3) reality of the rule in which there is an actual exercise of royal authority. Moreover, there are two aspects of the kingdom: it is not only universal and eternal, but also temporal, local, and mediated. Beginning with the angelic realm and proceeding to the sphere of the mediatorial kingdom on earth, Pentecost traces the kingdom of God through His appointed representatives including Adam, Moses, the kings, the prophets, and concluding with the millennial kingdom of Christ and the eternal state. This volume is an unusually helpful treatise in understanding the program of God on earth and what God is sovereignly and actively doing through His appointed representatives.

The Sermon on the Mount clarifies considerable misunderstanding over the dispensational interpretation of the Sermon on the Mount. False accusations have frequently been hurled at dispensationalists suggesting they reject the Sermon on the Mount as having any present-day application. *The Sermon on the Mount* dispels this notion, showing dispensationalists indeed do apply the Sermon to life today. But Pentecost first interprets it, showing that "it is a revelation of the righteousness of God and reflects the demands that the holiness of God makes upon those who would walk in fellowship with Him" (p. 17). Pentecost shows "how this sermon of Christ affects the conduct of those who would walk with God and thus how we can 'use the law lawfully'" (p. 17).

Also helpful in maintaining the distinction between Israel and the church is Pentecost's exposition of Hebrews, *A Faith That Endures*. Hebrews is addressed to Jews that had been identified with Christ through baptism and for this reason were cut off from the commonwealth of Israel and were experiencing persecution. For this reason the author exhorts them to patient endurance amid their circumstances. The author of Hebrews warns the believers against neglecting God's revelation in Christ and spiritual regression. While there are difficult passages in Hebrews, *A Faith That Endures* expressly interprets the book in its historical context and avoids the confusion of so many commentaries.

Pentecost reinforces the distinction between Israel and the church, illuminating the uniqueness of the Holy Spirit's work in the church age in *The Divine Comforter*. This knowledge is key not only as doctrinal truth, but also for spiritual living.

Having authored over twenty volumes, Pentecost's expositions have illuminated the Scriptures for the Christian public in a clear, nontechnical way, helping believers understand them in their historical context, properly distinguishing Israel and the church.

See also KINGDOM, UNIVERSAL AND MEDIATORIAL.

Paul P. Enns

J. Dwight Pentecost, *Design for Discipleship* (Grand Rapids: Zondervan, 1971), *Designed To Be Like Him* (Grand Rapids: Discovery House, 1994), *The Divine Comforter* (Chicago: Moody, 1963), *A Faith That Endures* (Grand Rapids: Discovery House, 1992), *The Glory of God* (Portland: Multnomah, 1978), *The Harmony of the Words and Works of Jesus Christ* (Grand Rapids: Zondervan, 1981), *The Joy of Fellowship* (Grand Rapids: Discovery House, 1995), *The Joy of Living* (Grand Rapids: Kregel, 1996), *Man's Problems/God's Answers* (Chicago: Moody, 1972), *The Parables of Jesus* (Grand Rapids: Zondervan, 1982), *Prophecy For Today* (Grand Rapids: Zondervan, 1961), *Sermon on the Mount* (Portland: Multnomah, 2nd. ed., 1980), *Things Which Become Sound Doctrine* (Grand Rapids: Kregel, 1996), *Things to Come* (Grand Rapids: Zondervan, 1958), *Thy Kingdom Come* (Wheaton: Victor, 1990), *Will Man Survive?* (Chicago: Moody, 1971), *The Words and Works of Jesus Christ* (Grand Rapids: Zondervan, 1981), and *Your Adversary the Devil* (Grand Rapids: Zondervan, 1969).

PENTECOST, THE FEAST OF

The Feast of Weeks *(Hag Ha Shavuot)* was also called the Feast of Pentecost, the Greek name for this Old Testament feast. God set Israel's feast times (Lev. 23:4: *moed,* "an appointed meeting"), and the seven feasts of Moses are both commemorative and prophetic (Matt. 5:17; Rom. 15:4; Col. 2:16–17). They are described in Leviticus 23, Numbers 28–29, and Deuteronomy 16.

Three were to be observed in the first month (Nisan): Passover, Feast of Unleavened Bread, and Feast of Firstfruits. The last three fall in the seventh month (Tishri): the Feast of Trumpets (*Yom Teruah*), the Day of Atonement (*Yom Kippur*), and the Feast of Tabernacles (*Succoth*).

The Feast of Weeks comes between these two feast periods. It was celebrated the day following the "counting of the omer" (Lev. 23:15–22), which would be fifty days after the Feast of Firstfruits; thus, the word *pentekonta* was used in the Septuagint to translate the word *fifty*. It is also known as "the first harvest" *(Hag Ha Kazir),* the Feast of Harvest.

The feast was proclaimed as a "holy convocation" (*mikraw*, "rehearsal") on which no servile work was to be done and at which every male Israelite was required to appear at the sanctuary (Lev. 23:21). It was one of three convocations that were obligatory for all male Jews (Deut. 16:16).

Two baked loaves of new, fine, leavened flour were brought by the worshippers and waved by the priest before the Lord, together with the offerings of animal sacrifice for sin and peace offerings (Lev. 23:17–20); this is the only feast that involves the use of leavened bread, leaven being a Levitical symbol of sin.

Pentecost was a day of joy and celebration. The devout Israelites expressed gratitude for the blessings of the grain harvest and experienced heartfelt fear of the Lord (Jer. 5:24). But it was the thanksgiving and fear of a redeemed people for the feast included sin and peace offerings and was a reminder of their deliverance from Egypt (Deut. 16:12) as God's covenant people (Lev. 23:22). The acceptance of the offering presupposes the removal of sin and reconciliation with God.

Rabbinic Traditions

This date of the feast, the sixth of Sivan, is viewed as the day of the birth of the nation Israel by rabbinical reckoning from Exodus 19.

There also appears to be a tradition, possibly from cabalistic grounds, that Enoch was born and also translated on the sixth of Sivan, the same day the Feast of Pentecost is celebrated.

This feast is also closely associated with the book of Ruth, which is traditionally read on this date.

Prophetic Implications

The first three feasts of the Jewish year appear to be prophetic of the First Coming of Jesus Christ: Passover, Feast of Unleavened

Bread, and Feast of Firstfruits. Their prophetic role also involved their fulfillment on the very day they were being celebrated. The last three feasts are generally associated with the second coming of Christ.

The church, the Spirit-indwelt body of Christ, began on this feast day (John 14:25–26; Acts 1:8; 2:1–47). The disciples were gathered in a house in Jerusalem and were visited with signs from heaven. The Holy Spirit descended upon them, and new life, power, and blessing were evident.. The fact that this feast was one of the obligatory feasts explains why so many foreign visitors were in Jerusalem and heared the disciples speaking in the visitor's own languages.

The use of *leavened* bread is also suggestive of a non-Jewish character. The use of two loaves and two lamb is sometimes associated by some with the birth of the nation (or the giving of the Law) and the birth of the church. It is interesting that the book of Ruth, a remarkable presentation of the kinsman-redeemer taking a Gentile bride, is associated with this feast.

There are some that find the association of both the day of Enoch's birth and his translation (rapture?) with this day provocative. The "trumpet of God" appears only twice in the Bible: at the giving of the Law at Sinai, (Exod. 19:13, 16) and the rapture (1 Thess. 4:16).

See also HOLY SPIRIT, BAPTISM OF THE; HOLY SPIRIT IN THE CHURCH AGE.

Charles W. Missler

Richard Booker, *Jesus in the Feasts of Israel* (Shippensburg, Penn.: Destiny Image Publishers, 1987); Victor Buksbazen, *The Feasts of Israel* (Ft. Washington, Penn: CLC, 1954); Abraham Chill, *The Minhagim* (New York: Sepher-Hermon Press, 1979); Alfred Edersheim, *The Temple: Its Ministry and Services* (Grand Rapids: Eerdmans, 1958); Daniel Fuchs, *Israel's Holy Days* (Neptune, N.J.: Loizeaux Bros., 1985); J. H. Hertz, *Pentateuch & Haftorahs* (London: Soncino Press, 1989); Rabbi Aryeh Kaplan, *The Living Torah* (Jerusalem: Maznaim Publishing Corp., 1981); Chuck Missler, *The Feasts of Israel* (Coeur d'Alene, Idaho: Koinonia House, 1993).

PEOPLE OF GOD, THE

The term *the people of God* (PG) is closely connected with the biblical covenants, particularly the administrative covenants (old/Mosaic and new covenants). Membership in PG is determined on the basis of participation in an administrative covenant structure. In the OT economy, this was an ethnic/national category based on the exodus redemption and the ensuing old/ Mosaic covenant. As it relates to the present and future, this involves the new covenant. This covenant promises that Israel will be restored to a position as PG in the future regathering. Since the church also participates in the new covenant [see NEW COVENANT, THEOLOGY OF], it is on that basis that the church becomes a part of PG. The church does not replace Israel as God's people. Rather, the category PG is a larger term that encompasses OT Israel, the NT church, and others in the future. This does not obviate distinctions within the larger category—Israel and church remain distinguishable as separate vehicles for accomplishing God's purposes in the world. PG should not be viewed as "all the redeemed of all ages," for such a definition makes PG a soteric category rather than a covenantal one. There is a shift in the composition of PG at the Cross because at that point there is a shift in covenants. It is the difference in the structure and provisions of the two covenants involved (old and new) that accounts for the shift from an ethnic/ national group to a group presently composed of believers. Since the old covenant was an administrative covenant that governed the life of a body politic, it included all persons under that jurisdiction in its scope. The new covenant, by contrast, is an administrative, pneumatological covenant that presently governs the lives of all those who are true believers on the basis of the internal work of the Spirit applying God's law to human hearts. In its future role in the millennial kingdom, the new covenant will once again administer political affairs as well as continue its pneumatological role in the lives of believers.

The term PG raises numerous theological questions pertaining to the relationships of various groups of people in the accomplishment of God's purposes in the world. This is particularly true of questions regarding the relationship between Israel and the church. Some argue that the church replaces Israel as PG. Others see a continuity in PG with believing Gentiles being added and unbelieving Jews removed. Some also argue for a dichotomous definition of PG: in the OT, Israel was elected as PG in a revelatory sense; in the NT, election as PG is defined in soteric terms and is open to both Jews and Gentiles. PG can also be defined as a unitary, umbrella category that encompasses distinguishable subgroups. Others argue for two separate PG: Israel and the church. Although not exclusively a dispensational view, the two people-of-God position is perhaps best known from classic dispensationalism's contention of an earthly and a heavenly people with differing purposes and destinies.

The exact phrase "people of God" (*'am 'elohim* and *laos theou*) occurs only five times in Scripture: Judges 20:2; 2 Samuel 14:13; Hebrews 4:9; 11:25; and 1 Peter 2:10. This is not, however, the full extent of the relevant biblical data. The words *'am* or *laos* alone may carry the same semantic value. The phrases *Lord's people, your people, his people, my people,* etc. are often the equivalent of *'am 'elohim* and *laos theou.* Such phrases refer to PG approximately four hundred times in Scripture. There are numerous related terms that could increase this number considerably (e.g., God of Israel, family of God, etc.).

Exodus 5:22–6:8 is a programmatic statement regarding PG at a crucial point in God's providential working in history. The significance of the passage for defining PG lies in the connection with God's taking the Israelites for the purpose of establishing a community that would be His possession and would have a special relationship with Him. This statement is anticipatory of what God was about to do in the great deliverance of the Exodus, culminating in the events of Sinai shortly thereafter. The concept of redemption in relation to God's people is introduced in Exodus 6:6 and is frequently associated with Israel's peoplehood status thereafter. This describes God's physical deliverance of the people from slavery, not their spiritual regeneration. In reference to this event, David describes *your people* as (1) a nation, (2) delivered from Egypt, (3) for God's glory, and (4) established in a special relationship with God (2 Sam. 7:23–24). The span of David's paean covers not only the Exodus proper, but also Sinai and the conquest. Although it is not mentioned directly, the covenantal idea seems to be the underlying concept here that forms the basis for Israel's national existence and relationship to God. It is also the focal point of the redemptive epoch to which David points. The emphasis on redemption (deliverance from Egyptian slavery) suggests that this is the basis on which the peoplehood relationship is based and on which God stakes His claim of Israel as His own people.

Peoplehood may also be expressed in elective terms (election in the OT is not personal or soteric but covenantal). Deuteronomy 7:6–8 is the *locus classicus* regarding Israel's election. Israel's status as the chosen PG sets them apart from all other ethnic groups on earth and establishes them as God's treasured possession. Moses' emphasis here is the basis of their election. It is not election based on merit, value, or status but is unconditional—based solely on God's love and His loyalty to His oath that upholds the Abrahamic covenant. Of greatest significance is the statement that "the LORD has chosen you . . . to be his people." The purpose of God's choice was to establish Israel as his people.

Beginning in Exodus 6:7 the formula, "I will be your God, and you shall be my people," becomes a refrain throughout the OT. The initial reference looks forward to what God will do. Later references (e.g., 1 Chron. 17:22; Jer. 7:23; 11:4) look backward to an accomplished event. Although the formula does not occur explicity in the record of the Sinai events, it is probably the establishment of the old covenant that anchors this transaction. This is substantiated not only by the forward and backward references that center on Sinai, but also on the nature of the statement itself, for this recurrent formula is the *Bundesformel* (declaration formula) of the OT. This literary expression declares the covenantal relationship between the parties of a covenant. The formula occurs some two dozen times in Scripture: in the OT, five times in reference to the old covenant, seventeen times in reference to the new, and three times in the NT.

The ancient Near Eastern covenants used a standard formula known as *die Bundesformel* that establishes, or at least declares, the relationship that will exist between the two parties (see Kalluveettil). In some sense the relationship may already exist, but it is the declaration formula that officializes the legal relationship. The parallels with the OT formula provide a helpful basis for understanding the significance of the covenant formula: it establishes and defines the nature of the relationship between the parties in the covenant. Just as Iatar-Ami declares "Zimri-Lim is my father," and the king's representative replies "Iatar-Ami is [a] devoted son" (Dossin, *RA* 35,120; cited by Kalluveettil, 95), even so the OT formula declares that God is Israel's God and Israel is God's people. This would suggest that the your God-My people relationship is established on the basis of covenant. By entering into covenant relationship with God, the human party becomes (part of) PG.

Just as the old covenant provides the basis for peoplehood in the OT, the new covenant prophecies relate people-of-God status to the administrative covenant that would one day replace the old. In Jeremiah 31, the prophet flows directly from the internalization of the law to the standard covenant formula: "I will be their God, and they will be my people" (v. 33; see also 32:38). Ezekiel frequently employs the declaration formula in connection with the new covenant (11:20; 34:25–31; 36:28; 37:23, 27) as does Zechariah (8:8; 13:7–9).

Peoplehood, though almost exclusively related to Israel in the OT, is not totally so. There are several passages that specifically prophesy the future inclusion of Gentiles with Israel as PG, including Psalm 87:5; Isaiah 19:25; Jeremiah 12:16; and Zechariah 2:11. Although not a major theme, it is clear that the OT anticipates an eschatological expansion of peoplehood. Since the crux of peoplehood throughout the OT is the covenant relationship, expressed so clearly in the covenant formula, and since that same relationship and formula play so heavily in the new covenant texts, it would seem to be a fair conclusion that this future expansion of PG will also be on a covenantal basis. Those who are so included are incorporated as part of PG and participants in the new covenant.

PG occurs much less frequently in the NT than in the OT. In Romans 9, Paul discusses God's sovereign election of Israel, arguing that Israel's failure to respond positively to Messiah's ministry is not an indication that God's word has failed. It is God's mercy that has now extended the riches of his glory to both Jew and Gentile. It is in support of this extension argument that Paul appeals typologically to Hosea 1:10 and 2:23 to demonstrate that the church is now part of PG. This is not simply a statement that the church occupies a similar position (analogy), but that they are indeed God's people. People with no previous covenant relationship with God become His covenant people by participation in the new covenant. In other words, the church does participate in the new covenant and becomes PG on that basis.

Second Corinthians 6:16 proposes a similar argument by citing Ezekiel 37:27. The use of the *Bundesformel* in relation to the Corinthian believers is significant. Paul calls NT believers PG. A composite allusion to OT peoplehood is used in 1 Peter 2:9–10. Peter draws from Exodus 19, Isaiah 43, and Hosea 1–2, texts united by the term *people* found in each context. This triple application of *laos* to Christians, especially the explicit *nun de laos theou* in verse 10, leaves little doubt that Peter considers believers who are part of the church to also be part of PG.

Acts 15 is a debated text; the points on which there is agreement may be summarized as follows. In the Jerusalem council's deliberation of the place and responsibilities of Gentiles in the church, James adduces OT evidence regarding God's inclusion of Gentiles in His program (Amos 9:11–12). He relates this to Peter's earlier account of God's taking from the Gentiles a people for His name (Acts 15:14). This refers back to verses 7–11, in which Peter recounts his experience of taking the Gospel to the Gentiles—a reference to the Cornelius experience in Acts 10. Although James's words in verse 14 are not an OT quotation, they do echo the wording of several OT peoplehood passages (Exod. 6:7; 2 Sam. 7:23). The fact that James used OT language to describe the spread of the Gospel to the Gentiles is significant. It seems inescapable that James understands the Gentile's position in OT people-of-God terms. This suggests some continuity between PG in the OT and NT.

Titus 2:14 describes Jesus as the one "who gave himself for us to redeem us from all wickedness and to purify for himself a people that are his very own [*laos periousion*], eager to do what is good." This phrase is a distinctive OT designation for PG (Exod. 19:5; Deut. 7:6; 14:2; 26:18). That Paul uses it here establishes the validity of NT believers being a part of PG.

The final occurrence of *laos* in the NT occurs in John's vision of the new heavens and new earth. At the commencement of this eternal state the announcement from the throne is: "They will be his people, and God himself will be with them and be their God" (Rev. 21:3). The inclusion of the covenant formula at this cusp between history and eternity suggests that this is the goal toward which God has been moving in His providential, theocratic plan.

The NT concept of peoplehood reflects its OT origins. A number of passages cite specific people-of-God texts from the OT and several others reflect OT phraseology or allusions. The covenantal basis of personhood is clearly evident here, particularly by the use of the covenant formula. Church believers are described as and included in PG on the basis of the new covenant. This is not presented as a dual category (Israel and the church), nor is the church described as the new PG that replaces the old people. Also seen are references to PG in an eschatological context that stretches peoplehood beyond the earthly history of the church; indeed, PG are described in the eternal state as enjoying the covenantal relationship.

See also COVENANTS, THE; NEW COVENANT, THE.

Rodney Decker

W. E. Glenny, "Dispensational Hermeneutics and the People of God in Romans 9:25–26" in *Bib Sac* 152:42–59 (1995); W. Kaiser Jr., "Israel as the People of God" in *The People of God: Essays on the Believers' Church* (Nashville: Broadman, 1991), 99–108; P. Kalluveettil, *Declaration and Covenant* (Analecta Biblica 88, Rome: Biblical Institute Press, 1982); P. Leonard, "Two Peoples of God" in *Handbook to Biblical Prophecy* (Grand Rapids: Baker, 1977), 221–30; A. Millard, "Covenant and Communion in 1 Corinthians" in *Apostolic History and the Gospel* (Grand Rapids: Eerdmans, 1970); P. Richardson, *Israel in the Apostolic Church* (SNTSMS 10, Cambridge: Cambridge Univ. Press, 1969); J. Shaw, "The Concept of 'The People of God' in Recent Research" (Th.D. diss., Princeton Theological Seminary, 1958); H. Strathmann and R. Meyer, "*laos*" in *TDNT* 4:30–57; H. Taylor, "Continuity of the People of God in the Old and New Testaments" in *Scottish Bulletin of Evangelical Theology,* 3:13–26 (1985); B. Ware, "The New Covenant and the People(s) of God" in *Dispensationalism, Israel, and the Church* (Grand Rapids: Zondervan, 1992), 68–97.

PETER, 1 & 2, ESCHATOLOGY OF

There is little doubt that the apostle Peter is the author of both of these epistles. Most believe 1 Peter was written around A.D. 63, and 2 Peter probably around A.D. 66. One year later, many believe, the apostle was martyred in Rome. The first letter right up front addresses the "aliens, scattered" that is, believing Jews living in Asia Minor and elsewhere. The second letter has a more typical salutation. Also, it deals head-on with many more heavy eschatological issues than

1 Peter. The theme of 1 Peter seems to be the grace of God applied to many tough issues about living the Christian life. Second Peter reminds Christians to oppose heretics and false teachers, to realize that God has reserved fire for the day of judgment and destruction of the ungodly.

First Peter has many prophetic passages, but most are subtle and limited to phrases or sentences. The apostle writes of a future inheritance imperishable, "reserved in heaven for you" (1:4 NASB) and about a salvation ready to be revealed in the last time (1:5). He speaks of coming praise and glory at the revelation of Jesus Christ (1:7), and the future outcome of the believers' faith which is "the salvation of your souls" (1:9). He urges Christians to fix their hope on the coming grace "brought to you at the revelation of Jesus Christ" (1:13). But he also reminds the flock that the Father will impartially judge according to each one's work. This judgment should cause the children of God to watch their behavior so that the Lord may be glorified in the coming day of visitation (2:12; 4:13).

Several times Peter refers to the present suffering that leads to a sharing in the glory to come. The Christian then is a partaker also of the glory that is to be revealed and is called to God's eternal glory and is to receive, when Christ appears, the unfading crown of glory (5:4). From Isaiah 8, 28, and other Old Testament passages, the apostle builds a prophetic profile of Jesus as the precious corner stone, the stone of stumbling, the rock of offense (2:6–8). Because of Israel's rejection of Christ, Peter focuses on these prophecies and even argues that his generation of Jews were appointed to stumble and be doomed because of their disobedience to the Word (2:8).

In a future context in 2 Peter, the apostle refers to the entrance into the eternal kingdom of our Lord (1:11). He writes prophetically of his own departure from earth, "knowing that the laying aside of my earthly dwelling is imminent" (1:14). He reminds believers to pay attention to the prophetic word and be alert "until the day dawns and the morning star arises in your hearts" (1:19), which is probably a reference to Christ's Second Coming (Ryrie).

In 2 Peter the apostle predicts the coming of false prophets and teachers who will malign the way of truth (2:2). He speaks of the fallen angels confined to the pits and reserved for future judgment (2:4). As well, he writes of mockers coming forth in the last days who say, "Where is the promise of His coming? For ever since the fathers fell asleep, all continues just as it was from the beginning of creation" (3:4). Peter then reminds his readers that the heavens and earth are stored up for the day of judgment and destruction of the ungodly (3:7). He warns that the Lord waits, not wishing for any to perish but for all to come to repentance (3:9). Sounding like the apostle Paul (1 Thess. 5:2), Peter speaks of the Day of the Lord coming like a thief. He writes of the day of God in which the elements will melt and there will follow the new heavens and a new earth, in which righteousness dwells (3:13).

These prophetic realities should cause the believer in Christ to live a diligent Christian life, in peace, spotless and blameless (3:14). And since these events have not occurred yet, this proves "the patience of our Lord to be salvation" (3:15).

The book of Jude, written probably around A.D. 70–80, borrows heavily from the words of 2 Peter. Jude (or James, the half brother of Christ), felt Peter's words appropriate for his audience. Obviously, skeptics came forward denying a judgment and the dramatic climax and end of the universe. Jude simply reinforces the authoritative words of the apostle Peter.

In Peter's two letters, there is no systematic or chronological flow of eschatology. He uses prophecy in a very practical way as an encouragement to believers and as a warning to the lost. The apostle is not attempting to lay out a chronological plan of future events. In some ways this is true of Paul also. It was the apostle John who was given by the Lord Himself a more comprehensive and complete scenario of end-time events, through the book of Revelation. Yet Peter's words are dramatic and sobering as he describes the priorities of living and the fact of the shortness of history itself.

See also DAY OF THE LORD; JUDE, ESCHATOLOGY OF.

Mal Couch

Charles C. Ryrie, *Ryrie NAS Study Bible*, expanded ed. (Chicago: Moody Press, 1995).

PETERS, GEORGE N. H.

George N. H. Peters (1825–1909) is one of the most mysterious and fascinating premillennial scholars of the nineteenth century. Giving most of his life to a study of the return of the Lord, he penned the classic three-volume work, *The Theocratic Kingdom*. The title actually continues: . . . *of our Lord Jesus, The Christ, as Covenanted in The Old Testament and Presented in The New Testament.* Why he was so driven in his premillennial convictions (yet being a Lutheran), is not fully known, except he was apparently influenced by the great Lutheran prophecy scholar, Dr. S. S. Schmucker. Schmucker also taught and inspired Joseph A. Seiss.

Peters attended and later graduated from Wittenberg College in Springfield, Ohio, in 1850. He held pastorates in Xenia and Springfield. How and when he began writing *The Theocratic Kingdom* is not clear. But he must have read hundreds, if not thousands, of references in theology (especially prophecy), history, science, and literature. Years must have passed before the 2,100 pages (some in small print) were completed. Amazingly, Peters has over four thousand quotes in this work. The "author lived and worked in an oblivion that seems almost mysterious, and experienced so little recognition at the time of the [first] publication of his work that one must almost believe that there was an organized determination to ignore its appearance" (Smith).

Though Peters lived during a period when there was an explosion of interest in Bible prophecy both in America and England, there was great opposition to such studies in the circles within which he lived. Peters writes of "deep despondency" because of criticism from brethren who opposed him. For many years in Springfield, a hundred laymen and pastors met for weekly prophecy studies. But he writes, his love of the prophetic Word brought upon him bitter and unrelenting abuse. Peters never fully explains the nature of the opposition. He writes that "his motive is assailed, his piety is doubted, his character is privately and publicly traduced, his learning and ability are lowered." All in "the defense of the truth."

In the introduction to *The Theocratic Kingdom*, Peters writes that all things are "tending toward the kingdom to be hereafter established by Christ, that the dispensations from Adam, to the present are only preparatory stages for its coming manifestation." He adds "that we cannot properly comprehend the Divine economy . . . unless we . . . consider the manifestation of its ultimate result as exhibited in this [coming] kingdom." Peters believed that modern rationalists had given untrustworthy definitions to the kingdom and we must return "to accept of the old view of the kingdom as the one clearly taught by the prophets, Jesus, the disciples, the apostles." Finally, Peters writes, after long investigation he was compelled with a sense of duty to publish his work. He notes he tried to set forth "the Millenarian views of the ancient and modern believers, and [to be] paving the way for a more strict and consistent interpretation of the kingdom, this itself would already be sufficient justification for its publication."

The Theocratic Kingdom may be one of the most complete compilations of quotes from all the writings of the last two thousand years dealing with the kingdom and the literal return of Christ to earth.

See also THEOCRATIC KINGDOM.

Mal Couch

George N. H. Peters, *The Theocratic Kingdom* (Grand Rapids: Kregel, 1957).

PETTINGILL, WILLIAM T.

William T. Pettingill (1866–1950) was an early-twentieth-century educator, pastor, and author. Pettingill was a member of the editorial staff of the *Scofield Reference Bible*, a reference Bible that has become a standard of conservative and premillennial interpretation. For twenty-five years, he served as a pastor in Wilmington, Delaware and was closely associated with C. I. Scofield in educational work, serving for many years as dean of the Philadelphia School of the Bible, founded by Scofield. Pettingill was the editor of several periodicals, including *Serving and Waiting* and *Just a Word*. The author of numerous books, he was known throughout the world for his expositional and prophetical writings. His writings include *God's Prophecies for Plain People*; *Simple Studies in Daniel*; *Simple Studies in Matthew*; *Simple Studies in Romans*; *Simple Studies in the Revelation*; *Israel: Jehovah's Covenant People*; and *Is Heaven a Real Place?* A popular conference and prophecy speaker, Pettingill travelled and ministered in England, Europe, Central America, Canada, and throughout the United States.

Pettingill's writing style was spiritually edifying, showed an acquaintance with the classical and scholarly literature and biblical languages, was sometimes quick to the point and was always written to bring a response from the heart.

His theological stance was dispensational, solidly premillennial, and in agreement with the pretribulational rapture.

See also SCOFIELD, C. I.

Lonnie L. Shipman

George W. Dollar, *A History of Fundamentalism in America* (Greenville, N.C.: Bob Jones University Press, 1973); William L. Pettingill, *Simple Studies in the Revelation* (Wilmington, Del.: Just a Word Inc., 1933), *God's Prophecies for Plain People* (Philadelphia: Philadelphia School of the Bible, 1923); Timothy P. Weber, *Living in the Shadow of the Second Coming: American Premillennialism, 1875–1925* (Grand Rapids: Zondervan, 1983).

PHILIPPIANS, ESCHATOLOGY OF

There is little doubt as to the authorship of Philippians. It was clearly written by the apostle Paul. Paul wrote this epistle while in prison, probably in Rome (A.D. 62). Philippians is known as Paul's love letter to the saints because it expresses his love and gratitude to those saints at Philippi.

The Day of Christ (Phil.1:6, 10; 2:16)

The Day of Christ is to be distinguished from the Day of the Lord, which normally has in view God's dealing in judgment in the world (1 Thess. 5:11). Rather, the Day of Christ refers to the Rapture and the immediate results of the believers being instantly taken home to be with the Lord (Walvoord).

In Philippians 1:6, Paul is anticipating the judgment seat of Christ, following the Rapture, in heaven where the believers' works will be examined and rewarded (2 Cor. 5:10). Thus in verse 10, the goal in view is that Paul's readers will live sincerely and without offense and hence give a good accounting on that day of reckoning. And in 2:16 Paul expresses his hope that he will be rejoicing on that occasion, the Day of Christ, in seeing the Philippians rewarded for their faithfulness as light-bearers in holding forth the word of life.

The Exaltation of Christ (Phil. 2:9–11)

The mind of God expressed in Philippians 2:9–11 is that, after Christ's awesome humiliation in His incarnation and crucifixion, God "also hath highly exalted him, and given him a name which is above every name: that at the name of Jesus every knee should bow, of things in heaven [holy angels and saints in glory], and things in earth [people still living on earth in their mortal bodies], and things under the earth [Satan, the world of demons, and the souls in hell], and that every tongue should confess that Jesus Christ is Lord, to the glory of God the Father. This the apostle Paul predicts will occur throughout eternity (Walvoord).

Escaping the Resurrection of the Dead (Phil. 3:11)

After Paul expressed his own heart to know experientially the power of Christ's resurrection, he paused to express his personal hope that he would be alive when the Rapture occurs. By using the Greek *ei pos* (if perhaps) he was expressing a doubt, not regarding the fact of the future resurrection, but of its timing, that is, would he be alive when this "partial resurrection out from among other corpses, literally an 'out resurrection" will occur (Lightner). Paul eagerly longed to share in this going-home experience (1 Thess. 4:13–18).

The Believer's Resurrection Body (Phil. 3:20–21)

When Christ returns at the Rapture, He will "change the outward form of believers' mortal bodies, so that they will conform to the character of his resurrection body." Our present lowly bodies Paul describes as vile, as bodies "of weakness and [susceptible] to persecution, disease, sinful appetites, and death" (Kent). Furthermore, these bodies "will be fashioned whether by resurrection of the dead or by rapture of the living, and believers will be transformed and receive glorified bodies that will adequately display their essential character (*summorphon*) as children of God and sharers of divine life in Christ" (Kent). This sharing the apostle Paul predicts will occur throughout eternity (Walvoord).

Alden Gannett

Homer A. Kent Jr., "Philippians" in *The Bible Expositor's Dictionary,* ed. Frank E. Gaebelein, vol. 11 (Grand Rapids: Regency Reference Library, 1978); Robert Lightner, "Philippians" in *The Bible Knowledge Commentary,* eds. John F. Walvoord and Roy B. Zuck, vol. 2 (Wheaton: Victor Books, 1983); John F. Walvoord, *The Prophecy Knowledge Handbook* (Wheaton: Victor Books, 1990).

PHILO JUDAEUS

Philo Judaeus (ca. 15/10 B.C.–A.D. 45/50), also called Philo of Alexandria, was the most important representative of Hellenistic Judaism. His writings compose the largest repository of Jewish law before the completion of the Talmud around A.D. 600. Philo's life overlapped the ministry of Jesus. Although conversant with Hellenistic culture and writing in Greek, Philo was clearly an observant Jew who was thoroughly familiar with the Scriptures and traditions of his people.

The one identifiable event in Philo's life occurred around A.D. 39, when he headed an embassy of Alexandrian Jews to the emperor Caligula. There he pleaded the cause of Jewish rights in Alexandria, which had been breached by recent anti-Jewish pogroms in the city. Although Philo was cut short by Caligula, the Jewish rights were later restored following the assassination of the emperor.

Philo's writings are of three types:

1. Essays and homilies on the Pentateuch. The most important are *Allegories of the Laws*, a commentary on Genesis, and *On the Special Laws*, an exposition of the laws found in the Pentateuch.

2. General philosophical and religious essays. He wrote of Stoic philosophy (*That Every Good Man is Free*), a mystical Jewish sect called the Therapeutue (*On the Contemplative Life*), as well as an apologetic defense of the Jews (*Hypothetica*).

3. Essays on contemporary subjects. *Against Flaccus* and *On the Embassy to Gaius* expose the hostility of the Romans and describe his unsuccessful embassy to the Roman emperor.

Philo's basic philosophical outlook is Platonic. The church father Jerome quoted the widespread saying, "Either Plato philonizes or Philo platonizes." He reconciled his Jewish theology with Plato's theory of Ideas in an original way: he posited the Ideas as God's eternal thoughts, which God then created as real beings before He created the world.

Philo saw the cosmos as a great chain of being presided over by the Logos, a Greek philosophic term, which is the mediator between God and the world. He called the Logos the first-begotten Son of God, the image of God, and second to God. In this he anticipated Johannine theology, which would later wed the Hellenistic concept of Logos to the Hebrew concept of the Word as the description of the role of Jesus in the divine cosmic plan.

Philo was also a mystic. Like Plato, he regarded the body as the prison house of the soul. He yearned for a direct experience of God by a flight from the self that would lead him out of the material into the "sober intoxication" of the eternal world. Because of the later rabbinical resistance to Greek authors and Hellenistic thought, Philo's writings were preserved by Christians. Early church fathers, particularly those in Alexandria, were greatly influenced by his thought.

In his many commentaries on the Pentateuchal books, Philo of Alexandria employed a hermeneutical method known as allegory. The basic meaning of the term *allegory,* is "to say another thing." In the interpretation of the Scriptures, allegory is the assertion that texts are not saying what they appear, but saying something different. Allegory is the direct opposite of *literal.* Allegory assigns a special meaning to a passage, which meaning is not present on the surface of the passage.

A few examples of Philonic allegory will illustrate. Philo interprets the conflict between Cain and Abel to be that of two types of persons. Cain represents the person fluent in speech but deficient in content, while Abel is the person whose content is solid but where speech is halting. A fluent person can "kill" a person of halting speech, as Cain killed Abel. Nothing in the scriptural account justifies such as interpretation. Throughout his writings, Philo transforms biblical characters or place names into universal types of people or characteristics of humankind.

The laws of Moses, as well as the narrative portions of the Pentateuch, are also interpreted allegorically. Thus, Passover symbolizes the passing of the soul out of its domination by the body (a Platonic concept). Circumcision prunes passion from the body, while abstinence from pork instructs in self-control (Stoic concepts).

Another aspect of Philo's allegorical method is that he makes much of numbers, such as the seven branches of the menorah and the ten commandments. In this he shows an indebtedness to earlier Pythagorean writers.

In his use of allegory, Philo sought to invest meanings in Scripture so as to find proof for his own novel insights. Therefore, while the assumption and loyalties of Philo are Jewish, the basic context of his thought is Greek. Allegory binds them together.

Philo was the culmination of a literary tradition within Alexandrian Judaism. His legacy, however, fell to some early church fathers who also labored in his hometown, particularly Clement of Alexandria and Origen. The hermeneutical principle of these two provided the conduit through which Philo's allegorical method entered the early church. Alexandrian allegorical exegesis was opposed by Antiochene literal method in the fourth century. The Alexandrian method greatly influenced medieval hermeneutics and resulted in the displacement of premillennialism with amillennialism after Augustine.

While most of evangelical hermeneutics has abandoned the Alexandrian allegorical method as applied to the narrative portions of Scripture, it is still inconsistently applied to the prophetic portions of the Old Testament, resulting in spiritualized interpretations of such terms as *Israel, Jerusalem,* and *Zion.* On a more popular level, many sermons unconsciously reflect the Philonic emphasis or number symbolism and illegitimate spiritual interpretations of texts.

William Varner

Peder Borgen, "Philo of Alexandria" in *Anchor Bible Dictionary*, vol. 5 (New York: Doubleday, 1992), 333–42; E. R. Goodenough, *An Introduction to Philo Judeaus* (New Haven, Conn.: Yale University Press, 1940); Samuel Sandmel, *Philo of Alexandria: An Introduction* (New York: Oxford University Press, 1979); C. D. Yonge, *The Works of Philo* (Peabody, Mass.: Hendrickson, 1993).

PINK, ARTHUR

Arthur Pink (1886–1952) was a deep spiritual writer, teacher, and Bible scholar with great ability. In his most productive years he wrote volumes of material in devotional commentaries and personality studies on the life of Moses, David, Elijah. Many of his books have been reprinted and are still in print, including his classic, *The Sovereignty of God.* In the 1920s Pink began a series of subscription studies entitled *Studies in the Scriptures.* Many of his works were first published in this study magazine that was sent worldwide.

Pink was born in Nottingham, England. In his early twenties, in 1908, he accepted Christ while alone in his bedroom. Early on he decided to attend Bible school or seminary but felt that most institutions of biblical learning were defiled with doctrinal "filth." But, at twenty-two, Pink changed his mind and came to America and attended Moody Bible Institute. He felt he "was wasting his time" and left the school in six weeks. He explained that he felt the teaching was pitched to a rather "immature" level. Armed with the *Scofield Reference Bible*, he immediately landed a pastorate in Colorado and later elsewhere. In 1916 he married his lifelong companion, Vera Russell. She was Pink's right-hand help and guide throughout his ministry. In later years, facing a lot of rejection, the two virtually walked alone, with few supporters and friends. Vera put into publishing form his writings after Arthur's death.

The Change

Pink's early views were "both Premillennial and, to some extent, Dispensationalist" (Murray). Though some spuriously believed dispensationalists taught different ways of salvation, an Old Testament and a New Testament way, Pink denied this. In actuality, dispensationalists never preached such a view, but it was claimed so by its enemies. Around 1929 Pink began to say dispensationalism negated Christian living. Because some date-setters were claiming Hitler was the Antichrist bringing on Armageddon, Pink reacted. He felt the message of personal repentance was being neglected. He felt dispensationalists "fiddled while Rome was burning!" To prove his point Pink latched onto extreme dispensational teachings. For example, Isaac M. Haldeman was preaching the Lord's Prayer has no more place in the Christian church than the thunders of Sinai or the offerings of Leviticus. From such extreme statements, Pink concluded by 1933 that dispensationalism was demonic (Murray). He wrote in the *Studies* that it was subversive to faith and reduced God's Word to a dead letter. He further felt it relieved the "Christian of repentance, obedience and cross-carrying."

Pink clearly was influenced by radical dispensational statements that few knowledgeable dispensationalists today (or even at that time) would agree with. He felt such teachings were carnal and shallow. But Pink may be guilty of throwing the baby out with the bath water! There were many solid, godly premillennial dispensational teachers who were mature in their teachings and in their Christian walk. Pink clearly overlooked them. He gravitated toward being a recluse and "an opinionated individualist" (Murray). He came to believe the only balanced biblical teaching came from the Reformation and the Puritan era. Pink apparently never researched the history of amillennial hermeneutics. In denouncing premillennialism he threw away the prophetic proclamations made by the early church about the literal, earthly return of the Lord.

Pink had trouble being accepted in the pastorate. He went from America to Australia and Great Britain seeking a stable pulpit ministry. It never happened for him. Pink lived out his final years in the Scottish Hebrides, monthly publishing his *Studies* newsletter for a few subscribers. He died unnoticed by the world.

The Antichrist

Before Pink rejected dispensationalism, he wrote what is considered the classic work on the end times, *The Antichrist.* This could easily be called the most complete work on the subject. The book sweeps both the Old Testament and New Testament and handles with exceptional merit all the passages about the coming Man of Sin. At the time Pink wrote the book he firmly believed the Day of the Lord could not come until after the period of church apostasy and after the Rapture. He believed the appearing of the Antichrist would herald the Day of the Lord. As well, Pink taught the Holy Spirit is now preventing the full and final outworking of the mystery of iniquity and the manifestation of the Antichrist. He also felt that, taken in their normal meaning, the Scriptures clearly taught this future coming of such an evil personality controlled by Satan. Pink urged that his readers "be stirred within" and "not hesitate to lift up our voices in warning. The world is in complete ignorance of what awaits it." Sometime later, Pink departed from his position of a consistent biblical hermeneutic and almost turned away completely from all prophetic teachings.

See also SCOFIELD, C. I.

Mal Couch

Iain H. Murray, *The Life of Arthur W. Pink* (Carlisle, Pa.: The Banner of Truth Trust, 1981); Arthur W. Pink, *The Antichrist* (Grand Rapids: Kregel, 1988).

POSTMILLENNIALISM

Simply put, postmillennialism is a view of eschatology teaching that Christ's return to earth will occur at the end of the Millennium.

Contemporary reconstructionist postmillennialist Kenneth L. Gentry gives the following seven characteristics of evangelical postmillennialism:

1. Postmillennialism "understands the messianic kingdom to have been founded upon the earth during the earthly ministry and through the redemptive labors of the Lord Jesus Christ. . . . the church becomes the transformed Israel."

2. "The fundamental nature of that kingdom is essentially redemptive and spiritual . . . Christ rules His kingdom spiritually in and through His people in the world (representation), as well as by His universal providence."

3. Christ's "kingdom will exercise a transformational socio-cultural influence in history. This will occur as more and more people are converted to Christ."

4. "Postmillennialism, thus, expects the gradual, developmental expansion of the kingdom of Christ in time and on earth. . . . Christ's personal presence on earth is not needed for the expansion of His kingdom."

5. "Postmillennialism confidently anticipates a time in earth history (continuous with the present) in which the very gospel already operative in the world will have won the victory throughout the earth in fulfillment of the Great Commission. . . . During that time the overwhelming majority of men and nations will be Christianized, righteousness will abound, wars will cease, and prosperity and safety will flourish."

6. There are "two types of postmillennialism today: pietistic and theonomic postmillennialism. . . . Pietistic postmillennialism . . . denies that the postmillennial advance of the kingdom involves the total transformation of culture through the application of biblical law. Theonomic postmillennialism affirms this."

7. "Possibly 'we can look forward to a great golden age of spiritual prosperity continuing for centuries, or even for millenniums. . . .' After this . . . earth history will be drawn to a close by the personal, visible, bodily return of Jesus Christ (accompanied by a literal resurrection and a general judgment) to introduce His . . . consummative and eternal form of the kingdom."

While many of the basic elements of postmillennialism remain the same, distinction should be made between liberals who promote a postmillennialism through humanism (i.e., the social Gospel of the past) and evangelical postmillennialism that promote progress through the church's preaching of the gospel and application of Mosaic Law. Both adhere to a gospel combined with social change as the agency of change and progress. Thus, in a sense, evangelical postmillennialists believe that many nineteenth-century postmillennialists went astray by adopting humanistic liberalism; instead they should have relied upon a more traditional, conservative approach.

The historical rise and development of postmillennialism has been the object of some dispute, partly because of some similarities between it and amillennialism. Amillennialism and postmillennialism, for example, would have Gentry's points (1), (2), and (4) in common. Thus, because of points of similarity, some have confused amillennialism and postmillennialism. Because of these similarities, it may be difficult at times to clearly distinguish postmillennialism and amillennialism in history. It is the differences that are significant, in spite of similarities. Both are clearly anti-premillennial.

It is generally thought that Daniel Whitby (1638–1725) developed systematic postmillennialism as a clearly distinct form of millenarianism. This does not mean that elements of systematic postmillennialism did not exist prior to Whitby, for they clearly did. However, it seems best to understand the maturity of postmillennialism into a distinct system as post-Reformational and in a sense an optimistic form of amillennialism. Thus, postmillennialism's development is dependent upon amillennialism.

Only a handful of partisan polemicists would attempt to argue that postmillennialism has a postapostolic presence. "All seem to agree that postmillennialism is quite foreign to the apostolic church. There is no trace of anything in the church which could be classified as postmillennialism in the first two or three centuries."

The rise of figurative interpretation and Augustine's millennial interadvent theory began to lay a foundation for the later development of postmillennialism. Augustine "held that the age between the first and second advents is the millennium of which the Scriptures speak and that the Second Advent would occur at the end of the Millennium. This is definitely a postmillennial viewpoint as it places the Second Advent *after* the millennium." However, it is also at the same time an amillennial viewpoint. Augustine and his eschatology is best classified as amillennial because he lacked the optimism required for a true postmillennial viewpoint.

Another development that contributed to the development of systematic postmillennialism is the rise of Christendom and the merger of church and state with Constantine's declaration that Christianity was the new religion of the Roman Empire (A.D. 313). Before Constantine it is estimated that only 8 to 10 per cent of the Empire was Christian. However, as the fourth century neared its end, virtually all identified themselves as Christian. This development lead to a form of victory and optimism about the spread of Christianity and its ability to overcome even a hostile state like the previously evil Roman Empire. However, such optimism was tempered by the loss to Christendom of North Africa in the fifth century and the rise of militant Islam a few centuries later.

Joachim of Fiore's rise to prominence in the twelfth century certainly was a watershed event in the development of eschatology. He not only laid the foundation for the historicist interpretation of prophetic literature, but his optimism is seen by some as contributing to the development of postmillennialism. Whether or not he can be classified as a clear postmillennialist, he certainly contributed to an optimistic view of history. E. Randolph Daniel notes, "the twelfth century was optimistic about history and the future. The Gregorian reformers certainly believed that they could dramatically reform and purify the church on earth. Joachim, who was clearly Gregorian in his sympathies, believed that history was evolving toward the status of the Holy Spirit . . . when the church would enjoy a historical era of peace and spiritual attainment that would far surpass anything achieved in the past."

While Joachim helped prepare the way for the later development of postmillennialism, it is best not to classify him as a millennialist.

Joachim's third *status* has often been described as chiliastic or millennial, which implies that it constitutes a new beginning, the emergence of a spiritual church that would replace the corrupt clerical church. Certainly the Millennium as depicted in Apocalypse 20 is a new beginning, but Joachim's status of the Holy Spirit is not millennial in this sense. . . . Joachim's thinking is evolutionary, not revolutionary. He was a reformer, not a millennialist.

Joachim helped prepare the way for postmillennialism by contributing an idea of optimism that was to be continuous with the course of the present age. His belief that it was to be an age of the Holy Spirit was often adopted by later postmillennialists.

The Reformation sprang out of an attitude of pessimism and despair. Marjorie Reeves notes, "E. L. Tuveson has argued that the classical attitude of Protestant reformers towards history was one of pessimism: all things must decline; decay is the essential fact of history." Robin Barnes says, "in the eyes of many Lutherans in the late sixteenth century, the entire social order appeared to be falling apart."

John Calvin, while not reaching the depths of Luther's despair, cannot be claimed for postmillennialism as some have done just because he utters statements of optimism. Such statements need to be optimism within the context of a postmillennial creed. Calvin also made pessimistic statements: "There is no reason, therefore, why any person should expect the conversion of the world, for at length–when it will be too late, and will yield them no advantage." Nevertheless, "despite Calvin's Augustinian avoidance of historically oriented eschatology, the hint of progressivism in his thought left the way open for the frank meliorism and chiliasm of many later Calvinist thinkers."

It would be left to the post-Reformation era for developments to spring forth into what can rightly be called postmillennialism. Joachim's idea of progress was recast into a "new interpretation of the Apocalypse and of the eschatological pattern which looked forward to some great transforming event rather than to inevitable decay." Postmillennialism came into flower in the 1600s as the "idea of novelty rather than return is seen in the excited references to all the new manifestations of the age—the new lands, the new learning, the new books, the new missionaries." This was aided by the gains of Protestantism over Catholicism in Europe as the new continued to gain over the old.

The postmillennialism of the seventeenth century consisted mainly of those who believed in the success of the preaching of the Gospel and correspondingly the conversion of the Jews. The latter belief was one held in common with premillennialism. Yet, even though there were a few prominent postmillennialists in the seventeenth century, the position exploded into popularity as a result of Whitby's "new interpretation" of Revelation 20 at the dawn of the eighteenth century.

Contemporary reconstructionist postmillennialists usually bristle at the reminder of Whitby's key role in postmillennial history. Their defensiveness likely stems from the fact that Whitby was a less-than-orthodox Unitarian. Nevertheless, it was as the result of the efforts of Whitby, who provided exegetical and theological definition for postmillennialism, that the position began to gain ground and become the dominant eschatology in Europe and eventually North America before its decline.

Walvoord notes the following concerning Whitby: "He was a liberal and a freethinker, untrammeled by traditions or previous conceptions of the church. His views on the millennium would probably have never been perpetuated if they had not been so well keyed to the thinking of the times. The rising tide of intellectual freedom, science, and philosophy, coupled with humanism, had enlarged the concept of human progress and painted a bright picture of the future. Whitby's view of a coming golden age for the church was just what people wanted to hear. It fitted the thinking of the times. It is not strange that theologians scrambling for readjustment in a changing world should find in Whitby just the key they needed. It was attractive to all kinds of theology. It provided for the conservative a seemingly more workable principle of interpreting the Scripture. . . . Man's increasing knowledge of the world and scientific improvements which were coming could fit into this picture. On the other hand, the concept was pleasing to the liberal and skeptic. If they did not believe the prophets, at least they believed that man was now able to improve himself and his environment. They, too, believed a golden age was ahead.

After gaining dominance in Europe and America among both conservatives and liberals, postmillennialism began a decline into near extinction. Fallout from the French Revolution in Europe dealt a severe blow to postmillennial optimism. Later, in the States, postmillennial decline awaited the turn of the century and was dealt a near-fatal blow by WWI and WWII and identification with the social gospel and liberalism. Only since the 1970s has postmillennialism begun to reassert itself, primarily through the reconstructionist movement. While postmillennialism has made some gains in recent years, it is still a minor position in the overall field of eschatology.

Objections to Postmillennialism

Basic to postmillennialism's failure to match up with Scripture is its lack of a consistent hermeneutic. At key points, postmillennialism must abandon the literal hermeneutic of the historical, grammatical, and contextual approach for some degree of spiritualization.

The postmillennial idea of progress is not found in any particular text of the Bible. Rather, it appears to be an idea brought to the pages of Scripture. Postmillennialism is inconsistent with the biblical fact that the cataclysmic return of Christ, not the preaching of the Gospel and gradual human progress, brings in the kingdom (Rev. 19–20). Gospel preaching in the current age is for the purpose of gathering out the elect for the future kingdom. Postmillennialism confuses Israel and the church and requires that the church takes over the fulfillment of promises made to national Israel so that they may posit a present kingdom.

While it is true that the Bible predicts an increasing spread of the proclamation of the Gospel, this does not support the notion of postmillennial progress. In addition, the Bible speaks frequently in catastrophic and interventionist language of Christ's return to earth as the cause of millennial conditions. Specific statements of gradualism are lacking in the Bible. Postmillennialism also denies the New Testament teaching that Christ could return at any moment, known as imminency.

If a viewpoint truly represents Scripture then it is not too much to ask it to be able to correspond to history. Postmillennialism teaches that this current age will be a time of steady and upward growth. However, this is impossible to defend from history. While the Gospel frequently expands to new territories, at the same time in so many areas where the gospel has dominated society and culture there has been regression and relapse, not progress. It appears that wherever Christianity has come to dominate the culture and has lost that dominance, it has never been revived as a significant force. This is not progress, it is regression.

Postmillennialism fails to account for the fact that if there is going to be a fulfillment of millennial conditions predicted in the Bible, it is going to be only as a result of a revolutionary intervention of Jesus Christ at His Second Coming in order to introduce new factors that are dicontinuous with the present age. It will require the personal presence of Jesus Christ Himself. Only the premillennial model provides the changes necessary to implement a millennial golden age.

See also RECONSTRUCTIONISM, CHRISTIAN.

Thomas D. Ice

Loraine Boettner, *The Millennium*, revised ed. (Phillipsburg, N.J.: Presbyterian and Reformed, 1984); John Jefferson Davis, *Christ's Victorious Kingdom: Postmillennialism Reconsidered* (Grand Rapids: Baker, 1986); Kenneth L. Gentry Jr., *He Shall Have Dominion: A Postmillennial Eschatology* (Tyler, Tex.: Institute for Christian Economics, 1992); H. Wayne House and Thomas Ice, *Dominion Theology: Blessing or Curse?* (Portland: Multnomah, 1988); Layton MacDonald Talbert, "The Theonomic Postmillennialism of Christian Reconstruction: A Contrast with Traditional Postmillennialism and A Premillennial Assessment" (Ph.D. diss., Bob Jones University, 1992); John F. Walvood, *The Millennial Kingdom* (Grand Rapids: Zondervan, 1959).

PREMILLENNIALISM

Of the three views concerning the Millennium, the premillennial view is the oldest. Some of the earliest adherents to the premillennial view included: Clement of Rome, who lived about A.D. 40–100; Ignatius of Antioch, who lived about A.D. 50–115; Hippolytus, who lived about A.D. 160–240. During the first three centuries of the church one could find very few who disagreed with the premillennial view. Oswald T. Allis and Daniel Whitby, an amillenarian and a postmillennialist, make the following comments: "[Premillennialism] was extensively held in the Early church" (Allis); "The doctrine of the Millennium, or the reign of the saints on earth for a thousand years . . . passed among the best Christians, for two hundred and fifty years, for a traditional apostoical; and, as such, is delivered by many Fathers of the second and third century" (Whitby).

In its simplest form, the premillennial view holds that Christ will return to earth, (this return is also known as the Second Coming) literally and bodily, before the millennial age begins and that, by His presence, a kingdom will be instituted over which He will reign (Pentecost). It is during this reign that Israel will see the fulfillment of its covenants that were unconditionally promised in the Old Testament. Other aspects of the kingdom are found in various Old Testament books. It will be a time of peace (Mic. 4:2–4), joy (Isa. 61:7, 10), and no poverty or sickness (Amos 9:13–15; Isa. 35:5–6) (Enns). Premillennialism holds that Christ's reign will last one thousand years, as recorded in Revelation 20. At the end of this reign the unsaved dead, along with Satan, the Antichrist, and the False Prophet, will be cast into the lake of fire. After this the eternal state will begin for all believers.

Premillennialism is based on two concepts that are unique to it.

1. Literal interpretation is also known as the literal, grammatical-historical method of interpretation (Walvoord). Bernard Ramm defines this method of interpretation as follows: "The literal meaning of a word is the basic, customary, social designation of that word . . . To interpret literally means nothing more or less than to interpret in terms of normal, usual, designation." Dr. Walvoord adds concerning amillennial interpretation, "Amillenarians use the literal method theology as a whole but spiritualize Scripture whenever its literal meaning would lead to the premillennial viewpoint." Only the premillennial viewpoint relies on literal interpretation exclusively.

2. The premillennial interpreters recognize a distinction between Israel and the church. This distinction has been evident throughout history and will continue through the Millennium. Prophecies given to Israel are for Israel and cannot be usurped by the church. In this present age, Israel has been set aside, its promises held in abeyance (Walvoord). Such a postponement is not a denial of God's Word to Israel. Such a postponement can be seen in the forty-years wandering in the desert after leaving Egypt. God's promises have been made to Israel, and they will find their fulfillment in the Millennium.

Adherents to premillennialism hold that the return of Christ to reign is but the second part of a two-part plan. The first part is called the Rapture. The Rapture is taught in John 14:1–3; 1 Corinthians 15:51–57; and 1 Thessalonians 4:13–18. Separating the Rapture and the Second Coming is a seven-year time period known as the Tribulation. The purpose of the Tribulation is to bring judgment upon an unbelieving world. At the end of the seven years the entire armies of the world will be fighting the greatest world war that has ever been known. It is during this world war that Christ will return with the raptured saints. He will depose the earthly rulers and will begin His millennial reign.

See also RAPTURE, DOCTRINE OF THE; WALVOORD, JOHN.

Bobby Hayes

Paul Enns, *The Moody Handbook of Theology* (Chicago: Moody Press, 1989), 389–94; J. Dwight Pentecost, *Things to Come* (Grand Rapids: Zondervan, 1958), 9, 11, 374–82; John F. Walvoord, *The Millennial Kingdom* (Grand Rapids: Zondervan, 1959), 4–6, 128–31.

PRESENT AGE, THE COURSE OF THIS

The age in which we presently live is the sixth of seven dispensations, the age of grace. In the Old Testament, God was concerned with Israel, His chosen people, and through them He related to the world. In this age, however, God is dealing not with the nation Israel, but with the Gentile nations and is using His church to carry out the Great Commission (Matt. 28:18–20). During this age, then, God is gathering a people for Himself through individual conversions (Titus 2:14). At the same time, the mystery of the church is being unfolded (Eph. 2:11–16; 3:3–10; Col. 1:24–29).

Sometimes this dispensation is referred to as the age of the Holy Spirit because of the unique ministry of the third person of the Trinity both in the world and in the believer during this period. This does not, however, mean this age is perfect in any sense. The Scriptures describe it as an evil age (Gal. 1:4; 2 Cor. 4:4; Eph. 2:2), an age of darkness (Eph. 6:2), an age marked by ungodliness (Eph. 2:1–3; Titus 2:12), and an age of apostasy (1 Tim. 4:1–3; 2 Tim. 3:1–14; 4:3–4; 2 Peter 2:1–3, 12–22; Jude 4, 8, 10).

It is an age that denies rather than affirms the things of God. Commenting on conditions at the end of this age, Pentecost suggests, "These conditions center around a system of denials. There is a denial of God (Luke 17:26; 2 Tim. 3:4–5), a denial of Christ (1 John 2:18; 4:3; 2 Peter 2:6), a denial of Christ's return (2 Peter 3:3–4), a denial of the faith (1 Tim. 4:1–2; Jude 3), a denial of sound doctrine (2 Tim. 4:3–4), a denial of the separated life (2 Tim. 3:1–7), a denial of Christian liberty (1 Tim. 4:3–4), a denial of morals (2 Tim. 3:1–8, 13; Jude 18), a denial of authority (2 Tim. 3:4). This state at the close of the age is seen to coincide with the state within the Laodicean church, before which Christ must stand to seek admission. In view of its close it is not surprising that the age is called an 'evil age' in Scripture."

Two passages of Scripture are generally held to present a prophetic history of the major trends of this age. When Jesus gave His kingdom parables, some commentators believe He was chronologically outlining the characteristics of this present age. Later, as Jesus evaluated the seven churches of Asia (Rev. 2–3), He may have also presented a second clue concerning the future history of this church age.

Kingdom Parables

Matthew 13 records seven parables in which Jesus sought to teach His disciples the mysteries of the kingdom of heaven (Matt. 13:11). Here, Jesus outlined the progress of this current age. Concerning these parables, Walvoord writes, "The Old Testament reveals, in clear terms, the earthly reign of Christ when He comes as King to reign on the throne of David (which truths are not mysteries). Matthew 13 introduces a different form of the kingdom, namely the present spiritual reign of the King during the period He is physically absent form the earth, prior to His Second Coming. The mysteries of the kingdom, accordingly, deal with the period between the First and Second Advent of Christ and not the millennial kingdom which will follow the Second Coming."

The entire chapter records seven parables of the mysteries of the kingdom and has been outlined in various ways by different expositors. One such interpretive outline sees verse 52, where Jesus speaks of things new and old as the key to interpreting the chapter. According to Scroggie, "It appears to me that the key to the interpretation of these parables is in verse 52 of this chapter: 'Every scribe which is instructed into the kingdom of heaven is like unto a man that is an householder, which bringeth forth out of his treasure things new and old.' These words are spoken of the things which precede, and surely speak of the parables as some new and some old. . . . Assuming this, the present Age is presented to our view in a series of seven progressive pictures, describing the course of the kingdom in mystery."

The New Things

1. The seed and the soils: the proclamation of the kingdom.

2. The wheat and the darnel: false imitation in the kingdom.

3. The mustard tree: wide, visible extension of the kingdom.

4. The leaven in the meal: insidious corruption of the kingdom.

The Old Things

5. The treasure: the Israelitish nation.

6. The pearl: the Jewish remnant during the Tribulation.

7. The dragnet: the judgment of the nations at the end of the Tribulation.

In the gospel of Matthew, there is a distinction made between the kingdom of God and the kingdom of heaven. These two expressions indicate different aspects of the rule of God. Neither of these should be confused with the church. This is sometimes a difficult distinction to maintain because, whereas the church is not the kingdom of heaven, the church certainly does fall under the broader kingdom of heaven.

When studied in this light, perhaps the seven parables prophetically describe the course of this age. From our perspective at the end of the age, the accuracy of these predictions is apparently reflected in the record of church history. The following summarizes the course of this age as seen in the kingdom parables of Matthew 13.

1. Parable of the Sower (vv. 1–23): There will be a sowing of the gospel throughout the world.
2. Parable of the Tares (vv. 24–30): There will be a counter-sowing by Satan.
3. Parable of the Mustard Seed (vv. 31–32): There will be an outward growth of Christendom, but not necessarily the church.
4. Parable of the Leaven (vv. 33–35): There will be a permeation of the gospel into all areas of life.
5. Parable of the Hidden Treasure and Parable of the Pearl of Great Price (vv. 44–46): God will gather to Himself a peculiar people.
6. Parable of the Dragnet (vv. 47–51): God will end the age in judgment.

Churches of Revelation

When Jesus appeared to John on the Island of Patmos, the first part of His revelation was to dictate seven letters to the messengers of seven specific named churches in Asia (Rev. 2–3). There were far more than seven churches in that region, but only seven were chosen by Christ to receive messages. The order in which the messages are presented is also unusual. It is not the normal order in which these churches would be visited by a traveler. Some conservative scholars believe Christ selected these seven churches in this particular order to prophetically suggest the major trends in church history.

While not all dispensationalists hold to this view, many of the early dispensational writers of this century have. Summarizing this view of the seven churches as representing the seven ages of the church, Scott writes, "Ecclesiastical pretension and departure from first love characterized the close of the apostolic period—**Ephesus** (chap. 2:1–7). Next secceeded the martyr period, which brings us down to the close of the tenth and last persecution, under Diocletian—**Smyrna** (chap. 2:8–11). Decreasing spirituality and increasing worldliness went hand in hand from the accession of Constantine and his public patronage of Christianity on to the seventh century—**Pergamos** (chap. 2:12–17). The papal church. . . is witnessed in the assumption of universal authority and cruel persecution of the saints of God. Its evil reign covers 'the Middle Ages,' the moral characteristics of which have been well termed 'dark.' Popery blights everything it touches—**Thyatira** (chap. 2:18–29). The Reformation was God's intervention in grace and power to cripple papal authority, and introduce into Europe the light which for 300 years has been burning with more or less brilliancy. Protestantism, with its divisions and deadness, shows clearly enough how far short it comes of God's ideal of the church and Christianity—**Sardis** (chap. 3:1–6). Another Reformation, equally the work of God, characterized the beginning of last century—**Philadelphia** (chap. 3:7–13). The present general state of the professing church, which is one of lukewarmness, is one of the most hateful and nauseous of any yet described. We may well term this last phase of church history on the eve of judgment the Christless period—**Laodicea** (chap. 3:14–22)."

As both the kingdom parables and church epistles describe the course of this present age, it is reasonable to investigate the relationship between these two sections of Scripture. Both were recorded by disciples of Christ, one as the New Testament was first being written and the other as the canon was coming to a close. Contrasting these two passages, Gaebelein suggests the following outline:

THE SEVEN CHURCHES THAT ARE IN ASIA: REVELATION 2–3							
	2:1–7	2:8–11	2:12–17	2:18–29	3:1–6	3:7–13	3:14–22
City	Ephesus	Smyrna	Pergamum	Thyatira	Sardis	Philadelphia	Laodicea
Meaning of name of city	Let go. Desirable	Death. Myrrh	Tower. Marriage	Never tiring of sacrifice	Escaping one's remnant	Brotherly love	People's rights
Title	Patient Church	Persecuted Church	Polluted Church	Paganized Church	Peculiar Church	Pure Church	Passive Church
Church Age	First century	A.D. 100–316	316–500	500–1500	1500–1750	1750–1910	1910–?
Description of church	Holds 7 stars, walks in midst 7 lampstands	First and Last, was dead and is alive	Has sharp sword with 2 edges	Son of God, eyes like fire, feet like bronze	Has 7 Spirits of God and 7 stars	Holy, true, has key of David, opens and closes	Amen, faithful and true witness, beginning of the Creation of God
Positive	Works, toil, patience	Tribulation, apparent poverty, true wealth	Hold fast Name of Christ, did not deny faith	Love, faith, ministry, patience	Reputation of being alive	Set before thee an open door	
Negative	Left first love		Teaching of Balaam, fornication, Nicolatians	Jezebel	But really dead		Lukewarm, wretched, miserable, poor, blind, naked
Instructions to church	Remember, repent, do the first works	Be faithful unto death	Repent or I will come quickly and make war	Judge Jezebel	Be watchful, strengthen what remains, remember, hold fast, repent	Hold fast	Be zealous, repent, allow Christ in
Promise	Eat of Tree of Life	Not hurt in 2nd death	Hidden manna, white stone	Power over nations, Morning Star	White raiment, confessed before Father	Pillar in temple, new names	Right to reign

1. The parable of the sower. **Ephesus:** the apostolic age; the beginning with failure—leaving the first love.
2. The parable of the evil seed. **Smyrna:** meaning bitterness; the enemy revealed.
3. The parable of the mustard seed. **Pergamos:** meaning "high tower" and "twice married." The professing church becomes big, a state institution under Constantine the Great. The big tree and the unclean birds (nations) find shelter there.
4. The parable of the leaven. **Thyatira:** the one who sacrifices; Rome and her abominations; the woman Jezebel, the harlot, corresponds to the woman in the parable of the leaven.
5. The parable of the treasure hid. **Sardia:**

the Reformation Age; having a name to live, but being dead, and a remnant there; Israel, dead, but belonging to Him who has purchased the field.

6. The parable of the pearl. **Philadelphia:** the church—the one pearl; the one body of Christ and the removal of the church to be with Him.
7. The parable of the dragnet. **Laodicea:** judgment—"I will spew thee out of my mouth."

Similarly, Dwight Pentecost also sees a relationship between the seven churches and seven kingdom parables. In both cases he sees a similar development of evil as reflected in the chart below.

In both cases, one could argue that some parables or epistles may overlap, but the major theme illustrates the course of this present age. As one surveys the history of these last two millennia, it is possible to see how these prophetic allusions may have been fulfilled. God's final judgment is all that remains to be fulfilled in this age.

See also KINGDOM, PARABLES OF THE; REVELATION, INTERPRETIVE VIEWS OF; REVELATION, STRUCTURE OF.

Elmer Towns

A. C. Gaebelein, *The Gospel of Matthew: An Exposition* (New York: Publication Office, Our Hope, 1910); J. Dwight Pentecost, *Things to Come* (Grand Rapids: Zondervan, 1958); Walter Scott, *Exposition of the Revelation of Jesus Christ and Prophetic Outlines* (London: Pickering & Inglis, n.d.); W. Graham Scroggie, *Prophecy and History* (London: Marshall, Morgan & Scott, n.d.); John F. Walvoord, *Matthew: Thy Kingdom Come* (Chicago: Moody Press, 1974).

PROPHECY, DOUBLE FULFILLMENT OF

Generally prophecy of Scripture is viewed as referring to a specific future event. Messianic prophecies were fulfilled in the life, death, and resurrection of Jesus, while end-time prophecies speak of those things that will happen in relationship to the coming of Jesus Christ at His advent. At times, however, a given prophecy may have reference to more than one future event. When this is the case, the term often used to describe this phenomenon is *double fulfillment* or *double reference*. Other terms, dependent on the particulars, might be *multiple fulfillment,* with more than two instances in view, or *progressive fulfillment*, indicating that the

Matt. 13	Rev. 2–3	Meaning of the name	Approximate dates	Characteristics
Sower	Ephesus	Desired	Pentecost to A.D. 100	Time of sowing, organization, and evangelism
Wheat and tares	Smyrna	Myrrh	Nero to A.D. 300	Persecution. Enemy revealed
Mustard seed	Pergamos	Thoroughly married	300 to 800	Worldly alliance. Great external growth
Leaven	Thyatira	Continual sacrifice	800 to 1517	Papal domination. Doctrinal corruption
Treasure hid	Sardis	Those escaping	Reformation	Empty profession. Rise of the state church
Pearl	Philadelphia	Brotherly love	Last days	True church of the last days
Dragnet	Laodicea	People ruling	Last days	Apostasy

prophecy is not static but finds fulfillment in a succession of events. This should be distinguished from *typology*, in which points of commonalty between Old Testament events and symbols illustrate or foreshadow New Testament truths. For example, there are personality or spiritual characteristics in the life of Joseph that are found in our Lord; these may be viewed as types. Or aspects of the tabernacle or sacrifices may refer to the salvation work of Christ; these are also types. But when the prophecy and its fulfillments have direct connection between two events and they are understood as being one reality, then it is double fulfillment.

Double fulfillment, in specific, relates to a prophecy that has two stages of fulfillment in one prophetic statement, one near and one remote. Roman Catholic theologians have called this *compenetratation*, when an Old Testament more immediate meaning and the New Testament remote meaning so compenetrate that the passage at the same time and in the same words refers to the near and the remote New Testament meaning. Bernard Ramm explains, "Double reference is characteristic of all great literature, and the Bible being great literature contains it. Hence deeply buried in the events, persons, and words of the Old Testament are references to events, person, and words of the New Testament. An Old Testament prophecy may find a fulfillment in a pre-Christian event and later in the Christian period, such as the astonishment of the Jews (Hab.1:5–6), which was fulfilled in the Old Testament with the destructive armies of the Chaldeans and in the New Testament with the salvation of the Gentiles" (Ramm, 234).

An example of this type of fulfillment might be the prophecy of Daniel concerning the one who would desecrate the temple by an offering, possibly fulfilled in the unsuccessful attempt of Antiochus the Great or by the desecration by Titus at the fall of Jerusalem, but the epitome of this fulfillment will be the desecration by the Beast of the book of Revelation during the Tribulation period.

The idea of a prophecy having more than one dimension to its fulfillment may be foreign to the modern observer. The prophets saw no difficulty in a particular prophecy having different aspects to its fulfillment or in the fulfillments being separated by large spans of time. "They saw the future rather in space than in time; the whole, therefore, appears foreshortened; and perspective, rather than actual distance, is regarded. They seem often to speak of future things as a common observer would describe the stars, grouping them as they appear, and not according to their true positions" (Angus and Green; quoted in Pentecost, 46).

The prophet not only had a message for his own day but also for the future. The two events could be brought together into the scope of one prophecy due to this. Horne says, "The same prophecies frequently have a double meaning, and refer to different events, the one near, the other remote; the one temporal, the other spiritual or perhaps eternal. The prophets thus having several events in view, their expressions may be partly applicable to one, and partly to another, and it is not always easy to make the transitions. What has not been fulfilled in the first, we must apply to the second; and what has already been fulfilled, may often be considered as typical of what remains to be accomplished" (Horne, I:390).

Let me hasten to add that when I say double fulfillment, this is not the same as double meaning. The meaning includes the elements that make up the multiple fulfillment, though they might not be obvious to the ones who received the first fulfillment. God's meaning included other aspects that were not originally understood.

Pentecost believes that it was the purpose of God in giving this near and remote view to assure, by the fulfilling of the one, the ultimate fulfillment of the other. He quotes Girdlestone, "Yet another provision was made to confirm men's faith in utterances which had regard to the far future. It frequently happened that prophets who had to speak of such things were also commissioned to predict other things which would shortly come to pass; and the verification of these latter predictions in their own day and generation justified men in believing the other utterances which pointed to a more distant time. The one was practically a 'sign' of the other, and if the one proved true the other might be trusted. Thus the birth of Isaac under the most unlikely circumstances would help Abraham to believe that in his seed all the families of the earth should be blessed" (Girdlestone, 21).

Double fulfillment must be especially seen in light of the promises of God. Often these promises specify more than one historical reference, capable of multiple partial fulfillments before culminating in the final realization of the commitment God has made. Beecher explains this sense of God's promise: "God gave a promise to Abraham, and through him to mankind; a promise eternally fulfilled and fulfilling in the history of Israel; and chiefly fulfilled in Jesus Christ, he being that which is principle in the history of Israel" (Beecher, 163). The fulfillments to and through Isaac, Jacob, Joseph, David, and Israel only receive a limited fulfillment. Jesus Christ is the primary fulfillment through whom, then, the Gentiles would also be included in the blessing of God.

See also PROPHECY, LITERAL INTERPRETATION OF.

H. Wayne House

R. B. Girdlestone, *The Grammar of Prophecy* (London: Eyre and Spottiswoode, 1901); Thomas Hartwell Horne, *An Introduction to the Critical Study and Knowledge of the Holy Scriptures,* 2 vols. (New York: Robert Carter and Brothers, 1859); Elliott E. Johnson, *Expository Hermeneutics: An Introduction* (Grand Rapids: Zondervan, 1990); J. Dwight Pentecost, *Things to Come* (Grand Rapids: Zondervan, 1958); Bernard Ramm, *Protestant Biblical Interpretation* (Boston: W. A. Wilde Company, 1956).

PROPHECY, LITERAL INTERPRETATION OF

The major difference between the various millennial positions in the prophetic debate and in the differing interpretations of the book of Revelation is in hermeneutical approach. Ramm in his discussion on the interpretation of prophecy notes, "The real issue in prophetic interpretation among evangelicals is this: Can prophetic literature be interpreted by the general method of grammatical exegesis, or is some special principle necessary?" Similarly, Allis, an amillennialist, acknowledges this as a fundamental issue relating to the difference between his views and those of premillennial teachers. He writes, "One of the most marked features of Premillennialism in all its forms is the emphasis which it places on the literal interpretation of Scripture. It is the insistent claim of its advocates that only when interpreted literally is the Bible interpreted truly; and they denounce as 'spiritualizers' or 'allegorizers' those who do not interpret the Bible with the same degree of literalness as they do. None have made this charge more pointedly than the Dispensationalist. The question of literal verses figurative interpretation is, therefore, one which has to be faced at the very outset."

In the field of prophecy, the two basic approaches to interpreting Scripture are identified as the literal, or historical-grammatical, approach and the allegorical, or mystical or spiritual, approach.

"Allegorical interpretation believes that beneath the letter (*rhete*) or the obvious (*phanera*) is the real meaning (*hyponoia*) of the passage. Allegory is defined by some as an extended metaphor. There is a literary allegory which is intentionally constructed by the author to tell a message under historical form. . . . But if we presume that the document has a secret meaning (*hyponoia*) and there are no clues concerning the hidden meaning, interpretation is difficult. In fact, the basic problem is to determine if the passage has such a meaning at all. The further problem arises whether the secret meaning was in the mind of the original writer or something found there by the interpreter. If there are no clues, hints, connections, or associations which indicate that the record is an allegory, and what the allegory intends to teach, we are on very uncertain grounds" (Ramm).

Concerning the other approach to the interpretation of prophecy, Pentecost writes, "The literal method of interpretation is that method that gives to each word the same exact basic meaning it would have in normal, ordinary, customary usage, whether employed in writing, speaking or thinking. It is called the grammatical-historical method to emphasize the fact that the meaning is to be determined by both grammatical and historical considerations."

The tendency of allegorical interpretation is to try to make the Bible say something that it may or may not otherwise state. Many conservative Bible scholars will interpret the Scriptures literally until they come to a prophetic passage. Then they begin to interpret it allegorically, giving undue consideration to names, numbers, and hidden meanings of symbols. These are important considerations as God will sometimes use these to teach important truth, but we should not allow this emphasis to destroy the use of a consistent, literal interpretation of Bible prophecy. This literal approach to interpreting prophecy is the basis of the premillennial interpretation.

According to amillennial writer Hamilton, "Now we must frankly admit that a literal interpretation of the Old Testament prophecies gives us just such a picture of an earthly reign of the Messiah as the premillennialist pictures. That was the kind of a messianic kingdom that the Jews of the time of Christ were looking for, on the basis of a literal interpretation of the Old Testament promises. That was the kind of kingdom that the Sadducees were talking about when they ridiculed the idea of the resurrection of the body, drawing from our Lord the clearest statement of the characteristics of the future age that we have in the New Testament, when He told them that they erred 'not knowing the Scriptures nor the power of God' (Matt. 22:29) . . . the Jews were looking for just such a kingdom as that expected by those premillennialists who speak of the Jews holding a preeminent place in an earthly Jewish kingdom as that expected by those premillennialists who speak of the Jews holding a preeminent place in an earthly Jewish kingdom to be set up by the Messiah in Jerusalem."

The Bible was revealed, inspired, and written by the ordinary use of words and thoughts that were expressed in the language of the day. Therefore, it is expected that Scripture will be interpreted by the same method it was given. Most contemporary Bible students follow the advice of Cooper in his "golden rule of interpretation." When the plain sense of Scripture makes common sense, seek no other sense, but take every word at its primary literal meaning unless the facts of the immediate context clearly indicate otherwise.

This statement is popular and will usually guide the Bible student into a correct understanding of Scripture. However, be careful of the crack in the door that allows for some other form of interpretation when the student gets stuck on a difficult passage. If we allow even one verse to be interpreted allegorically, the whole argument breaks down. When we come to metaphors, symbols and figures of speech, we must be consistent in applying the literal method of interpretation. We must interpret according to the literal meaning in the mind of the author and never seek to read any other meaning into a passage. This is more than an attitude or a philosophy, it is a principle of interpretation. Stevens calls it a law. "It is reasonable to suppose that there is a method of interpreting God's Word that makes the Bible harmonious and produces unity the world over among those who read and believe the same Book. There are certain laws peculiar to various fields of operation. Unless these laws are adhered to, no knowledge can be gained. . . . The Bible has its own laws set forth clear and unmistakable. To follow these laws is to behold the unsullied light of the truth of God. When we interpret the Bible in the light of itself, we recognize its sufficiency; we discover its divinity; we become acquainted with its mighty power."

The literal method of interpretation is an attempt to give the same meaning to a word as the author who wrote the passage. This means we do not try to think up an interpretation for the book of Daniel, but to seek the author's meaning of words and passages. By literal interpretation we mean the normal meaning of words and terms. Obviously, when Jesus is called the Lamb in the Bible, the writer does not mean Jesus had four legs and was covered with wool. *Lamb* in this case is a figure of speech and must be interpreted with the meaning John the Baptist had in mind when he said, "Behold, the Lamb of God" (John 1:29, 36). John the Baptist meant that Jesus was the fulfillment of the typical paschal lamb in the Passover supper. This literal approach is the most secure method of determining what God intended to say. It simply asks, In the light of the historical context of this passage and the basic rules of grammar as we understand them, what was the writer saying? But since all Scripture has dual authorship (God and human) we must seek the mind of both authors in interpreting Scripture.

Symbols are an important part of the prophetic Scriptures, but the Christian does not have to rely upon imagination to interpret them. The Bible often reveals the meaning of a symbol within the context of the passage. This is illustrated in the first chapter of Revelation. The symbols of stars and candlesticks are used, and they are identified as the churches and messengers of the seven churches in Asia (Rev. 1:20). Sometimes a parallel passage can be used to determine the divine interpretation of a symbol otherwise not understood. This can be illustrated by comparing parallel accounts of the same discussion between Jesus and the Pharisees concerning the casting out of demons. According to Luke, Jesus spoke of casting out demons with the finger of God (Luke 11:20). Comparing Matthew's record of the same discussion, it becomes obvious that the "finger of God" is symbolic of the Holy Spirit (Matt. 12:28).

One of the implications of literal interpretation is that the author has a literal meaning in mind, and only one meaning, for a word or passage. However, there is one place where it seems the writer has a double meaning. This is when a prophecy has a double fulfillment. The author, by control of the Holy Spirit, makes a prediction that has two fulfillments.

When Isaiah predicted the Messiah would be born of a virgin (Isa. 7:14), he spoke to an immediate setting (Isa. 7:1–14), but he also predicted the birth of Christ (Matt. 1:21–22). This is not speculation—Matthew says as much. The double fulfillment is also seen when Joel predicted, "I will pour out my spirit upon all flesh" (Joel 2:28). This applies to the outpouring of the Holy Spirit on the Day of Pentecost (Acts 2:16–21) and to the end times. The problem of double fulfillment is answered in that the author had one meaning in mind, which was to communicate that one prophecy could have two literal fulfillments. The writer was not being double-minded but was further revealing the supernatural nature of Scripture. This does not question the literal method of interpretation, but supports it.

See also HERMENEUTICS, CONTEMPORARY BIBLICAL.

Elmer L. Towns

Oswald T. Allis, *Prophecy and the Church* (Philadelphia: Presbyterian and Reformed Publishing Co., 1945); David L. Cooper, cited by Tim LaHaye, *How to Study the Bible for Yourself* (Eugene, Oreg.: Harvest House, 1976); Floyd E. Hamilton, *The Basics of Premillennial Faith* (Grand Rapids: Eerdmans, 1942); J. Dwight Pentecost, *Things to Come* (Grand Rapids: Zondervan, 1958); Bernard Ramm, *Protestant Biblical Interpretation* (Grand Rapids: Baker, 1974); Charles H. Stevens, "How Shall We Interpret the Bible?" in *The Sure Word of Prophecy*, ed. John W. Bradbury (New York: Revell, 1943).

PSALMS, ESCHATOLOGY OF

The Psalms is a collection of hymns of praise and worship that were widely used by Israel in their temple and synagogues. The Psalms have a universal quality that come from the individual personalities of those who wrote them. Their motivation for writing was the inherent desire to respond to the living God by expressing their deepest feelings. The book of Psalms is therefore applicable in every age.

The Psalms were written by different authors and at different time periods. David is recognized as the author of seventy-three psalms; Solomon, two; the sons of Korah, twelve; Asaph, twelve; Heman, one; Ethan, one; and Moses, one. The remaining psalms specify no authors. The majority of psalms were written in the tenth century B.C. during the time of David and Solomon. The period of time covered by all of the psalms extends from Moses to the return from captivity.

Although the book is the recorded prayers, experiences, and worship of the psalmists, they contain prophetic expectations of the future. Psalmic themes include: the surety of God's loving care and faithfulness (12:7; 27:1–4; 100; 102:25–28); God's judgment on the wicked (1:1–6; 6:8–10; 125; 145:1–21; 147:6); God's reward for the righteousness (1:1–6; 15:1–5; 18:1–50; 25:1–22; 73:24; 121:1–8).

The distinctly messianic psalms are 2, 16, 22, 40, 45, 69, 72, 89, 110, and 118. Then there are some psalms that are not specifically included in the messianic list but contain messianic references.

Psalms 96–99 refer to the enthronement of the King; 2:1–21 describes God's purpose to put His Son as King on Mount Zion; 8:1–4 contrasts human triviality against the supernatural work of creation; 8:5–8 contrasts Christ's earthly existence with the glory that was His upon His return to heaven; 9:1–20 foresees the coming rule of Christ; 10:1–18 predicts the future reign of Christ on the earth; 14:7 envisions the restoration of Israel at the time of the Second Coming; 16:1–11 expresses faith in the fact of the resurrection of those who died in their faith; 24:1–10 anticipates the Lord's coming to claim the earth at His Second Coming; 45:6–7 refers to the everlasting throne of David; 46:4–10 looks to Christ's Second Coming when wars shall end and He shall be exalted among the nations; 72:1–20 looks forward to Christ's reign in the millennium and finally His eternal reign; 78:2 foretells of the coming Messiah; 89:1–37 expresses confirmation that the Davidic covenant will continue forever; 96:1–13 foresees the time when the Lord reigns over the earth and judges the people with justice; 97:1–12 the millennial reign; 98:1–9 when Christ judges the world in righteousness and justice; 99:1–9 pictures Christ as King in Zion; 102:12–28 the future kingdom on the earth; 105:5–11 confirmation of the eternal state of the Abrahamic covenant; 110:1–7 references Christ as King and the beginning of the millennial kingdom; 118:2–29 Christ, once rejected as king will come again as the King of Kings and exercise His authority over the whole earth; 145:13–14 reassurance that the promises made by God will all be fulfilled, and He will possess His kingdom for all eternity.

See DAVIDIC COVENANT; PSALM 2; PSALM 8; PSALM 16; PSALM 22; PSALM 89; PSALM 110.

Rick Bowman

Merrill F. Unger, *Unger's Bible Dictionary* (Chicago: Moody Press, 1966); John F. Walvoord, *The Bible Prophecy Handbook* (Wheaton: Victor Books, 1990); John F. Walvoord and Roy B. Zuck, eds., *The Bible Knowledge Commentary* (Wheaton: Victor Books, 1985).

PSALM 2

Written by David (Acts 4:25), this indirectly messianic psalm describes royal activities in general. (Other royal psalms are 18, 20–21, 45, 72, 89, 101, 110, 132, and 144.) Psalm 2 describes a celebration at the coronation of the Davidic king despite opposition by rebellious people in surrounding territories. The general character of this psalm allows it to be applied to a variety of circumstances. The NT writers quote Psalm 2 (vv. 1–2 in Acts 4:25–26; v. 7 in Acts 13:33, Heb. 1:5 and 5:5; v. 9 in Rev. 2:26–27) and allude to it (Matt. 3:17, 17:5, 2 Peter 1:17, Rev. 12:5, 19:15) so often that its application to Jesus' messianic office and His expected return to rule in glory and power cannot be denied.

Acts 13:33 cites Psalm 2:7, "Thou art My Son. Today I have begotten Thee," in the context of Jesus' resurrection. The resurrected Messiah who will never die again is God's way of accomplishing the Davidic covenant promise to provide a ruler from David's seed who will sit on David's throne forever. The covenant mercies are sure (Acts 13:34 cites Isaiah 55:3, which in turn alludes to the Davidic covenant in 2 Sam. 7:12–16) because

Messiah will never see decay (Acts 13:35 cites Ps. 16:10). The father-son language of Psalm 2:7 is an adoption formula that legitimizes the right of a king to reign (cf. 2 Sam. 7:14 and 1 Chron. 28:6). By His resurrection and exaltation, Messiah Jesus is declared to be the legitimate Davidic ruler (cf. Rom. 1:4).

Whereas Hebrews 1:5 pairs Psalm 2:7 with 2 Samuel 7:14 to highlight Messiah's right to rule, Hebrews 5:5–6 pairs Psalm 2:7 with Psalm 110:4 (another royal psalm) to emphasize Messiah's mediatorial role. Jesus' dual role as the king-priest fits consistently with the language of Psalm 2. Furthermore, the scenario that develops from this psalm understood with its NT citations is premillennial, although Psalm 2 does not speak of Messiah going away and returning. Based on the secure Davidic promises, God's people have longed for a time when a ruler from David's lineage will bring in an era of peace and prosperity of universal proportions (Ps. 2:8: "nations . . . the ends of the earth"; cf. Isa. 2:2–4, 9:2–7, Jer. 23:5–6, 33:14–16, Ezek. 37:24–28). When Messiah comes to sit on Zion's hill (Ps. 2:6), He will extend His rule to the ends of the earth by subjugating all rebellious nations (2:9: "break them . . . dash them in pieces"; cf. Rev. 19:15). In the meantime, the nations are admonished to put their trust in or, take refuge in Him (Ps. 2:12) so that they will not experience His wrath. Those who have come to God by the mediatorship of Jesus will be safe when He comes as King Jesus.

Floyd S. Elmore

Derek Kidner, *Psalms 1–72* (Downers Grove, Ill.: InterVarsity Press, 1973); Allen P. Ross, "Psalms" in *The Bible Knowledge Commentary* (Wheaton: Scripture Press, 1985); Willem A. VanGemeren, "Psalms" in *The Expositor's Bible Commentary*, vol. 5 (Grand Rapids: Zondervan, 1991).

PSALM 8

Psalm 8 is a hymn of praise that exalts the Lord's character through His majestic creative abilities and product. The psalm possesses the normal motifs of this kind of hymn:

1. The call to praise (8:1)
2. The reasons to praise (8:1–8)
3. The renewed call to praise (8:9)

Other psalms using creation as a key component include Psalms 19, 29, 104, 139 and 148.

The essence of Psalm 8 lies in the fact that the glorious Lord of heaven whose name is excellent should graciously use humankind in the dominion of the earth. Further, the psalm reveals the still existing dignity of fallen humankind in its role as God's representative on earth. God's use of frail humanity in accomplishing His purposes also displays God's condescension, another quality of God that the psalmist praises.

Authorship is ascribed to David as seen in verse 1 of the Hebrew text (the title section in English Bibles), "for the choir director; upon the gittite. A psalm of David." The dating of the psalm has been difficult for scholars as the creation motif of the psalm could have been employed by David anytime during his tenure as a writer. Additionally, the psalm itself contains no historical or situational citations helpful in pinpointing an exact date. Of note is the required musical accompaniment for the psalm. The Hebrew term translated "gittite" refers to a lyre, a small stringed harp that provided melody for the psalm/hymn. Since the primary content of the psalm (creation) is so central to the Israelite tradition, there would have been many occasions when Psalm 8 would be appropriate.

The Call to Praise (8:1)

The first two lines of verse 1 in English versions are an exclamation of praise to the Lord for His magnificent display of His character as revealed in His creation and His condescension. The psalmist immediately employs the Hebrew term YHWH (Jehovah) to emphatically identify the recipient of praise by His special covenantal name. Further, David ascribes to YHWH His title "Lord," an important reminder that He indeed is our Lord (Heb. *Adonai*, "sovereign, master, lord").

The Reasons to Praise (8:1–8)

The last line of verse 1 and all of verse 2 introduces the two main reasons to praise YHWH: His creation (8:1) and His condescension to include fallen humanity (8:2).

The expansion of these two themes comprises the remainder of this section dealing with the reasons to praise YHWH. After first observing the great work of God seen in His creation (v. 3), the psalmist next (v. 4) expresses amazement that humankind has been given the awesome responsibility over the creation! David's amazement is captured in his use of the rhetorical question, "What is man . . . ?" Verse 5 answers this question by stating that humankind was created by God to serve with power and dignity. Humanity was made a little lower than *God* (Heb. *elohim*, "God or mighty ones"). Some translations render this "angels." Though the term *elohim* could refer to angels, its predominant use in the Old Testament is "God," which seems best here so to display the idea that humankind was created as God's representative to rule over His creation and is subordinate only to God Himself in the created order. Further, humankind was crowned with "glory" (importance) and "majesty" (honor).

In verses 6–8, David marvels that the author of such a vast creation should so condescend by elevating such relatively insignificant creatures as humans over all the rest of His earthly creation. These verses clearly refer to God's original mandate given to the original couple: subdue and rule over (Gen. 1:26–28). We are still sovereignly commanded by God to rule over the works of His hands (Ps. 8:6).

The Renewal Call to Praise (8:9)

The psalm closes with the same expression of praise for God's majestic character with which it began. This verse provides the reader with a final reminder that our master, YHWH Himself, has graciously included humankind in the dominion of the earth—a fact that should invoke the whole world to extol the majestic name of God!

Robert G. Anderson Jr.

Peter C. Craigie, *Word Biblical Commentary* (Waco: Word Publishers, 1983); Donald R. Glenn, *Walvoord: A Tribute*, ed. Donald K. Campbell (Chicago: Moody Press, 1982); Allen P. Ross, *The Bible Knowledge Commentary*, eds. John F. Walvoord and Roy B. Zuck (Wheaton: Victor Books, 1985); Leopold Sabourin, S. J., *The Psalms: Their Origin and Meaning* (New York: Alba House, 1974); Claus Westermann, *Praise and Lament in the Psalms* (Atlanta: John Knox Press, 1981).

PSALM 16 PROPHECIES

Psalm 16 contains the most important prophecy of the resurrection of Christ in the Old Testament. It is one of the three passages (together with Psalm 22 and Isaiah 53) that predict more about the death and resurrection of the Messiah than anywhere else in the Hebrew Scriptures. The significance of Psalm 16 becomes apparent in light of the fact that the two major apostles, Peter and Paul, both utilized this passage in their messages to Jewish audiences, in Acts 2 and 13, to prove that the Messiah had to rise from the dead. In fact, this is the main passage the apostles use from the Old Testament to prove the resurrection of the Messiah. It is difficult, then, to overestimate the importance of this psalm in the original proclamation of the Gospel.

The argument by Peter in Acts 2 on the Day of Pentecost was that King David prophesied that the "Holy One" (*Chasid*, the sanctified one) would not see corruption. "Whom God hath raised up, having loosed the pains of death: because it was not possible that he should be holden of it. For David speaketh concerning him, I foresaw the Lord always before my face, for he is on my right hand, that I should not be moved: Therefore did my heart rejoice, and my tongue was glad; moreover also my flesh shall rest in hope: Because thou wilt not leave my soul in hell, neither wilt thou suffer thine Holy One to see corruption. Thou hast made known to me the ways of life; thou shalt make me full of joy with thy countenance." (Acts 2:24–32 KJV).

Since David had been dead for a thousand years, his body had long since been corrupted, and the memorial of the tomb of David was visible to Peter's listeners, it was clear that David could not have been prophesying about himself. Rather, David must have been prophesying about his future descendant, the Messiah. On the basis of this reasoning, Peter argued that the Messiah would die and would be buried. His soul would be in sheol and His body would be in the grave. However, before the body of the Holy One corrupted, He would see the path of life. Thus, not only would the Messiah be raised from the dead, the event would have to take place before the corruption of the body, or within a few days after entombment. This argument was so powerful that three thousand Jews received Christ that day, in part because of the force of this fulfilled prophecy.

The apostle Paul used Psalm 16 in a similar manner when he presented his evangelistic sermon in the synagogue in Pisidian Antioch: "Wherefore he saith also in another psalm, Thou shalt not suffer thine Holy One to see corruption. For David, after he had served his own generation by the will of God, fell on sleep, and was laid unto his fathers, and saw corruption: But he, whom God raised again, saw no corruption."

King David, he reasoned, long ago went to sleep (died) in his own generation, and his body saw corruption. But the Holy One, whom God would raise from the dead, would see no corruption. Thus, the Messiah had to rise from the dead before His body saw corruption, and this was fulfilled in Jesus, who arose on the third day (Acts 13:35–37).

It is eminently clear, then, that the apostles considered Psalm 16 absolutely central to the biblical proof that the Messiah had to be raised from the dead within days after His death and that Jesus Christ fulfilled this prophecy precisely.

The Resurrection Prophecy

The passage the apostles concentrate on in Psalm 16 is the section from verses 8–11, the last four verses of the psalm: "I have set the LORD always before me: because he is at my right hand, I shall not be moved. Therefore my heart is glad, and my glory rejoiceth: my flesh also shall rest in hope. For thou wilt not leave my soul in hell; neither wilt thou suffer thine Holy One to see corruption. Thou wilt shew me the path of life: in thy presence is fullness of joy; at thy right hand there are pleasures for evermore."

There are several key words in this segment of Psalm 16 that are essential to understanding the prophecy and how both Peter and Paul applied it to Christ.

My Flesh

The speaker is speaking as one who has died, and the flesh (v. 9) of the speaker rests in hope in the grave. What hope does the flesh have after physical death? Our natural senses only see the corruption of the flesh into the dust of the earth. There is not much hope in that. However, the Word of God promises a resurrection of the flesh from the dead. This is the basis of hope. The reason the speaker's flesh rests in hope is because the speaker believes in the promise of the Word of God that there will be a resurrection of the body (Job 19:26; Dan. 12:1–2). This is true of any believer, but the prophecy becomes more particular as it goes on because of the specified time factor of the resurrection.

My Soul in Hell

Not only is the flesh of the speaker seen to be in the grave, but the soul is described to be in hell (v. 10), or more particularly, in sheol. Hell is a poor translation of *sheol* because it has the connotation of being the abode only of the wicked dead souls. However, in the Old Testament circumstances, sheol was the abode of the souls of both the righteous and the wicked dead. This is intimated in the Old Testament and is clarified in the account given by the Lord in Luke 16. There, He describes both the righteous and the wicked dead as being in hades (the Greek equivalent of the Hebrew *sheol,* but separated by a great gulf fixed between them. The righteous poor man was on the bosom-of-Abraham side, while the wicked rich man was on the side where there was perpetual torment. The speaker rejoices that his soul will not be left in sheol.

Corruption

The key phrase in the entire passage is the declaration by the speaker that God would not allow the Holy One (*chasid*) to see corruption (*shachath*). While some translations render this as some kind of pit or grave, this does not fit the context, and the Septuagint translation of *diaphthoran*, which is reflected in the New Testament quotations, connotes the concept of physical corruption. Here, the reality that King David, the writer, is speaking prophetically of his great descendant, the Messiah, is driven home.

The Messiah, the *chasid* or "Holy One," would die. His body would be laid in the grave, but his flesh would rest in hope of the resurrection. His soul would descend to sheol, but would not be left there. In fact, his body would remain so little a time in the grave that it would not see corruption, would not decay.

Jewish burial custom did not then, nor does it now, utilize any embalming procedures in preparation of the dead. Therefore, physical corruption sets in very quickly, and the body begins to decay within a few days following death. For this prophecy to be fulfilled, then, the body of the speaker would have to be raised from the dead within a few days after his death, so that his body would not see corruption.

While all believers rest in the assurance that their bodies will be reunited with their souls in the resurrection of the dead, only the Messiah had the promise that His body would not be in the grave long enough to see corruption.

Path of life; In thy presence

Not only would the Messiah's dead body not see corruption, and not only would His soul be reunited with His body in resurrection by leaving sheol and finding the path of life (v. 11), but He would then be transferred from sheol to the presence of the Lord forever. Thus, the Messiah is the first human promised access to the presence of God in a resurrection body.

Before the death and resurrection of Christ, human souls were somewhat restricted in sheol, away from the direct presence of the Almighty in heaven. Their sins were covered, but had not actually been paid for by the blood of the Messiah. After the Lord died for our sins, and the one true sacrifice was finished, then He could take captivity captive (Eph. 4:8; Ps. 68:18), and carry the souls of the righteous from sheol to the third heaven, the abode of God.

Therefore, no human before Christ was permitted access into the presence of the Lord in heaven after death. However, when Christ died, accomplishing the complete atonement, then He as the first resurrected human could Himself ascend to the Father and transfer paradise from sheol to heaven. Now when believers die, their souls do not go to sheol, but rather directly to heaven, to be absent from the body and to be present with the Lord (2 Cor. 5:8). The wicked dead, though, still go to sheol, the place of torment, awaiting the Great White Throne judgment described in Revelation 20.

No wonder the apostles considered Psalm 16 so crucial to the presentation of the Gospel. In it are contained the promises related to the specific and unique resurrection of the Messiah Himself and its implications with regard to the resurrection of believers of all ages.

See also RESURRECTIONS, VARIOUS.

Thomas S. McCall

PSALM 22

This psalm is usually classified as lament in verses 1–21 and in verses 22–31 as praise and thanksgiving. Some have also argued that this is a royal psalm (see Ps. 89) because of the humiliation of the king and his restoration (A. A. Anderson, 1:184). However, the most debated aspect of this psalm is how to characterize its nature. How does this psalm relate to Christ? There have been five basic views: (1) It relates only to the person of David. It does not apply to Christ. (2) The national approach would refer the details of the psalm to the nation of Israel, particularly in the exile. This interpretation would not connect it with Christ. (3) The ideal interpretation claims that the psalm is not the record of any one individual but describes the experience of the ideal righteous person.

Therefore, this can be applied to Christ. (4) The predictive approach regards the entire psalm to be prophetic about Christ Himself. Therefore, the author was conscious that he was prophesying about Christ. (5) The typical, prophetically messianic approach understands this psalm to be typological of the death of Christ. "Gospel writers also saw connections between some of the words in this psalm (vv. 8, 16, 18) and other events in Christ's Passion. Also Hebrews 2:12 quotes Psalm 22:22" (Ross, 809). Thus David used many figurative terms to portray his sufferings, but these poetic words became literally true of the sufferings of Jesus Christ. The last two interpretative views present the best approaches and the typico-prophetic view seems to be the strongest.

The contribution that this psalm gives to our understanding of the future kingdom is found in verses 27–31. In the theocratic kingdom we see all the ends of the earth and all the families of the nations turning to the Lord in worship and the Lord and His kingdom ruling over the nations. Those Gentiles who were converted out of all the nations (Rom. 11:25; Rev. 5:9) remember and worship the Lord and God establishes a world government (Dan. 7:27; Rev. 2:26–27, 19:15) under Christ (Peters, 1:536, 3:215). God also promises a posterity that will testify to the generations to come the righteousness that God has performed.

See also THEOCRATIC KINGDOM.

Steve P. Sullivan

A. A. Anderson, "The Book of Psalms" *in The New Century Bible Commentary* (Grand Rapids: Eerdmans, 1981), 1:184–95; E. W. Hengstenberg, *Commentary of the Psalms* (Edinburgh: T & T Clark, 1858), 1:355–97, *Christology of the Old Testament* (Grand Rapids: Kregel, 1970), 78–90; H. C. Leupold, *Exposition of the Psalms* (Grand Rapids: Baker, 1969); George N. H. Peters, *The Theocratic Kingdom*, 3 vols. (Grand Rapids: Kregel, 1978), 1:478, 536, 3:215; Allen P. Ross, "Psalms" in *The Biblical Knowledge Commentary*, eds. John F. Walvoord and Roy B. Zuck (Wheaton: Victor Books, 1985) 1:809–11.

PSALM 89

The author of Psalm 89 is Ethan, who, according to 1 Chronicles 6:44 and 15:17, 19, was appointed as one of the leaders of the temple music by David. Some believe that Ethan's name was changed to Jeduthun because Jeduthun is associated with the families of musicians Asaph and Heman, whom David appointed for music leadership (see 1 Chron. 25:1, 3, 6). As far as we know Ethan contributes only one psalm to the collection found in Holy Scripture.

This psalm is usually called a royal psalm or a royal lament psalm. A royal psalm brings to the foreground the anointed king, some high point in the career of the monarch, or some aspect of the Davidic covenant. Psalm 89 is a prayer that God will honor the Davidic covenant; however, it is set in the context of a lament (vv. 38–51). The exact occasion of the psalm is unknown. The context conveys the setting where the affliction and defeat of David or the anointed Davidic king caused Ethan to pray that the Lord would remember His covenant to David and end the disaster.

The outline of the Psalm is as follows:

- I. Introduction: Praise to the Lord for His faithfulness and lovingkindness in establishing the covenant (vv. 1–4)
- II. The Character of the Covenant God: Praise the character of the Lord who has established the Davidic covenant (vv. 5–18)
- III. The Remembrance of the Covenant Promise: The promise of the Davidic covenant recited (vv. 19–37)
  - A. The promise detailed (vv. 19–29)
  - B. The provisions are certain even if discipline is needed (vv. 30–34)
  - C. The permanence of the covenant (vv. 35–37)
- IV. The Lament Concerning the Covenant: The lament over the affliction and defeat of the king and his concern over the promises of the Davidic covenant (vv. 38–51)
- V. Doxology: The closing praise (v. 52)

The heart of the psalm and its contribution to eschatology is in verses 19–37. Here we have another confirmation of the Davidic covenant, which is detailed in 2 Samuel 7 and 1 Chronicles 17. Notice the provisions of the Davidic covenant affirmed by Psalm 89.

1. David's descendants will be established forever (vv. 4, 29, 36).

2. The throne of David will be established forever—to all generations (v. 4), as the days of heaven (v. 29), as the sun before Me (v. 36), like the moon, and the witness in the sky is faithful (v. 37). This promise gives David's descendants the right to rule over the kingdom.

3. This eternal covenant is immutable. The word "forever" is used to describe parts of the promises of the covenant (vv. 4, 28–29, 36–37). The psalmist warns in verses 30–32 that if any individual in the Davidic line is disobedient they will be disciplined and could lose their personal and individual benefits of the covenant. But, in verses 33–37, the psalmist reassures the unconditionality of the covenant. Even this disobedience cannot break off or violate the covenant. This is a powerful statement. If the descendants of David had yielded obedience, David's throne would never have been vacated until the Seed, Jesus Christ, came. The unconditional promise is not that there must be someone always ruling on the Davidic throne, but that the "the lineage, royal prerogative, and right to the throne be preserved and *never lost*, even in sin, captivity and dispersion" (Walvoord, 201).

The line continued until Jesus of Nazareth appeared and He was declared *the* Seed of the Davidic covenant (Luke 1:26–33). At His death the line came to an end. But in His resurrection Jesus succeeds Himself. In His resurrection the words of 2 Samuel 7:14 and Psalm 2:7 (cp. Ps. 89:24–27) are realized in Him (Acts 13:30–37; Heb.1:5; 5:5). "He who is the eternal Son of God (as the second member of the Holy Trinity), is the adopted royal Son of God (in fulfillment of the Davidic covenant)" (Allen, 72). He waits at the right hand of His Father for the proper time to come again and establish His kingdom and fulfill the Davidic covenant (Rev. 20:1–6). The plain grammatical sense of the promises of the Davidic covenant indicate that this covenant must be fulfilled by a visible, external kingdom that embraces spiritual and divine things (Peters, 1:343–44). The Davidic covenant was not fulfilled in the Old Testament nor is it being fulfilled now in this present age (Benware, 61–67). God will fulfill His covenant to national Israel through Jesus Christ at the Second Coming in the millennial (messianic) kingdom. The second phase of the kingdom will have an eternal duration in the new heavens and the new earth (1 Cor. 15:24; Rev. 20–22).

See also DAVIDIC COVENANT.

Steve P. Sullivan

Ronald B. Allen, "Evidence from Psalm 89" in *A Case For Premillennialism,* eds. Donald K. Campbell and Jeffrey L. Townsend (Chicago: Moody Press, 1992), 55–77; Paul N. Benware, *Understanding End Times Prophecy* (Chicago: Moody Press, 1995); Walter C. Kaiser Jr., *Toward and Old Testament Theology* (Grand Rapids: Zondervan, 1978), 143–64; J. Dwight Pentecost, *Things to Come* (Grand Rapids: Zondervan, 1958), 100–115; George N. H. Peters, *The Theocratic Kingdom,* 3 vols. (Grand Rapids: Kregel, 1978), 1:313–19, 342–51; John F. Walvoord, *The Millennial Kingdom* (Grand Rapids: Zondervan, 1959), 194–207.

PSALM 110

Psalm 110 prophesies the ministry of a waiting King-Priest after the pattern of Melchizedek (v. 4), who from heaven (v. 1) directs affairs on a hostile earth (v. 2) mediately through His army of volunteer priests (v. 3). The time of His waiting in heaven will come to a close at the Battle of Armageddon when He returns to earth to shatter kings in the day of His wrath (v. 5). The enemies are judged (v. 6), and He receives a final exaltation (v. 7) that paves the way for His being seated on the throne of David to rule directly on the earth in the promised millennial kingdom.

The Unity of the Psalm

There are two prevailing themes to this psalm: king and priest. Some have seen these as unrelated ministries: the kingly as Davidic, the priestly as Melchizedekian. However, the psalm displays an obvious unity and suggests that these two ministries are more closely related. An understanding of the structure of the psalm helps in the interpretation. One approach is to see millennial-reign themes in the first section and Second Advent themes in the second, with the present high priestly ministry of Christ in between. In an attempt to understand the psalm as a whole, reformed theologians and progressive dispensationalists suggest that the psalm reflects not only the Davidic covenant, but also David as a Melchizedekian King-Priest.

Central Message of the Psalm

David is allowed to see a prophetic vision of how the Messiah will begin His reign from Zion. This reign will be mediated through volunteer people carrying out His orders in the midst of the Messiah's enemies while He is seated in heaven. The reign will then continue to a time when Messiah will act as a Melchizedekian priest leading the armies of the Lord in a holy war until His enemies are defeated and He is victorious.

The outline of the psalm is as follows:

I. The Oracle of the Lord for David: The Messiah will begin His reign from heaven through holy warriors (vv. 1–3)
   A. David's Lord is exalted to a heavenly throne until, after the defeat of His enemies, it can be established on earth (v. 1)
   B. Jehovah begins the Messiah's reign in Zion even in the midst of His enemies (v. 2)
   C. Jehovah promises that His people will offer themselves as free-will offerings to the Messiah in holy array (v. 3)

II. The Oath of the Lord for the Messiah: The Messiah will establish His reign on earth through holy war (v. 4–7)
   A. Jehovah swears to make the Messiah a priest after the pattern of the "holy-war" priest Melchizedek (v. 4)
   B. The Messiah, acting as a "holy-war" priest, assures His troops that Jehovah will be their strength, shattering kings in the day of His wrath (v. 5)
   C. Jehovah will utterly destroy all those who oppose Him (v. 6)
   D. Completely confident in battle, He goes; therefore, He will lift up His head in victory (v. 7)

Authorship

The Davidic authorship of the psalm is amply supported by (1) its title and (2) its understanding by those in New Testament times. During New Testament times this is so universally understood as being written by David that Jesus can state it and the scribes will not argue against it (Matt 22:43–46).

Psalm 110 and the Davidic Covenant

The question of whether any part of Psalm 110 may be taken as related to the Davidic covenant has to consider Jesus' interpretation of the psalm. Mark's account of an encounter between Jesus and the Pharisees regarding the interpretation of this psalm is of great importance (Mark 12:35–37), especially as seen in contrast to the other synoptics. The force of the Greek word *pothen* is unique to Mark's account. Jesus' question to the scribes, the Jewish interpreters, is, "Whence" ("from where," i.e., from what passage) is the Messiah the son of David? *Pothen* is used here with the sense of "from what source of authority" (cf. Mark 6:1–2; Luke 20:7). Mark's version of Jesus' response to the scribes' teaching about the Messiah being David's Son in 12:35–37 focuses on the source of authority for making such a claim. The scribes appear to have used Psalm 110:1 as a proof text for their point. Jesus does not deny that Messiah is to be a descendent of David, but He does take issue with the scribes' interpretation of Psalm 110. We might paraphrase Jesus' response as follows: "You say that Messiah is David's Son? Fine, but on what authority do you make that assertion? Psalm 110? Impossible! For in that psalm David addresses Messiah as his Lord, not his son."

The Throne of the Messiah

In considering the throne of the Messiah in Psalm 110:1, several things must be taken into consideration: the location of the throne, the reason for the honor, and the authority of the throne.

1. What might seem to be obvious about the location of the throne some have complicated. The Messiah is told to sit at the right hand of the Lord (Jehovah). It should be, therefore, a celestial throne, that is, in heaven. Some have tried to link it up with the throne of the Lord (Jehovah) as seen in 1 Chronicles 28:5; 29:23 and 2 Chronicles 9:8. But the contemporaries of the psalm are familiar with the difference between the throne of the king and the throne of someone, like the queen mother, on his right hand (cf. 1 Kings 2:19). If the throne of the Messiah were an earthly throne it would be lower than the Davidic throne! Surely no one, of that time period at least, would hear the words spoken by Jehovah to the Messiah, "Sit at my right hand" and confuse it with the Davidic throne. On the contrary, it would conjure up thoughts of a throne in heaven, literally at the right hand of Jehovah. Finally, it was not only the understanding of the members of the Sanhedrin that Psalm 110:1 spoke of a heavenly throne (cf. Luke 22:66–71; especially v. 69), but it is the universal understanding of the New Testament, including that of our Lord Jesus Christ, that the Messiah is now seated in heaven at the right hand of the Father, in fulfillment of Psalm 110 (cf. Mark 16:19; Acts 2:34–35; Rom. 8:34; Eph. 1:20; Col. 3:1; Heb. 1:3; etc.).

2. Consider the reason for the honor. The double reference to the Messiah's enemies (*oy[e]beka*) is instructive. In a holy war, the warriors and the deity share a common enemy to be defeated. Here the Lord considered the Messiah's enemies worthy of being His own enemies due to the Messiah's previous conduct. Jesus clarifies what He did to deserve the honor of sitting at the right hand of Jehovah in Revelation 3:21, "He who overcomes, I will grant to him to sit down with Me on My throne, as I also overcame and sat down with My Father on His throne." The Messiah judged the spiritual leaders of wickedness (cf. John 12:31; 16:11) and overcame the enemy. Thus He is worthy of exaltation to Jehovah's throne.

Lastly, consider the authority of the throne. This is expressed by the two phrases of verse 2. It is the Lord who stretches out the strong scepter of the Messiah, and it is the Lord who commands the Messiah to rule. In short, it is the Lord who initiates the rule of the Messiah. The authority of the Messiah is derived solely from the Lord (Cf. Dan. 7:14; Matt. 28:18).

That this authority stretches out from Zion in no way limits the Messiah's authority to those environs. Rather, it stretches out to the midst of the enemies, as the second phrase states. This authority begins in Zion and reaches out from there to the enemies around about.

Progressive dispensationalists see the Davidic throne in Psalm 110. They refer to such verses as 1 Chronicles 29:23 and 2 Chronicles 9:8. But these passages refer to the throne as "of the LORD" not by virtue of the fact that the Lord sits on it but rather by virtue of the fact that He controls who sits on it. The throne in Psalm 110:1 is that of the Lord by virtue of the fact that He does sit on it. The first one is earthly, situated in Jerusalem; the second is celestial, situated in heaven.

See also DAVIDIC COVENANT; THRONE OF DAVID.

George Gunn and Jerry Neuman

Craig Blaising, *Progressive Dispensationalism* (Wheaton: Victor Books, 1993); Darrell Bock, "The Reign of the Lord Christ" in *Dispensationalism, Israel, and the Church,* eds. C. A. Blaising and D. L. Block (Grand Rapids: Zondervan, 1992) and "Evidence From Acts" in *A Case for Premillennialism,* eds. D. K. Campbell and J. L. Townsend (Chicago: Moody Press, 1992); Jay Butler, "An Exegetical Study of Psalm 110" (Master's thesis, Dallas Theological Seminary, May 1980); C. F. Keil and F. Delitzsch, *Commentary on the Old Testament,* vol. 5 (Grand Rapids: Eerdmans, 1867); Derik Kidner, *Psalms* (London: InterVarsity Press, 1975); J. J. Stewart Perowne, *Commentary on the Psalms* (Grand Rapids: Kregel, 1989); John H. Sailhamer, *The Pentateuch as Narrative* (Grand Rapids:

Zondervan, 1992); Robert Saucy, *The Case for Progressive Dispensationalism* (Grand Rapids: Zondervan, 1993); W. VanGemeren, *The Expositor's Bible Commentary,* ed. Frank E. Gaebelein, vol. 5 (Winona Lake, Ill.: BMH Books, 1991).

PSEUDO-EPHRAEM

Pseudo-Ephraem as a Historical Source

An apocalyptic sermon containing two protorapture statements, Pseudo-Ephraem, is known today as *Sermon on the End of the World,* with extant copies in Syriac, Greek, and Latin. The sermon claims the authorship of the Syrian church father Ephraem of Nisibis (306–73), the most important and prolific of the Syrian fathers and a witness to Christianity on the fringes of the Roman Empire. He was well known for his confrontations with the heresies of Marcion, Mani, and the Arians. His works became so popular that in the fifth and sixth centuries he was adopted by several Christian communities as a spiritual father and role model. It is not at all unreasonable to expect that a prolific and prominent figure such as Ephraem would have writings ascribed to him. While there is little support for Ephraem as the author of the *Sermon on the End of the World*, Pseudo-Ephraem was greatly influenced by his writings.

The exact date of the original sermon is uncertain and dates range from as early as 373 to as late as 565–627. While a late date (seventh century) seems to have the consensus of support, any reasonable date is acceptable in relation to the history of the Rapture and premillennialism.

Eschatology

"All the saints and elect of God are gathered together before the tribulation, which is to come, and are taken to the Lord, in order that they may not see at any time the confusion which overwhelms the world because of our sins."

These words, along with an earlier similar statement, proclaim a divine act of mercy and intervention enacted upon believers prior to a time of great calamity. The chronology of events in Byzantine apocalyptic texts such as Pseudo-Ephraem was fairly standard, although Pseudo-Ephraem does offer some minor differences. Several motifs appear in varying degrees and stages throughout the apocalyptic texts. Among these are: Gog and Magog, the last Roman Emperor, and the rise and fall of the Antichrist. Through the centuries different emphases were extolled as Christians responded to emerging political structures and to human and natural disasters. Biblical texts were often paraphrased or only alluded to, and frequently several apocalyptic traditions were striving for acceptance at the same time.

However, the present text is much less complex than many of the medieval texts and contains only one of the three major themes: the rise and fall of the Antichrist. Additionally, the sequence of events in its eschatology is straightforward and simple to discern.

Pseudo-Ephraem believed Christians were living in the last days and would soon experience a gathering, or rapture, of believers prior to a forty-two month period of tribulation in which the Antichrist would reign. These months would culminate in the return of Christ, final judgment, and the eternal punishment of the Antichrist and Satan.

The sermon is unlike most Byzantine apocalypses that have some shortening of the time intervals by God during the rule of the Antichrist. Instead, it has Christians being removed from the time of tribulation, even though it is a three and one-half rather than a seven-year Tribulation.

The protorapture statements and chronology are very clear, although there are obvious shortcomings in some of its particulars from a contemporary pretribulational perspective. What is most important, however, for contemporary readers are not the differences but the similarities of its perspective with pretribulationism. The sermon proclaimed expectation of the removal of Christians from the earth prior to a specific period of tribulation.

Timothy J. Demy

Paul J. Alexander, *The Byzantine Apocalyptic Tradition* (Berkeley: University of California

Press, 1985); Timothy J. Demy and Thomas D. Ice, "The Rapture and an Early Medieval Citation" in *Bib Sac,* 152:306–17 (1995).

PURITAN ESCHATOLOGY

The English and American Puritans were part of the tradition of the Protestant Reformation and their eschatological ideas developed in that context. Following the earlier writings of John Wycliffe (1329–1384), Martin Luther (1483–1546) and Philip Melancthon (1497–1560) began to formulate the rudiments of Protestant eschatology which generally viewed the Catholic pope as the Antichrist, Gog and Magog as the Moslem Turks, and the end times as underway, giving rise to a postmillennial vision of the church bringing in the kingdom of Christ on earth. While John Calvin (1509–1564) moderated these views, John Knox (1514–1572) and the English Puritans took them to further extremes.

Knox's influence was particularly strong among the English Puritan exiles at Geneva, Switzerland, who produced the *Geneva Bible*, with its extensive eschatological annotations, in 1560. The popularity of the new Puritan study Bible, coupled with the publication in 1563 of John Foxe's *Actes and Monuments* (popularly known as *Foxe's Book of Martyrs*), gave rise to eschatological excitement about the coming of Christ and the end of the age.

The Puritans were known for their God-exalting and Christ-honoring scholarship that produced a series of great theologians as well as a host of eschatologists. Early Puritan writers included John Bale (1495–1563), who developed a concept of seven ages of human history, similar to the seven dispensations of later dispensationalists, and John Napier (1550–1617), the Scottish scholar who invented logarithms and wrote a commentary on Revelation in 1593. His commentary was later abridged and reissued as *The Bloody Almanac* (1643) and became the most popular tract in England during the English Civil Wars (1640–1660).

Hugh Broughton (1549–1612), Hebrew professor at Cambridge, wrote commentaries on Daniel (1596) and Revelation (1610) in which he emphasized the distinction between Israel and the church. Thomas Brightman (1557–1607) wrote a massive commentary on Revelation in which he foresaw a Jewish kingdom, separate from the church, arising from the conversion of the Jews into a literal kingdom on earth. He also suggested the seven churches of Revelation were prophetic of the seven ages of church history. Joseph Mede (1586–1638), Greek professor at Cambridge, became the father of English premillennial eschatology. His *Key to the Revelation* (1627) took the English public by storm. Mede also exercised considerable influence on the Westminster Assembly of Divines, including Thomas Goodwin, Jeremiah Burroughs, William Bridge, Stephen Marshall, and William Twisse—all of whom became ardent premillennialists. Mede also personally taught John Milton, Isaac Newton, and Nathaniel Holmes and carried on extensive correspondence with Anglican bishop James Ussher.

The turning point in Puritan eschatology came shortly after the Cromwellian revolution during the English Civil Wars. John Owen (1616–1683) was appointed vice-chancellor of Oxford University by Cromwell in 1651. Owen's early eschatological views that the fall of Babylon was fulfilled in the fall of the British monarchy were taken to extremes by the radical Fifth Monarchy Movement, which Owen openly condemned. By 1652, Owen began emphasizing the spiritual nature of Christ's kingdom and moderated his earlier premillennial views. Richard Baxter (1615–1691) went even further emphasizing the heavenly nature of Christ's kingdom in *The Saints' Everlasting Rest* (1650). Baxter looked for an eternal rest beyond the conflicts and quarrels of his time.

After Cromwell's death in 1658, the monarchy was restored, Charles II was recalled as king, and in 1662 the Act of Uniformity (known as the "Great Ejection") removed two thousand Puritan pastors from their pulpits. Militant premillennialism declined among the Puritans thereafter, but the premillennial tradition remained popular with the general public and was held by such notables as Charles Spurgeon (1834–1892).

Among American Puritans, the post-millennialism of Jonathan Edwards (1703–1758) was the dominant viewpoint in colonial New England. Eighteenth- and nineteenth-century American Puritans were generally optimistic about the success of world evangelism and the coming golden age of the church. Cotton Mather (1663–1728) of Harvard and Timothy Dwight (1752–1817) of Yale (Edwards' grandson) were among the leading American post-millennialists. Both believed the church was succeeding in bringing in the kingdom of Christ on earth, which Dwight believed would culminate in A.D. 2000. American postmillennialism was later popularized by theologians such as Charles Hodge (1797–1878) at Princeton.

See also BALE, JOHN; EDWARDS, JONATHAN; MATHER, RICHARD, INCREASE, AND COTTON; MEDE, JOSEPH.

Edward Hindson

Paul Christianson, *Reformers and Babylon* (Toronto: University of Toronto Press, 1978); K. R. Frith, *The Apocalyptic Tradition in Reformation Britain 1530–1645* (Oxford: Oxford University Press, 1979); Christopher Hill, *Antichrist in Seventeenth-Century England* (Oxford: Oxford University Press, 1971); Edward Hindson, *Puritans' Use of Scripture in the Development of an Apocalyptical Hermeneutic* (Pretoria: University of South Africa, 1984).

R

RAPTURE, BIBLICAL STUDY OF THE

Believers of every generation have had a longing for Jesus Christ's return. It was generally understood that Christ would come back to the earth and end all human sorrow. After a general resurrection and judgment, He would initiate a new heaven and a new earth, eternity itself. While the details of how the Lord would come back may not have been defined, a belief in the Second Coming has been held by nearly all Christians.

With the resurgence of the study of Bible prophecy at the beginning of the nineteenth century, students of the prophetic Word noticed that in 1 Thessalonians 4:13–18 the apostle Paul first speaks of a resurrection of those who have died in Christ and then of those caught up together to meet the Lord in the air. Most prominent amillennial scholars ignored the idea that 1 Thessalonians 4 could be any different from other passages that speak of "the coming" (*parousia*) of Christ. In fact, to them the word *parousia* seemed to sum up the doctrine of only one return of Jesus.

Toward the end of the nineteenth century, a greater attention to sound hermeneutics led scholars of prophecy to a better understanding of: 1) how God providentially worked differently in various ages of biblical history; 2) how the end of history had a larger prophetic scheme of things than originally thought; and 3) how important a role that interpreting by context played in comprehending the full scope of prophetic truth.

In time it became clearer to some that, by contextual study, the coming of Christ to "rapture" away the church saints was an entirely different event than was His coming to judge sinners and to rule and reign for a thousand years. Many great Bible teachers of the period saw that both events were to be taken as distinct, literal comings and could not simply be spiritualized away.

By studying various passages, it can be shown that there are two distinct resurrections connected to the Lord's return. There is the resurrection for those in Christ, who will be taken to glory before the Tribulation begins. There is also a raising of the Old Testament saints and the Tribulation-martyred believers to enjoy the blessings of the Lord's one-thousand-year literal kingdom reign. Eleven key elements appear in such passages.

1. Resurrection. Though the resurrection is mentioned in Second Coming passages, these verses and sections of verses reveal certain special elements when they prophesy about those who will be coming forth from the grave (1 Cor. 15:23–24, 51–52; 1 Thess. 4:13–18; 5:1–11).

2. Hope and comfort. These passages give a particular hope and comfort because believers in Christ will be caught away to be at home in heaven with their Lord (John 14:1–3; 1 Cor. 15:51–52; Phil. 3:20–21; 1 Thess. 1:9–10; 2:17–19; 4:13–18; 5:1–11; 2 Thess. 2:1–2; James 5:7–9; 1 John 3:2–3).

3. Change. A new body is given to those who are resurrected as well as to those who are alive who will suddenly be transformed so that they can go home to be with the Lord in heaven (1 Cor. 15:51–52; Phil. 3:20–21; 1 Thess. 4:13–18; 5:1–11; 1 John 3:2–3).

4. Return to Heaven (John 14:1–3; Phil. 3:20; 1 Thess.1:9–10; 3:13; 4:13–18; 5:1–11; 2 Thess. 2:1).

5. Taken Directly by the Lord Himself or, Intimacy Facing Christ at His Coming (John 14:1–3; 1 Thess. 1:9b–10; 2:17–19; 4:13–18; 5:1–11; 2 Thess. 2:1–2; Phil. 3:20–21; James 5:7–9; Titus 2:13; 1 John 2:28, 3:2–3).

6. His people live differently than others because He is coming (1 Thess. 5:1–11; 5:23;

1 Tim. 6:14; Titus 2:12–14; James 5:7–9; 1 John 2:28; 3:2–3).

7. Imminence. The pronouns *we, you,* and *us* are proof that the Rapture could have happened in Paul's own generation (John 14:1–3; 1 Cor. 15:51–52; Phil. 3:20–21; 1 Thess. 1:9–10; 2:17–19; 3:13; 4:13–18; 5:1–11; 5:23; 2 Thess. 2:1–2; 1 Tim. 6:14; Titus 2:13; James 5:7–9; 1 John 2:28; 3:2–3).

8. The term *parousia* is used to describe the Rapture (1 Thess. 2:17–19; 3:13; 4:13–18; 2 Thess. 2:1–2; 1 Cor. 15:23–24; James 5:7–8; 1 John 2:8; 3:2–3).

9. Other Expressions for the Coming (John 14:1–3; 1 Thess. 4:16; 5:23–24; 2 Thess. 2:1–2; Titus 2:13; James 5:7–9; 1 John 2:8; 3:2–3).

10. Being taken to the Father (John 14:1–3; 1 Thess. 3:13; Titus 2:13).

11. Those in Christ or allusions to the church. 1 Thess. 2:17–19; 4:13–18; 5:1–11; 2 Thess. 2:1–2; 1 Cor. 15:23–24; 15:51–52; Titus 2:13.

Resurrection and the the Rapture

The resurrection that takes place at the rapture has to do with the "dead in Christ," that is, deceased believers who became a part of the spiritual body of Christ in this dispensation.

Four distinct passages link the resurrection of church saints to the Rapture. In the most-inclusive rapture passage, 1 Thessalonians 4:13–18, the apostle Paul addresses the issue of those who have fallen asleep in Jesus (4:14). He ties together this "catching away" *(harpazo),* or the rapture of living believers, with the resurrection of church saints or those in Christ: "But we do not want you to be uninformed . . . about those who are asleep. . . . God will bring with Him those who have fallen asleep in Jesus. . . . The Lord Himself will descend . . . and the dead in Christ shall rise first. Then we who are alive and remain shall be caught up together with them in the clouds to meet the Lord in the air (vv. 13–14, 16–17).

The Thessalonian church seems to have been concerned about the death of those who had accepted Christ as Savior. Will they live again? This question had not been answered, and they were grieving as the pagans who had no guarantees about an afterlife (v. 13). The answer is that those believers who have died will in no way miss out on the blessing of the Lord's coming.

Paul states, "In no way, not even, should we proceed the ones who have been put to sleep" (v. 15 trans. mine). The word "proceed" (*phthasomen*) has a double negative that carries the force of an extra emphatic, "We should *absolutely not* proceed those who have been put to sleep!" This is a Greek idiom that effectively takes away any apprehension about the dead in Christ being left out. This idiom has the sense of an emphatic future, "when the time comes this is the sequence of events." The dead in Christ shall rise first.

Those Awake and Asleep Will Live Together with Christ

In 1 Thessalonians 5:1–11 the apostle Paul writes about the coming Day of the Lord (v. 2) or the wrath (v. 9) that will fall on the lost who are proclaiming peace and safety (v. 3). In verses 2–7 the apostle pictures the birth pangs of trouble and pain that fall suddenly on the lost. They are in spiritual darkness, and they will not escape the terror that will overcome them like a thief (vv. 3–4).

In 5:9–10 Paul comes back to the issue of the Rapture that he began writing about in 4:13–17. He summarizes and restates the fact that both those who are asleep (the dead in Christ) and those awake will live together with Jesus. This was meant to calm their fears during their trials and to correct an error that seems to have arisen that those who were found alive when He returns would have some priority over those who were dead.

Verse 10 reads: "[Christ] died for us, in order that whether we should right now be fully awake or whether we should right now be sleeping, we shall in the future, [and] all at once at the same time, be alive together with Him" (trans. mine).

The expression "in the future . . . be alive" prophetically sees the resurrected saints in Christ and those raptured believers together someday living with Him. The force of the verb could also mean "now and forever" we shall live with Him. The expression "all at once at the same time" sheds even more light on this resurrection and the Rapture. Actually, this represents two expressions joined together: "Together with" (*hama*) and "with Him" (*sun auto*). Barnes interprets this as "those who are alive and those who are dead—meaning that they would be *together* or would be with the Lord *at the same time*." Hendricksen adds: "Those who are *awake* are those who are *alive*, the survivors, the ones who according to 4:15 are 'left until the coming of the Lord.'"

Two Resurrections or More?

Even some of the earlier Bible scholars who do not accept a dispensational rapture see two resurrections in 1 Corinthians 15:23–24. In the full context, Paul promises a resurrection in which in Christ all shall be made alive (v. 22). "To explain, each [will be resurrected] in his own order: Christ the firstfruits; next after that, those [believers] who belong to Christ at His coming; after this [will come] the consummation whenever [Christ] [in the future] will be handing over the kingdom to the God and Father [including] whenever He abolishes all rule and all authority and power" (trans. mine).

The whole context is governed by "in Christ . . . made alive." Dispensationally, verse 23 clearly has the church saints in mind and is not describing Jesus' coming to reign over Israel as the Son of Man nor His coming to judge the world. He is returning to take the church. Since the kingdom is unquestionably separated in verse 24 from verse 23, the rapture resurrection is the only explanation for this passage.

"There is to be a sequence in the resurrection of the dead, and St. Paul explains this by the three groups: (1) Christ Himself, the first fruits; (2) the faithful in Christ at His coming; (3) all the rest of mankind at the end, when the final judgment takes place. The interval between these two—its duration, or where or how it will be spent—is not spoken of here. The only point the apostle makes concerns the order of the resurrection (Ellicott's *Commentary*).

Alford writes: "The resurrection of the rest of the dead, here veiled over by the general term *to telos* [the end]—that resurrection not being in this argument specially treated, but only that of Christians . . . It ought to be needless to remind the student of the distinction between this parousia [the coming] for those in Christ and the final judgment; it is here peculiarly important to bear in mind."

Robertson and Plummer also believe this passage is open to be interpreted as Christ coming exclusively for His own, the church saints, as separate from another coming in which He raises other dead: "Of these *tagamata* [each in his own order] there are two, clearly marked, in the present passage; Christ, who has already reached the goal of Resurrection; and Christ's Own [the church], who will reach it when He comes again. Perhaps St. Paul is thinking of a third *tagamata* [order], some time before the End. But throughout the passage, the unbelievers and the wicked are quite in the background, if they are thought of at all."

Christ's own, the church saints who have died, are still waiting for the resurrection. This passage shows a sequence in the unfolding of the final events concerning that resurrection. Since Paul was addressing the church, he was not concerned with detailing all future resurrections. He concentrated instead on the church saints who are asleep and on their place in the scheme of things.

Hope and Comfort

Almost all of the rapture passages speak of the blessing of the Lord's return for His own, or more specifically, the return of Jesus Christ to take His children home to heaven. This is the hope and comfort, and it is a different scenario than that of Jesus coming back to judge the earth, to reign and rule as Messiah. In fact a key to most rapture passages is this going-home joy and anticipation.

Going Home!

In John 14:1–3, Jesus promised His disciples that He was going to prepare a place for them. From the Greek text the passage could read: "Let not the heart of each of you be disturbed. All of you together are believing in God; in the same way, all of you continue to trust in Me. In My Father's house are many dwelling places, but if not, I would have told you, because I go to prepare a room for you [to live in]. And if I am going and preparing a room for you, I will be coming again and taking you along [to My own home], that where I am, I and you [will be together]" (trans. mine).

The hope and comfort in this passage is stated in a kind of a negative, "Let not the heart be disturbed." The reason: Christ is going to prepare a place for them, and He will come again for them and receive them to Himself. This is a rapture passage because it implies that His coming could have taken place while they were alive. Though death could overtake them (as it did), their new bodies would be taken home by the resurrection at the time of the Rapture.

The Father's "house" (*oikos*) could not be the location of the earthly kingdom in which Jesus will reign. Jesus would be going soon to His Father's house. He will come for His own and take them back to a location He has prepared. Jesus is not saying that His disciples will simply die and go to the Father's house (although that would be true of their souls if they died before He came for them). Therefore, His coming for them must refer either to the Rapture while they are living or the bodily resurrection that takes place simultaneously. "The dead in Christ shall rise first. Then we who are alive and remain shall be caught up together with them in the clouds to meet the Lord in the air, and thus we shall always be with the Lord" (1 Thess. 4:16–17).

Waiting Steadfastly

James 5:7–9 may be one of the earliest references to the rapture, apart from Christ's words in John 14:1–3. Regarding hope and anticipation, verses 7–9 could read from the Greek text: "Be waiting steadfastly then, until the time of the visitation [*parousia*] arrives. Behold, the farmer waits for the precious fruit of the ground, waiting patiently concerning it. . . . You too, be waiting steadfastly, firmly stabilize your emotions, because the visitation of the Lord has progressively been drawing near."

The phrase "be waiting steadfastly" refers to patience and forbearance. In illustration, it is said that the farmer also "waits." This verb *ekdechetai* has the idea of eager expectation. James urges his readers not only to wait eagerly with expectation for the Lord's coming but also to firmly stabilize their emotions (*kardia*).

This rapture passage gives confidence and hope despite persecutions falling on the early church. The farmer waits hopefully for the refreshing rains that herald the coming of new crops. So believers can look for the Lord coming for them. Barnes writes, "In due time, as [the farmer] expects the return of the rain, so you may anticipate deliverance from your trials."

Rescued from the Coming Wrath

First Thessalonians 1:9–10 is a powerful rapture passage that further speaks of an "eagerly waiting" kind of hope. It gives this comfort or hope because it speaks of believers being dragged away from the terror of the wrath that is on its way to this world. In regard to this hope the Greek text could read: "You turned . . . to presently be serving a living and true God, and to presently be eagerly waiting for His Son from the heavens, whom [God] raised from the dead, Jesus, who [will be] dragging (rescuing) us [to Himself] from the wrath which is coming!"

The verb "be eagerly waiting" (*anameno*) is given intensity with the preposition *ana*. And it has a continual, or linear, idea, "to keep on waiting." On this hopeful anticipation Hendricksen adds: "The force of the verb to wait must not be lost sight of. It means to look forward to with patience and confidence. . . . It implies (both in Greek and in English) being ready for His return. . . . The thought of His coming does not spell terror for the believer . . . For it is this Jesus rescues (is rescuing) us from the wrath to come (the coming wrath).

Barnes says: "The hope of his return to our world to raise the dead, and to convey his ransomed to heaven, is the brightest and most cheering prospect that dawns on man, and we should be ready, whenever it occurs, to hail him as our returning Lord and glorious Redeemer."

Our Hope When He Comes

Paul writes in 1 Thessalonians 2:19: "For what is our hope [anticipation] or joy or crown of rejoicing? Is it not even you in the presence of our Lord Jesus Christ at His coming?" This is an unusual way of speaking about hope and comfort. But Paul is telling the believers at Thessalonica how much he rejoices in their stand for the Gospel. In fact their suffering and persecution for the name of Christ was almost overwhelming. When the Rapture occurs, those saints of the Lord will be at that moment Paul's great rejoicing when he stands literally before the face of Jesus. It is with this coming that the Thessalonian believers will be presented as Paul's joy. This is not the coming of Christ to deliver worldwide judgment. This is the Lord taking His own home to be with Him—clearly the Rapture!

Comforting One Another

In the most important rapture passage (1 Thess. 4:13–18), the apostle Paul writes to the Thessalonian church about this great miracle event so that they might not grieve as do the rest who have no hope (v. 13). This should be translated "might not be made to grieve." Paul tells believers that if they grieve, it is because they allow grief about their relatives who are asleep to overtake them, thereby acting as the unsaved who look upon death as final destruction. Trying to correct this erroneous thinking, he pictures the pagan world as having no hope, and he tells of the Christian blessed assurance of resurrection to glory with the Lord Jesus Christ.

In verse 18, Paul exhorts the believers to find and give comfort in these words from the Lord about the Rapture and the accompanying resurrection. At its root the word "comfort" (*parakaleo*) can mean to call alongside or to counsel. "Likewise, be counseling one another by these words." The present tense and active voice in Greek are used to emphasize that they need to be comforting each other right now and until the Lord comes. This is an exercise in faith in order to recognize the certainty of ultimate triumph.

After writing about the Day of the Lord (5:2) and the wrath to come (5:9), the apostle concludes with the same command to comfort one another because God will not put His own through these days of horror that will come on the world. From the Greek text, Paul writes in 5:11: "Therefore, be continually comforting one another and building up one another, even as [I know] you presently are doing."

Some believers had fallen asleep in Jesus (4:14–15). Some will be alive when the Rapture takes place (4:17), and they will assuredly miss the terrible Day of the Lord that is coming on the earth (5:9). Thus, the larger hope is that believers will be with their Savior, whether by the Rapture or by resurrection.

The Day of the Lord Has Not Come

Most believe 2 Thessalonians 2:1 is a reference exclusively referring to the Rapture. From the Greek it could read: "Now I am begging you, brothers, concerning the coming of our Lord Jesus Christ even [concerning] our gathering together up to Him."

A. T. Robertson sees the entire verse as "referring to the rapture, mentioned in 1 Thessalonians 4:15–17." Paul often writes, that you may not be quickly shaken from your composure." (2:2). Though the words *hope* or *comfort* are not used here, the apostle is comforting the Thessalonians by saying that the Day of the Lord has not come. The apostasy must come first and the Antichrist (the man of lawlessness) must be revealed (2:3–4).

Paul gives comfort by using two negatives: "Do not totter or waver" *(saleuo)* in your mind, nor "be terrified" *(throeo)*, to the effect that the Day of the Lord has come (v. 2). Paul is referring to the Rapture in 1 Thessalonians 4:15–17 and amplifying the assurance that believers will escape the wrath.

Christ's Resurrection Gives Hope

In 1 Corinthians 15, Paul argues that we have no hope if Jesus was not raised from the dead. "Those also who have fallen asleep in Christ have perished. If we have hoped in

Christ in this life only, we are of all men most to be pitied" (vv. 18–19). He gives the great assurance to church saints: "in Christ shall all be made alive" (v. 22). And following Christ's resurrection comes the resurrection of the believers at the Rapture, "after that [the resurrection of Jesus] those who are Christ's at His coming" (v. 23 NASB). As He promised (John 14:2–3) Christ will return for those who compose the church and the dead in Christ will be raised (1 Thess. 4:16).

In 1 Corinthians15:49, Paul continues his anthem of hope in regard to the resurrection, "as we have borne the image of the earthy, we shall also bear the image of the heavenly." He follows this with the hopeful declaration: "Behold, I am telling you something not before revealed, we shall not all be put to sleep, however, we shall all be changed, in a moment, at a blink of an eye, with the last trumpet; for the trumpet will sound, and the dead ones will be raised imperishable, and we shall all be changed" (15:51–52, author's translation).

These verses truly express a hope and comfort. Saying "behold," the apostle uses a forceful exclamatory to point the reader's attention to a "momentous revelation . . . to which he calls our earnest attention," This is an "emphatic introduction of information of great moment." Paul twice says we shall be changed at some point in the future. The Greek word used has the force of "to alter," or in other contexts, "to change the customs." As well, "to take a new position, one thing for another, to alternate."

Because of the unique dispensation of the church and the fact that living believers in Christ will be changed and translated before the coming wrath, Paul proclaims with great joy this blessed "new" revelation. "That [Paul] did not refer only to those whom he was then addressing, is apparent from the whole discussion. The argument relates to Christians—to the church at large."

A New Citizenship

One of Paul's most hopeful proclamations is found in the Greek of Philippians 3:20–21: "For our citizenship really exists in heaven, out of which we are waiting expectantly [to welcome] a Savior, the Lord Jesus Christ, who will alter the configuration of our body [that has] a limitation" (author's translation).

We are waiting "expectantly" (*apekdechomai*). This word can mean "receive, welcome." Paul includes himself in that anticipation. "We wait for, expect, till the event arrives. . . . Paul's heart is in heaven. We wait for . . . vividly pictures Paul's eagerness for the . . . coming of Christ as the normal attitude of the Christian colonist whose home is in heaven" (Alford).

Great Expectations

Paul almost shouts his excitement about the possibility of the Rapture in Titus 2:13. From Greek the passage can read: "[We are] excitedly expecting continually the joyous prospect, even [the] glorious appearance of our great God, even [our] Savior, Christ Jesus!" (author's translation).

"Excitedly expecting continually" is often translated simply "looking for" (*prosdechomai*). And indeed, the present tense makes this "expecting" a continual hope. "This expectation [is] an abiding state and posture." But the word also has the force of "welcome, wait for, expect." The "blessed hope" might be translated "the joyous anticipation." There is no question about this expectation. It is going to come about, and it produces a great joyousness that looks forward to ultimate redemption. "This describes the great expectancy which is the ruling and prevailing thought in the lives of men looking for their Lord's return."

Having Confidence When He Comes

Christ could reveal Himself by the Rapture at any time. The apostle John expresses similar thoughts to Paul's in his personal love letter, 1 John. In two different contexts he speaks of confidence and hope in regard to Jesus' coming. From the Greek text: "However, now [I want you to specifically] keep on sticking with Him, so that whenever He should be revealed, we might have confidence and not shrink away from Him in shame at His coming" (2:28). ". . . We shall be like-ones with Him, because we shall see Him as He is. And everyone who is having this anticipation on Him, is purifying himself, as that One is [existing as] pure!" (3:2).

Sometimes "confidence" (*parousia*) can be translated "joyousness," "courage," or "boldness." By using "we" John implies that even he himself may be alive when Jesus comes and that his generation of believers may not have to die. He encourages them to live the Christian experience by something that could happen while he is alive.

In 3:2, John declares that when a believer anticipates or hopes for the Lord's return it produces a purifying effect within. "One who sets his hope by faith on the Son of God experiences an inward purification that is as complete as Christ's own purity."

The Change

When the Rapture takes place, believers will instantly receive new, glorified bodies like Christ's, and the resurrection of those asleep in Jesus takes place. This change affects both the living and the dead, in order that they may be brought into the very presence of the living God and His Son. By implication Paul first addresses this in 1 Thessalonians 4:13–18.

Meeting the Lord in the Air

It is clear the dead in Christ could not be raised (4:16) and that we who are alive could not "be caught up together with them in the clouds to meet the Lord in the air" (4:17) unless we had glorified bodies. The apostle seals this issue with his conclusion, "Thus we shall always be with the Lord" (v. 17 NASB).

We May Live Together with Him

Since believers in Christ are not destined for the wrath (1 Thess. 5:9) but are to obtain salvation through His sacrifice, they are raptured to "live together with Him" (5:10). This thought continues the fact that Christians must be changed in order to exist with the Lord.

Those Who Belong to Christ

After thoroughly explaining the need for the resurrection (1 Cor. 15:12–21), Paul summarizes by saying that "in Christ all shall be made alive" (v. 22 NASB). He then adds (Greek): "To explain, each [will be resurrected] in his own order: Christ the firstfruits, next after that, those [resurrected] who belong to Christ at His coming" (v. 23). Again, the change is specifically the resurrection. But in 15:51–54, it also includes a transformation physically of the living believers in Christ: "We shall not all sleep [physically die], but we shall all be changed . . . The dead will be raised imperishable, and we shall be changed. For this perishable must put on the imperishable, and this mortal must put on immortality (vv. 51–53).

The word *change* in Greek (*allasso)* can mean "to take a new position, one thing for another, to alternate."

Conforming Our Bodies

From the Greek, Philippians 3:21 forcefully explains this needed and dramatic change to our bodies: "[Christ] will alter the configuration of our body [that has] a limitation, into a together-forming with the body of His glory." He does this by the "energizing of His power, even [the ability] to subject all things to Himself."

The word *alter,* often translated "transform" *(metaschamatizo)* can literally mean to "alter the schematics." Jesus will "turn about" the present body into something new. The word can mean to change the form of a person or thing, to be changed in form, change configuration, change of position or posture.

Limitation is often translated "humble state" *(tapeinoseos)*. The word can mean to lower, reduce, to humble, abase, or a lessening. Paul is speaking about a body that is now less than "the body of His glory." It is earthly, natural, fleshly, perishable (1 Cor.15). Sin controls, condemns, and brings about a groaning for release. Thus, we groan "within ourselves, waiting eagerly for our adoption as sons, the redemption of our body" (Rom. 8:23 NASB).

The word *together-forming,* often translated "conformity" *(summorphon)*, can literally mean "together-formed." Homer Kent writes: "The present body is described literally as 'the body of lowliness' . . . a description calling attention to its weakness and susceptibility to persecution, disease, sinful appetites, and death. At Christ's coming, however, the earthly, transient appearance will be changed, whether by resurrection of those dead or by rapture of the living, and believers will be transformed and will receive glorified bodies that will more adequately display their essential character . . . as children of God and sharers of divine life in Christ."

Being Like Jesus

Though it is hard to fully fathom, John says, "We know with certainty that, whenever He should be revealed, we shall be like ones with Him, because we shall see Him as He is" (1 John 3:2, Greek). "'Whenever' sounds uncertain but the grammar construction implies certainty." The Greek grammar literally says "likeones with Him we shall be." We shall have a body and constitution just like Him! "It is clearly implied here that there will be an influence in beholding the Savior as he is, which will tend to make us like him, or to transform us into his likeness."

A Return to Heaven

Many of the rapture passages imply or speak directly of a return to heaven. In fact, seven specific contexts let us know our destiny is above. These "catching away" passages are rapture verses.

To My Father's House

Jesus said to His disciples: "In My Father's house are many dwelling places. I go to prepare a room for you [to live in]. I will be coming again . . . where I am, I and you [together]!" (John 14:2–3, Greek). Christ actually said, "Again I am coming."

By context, this should be taken as a future present. "I will be coming again." This event "is regarded as so certain that in thought it may be contemplated as already coming to pass."

Rescued from the Wrath

In 1 Thessalonians 1:9–10, Paul says we wait for God's Son from heaven, "who delivers us from the wrath to come." The implication is that we are taken up so that "we shall always be with the Lord" (4:17 NASB). This has to mean we are taken to heaven. Again, this is not the Son of Man coming to reign on earth but to deliver us out of the way when God afflicts earth's inhabitants with an unparalleled series of physical torments.

Taken Before the Father

In 1 Thessalonians 3:13 the apostle further argues that our hearts will be established unblamable in holiness before our God and Father at the coming of our Lord Jesus with all His saints. As in 2:19 (the presence of our Lord Jesus at his coming), "before" is used of a face-to-face encounter. Note the parallel: "Before (the presence of) our Lord Jesus" (2:19), and "before (the presence of) our God and Father" (3:13). This has to be in heaven.

Always with the Lord

Few would argue that when Paul says thus we shall always be with the Lord, he must be referring to heaven. Bible scholars of all prophetic persuasions have always held this means going home to heaven. This passage in Greek even more strongly suggests this: "We shall be snatched (raptured) into the clouds into the meeting place of the Lord in the air. Thus, altogether we shall ourselves be together with the Lord." Also, Bible teachers concur that Paul is alluding to heaven when he writes: "whether we are awake or asleep, we may live together with Him" (1 Thess. 5:10).

Gathered to Him

Many believe when the apostle writes of "the coming of our Lord Jesus Christ, even our gathering together to Him," he is still speaking of our going home to heaven (2 Thess. 2:1). Some have called this the muster of the saints to heaven! In fact, the phrase "to him" can be translated "up to him."

Citizenship in Heaven

There is no question about what Paul is saying in Philippians 3:20. Christians, while living on earth, have their citizenship elsewhere—in heaven. This contrasts with those who set their minds on earthly things (3:19). "Their mind [the world's] is on earth; our country is in heaven, and to it our affections cling, even during our earthly pilgrimage."

Taken Directly to the Lord or Intimately Facing Christ at His Coming

This "taking" is not before Jesus as the King of Israel, the Messiah, when He begins His earthly rule. All the contexts of the rapture passages either explicitly state or imply going home to be with the Lord in heaven. But they also indicate believers will see Jesus instantly by the dynamic Rapture and change upon those living or by the resurrection of the church saints. The purpose for this catching away of the living is so that the wrath may fall on the earth. When He comes to reign in His Second Coming, church saints return with Him.

Where Jesus Is, We Are

In John 14:3 Christ states it clearly: "I will be coming again and take you along [to my home], that where I am, I and you [together]" (author's translation). The Lord's disciples could have been raptured while living, but they died and their souls were taken to heaven. So Christ's coming back with their souls will bring about the bodily resurrection whereby their souls will be joined to their bodies. The disciples will then receive their new bodies. But they could have been snatched away while living and suddenly have met Him in air.

Waiting for God's Son

Believers are to be eagerly waiting for the return of the resurrected Jesus, God's Son from heaven (1 Thess. 1:10). They will see Him face-to-face! The word "wait" (*anameno*) could be translated "to keep on waiting up for His Son." "The force of the verb to wait must not be lost sight of. It means to look forward to with patience and confidence . . . being ready for his return . . . The thought of his coming does not spell terror for the believer" (Hendrickson).

The Judge Is Approaching

When the apostle James writes of Christ as an approaching Judge (James 5:9), he is not referring to a judgment of our eternal destiny but of the bema judgment for works. "For we must all appear before the judgment seat [*bematos*] of Christ, that each one may be recompensed for his deeds" (2 Cor. 5:10). From the Greek text, James actually says: "The coming of the Lord has progressively been approaching, coming nearer [at hand]" (5:8). Thus, Christ our judge is brought near, He is at the point of appearing.

Jesus Who Drags Us Away

Paul writes of "Jesus, who delivers us from the wrath coming" (1 Thess. 1:10). The deponent Greek word *ruomai* has the idea to deliver, rescue. In some contexts it is translated "saved from the jaws of the lion" (2 Tim. 4:17) and "delivered from the power of darkness" (Col. 1:13). Some see this as descriptive of Christ's office, Our Deliverer. Also, it could be a timeless substantive denoting one of Jesus' characteristics, Jesus who will return as rescuer. In classical Greek the word *erruo* can be translated "drag" or "draw away." Vincent translates *ruomai* with the force of the middle voice, "to draw to one's self" with the specification from evil or danger. The word can also have the force of a prophetic future, "The One who will drag us away [to Himself]" from the wrath that is coming.

Snatched Away

First Thessalonians 4:17 reads, from the Greek text: "We shall be snatched into the clouds into the meeting place of the Lord in the air." The word *rapture* comes from the Greek *harpazo*, which indicates being suddenly swooped away by a force that cannot be opposed. Believers are going to meet the Lord in an appointed place in the air. The term "meeting place" (*apantesin*) has a technical meaning in the Hellenistic world in relation to the visits of dignitaries. Visitors would be formally met by the citizens, or a deputation of them, who had gone out from the town for this purpose. The dignitary would then be ceremonially escorted into the city. In the Rapture, Christ will rescue us (1:10) and snatch us away to the meeting place in the sky, before the wrath of God falls on the earth (5:1–9).

Other passages speak of that face-to-face encounter with the Lord (1 Thess. 2:19). And "we shall always be with the Lord" (4:17). Other like phrases make it clear that when the Rapture comes, we are indeed to be with Him! "Whether we are awake or asleep, we may live together with Him" (5:10). "Our gathering together to Him" (2 Thess. 2:1). "We eagerly wait for a Savior, Christ Jesus" (Titus 2:13). Stay with Him, "so that when He appears, we may have confidence and not shrink away from Him [from His face] in shame at His coming" (1 John 2:28). "We shall see Him just as He is" (3:2).

His People Live Differently

In six distinct passages, godly living is tied to the rapture hope. Critics of the Rapture often claim this doctrine is but an escape for those who teach it. But the apostles James and Paul both make it an incentive for living because He could appear to take us to Himself at any moment.

Do Not Complain Against Another

James pleads: "Do not complain, brethren, against one another, that you yourselves may not be judged; behold the judge is standing right at the door" (James 5:9). James further warns against swearing and being flippant or profane. The Lord could come at any moment: "Above all . . . do not swear . . . let your yes be yes, and your no, no; so that you may not fall under judgment [when the judge comes]" (5:12).

Do Not Sleep, Be Sober

After Paul's great teaching on the Rapture and the accompanying resurrection of church saints, he reminds believers in Christ they are not destined for wrath (1 Thess. 5:9). The saints will escape the Day of the Lord (5:2) which will fall with sudden destruction on "them," those who have not trusted in Christ and who are in darkness (5:3–7). But with this reminder, Paul wants the believers to live godly lives. He writes: "We are of the day, let us be sober, having put on the breastplate of faith and love, and as a helmet, the hope of salvation" (5:8 NASB). The apostle says the children of light are not to sleep. We must be sober (5:5–6). Paul clearly is talking about how we are to live in the light of His any-moment return for those in Christ.

Paul further prays that God will sanctify the whole person, preserved morally intact and undiminished in light of Christ's return: "Now may the God of peace Himself sanctify you entirely' and may your spirit and soul and body be preserved complete, without blame at the coming of our Lord Jesus Christ" (5:23).

The word "entirely" could read "quite complete" or "through and through." To concentrate, to separate from things profane. . . . Here alone in the New Testament it means the whole of each of you, every part of you 'through and through' (Luther) qualitatively rather than quantitatively."

Living Without Stain

Paul urges those in Christ to "keep the commandment without stain or reproach until the appearing *(epiphaneias)* of our Lord Jesus Christ" (1 Tim. 6:14). The word "stain" can refer to a hidden reef or a soiled blemish. "Without reproach" carries the idea of irreproachable conduct. In the context, the apostle seems to be referring to the issues of money and wealth. Quite clearly he has in view proper moral living in regard to the proper use of material things in order to stand spiritually tall when Jesus comes.

The Blessed Hope and Christian Living

The grace of God and its accompanying salvation should cause us to be instructed and to be looking for the blessed hope (Titus 2:12–13). This salvation should assist in denying ungodliness and worldly desires and help us live sensibly, righteously and godly in the present age. And it should produce a welcoming and an expectation of the Lord's soon return. On the two participles "instructing" (v. 12) and "looking" (v. 13): together they would read "The grace of God has appeared . . . *instructing* us [that we might live sensibly] . . . [as we are] *looking* for the blessed hope."

Do Not Shrink Back

Like Paul, the apostle John urges believers to have confidence and not shrink away from Him in shame at His coming (1 John 2:28). As with us, it may have been easy for the early Christians to forget their Savior. For many, their lives must have been imperfect. John (and Paul) tie the believers' lives to the hope of the Rapture so that they might not shrink away from His face with guilt when He arrives.

John adds that just fixing hope on Jesus' return has a purifying effect on the child of God: "Everyone who has this hope fixed on Him purifies himself . . . One who sets his hope by faith on the Son of God experiences an inward purification that is as complete as Christ's own purity."

Imminence

Without doubt, the early church and the apostles hoped for Christ's soon return. The use of the terms "we, you, and us" are proof that the Rapture could have happened in Paul's own generation. As with some engagements, a wedding date may not have been set, yet the bride and groom long for and anticipate their coming union. The disciples had this longing but were given no hint as to the time of the Rapture. Since it did not come upon them, we do not question their hope nor the Lord's revelation about the doctrine itself. It simply means that it is yet to come.

The Use of the Technical Term *Parousia* to Describe the Rapture

It is not the purpose of this section to give a complete study on the word *parousia* except to simply say that the word can be applied to the rapture of the church or to the coming of Christ to establish the millennial kingdom. Context is the key issue in determining which coming is in view. It is also important to note that the word does not mean simply "a coming." It may, by context, mean a presence, an arrival, a situation, or simply the coming of a dignitary for an official visit.

Thus, when the word *parousia* is used in rapture passages, it in no way has to be understood as a coming to stay. Nor does the word automatically have to relate to the second coming of Christ; that is, His coming to earth to reign on the throne of David. By context, then, it may just be translated the "event," the "appearance," or the "visit." In light of this, the following selected passages are translated from the Greek text.

James 5:7–9: "Be waiting steadfastly then, until the time of the *visitation* arrives. Be waiting steadfastly . . . because the *visitation* of the Lord has progressively been drawing near."

First Thessalonians 2:17–19: "Are not you in fact [our joy] when we face our Lord Jesus at [the time of] His appearance."

First Thessalonians 3:13: "That [He may] firm up the hearts of you faultless, . . . in the [very] presence of the God and Father of us with the *arrival* of our Lord Jesus.

Other Expressions for the Coming

Besides *parousia,* other words and phrases describe the idea of Christ's rapture return to catch His own away. These words add weight and confirm this doctrine.

"I Will Return"

Jesus said, "I will come again, and receive you to Myself" (John 14:3). Actually it reads, "Again I am coming" *(palin erchomai).* By context and because of the "again," this should be taken as a future present. "I will be coming again." This should be taken as a definite promise. "This use of the present tense denotes an event which has not yet occurred, but which is regarded as so certain that in thought it may be contemplated as already coming to pass." Since He was addressing the apostles, this return could have even taken place while these disciples were alive.

The Lord's Coming Is Imminent

Besides using the word *parousia,* James adds, this coming is at hand (James 5:8). From the Greek the expression, "is at hand" *(engizo)* could read, "The coming of the Lord has progressively been approaching, coming nearer, drawing nearer. The word has the idea 'to be imminent' and can be translated 'to be at the point of.' The word *engizo* is related to the noun that has the idea of "in the vicinity of, close by."

James further sees Jesus the Judge standing right at the door (5:9). Christ has come right up to the door. By using the perfect tense, the apostle is saying, "He is, as it were, even now approaching the door."

The Lord Descends from Heaven

In 1 Thessalonians 4:16, the word "descends" means "to come down" *(katabaino)*. He will (future tense) come down from heaven." The result is that the dead in Christ shall rise first, then we who are alive and remain shall be caught up. But notice, He does not stay here on earth. In fact, *we*, along with the resurrected, are taken up to Him. This is one of the most important characteristics of the door."

Gathering Together up to Him

In 2 Thessalonians 2:1, though the apostle Paul uses the word *parousia* to describe the rapture coming of Christ he then adds "and our gathering together with him." Several Greek scholars feel the "coming" and the "gathering" are the same event and thus the passage should read "the coming, *even* the gathering together." Ellicott sees this "gathering" the same as the "taking up" in 1 Thessalonians 4:14–17. A. T. Robertson adds: "Paul is referring to the rapture, mentioned in 1 Thess. 4:15–17, and the being forever with the Lord thereafter."

The Blessed Hope and Appearing

Though the noun "appearing" *(epiphaneia)* can refer to the Second Coming of Jesus (2 Thess. 2:8), twice it refers to the rapture coming of our Lord (1 Tim. 6:14; Titus 2:13). As a verb, "appear" is used twice in 1 John to refer to the Rapture (2:28, 3:2), "when he appears."

In Titus 2:13 Paul says we are looking for this appearing of the glory of our great God and Savior, Jesus Christ. "The glory" is a descriptive genitive, translated as an adjective, thus, "the glorious appearance." The "and" between the two phrases "is explanatory, introducing the definition of the character of the thing hoped for. Looking for the object of hope, *even* the appearing of the glory. The Greek connects 'the blessed hope and glorious appearing' under one article, suggesting that the reference is to one event viewed from two aspects." The reference to the Lord should read, "the great God *even* Savior, Christ Jesus."

Being Taken to the Father

Three main passages refer directly to our being raptured to the Father. The first is John 14:1–3. "In My Father's house are many dwelling places . . . I go to prepare a place for you" (v. 2). This house could not be the location of the earthly kingdom in which Christ will reign. Jesus is going *now*, in the historical context of this passage and in reference to the near event of His death, to His Father's house. He will come for His own and take them back to a location in heaven He has prepared.

Thus, this is a specific and personal promise concerning the new dispensation of the church. His coming for them will either be the bodily resurrection or the bodily Rapture. We know now, of course, that they died. They now await the resurrection of their new bodies and the joining of their souls to those bodies.

First Thessalonians 3:13 pictures believers in Christ as kept "in holiness before [in the very presence of] our God and Father at the coming of our Lord Jesus Christ with all His saints." Paul is arguing for the believers' maturity, spiritually and morally, so that they may stand before God *uncensored* by the way they lived.

In a powerful passage on the Trinity and the deity of Christ, Paul writes about the appearing of the glory of our great God and Savior, Jesus Christ (Titus 2:13). Though the Father and the Son are separate persons in the Godhead, they share the same essence and attributes. We are raptured by God the Son and taken to the very presence of God the Father. In the same epistle, Paul says, "God [is] our Savior" (3:4) and "Christ [is] our Savior" (3:6).

Those in Christ or Allusions to the Church

The Rapture has to do with the dispensation of the church, or those "in Christ." The church age is a unique period with special promises. Those with Him now by faith will not face the coming wrath (1 Thess. 5:9). There was nothing like the Rapture for Old Testament saints, and there will be nothing similar for Tribulation believers.

Most of the rapture passages mention the believers' relationship to Jesus. Paul speaks of our Lord Jesus at His coming (1 Thess. 2:19) and of the dead as those who have fallen asleep in Jesus (4:14), who are now called "the dead in Christ" and who will rise first (4:17). The reason for the Rapture, Paul says, is so we might escape the coming wrath and obtain salvation through our Lord Jesus Christ (5:9). Awake or asleep we will live together with Him (5:10). The apostle continues to punctuate this relationship with our Redeemer when he reminds the confused Thessalonians of this coming of our Lord Jesus Christ and our gathering together to Him (2 Thess. 2:1).

In Paul's great resurrection and rapture section, 1 Corinthians 15:12–28, both events are tightly tied to believers' spiritual position in Christ. In Christ all shall be made alive, he says (15:21). Jesus is the firstfruits of the resurrection and then those who are Christ's at His coming (25:23). And following the apostle's great description of believers' change at the Rapture and the resurrection of the dead, he concludes with this triumphant statement, "thanks be to God, who gives us the victory *because of* our Lord Jesus Christ" (15:57, emphasis mine).

In Titus, Paul calls the Lord "our great God and Savior, Jesus Christ" (2:13). He gave Himself for us, and thus redeems and purifies a people for His own possession (2:14).

These statements are important because they reveal the unique position the church now has with its Savior that spares it from coming wrath. "When God vents his anger against earth dwellers (Rev. 6:16–17), the body of Christ will be in heaven as the result of the series of happenings outlined in [1 Thess.] 4:14–17 (cf. 3:13). This is God's purpose" (Thomas).

"At Christ's coming . . . the earthly, transient appearance will be changed, whether by resurrection of those dead or by rapture of the living, and believers will be transformed and will receive glorified bodies that will more adequately display their essential character . . . as children of God and shares of divine life in Christ" (Kent).

Conclusion

These rapture passages form webs of related themes that can be identified and cataloged. Key verses interface with each other and give patterns that are undeniable. All the accumulated rapture data strengthens the doctrine and gives believers assurance. These verses spell out that the living believers in Christ will be changed and taken home by the Lord before the terrible period of the wrath begins, and they reveal that the dead in Christ will be resurrected to receive a new, eternal body. Together we go home with the Lord and are presented to God our Father.

See also RAPTURE, HISTORY OF THE.

Mal Couch

Thomas Ice and Timothy Demy, *When the Trumpet Sounds* (Eugene, Oreg.: Harvest House, 1995), 26–56.

RAPTURE, HISTORY OF THE

A history of the doctrine of theRapture is of necessity a history of pretribulationism, since most other views do not distinguish between the two phases of Christ's return—the Rapture and the Second Advent. The partial rapture idea and midtribulationism have been developed only within the past one hundred years.

That the earliest documents (in addition to the New Testament canon) of the ancient church reflect a clear premillennialism is generally conceded, but great controversy surrounds the early understanding of the Rapture in relation to the Tribulation. Pretribulationists point to the early church's clear belief in imminency and a few passages from a couple of documents as evidence that pretribulationism was held by at least a few from the earliest times.

As was typical of every area of the early church's theology, views of prophecy were undeveloped and sometimes contradictory, a seedbed out of which developed various and diverse theological viewpoints. It is hard to find clear pretribulationism spelled out in the fathers; there are found clear pretribulational elements that, if systematized with their other prophetic views, contradict posttribulationism and support pretribulationism.

Since imminency is considered to be a crucial feature of pretribulationism by scholars such as John F. Walvoord, it is significant that the apostolic fathers, though posttribulational, at the same time just as clearly taught imminence. Since it was common in the early church to hold contradictory positions without even an awareness of inconsistency, it would not be surprising to learn that their era supports both views. Larry Crutchfield notes, "This belief in the imminent return of Christ within the context of ongoing persecution has prompted us to broadly label the views of the earliest fathers, 'imminent intratribulationism.'"

Expressions of imminency abound in the apostolic fathers. Clement of Rome, Ignatius of Antioch, The Didache, The Epistle of Barnabas, and The Shepherd of Hermas all speak of imminency. Furthermore, the Shepherd of Hermas speaks of the pretribulational concept of escaping the Tribulation: "You have escaped from great Tribulation on account of your faith, and because you did not doubt in the presence of such a beast. Go, therefore, and tell the elect of the Lord His mighty deeds, and say to them that this beast is a type of the great Tribulation that is coming. If then ye prepare yourselves, and repent with all your heart, and turn to the Lord, it will be possible for you to escape it, if your heart be pure and spotless, and ye spend the rest of the days of your life in serving the Lord blamelessly."

Evidence of pretribulationism surfaces during the early medieval period in a sermon some attribute to Ephraem the Syrian entitled "Sermon on the Last Times, the Antichrist, and the End of the World." The sermon was written sometime between the fourth and sixth centuries. The rapture statement reads as follows: "Why therefore do we not reject every care of earthly actions and prepare ourselves for the meeting of the Lord Christ, so that he may draw us from the confusion, which overwhelms all the world? . . . For all the saints and elect of God are gathered, prior to the Tribulation that is to come, and are taken to the Lord lest they see the confusion that is to overwhelm the world because of our sins."

This statement evidences a clear belief that all Christians will escape the Tribulation through a gathering to the Lord. How else can this be understood other than as pretribulational? The later Second Coming of Christ to the earth with the saints is mentioned at the end of the sermon.

By the fifth century A.D., the amillennialism of Origen and Augustine had won the day in the established church—East and West. It is probable that there was always some form of premillennialism throughout the Middle Ages, but it existed primarily underground. Dorothy de F. Abrahamse notes: "By medieval times the belief in an imminent apocalypse had officially been relegated to the role of symbolic theory by the church; as early as the fourth century, Augustine had declared that the Revelation of John was to be interpreted symbolically rather than literally, and for most of the Middle Ages church councils and theologians considered only abstract eschatology to be acceptable speculation. Since the nineteenth century, however, historians have recognized that *literal apocalypses did continue to circulate in the medieval world* and that they played a fundamental role in the creation of important strains of thought and legend" (emphasis added).

It is believed that sects like the Albigenses, the Lombards, and the Waldenses were attracted to premillennialism, but little is known of the details of their beliefs since the Catholics destroyed their works whenever they were found.

It must be noted at this point that it is extremely unlikely for the Middle Ages to produce advocates of a pretribulation rapture when the more foundational belief, premillennialism, is all but absent. Thus, the rapture question is likewise absent. This continued until the time of the Reformation, when many things within Christendom began to be revolutionized.

Premillennialism began to be revived as a result of at least three factors.

1. The Reformers went back to the sources, which for them were the Bible and the apostolic fathers. This exposed them to an orthodox premillennialism. Specifically significant was the reappearance of the full text of Irenaeus's *Against Heresies,* includinged the last five chapters that espouse a consistent futurism and cast the Seventieth Week of Daniel into the future.

2. They repudiated much, not all, of the allegorization that dominated mediaeval hermeneutics by adopting a more literal approach, especially in the area of the historical exegesis.

3. Many of the Protestants came into contact with Jews and learned Hebrew. This raised concerns over whether passages that speak of national Israel were to be taken historically or continue to be allegorized in the tradition of the Middle Ages. The more they were taken as historical, the more the Reformers awakened to premillennial interpretations, in spite of the fact that they were often labeled "Judaizers."

By the late 1500s and the early 1600s, premillennialism began to return as a factor within the mainstream church after more than a thousand-year reign of amillennialism. With the flowering of biblical interpretation during the late Reformation period, premillennial interpreters began to abound throughout Protestantism and so did the development of related issues like the Rapture.

It has been claimed that some separated the Rapture from the Second Coming as early as Joseph Mede, who is considered the father of English premillennialism, in his seminal work *Clavis Apocalyptica* (1627). Paul Boyer says that Increase Mather proved "that the saints would 'be *caught up into the Air*' beforehand, thereby escaping the final conflagration—an early formulation of the Rapture doctrine more fully elaborated in the nineteenth century." Whatever these men were saying, it is clear that the application of a more literal hermeneutic was leading to a distinction between the Rapture and the Second Coming as separate events.

Others began to speak of the Rapture. "Peter Jurieu in his book *Approaching Deliverance of the church* (1687) taught that Christ would come in the air to rapture the saints and return to heaven before the battle of Armageddon. He spoke of a secret Rapture prior to His coming in glory and judgment at Armageddon. Philip Doddridge's commentary on the New Testament (1738) and John Gill's commentary on the New Testament (1748) both use the term *rapture* and speak of it as imminent. It is clear that these men believed that this coming will precede Christ's descent to the earth and the time of judgment. The purpose was to preserve believers from the time of judgment. James Macknight (1763) and Thomas Scott (1792) taught that the righteous will be carried to heaven, where they will be secure until the time of judgment is over" (Benware).

Frank Marotta believes that Thomas Collier, in 1674, makes reference to a pretribulational rapture but rejects the view, thus showing his awareness that such a view was being taught.

Perhaps the clearest reference to a pretribulation rapture before Darby comes from Baptist Morgan Edwards (founder of Brown University) who, in 1742–44, saw a distinct rapture three and a half years before the start of the Millennium.

As futurism began to replace historicism within premillennial circles in the 1820s, the modern proponent of dispensational pretribulationism arrived on the scene. J. N. Darby claims to have first understood his view of the Rapture as the result of Bible study during a convalescence in December 1826 and January 1827. He is the fountainhead for the modern version of the doctrine.

The doctrine of the Rapture spread around the world through the Brethren movement with which Darby and other like-minded Christians were associated. It appears that either through their writings or personal visits to North America, this version of pretribulationism was spread throughout American evangelicalism. Two early proponents of the view include Presbyterian James H. Brookes and Baptist J. R. Graves.

The rapture doctrine was further spread through annual Bible conferences such as the Niagara Bible Conference (1878–1909); turn-of-the-century publications like *The Truth* and *Our Hope;* popular books like Brookes's *Maranatha*, William Blackstone's *Jesus Is Coming*, and *The Scofield Reference Bible* (1909). Many of the greatest Bible teachers of the first half of the twentieth century help spread the doctrine, men such as Arno Gaebelein, C. I. Scofield, A. J. Gordon, James M. Gray, R. A. Torrey, Harry Ironside, and Lewis S. Chafer.

In virtually every major metropolitan area in North America a Bible institute, Bible college, or seminary was founded that expounded dispensational pretribulationism. Schools like Moody Bible Institute, the Philadelphia Bible College, Bible Institute of Los Angeles (BIOLA), and Dallas Theological Seminary taught and defended these views. These teachings were found primarily in independent churches, Bible churches, Baptist churches, and a significant number of Presbyterian churches. Around 1925, pretribulationism was adopted by many Pentecostal denominations such as the Assemblies of God and the Foursquare Gospel denomination. Pretribulationism was dominant among charismatics in the 1960s and 1970s. Hal Lindsey's *Late Great Planet Earth* (1970) furthered the spread of the pretribulation rapture doctrine as it exerted great influence throughout popular American culture and then around the world. Many radio and TV programs taught pretribulationism as well.

Although still widely popular among evangelicals and fundamentalists, dominance of pretribulationism began to wane first in some academic circles in the 1950s and 1960s. A decline among Pentecostals, charismatics, and evangelicals began in the 1980s as the result of a shift toward greater social concern. Pretribulationism is still the most widely held view of the day, but it cannot be taken for granted in many evangelical, charismatic, and fundamentalist circles as it was a generation ago.

The doctrine of the Rapture has not been the most visible teaching in the history of the church. However, it has had significant advocates throughout the last two thousand years. It has surfaced wherever premillennialism is taught, especially with literal interpretation, futurism, dispensationalism, and a distinction between Israel and the church. Regardless of its history, belief in the Rapture has been supported primarily by those who attempt a faithful exposition of the biblical text.

See also RAPTURE, DOCTRINE OF THE.

Thomas D. Ice

Roy A. Huebner, *The Truth of the Pre-Tribulation Rapture Recovered* (Millington, N.J.: Present Truth Publishers, 1976); Thomas D. Ice, "Why the Doctrine of the Pretribulational Rapture Did Not Begin with Margaret Macdonald" in *Bib Sac* (April–June 1990), 155–68; Thomas Ice and Timothy Demy, eds., *When The Trumpet Sounds* (Eugene, Oreg.: Harvest House, 1995); Frank Marotta, *Morgan Edwards: An Eighteenth Century Pretribulationist* (Morganville, N.J.: Present Truth Publishers, 1995); *Precious Truths Revived and Defended Through J.N. Darby*, vol. 1 (Morganville, N.J.: Present Truth Publishers, 1991); Richard R. Reiter, "A History of the Development of The Rapture Positions" in *The Rapture: Pre-, Mid-, or Post-Tribulational?,* ed. Richard R. Reiter (Grand Rapids: Zondervan, 1984), 11–44; Charles C. Ryrie, *Come Quickly, Lord Jesus: What You Need to Know about the Rapture* (Eugene, Oreg.: Harvest House, 1996); John F. Walvoord, *The Blessed Hope and the Tribulation* (Grand Rapids: Zondervan, 1976); John F. Walvoord, *The Rapture Question*, revised ed. (Grand Rapids: Zondervan, 1955).

RAPTURE , PARTIAL-

The partial-rapture theory, a minority view among pretribulationists, affirms that the rapture/resurrection of believers is for those only who are watching and waiting for Christ's return. Not all believers will be raptured; only those who have some degree of spiritual attainment that makes them worthy of the Rapture. Thus, the *subjects*, not the *timing*, of the Rapture is at issue. And genuine, not merely professing, Christians are its subjects. The Rapture is viewed as a reward, not a privilege.

After the initial Rapture of all prepared believers at Christ's return in the air, several groups will be raptured during the Tribulation—as they become spiritually prepared. The Tribulation will purge the remaining believers from their sin and carnality (based on Rev. 7:9–14; 12:5; 16:15). However, if such believers do not change at all during the Tribulation, they will even miss the Second Coming and the Millennium—to be resurrected at the end of the Millennium (Rev. 20:5).

One major purpose of the Tribulation is the testing of lukewarm, shallow, Laodicean Christians. Like the foolish virgins, they were left behind, because they were not watchful.

This restrictive view of the rapture was first articulated in the mid-nineteenth century by a small group of pretribulationists in England. Their main publication was the *Dawn*. The first proponent of the modern theory of partial rapture was Robert Govett (1853), but its ablest proponent was G. H. Lang. Leaders such as D. M. Panton (editor of the *Dawn*), Govett, G. H. Pember, J. A. Seiss, Austin Sparks, and a few others sincerely taught and wrote. But they were mostly considered heterodox by other pretribulationists.

Some proof texts of the partial rapturists are: (1) Matthew 24:41–42, Two women shall be grinding, one shall be taken; (2) Luke 21:36, Watch, that ye may be accounted worthy to escape; (3) 1 Corinthians 15:23, Every man in his own order, showing a division in the ranks of believers; (4) Philippians 3:11, where even Paul expresses doubt about his own resurrection; (5) 2 Timothy 4:8, to all that love His appearing; (6) Hebrews 9:28, to them that look for Him shall He appear the second time; (7) Revelation 3:10, because thou hast kept the word, I also will keep from the hour.

Most evangelicals reject the partial-rapture theory for the following reasons.

Most of the proof texts are wrongly interpreted to deal with the Rapture instead of the Second Coming; other texts simply describe the positional sanctification of every believer; the Philippians passage describes Paul's desire to excel (not just to be present) at the rapture.

The partial-rapture theory, based on a works principle, adversely affects the doctrine of soteriology (salvation). Evangelicals usually carry over to the rapture experience the strong belief of salvation by grace alone.

The Scripture pictures the Body of Christ as one unit. And if division is indicated, it is usually between true and professing (false) believers. But partial rapturists further divide the former into worthy and unworthy believers. This splits the body of Christ.

The Rapture passages pictures an all-inclusive coverage: 1 Corinthians 15:51, we . . . all; 1 Thessalonians 4:14, if we believe Jesus died and rose again: a cardinal belief; verse 16, dead in Christ; 1 Thessalonians 1:9–10; 2:19; 5:4–11.

First Thessalonians 5:9–10, Whether we wake or sleep, could be contextually translated as whether we watch or are unwatchful.

If unprepared living believers must go through the Tribulation, then, logically, unprepared dead believers must also be in some sort of purgatory. And nowhere does the Bible teach a purgatory.

See also RAPTURE, DOCTRINE OF THE.

Paul Lee Tan

R. Govett, *Entrance into the Kingdom* (London: Charles J. Thynne, 1923); G. H. Lang, *Firstborn Sons Their Rights and Risks* (London: Oliphants Ltd., 1943); D. M. Panton, *The Letters to the Seven Churches* (London: R. F. Hunger Printer, 1912); G. H. Pember, *The Great Prophecies* (London: Revell, 1912); George L. Rose, *Tribulation Till Translation* (Glendale, Calif.: Rose Publishing, 1943); Charles H. Welch, *The Testimony of the Lord's Prisoner* (London: Fred P. Brininger, n.d.).

RAPTURE, POSTTRIBULATIONAL VIEW OF

Good people have studied the prophetic Scriptures and arrived at different conclusions concerning when the Rapture occurs in relation to the Great Tribulation. Some claim the Rapture occurs after the Tribulation is over because the church is promised tribulation on earth (John 16:1–2; Rev. 12:12). This view is known as *posttribulationism,* although it is also sometimes referred to as *covenant* or *historic premillennialism.* Others claim that Christians will pass through the first half of the Tribulation, but be raptured prior to the last three and a half years. This view is known as midtribulationism. A third view holds to a pretribulation Rapture, claiming that there are several biblical arguments suggesting the rapture comes at the beginning of the Great Tribulation.

Most of the debate over the Rapture in premillennial circles today exists between the posttribulation and pretribulation positions. (Unfortunately, this debate has often degenerated into unjustified and sometimes slanderous charges between the differing sides.) Contrasting the basic statements of the pretribulation and posttribulation views, Ryrie has prepared the following chart.

Posttribulation Rapture

Posttribulationism is that view which anticipates the church will endure the Great Tribulation and be raptured at its conclusion. The rapture and Second Coming of Christ is viewed as one and the same. "The church of Christ will not be removed from the earth until the Advent of Christ at the very end of the present Age: The Rapture and the Appearing take place at the same crisis; hence Christians of that generation will be exposed to the final affliction under Antichrist" (Reese).

Posttribulation writers suggest several proofs for their theory. It should be noted that not every writer holding this view would necessarily agree with all the arguments listed, but the following list identifies the major arguments by leading speakers in this theological camp.

	PRETRIBULATIONISM		POSTTRIBULATIONISM
1.	Rapture occurs before the Tribulation.	1.	Rapture occurs after the Tribulation.
2.	Church experiences Revelation 3:10 before the Tribulation.	2.	Church experiences Revelation 3:10 at the end of the Tribulation.
3.	Day of the Lord begins with the Tribulation.	3.	Day of the Lord begins at the close of the Tribulation.
4.	1 Thessalonians 5:2–3 occurs at beginning of the Tribulation.	4.	1 Thessalonians 5:2–3 occurs near the end of the Tribulation.
5.	144,000 redeemed at start of Tribulation.	5.	144,000 redeemed at conclusion of Tribulation.
6.	Rapture and Second Coming separated by 7 years.	6.	Rapture and Second Coming are a single event.
7.	Living Israelites judged at Second Coming.	7.	No such judgment.
8.	Living Gentiles judged at Second Coming.	8.	Living Gentiles judged after Millennium.
9.	Parents of Millennial population come from survivors of judgments on living Jews and Gentiles.	9.	Parents of Millennial population come from 144,000 Jews.
10.	Believers of church age judged in heaven between Rapture and Second Coming.	10.	Believers of church age judged after Second Coming or at conclusion of Millennium.

Historical Argument

One argument advanced by post-tribulation writers is that the early church held their view. For this reason they sometimes refer to themselves as historic premillennialists. This argument has both a positive and negative emphasis. The positive argument is stated by Gundry: "Until Augustine in the fourth century, the early church generally held to the premillennarian understanding of Bible eschatology. The chiliasm entailed a futuristic interpretation of Daniel's Seventieth Week, the Abomination of Desolation, and the personal Antichrist. And it was posttribulational. Neither mentioned nor considered, the possibility of a pretribulational rapture seems never to have occurred to anyone in the early church."

There are two points that need to be observed in relation to these criticisms of the pretribulation position.

1. It is questionable if anyone can demonstrate that there was a finely developed eschatological position taught by the early church. This means the early church was not clearly pretribulational nor posttribulational. "The early church believed in Tribulation, the imminent coming of Christ, and a Millennium to follow. The early church was clearly premillennial but not clearly pretribulational, nor was it clearly posttribulational when measured against today's developed pre- or posttribulation teachings" (Ryrie).

2. The time of the Rapture was not an issue with early church fathers. They knew Christ was coming imminently. It was not until a hundred years ago that the Rapture became an issue. Someone has said that each generation fights its own theological battles. By this is meant that the church does not deal extensively with an issue until a need arises that demands attention. Then the issue is debated until it becomes systematically formulated. It seems that at different periods in church history, different doctrines have been at issue. In the two centuries following Christ's appearance on earth, the issue was Christology. In the early 1500s, debate over the doctrine of justification was renewed by Martin Luther. During the eighteenth century, sanctification was emphasized by John Wesley. In the twentieth century, the doctrine of eschatology has been the focal point of theological discussion; therefore, it is only natural that the timing of events has been closely analyzed as never before in Christian history.

Pentecost supports this conclusion, "It should be observed that each era of church history has been occupied with a particular doctrinal controversy, which has become the object of discussion, revision, and formulation, until there was general acceptance of what Scripture taught. The entire field of theology was thus formulated through the ages. It was not until the last century that the field of eschatology became a matter to which the mind of the church was turned."

Argument Against Imminency

One cannot read the New Testament and conclude the writers believed in other than an imminent return of Christ. Christians are exhorted to keep watching for it (1 Thess. 5:1–8; 2 Peter 3:8–10) and to wait for it (1 Cor. 1:7; 1 Thess. 1:9–10; Titus 2:13). These commands were as meaningful and applicable in the first century as they are today. Even if there are implied signs concerning the end time, that does not preclude the belief in the imminent return of Christ. Signs are not absolute measurements of time concerning His return, but relate to general conditions on earth when He returns. Imminency means He can come at any time.

The argument against the imminent return of Christ is normally based on a number of signs that had to be accomplished before He could return. It is also argued that certain events, such as the fall of Jerusalem or the death of Peter, had to happen before Jesus could return; therefore, He could not have returned before these things happened and was not expected by the church prior to these events. MacPherson lists the following twelve arguments against imminence.

1. The Great Commission fulfillment implies a long period of time.
2. Seed growth in Matthew 13 is a time-consuming process.
3. Paul expected death, not rapture, in 2 Timothy 4:6–8.

4. Jesus predicted Peter's martyrdom in John 21:18–19.
5. The Matthew 24 signs must come first.
6. A big interval between Christ's ascension and return expected: Jewish dispersion into all nations (Luke 21); a man travelling into a far country, after a long time the lord of those servants comes (Matt. 25).
7. Apostasy of the last days takes time to develop.
8. The bridegroom tarried in the parable of the virgins.
9. The Pastoral Epistles teach the church's continuing ministry, which involves time.
10. Paul says Christ's coming is not imminent (2 Thess. 2:1–3), for apostasy and the Antichrist must come first.
11. The view of seven phases of church history (seven churches of Revelation) involves a large lapse of time and imminence difficulties for pretribulationists; could Christ have come before the last phase?
12. Exhortations to watch and be ready are tied to so-called second stage in Matthew 24 and 25, 1 Corinthians 1:7, Colossians 3:4, 1 Thessalonians 3:13, 2 Thessalonians 1:7–10, 1 Peter 1:13, 1 Peter 4:13, and 1 John 2:28.

At first glance, the arguments may appear conclusive, but in light of the biblical teaching on imminence, they require closer evaluation. When this is done, the list reveals at least seven fundamental errors in interpretation.

1. MacPherson fails to interpret the Scriptures in the context of revelation. Conservative scholars are generally agreed the prophecy concerning Peter's martyrdom was recorded by John perhaps as much as thirty years after Peter was killed. How this could discourage the early Christians who first read this gospel from believing in the imminent return of Christ is difficult to comprehend. The context in which this prophecy exists suggests some readers may have believed Christ would return even before the death of the aging apostle John (John 21:23).

2. A second hermeneutical problem apparent in the list is evident in the failure to interpret a verse within its biblical context. This is particularly evident in the claim that Paul anticipated death, not rapture. It was Paul who most fully developed the doctrine of an imminent rapture of the church (1 Cor. 15; 1 Thess. 4). If toward the end of his life, he spoke of death as a very real possibility, it does not necessarily mean he was denying the doctrine of imminency.

3. MacPherson assumes certain conclusions that the early church would not have assumed. The fulfillment of the Great Commission does not necessarily imply a long time. Within their generation the early Christians were accused of having turned the world upside down (Acts 17:8). Paul himself claimed the Gospel had been preached "in all the world" during his lifetime (Col. 1:5–6). While MacPherson might believe apostasy takes time to develop, that was neither the experience nor conviction of the early church. Even before the Gospel was preached outside the city limits of Jerusalem, the church had to deal with the problem of deterioration (Acts 5:1–11). The whole emphasis of the biblical teaching concerning apostasy is that its growth is rapid (cf. 2 John 8; Jude; 1 Cor. 15:33f.; Gal. 3:1–5).

4. A fourth problem with the list is its dependence upon parables. MacPherson makes parables teach more than they may have been intended to teach. Jesus did not teach the parable of the ten virgins to convince His listeners that the bridegroom intends to be late arriving but to teach them to watch because he might come at any moment. Also, Jesus did not teach the parable of the sower to discuss the time it takes for germination but to teach the certainty of the harvest (judgment).

5. Posttribulationists tend to ignore the distinction between the Rapture and Second Coming. This is evident in arguments 5, 10 and 12 in the preceding list. The biblical distinction between the Rapture and Second Coming of Christ is a major argument for the pretribulational view.

6. Another error in MacPherson's list is his misunderstanding of the doctrine of imminence and its application to the Christian life. There can be no question that imminence

is taught in Scripture and was believed by the early church.Those believers, who understood that Christ could return at any moment, did not go to the mountains in white robes to wait for the Rapture. Rather, Christians obeyed the exhortation to be diligent in their labors that they might be found working when he returned. "The doctrine of imminency is taught in Scripture in such passages as John 14:2–3; 1 Corinthians 1–7; Philippians 3:20–21; 1 Thessalonians 1:9–10; 4:16–17; 5:5–9; Titus 2:13; James 5:8–9; Revelation 3:10; 22:17–22. . . . the early church held to the doctrine of imminency" (Pentecost).

When properly understood, none of the objections listed by MacPherson are effective except his eleventh argument involving the historical interpretation of the seven churches in Revelation 2–3. This interpretation, however, is not the only view held by premillennialists (the *Ryrie Study Bible* presents them as "types of churches in all generations"). It is a weak foundation upon which to erect a denial of a clearly taught biblical doctrine. This typical interpretation has become popular only in the twentieth century, and not many theologians would dream of building a theology or any part of it upon this one interpretation.

The Church in the Tribulation

Another argument of the posttribulationist is that the church will endure the Great Tribulation. Verses are cited such as Job 15:17–19; John 16:1–2, 33; Acts 8:1–4; Romans 12:12, noting that tribulation is promised to the Christian, not escape from tribulation. Those holding this position argue that this tribulation is simply the trials experienced over the years by Christians, so they equate suffering with the Great Tribulation. Others agree there is a coming Tribulation and that Christians will suffer during this period but they are not subject to the wrath of God. This appears to be the majority belief of contemporary posttribulational teachers. "It is not a point of disagreement whether the church will ever suffer God's retributive wrath. She will not (John 3:36; 5:24: Rom. 5:9; 8:1; Eph. 2:3; 5:6; 1 Thess. 1:10; 5:9). And there are clear indications in the book of Revelation that the bowls of divine wrath will not touch saints, indications in addition to the theological necessity that God's wrath not touch a saved person. . . . As now, the church will suffer persecution during the Tribulation, but no saint can suffer divine wrath" (Gundry).

Similarly, Harold Ockenga argues the church will endure the Tribulation. Further, he recognizes the nature of this argument must deny the identification of the Tribulation with the wrath of God. "The church will endure the wrath of men, but will not suffer the wrath of God. This distinction which has been of great help to me is generally overlooked by pretribulationists. . . . Pretribulation rapturists identify the Tribulation with the wrath of God. If this cannot be disproved, we must believe that the church will be taken out of the world before the Tribulation, for there is no condemnation to them which are in Christ Jesus."

This line of argumentation fails to recognize at least three distinctions between the use and interpretation of the word *tribulation* and the Great Tribulation as described in Scripture.

1. First is the argument of intention and fulfillment. When the Great Tribulation and the suffering of saints is confused, it logically demands that every generation experience its own Great Tribulation. Commenting on John 16:33, Mauro notes: "If the Lord meant that the Great Tribulation was the portion of His saints, then there would needs be about three 'great tribulations' every century—upwards of fifty to the present time—in order to meet the requirements of the case."

2. The next argument notes that the Great Tribulation is everywhere in Scripture discussed as largely Jewish in character and characterized not by human wrath so much as by the wrath of God. "It will help a great deal if we see at the very beginning that the Great Tribulation is the time of Jacob's trouble, not the time of the Church's trouble. It cannot begin until after that parenthetic period that comes in between Daniel's sixty-ninth and seventieth weeks, for during all this age God makes no distinction between the

Jew and the Gentile. It will be after the church is taken out of this scene that He will recognize Israel again as a nation in special covenant relationship with Himself. Then their time of final trial will begin" (Ironside).

Further summarizing the character of the Great Tribulation, Thiessen notes, "We know, of course, that believers must through 'much tribulation enter into the kingdom of God' (Acts 14:22); but there is besides this common experience of Christians a future *period* of tribulation. In Dan. 12:1 it is spoken of as a 'great tribulation;' Luke 21:34–36 refers to it as 'that day,' depicted in the preceding part of the chapter; Rev. 3:20 speaks of it as 'the hour of trial, that hour which is come upon the whole world, to try them that dwell upon the earth;' and in Rev. 7:14 we read of a great multitude who had come 'out of great tribulation.' In the Old Testament it is referred to as the 'day of Jacob's trouble' (Jer. 30:4–7) and is the time of God's indignation with the inhabitants of the earth (Isa. 24:17–21; 26:20, 21; 31:1–3; Zech. 14:1–3). That the Tribulation period will come between the two phases of Christ's coming appears from a study of the whole program of the future. Note particularly that Matt. 24:29 declares that it will close with Christ's return in glory, i.e., with His Revelation."

Daniel 9:24–27

Some posttribulationists hold to an historic fulfillment of Daniel 9:24–27, including the Seventieth Week of that prophecy. They believe the seventy weeks are a continuous, successive, unbroken period of years that ends with the death of Stephen or the destruction of Jerusalem. Typical of this interpretation, Rose writes, "If there were 'gaps' and 'intermissions' the prophecy would be vague, misleading and deceptive. . . . The '62 weeks' joined immediately unto the '7 weeks,' and their combined '69 weeks' reached 'Unto Messiah.' Beyond HIS birth, but not to his 'triumphal entry;' only 'Unto' His public anointing. There was no 'gap' between the sixty-ninth and the seventieth weeks. . . . The 'one week' of prophetic 'Seventy weeks' began with John the Baptist; from his first public preaching the kingdom of God, the gospel dispensation commenced. These seven years, added to the 483 years, completes the 490 years . . . so that the whole of the prophecy from the times and corresponding events, has been fulfilled to the very letter. . . . All the evidence of the New Testament and of Christian experience agree with the greatest teachers of the Christian church that the Seventieth Week of Daniel's prophecy has all been fulfilled more than 1900 years ago. This leaves no future seventieth seek yet to be fulfilled in 'the great tribulation' after the rapture."

It should be here noted that not all posttribulationists hold to a historic fulfillment of Daniel's Seventieth Week. In a rebuttal of posttribulationism of J. Barton Payne, Gundry emphasizes the futurity of the Seventieth Week, noting in part, "We cannot spiritualize the phrase 'your people' (v. 24) into a spiritual Israel inclusive of the Gentiles without doing violence to the plain sense of the passage. For example, the destruction of Jerusalem, spoken of prominently in the prophecy, deals with Israel the *nation*. And yet, since in the seventy weeks the goals listed in verse 24 were to be accomplished, the seventy weeks cannot have entirely elapsed, for the finishing of Israel's transgression, the purging of her iniquity, and the bringing in of her everlasting righteousness have not reached completion. Paul writes of these as still in the future for Israel (Rom. 11:25–27)."

There are five major schools of interpretation surrounding the issue of Daniel's Seventieth Week. Pretribulationists are futurists in interpreting this passage. Walvoord summarizes the other views: "In opposition to the futurist interpretation, at least four other views have been advanced: (1) the liberal view that the seventieth seven is fulfilled in the events following the Maccabean persecution just as the preceding sixty-nine sevens were; (2) the view of Jewish scholars that the Seventieth Week is fulfilled in the destruction of Jerusalem in A.D. 70; (3) the view that the Seventieth Week of Daniel is an indefinite period beginning with Christ but extending to the end, often held by amillennarians such as Young and Leupold;

(4) that the seventieth seven is seven literal years beginning with the public ministry of Christ and ending about three and a half years after His death."

The Doctrine of the Resurrection

Probably the strongest argument presented by posttribulationists is the doctrine of resurrection. According to this argument, the Rapture must be posttribulational because the resurrection occurs after the Tribulation. The importance of this argument is seen in various statements made by posttribulation writers. According to MacPherson, "Clearly the resurrection of the holy dead takes place at the rapture of the church (1 Thess. 4:16). Therefore, 'wheresoever the resurrection is, there will be the Rapture also.' Upon examination of passages that speak of the resurrection of the holy dead, which is the first resurrection (Rev. 20:5–6), we find that this first resurrection is associated with the coming of the Lord (Isa. 26:19), the conversion of Israel (Rom. 11:15), the inauguration of the kingdom (Luke 14:14–15; Rev. 20:4–6), the giving of rewards (Rev. 11:15–16), the Great Tribulation coming before it (Dan. 12:1–3)."

Ladd views this argument as the only one based upon an explicit statement of Scripture, explaining, "With the exception of one passage, the author will grant that the Scripture nowhere explicitly states that the church will go through the Great Tribulation. God's people are seen in the Tribulation, but they are not called the church but the elect or the saints. Nor does the Word explicitly place the Rapture at the end of the Tribulation. Most of the references to these final events lack chronological indications. . . . However, in one passage, Revelation 20, the Resurrection is placed at the return of Christ in Glory. This is more than an inference."

This argument is based on the conclusion that the resurrection of Revelation 20:5–6, which is there called "the first resurrection," is the same resurrection referred to in 1 Thessalonians 4:16. Probably the most systematic of the presentations of this argument is that of Reese. Summarizing this position, Stanton writes: "Reese's argument takes on the form of a syllogism, the major premises being (1) the Old Testament Scriptures prove that the resurrection of the Old Testament saints is at the revelation of Christ, just prior to the millennial kingdom; the minor premise being (2) all Darbyists agree that the resurrection of the church synchronizes with the resurrection of Israel; hence, the conclusion is drawn (3) therefore the resurrection of the church sets the time of the rapture as posttribulational."

The major weakness of this argument is the equating of the first resurrection (Rev. 20:5–6) or the resurrection of the Old Testament saints with that resurrection occurring at the Rapture. The Scriptures identify at least four distinct resurrections, the first chronologically being the resurrection of Christ (Matt. 28:1–7). The expression "first resurrection" can therefore be understood only within the immediate context of the passage since Christ's resurrection was first. The resurrection mentioned in Revelation 20 is first in that it comes one thousand years prior to the fourth and final resurrection, but it is also third in that it follows the resurrection of Christ and the resurrection of saints that accompany the Rapture.

Questioning Darby's wisdom in making such a statement, Walvoord, for instance, suggests, "The Old Testament saints are never described by the phrase 'in Christ.' The fact that the 'voice of the archangel'—Israel's defender—is heard at the rapture is not conclusive proof that Israel is raised at that time. The tendency of followers of Darby to spiritualize the resurrection of Daniel 12:1–2 as merely the restoration of Israel, thereby refuting its posttribulationism, is to forsake literal interpretation to gain a point, a rather costly concession for premillennarians who build upon literal interpretation of prophecy. The best answer to Reese and Ladd is to concede the point that the resurrection of Old Testament saints is after the Tribulation, but to divorce it completely from the translation and resurrection of the church. Reese's carefully built argument then proves only that Darby was hasty in claiming the resurrection of the Old Testament saints at the time of the translation of the church. If the translation of the church is a different event entirely, Reese proves nothing by his argument."

Finally, perhaps the word "first" did not mean first in time but first in kind, that is, the resurrection was of God's people (whether before or after the Tribulation). The second of a different kind, involved the unsaved.

Parable of the Wheat and the Tares

An additional argument based upon the parable of the wheat and the tares is sometimes used to defend the posttribulational cause. They suggest that Christ spoke of the wheat and the tares together until the harvest (Matt. 13:30) and suggest a general judgment at the end of the age.

"The period of Christ's Second Coming, and of the judicial separation of the righteous and the wicked. Till then, no attempt is to be made to effect such separation. But to stretch this so far as to justify allowing openly scandalous persons to remain in the communion of the church, is to wrest the teaching of this parable to other than its proper design, and to go in the teeth of apostolic injunctions (1 Cor. 5)" (Brown).

It must be remembered, however, that the purpose of the kingdom parables in Matthew 13 is not to record the history of the church but rather the history of the kingdom in mystery form, that is, Christendom.

"In this series of parables, Jesus explained the course of the gospel in the world. If Israel had received Him as King, the blessings would have flowed out from Jerusalem to the ends of the earth. But the nation rejected Him, and God had to institute a new program on earth. During this present age, 'the kingdom of heaven' is a mixture of true and false, good and bad, as pictured in these parables. It is 'Christendom,' professing allegiance to the King, and yet containing much that is contrary to the principles of the King" (Wiersbe).

Conclusion

The most important event of the age of grace is yet to occur. While there are arguments that this event will take place at the end of this age, specifically at the end of seven years of Tribulation, a close study reveals there are problems in interpretation of the data to support this position. While people of good will differ in interpretation, all agree it is the blessed hope, and all pray, "even so come Lord Jesus."

See also RAPTURE, DOCTRINE OF THE.

Elmer L. Towns

David Brown, *The Four Gospels* (London: Banner of Truth Trust, 1969); Robert Gundry, *The Church and the Tribulation* (Grand Rapids: Zondervan, 1973); Harry A. Ironside, "Why the Church Will Not Go Through the Great Tribulation" in *The Sure Word of Prophecy*, ed. John W. Bradbury (New York: Revell, 1943); George E. Ladd, *The Blessed Hope* (Grand Rapids: Eerdmans, 1956); Norman S. MacPherson, *Triumph through Tribulation* (Otego, N.Y.: self-published, 1944); Philip Mauro, *Looking for the Savior* (London: Samuel E. Roberts, Publishers, n.d.); Harold J. Ockenga, "Will the Church Go Through the Tribulation? Yes" in *Christian Life* (February 1955); J. Dwight Pentecost, *Things to Come* (Grand Rapids: Zondervan, 1958); Bernard Ramm, *Protestant Biblical Interpretation* (Grand Rapids: Baker, 1974); Alexander Reese, *The Approaching Advent of Christ* (London: Marshall, Morgan & Scott, n.d.); George L. Rose, *Tribulation till Translation* (Glendale, Calif.: Rose Pub. Co., 1943); Charles C. Ryrie, *What You Should Know about the Rapture* (Chicago: Moody Press, 1981); Gerald B. Stanton, *Kept from the Hour* (Grand Rapids: Zondervan, 1956); John R. W. Stott, *Guard the Gospel: The Message of 2 Timothy* (London: InterVarsity Press, 1973); Henry Clarence Thiessen, *Lectures in Systematic Theology* (Grand Rapids: Eerdmans, 1951); John F. Walvoord, *The Rapture Question* (Grand Rapids: Zondervan, 1972); Warren W. Wiersbe, *Meet Your King* (Wheaton: Victor Books, 1980).

RAPTURE, THE PREWRATH

A Description of the View

The prewrath rapture view teaches that the Seventieth Week of Daniel 9 will have three divisions.

1. The first division will consist of the beginning of birth pangs (Matt. 24:4–8), or first four seals (Rev. 6:1–8) and will cover the first half of the Seventieth Week.

2. The second division will consist of the Great Tribulation (Matt. 24:21), or fifth seal (Rev. 6:9–11), will begin in the middle of the Seventieth Week, and will end sometime between the middle and end of the Seventieth Week. The sixth seal, with its great cosmic disturbances and major earthquake, will be a forewarning to the unsaved that the third division, the Day of the Lord, is about to begin (Rev. 6:12–17). The church (the great multitude of Rev. 7:9–17) will be raptured from the earth between the sixth and seventh seals (after the Great Tribulation and before the Day of the Lord) when Christ will come from heaven in His glorious Second Coming. Thus, the Rapture will not be a separate event from the Second Coming.

3. The third division of the Seventieth Week will consist of the Day of the Lord, will begin with the breaking of the seventh seal (Rev. 8:1), and will continue to the end of the Seventieth Week. Thus, the Day of the Lord will not begin until the breaking of the seventh seal sometime between the middle and end of the Seventieth Week. The beginning of birth pangs (seals 1–4) and Great Tribulation (fifth seal) will contain no wrath of God. They will be characterized totally by human wrath. Thus, there will be no divine wrath throughout the entire first half and a significant part of the second half of the Seventieth Week. The wrath of God will not begin until the Day of the Lord begins with the breaking of the seventh seal between the middle and end of the Seventieth Week. The church will be on earth throughout the whole first half of the Seventieth Week and the entire Great Tribulation. This means that it will be exposed to human wrath, including that of the Antichrist, contained in the beginning of birth pangs, or first four seals plus the Great Tribulation. The church, however, will not be exposed to the wrath of God. It will be raptured from the earth before the Day of the Lord will begin with its outpouring of God's wrath. Thus, the church will experience a prewrath rapture.

Problems with the View

The prewrath rapture view has a number of problems.

Concerning the Tribulation and the Day of the Lord

1. The view requires a complete distinction between the Great Tribulation and the Day of the Lord, insisting there is no overlapping of the two, that the Great Tribulation contains only human wrath, that the Day of the Lord contains the wrath of God, and that the Scriptures never associate Tribulation with the Day of the Lord's wrath. There are at least three difficulties with this distinction, (1) the Bible associates both the Day of the Lord (Joel 2:1–2) and the Great Tribulation (Dan. 12:1; Matt. 24:21) with the unparalleled time of trouble. Since there can be only one unparalleled time of trouble, this common association prompts the conclusion that the Great Tribulation cannot be totally separate from the Day of the Lord. (2) Certainly God's wrath is far worse than human wrath. In light of this, how can the great Tribulation be the unparalleled time of trouble if it will contain only human wrath? (3) The Scriptures associate Tribulation with the Day of the Lord's wrath. The same Hebrew word that communicated the concept of Tribulation or trouble was used for both the Great Tribulation (Dan. 12:1) and the Day of the Lord (Zeph. 1:15). Paul associated Tribulation with "the day of wrath and revelation of the righteous judgment of God" (Rom. 2:5–9).

Concerning the Sixth Seal

The prewrath view claims that the sixth seal will be a forewarning to the unsaved that the Day of the Lord is about to begin. By contrast, Paul declared that the Day of the Lord will come as a thief in the night (1 Thess. 5:2). Just as a thief gives the intended victim no forewarning, so the unsaved will be given no forewarning concerning when the Day of the Lord will begin.

Concerning the Great Multitude

The prewrath view asserts that the great multitude from all nations, kindreds, people, and tongues is the church, which has just been raptured in conjunction with the second coming of Christ during the time between the sixth and seventh seals. There are two problems with that identification.

1. One of the twenty-four elders indicated that the people who make up the great multitude come out of the Great Tribulation (Rev. 7:13–14). This means that all the people who make up the great multitude will be on earth during the Great Tribulation, making this a partial rapture of the church. It would include only those church saints living on earth during the Great Tribulation. It would not include all the church saints who live and die before the Great Tribulation, and who, therefore, will never be in it. By contrast, the Bible indicates that all church saints will be raptured together as one body at the same time (1 Thess. 4:13–18).

2. The Greek present tense of the main verb in the elder's statement indicates that the people who make up the great multitude do not come out of the Great Tribulation as one group at the same time, but one by one, continuously, throughout the course of the Great Tribulation, apparently through death. This again contrasts with the manner in which the church will be raptured from the earth.

Concerning the Rapture and the Second Coming

The prewrath view teaches that the church will be raptured in conjunction with the second coming of Christ. Therefore, the Rapture will not be a separate event from the Second Coming. By contrast, Jesus' teaching indicated that the order of things at His Second Coming will be the reverse of the order of things at the Rapture. At the Rapture all believers will be removed from earth and taken to heaven, and all living unbelievers will be left on earth to go into the next period of history. At Christ's Second Coming all living unbelievers will be removed from earth in judgment, and all living believers will be left on earth to go into the next period of history (the Millennium). Jesus taught this order of events at His Second Coming more than once. For example, in His parables of the tares (Matt. 13:24–30, 36–43) and of the dragnet (Matt. 13:47–50) He indicated that at the end of this age He will send His angels into the world to remove all the tares, or bad fish, (the unsaved) from the earth and to cast them into a terrible place of judgment, but the wheat, or good fish, (the saved) will be left to be part of the kingdom. In the Olivet Discourse Jesus taught that the order of things at His Second Coming immediately after the Great Tribulation will be the same as the order in the days of Noah (Matt. 24:21, 29–30, 37–39). Just as in Noah's days the flood took all the unsaved from the earth in judgment, and the saved (Noah and his family) were left on the earth to enter the next period of history, so it will be at Christ's Second Coming. Jesus gave two illustrations of this. Of two people in the field, the unbeliever will be taken from the earth in judgment, but the believer will be left in the field. Of two grinding at the mill, the unbeliever will be taken in judgment, but the believer will be left at the mill (Matt. 24:40–41). Those that were removed will be taken into the realm of death, where their bodies will be eaten by flesh-eating fowl (Luke 17:37).

Concerning Imminence

The prewrath view denies the imminence of Christ's return. By contrast numerous scholars, even many who do not advocate the pretribulation rapture view, assert that the New Testament teaches that Christ could return at any moment. They also claim that God intends this teaching to be great incentive for godly living and aggressive ministry. As many as sixteen imminency-related passages have been identified in the New Testament. One of them indicates that the Thessalonian believers continuously had the attitude of expecting or waiting up for Christ to return from heaven because they were confident that He could come at any moment (1 Thess. 1:10). Through the use of the Greek perfect tense in the verbs (James 5:8–9), James indicated two things.

1. The coming of the Lord drew near before James wrote his epistle, and His coming continues to be near (v. 8).

2. Christ as judge began to stand before the door of heaven before James wrote, and He continues to stand there (v. 9). The implication is that Christ could step through the door of heaven at any moment and cause church saints to stand before Him at the judgment seat of Christ. Thus, Christ's coming from heaven is imminent.

Concerning the Seals and the Saints

The prewrath view asserts that the seals of Revelation 6 have the function of providing security for the church saints on earth at that time. It is true that seals often have the function of making an object secure, but two things should be noted. (1) Seals provide security only for the object to which they are applied. The seals were applied to the scroll that God held in His hand (Rev. 5:1–9), not to people. Thus, the seals of Revelation 6 provide security for that scroll, not for church saints. (2) Seals provide security for an object only as long as the seals are kept intact. Christ (Rev. 6) breaks the seals, thereby ending their function of security.

Concerning Seals and the Wrath of God

The prewrath view insists that Day of the Lord's wrath will not begin until the breaking of the seventh seal (Rev. 8:1) and that, therefore, there will be no wrath of God in the first six seals, which will cover the first half plus the Great Tribulation of the Seventieth Week. Only human wrath will be contained in those seals.

1. One major problem with this teaching is that it is Christ who breaks the seals unleashing the things contained in the them. The prewrath view counters this objection in two ways. First it claims that the breaking of the first seal (Rev. 6:1–2) sets the Antichrist loose upon the world. Then it argues that certainly Christ would not turn the Antichrist loose since the Antichrist will be energized and controlled by God's great enemy, Satan. Such action by Christ would be counterproductive to God. However, this action by Christ would not be counterproductive to God if it would serve His sovereign purpose, for example, did not God have a sovereign purpose for raising up the pharaoh who severely abused Israel (Exod. 9:16; Rom. 9:17) and for hardening that ruler's heart so that he refused to obey God's command to let Israel go (Exod. 9:1, 12; 10:1)? Also, God declared (Zech. 11:15–17) that He will bring upon the world scene the foolish, idol shepherd (the Antichrist) who will desolate the people of Israel for his own selfish purposes (cf. Dan. 9:27; Matt. 24:15–23).

Second, the fifth seal (Rev. 6:9–11) involves the martyrdom of saints. The prewrath view then argues that surely Christ would not instigate the killing of His own saints. However, when Christ broke the fifth seal John did not see saints being martyred, but the disembodied souls of saints who had been slain before the fifth seal was broken. The Greek perfect tense of the verb translated "were slain" indicates that the slaying of this group of saints had already been completed before John saw their souls under the altar. When Christ breaks the fifth seal, He does not instigate the martyrdom of His saints.

2. There is another problem with the prewrath teaching that there will be no Day of the Lord wrath of God in the first six seals. Several biblical factors indicate that those seals will involve an outpouring of God's Day of the Lord wrath, beginning with the first seal.

First, Paul taught that the Day of the Lord will come suddenly with wrathful destruction at the same time that the unsaved are saying, Peace and safety (1 Thess. 5:2–3). Clearly, the Day of the Lord will begin at the time that the world is convinced that there will be no more war. The world's confidence concerning no more war will be shattered with the breaking of the first seal. That sets loose a powerful warrior who will go forth conquering and to conquer (Rev. 6:1–2). The breaking of the second seal will cause peace to be removed from the earth, with people killing one another (Rev. 6:3–4). The Scriptures indicate that wars of nations are often the weapons of God's wrath (Isa. 10:5–6; Jer. 50:9–13, 25) and that once the seals begin to be broken (Rev. 6–20), there will be no peace and safety for the world until Christ establishes the millennial kingdom after His

Second Coming to earth. In light of these things, it appears that the Day of the Lord with its outpouring of God's wrath will begin with the breaking of the first seal.

Second, the breaking of the third seal will cause famine on earth (Rev. 6:5–6). It is important to note that it is either God or Christ (one who speaks from the midst of the four beasts; compare Rev. 4:6–5:6), who will administer this famine. He will determine the price of food and extent of the famine. Scripture teaches that God uses famine as an expression of His wrath (Jer. 42:17–18; 44:8, 11–13; Ezek. 5:11–17; 7:14–15).

Third, when Christ breaks the fourth seal, one-fourth of the world's population will be killed through sword, famine, pestilence, and wild beasts (Rev. 6:7–8). In Ezekiel God declared that He sends famine, beasts, pestilence, and sword as expressions of His anger and fury (5:15–17), and He called these means of death "my four sore judgments" (14:21).

Fourth, since the breaking of the fifth seal will display the disembodied souls of martyred saints (Rev. 6:9–11), it thereby will reveal another reason why Satan's forces will deserve more divine wrath poured out on them through the remaining seals, trumpets and vials.

Fifth, the magnitude of the cosmic disturbances and earthquake that will be caused by the breaking of the sixth seal (Rev. 6:12–17) prompts the conclusion that this will be an awesome expression of God's wrath, not the work of humans. The response of the unsaved to these phenomena indicates that they will recognize this as an expression of God's wrath. In addition, Isaiah foretold the sixth seal (Isa. 2:10–22) and associated it with the Day of the Lord (v. 12). He thereby indicated that the sixth seal will involve the Day of the Lord wrath. Jesus described conditions (Matt. 24) that will exist in the world before the Abomination of Desolation in the middle of the Seventieth Week, and He called those conditions "the beginning of birth pangs" (vv. 4–8). The fact that Jesus referred to these birth pangs before the midweek Abomination of Desolation indicates that the beginning of birth pangs will take place during the first half of the Seventieth Week. A comparison of the beginning of birth pangs with the first four seals of Revelation 6 demonstrates that they are the same thing. Thus, since the beginning of birth pangs will take place during the first half of the Seventieth Week, then the first four seals must also take place then.

Since, as noted earlier, the first four seals will involve an outpouring of God's wrath and since those seals will take place during the first half of the Seventieth Week, then, contrary to the prewrath view, it can be concluded that the first half of the Seventieth Week will be characterized by an outpouring of God's wrath.

See also RAPTURE, DOCTRINE OF THE.

Renald E. Showers

Tim LaHaye, *No Fear of the Storm* (Sisters, Oreg.: Multnomah Press, 1992); Marvin J. Rosenthal, *The Pre-Wrath Rapture of the Church* (Nashville: Thomas Nelson, 1990); Renald E. Showers, *Maranatha, Our Lord, Come!* (Bellmawr, N.J.: The Friends of Israel Gospel Ministry, 1995); Gerald B. Stanton, *Kept From The Hour* (Miami Springs: Schoettle Publishing Co., 1992); Robert VanKampen, *The Sign* (Wheaton: Crossway Books, 1992).

RECONSTRUCTIONISM, CHRISTIAN

The Christian reconstruction movement began to develop in the 1960s within the conservative branch of Reformed theology or Calvinism. The movement's goal is to reconstruct society in accordance with its understanding of certain New Testament principles and the Mosaic Law. Founder of the movement is Rousas John Rushdoony. Prominent contributors include historian-economist Gary North, Greg Bahnsen, Kenneth L. Gentry, Gary DeMar, David Chilton, and many others who identify with the movement to varying degrees.

Andrew Sandlin of Rushdoony's Chalcedon Foundation has composed "The Creed of Christian Reconstruction." He lists Calvinism, theonomy, presuppositionalism, postmillennialism, and dominion as the distinctives of Reconstructionism. None of these alone distinguishes reconstructionism; however, held in concert with one another, they comprise Christian reconstructionism. Theonomy and postmillennialism are two aspects that set Christian reconstructionism apart from other traditions of Reformed theology. Normally if one adopts theonomy and postmillennialism, the other three beliefs have already been adopted.

Being a Calvinist does not make one a reconstructionist. Some of the strongest criticism of the movement comes from nonreconstructionist Calvinists. Calvinism includes a whole array of beliefs, but one aspect of Reformed theology featured in Reconstructionism is covenant theology, especially that feature of replacement theology (i.e., the church replaces Israel).

If there is any one feature unique to modern reconstructionism it would have to be theonomy (Gk. *theos*, God; *nomos*, law; thus, "God's law"). Theonomy describes the belief that, "The Christian is obligated to keep the whole law of God as a pattern for sanctification and that this law is to be enforced by the civil magistrate where and how the stipulations of God so designate." Rushdoony declares, "man grows in grace as he grows in law-keeping, for the law is the way of sanctification." Reconstructionists believe that the Law of Moses is still in force today, in spite of the many New Testament statements to the contrary (Rom. 6:14–15; 7:1–6; 1 Cor. 9:20–21; 2 Cor. 3:7–11; Gal. 4:1–7; 5:18; Eph. 2–3; Heb. 8:6–7, 13; 10:9). Even during the Mosaic era, the Law was given exclusively to Israel (Exod. 34:27; Deut. 4:6–8; Ps. 147:19–20; Eph. 2:14–15) for the purpose of separating and keeping Israel distinct from the nations (Exod. 19:5–6, 10, 14; Lev. 19:2; Deut. 7:6; 14:2). The New Testament church-age believer is not lawless, but is under the Law of Christ (1 Cor. 9:21; Gal. 6:2), which consists of hundreds of imperatives found in the New Testament epistles. Reconstructionists often speak of biblical law as if every law ever given by God always applies to all humanity regardless of jurisdictional factors like Israel and the church.

The presuppositional apologetics of Cornelius Van Til is said to be central to reconstructionism, even though Van Til distanced himself from many reconstructionist beliefs and emphasis. While Van Til's apologetic is as fine a system as ever developed to defend the faith, reconstructionists believe that it gives them the philosophical basis for maintaining a distinctly biblical approach to every area of life. They believe that Van Til's epistemology (theory of knowledge) should protect them from the inroads of humanistic thought that has so often plagued Christianity in the past. Van Til's thought is seen by many Reconstructionists as a development that will enable the Christianization of the whole world as they seek to apply the Bible in every sphere of life without sinking into the pitfalls of humanism, as did the Reformers and Puritans before them. It is seen as a tool that will facilitate the outworking of theonomy and postmillennialism. There are many who follow Van Til that are not reconstructionists, but reconstructionists tend to be his most rabid propagators and defenders.

It would be hard to conceive of the Christian reconstruction movement without postmillennialism. Without a doubt, postmillennialism provides the motivation and goal that drives the reconstructionist. Sandlin's vision of postmillennialism is as follows: "He believes Christ will return to earth only after the Holy Spirit has empowered the church to advance Christ's kingdom in time and history. He has faith that God's purposes to bring all nations, though not every individual, in subjection to Christ cannot fail. The Christian Reconstructionist is not utopian. He does not believe the kingdom will advance quickly or painlessly. He knows that we enter the kingdom through much tribulation. He knows Christians are in the fight for the 'long haul.' He believes the church may yet be in her infancy. But he believes the Faith will triumph. Under the power of the Spirit of God, it cannot but triumph."

To the reconstructionist, premillennialism is viewed as unjustified pessimism, even though the current course of history does not appear to support reconstructionist optimism.

In fact, Rushdoony sees premillennialism as a heresy in the church, because it impedes prescribed postmillennial progress. Reconstructionists tend to see contemporary downturns in society as a phase of God's judgment out of which will come a growing remnant who will rebuild Christendom upon the current rubble. They believe that precedent for such a view is that medieval Christendom and the Reformation advanced God's kingdom as they replaced pagan Rome and an apostate Christianity. With the aid of the Holy Spirit, they believe, it is already beginning to turn around and will be a matter of time before progress toward the Millennium begins to bloom in society again.

Such visions of optimism are not taught in Scripture as occurring until after the return of Christ to reign and rule upon earth from Jerusalem. Postmillennialism confuses not only the timing of the Millennium, but the agency. While it is true that God is pleased for the gospel to spread through the church's mediation; the progress of the millennium will not be through a similar agency. Postmillennialism romanticizes this present age and the Millennium because it improperly blends the age to come with this present evil age. Two major objections to equating this current age with the Millennium should be raised at this point. (1) The interaction between group, individual, and environment evidently is a lot more profound than even sociologists are willing to admit, so profound, in fact, that a catastrophic alteration is required for the perfect social order. (2) This being the case, even total regeneration of the human race would not be far-reaching enough to establish the millennial vision. The physical environment must be totally changed (Rom. 8:19–22).

Only premillennial futurism does justice to taking the text literally when it describes the radical changes that Christ's kingdom will truly bring. Only premillennialism handles passages that speak of the future Eden in the same way that the original Eden in Genesis is pictured.

Related to postmillennialism, for the reconstructionist, is its view of dominion. Sandlin says in his creed, "The Christian Reconstructionist believes the earth and all its fullness is the Lord's: that every area dominated by sin must be 'reconstructed' in terms of the Bible."

Premillennialists believe in dominion, but not in the same way as the reconstructionist. Premillennialists agree that the cultural mandate of Genesis 1:26–28 is the basis throughout history for cultural involvement. It is a creation ordinance given to all humanity. It has not been revoked. It has been affected by the Fall so that human dominion is infected with evil. But as David notes in Psalm 8:6, "Thou dost make him to rule over the works of Thy hands"; man is currently exercising dominion. It is precisely this kind of evil dominion that must be judged at Christ's Second Coming and replaced with His rule. Note the difference between a premillennial view of dominion and that of postmillennial dominion.

A major insight of dispensational premillennialism is the picture it gives of the dynamics of evil. There are three factors involved: (1) the impact of regenerated and spiritually active people relative to the impact of the remainder; (2) the restraining ministry of the Spirit during the church age in suppressing total evil domination of basic social structures; (3) all pervading domain of Satan over both the social order and its physical environment. Factor (2) is relatively stable and factor (3) in the realm of the social order appears to vary approximately inversely with factor (1). As is commonly recognized, then, the basic variable is the impact of the church.

But the unique contribution of this eschatology is how it establishes realistic upper and lower limits on the variation of satanic domination in the present social order. The upper limit of which the pretribulational rapture is an integral part states, in effect, that no matter how small the church is in the world the general social order of the world will be graciously kept from total satanic control until the rapture. Satan's plans are held in temporary suspension while the human race is given opportunity to trust Christ (2 Peter 3:9). The lower limit of which Satan's reign over physical creation is an integral part states, in effect, that no matter how many are won to Christ in the world the general social order of the world will still remain under the influence of a corrupt physical environment. Christ must return and redeem physical creation for elimination of this influence. . . . Thus dispensational premillennialism sets forth data from which it is possible to deduce a realistic picture of the working of evil in the social order today and why the "perfect" social order must be future to a supernatural realignment of the basic factors.

Dispensational premillennialists believe in victory in history in every sphere of life. Just as salvation is accomplished immediately by Christ's work as the author of a whole new race, so will the consummation be immediate, not mediate as, reconstructionists preach. Alva J. McClain notes that there is also a carryover of many accomplishments during the church age into the kingdom.

The premillennial philosophy of history makes sense. It lays a biblical and rational basis for a truly optimistic view of human history. Furthermore, rightly apprehended, it has practical effects. It says that life here and now, in spite of the tragedy of sin, is nevertheless something worthwhile; and therefore all efforts to make it better are also worthwhile. All the true values of human life will be preserved and carried over into the coming kingdom; nothing worthwhile will be lost. Furthermore, we are encouraged in the midst of opposition and reverses by the assurance that help is on the way, help from above, supernatural help—"Give the king thy judgments, O God. . . . In his days shall the righteous flourish . . . all nations shall call him blessed" (Ps. 72:1, 7, 17).

Since the present age is not the kingdom and the kingdom is yet future, the biblical premillennialist is watching and waiting for the coming King while going about the tasks He has commissioned, praying, "Come, Lord Jesus!"

Reconstructionism has greatly impacted the religious right in the development of its social and political direction. Reconstructionists have often been at the forefront in Christian day schools and in home schooling. They have also lead a revival of postmillennialism and the preterist interpretation of Bible prophecy. Reconstructionism has expanded beyond its Reformed birthplace and is increasingly making inroads into various aspects of the charismatic movement. Reconstructionism has spread considerably throughout the English-speaking world and also has a number of German and Dutch converts.

Christian reconstructionism is a movement that attempts to prematurely deploy Christ's kingdom. Thus, some of its errors include: wrongly replacing Israel with the church, spiritualizing the Bible at key points, putting believers under the Mosaic Law, teaching that Christ's return is not imminent but will occur only after the church has been the instrument of millennial bliss.

See also POSTMILLENNIALISM.

Thomas D. Ice

Greg L. Bahnsen, *Theonomy in Christian Ethics* (Phillipsburg, N.J.: Presbyterian & Reformed Publishing Co., 1977); William S. Barker and W. Robert Godfrey, eds., *Theonomy: A Reformed Critique* (Grand Rapids: Zondervan, 1990); David Chilton, *Paradise Restored: An Eschatology of Dominion* (Tyler, Tex.: Reconstruction Press, 1985); Kenneth L. Gentry Jr., *He Shall Have Dominion: A Postmillennial Eschatology* (Tyler, Tex.: Institute for Christian Economics, 1992); H. Wayne House and Thomas Ice, *Dominion Theology: Blessing or Curse?* (Portland: Multnomah, 1988); Rousas John Rushdoony, *The Institutes of Biblical Law* (Phillipsburg, N.J.: Presbyterian & Reformed Publishing Co., 1973).

RESURRECTIONS, THE

In the Old Testament

The doctrine of the resurrection in the Old Testament is rather limited in its development. But there are several very important key verses that support this doctrine and promise a new body at some glorious future day. Abraham and others were told they would go to their fathers in peace (Gen.

15:15), which may imply a future awakening to a new physical life. Psalm 73:24 makes it clear that the souls of the righteous go to be with the Lord upon death. "With Thy counsel Thou wilt guide me, and afterward receive me to glory." Resurrection was more specified in the revelation given to Job in chapter 19 of his poem. He uttered the words of hope, "I know that my Redeemer (*goel*) lives, and at the last He will take His stand on the earth. . . . Yet from my flesh I shall see God" (vv. 25–26). Since God does not have a body this must refer to the future messianic reign of Christ. As well, the verses loudly herald the promise of a new physical body that will "see" again.

Other Old Testament verses point to a resurrection. King David will be raised to "feed" the Jewish remnant in the kingdom. For God says, "I, the LORD, will be their God, and My servant David will be prince among them" (Ezek. 34:24). Some take this typologically as speaking of Christ, but most premillennialists hold that it refers to the resurrected patriarch himself. In the midst of a passage predicting the future kingdom, Isaiah says "Your dead will live; their corpses will rise. You who lie in the dust, awake and shout for joy. . . . And the earth will give birth to the departed spirits" (26:19).

It is the prophet Daniel who predicts the resurrection of the righteous following the terrible world Tribulation. He writes: "There will be a time of distress such as never occurred since there was a nation until that time; and at that time your people, everyone who is found written in the book, will be rescued. And many of those who sleep in the dust of the ground will awake, these to everlasting life, but the others to disgrace and everlasting contempt" (Dan. 12:1–2).

Two Greek words describe resurrection in the New Testament, *egiro,* "to raise," and *anisteemi,* "to stand up." Both words are used in a flurry of verses to thoroughly flesh out and mature the doctrine. There are several illustrations of resurrection that give a foretaste of this blessed hope. Lazarus was commanded by Jesus to come forth after being dead four days (John 11). Jesus had said, "I am the resurrection and the life; he who believes in Me shall live even if he dies" (v. 25). And when the Lord died on the cross, Matthew records, "the tombs were opened; and many bodies of the saints who had fallen asleep were raised" (27:52). Some have called these resuscitations rather than resurrections because those who came forth would have to die again. Too, they were not given new bodies but came forth in their old shells. The word *resuscitate* means "to revive when unconscious" (Webster) and therefore does not describe the true miracle of the event. Thus, these are more like foreshadowings, types, and pictures of what is to come. Final and ultimate resurrection will be without decay. In this, Christ sets the pattern for the saints. "[God] raised Him up from the dead, no more to return to decay" (Acts 13:34).

Resurrection of course is made possible because of the death, burial, and resurrection of Christ. He leads the way for those related to Him by faith. He makes new life possible for Old Testament saints who have gone before. The Trinity is involved in Christ's resurrection. Jesus told the Jews that He Himself would raise it up if they destroyed His body (John 2:19). As well, God the Father raised the Lord (Rom. 4:24), as also the Holy Spirit (Rom. 8:11). In a positional sense, God has already raised believers in Jesus. Paul describes how believers in this dispensation are raised up with the Lord in this spiritual way (Eph. 2:6; Col. 2:12; 3:1). This union with Him is what gives us this new eternal life.

But actual physical resurrection is the cornerstone of Paul's theology. "If Christ has not been raised, your faith is worthless; you are still in your sins" (1 Cor. 15:17). He goes on to describe true resurrection. The body is sown in the ground perishable, dishonored, in weakness, and natural (1 Cor. 15:42–44). It is raised imperishable, in glory, in power, and spiritual. It is still physical, with flesh and blood, yet impervious to sin and sickness. It is like Christ's new body. "We know that, when He appears, we shall be like Him, because we shall see Him just as He is" (1 John 3:2). The new body is not simply a floating spirit or apparition. It is actually a new, resurrected body.

Amillennialists and covenant theologians generally see only one resurrection in Scripture. For example, besides the resurrection of Christ, A. A. Hodge takes all the resurrections mentioned in the Bible as one. But dispensationalists, studying contexts, note the difference between the resurrection of those asleep in Jesus and the general resurrection of Revelation 20:5. "Those in Jesus" refers to those who have died in this dispensation and who will be raised when the trumpet sounds. The first resurrection of Revelation 20:5 points to the resurrection of those martyred in verse 4 but also ties it to the promises of the Old Testament of being raised for the kingdom. Thus it is inclusive of the resurrection of the just (Luke 14:14; Acts 24:15), the resurrection from among the dead (Luke 20:34–36), the resurrection of life (John 5:29), and the resurrection to everlasting life (Dan. 12:2; Thomas).

There is also the resurrection of all unrighteous dead for the Great White Throne judgment (Rev. 20:11–15). The lost of all dispensations are judged on the basis of their deeds (20:13). Everyone is judged with no possible appeal. They are without the imputed righteousness of Christ and thus stand clothed only with their own sinful self-works. They are condemned to the second death, the lake of fire (20:14) because their names were not written in the book of life (20:15).

See also JUDGMENTS, VARIOUS.

Mal Couch

Lewis Sperry Chafer, *Systematic Theology*, vols. 2, 4 (Grand Rapids: Kregel, 1993); David B. Gurainik, ed., *Webster's New World Dictionary* (New York: Simon and Shuster, 1980); A. A. Hodge, *Outlines of Theology* (Carlisle, Pa.: The Banner of Truth Trust, 1991); Robert L. Thomas, *Revelation 8–22* (Chicago: Moody Press, 1995).

REVELATION 11, THE TWO WITNESSES OF

The two witnesses in Revelation 11 appear suddenly, without extensive biographical information other than the fact that they are prophets of God (11:3–4, 10). Godet goes to the point of saying they are the "most startling feature of the book"—which is an overstatement considering the subject matter of the book. However, the witnesses do accomplish an important ministry for God during the Tribulation.

Who Are the Two Witnesses?

The identification of these witnesses has been a major issue among scholars. There are at least seven formal opinions and several suggestions as to the identity of these two prophets. The following is a brief survey of the most popular opinions.

1. Moses and Elijah. This is the most popular view over the past century. The arguments for this position are: a) Malachi 4:5–6 seems to predict that Elijah will reappear before the Day of the Lord to turn Israel to God and to curse the land; b) the type of miracles that the two witnesses do are described (Rev. 11:6) in terms like those of Moses and Elijah, namely, being able to cause droughts by causing it not to rain and turning water to blood; c) Moses and Elijah appeared with Jesus at the Transfiguration, therefore they must symbolize or represent in some way believers who experience death and those who do not; d) Tenney notes that Elijah is taken up into heaven as recorded in 2 Kings 2:11 and the assumption of Moses is referred to by Origen and Clement of Alexandria; e) Moses and Elijah were dominant in the Old Testament for standing against great opposition, Moses versus Pharaoh and the children of Israel and Elijah versus Ahab, Jezebel, and the eight hundred prophets of Baal and Asherah; and f) some believe that Moses and Elijah represent deliverance from spiritual and physical bondage, thus making it fitting for their reappearance during the time of the Tribulation or Jacob's Trouble.

2. Enoch and Elijah. The next most common view is that the two translated prophets of the Old Testament will be the final two prophets before the Second Coming of Christ. The arguments for this position are: a) Since neither Enoch nor Elijah died but were translated to heaven, perhaps they have a future ministry before they face death at the hands of the Antichrist; b) they were both judgment prophets and appear to fit the

situation the two witnesses will face in Revelation 11; c) this was the view of the Gospel of Nicodemus. "I am Enoch who pleased God and was translated by Him. And this is Elijah the Tishbite. We are also to live to the end of the age: but then we are about to be sent by God to resist the Antichrist and be slain by him and to rise after three days and to be caught up in the clouds to meet the Lord."

3. True church. Some who hold to a midtribulation or posttribulation rapture believe that the two witnesses are a symbol or figure of the church or church-age martyrs in the Tribulation, based on the two olive trees and two lampstands in 11:4 and Zechariah 4:1–4.

4. Two testaments. Another opinion is that the two witnesses are figures of the work of the Word of God or the two testaments.

5. Elijah and John the Baptist. As John the Baptist, in a ministry that resembled Elijah's, prepared the way for the First Advent of Jesus Christ, perhaps they will reappear together to prepare the way for the Second Advent.

6. Figure of testimony. This view holds that the two witnesses are to be interpreted as a figure of speech representing large testimony against the Antichrist in Jerusalem during the Tribulation.

7. Two Tribulation saints. The two witnesses who appear as prophets against the Antichrist in Revelation 11 are real individuals who have not lived previously. The arguments are: a) Since they are killed and resurrected it would be hard to identify them with glorified prophets of the past; b) all the arguments for being prophets from the past is very circumstantial and unconvincing; c) their identity as real people and not a figure or symbol of something else is taken from a normal reading of the text, the use of the Greek definite article with the two witnesses in 11:3, and the fact that what they do is consistent with the actions of real prophets; and d) they will demonstrate power and miracles comparable to those performed by Moses and Elijah.

The two-tribulation-saints view appears to be the best answer for the evidence since: a) Enoch was a Gentile, while Revelation 11 seems to demand an Israelite; b) being translated into heaven does not demand a future ministry for an individual on earth; c) their types of ministry and miracles are compared to Moses and Elijah in 11:6, but this is done elsewhere in Scripture (Matt. 11:10–14 and Luke 1:13–17) as a point of comparison not identification; d) a second coming of Moses is not promised in Scripture and the prophetic statement in Malachi 4:5–6 that appears to indicate a reappearance of Elijah in the future was fulfilled by John the Baptist (Matt. 11:10–14, 17:10–13; Luke 1:13–17); and e) simply speaking, the ministry of the two witnesses will have a greater intensity and impact on the world than the ministries of Moses and Elijah in the Old Testament.

Where Will the Two Witnesses Minister?

The focus of their ministry will be in Jerusalem. The apostle John informs us that they will confront the Beast or Antichrist for 1260 days, or for forty-two months (three and one-half years) in 11:2–3. However, the impact of their ministry will be worldwide as they stand nose to nose with the Antichrist (11:9–10). Finally, after they have accomplished what God has for them to do, the Antichrist will wage war with them and kill them in Jerusalem (11:8).

When Will the Two Witnesses Minister?

They will minister during the Tribulation and more specifically, it appears from the evidence, during the last half of the Tribulation, referred to as the Great Tribulation, when the Antichrist turns against Israel. Their ministry of divine judgment and the need for divine protection resembles the time of the Tribulation referred to in 11:1–2, Daniel 9:27 and the time just before the seventh trumpet that contains the seven bowls of judgment (Rev. 11:15–16:1).

What Will the Two Witnesses Do in Their Ministry?

The character of their ministry is symbolized by the type of clothing that they will wear. The apostle John states that they will wear sackcloth (11:3) which is symbolic of a time of great distress, doom, and mourning when people should seek the Lord (Jonah 3:6, Isa. 37:1–5, Dan. 9:30). Their powerful miracles are divine and comparable to those of Moses and Elijah, but also different in that they can kill opponents by fire coming out of their mouths! Their major endeavor will be to stand as witnesses against the Beast (11:3–7, 13:1ff.), who is the Antichrist. Apparently, they proclaim that this popular world leader is the Antichrist prophesied in Scripture. They cause a tremendous drought to occur during the time of their work (11:6) and afflict the earth with several plagues. When they are killed, the Antichrist and their opponents do not allow their bodies to be buried, but they must lie on a street in Jerusalem where they died. For three and a half days, the people of the world will view their corpses, probably by television and news paper. World leaders will exchange gifts and have parties celebrating their deaths. However, two magnificent events happen at the end of these few days: God resurrects the two witnesses in public view and they ascend into heaven, also in public view (11:11–12). Finally, a horrific event follows their ascent into heaven as a powerful earthquake strikes Jerusalem and seven thousand people are killed. This event causes a twofold reaction among the people, terror and giving glory to God (11:13).

Eugene Mayhew

Arno C. Gaebelein, *Revelation* (New York: Our Hope Publication, 1915); Herman Hoyt, *An Exposition of the Book of Revelation* (Winona Lake, Ind.: Brethren Missionary Herald Co., 1966); Leon Morris, *The Revelation of St. John* (Grand Rapids: Eerdmans, 1969); J. Dwight Pentecost, *Things to Come* (Grand Rapids: Zondervan, 1958); Merrill C. Tenney, *Interpreting Revelation* (Grand Rapids: Eerdmans, 1957); John F. Walvoord, *The Revelation of Jesus Christ* (Chicago: Moody Press, 1966).

REVELATION, DATING THE BOOK OF

The majority of authorities in both the early and contemporary church date the writing of Revelation in the last decade of the first century, in about A.D. 95. A small minority of voices in the late twentieth century have opted for an earlier date, before or just after the death of Nero in the late sixties of the first century. Proponents of reconstructionism—a movement with an optimistic view of Christianity's ability to control secular society—constitute this small minority for the most part. Reconstructionism cannot fit a future fulfillment of Revelation's prophecies into its optimistic scheme, so it relegates Revelation's writing to the 60s and explains the book's fulfillment by the events prior to and including the destruction of Jerusalem in A.D. 70. Reconstructionism sees that destruction as fulfillment of Christ's promised coming (Rev. 1:7), a so-called cloud coming, but most reconstructionists think another coming of Christ is yet future.

The unanimous witness of the early church fathers, including Irenaeus, Clement of Alexandria, Origen, Victorinus, Eusebius, and Jerome, fix the date in the 90s, during the reign of Roman emperor Domitian. The contents of the book confirm this dating.

1. The condition of the churches of Asia to which John addresses the book is significantly different from that of those same churches in the 60s, as represented in Paul's epistles of Ephesians, Colossians, and 1 and 2 Timothy. Spiritual deterioration and doctrinal apostasy had become far worse.

2. The fact that John the apostle, who wrote Revelation, did not arrive in Asia to begin a ministry there until the late 60s shows that he could not have written to the churches there before A.D. 70. He hardly had time to settle in Asia, replace Paul as the respected leader of the Asian churches, and enter exile on Patmos before Nero's death in A.D. 68, the date usually cited by reconstructionists as the latest John could have written the book.

3. Another reason for not dating the book in the 60s is an earthquake that demolished the city of Laodicea, one of the seven cities addressed in Revelation, in A.D. 60 or 61. The earthquake had a long-term effect in Laodicea which was deeply involved in rebuilding for the rest of Nero's reign and shortly thereafter. Revelation 3:14–22

pictures the city as materially prosperous, not as struggling for existence. The best dating of the book is approximately A.D. 95 when the persecution under Domitian had spread as far as Asia, creating the need to encourage suffering Christians. To meet that need, the book details the promise of Christ's Second Advent and happenings surrounding that advent.

See also REVELATION, INTERPRETIVE VIEWS OF; RECONSTRUCTIONISM, CHRISTIAN.

Renald L. Thomas

Donald Guthrie, *New Testament Introduction* (Downers Grove, Ill.: InterVarsity Press, 1990), 948–62; Renald L. Thomas, *Revelation 1–7* (Chicago: Moody, 1995), 20–23, "Theonomy and the Dating of Revelation" in *The Master's Seminary Journal,* 5/2:185–202 (Fall 1994).

REVELATION, THE FALSE PROPHET IN

The False Prophet first appears in Revelation 13:11–17 as "another beast," following John's description of the beast of 13: 1–10. The first beast is said to have come out of the sea but the second is said to come out of the earth. The "sea" generally refers to the Gentile nations and indicates that the first beast came out of the nations but the second beast comes out of the "earth," which indicates, according to Walvoord, "that this character, who is later described as a false prophet (Rev. 19:20), is a creature of earth rather than heaven." Several important facts may be observed from Revelation's description of the person and work of the False Prophet.

1. He has two horns like a lamb. Most scholars agree that this holds some religious significance and probably relates to his influence in religious affairs since he is later referred to as a prophet (13:11; cf. 19:20).

2. It is said that he spoke as a dragon. The dragon is Satan and thus the beast derives his power from Satan (13:11; cf. 16:13, 20:2).

3. He exercises all the power of the first beast that was delegated to him (13:12).

4. We see that the beast is a supporting character to the first beast as he causes, through satanic deception, the people of the earth to worship the first beast who had been healed (13:12; cf. 13:3).

5. It is revealed that he will perform great signs to deceive the people and authenticate his ministry (13:12–13).

6. The False Prophet will instruct the people to create an image to the beast, to whom he appears to impart life. His main purpose seems to be to convince the people to give full allegiance and worship to the first beast and his image (13:14–15).

7. He will have the power to control the economic system by requiring a mark on the right hand or on the forehead that determines people's ability to buy or sell in the one-world economy (13:16–17).

8. The mark on the beast worshipers will be either the name of the beast or the number of his name, which is 666 (13:18).

Walvoord states the following about these two beasts revealed to us in Revelation 13: "Chapter 13, taken as a whole, is one of the great prophetic chapters of Scripture and is the only passage which presents in any detail the two principal evil characters of the end of the age who form with Satan an unholy trinity. Here is clearly presented the fact that the head of the revived Roman Empire ultimately becomes the ruler of the entire world. Dominated by Satan, he is Satan's masterpiece and substitute for Christ, and is aided and supported by the second beast called the false prophet."

The name False Prophet is mentioned three times in the book of Revelation (16:13–14; 19:20; 20:10). In chapter 16, John sees a vision of the Dragon, the Beast, and the False Prophet; coming out of their mouths are three unclean spirits like frogs (16:13). Verse 14 makes it clear that these are spirits or demons who are able to perform signs and direct the kings of the earth to gather together for the war of the great day of God, the Almighty (16:14). Walvoord comments, "While many commentators have agreed that this is the prelude for the great battle climaxing in the second coming of Christ, some have been confused as to the details. The battle (Gk., *polemos*) is probably better translated 'war' in contrast to *mache,* which is properly a battle or fighting (cf. James 4:1 where both are used). It is rather a major war. The evidence, however, seems to point to the conclusion that this is a climax of a series of military events described in Daniel 11:40–45, where the reference to the 'tidings out of the east' (Dan. 11:44) may have this invasion in view."

The next passage in which we see the False Prophet is Revelation 19:20. In 19:19–21, the Beast and the armies of the earth that have been deceived into gathering together against Christ and His army are soundly defeated. The return of Christ and His victory over the forces of evil at the Battle of Armageddon will spell doom for the Beast and the False Prophet. The Beast (13:1–10) and the False Prophet (13:11–17) "who performed the signs in his presence, by which he deceived those who received the mark of the beast and those who worshipped his image. . . . were thrown into the lake of fire which burns with brimstone." Walvoord states, "the lake of fire thus introduced is mentioned again in 20:15. By comparison with other scriptures, it seems that the beast and the false prophet are the first to inhabit the lake of fire. Unsaved who die prior to this time are cast into Hades, a place of torment, but not into the lake of fire, which is reserved for those who have been finally judged as unworthy of eternal life."

The False Prophet is only mentioned once more and here only in reference to the lake of fire and brimstone, when the Devil is finally judged and thrown in with him and the Beast. The punishment they receive is said to involve torment day and night forever and ever (Rev. 19:10).

See also ANTICHRIST.

Donald Perkins and Russell L. Penney

Donald Perkins, *The False Prophet of the Book of Revelation* (Lemon Grove, Calif.: According to Prophecy Ministries, 1996); J. Dwight Pentecost, *Things to Come* (Grand Rapids: Zondervan, 1958); John F. Walvoord, *The Revelation of Jesus Christ* (Chicago: Moody Bible Institute, 1966).

REVELATION, INTERPRETATIVE VIEWS OF

One of the most important, but seemingly little recognized, aspects of proper interpretation of the book of Revelation and all Bible prophecy is the role of timing. When will a prophecy be fulfilled in history? There are four possibilities. The four views are simple in the sense that they reflect the only four possibilities in relation to time—past, present, future, and timeless.

The *preterist* (past) believes that most, if not all prophecy has already been fulfilled, usually in relation to the destruction of Jerusalem in A.D. 70. The *historicist* (present) sees much of the current church age as equal to the Tribulation period. Thus, prophecy has been and will be fulfilled during the current church age. *Futurists* (future) believe that virtually all prophetic events will not occur in the current church age but will take place in the future Tribulation, Second Coming, or Millennium. The *idealist* (timeless) believes that the Bible does not indicate the timing of events and that we cannot determine their timing in advance. Therefore, idealists think that prophetic passages mainly teach great ideas or truths about God to be applied regardless of timing.

Preterist History

Antimillennialism provided the motive for the nonliteral interpretation in preterism, historicism, and idealism. A preterist interpretation of the Olivet Discourse began to appear in writers such as Eusebius (263–339) in his *Ecclesiastical History* and *The Proof of the Gospel*. However, he did not apply it to the book of Revelation. An A.D. 70 fulfillment of the Olivet Discourse is often held by preterists, historicists, and idealists. "The first systematic presentation of the preterist viewpoint originated in the early seventeenth century with Alcazar, a Jesuit friar." Alcazar's work first appeared in 1614 and influenced the first Protestant preterist, Hugo Grotius of Holland, who published his work in 1644. Preterism first appeared in England through a commentary by Henry Hammond in 1653. These early forms of preterism were mild and undeveloped by today's standards. They saw Revelation as "descriptive of the victory of the early church, as fulfilled in the downfall of the Jewish nation and the overthrow of pagan Rome, and in this way limited their range to the first six centuries of the Christian Era, and making Nero the Antichrist." In contrast, current forms of preterism concentrate the whole fulfillment of the book of Revelation around the A.D. 70 destruction of Jerusalem. Thus, preterist David Chilton writes, "The book of Revelation is not about the second coming of Christ. It is about the destruction of Israel and Christ's victory over His enemies in the establishment of the New Covenant Temple."

Historicist History

The preterist and historicist interpretations both emphasize historical fulfillment in the present church age. Though they are sometimes confused with each other, preterists usually limit historical fulfillment to the first century because they believe that prophecy has already been fulfilled. On the other hand, historicists usually view the whole of church history as fulfilling Revelation, leading up to the yet-future Second Advent. Thus, while most of Revelation has already been fulfilled, the historicist believes that a few passages and events are awaiting future fulfillment. They also believe, more than other viewpoints, that prophecy can be fulfilled in our own day since they think the church has been in the Tribulation for over fifteen hundred years.

Early forms of historicism surfaced around the fourth century when some interpreters began to see current events as fulfilling biblical prophecy. Later, Joachim of Fiore (1135–1202) accelerated development of the historicist approach by dividing church history into three ages. First, the Old Testament age under the law and Moses was the age of God the Father. Second came the New Testament age of Christ and the grace of Paul, until 1260. The third age, of the Holy Spirit (to begin in 1260), would be a time of love, until the whole world would be won to Christ. Historicism developed more fully when Joachim's scheme was reworked and associated with fulfillment of the book of Revelation. The Reformers were especially attracted to historicism as they taught that the pope was the Antichrist and saw themselves as the godly remnant being persecuted by Rome. Historicism became so dominant during the Reformation and into the nineteenth century that it was accepted as the Protestant interpretation.

Shortly after reaching its height of popularity in the early 1800s, historicism began a decline from which it has never recovered. The decline of historicism was the result of a number of factors. As eighteen hundred years of church history elapsed, historicist belief that the Second Coming was very near reached almost fever pitch. American William Miller set the date of Christ's return on the basis of historicist principles for 1843 and then revised it for 1844. This kind of date setting helped destroy confidence in the system. Another factor was related to historicism's view that the Roman church was the anti-Christ because of its departure from the faith. By the mid-1800s, Protestantism was being threatened by the rise of liberalism, which evangelicals saw as a more pressing threat. Finally, the rise of the more literal approach to prophecy produced a revival of futurism, which made more sense to evangelical premillennialists. Today, if it were not for Seventh-day Adventists, historicism would have virtually no proponents.

Futurist History

While its view was not as consistently developed as modern futurism, the early church outlook would have to be classified as futurist, more than any thing else. With a few exceptions, the early church believed that events of the Tribulation, Millennium, and Second Coming were to take place in the future. As antimillennial views begin to arise in the third century and the Christianization of the Roman Empire through Constantine was spreading in the fourth century, futurism began to be displaced. As the fourth century turned into the fifth, Jerome and Augustine's influence against futurism drove it underground during the thousand-year era of medievalism. But there remained during this time pockets of futurism scattered throughout a number of the groups who refused to come under Roman Catholic authority. Further, there have been discoveries of medieval apocalypticism during this time written from varying degrees of futurism.

The Reformation brought a return to a study of the sources. In northern Europe those sources included the early church writers and aided in a renewal of the study of prophecy from a futurist perspective within the Roman Catholic and then the Protestant churches. The Jesuit Francisco Ribera (1537–1591) was one of the first to revive an undeveloped form of futurism, around 1580. Because of the dominance of historicism, futurism made virtually no headway in Protestantism, until the 1820s through Church of England scholar S. R. Mainland in 1826. In the late 1820s, futurism began to gain converts and grow in the British Isles, often motivated by a revived interest in God's plan for Israel; during this time it gained one of its most influential converts in John Nelson Darby. Through Darby and other Brethren expositors, futurism spread to America and throughout the evangelical and later the fundamentalist world. The last 150 years have seen, for the first time, the full development of consistent futurism. This has lead in turn to the formulation of modern dispensationalism and a clearer understanding and more consistent presentation of the pretribulational vew of the rapture of the church.

Idealist History

Idealism is the least systematic of the four approaches. Therefore, it is more difficult to classify as to specific characteristics. But most likely it had its beginnings during the fourth and fifth centuries through those who were antipremillennial and antiliteral in their understanding of prophecy. From that time until the present, there have been within the church those who have not dealt with the timing of biblical prophecy, even though they have usually been a small minority. The most vigorous debate has been between the three approaches that advocate a specific timing of the fulfillment of Bible prophecy.

Support for Futurism

Futurism is the only approach that can consistently apply literal interpretation, that is, the historical, grammatical, contextual hermeneutic. Other approaches must supply key elements of their system from outside of the text of Scripture.

Futurism is supported by considering that God gave an outline of Israel's history before they ever set foot in the Promised Land. Deuteronomy 4:25–31 cites the following key events prophesied concerning Israel: (1) Israel and their descendants would remain long in the land; (2) they would act corruptly and slip into idolatry; (3) they would be kicked out of the land; (4) the Lord would scatter them among the nations; (5) they would be given over to idolatry during their wanderings; (6) while dispersed among the nations, they would seek and find the Lord when they searched for Him will all their heart; (7) there would be a time of tribulation said to occur in the latter days, during which time they would turn to the Lord. "For the LORD your God is a compassionate God; He will not fail you nor destroy you nor forget the covenant with your fathers which He swore to them" (Deut. 4:31).

A similar, but more detailed, outline of Israel's history is included in Deuteronomy 28–32. Israel is promised restoration from captivity (Deut. 30:3–5); unbelief will be turned into obedience (Deut. 30:6); and the Lord will curse Israel's enemies (Deut. 30:7) and in the end prosper Israel more than it has ever experienced (Deut. 30:8–9). This final blessing is no doubt millennial.

This prophetic outline from Deuteronomy supports futurism in that nowhere is there said to be a change in God's people (from Israel to the church), thus, the whole outlined program is for Israel, not Israel and then the church. This is clear, since those who were once cursed are the same people who are later blessed. Since national Israel has never experienced these blessings, they must be in the future. This would mean that dozens of passages from the Old Testament prophets have yet to be fulfilled for Israel. Romans 9–11 teaches that while Israel has been temporarily set aside because of current disobedience (except for a remnant), it will yet in the future fulfill its destiny. This then means that Matthew 24–25 and the book of Revelation foretell a similar story relating to Israel. Thus, they also are still future, since Israel has never experienced widespread belief in the Lord and blessing from His hand.

The only way to escape the implications of the text of Scripture is to attempt to change horses in midstream, as do those who teach that while Israel experiences the curses of the Old Testament, it does not receive its equally clear prophecy of blessings; instead the church is said to receive the blessing. Such a view is not supported from the text of the Bible; in fact it is contradicted by Scripture. It is a view that must import into the process the idea that the church replaces Israel. Thus, if the blessings promised to Israel from the outset are going to be fulfilled for Israel as Israel, then it must be concluded that they have not yet happened and will occur in the future. Thus, great portions of the Bible are yet future, establishing the futurist approach to Bible prophecy.

See also REVELATION, DATING OF.

Thomas D. Ice

Arnold G. Fruchtenbaum, *Israelology: The Missing Link in Systematic Theology* (Tustin, Calif.: Ariel Ministries Press, 1993); David Larsen, *Jews, Gentiles, & the Church: A New Perspective of History and Prophecy* (Grand Rapids: Discovery House, 1995); Charles C. Ryrie, *Dispensationalism*, revised and expanded (Chicago: Moody Press, 1995); Wilber B. Wallis, "Reflections on the History of Premillennial Thought" in *Interpretation & History: Essays in Honour of Allan A. MacRae*, eds. R. Laird Harris, Swee-Hwa Quck, and J. Robert Vannoy (Singapore: Christian Life Publishers, 1986), 225–51.

REVELATION, PROGRESSIVE

If special revelation is God's message in what was codified in the Bible (Ryrie), then progressive revelation is the historic unfolding of the expression of that message. As such, God chose to disclose Himself and His plan for humanity on earth through the developing history of His chosen people, Israel.

In the gradual unfolding of the message, the initial expressions are true in a comprehensive sense, but they are not yet complete in a particular and historic sense. These initial expressions feature God's message comprehensively expressed as a seed; that seed will grow, flower, and mature and yet not change in essential identity. Thus, the unfolding growth of the message develops truths implicit within the comprehensive boundaries of that initial message. Thus, as an example, the source of God's provision of deliverance is the seed of the woman . . . the seed of Abraham . . . the seed of David . . . The identity of this deliverer unfolds within the boundary of the narrowing promise yet becomes historically and potentially known in each generation, in the progression of revelation. It may have been Noah. It may have been Solomon. In fact, it is only Jesus, the son of David, the son of Abraham, the son of Adam.

There are four distinct but related comprehensive messages that are introduced and when completely unfolded will combine into a unified comprehensive message. These four messages include God's permission of sin in the human race (Gen. 3:1–6) and three promises that announce God's remedy for sin: (1) God's just judgment of sin (Gen. 3:7–24), (2) God's merciful provision of deliverance from judgment for the elect, (Gen. 3:15), and (3) God's gracious blessing of those delivered (Gen. 12:1–3, 7). The comprehensive, unifying message affirms that God will reestablish His rule over Man and then through Man over evil, all humanity, and all the earth. This will be fulfilled in the millennial kingdom of God.

This gradual unfolding is conditioned upon the developing history of Israel. This development is largely related to the revelation of the Law. While the initial expression of the Law is both comprehensive and complete in principle, the unfolding revelation relates to Israel's historic responses as demanded by the Law. That development reflects repeated sinful responses from the very beginning (Exod. 32–34). The unstated but necessary implication to be recognized in the repeated sinful responses is that what God promised to provide through Israel (Gen.12:3), God must Himself provide for and with Israel—as He would in Jesus, the promised Messiah. In Christ, the demands of the Law are satisfied and the promised provision is fulfilled. In this fulfillment, God's rule over humanity is accomplished in Christ's death so that God's righteous rule may be realized through Christ's resurrection and reign on earth.

The character of progressive revelation impacts one's hermeneutic and one's model of biblical theology. In a hermeneutic, the issue concerns the relationship between the statement of the message in the Old Testament and in the New Testament. This relationship may be likened to a foundation, the initial statement upon which subsequent statements are the superstructure. As such, the New Testament statements about Christ and the church don't replace promises made to Israel but rather Christ is the Israel, the Representative through whom Israel, the nation, will find fulfillment and also the Savior in whom the church is blessed. Historically particular statements in the New Testament don't expand the boundaries, nor alter, reverse, or contradict the original comprehensive statements of the truth. Rather, these subsequent statements are compatible with and comprehended within the original statements of the Old Testament, in the unfolding revelation.

In relation to a model of biblical theology, progressive revelation reflects both a unity of message and purpose of God and a diversity in the developing history of God's people. A biblical theology must also reflect such unity and diversity. A dispensational theology reflects such unity of purpose in the revelation of God's glory in the reestablishment of the mediatorial kingdom on earth. In addition, it reflects a diversity in the successive stages in God's administration of this purpose (promise, law, gospel, kingdom) in the developments of history.

Elliott Johnson

A. J. McClain, *The Greatness of the Kingdom* (Winona Lake, Ind.: BMH Books, 1979); Charles C. Ryrie, *Dispensationalism* (Chicago: Moody Press, 1995).

REVELATION, STRUCTURE OF THE BOOK OF

The book of Revelation is important because it is the last book of the Bible to be written, and it contains the final revelation of the second coming of Christ. The events depicted in the Revelation lead into the eternal state of perfect fellowship with God. There are four indications from internal evidence about the author of Revelation: (1) his name was John, (2) he was a Palestinian Jew, (3) he was on the island of Patmos, (4) he demonstrated a great deal of authority over the churches of Asia Minor. This evidence argues for John, the beloved disciple of Jesus, as the author.

Revelation was written and recorded by John while he was in exile on the island of Patmos. It was probably written around A.D. 95–96, when John was in his early eighties. The Revelation was given to him by God. God sent the message through Jesus Christ who mediated the message through an angel to John. The primary recipients of the book were the seven churches of Asia that are referred to in chapters 2–3. See books by Robert L. Thomas for a very thorough discussion of introductory matters.

The purpose of the book is manifold. It was written to (1) reveal the glorified Christ and show that He is the King of Kings and the Lord of Lords, (2) correct the churches in Asia, (3) encourage Christians who were under persecution, (4) show the completion of Old Testament prophecy, including God's program for the nation of Israel, (5) show the righteous and sovereign judgment of God on sin, and (6) to warn people to repent of their evil deeds and unbelief lest they be judged. God is seen as righteously vindicating the Godhead and the saints as He judges a world controlled by Satan.

The Rapture in the Book of Revelation

There are expositors who argue that Revelation supports a pretribulational rapture of the church. They cite the following arguments: (1) the promise of exemption from tribulation that was given to the church at Philadelphia (Rev. 3:10); (2) John's spiritual translation to heaven as an indication of the Rapture (Rev. 4:1–2); (3) the presence of the twenty-four elders in heaven which indicates that the church is removed during the Tribulation (Rev 4:4ff); (4) the absence of any reference to the church in Revelation 4–18; (5) the marriage supper of the Lamb coming down with Christ at His Second Coming (Rev. 19:7–90); (6) The complete absence of any statement of rapture in the closing days of the Tribulation.

The Structure of Revelation

There are four major principles that define the structure of Revelation and show that its structure is both chronological and sequential. The Apocalypse unfolds according to a prophetic timetable as well as a literary sequence of events that reveals more precise definition and detail about the closing events of a period that is called the "Great Tribulation."

The First Principle

The first principle is the recognition of the epistolary nature of the book. Revelation begins with a prologue (1:1–8) and closes with an epilogue (22:6–21). The book contains seven exhortations to seven churches in Asia Minor. Although other common elements of epistolary literature are absent from the Apocalypse, these missing elements should not dissuade a person from acknowledging this aspect of the structure.

The Second Principle

The second principle is stated in Revelation 1:19: "Write therefore the things which you have seen, and the things which are, and the things that shall take place after these things."

The Revelation is structured in part by the three time periods that are mentioned in this verse: (1) the things that you have seen; (2) the things that are; (3) the things that shall take place after these things.

This threefold division does not control the major content of the book as evidenced by the disproportional character of the three sections (1:1–20; 2:1–3:22; 4:1–22:5). The "things which you have seen" are recorded in chapter 1. John recorded the initial vision of the glorified Jesus Christ in which he was commissioned to write the entire book of Revelation. Chapters 2 and 3 contain the "things which are." This is evidenced by the command to John: "Write in a book what you see" (Rev. 1:11), indicating the existence of these churches in John's day and the present aspect of the "things which are." This section closes with the opening of the third section, "the things which shall take place after these things." Revelation 4–21 comprises this third section as indicated by chapter 4 and verse 1: "After these things I looked, and behold, a door standing open in heaven, and the first voice which I had heard, like the sound of a trumpet speaking with me, said, Come up here, and I will show you what must take place after these things." John clearly provided a chronological division to the book with this threefold segmentation.

The Third Principle

The third principle concerns the sequential nature of the three septet judgments (seals, trumpets, bowls) of Revelation. The structure of the Apocalypse is determined, in part, by one's understanding of whether the three septet judgments are sequential or simultaneous. The sequential view understands the seals, trumpets, and bowls as successive judgments that proceed out of each other. The simultaneous view sees a recapitulation of the septets in which the judgments are parallel to each other. Each recapitulation reviews previous events and adds further details.

This article argues for the successive view of the septet judgments, that is, the trumpets sequentially follow the seals, and the bowls sequentially follow the trumpets. The successive structure does not negate a recapitulation of other visions in that the writer does portray visionary scenes that preview eschatological events to come (Rev. 7:9–17; 14:8–13).

There is continuity between the septets

as evidenced by similar patterns of devastation. Each set of judgments is more intense and destructive than the previous ones. The second trumpet destroys one-third of seas while the second bowl turns all of the seas into blood (Rev. 8:8–9; 16:3). The third trumpet pollutes one third of the rivers and springs while the third bowl transforms all of the rivers and springs to blood (Rev. 8:10–11; 16:4–7). The fourth trumpet smites one third of the sun, moon, and stars while the fourth bowl causes the sun to intensify and scorch the people of the earth (Rev. 8:12–13; 16:10–11).

Although there are many similarities between the septets, the differences are more crucial and determinative. The seals generally differ in content from the trumpet and bowl plagues. There is no parallel alignment between the first, fifth, and seventh judgments of the septets.

A first-impression reading of the book suggests that the septets are sequential. The two Greek phrases καὶ εἶδον and μετὰ ταῦα indicate a sequential movement of the visions beyond just the reception of these visions by John. It should also be admitted that these phrases indicate a chronological movement as seen in the contexts of Revelation 1:19; 9:12; 15:15; 19:1; 20:3; (μετὰ ταῦα) 5:1–2, 6, 11; 6:1–2, 5, 12; 7:2; 8:2; 9:1; 15:1–2; 17:3, 6; 19:11, 17, 19; 20:1, 4, 11–12; 22:1 (καὶ εἶδον).

The seven seals are followed by the seven trumpets, and the seven bowls follow the seven trumpets (Rev. 6:1–17; 8:1–9:21; 16:1–21). The bowls evidence a sequential pattern as they are called "the last, because in them the wrath of God is finished" (Rev. 15:1). Sequential character is manifested within each septet. The ordinal numbers indicate succession: δευτέραν, τρίτην, τετάρτην, πέμπτην, ἕκτην, ἑβτόμην. There is a successive building within each septet to a climax. Sequential progression is also noted by the parallels between the three woes and the fifth, sixth, and seventh trumpets (Rev. 8:13; 9:12; 11:14).

The successive nature of the judgments is evidenced in the breaking of the seventh seal: "And when He broke the seventh seal, there was silence in heaven for about half an hour. And I saw the seven angels who stand before God; and seven trumpets were given to them (Rev. 8:1–2)." The seven angels then execute the seven trumpet judgments, bringing an intensification of destruction on the earth (Rev. 8:7–9:21).

The seventh trumpet is linked to the seven bowls. John states that when the seventh angel sounds the trumpet, "then the mystery of God is finished" (Rev. 10:7). At the introduction and conclusion of the bowl judgments, the writer emphasizes that in them the wrath of God is finished (Rev. 15:1, 8; 16:17). The seventh trumpet brings forth the execution of the seven bowls and the completion of God's wrath.

The 144,000 people are an example of an event under a trumpet judgment following a seal judgment. One hundred and forty-four thousand people are protectively sealed on their foreheads after the sixth seal and before the release of the plague by the four angels (Rev. 7:1–8). The fifth trumpet brings a demonic plague on humankind and torments "only the men who do not have the seal of God on their foreheads" sixth seal proceeds the demonic plague of the fifth trumpet.

In summary, the crucial differences between the judgments include: the prima facie reading of the text, the sequential character within each septet, the use of ordinal numbers, the sequential aspect of the seventh part of each septet, and the contextual clues of progression all argue for the successive approach.

The Fourth Principle

The fourth principle for understanding the structure of Revelation is the correlation of the Seventieth Week of Daniel 9:27 with the synoptic eschatological discourses of Matthew 24, Mark 13, Luke 21, and Revelation 4–19. Thematic parallels between the birth pangs of the synoptics (Matt. 24:4–8; Mark 13:5–8; c.f. Luke 21:8–19) and the first six seals of the Apocalypse (Rev. 6:1–11) show a definite correlation between the events described in the passages.

An analysis of eschatological sections in

Luke (Luke 21:22–23; 23:28–31) argues that the structural benchmark for the midpoint of Daniel's Seventieth Week is the sixth seal of Revelation 6, which leads up to the Abomination of Desolation, which is the midpoint of Daniel's Seventieth Week (Dan. 9:27).

Luke intersperses eschatological statements throughout the closing chapters of his work (Luke 17:20–37; 19:41–44; 21:5–38; 23:26–31). The last disclosure of eschatological teaching (Luke 23:26–31) is set in the context of the crucifixion of Jesus Christ. Luke states: "And there were following Him [Jesus] a great multitude of people, and of women who were mourning and lamenting Him. But Jesus turning to them said, 'Daughters of Jerusalem, stop weeping for Me, but weep for yourselves and for your children. For behold, the days are coming when they will say, Blessed are the barren, and the wombs that never bore, and the breasts that never nursed'" (Luke 23:27–29).

It appears the blessedness of this situation is the freedom from pregnancy and caring for small children during a time of trouble. Christ ironically states positively as a blessing (Luke 23:29) what He previously stated negatively as a warning (Luke 21:23). Each of the synoptic writers records the negative version of this teaching: "Woe to those who are with child and to those who nurse babes in those days" (Matt. 24:19; Mark 13:17; Luke 21:23).

This admonition is in view of the persecution that results from the Abomination of Desolation and the destruction of Jerusalem (Matt.24:15–24; Mark 13:14–23; Luke 21:20–24). The people of Jerusalem are warned to flee to the mountains of Judea in order to protect themselves from the impending persecution. A woe is pronounced over pregnant women and women with small children because their flight will be impeded by their responsibilities and concerns for others. Blessed are the women who are free from these burdens because their flight will be quicker and easier. It appears that Luke has the time frame of the destruction of Jerusalem in mind when he records this declaration (Luke 23:29, cf. 21:23).

A second event in this discourse describes the reaction of some people to the resulting tribulation: "Then (τότε) they will begin to say to the mountains, 'Fall on us,' and to the hills, 'Cover us'" (Luke 23:30). Τότε, which can be translated, "at that time," indicates the sequential proximity of these two events. People who flee to the mountains will cry out for the mountains and hills to hide them.

A comparison of Luke 23:30 with the sixth seal of Revelation 6:12–17 demonstrates a further correlation. Revelation 6:15–17 states: "And the kings of the earth and the great men and the commanders and the rich and the strong and every slave and free man, hid themselves in the caves and among the rocks of the mountains; and they said to the mountains and to the rocks, 'Fall on us and hide us from the presence of Him who sits on the throne, and from the wrath of the Lamb; for the great day of their wrath has come; and who is able to stand?'"

An integration of these correspondences with the synoptics suggests the prophetic sequence would be (1) the Abomination of Desolation and the destruction of Jerusalem at the midpoint of Daniel's Seventieth Week (Matt. 24:15; Mark 13:14; Luke 21:20); (2) people flee to the mountains (Matt. 24:16–18; Mark 13:15–16; Luke 21:21; and (3) people cry for the mountains and rocks to fall on them and hide them from the wrath of God and the Lamb (Luke 23:30; Rev. 6:15–17).

A mathematical formula may help to illustrate this analogy. Mathematics teaches that if A=B and B=C and C=D, then A=D. Applying this logic to the texts, if the time sequence of A (the Abomination of Desolation at the midpoint of the Seventieth Week of Daniel and the tribulation of the synoptics), equals B (at this time the people flee to the mountains and women are warned about impending dangers); and the time frame of B equals C (the people cry out for the mountains to fall on them); and reference C equals D (the sixth seal of Revelation when the wrath of God and the Lamb initiate the great day of their wrath, and people cry for the mountains to fall on them), then A (the Abomination of Desolation at the midpoint of Daniel's Seventieth Week), equals or occurs at the time as D (the time of the sixth seal of the

Apocalypse). Textual correlations that develop the expansion and chronological framework of the Seventieth Week of Daniel are:

1. The Abomination of Desolation: Daniel 9:27 equals Matthew 24:15–19, Mark 13:14–17, and Luke 21:20–21

2. People flee from persecution: Matthew 24:15–19, Mark 13:14–17, and Luke 21:20–21 equals Luke 23:29–31

3. People cry for the rocks to hide them: Luke 23:29–31 equals Revelation 6:12–17

4. Therefore, Daniel 9:27 equals Revelation 6:12–17.

If this correlation is correct, then a structural benchmark is established. The benchmark is that the sixth seal is the midpoint of the Daniel's Seventieth Week. The Apocalypse has amplified on this framework as expanded on by the synoptic writers in Matthew 24, Mark 13, and Luke 21. The first five seals are parallel and sequential to the birth pangs of the synoptics, therefore it is suggested that the sixth seal can be accepted as the dividing point of the Seventieth Week of Daniel.

Structural Outline

The following structural outline represents a descriptive view of the development of the Apocalypse. This progressive disclosure is like a spiraling conical staircase. The climax of the Apocalypse is the coming of the Son of Man. The major motif that leads up to the parousia is the intensification of the septet judgments (4:1–19:21). The septets unfold out of each other until the climax of worldwide destruction. The writer intermittently suspends the progressive movement and disclosure of the septets in order to introduce pertinent information. The information is inserted by narrative previews or narrative synopses. Narrative previews prophetically amplify major characters or events that are enunciated later in the Apocalypse. Narrative synopses provide apocalyptic scenes that review past events and lead the reader to future episodes.

Structural Outline of the Apocalypse of John

I. Prologue: "Things Which You Have Seen," 1:1–20

II. Letters to the Seven Churches: "Things Which Are," 2:1–3:22

III. God's Wrath\Great Tribulation: "Things Which Shall Take Place After These Things," 4:1–19:21

- A. Introduction to the Seven Seal Judgments 4:1–5:14
  1. Throne of God in heaven 4:1–11 First Half of the Tribulation
  2. The Scroll of the Lamb 5:1–14
- B. The Six Seal Judgments 6:1–7:17
  1. First Seal: White horse 6:1–2
  2. Second Seal: Red horse 6:3–4
  3. Third Seal: Black horse 6:5–6
  4. Fourth Seal: Ashen horse 6:7–8
  5. Fifth Seal: Martyrs under the altar 6:9–11
  6. Sixth Seal: Great day of God's wrath 6:12–17, Mid-point
  7. Narrative Preview: Redeemed of God, 7:1–17
     - a. Sealing of the 144,000 7:1–8
     - b. Martyrs from the great Tribulation 7:9–17
- C. The Seventh Seal: Seven Trumpets, 8:1–18:24, Second Half
  1. Breaking Seventh Seal: intro. to the Seven Trumpets 8:1–6
  2. First Trumpet: one-third of the earth destroyed 8:7
  3. Second Trumpet: one-third of the sea destroyed 8:8–9
  4. Third Trumpet: one-third of the water destroyed 8:10–11
  5. Fourth Trumpet: one-third of the celestial destroyed 8:12
  6. Introduction of the Three Woes 8:13
  7. Fifth Trumpet, First Woe: Men tormented 9:1–12
  8. Sixth Trumpet, Second Woe:one-third of mankind 9:13–11:14
     - a. Sixth Trumpet, one-third of mankind destroyed 9:13–21
     - b. Narrative Preview: Little Scroll Final Judgment 10:1–11
     - c. Narrative Synopsis: Witnesses' Persecution 11:1–14
  9. Seventh Trumpet: The Seven Bowls, Third Woe 11:15–18:24
     - a. Seventh Trumpet, proclamation of God's kingdom 11:15–19

b. Narrative Synopsis 12:1–14:13
   1) A Woman, Male child, Satan in conflict 12:1–6
   2) Angelic war in heaven 12:7–12
   3) War on earth 12:13–17
   4) Beast out of the sea 13:1–10
   5) Beast out of the earth 13:11–18
   6) Narrative Preview 14:1–13
c. Introduction of the Seven Bowls 14:14–15:8
   1) Son of Man with a sickle 14:14–16
   2) Wine press of God's wrath 14:17–20
   3) Seven angels of the Seven plagues 15:1
   4) Worship of God and the Lamb 15:2–4
   5) Seven angels receive the Bowls 15:5–8
d. Seven Bowl Judgments: The End 16:1–18:24, Closing Days
   1) First Bowl: malignant sores 16:1–2
   2) Second Bowl: sea destroyed 16:3
   3) Third Bowl: rivers destroyed 16:4–7
   4) Fourth Bowl: scorching heat 16:8–9
   5) Fifth Bowl: darkness 16:10–11
   6) Sixth Bowl: preparation for war 16:12–16
   7) Seventh Bowl: worldwide destruction 16:17–21
   8) Narrative Synopsis 17:1–18:24
      a) Description and Destruction of the Harlot 17:1–18
      b) Condemnation and Destruction of Babylon 18:1–24

D. The Advent of Jesus Christ 19:1–21 End of the Tribulation
   1. Introduction and praise of the advent 19:1–10
   2. Parousia of Jesus Christ 19:11–16
   3. Judgment of the beast, false prophet, and people 19:17–21

IV. Millennial Kingdom: "Things Which Shall Take Place After These Things," 20:1–15
   A. Satan is bound in the abyss 20:1–3
   B. Saints are resurrected 20:4–6
   C. Final judgment of Satan 20:7–10
   D. Final judgment of humankind 20:11–15

V. The New Jerusalem 21:1–22:5

VI. Epilogue 22:6–21

See also REVELATION, DATING OF; REVELATION, INTERPRETIVE VIEWS OF.

John A. McLean

Gary Cohen, *Understanding Revelation* (Chicago: Moody Press, 1978); John A. McLean, "The Structure of Revelation" in *When the Trumpet Sounds* (Eugene, Oreg.: Harvest House, 1995); Robert Thomas, *Revelation 1–7* (Chicago: Moody Press, 1992).

REVELATION, TWENTY-FOUR ELDERS OF

The telders are a prominent group mentioned twelve times in chapters 4–19 (4:4, 10; 5:5, 6, 8, 11, 14; 7:11, 13; 11:16; 14:3; 19:4) of Revelation. They are first seen enthroned around the throne of God in heaven. They praised God for His work of creation and governance (4:10–11), praised Jesus Christ for His work of redemption (5:8–12), praised God for the entrance of redeemed people into heaven out of the Great Tribulation (7:9–14), praised God for His sovereign right to judge the wicked and to initiate the kingdom of God on earth (11:15–19), and praised God for His destruction of wicked Babylon (19:4). There is much debate over the identity of this group. Do the elders symbolize angels or humans? If they represent humans, do they symbolize Old Testament believers, New Testament believers, or both? The biblical description seems to point to believers of this present church age. They are already in heaven (chaps. 4–5) before the opening of the seal judgments (chap. 6). They are sitting on thrones before God (4:4). Angels never sit in the presence of God. However, Christ promised church-age believers that they would sit with Him on His throne (Rev. 3:21). God positionally has made all believers today sit together in the heavenly places in Christ (Eph. 2:6). The elders are clothed in white robes (4:4). Church-age believers are promised such pure clothing (Rev. 3:5, 18; 19:7–8). The elders have crowns of gold on their heads (4:4). These crowns (*stephanous*) indicate achievement and victory. Believers in the churches were promised such crowns (Rev. 2:10; 3:11). In the Epistles, believers are also promised crowns for spiritual accomplishments (1 Cor. 9:25; 1 Thess. 2:19; 2 Tim. 4:8; James 1:12; 1 Peter 5:4). Holy angels do not wear crowns, but believers can and will wear them. The numerical adjective *twenty-four* is significant. King David divided the Levitical priesthood into twenty-four orders (1 Chron. 24). Each order represented the entire priestly tribe and the whole nation of Israel as it functioned before God. The number thus represents a larger, complete group. It does not refer to twenty-four specific individuals. The elders acknowledged that they were kings and priests (5:10). Church-age believers are a royal priesthood (1 Peter 2:9; Rev. 1:6). Since Jesus Christ is a King-Priest according to the order of Melchizedek (Heb. 5–7), believers who are in Christ are also king-priests.

The elders are set in contrast to angels (5:11). The term *presbuteros* (elder) is never used of angels in the Bible. The word denotes maturity and growth. Holy angels could not be designated with this term because they were all created at the same time. The term, however, is often used of the leaders and representatives of the churches (Acts 20:17; 1 Tim. 3:1–7; Titus 1:5–9). The more plausible explanation of the twenty-four elders is that they represent the redeemed of this present church age. Since they are in heaven before the onset of the Tribulation judgments (Rev. 6–16), then they were raptured into heaven before the Tribulation began.

Robert G. Gromacki

RIBERA, FRANCISCO

Francisco Ribera (1537–1591) of Salamanca, Spain, was a Catholic Jesuit scholar who was born in Villacastin, Spain and educated at the University of Salamanca, where he earned a doctorate in theology. He was a specialist in biblical studies, Latin, Greek and Hebrew. He taught many years at the university and began writing commentaries on the Bible in 1575. Ribera's notoriety in our day revolves around his five-hundred-page commentary on Revelation completed in 1590, shortly before his death, in which he is said to have revived the futurist interpretation of the book.

It is possible that Ribera revived a mild form of futurism, but he hardly can be considered the father of futurism, as suggested by critics. Ribera remained an Augustinian amillennialist but differed from Augustine in that he placed the saints' reign in heaven, not on earth. He did not believe in a literal thousand-year millennium. The extent of his futurism revolved around his understanding that "the Antichrist would be a single individual, who would rebuild the temple in Jerusalem, abolish the Christian religion, deny Christ, be received by the Jews, pretend to be God, and conquer the world—and all in this brief space of three and one-half literal years. . . . Ribera also believed that at that time Christian Rome would be overthrown because of her sins" (Froom). Other than a personal Antichrist and a future ten-horn kingdom, Ribera tended to interpret the rest of Revelation from the perspective of the historicism so common in his day.

Some have tried to taint the modern futurism of dispensational premillennialism by ascribing it to "that Catholic Jesuit, Ribera, who adopted futurism to avoid the historicist view that Romanism and the Pope are the Antichrst." It may be true that Ribera's motive for adopting futurism was to deflect Protestant criticism away from Rome. However, Ribera's futurism hardly compares to modern versions, let alone the futurism of the early church. In fact, Ribera's futurism is mild indeed compared to Irenaeus's of the second century. Irenaeus is more responsible for the revival of futurism within both Catholicism and Protestantism, because around 1570 the last five chapters of Irenaeus's *Against Heresies* were rediscovered after over a thousand years of suppression during the Middle Ages. These chapters contained Irenaeus's system of premillennial futurism. "We may feel that the intensive Bible study of the Reformation, combined with the knowledge of antiquity, was beginning to swing the pendulum back to the primitive premillennialism of Irenaeus which had been rejected by Augustine (Wallis).

Ribera, along with a few Protestants (i.e., Joseph Mede and Henry Alsted), began to revive futurism. However, the development of a futurism that would surpass that of Irenaeus had to await developments of the early 1800s.

Thomas D. Ice

Le Roy E. Froom, *The Prophetic Faith of Our Fathers*, vols. 2–3 (Washington, D.C.: Review and Herald, 1945–54); Wilber B. Wallis, "Reflections on the History of Premillennial Thought" in *Interpretation & History: Essays in Honour of Allan A. MacRae,* eds. R. Laird Harris, Swee-Hwa Quck, and J. Robert Vannoy (Singapore: Christian Life Publishers, 1986).

RILEY, WILLIAM BELL

William Bell Riley (1861–1947) was born in Green County, Indiana and very early aspired to be a lawyer. Finances kept him from this goal, but in 1885 he attended Southern Baptist Theological Seminary in Louisville and finished the seminary program in three years. He pastored small churches in Kentucky, Indiana, and Illinois. Moving to Chicago in 1893, by hard work and energy he increased the membership of Calvary Baptist Church from sixty to five hundred in just four years.

Riley considered himself first a pastor but also a revivalist, a civic reformer, an educator, and an ecclesiastical politician. He was also a thorough fundamentalist who saw liberalism creeping into the churches and into the Northern Baptist Convention. Forming the Fundamentalist Fellowship, he and others tried to stem the tide. By 1930, he realized the task was impossible. In his later years, he and other well-known Bible teachers spent time fighting what turned out to be a forgery, "The Protocols of the Elders of Zion," a publication purporting to outline a plot to destroy Christian civilization and also supposedly advocating an international Jewish conspiracy. This proved to be the dark side of his energetic career.

Though Riley lived a controversial life, he had established his Northwestern Schools, a series of biblical study centers scattered across the Upper Midwest. Near his death in August 1947, he appointed young Billy Graham to take over this teaching network. At his death, he was called "a prima donna of fundamentalism" and Harry Ironside called him one of the greatest leaders ever.

Riley stood strongly for two major biblical doctrines: inerrancy of Scripture and dispensational premillennialism. He taught a coming apostasy, the premillennial rapture of the church, the Tribulation, the Antichrist, Armageddon, and the coming kingdom reign of Christ. He was popular in teaching at prophetic conferences and so knowledgeable on prophetic issues that C. I. Scofield asked him to contribute to the *Scofield Reference Bible,* published in 1909. He declined because of other pressing duties.

Riley worked hard fighting liberalism and evolution in the school systems and in the denominations. Though in a sense he lost the struggle, he has to be admired for his passion and persistence. At the time of his death, seventy percent of Baptist pastors in Minnesota were alumni of his Northwestern Schools. Though modernism had already taken hold of the educational process and denominational power, Riley had the most influence, at least for awhile, with the people and the pastors.

Mal Couch

Timothy George and David S. Dockery, eds., *Baptist Theologians* (Nashville: Broadman Press, 1990).

ROMANS, ESCHATOLOGY OF

The epistle to the Romans was written by the apostle Paul to the Christians at Rome around A.D. 57. Corinth is the probable place of writing. Differences of opinion regarding how chapters 5–8 and 9–11 fit in the epistle have resulted in a variety of suggestions for both the subject and theme. The subject is justification by faith. The theme is straightforward: Salvation is for all, both Jew and Gentile, by faith in Jesus Christ and not by the Mosaic Law or any works. Romans is replete with descriptions of the personal future prospects for believers, but certain passages are significant for eschatology in the usual sense of future historical events still to occur and the program of God that brings them to pass. These passages are Romans 3:1–4; chapters 9–11; 13:11; and possibly 16:25–27 (14:24–26, Majority Text).

Romans 3:1–4

The eschatological significance of 3:1–4 is generally unrecognized but is very significant for premillennialism. The passage says, "Then what is the advantage of the Jew or what is the profit for the circumcision? Much in every way. First, because the oracles [*logia*] of God were committed to them. For, what if some disbelieved, their disbelief will not nullify God's faithfulness, will it? No! Not at all. Rather, God be true but every man a liar, just as it is written, "In order that you be justified by your words and be victorious when you are judged."

The question in the first line, What is the advantage of the Jew or the profit for the circumcision, arises from Paul's argument in the previous chapter that the Jew and Gentile will both be judged impartially according to their deeds. He specifically argued that the individual Jew, although having the Mosaic Law, will be shown no partiality in the judgment over the Gentile who does not have the Law. Since the Old Testament presents Israel as God's chosen nation and recipients of the covenants, promises, and blessings, the statement that Jews have no advantage individually regarding salvation and condemnation naturally gives rise to the question, What then is the advantage for the Jew? The question does not concern believing Jews only but all Jews in contrast to Gentiles, that is, Jews ethnically as a group, as the nation Israel. This is basically the same question discussed in the major eschatological passage, chapters 9–11. Also significant is the fact that the question concerns an advantage in existence at the time Paul is writing, that is, an advantage for the Jew not available to Gentiles during this church age. However, the question also indicates that this advantage was in existence previously; thus, it is an advantage for all Jews in contrast to Gentiles which existed before the church and is still in effect now that the church is in existence. This is an advantage that neither the Gentiles nor the church have but all Jews, even unbelieving Jews have solely because they are Jews. The apostle Paul answers, *they* (plural) were entrusted with God's oracles, and What if *some* (some out of the whole) disbelieved? thus showing that the passage refers to the whole of Israel, to Israel as a nation. The disbelief referred to here is the same disbelief that is referred to throughout this epistle, that is, Israel's refusal to believe its own Messiah.

The advantage, according to Paul's answer, consists chiefly in the fact that the oracles, *logia*, of God were entrusted to Israel. *Logia* is not the word *logos* (word) or *graphe* (scripture), but refers to the sayings of a deity and could refer to part or the whole of God's sayings. It cannot refer to the promise of the Gospel, to the church, or to salvation since the Gentiles, as well as the church have these as much as Israel. It cannot refer to the Mosaic covenant or Law since chapter 2 has just shown that not only does the Jew have no advantage relating to salvation, but that possessing the Law gives the Jew no advantage. In fact, Romans and Galatians regard the Law as more of a disadvantage than an advantage to those under it. The most common view, that it refers to the Old Testament scriptures as a whole, is also unacceptable. The verb *committed* may seem to imply that Israel was entrusted with the Scriptures as to a custodian, but this word is used several times in the New Testament in the same sense as here. This use means to entrust or commit to someone in order to accomplish the respective purpose, not to merely mke someone a custodian. In addition, the church is as much, if not more so, a custodian of both Old and New Testaments, thus ruling out this as an advantage specifically for Israel. Neither does this view fit with the statements of verses 3 and 4.

These verses show that Israel's advantage in having the *logia* committed to them is not merely in possessing them but in God's faithfulness to what He has said in the *logia.* The connection with verse 3 shows that the advantage lies in the fact that God will be faithful to His sayings, *logia*, in spite of Israel's unbelief in its Messiah. Verse 4 clarifies that God's faithfulness is in the fact that He does not and will not lie. Thus the connection of thought in the passage itself shows that the advantage for Israel in the *logia* is not in possession but that God will do what He has said He will do for Israel in contrast to others. This is confirmed by the question raised in verse 3 indicating that someone could think that God would not be faithful to His *logia* due to the fact that Israel disbelieved and rejected their Messiah. Only the national promises to Israel fit verses 3 and 4 as they are used in this context. Paul specifically says that if God does not keep His promises to Israel this would make Him a liar. Despite this statement of Paul's and that this is contrary to what we know of God's character, this is what the majority of Christians known as amillennialists have always believed. This explains also why so many commentators try to avoid the obvious fact that the *logia* are specifically the promises to Israel and not the Old Testament in general. This passage teaches that God will not renege on His promises to national Israel despite Israel's rejection of Christ. Even if someone does not admit that it refers specifically to the promises, the passage still teaches that God will be faithful and will not lie, particularly regarding Israel, and that Israel's rejection of its Messiah will not cause Him to be unfaithful to what He has said in His word. Thus this includes the promises to national Israel. Even though the church age is in effect, Israel is still Israel in contrast to Gentiles and the church and has a national future as prophesied in the Bible. The perspective of this passage is definitely premillennial and definitely contradicts amillennialism. The church and Israel are regarded as distinct, presently existing entities, each having a different relationship to God at the present time. Israel and the church are distinct now and in the future; thus, the passage also teaches a dispensational distinction.

Romans 9–11

This next eschatological section is a major portion of the epistle. It answers the same basic question raised in 3:1. The answer to 3:1, that God will be faithful to His promises to Israel, is also the answer basic to the argument of chapters 9–11. Paul opens his discussion by telling of the anguish in his heart concerning Israel, a nation that, although it has so many blessings and promises, is lost because it has refused to believe the Gospel. The question naturally arises, Since God has given the covenants and promises to Israel, then what has happened so that the nation as a whole is lost? Verse 6 gives the answer in its most basic form, The word of God has not gone astray. All those of Israel are not Israel. That is, all physical Israelites are not Israel in the sense of being children of God who will receive the blessings and promises. This does not say that Gentiles or the church are included in "Israel." It says just the opposite, not all Israel, only some of them are Israel. Paul does not broaden the term *Israel* to include others but narrows it to include only those who respond by faith. This narrowing is clear from his next two illustrations using first Isaac and Ishmael and then Jacob and Esau. In each case only one is in the line of promise. Verses 14–27 argue that God is free to save as He pleases; thus, He is free to save on the basis of mercy and grace and is not obligated to save due to works (the Law). The statement in verse 24 that God has called not only those out of the Jews but also out of the Gentiles does not imply that Israel's promises have been taken from it and given in a spiritual form to the church. The term *Israel* is not used. The only fact stated is that Gentiles have been called as vessels of mercy destined for glory as well as Jews. There is nothing regarding Israel's national promises. If this did refer to Israel's promises, it would indicate that Gentiles would share in Israel's national promises of a messianic kingdom. Paul ends chapter 9 by stating that the Gentiles have obtained righteousness by faith but Israel rather than obtaining righteousness has stumbled due to unbelief in Jesus Christ (9:30–33). Chapter 10 specifies that Israel has received from God everything necessary to be saved, that is, the proclamation of the Gospel message, but has refused to believe and is, therefore, lost.

In chapter 11:1–10, Paul, answering the question in verse 1, states that Israel is not completely rejected since some, including Paul himself, are saved. He argues that God has a remnant based on grace rather than works. The present situation of Israel is summarized in verse 7. The remnant obtained righteousness by faith, but Israel as a whole (the "rest") did not and are hardened. Thus far, Paul has shown that Israel's present condition is lost (9:1–5, 30–33; 10:1–3, 16–21; 11:1–10). The remainder of chapter 11 describes how this situation fits in God's overall plan. In answering the question of 11:11, Paul outlines God's plan for the world and for Israel. By Israel's offense (their present situation) God has brought salvation to the Gentiles. This, however, is designed to provoke Israel to jealousy (cf. 10:19) resulting in their salvation. This is not the goal, but when Israel is restored (its "fullness," v. 12) this will result in even greater blessing for the world at large. God's purpose for Israel is that it be a testimony, a means of reaching the world. Throughout this section only national Israel can be meant by the term *Israel* since the plan of God can hardly be to stumble an individual Jew to reach an individual Gentile; this, so that Gentile will then provoke the Jew to jealousy and, once restored, that individual Jew would reach more Gentiles. Israel's present condition is described in terms of its offense, loss (v. 12), needing salvation (v. 14), casting away (v. 15), fallen (v. 22), enemies (v. 28), and disobedient (v. 30). This same time is described with respect to the Gentiles as salvation (v. 11), the wealth of the Gentiles, the wealth of the world (v. 12), the reconciliation of the world (v. 15). This describes the present time. However, Paul also refers to a time described as Israel's fullness (v. 12), which will bring even greater riches to the world than this present time. That time is also described as Israel's reception (v. 15), as a time when Israel is grafted back in (v. 23), a time when all Israel will be saved (v. 25). According to the Scripture Paul uses as proof, this will be when the Deliverer, the Messiah, comes and converts the nation. Thus, Paul speaks of two different periods for Israel, the present period of loss and a different and future period of fullness, bringing blessing to the earth. The future description can only refer to the millennial kingdom. It is specifically stated that the present hardening will be removed from Israel and all Israel (the nation as a whole) will be saved (v. 25f). This is in total contrast to the description of its present state.

The final verses confirm this. In verse 28, Israel is described in its present condition as enemies, elect, and beloved. Even though enemies it is still elect and beloved from God's perspective. This is hardly a description of a nation from whom God has taken His promises due to its actions and given them to others (the church). Israel is beloved not for their own sakes but for the sake of the patriarchs, because the gifts and calling of God are not regretted. Their status as beloved is because God made certain promises to the fathers. Thus, whether God keeps the promises or not does not relate at all to the generation of Israel when their Messiah came. They will be kept because God made the promises to the patriarchs. Therefore, the fact that Israel rejected her Messiah cannot nullify promises made to Abraham, Isaac, and Jacob many years earlier (v. 28), nor will, in any case, God go back on His promises since this would make Him a liar (3:1–4). Paul then explains that now is Israel's disobedience so that it, just as the Gentiles who were disobedient previously, is now an object of God's mercy (v. 30–32).

This passage is distinctly premillennial in perspective. In addition, it is distinctly contrary to the amillennial concept that God has taken Israel's national promises from it and fulfilled them in the church so that there is no future kingdom for Israel as prophesied in the Old Testament. In this section, whether describing the present age or the future, Israel and the Gentiles are always distinct and different entities. Thus the outlook of this passage, as well as 3:1–4, is clearly dispensational.

Romans 13:11

This passage refers to an eschatological event, believers' future salvation. In saying that now our salvation is closer than when we first believed, Paul admonishes believers to live properly in view of the fact that each day brings them closer. This fits well with an imminent rapture that serves as a motivation to be ever on the alert for the Lord.

Romans 16:25–27 (14:24–26, Majority Text)

These verses do not refer to an eschatological event and so are not necessarily part of this discussion. They do, however, indicate that the present time is basically a Gentile time. They also state that the present church truths were kept silent in the Old Testament and are only now revealed in the New Testament age. Thus, they present a dispensational perspective in that the church was not in the Old Testament, and the present is a time primarily oriented toward Gentiles rather than toward Israel.

There is no question that the eschatology revealed in the epistle to the Romans is definitely premillennial and dispensational and harmonizes best with an imminent rapture.

See ISRAELOLOGY, DOCTRINE OF; JEWS, RETURN OF THE.

Thomas R. Edgar

C. E. B. Cranfield, *The Epistle to the Romans,* (Edinburgh: T &T Clark, 1975); James D. G. Dunn, *World Biblical Commentary,* vol. 38 (Dallas: Word Books, 1988); Joseph A. Fitzmeyer, "Romans" in *The Anchor Bible* (New York: Doubleday, 1992); S. Lewis Johnson, "Studies in Romans, Part VII: The Jews and the Oracles of God" in *Bib Sac,* 130 (1973); Douglas Moo, *The Wycliffe Exegetical Commentary, Romans 1–8* (Chicago: Moody Press, 1991).

RYLE, JOHN CHARLES

J. C. Ryle (1816–1900) was an Evangelical low-church Anglican, bishop of Liverpool, prolific writer best known for his *Expository Thoughts on the Gospels, Holiness,* and *Knots Untied.* He was born at Macclesfield and educated at Eton and Christ Church, Oxford. Ordained a priest in 1842, he pastored several churches, then in 1871 was made dean of Norwich. In 1880, he was nominated by Lord Beaconsfield as dean of Salisbury. However, before he had taken office he was made the first bishop of the newly created Anglican diocese of Liverpool, a position he held till shortly before his death. A strong evangelical, he wrote more than one hundred tracts and pamphlets on doctrinal and practical subjects, which enjoyed wide circulation. He authored a number of books of sermons and devotional literature and edited numerous books. Eschatology was not a major emphasis of Ryle's ministry. But nineteenth-century Anglican premillennialist that he was, he deserves mention in a dictionary of premillennial theology. He also appears to have been something of a dispensationalist.

On prophetic matters, Ryle was careful and conservative. He avoided speculation and especially so in the area of eschatology. He did not venture to fix dates or to settle the precise order or manner in which predictions of things to come are to be fulfilled. He did, however, hold firmly to the premillennial return of Christ to establish His millennial kingdom. In Ryle's preface to a volume of sermons on prophecy (*Coming Events And Present Duties*, 1867), he stated what he called the chief articles of his prophetical creed as follows (*Prophecy*, 6–9):

1. I believe that the world will never be completely converted to Christianity by any existing agency, before the end comes. In spite of all that can be done by ministers, churches, schools, and missions, the wheat and the tares will grow together until the harvest; and when the end comes, it will find the earth in much the same state that it was when the flood came in the days of Noah. (Matt. 13:24–30; 24:37–39.)

2. I believe that the widespread unbelief, indifference, formalism, and wickedness,

which are to be seen throughout Christendom, are only what we are taught to expect in God's Word. Troublous times, departures from the faith, evil men waxing worse and worse, love waxing cold, are things distinctly predicted. So far from making me doubt the truth of Christianity, they help to confirm my faith. Melancholy and sorrowful as the sight is, if I did not see it I should think the Bible was not true (Matt. 24:12; 1 Tim. 4:1; 2 Tim 3:1, 4, 13).

3. I believe that the grand purpose of the present dispensation is to gather out of the world an elect people, and not to convert all mankind. It does not surprise me at all to hear that the heathen are not all converted when missionaries preach, and that believers are but a little flock in any congregation in my own land. It is precisely the state of things which I expect to find. The Gospel is to be preached 'as a witness', and then shall the end come. This is the dispensation of election, and not of universal conversion (Acts 15:14; Matt. 24:14).

4. I believe that the second coming of our Lord Jesus Christ is the great event which will wind up the present dispensation, and for which we ought daily to long and pray. "Thy kingdom come," "Come, Lord Jesus," should be our daily prayer. We look backward, if we have faith, to Christ dying on the cross, and we ought to look forward no less, if we have hope, to Christ coming again (John 14:3; 2 Tim. 4:8; 2 Peter 3:12).

5. I believe that the second coming of our Lord Jesus Christ will be a real, literal, personal, bodily coming; and that as He went away in the clouds of heaven with His body, before the eyes of men, so in like manner He will return (Acts 1:11).

6. I believe that after our Lord Jesus Christ comes again, the earth shall be renewed, and the curse removed; the devil shall be bound, the godly shall be rewarded, the wicked shall be punished; and that before He comes there shall be neither resurrection, judgment, nor millennium, and that not till after He comes shall the earth be filled with the knowledge of the glory of the Lord (Acts 3:21; Isa. 25:6–9; 1 Thess. 4:14–18; Rev. 20:1, etc.).

7. I believe that the Jews shall ultimately be gathered again as a separate nation, restored to their own land, and converted to the faith of Christ, after going through great tribulation (Jer. 30:10–11; 31:10; Rom. 11:25–26; Dan. 12:1; Zech. 13:8–9).

8. I believe that the literal sense of the Old Testament prophecies has been far too much neglected by the Churches, and is far too much neglected at the present day, and that under the mistaken system of *spiritualizing and accommodating* Bible language, Christians have too often completely missed its meaning (Luke 24:25–26).

9. I do not believe that the preterist scheme of interpreting the Apocalypse, which regards the book as almost entirely *fulfilled*, or the futurist scheme, which regards it as almost entirely *unfulfilled*, are either of them to be implicitly followed. The truth, I expect, will be found to lie between the two.

10. I believe that the Roman Catholic Church is the great predicted apostasy from the faith, and is Babylon and the Antichrist, although I think it highly probable that a more complete development of the Antichrist will yet be exhibited to the world (2 Thess. 2:3–11; 1 Tim. 4:1–3).

11. Finally, I believe that it is for the safety, happiness, and comfort of all true Christians, to expect as little as possible from Churches or Governments under the present dispensation, to hold themselves ready for tremendous convulsions and changes of all things established, and to expect their good things only from Christ's Second Advent.

Ryle abstained from addressing certain particulars. He said: "About the precise time when the present dispensation will end, about the manner in which the heathen will be converted, about the mode in which the Jews will be restored to their own land, about the burning up of the earth, about the first resurrection, about the rapture of the saints, about the distinction between the appearing and the coming of Christ, about the future siege of Jerusalem and the last tribulation of the Jews, about the binding of Satan before the millennium begins, about the duration of the millennium, about the loosing of Satan at the end of the thousand years, about the destruction of Gog and

Magog, about the precise nature and position of the New Jerusalem, about all these things, I purposely decline expressing any opinion" (*Prophecy*, 10).

It is interesting to note that Ryle emphasized literal interpretation (article 8, above). This apparently led him to certain dispensational distinctions. Exactly where Ryle stood on the issue of dispensationalism is unclear. Very likely, he did *not* hold a developed form of dispensationalism. But he did make certain essential dispensational distinctions. He *did* distinguish the church from Israel in that he saw a national future for Israel (article 7, above). And he *did* distinguish "the present dispensation" from "all dispensations preceding our own" (*Prophecy*, 10). How many dispensations Ryle held is uncertain. He did, however, distinguish "the Christian dispensation" (which he apparently equates with "our own") from "the patriarchal" and "Mosaic dispensations" (Ibid., 11).

Steven L. McAvoy

F. L. Cross, ed., *The Oxford Dictionary of the Christian Church* (London: Oxford University Press, 1958); J. C. Ryle, *Prophecy* (Ross-shire, Scotland: Christian Focus Publications, 1991); Peter Toon and Michael Smout, *John Charles Ryle: Evangelical Bishop* (Swengel, Pa.: Reiner Publications, 1976).

RYRIE, CHARLES C.

Charles Caldwell Ryrie (b. 1925) is a graduate of Haverford College (B.A.), Dallas Theological Seminary (Th.M., Th.D.) and the University of Edinburgh, Scotland (Ph.D.). For many years he served as professor of systematic theology and dean of doctoral studies at Dallas Theological Seminary, where he challenged students to precision in theological speaking and writing. Dr. Ryrie is especially gifted in his ability to clarify profound theological truths in simple, precise language. He has enabled people to understand biblical truth that they would otherwise not readily comprehend and in this he has made an inestimable contribution to the Christian world.

Dr. Ryrie's writings have consistently been on the theological cutting edge, addressing the critical issues of the day and speaking on behalf of dispensational premillennialism. In his classic text, *Dispensationalism Today* (1965), and his recent update, *Dispensationalism* (1995), Ryrie clarifies many of the misunderstandings that opponents of premillennialism and dispensationalism have levelled. He notes that even Louis Berkhof, a covenant theologian, makes (dispensational) distinctions, differentiating the OT from the NT and seeing four subdivisions in the OT. Ryrie defines a dispensation as "a distinguishable economy in the outworking of God's purpose" (*Dispensationalism,* 28). In a dispensation God places people under a stewardship or responsibility, people invariably failing the test, with a corresponding judgment and change.

Ryrie clearly delineates the *sine qua non* of dispensationalism:

1. Dispensationalism keeps Israel and the church distinct. This is the most basic test of dispensationalism.
2. The distinction between Israel and the church is born out of a system of hermeneutics that is usually called literal interpretation. Dispensationalism interprets words in their normal or plain meaning; it does not spiritualize or allegorize the text. The strength of dispensationalism is its consistently literal, or plain, interpretation of Scripture.
3. The underlying purpose of God in the world is the glory of God (pp. 39–40). In contrast to covenant theology (which sees salvation as the underlying purpose) and progressive dispensationalism (which emphasizes a Christological center), dispensationalism sees a broader purpose—the glory of God. (This theme is developed in *Transformed By His Glory*.) For this reason, the number of dispensations is not the critical issue in dispensationalism—as long as one is true to the three essentials of dispensationalism. Three dispensations—law, grace, and kingdom—receive most of the treatment in Scripture; however, it is possible to recognize other dispensations and while the historic sevenfold scheme of dispensations is not inspired, they seem to be distinguishable economies in God's program.

Dr. Ryrie also interacts with progressive (revisionist) dispensationalism as held by Darrell Bock, Craig Blaising and Robert Saucy. This revisionist dispensationalism represents a major departure from normative dispensationalism. A major tenet of progressive dispensationalism is its belief that the Abrahamic, Davidic, and new covenants are already inaugurated and beginning to be fulfilled (already/not yet). They understand Christ as already seated and reigning on the throne of David in heaven. Ryrie questions, "Why is no mention made of an already inaugurated Palestinian covenant (Deut. 29–30)?" (p. 163). The revisionist teaching of "already/not yet" is not new. C. H. Dodd taught it early in the twentieth century; George Ladd, the covenant premillennialist, and amillennialists A. Hoekema and R. C. Sproul have taught variations of it. Even nondispensationalists recognize that progressive dispensationalism has changed to covenant dispensationalism and has moved closer to covenant theology. The revisionists' failure to make a clear and consistent distinction between Israel and the church and the teaching that Christ is currently reigning on the throne of David in heaven is assuredly closer to covenant theology than to normative dispensationalism.

Originally a doctoral dissertation, *The Basis of the Premillennial Faith* established the Old Testament foundation of premillennialism: "Holding to a literal interpretation of the Scriptures, [premillennialists] believe that the promises made to Abraham and David are unconditional and have had or will have a literal fulfillment. In no sense have these promises made to Israel been abrogated or fulfilled by the church, which is a distinct body in this age having promises and a destiny different from Israel's" (p. 12). With this foundation, Ryrie develops the Abrahamic covenant (Gen. 12:1–3), showing that this covenant awaits a literal, future fulfillment with the establishment of Israel in the Promised Land. This can only be properly understood when recognizing the distinction between Israel and the church (cf. 1 Cor. 10:32). The church does not receive the fulfillment of these promises; they were made to Israel and will be fulfilled to that nation.

Premillennialism is further established through the unconditional Davidic covenant (2 Sam. 7:12–16), which promises: (1) a posterity; (2) David's throne will be established forever; (3) David's kingdom will be established forever (p. 77). Many OT passages confirm the future fulfillment of the Davidic covenant (Ps. 89; Isa. 9:6–7; Jer. 23:5–6; 30:8–9; 33:14–21; Ezek. 37:24–25; Dan. 7:13–14; Hos. 3:4–5; Amos 9:11). Christ did not inaugurate this kingdom at His First Advent; it awaits His future return for fulfillment (p. 93).

Premillennialism also has a basis in the new covenant (Jer. 31:31–34), which provides unconditional grace, forgiveness, and restoration to the favor and blessing of God. While an aspect of it applies to the church, its complete fulfillment "requires the regathering of all Israel, their spiritual rebirth, and the return of Christ" (p. 111). Ultimately, "the new covenant is for Israel" (p. 124) and awaits fulfillment at Jesus' return.

While recognizing Ryrie's important contributions to many critical theological issues, perhaps his most noteworthy contribution is the *Ryrie Study Bible*, now in an expanded edition (1995).

See also DISPENSATIONALISM.

Paul P. Enns

Charles C. Ryrie, *Acts of the Apostles* (Chicago: Moody, 1961), *Balancing the Christian Life* (Chicago: Moody, 1969), *Basic Theology* (Wheaton: Victor, 1986), *The Basis of the Premillennial Faith* (Neptune, N.J.: Loizeaux, 1953), *The Best Is Yet to Come* (1976), *Biblical Answers to Contemporary Issues* (Chicago: Moody, 1991), *Biblical Theology of the New Testament* (Chicago: Moody, 1959), *Dispensationalism* (Chicago: Moody, 1995), *Dispensationalism Today* (Chicago: Moody, 1965), *Easy Object Lessons* (Chicago: Moody, 1949), *Easy-to-Give Object Lessons* (Chicago: Moody, 1954), *The Final Countdown* (Wheaton: Victor Press, 1969), *First & Second Thessalonians* (Chicago: Moody, 1959), *The Grace of God* (Chicago:

Moody, 1963), *The Holy Spirit* (Chicago: Moody, 1965), *Making the Most of Your Life* (Chicago: Moody, 1965), *The Miracles of Our Lord* (Nashville: Thomas Nelson, 1984), *Neo-Orthodoxy* (Chicago: Moody, 1956), *Revelation* (Chicago: Moody, 1968), *Ryrie Study Bible* (Chicago: Moody, 1995), *Ryrie's Concise Guide to the Bible* (San Bernadino, Calif.: Here's Life Publishers, 1983), *So Great Salvation* (Wheaton: Victor, 1989), *A Survey of Bible Doctrine* (Chicago: Moody, 1972), *Transformed by His Glory* (Wheaton: Victor, 1990), *What You Should Know about Inerrancy* (Chicago: Moody, 1981), *What You Should Know about the Rapture* (Chicago: Moody, 1981), *What You Should Know about Social Responsibility* (Chicago: Moody, 1982), and *You Mean The Bible Teaches That . . .* (Chicago: Moody, 1974).

S

SALVATION, DISPENSATIONAL VIEW OF

Salvation is the work of God with the purpose of delivering believers from the judgment and presence of sin. A dispensational view of salvation has been misunderstood when it was inferred that the administrations (dispensations) of law and of grace involved two ways of salvation. Charles Ryrie categorically answered this charge and clarified the dispensational view of salvation; "The *basis* of salvation in every age is the death of Christ; the *requirement* for salvation in every age is faith; the *object* of faith in every age is God; the *content* of faith changes in various dispensations." (*Dispensationalism*, 115). The content changes because what may be known of Christ and Christ's death grows in the progress of revelation in each dispensation.

Genesis 3:15 has been viewed by Christians as the *protoevangelium* that includes God's comprehensive promise (object) that the seed of the woman would suffer under the serpent (basis), but that seed would ultimately conquer the serpent (content). Such a promise simply required a faith response. That is what Adam did (Gen. 3:20). Under the development of the promise, the content of the promise was clarified to include the provision of blessing through Abraham's seed available for all nations (Gen. 12:1–3, 7). Thus the basic model of salvation emerged in Abraham's response to God's promise to him (Gen.15:6). Abraham believed (requirement) God (object) in terms of what God had just promised (content; Gen. 15:1–5, that God would raise up a son from the deadness of his own and Sarah's bodies). God then accounted Abraham's faith (requirement) to be righteousness (delivered from the condemnation of sin).

1. Under law, the basis of salvation was clarified in the revelation of redemption from Egypt and in the revelation of the covenant sacrificial system. The object of faith remained God. The content of God's work of salvation remained expressed in the promise as it was repeated in the ceremony of circumcision and as it was celebrated at the Passover (Exod. 12:3–13). In particular, the basis of salvation was a lamb, with God-determined qualifications, that was sacrificed as a substitute so that the blood covers the house over which the death angel would pass. The requirement was faith to place blood on ones doorway. This redeemed people then received a covenant that also provided a basis for continued forgiveness in the substitutionary sacrifice of animals for sin.

2. Under grace, the content of the promise received final historical expression in the Gospel. The seed of the woman and of Abraham is Jesus of Nazareth. The blow by the serpent was Jesus' death on the cross (the ultimate basis). The blow that defeated Satan is the resurrection of Jesus from the dead. The promised blessing now mediated for all nations is eternal life with all of the related blessings identified in the New Testament. Under the kingdom, salvation will remain unchanged but the experience of the blessings of salvation will reach a historical climax.

See also DISPENSATIONALISM.

Elliott Johnson

Charles C. Ryrie, *Basic Theology* (Wheaton: Victor Books, 1986), *Dispensationalism* (Chicago: Moody Press, 1995).

SAMUEL, 1 & 2, ESCHATOLOGY OF

These two books draw their names from the fact that Samuel is the principal character. The books carry on the Israelite history from the final years of the judges to the establishment of the Davidic kingdom. The death of Eli and his sons is recorded to indicate the moral decline of the priesthood. Samuel is presented as the founder of the office of prophet-judge and is the one who began schools for the prophets.

The author of part of the first book is thought to be Samuel, but there is no conclusive proof, although the first twenty-four chapters describe his life, his career, and his death. The writer of the remainder of book 1 and all of book 2 is a mystery. The date of their writing is about the tenth century B.C.

The prophecy in 1 Samuel concerns the promise of a future, faithful priest (1 Sam. 2:35–36). This will be fulfilled by Jesus Christ (Ps. 110:4; Heb. 5:6). There are other prophecies given in this book, but none as far-reaching as this one.

The great prophecy recorded in the book of 2 Samuel is that of the Davidic covenant (7:12–16). As the promises concerning the land are developed through the Palestinian covenant (Deut. 28–30), so the seed promises are expanded and validated in the Davidic covenant. The provisions of the covenant are that (1) David shall have a child who shall succeed him and establish his kingdom. (2) This son will be the one to build the temple, in David's place. (3) The throne of his, the son's, kingdom will continue forever. (4) Even though the sins of the son are great, the throne will not be taken from him. (5) David's house, throne, and kingdom will be established forever.

To uphold the future fulfillment of this covenant there are certain events that are required to take place. (1) Israel must be preserved as a nation. (2) Israel must occupy the land as a nation. (3) Jesus Christ, David's son, must physically and literally reign over the kingdom. (4) For the Messiah to reign there must first be a literal kingdom. (5) The kingdom must be eternal.

In order to understand future events as they unfold it is imperative to understand this covenant.

See also DAVIDIC COVENANT; THEOCRATIC KINGDOM.

Rick Bowman

J. Dwight Pentecost, *Things to Come* (Grand Rapids: Zondervan, 1958); John F. Walvoord and Roy B. Zuck, eds., *The Bible Knowledge Commentary* (Wheaton: Victor Books, 1985).

SCOFIELD, CYRUS INGERSON

C. I. Scofield (1843–1921) was an American Congregational/Presbyterian clergyman, writer, Bible conference speaker, defender of dispensational premillennialism, and editor of the *Scofield Reference Bible*. He was born on August 19 in Lenawee County, Michigan, the youngest of seven children, to a father that combined farming and lumbering to provide for his family. After his mother died, unable to recover from the birth of her son, his father remarried, so Cyrus was reared by a stepmother. His education, if any, is shrouded in a loss of the records; when he reappears in the historical record it is 1860, he is in Lebanon, Tennessee, in the home of his sister Laura and her husband. Scofield enlisted on May 20, 1861 in the Tennessee Infantry; though a minor, he claimed to be a twenty year old. He fought for the Confederacy on the eastern front at Richmond until he requested release from service in 1862; he claimed to be an alien—having residence in Michigan—and to have falsified his enlistment qualifications.

Scofield next appears in the record in St. Louis in 1865. Another sister, Emeline, had married Sylvester Pappin of a French family prominent in the world's fur market; Pappin was president of the St. Louis Board of Assessors. Scofield found employment in his brother-in-law's work and, advancing among the city's social elite, met Loentine Cerre; they married on September, 21 1866. Sometime later, Scofield, now a lawyer, moved to Atchison, Kansas, where he entered a career in politics and was elected in 1871 as a representative to the lower house of the Kansas legislature. In 1873 he was appointed by President Grant to the office of District Attorney for the District of Kansas; he resigned within six months under suspicion of misuse of his office for personal gain. Loentine gained a legal separation from her husband in 1877; the marriage dissolved, though the divorce did not become legal for several more years (1883). Scofield returned to St. Louis leaving behind his children. He appears to have sunken into a life of thievery and drunkenness, never to practice law again.

Scofield experienced an evangelical conversion in 1879, apparently through the witness of Thomas McPhetters, who was a member of James Hall Brookes's Walnut Street Presbyterian Church. Brookes, claimed Scofield, was his mentor in the faith. Scofield immediately became active in Christian work assisting in the campaign of Moody in St. Louis, 1879–80 and joined the Pilgrim Congregational Church. He was licensed to preach by the St. Louis Association of the Congregational Church shortly thereafter, then organized and pastored the Hyde Park Congregational church in the city. In addition, he worked under the auspices of the YMCA in East St. Louis. Enormous zeal for Christian work characterized his life from his conversion onward.

In 1882 Scofield accepted a call to a mission church of the denomination in Dallas where he was ordained in 1883. The small work grew rapidly; within the decade, the church reached a membership of four hundred from the fourteen when he first arrived; a larger church was erected in 1889. In 1884 he married a member of his congregation, Hettie Van Wark. In 1886 the Congregationalist D. L. Moody held a crusade, through Scofield's invitation, in the city, with Ira B. Sankey. Scofield became the acting missionary superintendent for his denomination in the Southwest (the American Mission Society of Texas and Louisiana). His church rose out of its former mission status to become vibrantly self-supporting. Scofield's sphere of influence increased rapidly. In 1887 he began to appear regularly in the Bible conferences (such as the Northfield and Niagara conferences), recognized for his teaching abilities. He was asked by his denomination to oversee mission work as far west as Colorado. In 1888, he published the immensely popular *Rightly Dividing the Word of Truth*, an explanation of the dispensational, pretribulational, and premillennial approach to interpreting the Bible. Further, Scofield directed the Southwestern School of the Bible in Dallas and was president of the board of trustees of the denomination's Lake Charles College in Lake Charles, Louisiana. His endeavors as pastor of the First Congregational Church seem to have been amazing, a witness to his enormous energy. In 1890, he founded the Central American Mission, having been inspired by J. Hudson Taylor the previous year at the Niagara Bible Conference. In the same year he started a self-study Bible program, called the Scofield Bible Correspondence Course (much of the material was placed in the Bible he edited). Further, the healthy growth of his church is evident in that two mission churches were started in the city, Grand Avenue Church and Pilgrim Chapel.

In 1895, Scofield accepted an invitation from D. L. Moody (who held a second campaign in Dallas that year) to the Trinitarian Congregational Church of Northfield, Massachusetts, leaving in Dallas a church that had reached a membership of over eight hundred. In addition to pastoral duties, Scofield presided over the Northfield Bible Training School (he served as president from 1900–1903), which Moody had established in 1890, and regularly attended the major Bible conferences. He witnessed the growing rift in the grand Niagara Bible Conference as the premillenarian assembly became divided over pre- and posttribulationalism, Scofield and A. C. Gaebelein favoring the former, with West and Cameron the latter. Though not the only issue in the demise of Niagara in 1899, it was a major factor. As a result, A. C. Gaebelein, Scofield, John T. Pirie and Alwyn Ball established the Sea Cliff Bible Conference on Long Island. At the conference in 1902, the idea of editing a reference Bible was first discussed, according to Gaebelein; it is there that the basic outline of the work was formulated, with Pirie's financial support.

Increasing preoccupation with editing the notes for the *Reference Bible* and the desire to be in a less hectic environment enticed Scofield to consider a return to his former pastorate in Dallas, where the promised assistant would allow for intense work on the new project. He returned in 1903 through 1909; however, work on the Bible took him away from Dallas after 1905. He apparently finished the initial draft of the notes in Montreux, Switzerland, in 1907, and edited them at his summer home in New Hampshire and in New York City in 1908. The Bible was published by Oxford University Press in 1909 and again with revisions in 1917. Scofield continued as pastor of the Dallas church, but appears to have been present only for periodic annual meetings. In 1908 the church withdrew from the Lone Star Association of the Congregational Church citing the rise of liberalism as the ground. In 1910, Scofield left the denomination also joining the Paris (Texas) Presbytery of the Presbyterian Church, USA (a strongly premillen-arian presbytery where Judge Scott was a firm financial supporter of Scofield's). Formally resigning from the church in 1909, he was granted the status of pastor emeritus from 1910–21. In 1923, the church was named in his honor, the Scofield Memorial Church during Chafer's pastorate.

After the publication of the *Reference Bible* in 1909, Scofield became evermore popular in the evangelical world. From his residence near New York City, he established the New York School of the Bible, which was more of a coordinating center than a school. From that office the Bible correspondence course was sent out and graded and Bible conferences and institutes were organized throughout the country. Scofield was asked by Oxford University Press to prepare another edition of the *Bible,* the Tercentenary Edition of 1911, later to revise the 1909 *Reference Bible* for republication in 1917. In 1914, Scofield, with William Pettingill and Chafer, established the Philadelphia School of the Bible; Scofield served as its president, though Pettingill oversaw the school's daily operations until failing health necessitated his resignation in 1918. In 1915, Scofield and several residents of Douglaston organized the Community Church; Scofield agreed to do the regular preaching. He continued to write extensively for Charles Trumbull's *Sunday School Times*. Notices of Scofield's declining health became a recurrent theme in the publications of the *Central American Bulletin*, the mission's journal after 1910; he resigned from the executive council of the mission in 1919. He died at his Douglaston residence on July, 24 1921; Hettie died there in 1923.

The contribution of C. I. Scofield to the development of the evangelical fundamentalist movement in the twentieth century has been enormous, particularly as it relates to premillennial dispensationalism. This can readily be demonstrated in several ways.

1. Scofield was profoundly influential in the development of the Bible conference movement (It must be understood that the appeal of this movement was to a popular audience, not the learned scholarly community. The vast majority of the voluminous literary output of this movement aimed at the nonprofessional). He was a regular speaker at the Niagara conferences in the 1880s and 1890s, as well as the Northfield conferences after 1887. Possessing the communicative skills to clearly and effectively teach the Bible, Scofield was significant in the ongoing of these conferences, as well as the important Sea Cliff conferences. Out of these conferences, a network developed of friendships with such leaders as Gaebelein, Brooks, James Martin Gray, W. H. Griffith Thomas, Chafer, and numerous others who cooperated in a wide variety of evangelical enterprises from conferences to missionary agencies to Bible institutes. Scofield influenced a younger generation of leaders, such as Chafer, to carry forth the Bible conference tradition.

2. Scofield was a major influence in the institutionalization of the Bible conference movement through educational institutions and missionary agencies. He was centrally prominent in the creation of several schools, beginning with the Southwestern School of the Bible during his first Dallas pastorate, then presiding over the Northfield Bible Training School, founding the New York School of the Bible, and, finally, establishing the Philadelphia School of the Bible (now Philadelphia College of Bible). In the field of missionary endeavor, he founded the Central American Mission and presided over its direction for nearly thirty years.

3. Scofield was a persistent contributor to

the massive literary production of the evangelical fundamentalist movement, particularly the dispensational and premillennial wing of it. What began as regular installments of Bible expositions in *The Believer,* a publication through the Dallas church in 1890, became the extremely popular Scofield Bible Correspondence Course and Bible leaflets. They sold in the thousands, providing self-study training for many pastors and Christian workers. The Dallas and the New York schools were correspondence centers, not resident schools. Along with the self-study course were numerous other publications that flowed from conference and pulpit addresses. These include such doctrinal works as *Plain Papers on the Holy Spirit* (1899), *No Room in the Inn and Other Interpretations* (1913), *New Life in Jesus Christ* (1915), *Where Faith Sees Christ* (1916), *Dr. C. I. Scofield's Question Box* (1917) and *In Many Pulpits with Dr. C. I. Scofield* (1920); expositional works such as *The Epistle to the Galatians* (1903); and eschatological works such as *The World's Approaching Crisis* (1913), *Addresses on Prophecy* (1914, messages that came out of the prophetic conference held at Moody Bible Institute), *Will the Church Pass Through the Tribulation?* (1917), *What Do the Prophets Say?* (1918), and *Things Old and New* (1922, a compilation by Gaebelein). Two other publications require particular note because of their wide influence in shaping the dispensational premillennial tradition. In 1888, Scofield wrote *Rightly Dividing the Word of Truth,* which attempted in pamphlet form to practically explain the dispensational, pretribulational, premillennial interpretation of the Bible. The hallmark of his literary production was the now-famous *Scofield Reference Bible* published in 1909 and revised in 1917. The *Reference Bible* is widely recognized as the most important literary production of the Bible conference/ institute movement. Scofield, by editing the text of the Bible with carefully placed notes, articulated the dispensational understanding of Scripture for the lay audience as never before accomplished. Generations of laity and pastors in the dispensational tradition learned the essence of the system from a careful study of the Scofield notes.

4. While Scofield was an advocate of a particular tradition, which he did much to create, he was an orthodox Presbyterian cleric who defended traditional orthodox interpretations of the Christian faith. He correctly commented to his longtime friend and colleague William Pettingill that eschatology, a doctrine that occupied so much of his time and interests, was not nearly so crucial as the central indisputable core of Christian truth that encompasses the doctrines of sin, Christ, and grace in redemption. In this sentiment Scofield stands in the continuum of the historic faith of the church universal. It is difficult to determine if Scofield was a fundamentalist since the movement did not coalesce definitely until the 1920s. He did not participate in the formation of the World Christian Fundamental Association in 1918 due to declining health. While it is not likely he would have embraced the more strident forms that fundamentalism later took, since he had quite a noncombative, irenic demeanor, he clearly was the ideological and practical source of many of its distinctive teachings.

5. Scofield had the ability, through his clear expositions of the Bible and personal charm, to inspire subsequent generations to continue the spirit of the Bible conference tradition within evangelical Christianity. The clearest example of his impact, perhaps, can be seen in his influence on Chafer, the founder of Dallas Theological Seminary, though it was certainly not limited to him. Having met Scofield for the first time at the Northfield Training School in 1901, Chafer was marked for life: "Until that time I had never heard a real Bible teacher. . . . It was a crisis for me. I was changed for life." What ensued was the closest relationship in which Scofield became Chafer's father figure. Writing shortly after Scofield's death, Chafer commented, "For twenty years, I have enjoyed the closest heart-fellowship with him, and the incalculable benefit of his personal counsel." The fruit of that mentoring relationship was the founding of Dallas Seminary as the fulfillment of a dream of Scofield's.

To Noel, Scofield's son, Chafer wrote, "You will be interested to know that the school, for which your father prayed and hoped for so many years for Dallas is going to be located here." Chafer's *Systematic Theology* (1948) was the culmination of Scofield's tutelage. The continued attraction of dispensational premillennialism, at least in part, has a root in the ability of leaders like Scofield, and later Chafer, to inspire a devoted following; in this, Scofield had a huge contribution to the movement.

See also CHAFER, LEWIS SPERRY.

John Hannah

William A. BeVier, "A Biographical Sketch of C. I. Scofield" (M.A. thesis, Southern Methodist University, 1960); Joseph M. Canfield, *The Incredible Scofield and His Book* (Ashville, N.C.: self-published, 1984); Arno C. Gaebelein, *The History of the Scofield Reference Bible* (New York: Our Hope Publications, 1943); Charles Gallaudet Trumbull, *The Life Story of C. I. Scofield* (New York: Oxford University Press, 1920).

SCROGGIE, W. GRAHAM

W. Graham Scroggie (1877–1958) was born in Great Malvern, England, and attended Spurgeon's Pastors' College. Doing battle with liberalism, he left his first two ministries. In time he took a pastorate in Edinburgh where large audiences came to hear his scholarly exposition of Scripture. The University of Edinburgh in 1927 conferred upon him the degree of doctor of divinity. His later years were spent in traveling and teaching throughout the English-speaking world. He was well accepted as a teacher at the English Keswick conventions and spent his final years lecturing at the Pastors' College in London.

Scroggie is best known in America for his classic and internationally known masterpiece *The Unfolding Drama of Redemption*. Originally published in three volumes, it is considered an unparalleled panorama of the greatest universal drama—God's undeterred plan of salvation for humankind.

It is probable that Scroggie did not often study the Bible in terms of its premillennial message. In *Drama of Redemption* he was far more interested in grasping the structure and themes of the Bible rather than its plan for the future. It is interesting, however, to see Scroggie struggle somewhere between a premillennial position and other views. Yet, over and over in this work, he substantiated his premillennial feelings.

For example, on Ezekiel's vision of the dry bones, Scroggie writes "it is the graveyard of the Jewish nation that the Prophet sees, the helpless, dismembered, denationalized people, whose return and restoration to the favour of God and to national unity are as resurrection from the dead." Scroggie sees Ezekiel and John in Revelation working "towards the same centre." By this Scroggie meant a future revelation about the city, the temple, the throne, Gog and Magog, and the glory of God enfolding all things. In Ezekiel, Scroggie sees the chosen people repossessing their inheritance, with a redistribution of the land, a rehabitation of the city of Zion, and a reconsecration of themselves to God.

In the Gospels, Scroggie recognizes "many references to the Messiah King who is yet to come, and Who will establish a kingdom which shall be universal and abiding." But it is in the book of Revelation that Scroggie seems confused. He writes that the book cannot be limited either to a future fulfillment or to supposing that the book deals only with the immediate and surrounding events of the apostle John. It has application in every age until Christ comes again. Scroggie concludes his comments on Revelation by saying there may be an element of truth in all the views about the book: preterist, historicist, and futurist. He summarizes his position: "I growingly feel that no one of these interpretations meets the demands of [Revelation], and, probably, there is a large element of truth in each of them. It may be that prophecy being slowly unfolded in the long course of history will be, in all its essential features, rapidly fulfilled within a strictly limited period at the end of the age."

Mal Couch

W. Graham Scroggie, *The Unfolding Drama of Redemption* (Grand Rapids: Kregel, 1994).

SEISS, JOSEPH A.

Joseph A. Seiss (1823–1904) has been labeled as one of the most able popular Lutheran preachers of the nineteenth century. Holding several pastorates, he was well-known and in demand as a speaker and author. He wrote over a dozen books; his most popular titles are: *The Apocalypse, The Gospel in Leviticus,* and *The Gospel in the Stars.* He also acted as editor of two magazines, *The Lutheran* and *Prophetic Times.*

His classic premillennial work is *The Apocalypse,* which is one of the most important studies ever written on the book of Revelation. It is called "an exhaustive, premillennial exposition" (Barber) and, "the most famous expository work on Revelation . . . sane, suggestive, reverent, . . . dependable" (Smith). Though a respected scholar in the Lutheran church, Seiss met much opposition for his millennial views. Seiss writes: "There is a widespread prejudice against the study of the Apocalypse." He added, "there are religious guides, sworn to teach 'the whole counsel of God,' who make a merit of not understanding [Revelation], and of not wishing to occupy themselves with it."

The key to Revelation, according to Seiss, is that the Apocalypse does not mean a communicated message, "but the coming, appearing, manifestation, uncovering, presentation, of Jesus Christ in person." He adds it is "His own personal manifestation and unveiling in the scenes and administrations of the great Day of the Lord."

Both Seiss and George N. H. Peters were brought to their premillennial convictions through the influence of one of the most outstanding Lutheran scholars of the nineteenth century, Dr. S. S. Schmucker. Schmucker has been called one of the most forceful exponents of biblical prophecy in America during that period (Smith).

See PETERS, GEORGE N. H.

Mal Couch

Joseph A. Seiss, *The Apocalypse* (Grand Rapids: Kregel, 1987).

SON OF DAVID

The humanity of the Lord Jesus Christ is specified often in the New Testament with regard to His being the son of David. The New Testament opens with the introduction of Jesus as the son of David, the son of Abraham (Matt. 1:1). His relationship to King David not only links Him to the human race, but also to the divinely ordained Davidic monarchy and the eternal and unconditional Davidic covenant (2 Sam. 7:4–17). In that covenant, God promised that David's royal dynasty would last forever and that David's son would be God's Son. This covenant has its perfect fulfillment in Christ.

Matthew and Luke, the two Gospels that deal with the details of the birth of Jesus, emphasize His genealogical descent from King David. A problem is that while both Matthew and Luke indicate the genealogy of Joseph, the names are different in the two lists from David to Joseph. This has led critics to assume that there are errors in the lists. However, the two lists can be reconciled by concluding that Matthew gave Joseph's genealogy, while Luke gives that of Mary (see the *New Scofield Reference Edition* for an explanation of the substitution of Joseph's name in Luke 3:23). Assuming, then, that Luke has Mary's genealogy, she was then a descendant of King David through his son Nathan. Joseph, on the other hand, descended from David through Solomon.

Inasmuch as Mary was the natural mother of Jesus, the fact that she was a descendant of David caused Jesus to be of the physical seed of David. In light of the Virgin Birth, though, what is the significance of Joseph's genealogy? As he was not the physical father of Christ, what difference does it make that he was also a descendant of David? First, the fact that Joseph was a descendant of David made it necessary for he and Mary to go from Nazareth to Bethlehem when Caesar's tax was taken; secondly, Joseph was thereby able to confer on Jesus, by adoption, the legal right to the throne of David.

Actually, if Israel had been an independent monarchy at the time, Joseph could have laid claim to being the king, since he was of the royal seed of the reigning kings of Jerusalem! Israel was not independent, but was under the rule of Rome. Also, the Lord Himself had pronounced a curse upon the Davidic dynasty, telling the last sitting king of the royal seed, Jeconiah, that none of his descendants would reign upon the Jerusalem throne (Jer. 22:28). Thus, by adoption, Joseph was able to convey the legal right to the throne upon Jesus, without passing on the curse of Jeconiah, while Mary conveyed physical descendance from David.

The New Testament attaches considerable importance to the fact that Jesus Christ is the son of David, and the Old Testament makes it clear that the Messiah would be the ancient king's descendant. It is through the Davidic royal dynasty that Jesus relates to the human race. The references to His descendence from King David are numerous:

1. Second Samuel 7:12, 14; your seed shall be My Son
2. Isaiah 11:1; a rod out of the stem of Jesse
3. Matthew 1:1; Jesus Christ, the son of David, son of Abraham
4. The genealogies of Joseph (in Matthew) and Mary (in Luke) from David
5. Acts 2:30; fruit of David's loins, Christ, to sit on his throne
6. Acts 13:34; Jesus is given the sure mercies of David
7. Romans 1:3; Christ was made of the seed of David according to the flesh
8. Revelation 5:5; the root of David has prevailed
9. Revelation 22:16; Jesus is the root and the offspring of David

The New Testament begins and ends with an emphasis on Jesus' relationship to the human race as the son of David. The personality of David, the promises to David, and the prophecies of David are central to this theme.

Personality of David

God, who is reticent about giving compliments to humans, lavishes on David the description that he is a man after God's own heart (1 Sam. 13:14). Paul picks up on this theme in his message to the Pisidian Antioch synagogue (Acts 13:22) and shows how God raised up both David and Jesus in their respective times. Christ also identified Himself with His honored ancestor when He defended His eating wheat from the fields on the Sabbath along with His disciples (Luke 6:1–5). In similar circumstances, David, the anointed of the Lord, was rejected and persecuted by King Saul and his army. David and his fellow fugitives stopped at Shiloh and ate the showbread reserved for the priests. The argument was that if God's anointed, David, could apparently violate the Law of Moses in a state of stress and rejection, surely God's anointed Son could do the same. Obviously, the Lord felt a great affinity with David.

Promises to David

In the Davidic covenant, God made several important promises to King David (2 Sam. 7:4–17) but the pertinent ones to our subject are that David would have a dynasty that would last forever and that David's son would be God's Son. These are promises made to no other monarch in history and, of course are fulfilled in the eternal reign of David's great son, Christ Jesus.

When Christ returns to the earth and establishes His millennial reign, He will rule Israel and the world on the throne of His father David.

Prophecies of David

The Psalms were the great vehicle of expression by David, as he was inspired by the Holy Spirit. They not only conveyed the worship of the Almighty, but also prophecies about the Messiah. Jesus used one Davidic prophecy in the Psalms to prove His own deity when He referred to Psalm 110:1, "The LORD said unto my Lord." He argued, if the Messiah is only David's son, why does David call Him his Lord?

Apostles Peter and Paul both used Ps. 16:10 to prove that the Messiah had to rise from the dead. King David had died long before and his body had corrupted in the tomb, but David was speaking of the resurrection of his great messianic son when he prophesied that "neither wilt thou suffer thine Holy One to see corruption." If the Messiah's dead body was not to see corruption, then

He would have to rise from the dead within three days, which, of course, is exactly what happened in the case of the risen Christ.

In this light, then, Jesus' title as the son of David must be understood as a central theme of the Scriptures.

See also DAVIDIC COVENANT.

Thomas S. McCall

SON(S) OF GOD

The designation "sons of God" is used in Scripture of humans who, by grace alone through faith alone in Christ alone, trust Him as their substitute for sin. It is used as well of holy angels and, some think, of wicked angels also in Genesis 6.

The Lord Jesus Christ is also referred to in Scripture many times as the Son of God. This name is far more than simply a designation or a mere title. Not all of the names ascribed to Christ are descriptive of His essence, but Son of God does reveal His divine essence and equality with the Father. This, in the main, has been the doctrine of the church since the Council of Nicaea in A.D. 325.

Christ Is the Eternal Son of God

There was never a time when Christ was not the Son of God, though there was a time when He was not human, Jesus, son of David, or son of Mary. He became these at His incarnation, but He was the Son of God always.

The eternal sonship of Christ, though a vital part of the historic orthodox faith, has been denied by some within orthodoxy. These have embraced what might be called the incarnational sonship of Christ as opposed to the eternal sonship of Christ. The deity and eternal existence of Christ are maintained in this view but not His eternal sonship. Son of God as applied to Christ is believed to be merely a title, not descriptive of His essence. F. E. Raven, an influential teacher among the Plymouth Brethren assemblies, rejected the doctrine of Christ's eternal sonship and was rejected by the leadership of this group because of his teaching. The denial also surfaced among some Baptists and prompted a defense of Christ's eternal sonship by J. C. Philpot, *The True, Proper, and Eternal Sonship of the Lord Jesus Christ, The Only Begotten Son of God* (England: Gospel Standard Baptist Trust, 1926 reprint). Respected theologian Ralph Wardlaw in his *Systematic Theology* also rejects the eternal sonship of Christ (Edinburgh: Black, 1857).

When the title Son of God is used of Christ, it has nothing to do with His birth or with Mary being His mother. He was Mary's child and son, but He was not God the Father's child. Christ is never called God's child *(teknos)* in Scripture, but He is called God's Son *(huios)* many times. As such He has an eternal relation with the Father.

Three things are signified by the term *son.* "It signifies that a son is a separate person from his father; a son is the heir, not the servant, of his father; and a son has the same nature as his father" (Zeller and Showers). Christ's sonship and deity go together. Consistency requires that to affirm either one is to affirm the other; to deny either one is to deny the other.

Scripture makes it very clear that the Son of God was present at Creation and had a vital part in it (Col. 1:13–17; Heb. 1:2). The Son of God is said to be in the Father's bosom (John 1:18; 1 John 1:1–2). Many times the Son of God is said to have been sent by God the Father to be the sinner's substitute for sin (Isa. 9:6; John 3:16; 20:21; Rom. 8:32; Gal. 4:4; 1 John 4:10, 14).

Robert P. Lightner

J. C. Philpot, *The True, Proper, and Eternal Sonship of the Lord Jesus Christ, the Only Begotten Son of God* (England: Gospel Standard Baptist Trust, 1926 reprint); John F. Walvoord, *Jesus Christ Our Lord* (Chicago: Moody Press, 1969); George W. Zeller and Renald E. Showers, *The Eternal Sonship of Christ* (Neptune, N.J.: Loizeaux Brothers, 1993).

SON OF MAN

The title "Son of Man" is used eighty-two times in the Gospels, once in Acts, once in Hebrews, and twice in the book of Revelation. New Testament usage is based on the Old Testament, where it occurs 107, times of which ninety-three are in Ezekiel. That the term refers to human beings is made clear, for example, in Psalm 8:4, "What is man, that Thou dost take thought of him? And the son of man, that Thou didst care for him?" The addition of the words *son of* emphasize the quality as the "children of the bridechamber" refers to the friends of the bridegroom (Matt. 9:15) and the phrase *son of the field* refers to a farmer. So the phrase *son of man* places special emphasis on the humanity of a person.

Thus, the phrase, as it is used for Jesus in the Gospels, stresses His genuine humanity. Hebrews 2:6 uses the phrase to show that the Son who was revealed as God in chapter 1 and so is greater than the angels, is also truly human and with His divinely given supervision of the earth is also greater than the angels. This God-Man defeated the devil and his power of death, made propitiation for the sins of the people, and is able to come to the aid of those who are tempted (Heb. 2:14–18).

However, Jesus clearly tied the use of the term to Daniel 7:13. Daniel sees a vision of "one like a son of man" come with the clouds of heaven to stand before the Ancient of Days, from whom he receives an eternal kingdom over all peoples and nations. Then this one like a son of man comes to earth to establish the eternal and universal kingdom of God promised so often in the Old Testament Scripture. This person, therefore, has much the same ministry as the promised seed of David (see SON OF DAVID), who also will bring in the promised eternal kingdom (2 Sam. 7: 12–16). The similarity and distinction between the two must be noticed: the seed of David is clearly a human but the one like a son of man is *like* a human, and the seed of David is the descendant of David on earth while the one like a son of man comes from heaven, thus emphasizing his supernatural origin.

Jesus used the term *to refer to Himself*, almost as a substitute for the pronoun *I*. He warned the man who volunteered to follow Him, "The foxes have holes, and the birds of the air have nests, but the Son of Man has nowhere to lay His head" (Luke 9:58). He used the term without the comparison shown by the word *like* and He used it to refer to Himself as without His own home—surely the future ruler of the nations should have His own home; the prospective disciple is warned of the sacrifices involved. When the cities of Galilee rejected Him and His message, He announced, "The Son of Man came eating and drinking, and they say, 'Behold, a gluttonous man and a drunkard, a friend of tax-gatherers and sinners!" (Matt. 11:19). The coming of the Son of Man the first time was far from glorious and world conquering.

Other times Jesus used the phrase Son of Man *to emphasize the authority of His claims and declarations:* His power to save in Luke 19:10, "For the Son of Man has come to seek and to save that which was lost"; His future resurrection as a sign, "For just as Jonah became a sign to the Ninevites, so shall the Son of Man be to this generation" (Luke 11:30); and for His future glorious judgment, "For whoever is ashamed of Me and My words, of him will the Son of Man be ashamed when He comes in His glory, and the glory of the Father and of the holy angels" (Luke 9:26). Having demonstrated His authority to heal, Jesus asserted His authority to forgive sin, the prerogative of God alone: "'But in order that you may know that the Son of Man has authority on earth to forgive sins'—then He said to the paralytic—'Rise, take up your bed, and go home'" (Matt. 9:6). Rebuked for allowing His disciples to pick grain on the Sabbath, He responded, "For the Son of Man is Lord of the Sabbath" (Matt. 12:8). Other passages on His authority as the Son of Man include Matthew 12:32; 13:37; 16:13; Mark 2:28;; Luke 6:5, 22; 22:48.

Frequently Jesus used the term to point to the series of events in His suffering, death, and resurrection. After the disciples confessed that He was the Christ, the Son of God, He informed them that He must "go to Jerusalem, and suffer many things from the elders and chief priests and scribes, and be killed, and be raised up on the third day" (Matt. 16:21). The other Synoptic Gospels also use the title Son of Man for this series of events. Mark 8:31 narrates: "And He began to teach them that the Son of Man must suffer many things and be rejected by the elders and the chief priests and the scribes, and be killed, and after three days rise again" (cf. Luke 9:22). Earlier in John's gospel Jesus informed Nicodemus about this same series of events, using the Son of Man title: "As Moses lifted up the serpent in the wilderness, even so must the Son of Man be lifted up" (John 3:14). Later, after His resurrection, as the women sought Him at the tomb, the angels reminded them, "Why do you seek the living One among the dead? He is not here, but He has risen. Remember how He spoke to you while He was still in Galilee, saying that the Son of Man must be delivered into the hands of sinful men, and be crucified, and the third day rise again" (Luke 24:5–7). Mark 9:31 and Luke 22:22 reveal similar announcements.

Some texts point more particularly *to the betrayal:* "the Son of Man is going to be delivered into the hands of men" (Matt. 17:22); "Are you sleeping and taking your rest? Behold, the hour is at hand and the Son of Man is being betrayed into the hands of sinners" (Matt. 26:45; see also Matt. 26:24; Mark 14:21, 41; Luke 22:22). Others passages make more of a point of His *suffering*: "So also the Son of Man is going to suffer at their hands" (Matt. 17:12); "Elijah does first come and restore all things. And how is it written of the Son of Man that He should suffer many things and be treated with contempt" (Mark 9:12; cf. Luke 9:44.)

Most important is Jesus' use of the phrase Son of Man in connection with *His creucifixion and death:* "Behold we are going up to Jerusalem; and the Son of Man will be delivered to the chief priests and scribes, and they will condemn Him to death" (Matt. 20:18; cf. Mark 10:33). The gospel of John declares the Lord's attitude toward His crucifixion as His time of glory: "Jesus answered them, saying, 'The hour has come for the Son of Man to be glorified'; when Judas left the twelve, Jesus said, Now is the Son of Man to be glorified, and God is glorified in Him" (John 13:31; cf. John 12:34).

The crucifixion and death of the Son of Man becomes so glorious because it is the means for *the redemption and salvation* of His people: "The Son of Man did not come to be served, but to serve, and to give His life a ransom for many" (Matt. 20:28; cf. Mark 10:45); "for the Son of Man did not come to destroy men's lives, but to save them" (Luke 9:56); "For the Son of man has come to seek and to save that which was lost" (Luke 19:10).

John's gospel emphasizes union with the Son of Man as the means of eternal life: "Do not work for the food that perishes, but for the food that endures to eternal life, which the Son of Man shall give to you, for on Him the Father, even God, has set His seal. . . . Truly, truly, I say to you, unless you eat the flesh of the Son of Man and drink His blood, you have not life in yourselves" (John 6:27, 53). One reason for the Lord's frequent reference to the betrayal, suffering and death of the Son of Man is the revelation of the cutting off of the Messiah in Daniel 9:26, just two chapters after the revelation of the coming of the One like the Son of Man in Daniel 7:13. The crucifixion had to take place before the exaltation.

Daniel's vision of the coming of the Son of Man to earth to judge and to establish the eternal kingdom undoubtedly must be understood as the foremost feature of Christ's message; thus, it is most necessary for the Son of Man to be resurrected and to ascend into heaven after His crucifixion and death so that He may come gloriously from heaven. Thus some of the Son of Man passages point most particularly *to His resurrection from the dead:* after rejection by the cities in Galilee, Jesus responded to the request by the scribes and Pharisees for a sign, "For just as Jonah was three days and three nights in the belly of the sea monster, so shall the Son of Man be three days and three nights in the heart of the earth" (Matt. 12:40). After the vision of transfiguration, He told the disciples, "Tell the vision to no one until the Son of Man has risen from the dead" (Matt. 17:9; cf. Mark 9:9). The apostle John bore testimony to the same reality with these words, "What then if you should behold the Son of Man ascending where He was before?" (John 8:28).

Though it is clear that Jesus taught very

frequently on the subject of the betrayal, death, and resurrection of the Son of Man, He taught even more often and with stronger emphasis *on the glorious coming of the Son of Man to judge and to reign.* Some sayings point to *the coming* of the Son of Man apart from the other features: "I tell you that He will bring about justice for them speedily. However, when the Son of Man comes, will He find faith on the earth?" (Luke 18:8); "For just as the lightening comes from the east, and flashes even to the west, so shall the coming of the Son of Man be" (Matt. 24:27); "For this reason you be ready too; for the Son of Man is coming at an hour when you do not think He will."

Other passages accentuate the *judgment* the Son of Man will exercise at His coming: "And He gave Him authority to execute judgment, because He is the Son of Man" (John 5:27); "The Son of Man will send forth His angels, and they will gather out of His kingdom all stumbling blocks, and those who commit lawlessness" (Matt. 13:41). "And then the sign of the Son of Man will appear in the sky, and then all the tribes of the earth will mourn, and they will see the Son of Man coming on the clouds of the sky with power and great glory. But when the Son of Man comes in His glory, and all the angels with Him, then He will sit on his glorious throne. And all the nations will be gathered before Him; and He will separate them from one another, as the shepherd separates the sheep from the goats" (Matt 25:30–32). "For whoever is ashamed of Me and My words, of him will the Son of Man be ashamed when He comes in His glory, and the glory of the Father and of the holy angels" (Luke 9:26; cf. Luke 21:36).

The final set of passages enunciated by the Lord Jesus about the coming of the Son of Man show forth the *glorious reign in the kingdom of the Son of Man.* With His chosen twelve before Him, "Jesus said to them, 'Truly I say to you, that you who have followed Me, in the regeneration when the Son of Man will sit on His glorious throne, you also shall sit upon twelve thrones, judging the twelve tribes of Israel" (Matt 19:28). In the parallel passage in Luke Jesus said, " And just as My Father has granted Me a kingdom, I grant you that you may eat and drink at My table in My kingdom, and you will sit on thrones judging the twelve tribes of Israel" (Luke 22:29–30).

Clearly Jesus promised that His future kingdom will have the presence of the people of Israel and of His disciples ruling together with Him and even eating together with Him at His table. This is exactly the kind of a kingdom the Old Testament promised—a literal kingdom on earth. Just as the details about His authority, about His betrayal, death and resurrection were literally intended and fulfilled by the Lord, so surely the details about His future return, judgment, and kingdom will also be fulfilled in the detail that He specified.

John H. Mulholland

O. Cullmann, *The Christology of the New Testament* (London: SCM Press, 1959); Seyoon Kim, *The Son of Man as the Son of God* (Grand Rapids: Eerdmans, 1985); D. E. Aune, "Son of Man" in *ISBE* (Grand Rapids: Eerdmans, 1988); C. Colpe, "Son of Man" in *TDNT* (Grand Rapids: Eerdmans, 1972).

SONG OF SOLOMON, ESCHATOLOGY OF

This part of the canon of Scripture has caused great controversy and confusion concerning the purpose of the book. The popular views are that it is (a) an allegory, (b) an extended type, or (c) a literary drama that involves two main characters. Those who hold the allegorical view see the book as a picture of the love of God for Israel or of Christ's love for His bride, the church. The extended type sees Solomon as typifying Christ and the beloved as a type of the church even though the Scriptures present no indication that portions of Solomon's life are meant as types of Christ. The literary view fails to take into account that the book cannot be divided into acts and scenes.

A better approach is to treat the song as a lyrical poem that is comprised of a series of fifteen reflections of a married woman as she recalls the events which lead to her marriage, wedding night, and the early years with her husband. The purpose is to commend human love and marriage.

The author is traditionally identified as Solomon, and it was most likely written during his reign between 971 and 931 B.C.

Rick Bowman

Joseph C, Dillow, *Solomon on Sex* (Nashville: Thomas Nelson, 1977); Merrill F. Unger, *Unger's Bible Dictionary* (Chicago: Moody Press, 1966); John F. Walvoord and Roy B. Zuck, eds., *The Bible Knowledge Commentary* (Wheaton: Victor Books, 1985).

SPURGEON, CHARLES HADDON

C. H. Spurgeon (1834–1892), famous London pastor, was born in Essex, England, and converted at age fifteen. He preached his first sermon at age sixteen and became a pastor the following year. By his early twenties, he was preaching to a congregation of more than ten thousand. Spurgeon's forty-two years of ministry resulted in sixty-three volumes of published sermons and earned him the title "prince of preachers."

Spurgeon believed that the personal return of Christ should be proclaimed dogmatically from the pulpit of the preacher and the lectern of the teacher. He was convinced that failure to preach the Second Advent would inevitably result in preaching and teaching that he described as "lame." His own sermons abound with the theme of hope, and central to this hope is the great hope of Christ's soon coming. A confession statement signed by Spurgeon and published in the *Sword and Trowel* explicitly states; "Our hope is the Personal Pre-Millennial Return of the Lord Jesus in Glory."

When preaching on eschatological matters, Spurgeon thought it proper to deal primarily with those things he perceived to be "clearly revealed." Thus, his eschatological preaching tended to focus upon imminency and the believer's response to the blessed hope. Some have taken Spurgeon's reluctance to meticulously systematize his eschatology as an opportunity to impose their own eschatological grid upon his teachings. Recently there have been attempts to redefine Spurgeon as a midtribulationist. However, Spurgeon's sermons, as well as his commentary on the gospel of Matthew, clearly demonstrate a posttribulational premillennial eschatology that is generally referred to as historic premillennialism.

Kevin Stilley

C. H. Spurgeon, "The Ascension and the Second Advent Practically Considered" in *Spurgeon's Expository Encyclopedia*, vol. 4 (Grand Rapids: Baker, 1951), 437–448, *The Gospel of Matthew* (Grand Rapids: Baker, 1987), "He Cometh With Clouds" in *The Treasury of the New Testament,* vol. 4 (London: Marshall, Morgan & Scott, n.d.), 663–69 and "Mr. Spurgeon's Confession of Faith" in *The Sword & The Trowel* (August 1891), 446–48.

STROMBECK, J. F.

John Frederick Strombeck (1881–1959) was born in Moline, Illinois, of a pioneer Swedish family. Coming to the Lord early, he always sought God's leading in his personal and business decisions. After graduating from Northwestern University in 1911, he founded the Strombeck-Becker Manufacturing Company specializing in wood products. Though a successful entrepreneur, Strombeck spent much of his life in speaking and teaching at various conferences nationwide and in publishing. As well, he gave generously to various Christian organizations such as Dallas Theological Seminary and Moody Bible Institute. Though not formally trained, Strombeck was a self-taught Bible scholar who could make deep truths plain and down to earth for the laity. Many beginning their Christian walk in the 1950s and before were greatly influenced by his books *Disciplined by Grace, So Great Salvation*, and *Shall Never Perish.*

But it was Strombeck's book *First the Rapture* that helped thousands of new Christians truly comprehend all the issues of Christ's return. Answering posttribulational views with biblical nsight and simplicity, he helped many understand the difference between the body of Christ and the Jewish nation. He wrote, "It is of the greatest importance to recognize the difference between the church and Israel. Both worship the One and only true and living God, but the church has a heavenly, while Israel has an earthly, calling. The two must not be confused. Christianity, the church, does not come out of Judaism . . . Christianity is a new thing, entirely distinct from Judaism. The church is a new creation in Christ (2 Cor. 5:17)." Strombeck lamented the poor quality of Bible teaching in this century. "What do the Scriptures say?" was his guiding rule of thumb whether teaching Bible prophecy or any other truth from the Word of God.

Mal Couch

J. F. Strombeck, *First the Rapture* (Grand Rapids: Kregel, 1992).

T

TABERNACLE, PROPHETIC TYPOLOGY OF THE

The tabernacle was revealed by God as an expression of the Mosaic covenant promise: "I will be your God and you shall be My people" (Exod. 6:6–7; Lev. 26:11–13). As such, the tabernacle reveals the person of Yahweh and the means of the people's access to Him in their covenant relationship. The pattern and the extensive details of the tabernacle (Exod. 25:9) included both the *symbolism* of the character of God and the *historic type* of a covenant relationship involving the same promise that would be completed in the future.

This combination of meanings alerts us to recognize that the details may communicate symbolic meaning, typological meaning or, in some cases, both. While the structure symbolized the historic relationship between God and Israel, it was in one sense only an introductory sketch of the covenant relationship. As an initial structure, the tabernacle, and sacrificial system anticipated and foreshadowed the final covenant relationship with God.

The tabernacle was a revelation of God (Exod. 25:8) to His people as expressed in its pattern (Exod. 25:9). "Every detail of the structure reflects one divine will and nothing rests on the *ad hoc* decision of human builders. There is no tension whatever between form and content, or symbol and reality" (Childs). The holiness of God is symbolized in the two courts and in the basic color, white. The association of the sanctity of the Sabbath (31:12ff and 35:1ff) with the sanctifying of the people who approach God in the tabernacle (Exod. 25:8) witnesses to God's rule over His people and His creation (Exod. 31:17). This function is associated with the cherubim, the ark of the covenant, and the colors of purple, gold, and silver. The tent structure symbolized the reality of God's presence as a temporary, earthly expression of God's glory. The tent constitutes the dwelling of Yahweh. No image of God appeared in the structure (Deut. 4:9–14), but His glory filled the Holy of Holies. God's presence was revealed by the cloud and pillar of fire that overshadowed the tent with glory and splendor.

In addition, the righteousness and mercy of God is revealed in the sacrificial system and the priestly representative covenant structure. The color of red that was woven into the fabric as a constant reminder of the blood as well as the elaborate regulations of the Day of Atonement (Lev. 16–17) reveal the demands of righteousness and the mercy available in approaching God.

While the tabernacle had a symbolic meaning in the Mosaic covenant relationship, the inherent limitations that became increasingly apparent in the progress of revelation implied typological meanings. These meanings are recognized in later revelation. Isaiah 7:14, as interpreted by Matthew 1:23, revealed that the name of Messiah would be Immanuel, "God with us." The essential purpose of the tabernacle, therefore, would be realized in the person and work of Jesus. The apostle John captured this truth as he described Jesus' life with the word *skenoo*, "to tabernacle" or "to pitch a tent"—"And the Word became flesh, and *dwelt* (tabernacled) among us" (1:14). The author of Hebrews applies the pattern of the tabernacle service to the priesthood of Christ, who "appeared as a high priest of the good things to come" (9:11), to anticipate His present heavenly ministry. Further the Mosaic covenant system is simply "a shadow (*skana*) of the good things to come" (10:1 NASB). These things to come include a new covenant ministry (8:7–9:15).

See also NEW COVENANT, THEOLOGY OF THE.

Elliott Johnson

B. Childs, *The Book of Exodus* (Louisville: Westminster, 1974); R. M. Davidson, *Typology in Scripture* (Berrien Springs, Mich.: Andrews University Press, 1981).

TEMPLE, HISTORY OF THE

The history of the Jewish temple begins and ends in prophecy. The sanctuary (a term inclusive of God's dwelling in all its forms) was proleptically revealed to Abraham in its sacrifical service and permanent location on Mount Moriah (Gen. 22:2, 14). Enlarging the Abrahamic revelation in similar terms, Moses receives prophetic instructions at the time of the Exodus for Israel's relationship to the sanctuary (Exod. 15:17). Later on Mount Sinai, he receives the heavenly blueprint for the sanctuary and its vessels (Exod. 25:8–9, 40). This verse is important in that it shows that the divine ideal for the sanctuary is God's manifest presence on earth among His people (v. 8; cf. its millennial expression, Zech. 2:10–12) and that the same celestial pattern (vv. 9, 40) was used for both the tabernacle and the temple (cf. 1 Chron. 28:11–19; cf. Rev. 15:5). The tabernacle is distinguished from the temple in that it was a portable and temporary dwelling place for God's presence (Exod. 40:36–38; cf. 2 Sam. 7:6), whereas the temple was to be a permanent and eternal habitation (2 Chron. 7:16; Ezek. 37:26–28). In token of their mutually prophetic purpose, when the first temple was built, the tabernacle/tent of meeting was apparently included within it (1 Kings 8:4; 2 Chron. 5:5).

It is King David who, meditating on the divine ideal (cf. Ps. 132), is moved to begin the process of building the first temple (2 Sam. 7:2; 1 Chron. 17:1). However, since the temple was designed to regulate the universal peace brought by God's presence on earth during the Millennium (David only understands the restricted concept, cf. 2 Sam. 7:1), it could only be completed by one who was a fitting representative of God's peaceful program (1 Kings 3:3–14; 5:3). Yet David was in prophetic succession to those to whom God had previously revealed the temple's program. This is seen in God's reminding David of the Abrahamic promise (2 Sam. 7:10) and repeating to him the Mosaic revelation (1 Chron. 28:11, 19). On this basis (as a founder, not a builder), David was qualified to make financial and material preparations for the temple (1 Chron. 29). Solomon [meaning, his peace] however, was to construct the temple based on the terms of his father's covenant (2 Sam. 7:12–13; 1 Kings 5:5; 6:12–13). In his prayer of dedication (1 Kings 8) is revealed both the temple's divine ideal as the place of God's presence (vv. 27–34) and its universal (millennial) function (vv. 41–43, 56–60).

The Davidic covenant, which provided for a permanent temple in Jerusalem, was nonetheless conditioned upon the nation's obedience. This meant that throughout Israel's future the temple could be removed and returned as often as Israel was fickle or faithful to the covenant. As history unfolded, the first temple was destroyed in 586 B.C. as a direct result of covenantal violations. The downward slide began already in the time of Solomon (1 Kings 11:1–13) and culminated with King Manasseh (2 Kings 21:7–14) and was especially prolonged with respect to violations of the Sabbath (2 Chron. 36:21).

Restoration began with the return and rebuilding of the second temple under Zerubbabel in 515 B.C. (Ezra 1–6), but because of continued covenant violations (cf. Ezra 9; Neh. 13; Mal. 1–4) the millennial restoration envisioned by the prophets (cf. Ezek. 40–48) was postponed (cf. Hag. 2:1–9). Half a millennia later, perhaps a decade before Jesus was born in Judea, the second temple was in such severe need of repairs that the reigning king, Herod the Great, refurbished it completely, even expanding its size. Although newly restored, it was still subject to the old terms of the covenantal contract, and with the nation's rejection of Jesus as Messiah the temple was again doomed to desolation. All of Jesus' pronouncements of the temple's destruction (Matt. 24:2; Mark 13:2; Luke 21:6, 20–24) must be viewed in this light and not as a rejection or replacement of the temple as a legitimate institution. In fact, joined immediately to Jesus' own pronouncement of the temple's desolation (Matt. 21:38) is His promise (in the word "until") of Israel's (and the temple's) restoration (Matt. 23:39). This and Jesus' positive statements concerning the temple elsewhere (Matt. 12: 4; 17:24–27; 23:16–21; John 2:16–17) and especially in His Olivet Discourse (Matt. 24:15; Mark 13:14) hold out the prophetic promise that the temple will be continued in the future

See also TEMPLE, FUTURE.

J. Randall Price

Meir Ben-Dov, *In the Shadow of the Temple: The Discovery of Ancient Jerusalem*, trans. Ina Friedman (San Francisco: Harper & Row, 1982); Joan Comay, *The Temple of Jerusalem* (New York: Holt, Rinehart and Winston, 1975); Alfred Edersheim, *The Temple: Its Ministry and Services* (Peabody, Mass.: Hendrickson Publishers, 1994) [evangelical, Jewish-Christian perspective]; Menahem Haran, *Temples and Temple Service in Ancient Israel* (Winona Lake, Ind.: Eisenbrauns, 1985) [Jewish, higher critical, perspective]; Flavius Josephus, "Antiquities of the Jews" and "Jewish Wars" in *The Complete Works of Josephus,* trans. William Whiston (Grand Rapids: Kregel, 1981); Mina C. Klein and H. Arthur Klein, *Temple Beyond Time: The Story of the Site of Solomon's Temple* (New York: Van Nostrand Reinhold Co., 1970); Benjamin Mazar, *The Mountain of the Lord* (New York: Doubleday & Co., 1975); Leibel Reznick, *The Holy Temple Revisited* (New Jersey: Jason Aronson Inc., 1993) [orthodox Jewish perspective].

TEMPLE, THE FUTURE

The prophecy of a future Jewish temple in Jerusalem (see TEMPLE, HISTORY OF THE) is part of the greater restoration promise made to national Israel. This promise, made at the close of the first temple period (cf. Isa. 1:24–2:4; 4:2–6; 11:1–12:6; 25–27; 32; 34–35; 40–66; Jer. 30–33; Ezek. 36–48; Amos 9:11–15; Joel 2:28–3:21; Micah 4–5; 7:11–20; Zeph. 3:9–20), made again by the prophets who prophesied after the return from captivity (cf. Dan. 9–12; Hag. 2:5–9; Zech. 8–14; Mal. 3–4), and reaffirmed in the New Testament (cf. Acts 3:19–26; Rom. 11:1–32) contained inseparably linked elements of fulfillment: the return of Israel to the land of Israel (in unbelief), the experience of the Time of Jacob's Trouble (Tribulation), the rebuilding of the temple, the return of Messiah, the redemption of Israel, and the restoration of Israel's glory (Millennium). Biblical texts that support this promise likewise generally support the future rebuilding of the temple.

The future temple is in view by the biblical writers throughout this period commencing with the Seventieth Week of Daniel's prophecy (see DANIEL'S SEVENTY WEEKS) and moving through the kingdom age. This is to be expected as the temple is the symbol of both Israel's national and spiritual existence and this future program involves both national desecration (Tribulation) and spiritual restoration (Millennium), which historically was experienced by Israel in relation to its temple (cf. desecration: 2 Kings 24:3–4; cf. Jer. 7:1–8:3; Ezek. 8:6–18; Zeph. 1:9; Ezra 5:11–12; restoration: 2 Chron. 36:20–23; Ezra 1:1–4; 6:14, 22; Hag. 1:7–9 with 2:15–19; Zech. 1:15–16; Mal. 3:7–12).

It is necessary to distinguish in the context of the Old Testament whether the future Tribulation or millennial temple is in view. The tribulation temple will be built by unbelieving Jews and desecrated by the Antichrist (Dan. 9:27; cf. 11:36–45). The millennial temple will be built by the Messiah (Zech. 6:12–13) and redeemed Jews, and as a particular sign of restoration, assisted by representatives from Gentile nations (Zech. 6:15; Hag. 2:7; cf. Isa. 60:10). It will be distinguished from the tribulation temple as the restoration temple by a return of the Shekinah Glory of God (Ezek. 43:1–7; cf. Ezek. 10:4,18–19; 11:22–23) and by Gentile worship (Isa. 60:6; Zeph. 3:10; Zech. 2:11; 8:22; 14:16–19). These traits also distinguish the millennial temple from any previous historical temple (the first temple lacked Gentile worshipers; the second temple lacked the Shekinah). In addition, the literal dimensions and architectural and ritual descriptions of the millennial temple are distinctly unique. The primary text in the Old Testament which speaks directly about the tribulation temple is Daniel 9:27 (cf. 12:11), although the temple's presence is stated or indirectly implied in other Tribulation contexts (cf. Isa. 24:2, 23; Mal. 3:1–3). Specific texts that speak about the millennial temple are Isaiah 2:2–4; Jeremiah 33:18; 60:7, 13; Ezekiel 37:26–28; 40–48; Haggai 2:9; Zechariah 6:12–13;14:20).

In continuity with the Old Testament program expected for Israel's restoration, Jesus and the New Testament writers likewise present a rebuilt temple in Jerusalem as part of their eschatological program. Basing His interpretation on Daniel's prophecy (Dan. 9:27), Jesus sets the temple as the signal event dividing the birth pangs of the Tribulation from the Great Tribulation (Matt. 24:15; Mark 13:14). Paul also builds upon Daniel's prophecy (Dan. 9; 11) in his account of the desecration of the Tribulation temple by the Antichrist (2 Thess. 2:4). In like manner, John, who understands a coming Antichrist (1 John 2:18), describes the desolation of the temple courts by Antichrist's Gentile forces during the last half of the Tribulation period (Rev. 11:1–2).

J. Randall Price

Dispensational premillennial perspective unless otherwise noted: Yisrael Ariel and Chaim Richman, *The Odyssey of the Third Temple* (Jerusalem: G. Israel Publications & Productions, Inc./The Temple Institute, 1994) [orthodox Jewish perspective]; Tommy Ice and Timothy Demy, *The Truth about the Last Days' Temple* (Eugene, Oreg.: Harvest House, 1995); Thomas Ice and Randall Price, *Ready to Rebuild: The Imminent Plan to Rebuild the Last Days Temple* (Eugene, Oreg.: Harvest House, 1992); Roger Liebi, *Jerusalem—Hindernis für den Weltfrieden?: Das Drama des jüdischen Tempels* (Berneck: Schwengeler-Verlag, 1994), 97–114; J. Randall Price, *The Desecration and Restoration of the Temple as an Eschatological Motif* (Ann Arbor, Mich.: UMI, 1993), *In Search of Temple Treasures* (Eugene, Oreg.: Harvest House, 1994); Shalom Dov Steinberg, *The Third Temple According to the Prophecy of Ezekiel,* trans. Moshe Leib Miller (Jerusalem: Moznaim Publications, 1994) [orthodox Jewish perspective]; Don Stewart and Chuck Missler, *The Coming Temple* (Orange, Calif.: Dart Press, 1991).

THEOCRATIC KINGDOM

The term *theocratic kingdom* refers to the demonstration of God's sovereignty and rule on the earth throughout the various epochs of biblical history. It finds its ultimate historical consummation in the future eschatological, or millennial, kingdom on the earth when God's sovereignty will be universally recognized. The expression is used in premillennial interpretation as an umbrella term to discuss the overall kingdom program outlined in the Bible. This program is the development of the manifestation of God's sovereignty throughout the various dispensations on earth through various chosen individuals and institutions.

Various emphases concerning the theocratic kingdom have been put forward by premillennial interpreters. Arno C. Gaebelein focused on the future aspect of the coming millennial reign of Christ in using the term. Alva McClain highlighted the human mediators through whom God demonstrated His sovereign rule throughout the stages of biblical history. This emphasis gave rise to his use of the term *mediatorial kingdom* to refer essentially to the same concept as theocratic kingdom. George N. H. Peters, in his massive three-volume contribution entitled *The Theocratic Kingdom* (1884), outlined in detail how earlier dispensations such as the Law with its theocracy presented a kind of earnest (down payment), introductory, or initiatory form of God's kingdom. These earlier glimpses of God's rule merely reflect in small ways the full revelation of the kingdom of God to come when Christ returns to establish His visible kingdom on the earth. J. Dwight Pentecost, in more recent times, unified all of these aspects in the term as described in the opening paragraph. All premillennial writers ground the fulfillment of this kingdom program in the biblical covenants, starting with the promises made to Abraham in Genesis 12 and, therefore, see national, political, and ethnic Israel at the center of God's demonstration of His rule on earth. Consequently, the national promises to Israel cannot be abandoned, as in amillennial and postmillennial interpretations.

Of special interest for the premillennial interpreter is the role that the church age, or present age, plays in the outworking of this kingdom program. Many premillennialists believe that the present age is discontinuous with the kingdom program and believe that the kingdom is held in abeyance during this present time. Therefore, references to the kingdom of God in relation to Christian believers are generally thought to refer to (1) the eternal kingdom of God rather than to the demonstration of God's rule in specific earthly governance, or (2) the relationship of the Christian believer to the future eschatological kingdom in light of hie believer's inheritance through Christ.

See KINGDOM OF GOD, OF HEAVEN; KINGDOM, UNIVERSAL AND MEDIATORIAL.

Michael D. Stallard

Arno C. Gaebelein, *The Harmony of the Prophetic Word* (New York: Revell, 1907); Alva J. McClain, *The Greatness of the Kingdom* (Winona Lake, Ind.: BMH Books, 1974); J. Dwight Pentecost, *Things to Come* (Grand Rapids: Zondervan, 1958); George N. H. Peters, *The Theocratic Kingdom*, 3 vols. (Grand Rapids: Kregel, 1988).

THESSALONIANS, 1 & 2, ESCHATOLOGY OF

First Thessalonians

The church at Thessalonica was established by Paul during his second missionary journey. The Thessalonians were in need of apostolic instruction because they were careless in their daily activities, because of their concern over believing friends who had died, and because of friction between church officials. The letter was written to encourage the Thessalonians to excellence in their conduct and to calm their fears over those that had died and to reaffirm the fundamental truths of the Gospel of Jesus Christ.

Authorship is attested in the epistle itself (1:1; 2:18) to be the apostle Paul. It was written shortly after Paul arrived in Corinth (Acts 17:1–10, 18:1). The date of writing is placed at A.D. 50–54.

The prophecy contained in this letter concerns the Lord's coming. The hope (anticipation) of the Lord's return is first spoken of in 1:3. Here Paul reminds the Thessalonians that their hope lies in the return of the Lord, and he encourages them to develop a stronger faith and to bear up under the burdens of day-to-day life. Paul reminds them (1:9) that they had once before turned from serving idols to serving the true God. He speaks of the future time when Jesus will deliver them from the wrath to come (1:10). Thus, their lives should be lived in light of His imminent return. The future punishment of the wicked is given in 2:15–16. Paul connects the believers' present lives with their future lives with the Lord (2:19–20) and exhorts them (3:13) to live blameless and holy lives. The believers are comforted concerning those who have died in the Lord (4:13–15). Paul deals with their confusion over this issue by teaching them what will occur at the Rapture, thus reassuring them that those believers who have experienced physical death will be included in this great event. The sequence of events will be (1) The Lord comes down from heaven. (2) A loud command (shout) will be given by Him. (3) The dead in Christ are the first to rise. (4) Those who are alive in Christ will then rise. (5) Both groups will meet the Lord in the air. Thus, every believer in the church age will be with the Lord forever.

Immediately following the Rapture the Day of the Lord begins (5:1–11). This period includes a time of trouble that precedes the second coming of Christ and the establishment of His earthly kingdom. The emphasis here is on how quickly this period will begin, as a thief in the night, and that believers will not take part in the events included in this prophecy. It is a period in which

God will deal with Israel and all those who are left upon the earth after the Rapture.

Second Thessalonians

The second epistle to the Thessalonians was written in response to the false notion that their persecutions were those of the Day of the Lord. These beliefs were causing false expectations concerning the Rapture. Once again the apostle comforts these people and cautions them to live productive and disciplined lives as they wait. Paul wrote this letter shortly after writing the first one.

Second Thessalonians contains further instructions about the Day of the Lord and prophecies about the Man of Lawlessness. The promise concerning the judgment on the wicked and the reward of the righteous (1:5–10) is given to comfort these believers. The Day of the Lord is addressed again (2:1–17) in relation to (1) the present time (vv. 1–2) in which the Thessalonian believers were upset by the false teaching concerning future events, (2) the apostasy (v. 3) which the general turning away from God signals, (3) the Man of Lawlessness (vv. 3–4) who will claim to be God, (4) the Holy Spirit who is the now the restraining force against the Antichrist, (5) the unbelievers (vv. 10–12) who have received a deluding influence from God as a result of their rejection of the truth, and (6) believers (vv. 13–17) who are exhorted to appropriate living in anticipation of that day. Paul corrects the doctrinal error of the false teaching and gives dreadful warnings of its consequences.

See also DAY OF THE LORD; RAPTURE, DOCTRINE OF THE.

Rick Bowman

J. Dwight Pentecost, *Things to Come* (Grand Rapids: Zondervan, 1958); John F. Walvoord and Roy B. Zuck, eds., *The Bible Knowledge Commentary* (Wheaton: Victor Books, 1985).

THOMAS, W. H. GRIFFITH

William Henry Griffith Thomas (1861–1924), scholar, writer, and preacher of wide reputation in England, Canada, and the United States, was a participant in many of the significant events that contributed to the emergence of fundamentalism in America. Born on January 2 in Oswestry, Shropshire, near the border of Wales, Thomas's conversion occurred when he was seventeen through the testimony of two friends from the Young Men's Society and his confirmation followed in May. At twenty-one Thomas became a curate at King's College, graduating and being ordained in 1885. He achieved an excellent record in his studies at King's College and Oxford, earned several academic prizes, and was awarded the Doctor of Divinity from Oxford in 1906. Largely on the merits of his academic achievements, in 1896 he became the first curate ever to be invited to present a paper at the Islington Clerical Conference. From 1896 to 1905 he served as vicar of one of the most influential evangelical Anglican congregations in London, St. Paul's of Portman Square. Thomas was also a popular speaker at the Keswick and Mildway conferences and was invited in 1903 to speak at D. L. Moody's Northfield summer conference. In 1905 he became editor of *The Churchman*, an important evangelical voice within Anglicanism, and he also served as principal of Wycliff Hall, Oxford, a center of evangelical learning of the first rank. While there his Sunday afternoon lectures were attended by T. E. Lawrence, among others. Also, in 1908 Thomas assisted R. A. Torrey in evangelistic meetings at Oxford. By 1910 Thomas had published more than a dozen widely read books including *The Work of the Ministry*, *Christianity Is Christ*; commentaries on Genesis and Romans; *The Catholic Faith*; *The Acts of the Apostles: Outline Studies in Primitive Christianity*; *The Apostle Peter*; *Life Abiding and Abounding* and *Methods of Bible Study*. His acceptance of a professorship at Wycliff College, Toronto caused much surprise and regret among his fellow English evangelicals and much enthusiasm in Canada and the United States. In 1913 Thomas was invited to deliver the L. P. Stone lectures at Princeton Theological Seminary, which were published later that year as *The Holy Spirit of God*, Thomas's most studied argument for the importance of the Holy Spirit in the contemporary church and world. He also enjoyed the hospitality of Charles G. Trumball, editor of the American *Sunday School Times* and Thomas wrote a weekly feature for the "International Sunday School Lesson" published in the *Times*. Later, as a speaker at the Oxford Conference of Philadelphia, a precursor to the victorious life conference of Princeton and Keswick, New Jersey, Thomas's influence helped formulate the organization that promoted these conferences, the Victorious Life Testimony. In May 1919, Thomas chaired the Resolutions Committee of the World's Christian Fundamentals Conference and helped frame its doctrinal statement. He held and propagated doctrines that fundamentalists from a variety of traditions shared. He saw clearly the major points of tension that fundamentalists felt and helped construct many of the ramparts they would defend.

Other noteworthy events include Thomas's trip in 1920 to Japan and China with Trumball. During this trip Thomas endeavored to encourage the missionaries through Bible teaching and the message of the victorious spiritual life, but he observed dangerous inroads of higher criticism among them and spoke openly against this upon his return. Harry Emerson Fosdick was called upon to speak for the modernist side and a warning was sounded among the evangelicals, resulting in the exodus of many of the Presbyterians and Congregationalists into the congregations of independent, fundamentalist churches. Thomas was also a friend to William Bell Riley and involved in the fundamentalist movement of the north. He was invited by C. I. Scofield to be a contributing editor to the *Scofield Reference Bible*. He declined but heartily recommended the study Bible. And Thomas's close association with Lewis Sperry Chafer resulted in Thomas's participation in the founding of the Evangelical Theological College, which later became the Dallas Theological Seminary.

In Thomas's epistemology, Baconian empiricism and Scottish common sense realism were moderated by the more romantic and idealistic traditions stemming from Kant. While defending biblical authority through well-framed and persuasive lines of empirical evidence and reasoning, Thomas ultimately rested on an appeal to spiritual experience. His soteriology, dispensationalism, and premillennialism demonstrated that he purposely avoided rigidly rational, "scientific" systems of theology. When dealing with the doctrines of Calvinism, Thomas held to predestination and total depravity but did not embrace limited atonement and was consistently silent about irresistible grace. His view of dispensationalism is, first of all Trinitarian: *the dispensation of the Father,* from Abel to John the Baptist, *the dispensation of the Son,* the period of the Lord's ministry on earth, and *the dispensation of the Spirit,* from Pentecost through the church age. Thomas believed these could be further divided into seven dispensations: the Edenic, the antediluvian, the patriarchal, the Mosaic, the Christian, the millennial, and the eternal. He also saw fuller divisions of the Mosaic dispensation into the theocracy, the monarchy, and the return, as well as the dividing of the Christian dispensation into the times before and after Pentecost. Thomas's view of premillennialism was already evidenced in England and was more fully expressed with his coming to America. In his sermon entitled "Our Lord's Second Coming," given in 1918, Thomas proclaimed that the Second Advent would be personal and premillennial, giving a standard premillennial view of biblical prophecy including the pretribulational rapture.

Thomas was committed to interpretation through the dual principle of biblical authority and the ministry of the Holy Spirit, and through his ministry and writings, his influence continues.

Lonnie L. Shipman

M. Guthrie Clark, *W. H. Griffith Thomas, 1861–1924* (London: Church Book Room Press, n.d.); George W. Dollar, *A History of Fundamentalism in America* (Greenville, N.C.: Bob Jones University Press, 1973); Richard A. Lum, *W. H. Griffith Thomas and Emergent Fundamentalism* (Ph.D. diss.,

Dallas Theological Seminary, 1994); John S. Reynolds, *Canon Christopher of St. Aldate's Oxford* (Oxford, England: Abbey Press, 1967); Ernest R. Sandeen, *The Roots of Fundamentalism: British and American Millenarianism, 1806–1930* (Chicago: University of Chicago Press, 1970).

THRONE OF DAVID

To gain a clear understanding of what the Scripture teaches concerning the throne of David a bit of background information is in order. In Genesis 12:1–3, God first gave to Abraham what is referred to as the Abrahamic covenant. The promises contained in this covenant are enlarged in some additional biblical covenants (see ABRAHAMIC COVENANT). The future implications of this covenant are found in the key words *land* and *seed*. The land promises are enlarged and confirmed in what is referred to as the Palestinian covenant (Gen. 12:7; 13:15; Gen. 17:7–8; Deut. 30:1–10; Ezek. 16:60–62) whereas the seed promises are enlarged and confirmed in what is called the Davidic covenant.

The Davidic covenant is stated in 2 Samuel 7:12–16. Dr. J. Dwight Pentecost points out that the provisions of the covenant include the following items:

1. David is to have a child, yet to be born, who will succeed him and establish his kingdom.
2. This son (Solomon), instead of David, will build the temple.
3. The throne of his kingdom will be established forever.
4. The throne will not be taken away from him (Solomon) even though his sins justify God's discipline.
5. David's house, throne, and kingdom will be established forever.

As Pentecost notes, "The term *throne* refers not so much to the material throne on which David sat as to the *right to rule*, the *authority as king* vested in him." This covenant is mentioned in other passages of Scripture and confirmed as being unconditional and eternal in nature (2 Sam. 7:13, 16, 23:5; Isa. 55:3; Ps. 89:3–4, 34–37; Isa. 9:6-7; Jer. 23:5–6; 30:8–9; 33:14–17, 20–21; Ezek. 37:24–25; Dan. 7:10–14; Hos. 3:4–5; Amos 9:11; Zech. 14: 4, 9).

It is clear from a careful examination of Scripture that the covenant will be fulfilled literally. From the preceding list of items that are contained in the covenant we see that items (1), (2), and (4) that deal with Solomon, the son yet to be born, were very literally fulfilled. This is strong evidence that the other items will be fulfilled literally as well. In addition, David interpreted the fulfillment of the covenant as literal. This is seen in passages such as 2 Samuel 23:5 and 1 Kings 1:30–37. Next, we see that the nation of Israel also believed that the covenant would be fulfilled very literally (see previous Scripture list).

Lastly, the New Testament references to the covenant made with David confirm the literal nature of the covenant. With fifty-nine references to David in the New Testament and many references to the present session of Christ, it is amazing, if the covenant be not literal, that not one reference can be found that connects Christ's present reign with the Davidic throne. In addition, Pentecost points out that "in all the preaching concerning the kingdom by John (Matt. 3:2), by Christ (4:17), by the Twelve (10:5–7), and by the seventy (Luke 10:1–12), not once is the kingdom offered to Israel as anything but an earthly, literal kingdom."

Based on the items already fulfilled, the interpretation of David, the interpretation of the Jews, and the New Testament revelation on the matter, it is clear there will be a literal reign of Christ on the throne of His earthly father, David (Matt. 1:1–17). This is "crystallized," as Walvoord puts it, in the announcement of Gabriel to Mary before Christ's birth. He stated, "And behold, you will conceive in your womb, and bear a son, and you shall name Him Jesus. He will be great, and will be called the Son of the Most High; and the Lord God will give Him the *throne* of His father David; and He will reign over the *house* of Jacob forever; and His *kingdom* will have no end" (Luke 1:31–33, emphasis added). The three key terms used in the Davidic covenant are here repeated and it is revealed that Mary's son will ultimately fulfill the covenant that God made with David.

The kingdom was legitimately offered to Israel in the Lord's First Advent but was rejected. But even then the apostles still believed that a literal kingdom would be set up. This is evident from their question at Christ's ascension. In Acts 1:6, they asked, "Lord, are you at this time going to restore the kingdom to Israel?" Christ had a golden opportunity to correct their "misunderstanding" of a literal kingdom here on earth, but He did not. The only explanation of this is that the kingdom will be literal and earthly.

The Scriptures are clear on the matter. The Davidic covenant is unconditional, eternal, and literal. The portion of the covenant that has already been fulfilled necessitates a literal fulfillment of the rest of the covenant. David, the nation of Israel, and the New Testament believers all believed the promises would be fulfilled literally. As Gabriel revealed to Mary, Christ will reign on David's throne, not the Father's throne (Luke 1:31–33; Rev. 20:4), and will reign over the nation of Israel (and the world), and He will have an eternal kingdom.

See also DAVIDIC COVENANT.

Russell L. Penney

J. Dwight Pentecost, *Thy Kingdom Come* (Grand Rapids: Kregel, 1995) and *Things to Come* (Grand Rapids: Zondervan, 1958); John F. Walvoord, *The Millennial Kingdom* (Grand Rapids: Zondervan, 1959) and *The Prophecy Knowledge Handbook* (Wheaton: Victor Books, 1990).

THRONE OF GOD

The Scriptures portray God's providential and sovereign rule over the universe as coming forth from the throne of God. In fact His heavenly temple and throne are equated. "The LORD is in His holy temple; the LORD's throne is in heaven" (Ps. 11:4). The Lord is pictured as seated and ruling from this eternal throne (Ps. 47:8), which is also called a throne of justice (Ps. 89:14). In a larger and more encompassing sense, Jesus spoke of heaven itself as the throne of God and the earth as His footstool (Matt. 5:34–35).

In contrast, the expression *throne of David* has a reference in the past and also represents the future earthly reign of David's son, the Messiah. It is always spoken of as literal, whether past or future. For example, Solomon mounted the throne after the death of his father David. "And Solomon sat on the throne of David his father, and his kingdom was firmly established" (1 Kings 2:12). In regard to its future, King Solomon himself noted: "But [I] King Solomon shall be blessed, and the throne of David shall be established before the L*ord* forever" (2:45). That this is not the providential throne of God is clear from Revelation 3:21, which clearly separates the two thrones: "He who overcomes, I will grant to him to sit down with Me on My throne, as I also overcame and sat down with My Father on His throne."

The throne of God has a specific place in the present and future work of the Lord Jesus. Many Bible scholars teach that upon the Son of God's ascension, He entered the throne room of the Ancient of Days and was presented to His Father as the victorious Son of Man (Dan. 7:9–28). *Son of Man* more than likely refers to the Son related to Mankind, because He became human and died for the sins of humanity. Interestingly, the throne of God in the Daniel 7 passage is said to be ablaze with flames, which would indicate that God's throne shows forth His righteous judgments (7:9).

Upon entering the throne room of God in heaven, Christ then seated Himself, waiting for His enemies to be made His footstool (Ps. 110). Those enemies seem mostly to be earthly but this cannot exclude the world of the fallen angels and demons. The Lord Himself will someday stretch forth His Son's "strong scepter from Zion, saying, 'Rule in the midst of Thine enemies'" (Ps. 110:2). This will be specifically the earthly Messianic rule from David's throne. While waiting for the enemies to be subdued, Jesus "was raised [from the dead], who is at the right hand of God, who also intercedes for us" (Rom. 8:34).

Besides Daniel 7, Revelation 4–5 gives an equally intimate view of the throne of

God. John was transported to glory where he saw a throne standing and the Lord God sitting on it (4:2). Around the throne were the twenty-four elders (4:4) and from it came flashes of lightning with sounds of thunder (4:5). John also describes angelic beings and saints numbering myriads of myriads and thousands of thousands proclaiming blessings to both God who sits on the throne and to the Lamb also seated with the Lord (5:11–12).

In the throne room of God in heaven is the altar before the Lord (Rev. 6:9). Underneath it are the souls of the martyrs slain because of the word of God and because of their testimony. In reference to the final days of the Tribulation, the heavenly temple is also seen associated with God's throne: "a loud voice came out of the temple from the throne, saying, 'It is done'" (16:17). Some see the final judgment throne, the Great White Throne, as God's throne (20:11–15), but more than likely it is a special and designated place used only for the judgment of the resurrected unrighteous.

From God's throne comes the declaration of the new heaven and new earth: "And He who sits on the throne said, 'Behold, I am making all things new'" (21:5). In the New Jerusalem there is "a river of the water of life, clear as crystal, coming from the throne of God and of the Lamb" (22:1). Here, as eternity begins, the heavenly throne becomes "the throne of God and of the Lamb" placed in the New Jerusalem (22:1, 3). And before the throne, the Lord's "bond-servants shall serve Him" (v. 3). From the throne shall come God's divine radiance whereby "the Lord God shall illumine [His servants]; and they shall reign forever and ever" (22:5).

One of the most controversial passages on the throne of God is Acts 2:29–36. Some progressive dispensationalists claim that Christ is now on the throne of David because He has been elevated to His Father's throne. The claim is that the throne of David is the heavenly throne. But a careful reading of these verses does not lead to this conclusion. Peter argues that the Christ (the Messiah) was not abandoned to the grave, nor did His flesh suffer decay (2:31). Since His body came forth from the grave, He has now been exalted to the right hand of God (2:33). But Peter goes on to make a separation in his thinking. "God has made Him *both* Lord and Christ—this Jesus whom you crucified" (2:36). "Made" (*poiew*) has the contextual force of "to designate, establish, declare." When Jesus was exalted to God's right hand He was (1) declared Lord; someday He will reign on David's throne as (2) the Christ (Anointed One). Thus, there are two specific time sequences, two unique thrones, and two different locations—one heavenly and one earthly.

See also DANIEL, ESCHATOLOGY OF.

Mal Couch

TIMOTHY, 1 & 2, AND TITUS, ESCHATOLOGY OF

First Timothy

This letter was written by the apostle Paul to Timothy in A.D. 64 to encourage him to oppose false teaching and false teachers. It also provided Timothy with credentials and gave him instructions on church management. Timothy was encouraged to be diligent towards his pastoral duties. The theme of this epistle is church order and conduct.

The book contains a prophecy that looks forward to the Rapture and the appearing of the Lord Jesus Christ (6:14–16).

Second Timothy

This is the last of Paul's writings, in A.D. 67, and contains his final message. The focus is on the personal walk of the true believer and the believer's testimony as a soldier of Christ living in a day of apostasy. Paul's appeal to Timothy is for loyalty to the Gospel and for endurance in ministry. He warns of the apostasy that will take place during the last days of the church age (3:1–9). In answer to this falling away the Scriptures are set forth as the only defense against it (3:10–13). The Rapture and the appearing of Christ are mentioned (4:1). Finally, the assurance of a rescue from death and a place in heaven is given to Paul and in the broader sense extends to all believers (4:18).

Titus

The condition of the Christian work on the island of Crete led Paul to write this letter in A.D. 65. The false teaching of legalism had become a problem on the island, and Paul wrote to encourage Titus in his ministry. The letter emphasizes the qualifications of elders and the need to stand strong against the false teachers.

The prophecy looks to the Rapture as the final stage of the believers' salvation (2:13). The anticipation of this event should bring joy.

See also RAPTURE, DOCTRINE OF THE.

Ervin R. Starwalt

Everett F. Harrison and Charles F. Pfeiffer, eds., *Wycliffe Bible Commentary* (Chicago: Moody Press, 1962); John F. Walvoord, *The Prophecy Knowledge Handbook* (Wheaton: Victor Books, 1990); John F. Walvoord and Roy B. Zuck, eds., *The Bible Knowledge Commentary* (Wheaton: Victor Books, 1985).

TRIBULATION, OLD TESTAMENT REFERENCES TO THE

The eschatological period of divine judgment preceding the time of national Jewish redemption and the establishment of God's kingdom on earth is known as the Tribulation period. This concept was part of Jesus' eschatological teaching and was a frequent theme of the apostles and the early church. The Tribulation doctrine developed from antecedent Old Testament usage. This is evident from the citations and allusions from the Old Testament in the principal New Testament eschatological texts, the Olivet Discourse and the book of Revelation. Therefore, the meaning and usage of OT Tribulation terms is essential to an understanding of the New Testament doctrine.

The Greek term commonly employed in the New Testament as a technical expression for the Tribulation period is *thlipsis* (wrath, tribulation). This may be observed in Luke's substitution of the phrase *anagke megale* (great distress), Luke 21:23, for Matthew's *thlipsis megale* (great tribulation), Matthew 24:21, to distinguish the days of vengeance (the Roman destruction in A.D. 70) from the eschatological Tribulation. The Greek translation of the Old Testament, the Septuagint, used *thlipsis* to render the Hebrew term *sar/sarah* (trouble, tribulation, distress). This Hebrew term was especially used in contexts in which curses based on violations of the Mosaic covenant were threatened or pronounced and appears in the principal Old Testament texts alluded to by the New Testament (e.g., Deut. 4:30; Jer. 30:7; Dan. 12:1).

Synonymous terms with supporting texts containing the concept of a future tribulation are:

1. Day of the Lord (*Yom YHWH*) Isaiah 2:12; 13:6, 9; Exekiel 13:5; 30:3; Joel 1:15; 2:1, 11, 31; 3:14; Amos 5:18, 20; Obadiah 15; Zephaniah 1:7, 14; Zechariah 14:1; compare: great and terrible Day of the Lord (*Yom YHWH hagadol* v^e*hanora'*) Malachi 4:5
2. Trouble, tribulation (*Sar/sarah*) Deuteronomy 4:30; Zephaniah 1:16
3. Time or day of trouble (*'Et/yom sarah*) Daniel 12:1; Zephaniah 1:15
4. Time of Jacob's Trouble (*'Et sarah hi'* l^e*ya'*^{a}*cov*) Jeremiah 30:7
5. Birth pangs (*Chil*) Isaiah 21:3; 26:17–18; 66:7; Jeremiah 4:31; Micah 4:10 (c.f. Jer. 30:6)
6. The day of calamity (*Yom 'edom*) Deuteronomy 32:35; Obadiah 12–14
7. Indignation (*Zaram*) Isaiah 26:20; Daniel 11:36
8. The [Lord's] strange work (*Ma'asehu zar*) Isaiah 28:21
9. Overflowing scourge (*Shot shotef*) Isaiah 28: 15, 18
10. Day of vengeance (*Yom naqam*) Isaiah 34:8; 35:4; 61:2; 63:4
11. Day of wrath (*Yom '*^{e}*vrah*) Zephaniah 1:15
12. Day of the Lord's wrath (*Yom '*^{e}*vrat YHWH*) Zephaniah 1:18
13. Day of distress (*Yom* m^e*suqah*") Zephaniah 1:15
14. Day of destruction (*Yom sho'ah*) Zephaniah 1:15
15. Day of desolation (*Yom* m^e*sho'ah*) Zephaniah 1:15

16. Day of darkness and gloom (*Yom hoshek u'^{a}pelah*) Joel 2:2; Amos 5:18, 20; Zephaniah 1:15
17. Day of clouds and thick darkness (*Yom 'anan u'arapel*) Joel 2:2; Zephaniah 1:15
18. Day of trumpet and alarm (*Yom shofar ut^{e}ru'ah*) Zephaniah 1:16
19. Day of the Lord's anger (*Yom 'af YHWH*) Zephaniah 2:2–3
20. [Day of] destruction, ruin from the Almighty (*[Yom] sod mishaddai*) Joel 1:15
21. The fire of His jealousy (*'Esh qina'to*) Zephaniah 1:18

Lesser expressions also are used to describe this period as a time when God arises to shake violently the earth (Isa. 2:19), to make the earth utterly emptied and ruined (Isa. 24:1, 3, 6), to break down and dissolve the earth (Isa. 24:19), or to punish the kings and the inhabitants of the earth for their iniquity (Isa. 24:21; 26:21).

These terms for tribulation are not necessarily in themselves *eschatological* expressions of tribulation. This is usually conveyed in the context by temporal phrases that may denote both an indefinite and definite sense of futurity. In some cases, such as the Day of the Lord, the idiomatic nature of prophetic speech allows for an immediate application (e.g., Assyrian or Babylonian destructions) or a more remote or ultimate application to a future event (Tribulation and Millennium). Another chronological expression of future time during which the Tribulation is predicted is indicated by the Hebrew phrase *b^{e}'ah^{a}rit hayyamim* (the latter days). The eschatological connotation of this formula is especially prominent in the biblical prophets (e.g., Isa. 2:2; Jer. 23:20; 34:20; 48:47; 49:39; Ezek. 38:16; Hos. 3:5; Mic. 4:1) and Daniel (2:28; 8:19, 23; 10:14; cf. 12:8), although it is by no means limited to them, and is found as early as the Pentateuch (e.g., Gen. 49:1; Num. 24:14; Deut. 4:29–31). When we examine the usage of the compound expression *latter days* in the Old Testament, we find that it is used in the general sense of "days to come" (cf. Gen. 49:1; Num. 24:14; Deut. 31:29) but more often has the more definite sense of a time in the future. This latter sense encompasses both near (historical) and far (eschatological) points of reference, some being of an immediate future and others spanning a comprehensive period from the author's vantage point until the messianic age. By contrast, the Hebrew expression *'et qetz* (end time) is distinct from the term *latter days*. While both are eschatological expressions, only *'et qetz* refers exclusively to the final eschatological period or event. In three texts (Lam. 4:18; Ezek. 7:2–3, 6; Amos 8:2), *qetz* is employed in the context of the Day of the Lord, with clearly eschatological intent. In Daniel 8:19; 9:26; 11:27, 45; 12:6, 13, it has eschato-logical significance or refers to the end of the age. The combined construction *'et qetz*, which appears uniquely in Daniel, and then in only the latter half of the book, is strictly eschatological (cf. Dan. 8:17; 11:35, 40; 12:4, 9). Here it appears eleven times as a chronological marker of a specific eschatological period (cf. Dan. 9:21, 25; 11:6, 13, 14,24; 12:11). In Daniel 12:1–2, especially, it assumes the character of an apocalyptic *terminus technicus* denoting the final period that culminates the divine program, including all the events of that time.

The nature of the Tribulation is revealed by the characteristic terms we have seen as descriptive of this period. A brief catalog of such expressions gives a clear picture of the severity of this period: wrath (Zeph. 1:15, 18), indignation (Isa. 26:20–21; 34:1–3), trouble, distress (Jer. 30:7; Zeph. 1:14–15; Dan. 12:1), destruction (Joel 1:15), darkness (Joel 2:2; Amos 5:18; Zeph. 1:14–18), desolation (Dan. 9:27; Zeph. 1:14–15), fire, burning (Zeph. 1:18; Isa. 24:6), punishment (Isa. 24:21), overflowing scourge (Isa. 28:15, 18), and vengeance (Isa. 34:8; 35:4; 61:2). The accumulation of such terms dealing with divine judgment is exceptional, and it was this characteristic above all that served to highlight and heighten these references and project them onto the eschatological stage. The exceptional nature of the Tribulation is earmarked by such phrases as: "that day is great, there is none like it" (Jer. 30:7), or "such as never occurred since there was a nation until that time" (Dan. 12:1). These expressions emphasize the uniqueness of this specific judgment, while the accompanying contextual descriptions of the effects such judgments have on both God and Israel affirm that this is a time unparalleled in Israel's previous history. Understanding the eschatological nature revealed by these Old Testament expressions of final judgment, Jesus likewise qualified the Tribulation of the end time with a language patterned after Daniel 12:1: "such as has not occurred since the beginning of the creation which God created, until now, and never shall" (cf. Matt. 24:21; Mark 13:19).

The nature of the Tribulation is also conveyed in related contexts by the use of a figure of intense suffering and expectation. Specifically, the *experience* of end-time judgment in the Tribulation is depicted by the travail of childbirth, Hebrew: *kayyoledah*, "as a woman giving birth" (Jer. 30:5–6). The eschatological Day of the Lord is often associated with the expression of birth pangs as well (cf. Isa. 13:8; 25:17–18; 66:7–8; Jer. 22:23; 48:41; Hos. 13:13; Zeph. 1:14–18; Mic. 4:9–10; 5:1[2]). The New Testament also makes this association (cf. 1 Thess. 5:2–3). The Hebrew expression for these pains is derived from the root *chil*, which has the basic meaning of "being in labor," with the resultant idea of "fear" and "trembling." From the use of this expression in the Olivet Discourse, it can be seen that the first half of the Tribulation is characterized by judicial beginning birth pangs (Matt. 24:8), while in the second half judgment comes to full term, hence the designation "Great Tribulation" (Matt. 24:21). Just as the woman must endure the entire period of labor before giving birth, so Israel must endure the entire seven-year period of Tribulation. The divisions of this period of Tribulation are also illustrated by the figure, for just as the natural process intensifies toward the expectation of delivery after the labor ends, so here the Tribulation moves progressively toward the Second Advent (vv. 30–31), which takes place "immediately after" the Tribulation ends (v. 29).

An explicit Old Testament passage for the Tribulation is Jeremiah 30:7. The reference to "Jacob" is to Israel as a national entity, and therefore the time of distress refers to a period of national trouble unlike any other. To what time of trouble was Jeremiah referring? Some have argued that the use of the Hebrew time marker *'et* (and its translation by the LXX as *chronos*), indicates a reference to a *specific* future time in contrast to a distant future. Interpreted literally, none of these elements could be fulfilled in these terms except in the future eschatological context (the days concluding and following the Tribulation period, cf. Matt. 24:29ff/Mark 13:24ff).

The premiere Tribulation text, cited by Jesus in the Olivet Discourse (Matt. 24:15; Mark 13:14), and alluded to by Paul in his Day of the Lord discourse (2 Thess. 2:4), is Daniel's prophecy of the Seventieth Week. Detailing the events of the seven-year period of Tribulation, this passage (Dan. 9:27) uniquely sets off the beginning, midpoint, and ending of the Tribulation. The beginning is designated as the time Israel enters into a covenant with the figure known as "the prince" (Hebrew *nagid*, "leader") that was predicted to come, and whose people (i.e., Gentiles [Romans]) destroyed the [Second] temple (v. 26). Daniel's prophecy depicts the entire Seventieth Week as a time of wrath (cf. Dan. 12:7). The exilie is understood as a punishment for transgression, sin, and iniquity, and this will continue as a decree of divine wrath against Israel until the end, when everlasting righteousness and the messianic consecration of the temple can take place (v. 24). The resolution of Daniel's concerns for his city and people will not be realized until after the Seventieth Week has concluded and its events of deception and desecration have passed (Dan. 9:27; 12:1). Furthermore, Daniel understood that the desolation that will occur from the middle of the Seventieth Week is connected with the covenant that also commenced this period. The covenant with the Antichrist (Dan. 9:27; Rev. 11:1) and the cessation of the sacrificial program as a result of the Abomination of Desolation (Dan. 9:27; Rev. 11:2) are signal events of the Tribulation (marking its beginning and midpoint). Therefore our Lord chose this text to warn a future Jewish generation that from the beginning of the birth pangs they were already in the eschatological Tribulation (Matt. 24:15; Mark 13:14; cf. 2 Thess. 2:4). The Seventy Weeks prophecy also evidences that Tribulation terms deal exclusively with a national Jewish context. The phrase "your people," that is, Daniel's nation (9:24), emphasizes this exclusivity. The context demonstrates this, describing the judgment as both the apex of punishment for national Israel and the judgment of Israel's Gentile oppressors. Tribulation contexts also contain the elements of judgment, repentance, and blessing *always* in relation to the land of Israel (cf. Rev. 11:18 with Dan. 9:27). Thus the application of Tribulation terms is limited to a period of national Jewish residency in the land and to the people that represent that resident population.

When we examine the common elements of Old Testament references to the Tribulation, in every case the expected fulfillment is at a time corresponding to the endtime. The scope of the judgment is in most cases unparalleled and required salvation (physical deliverance) as a sign of the severity of the event. Each context involves idolatry in some form, whether generally as false prophets or specifically as the Antichrist and the Abomination of Desolation, and each has in the context a reference to either the temple or a promise of theocratic restoration.

The Old Testament presents at least five purposes for the Tribulation.

1. The Tribulation will complete the decreed period of national Israel's judicial hardening as punishment for its rejection of the messianic program, which the partial return from exile did not remove and which culminated in the national rejection of Jesus (Isa. 6:9–13; 24:1–6; cf. John 12:37–41; Rom. 11:7–10).

2. It will produce a messianic revival among Jewish people scattered throughout the world (Deut. 4:27–30; cf. Rev. 7:1–4; Matt. 24:14).

3. The Tribulation will convince the Jewish nation of their need for the Messiah in order to produce a national regeneration (Dan. 12:5–7; Jer. 31:31–34; Ezek. 20:34–38; 36:25–27; 37:1–14; Zech. 12:9-13:2; Isa. 59:20–21). This will result in a massive return of Jews to the land of Israel (Zech. 8:7–8; Ezek. 36:24; 37:21).

4. It will end the time of the Gentiles and effect the deliverance of the Jewish people from Gentile dominion (Isa. 24:21–23; 59:16–20; cf. Matt. 24:29–31; Mark 13:24–27; Rom. 11:25).

5. The Tribulation will purge the earth of wicked people in order to establish the messianic kingdom in righteousness (Isa. 13:9; 24:19–20; Ezek. 37:23; Zech. 13:2; 14:9; Isa. 11:9). This violent reduction of the world's unbelieving population will result from the divine judgments unleashed throughout the Tribulation (Rev. 6–18), climaxing with the Battle of Armageddon under King Messiah (Rev. 19) and His purge of rebel Jews and oppressive Gentiles at the end of the Tribulation (Ezek. 20:33–38; Matt. 25:31–46).

See also TRIBULATION, THE GREAT; TRIBULATION, VARIOUS VIEWS OF THE.

J. Randall Price

Gleason L. Archer and R. Laird Harris, *Theological Wordbook of the Old Testament* (Chicago: Moody Press, 1979); Tommy Ice and Timothy Demy, *The Truth About the Tribulation* (Eugene, Oreg.: Harvest House, 1995), 8–12; J. Dwight Pentecost, *Things to Come* (Grand Rapids: Zondervan, 1958), 229–50; J. Randall Price, "Old Testament Tribulation Terms" in *When the Trumpet Sounds*, eds. Tommy Ice and Timothy Demy (Eugene, Oreg.: Harvest House, 1995), 57–83.

TRIBULATION, THE GREAT

In the New Testament, the Great Tribulation is mentioned as a technical expression but once (Matt. 24:21). The expression actually is *thlipsis megala*. Many take this as a special period that will be part of the final days of the last half of the Tribulation. In fact, some actually see that last three and a half years as the Great Tribulation itself. It is a period of trial never before experienced on earth. Many believe Jeremiah refers to it. "Alas! for that day is great, there is none like it; and it is the time of Jacob's distress" (30:7). Daniel, as well, seems to address it. "And there will be a time of distress (Heb., loud crying) such as never occurred since there was a nation until that time" (12:1). Jesus uses almost the same words as Daniel. "There will be a great tribulation, such as has not occurred since the beginning of the world until now, nor ever shall. And unless those days had been cut short, no life would have been saved; but for the sake of the elect those days shall be cut short" (Matt. 24:21–22).

Christ seems to continue to talk about that period when He says "But immediately after the tribulation of those days . . ." (24:29). He describes the coming of the Messiah, the Son of Man, in glory. But before this, it would seem as if the Great Tribulation has more to do with the move of the Antichrist and his attempt to deify himself. Walvoord believes this begins that most awful period. This coincides with Revelation 13 and the moment the Antichrist makes his move to enter the temple and proclaim himself as God (2 Thess. 2:4–9). Revelation 14 seems to highlight the Great Tribulation that God Himself will bring on the Beast and the people of earth for showing their allegiance to the Beast. The Antichrist is to drink "of the wine of the wrath of God, which is mixed in full strength in the cup of His [God's] anger" (Rev. 14:10), and Christ swings the sickle because the harvest of the earth is ripe (14:15) with sin. Thus the world will experience the Great Tribulation of the great winepress of the wrath of God (14:19).

See also TRIBULATION, OLD TESTAMENT REFERENCES TO THE; TRIBULATION, VARIOUS VIEWS OF THE.

Mal Couch

J. Dwight Pentecost, *Things to Come* (Grand Rapids: Zondervan, 1958); John F. Walvoord, *The Millennial Kingdom* (Grand Rapids: Zondervan, 1959).

TRIBULATION, VARIOUS VIEWS OF THE

The time of Tribulation on earth spoken of in the New Testament is variously interpreted as fulfilled at one of several different periods. The school of realized eschatology, begun by C. H. Dodd, holds that Jesus "suffered and died in the great Tribulation." They interpret every reference to tribulation as occurring during the lifetime, and particularly in the Passion, of Jesus. According to this interpretation, just as the eschatological expectation of tribulation was fulfilled in Christ's sufferings, so that of eschatological salvation (the general resurrection) was inaugurated with Christ's resurrection. The Reformed school (amillennialism and postmillennialism) interprets the Tribulation to take place just before the close of this age, which they hold is the Millennium. Their Tribulation is the period during which Satan is released to go out and deceive the nations (Rev. 20:7–9). This text is taken as synonymous in time with the Tribulation predicted in the Olivet Discourse (Matt. 24:14, 21) and the apostasy spoken of as occurring in the latter times (1 Tim. 4:1–3; see DANIEL'S SEVENTY WEEKS, AMILLENNIAL INTERPRETATION). The symbolical school interprets the Tribulation allegorically, so that the Tribulation and Millennium (including the new heaven and earth) are symbolic of Christian death and resurrection through baptism. Historicists hold that the Tribulation occurred in the experience of the church in the past, usually at some point during the history of Roman persecutions. The persecution by Nero, Caligula, or Domitian are usually the chief contenders; however there may be as many events located as there are historicists to posit them. The preterist school interprets the fulfillment of Daniel's seventy weeks by A.D. 70, with the events of the Seventieth Week taking place in the destruction of the Jerusalem temple by the Romans. More extreme preterists hold that the Second Advent also occurred at this time, in the Romans coming in judgment on the Jews.

While premillennialists agree that the Tribulation is future, they disagree on the duration of it and the identity of the future saints who will be present during the Tribulation and for what part of it. The duration of the Tribulation is variously accepted to be three and one-half years, three and one-half plus years, or seven years. These differences, in part, relate to the different degrees of intensity experienced during this period. If one only considers the more severe outpourings of God's wrath during the trumpet and bowl judgments, the Tribulation only encompasses this time (midtribulationism, prewrath view). However, if one considers the first six seal judgments at the beginning of Daniel's Seventieth Week as displays of divine wrath, the Tribulation covers this entire period (pretribulationists). Although posttribulationism generally holds that the Tribulation is seven years in duration, it is not as concerned with the extent because it holds that believers are protected from God's wrath whenever the wrath is outpoured. These differences derive from acceptance or rejection of dispensationalism. Pretribulationism, which alone maintains a dispensational commitment, sees those directly addressed in the Olivet Discourse to be exclusively Israel rather than inclusive of the church. The church (composed of Jews and Gentiles) is to be removed before the Seventieth Week commences with the signing of the covenant with Antichrist (Dan. 9:27). Therefore the Tribulation saints are Jews who are restored to Messiah and Gentile proselytes to this form of messianic Judaism.

Thus, the distinguishable difference between believers in the present age and during the Tribulation is the restoration of Israel as the focus of God's election; nondispen-sationalists, midtribulationists, prewrath advocates, and posttribulationists see the church in the Tribulation. Midtribulationism sees the church surviving the first half of the Seventieth Week to be removed before the Great Tribulation commences. The prewrath view also sees the church in the first half of this period but does not interpret it as the Seventieth Week. This, prewrath advocates believe, begins only after the temple is desecrated and the wrath of God begins to come upon earth. Thus, they take the church past the midpoint into the second half of the seven years, to be removed just prior to the descent of God's wrath. Posttribulationism continues the church until the end of the Seventieth Week, with the church's removal connected to the timing of the Second Advent.

See also TRIBULATION, OLD TESTAMENT REFERENCES TO THE; TRIBULATION, THE GREAT.

J. Randall Price

Dale C. Allison Jr., "The End of the Ages Has Come: An Early Interpretation of the Passion and Resurrection of Jesus" in *Studies of the New Testament and Its World*, ed. John Riches (Edinburgh: T & T Clark, 1985); Gary DeMar, *Last Days Madness* (Tyler, Tex.: Institute for Christian Economics, 1993); Kenneth Gentry Jr., *He Shall Have Dominion: A Postmillennial Eschatology* (Tyler, Tex.: Institute for Christian Economics, 1992); Robert Gundry, *The Church and the Tribulation* (Grand Rapids: Eerdmans, 1973); William Hendriksen, *More Than Conquerors* (Grand Rapids: Baker, 1971); Tommy Ice and Timothy Demy, eds., *When the Trumpet Sounds: Today's Foremost Authorities Speak Out on End-Time Controversies* (Eugene, Oreg.: Harvest House, 1995); William F. Kerr, "Tribulation for the Church—But Not the Tribulation" in *Understanding the Times*, eds. William Culbertson and Herman B. Centz (Grand Rapids: Zondervan, 1956), 98–106; Richard R. Reiter, ed., *The Rapture: Pre-, Mid-, or Post-Tribulational?* (Grand Rapids: Zondervan, 1984); Marvin Rosenthal, *The Pre-Wrath Rapture of the Church* (Nashville: Thomas Nelson, 1990); Renald Showers, *Maranatha: Our Lord Come!* (Bellmawr, N.J.: The Friends of Israel Gospel Ministry, 1995); Gerald B. Stanton, *Kept from the Hour: Biblical Evidence for the Pretribulational Return of Christ* (Miami Springs, Fla.: Schoettle Publishing Co., 1991); John F. Walvoord, *The Blessed Hope and the Tribulation: A Historical and Biblical Study of Posttribulationism* (Grand Rapids: Zondervan, 1976).

TYPOLOGY, ESCHATOLOGY AND

Dispensational hermeneutics has viewed typology as both a blessing and a bane in biblical interpretation. The latter is due, in part, to excessive use of typology to the point of abuse and to the difficulty in understanding what typology actually is. Is it a genre of biblical revelation, like a prophetic text, or is it simply a method of interpreting a text?

Any definition of typology must begin with the New Testament writers' use of *tupos* in reference to other textual passages. The term *tupos* is not used consistently as a technical term. At times, it is used to refer to an analogous illustration between the events or institutions or persons from two narrative texts so that the early text illustrates the later text (1 Cor. 10:11). Such an illustration provides instruction about the later text. At other times, *tupos* refers to an analogous prediction between the two events, institutions, or persons. The early narrative text announces an event that finds fulfillment in the later text (Rom. 5:14). This use has become the basis for the technical use that is further substantiated by the use of *antitupos*, as in 1 Peter 3:21. In this case, the New Testament experience (Spirit baptism) answers to or fulfills the Old Testament experience (Noah and his family put in the ark). The common element in both uses includes the meaning expressed in the original narrative text. So typology is first of all, the meaning expressed in a narrative text that is paradigmatic of God's dealing with humanity. Some of these paradigms are merely illustrative of God's working in a general way in history, while others are predictive of God's future working in a particular way. Typology is thus only secondarily a method of interpreting narrative texts.

Another question concerns the recognition of a *type* in a narrative text. If the meaning is in a narrative text, can a reading of the text alone be sufficient to identify the paradigm? As Christians read the Old Testament, it was natural to recognize analogies about Christ and other Christian experiences. Because so many inconsequential analogies were recognized, the practice came under severe criticism.

A number of conservative interpreters chose to follow the objective criteria of Bishop Marsh (*Lectures on Criticism and Interpretation of the Bible*), who proposed that an Old Testament narrative is only a *type* if the New Testament specifically designates it to be so. While these objective criteria are helpful, they are also outside the text of the Old Testament narrative. The New Testament reference alone recognizes the meaning. Is there no method that would allow the reader to recognize the paradigm from the original narrative text itself?

There are few, if any, clues in the text of the narrative to disclose that a particular work of God is intended to be paradigmatic or predictive. The normative intent of a paradigm is recognized if the narrative features the basic and repeated acts of God as He deals with people in history. Predictive intent is only recognized if the narrative is a paradigm of a prior promise of God. The narrative is then seen to be a paradigm of God's keeping what He promised to do because what God performed did not fulfill the complete scope of what He promised.

So the technical *predictive type* is the meaning expressed in a narrative text that is paradigmatic of God's future work because of what God had promised He would do. Understanding such types and antitypes contributes to a believers appreciation of the unity and progress in biblical revelation and enriches a believer's eschatological hope.

See also HERMENEUTICS, CONTEMPORARY BIBLICAL.

Elliott Johnson

R. M. Davidson, *Typology in Scripture* (Berrien Springs, Mich.: Andrews University Press, 1981); P. Fairbairn, *Typology of Scripture* (Grand Rapids: Kregel, 1995).

W

WALVOORD, JOHN FLIPSE

John F. Walvoord, theologian, writer, and teacher, seminary president; and defender of dispensational pretribulational premillennialism, was born on May 1, 1910, in Sheboygan, Wisconsin. Walvoord was raised in a home that valued education in general and religious training in particular. His father, John Garrett Walvoord, was a school teacher. During Mary Flipse Walvoord's difficult pregnancy, her doctors advised an abortion; however, because of their conviction that the child was a gift from the Lord, they brought John to term. The child proved to be robust, and Mary lived to be 102. The family were members of the First Presbyterian Church, his father an elder and Sunday school superintendent. His parents determined that their children would be reared on the Westminster Shorter Catechism and Scripture memory.

When John was fifteen, the family moved to Racine where his father was a junior high school superintendent. During his high school years, John excelled in academics and athletics but continued to have only a nominal interest in Christianity, although he had committed his life to Christian work when he was twelve. His family joined the Union Gospel Tabernacle (now the nondenominational Racine Bible Church). While attending a study of the book of Galatians, he became assured of God's mercy toward him. Three years later (1928), he entered Wheaton College. John continued to excel in academics and athletics, though he also distinguished himself as a member of the debate team that won state championships in 1930 and 1931. Additionally, he was president of the college's Christian Endeavor where he made a commitment to foreign missions. He completed his undergraduate degree in 1931 with honors having accelerated his progress due to summer school work at the University of Colorado.

Walvoord was counseled against entering seminary at Princeton, although he considered himself of Presbyterian heritage and expected a Presbyterian ministry for two reasons. First, he had been impressed by the ministry of Lewis Sperry Chafer, a man of Presbyterian affiliations and president of the Dallas Theological Seminary (then called the Evangelical Theological College). Second, J. Oliver Buswell Jr., president of Wheaton College, was also a Presbyterian and more institutionally and theologically attuned to Chafer's school than Princeton (both schools shared an aversion to modernism, an attachment to the Bible conference tradition, and a distaste for the fanaticism of fundamentalism in the 1920s and 30s).

He pursued a regular program of studies at Dallas Seminary and graduated in 1934, deeply impressed once more with the character and teaching skills of Chafer (as well as others such as Harry Ironside and Henry Theissen). He was drawn increasingly to the Bible conference tradition, but remembering his college pledge to foreign missions, he was active in Christian work on the weekends and during the summers while in seminary. Having an application for the China Inland Mission, he found no peace about completing it, though his mother had dreamed of such a calling for her son. Instead, he sought a pastoral charge. Due to Chafer's influence, he assumed the pastorate of the Rosen Heights Presbyterian church in Fort Worth (now the Northwest Bible Church), in the Presbyterian Church, USA. He was able to complete his Th.D. degree in 1936 at the seminary.

In the same year, Walvoord was appointed by Chafer as the seminary's registrar and associate professor of systematic theology, thus becoming Chafer's assistant in the classroom. He excelled as a teacher and administrator. In 1939 he married Geraldine Lungren, and the couple would eventually have four sons. Walvoord served as moderator of the Fort Worth Presbytery twice and permanent clerk for ten years. He also completed an A.M. degree in philosophy from Texas Christian University in 1945. He considered further doctoral studies at Princeton University, but the strain of increased duties at the seminary precluded the opportunity.

Chafer's increasingly poor health in the 1940s made him determined to bring his protégé into a more prominent role in the school. Though continuing in the pastorate, teaching at the seminary, serving as registrar, and being the secretary of the faculty, Walvoord became an administrative assistant to the president. He did most of the institutional correspondence, served as director of publicity, officiated as chairman of the faculty, and took on an increasing portion of Chafer's Bible conference work.

After Chafer's death in 1952, Walvoord became the institution's second president and was promoted to fill Chafer's chair as professor of systematic theology (1953). As a result of the new duties, he resigned from the Rosen Heights Presbyterian church after twenty-four years of service and subsequently withdrew from the Presbyterian Church, USA, joining the Independent Fundamental Churches of America. Walvoord lead the seminary until his retirement in 1986. In the midst of his duties and burdens associated with a growing institution, he also emerged as one of the foremost scholars and writers in eschatological studies. He was recognized for his professional achievements with both a D.D. from Wheaton College in 1960 and an Litt. D. from Liberty Baptist Seminary in 1984.

Contribution to Evangelicalism

First, Walvoord's tenure at Dallas Theological Seminary effected evangelicalism both nationally and internationally. He taught systematic theology at Dallas Seminary for over fifty years, and for over thirty of those years, he also served as the institution's president. Under his administration, the school emerged as a major evangelical seminary, sending out hundreds of graduates into pastorates, missions, and teaching posts throughout the world and becoming the largest independent seminary in the world. Walvoord was also committed to continuing Chafer's legacy with an ongoing emphasis on the Bible conference and Bible institute distinctives at a graduate seminary level. On the one hand, he sought to stabilize the school maintaining its distinctive educational emphases; on the other hand, he recognized the daunting task of preparing the seminary for a future that would be different from its past. Whereas Chafer was a visionary and founder, Walvoord was concerned with establishing and stabilizing the school in academic and professional excellence. Walvoord achieved a balanced budget, debt retirement, and the launching of building programs that transformed the campus. There was a continual move to acquire property and erect buildings. Academic programs also escalated, and the school attained accreditation in 1969 by the Southern Association of Colleges and Secondary Schools.

Second, in addition to directing an increasingly complex school, Walvoord emerged in the same decades as an eminent scholar in the realm of prophetic and eschatological studies and in defense of pretribulational premillennialism. His stature in the premillennial dispensational movement is evidenced by his service on the committee of scholars and churchmen who produced the *New Scofield Reference Bible* in 1967, a revision of Scofield's work of 1909 and 1917. Far more crucial in the defense of modern premillennialism (distinguished from historic premillennialism), however, has been his personal literary output. As president of the seminary, he also served as editor of the school's journal, *Bibliotheca Sacra*. From 1952–85, he directed the journal in the defense of evangelical theology in general and dispensational premillennialism in particular. In this work alone, he contributed a total of 127 articles, specializing in biblical eschatology. Walvoord also authored nineteen books: *The Doctrine of the Holy Spirit* (1943, revised in 1954 and 1958); *The Return of the Lord* (1955); *The Thessalonian Epistles* (1956); *The Rapture Question* (1957, revised in 1979); *The Millennial Kingdom* (1959); *To Live Is Christ: An Exposition of the Epistle of Paul to the Philippians* (1961, reissued in 1971 as *Philippians: Triumph in Christ*); *Israel in Prophecy* (1962); *The Church in Prophecy* (1964); *The Nations in Prophecy* (1967, the last three were published together in 1988 as *Israel, the Nations, and the Church in Prophecy*); *Truth for Today* (1963); *The Revelation of Jesus Christ* (1966, a commentary on the book of the Revelation); *Jesus Christ Our Lord* (1969); *Daniel, The Key to Prophetic Revelation* (1971); *The Holy Spirit at Work Today* (1973); *Matthew: Thy Kingdom Come* (1974); *Armageddon, Oil, and the Middle East Crisis* (1974, revised in 1990); *The Blessed Hope and the Tribulation* (1976); *The Prophecy Knowledge Handbook* (1990) and *Major Bible Prophecies* (1991).

He also edited several works such as *Inspiration and Interpretation* (1957); *Major Bible Themes* (1974, a revision of Chafer's 1926 volume by the same title); *The Bib Sac Reade*r (1983, a collection of articles that appeared in the journal between 1934 and 1983); *The Bible Knowledge Commentary* (1983, a two-volume work by the seminary's faculty); and *Systematic Theology* (1988, a two-volume abridgment of Chafer's eight-volume 1947–48 publication).

Third, Walvoord has made a significant contribution to the delineation and defense of dispensational premillennialism. A perusal of his writings makes it clear that his focus was not upon modern dispensationalism as a system, but upon its eschatological implications. He accepted the theological structure that dispensationalists placed upon the Bible (i.e., literal interpretation, progressive revelation, discontinuity between the covenants, and a sharp contrast between Israel and the church in the economy of God, i.e., two peoples, two programs, and two destinies). Embracing the tenets of modern dispensationalism as derived from Chafer (who was influenced by Scofield) and cogently expressed later by Charles Ryrie, Walvoord delineated the prophetic details of that system. Though not to be identified with the recent revisionist approach taken by progressive dispensationalists, Walvoord's dispensationalism does evidence a revision at some points of Scofield and Chafer, although some would judge these to be of minor significance. For example, Walvoord's understanding of the distinction between Israel and the church, a rather important issue for dispensationalists, has evidenced revision. In his earlier writings, he struggled with the relationship of the church to the new covenant (Jer. 31, Heb. 8) and concluded with Chafer that there must be two new covenants, one for each of the distinct peoples of God. More recently, he has come to Scofield's position of a single covenant with two separate fulfillments. With regard to the Davidic covenant (2 Sam. 7), however, he is, in contrast to Scofield and the progressive dispensationalists, unwilling to grant a fulfillment of it in the church era.

Fourth, Walvoord must be seen as a defender of the historic Christian faith. His writings on the themes of Christ and the Holy Spirit, for example, as well as the republishing of Chafer's *Major Bible Themes* and the abridgment of Chafer's *Systematic Theology* reveal him, like his mentor, to be a proponent of orthodoxy. While viewing Christianity through the grid of the Bible conference tradition (i.e., mildly Keswick relative to the doctrine of sanctification, Warfieldian in the defense of inerrancy, and eschatologically rooted in the tradition stemming from John Nelson Darby and the eighteenth-century Brethren movement), he defended the Augustinian, Calvinist interpretation of sin, Christ, redemption, and grace (though embracing, as did Chafer, unlimited Atonement).

John Hannah

Donald K. Campbell, "Walvoord: A Tribute" in *Kindred Spirit* 10:5–7 (Spring 1986); Michael Fluent, "John F. Walvoord: Staunch Conservative Retires from Dallas Seminary" in *Fundamentalist Journal* 5:61–63 (April 1986); Timothy G. Mink, "John F. Walvoord at Dallas Theological Seminary" (Ph.D. diss., North Texas State University, 1987); "Q &

A: An Interview with John Walvoord" in *Fundamentalist Journal* 3:47–49 (October 1984); Rudolf A Renfer, "A History of Dallas Theological Seminary" (Ph.D. diss., University of Texas, 1959); John A. Witmer, "'What Hath God Wrought:' Fifty Years of Dallas Theological Seminary" in *Bib Sac* 131:3–13 (January–March 1974).

WATTS, ISAAC

Isaac Watts (1674–1748), father of hymnology, nonconformist pastor, and theologian, was born in Southampton, England, to a nonconformist deacon who was twice imprisoned for his religious convictions. The eldest of nine children, Watts was schooled in Hebrew, Greek, and Latin in grammar school by John Pinhorne, rector of All Saints in Southampton. Watts's early genius in English verse induced the physician Dr. John Speed to offer him an education at the university for prospective ordination in the Church of England. But he refused and entered a nonconformist academy at Stoke Newington at sixteen under the direction of Thomas Rowe, the pastor of the Independent congregation at Girdler's Hall. He received excellent instruction in the classics, logic, Hebrew, and divinity e was admitted to communion in Rowe's Independent church at age nineteen.

After leaving the academy, Watts's next two years were spent at home where he wrote most of *Hymns and Spiritual Songs*, published in 1707–9 and sung in the Southampton Chapel. The hymn "Behold the Glories of the Lamb" is believed to have been the first he composed, written as an attempt to raise the standard of praise. The next six years of his life were spent in Stoke Newington as tutor to the son of an eminent Puritan, Sir John Hartopp. His study of theological and philosophical materials led to his subsequent published volumes but also declining health.

Watts preached his first sermon on July 17, 1698, at the age of twenty-four, and the following year was chosen assistant pastor to Isaac Chauncy of the chapel at Mark Lane where he was ordained pastor on March 18, 1702. The former pastors included the famous Joseph Caryl and John Owen and its members included many distinguished nonconformists. In 1703 his health began to fail, weakened by his earlier intense studies. Samuel Price was appointed his assistant and became copastor after an illness in 1712 shattered his the frail constitution. As his health diminished, he only reluctantly retained his pastorate and had scruples about taking any salary, but his congregation refused to break their association with the beloved and famous Watts. In 1728 the University of Edinburgh bestowed on him the degree of Doctor of Divinity. At his peaceful passing on November 25, 1748, Watts was buried in the Puritan resting place at Bunhill Fields, and a monument was erected to him at Westminster Abbey.

Watts was one of the most popular writers of his day. His educational manuals—the *Catechisms* (1730) and *Scripture History* (1732)—were still standard works for religious instruction in the middle of the nineteenth century. His philosophical books, especially *Logic* (1725), were in wide circulation and used as texts at Oxford. *The World to Come*, a devotional book, was translated into several languages. The *Horae Lyricae* made Watts a recognized religious poet, but Watts's poetical fame rests largely upon his hymns. By the beginning of the eighteenth century, the strict use of metrical psalms and canticles in music had been broken by the hymns of Mason, Keech, and Barton and by the free use of hymns among the Independents and Baptists. Watts's poetry spoke to the world with its spiritual devotion and the contemplation of God's glory in nature and his revelation in Christ that made hymn singing a fervent devotional force.

Notwithstanding the wealth of hymn production of Methodism, Watts's hymns were still reaching an annual output of fifty thousand copies in the nineteenth century. *Hymns* (1707) and the *Psalms of David* (1719) contain the majority of Watts's hymns, which include such classics as "Jesus Shall Reign Where'ere the Sun," "When I Survey the Wondrous Cross," "O God, Our Help in Ages Past," "Joy to the World," and "Alas, and Did My Saviour Bleed." Watts also wrote the first children's hymnbook, *Divine Songs* (1715), and his hymns characterize tender faith, joy, and serene piety.

The Arian controversy is an unusual study in the theological reasoning of Watts. His hymns include an entire book of doxologies modeled on the Gloria Patri. But at the minister's conference held in 1719 at Salter's Hall, Exeter, Watts voted with the minority and refused to impose acceptance of the doctrine of the Trinity on the independent ministers. In "The Christian Doctrine of the Trinity" (1722), "Dissertations Relating to the Christian Doctrine of the Trinity" (1724), "The Glory of Christ as God-Man Unveiled" (1746) and "Useful and Important Questions concerning Jesus, the Son of God" (1746), Watts held that the creed of Constantinople was only a human explication of the mystery of the Godhead. Not believing the doctrine was necessary for salvation, Watts believed that the human soul of Christ had been created preceding the creation of the world and united to the divine principle in the Godhead known as the Sophia, or Logos, and that the personality of the Holy Spirit was figurative rather than proper or literal.

In the work entitled "A Solemn Address to the Great and Ever Blessed God," Watts shows how deeply he was troubled and perplexed as he neared his death. He wrote, "Forbid it, oh! my God, that I should ever be so unhappy as to unglorify my Father, my Savior, or my Sanctifier. . . . Help me . . . for I am quite tired and weary of these human explainings, so various and uncertain." By the testimony of those most intimate with Watts, during his last hours, near death, he expressed his total dependence on the atonement of Jesus Christ (which is incompatible with unitarianism).

Watts believed in a mild form of Calvinism, not espousing the doctrine of reprobation. His tolerance moved him to propose uniting the Independents and the Baptists by surrendering the doctrine of infant baptism if the Baptists would give up immersion.

Dispensationalism was a key part of Watts's theology, as stated in his *Harmony of All the Religions Appointed by God.* Watts taught that there were seven dispensations:

(1) the dispensation of innocence: God's dealing with Adam in the garden

(2) the Adamical dispensation: God's dealing with Adam after the Fall

(3) the Noahical dispensation: God's covenant with Noah after the flood

(4) the Abrahamical dispensation: God's covenant with Abraham and his seed

(5) the Mosaical dispensation: God's dealing with Israel through the Law

(6) the peculiar covenant of Sinai: God's dealing with Israel through the monarchy

(7) the Christian dispensation: God's dealing with the church.

About future dispensations, Watts was silent, but his beliefs in the last judgment, eternal damnation of the lost, and eternal bliss of the redeemed are firmly reiterated in his writings and hymns.

Lonnie L. Shipman

Theron Brown and Hezekiah Butterworth, *The Story of the Hymns and Tunes* (New York: American Tract Society, 1906); John Julian, ed., *Dictionary of Hymnology* (Grand Rapids: Kregel, 1985); Harvey B. Marks, *The Rise and Growth of English Hymnody* (New York: Revell, 1938); Sir Leslie Stephen and Sir Sidney Lee, eds., *Dictionary of National Biography,* vol. 20 (London: Oxford University Press, 1921); Isaac Watts, *The Works of the Rev. Isaac Watts D.D.*, vols. 1–7 (London: Leeds, 1746).

WEST, NATHANIEL

Born in Sunderland, England, Nathaniel West (1826–1906) came to the U.S. and received his B.A. and M.A. from the University of Michigan. Later he also earned a doctorate from Allegheny Seminary. West quickly became an internationally recognized scholar in prophetic and interpretative studies. Though pastoring eight churches, he lectured at many prophetic conferences and was a noted speaker at popular prophecy seminars. His book *A Complete Analysis of the Holy Bible* became a classic guide and tool for pastors and scholars alike.

West's unsurpassed work *The Thousand*

Year Reign of Christ is called "one of the greatest volumes in many ways, the most learned work on this aspect of biblical prophecy ever to appear in the English language" (Wilbur Smith). In his preface, West has hard words for amillennialism: "A false spiritualizing, allegorizing, and idealizing, interpretation has contributed to rob the predictions concerning Israel of their realistic value. . . . The church does not understand the present age, nor its relation to the coming age, nor Israel's relation to both, and to the Nations, and to the church herself. And this blindness will continue until the false systems of interpretation, by which it has been caused, are rejected."

West went on to note that the antisemitism of his day was due to false systems of interpretation. He points out that the apostolic age, up to three hundred years after Christ, viewed premillennialism as a test of orthodoxy. Two of the most outstanding chapters in his book are "The Testimony of the Synagogue" and "The Apocalypse of John." His chapter, "The Cause of Error in Determining the 70 Sevens" is essential reading in understanding Daniel 9.

Mal Couch

Nathaniel West, *The Thousand Year Reign of Christ* (Grand Rapids: Kregel, 1993).

WITNESSES, 144,000

The 144,000 witnesses are mentioned twice in the Revelation, first in the parenthetical section between the sixth and the seventh seal judgments (7:4–8), and second, in the interlude between the trumpet judgments and the bowl judgments (14:1–5).

The number 144,000 is the sum of twelve thousand sealed servants out of the twelve tribes of Israel, namely: Judah, Reuben, Gad, Asher, Naphtali, Manasseh, Simeon, Levi, Issachar, Zebulun, Joseph, and Benjamin (7:5–8). The name of Joseph stands for the tribe of Ephraim, a son to Joseph and a brother to Manasseh. The tribal name of Dan is absent. Irenaeus, a second-century church father, mentioned a tradition that the Antichrist would come from the tribe of Dan (see Gen. 49:16–18). The tribe of Dan, however, will have a presence and an inheritance in the millennial kingdom (Ezek. 48:1, 32). For some unknown reason, Dan will not contribute any to this special service during the Seventieth Week of Daniel (Dan. 9:24–27).

The 144,000 are designated as the servants of God (7:3). The nature of their service is not given. There is some speculation that they will serve by preaching the Gospel of the kingdom on earth during the first three and a half years of the seven-year period that precedes the coming of Jesus Christ to the earth (Matt. 24:14). To accomplish their service, they will be sealed by holy angels for protection from natural disasters and satanic attacks. The nature of the seal is not mentioned. It could be either visible or invisible to the human eye (Ezek. 9:4–11; Eph. 4:30). The seal on their foreheads may be seen in contrast to the mark of the Antichrist upon the foreheads of his followers (3:16).

The 144,000 thus comprise literal, ethnic Jews. They reveal the presence, salvation, and service of ethnic Israelites in the future Day of the Lord. Just as Jesus Christ was literally a Jew out of the tribe of Judah (5:5), so these servants are literally Jews out of their respective tribes. Although modern Israel does not have a system of tribal division, that system will be in place in that future day.

Later, the 144,000 will be standing with Jesus Christ, the Lamb, on Mount Zion (14:1).

There is debate as to whether "Zion" refers to the heavenly city (Heb. 12:22) or to earthly Jerusalem (2 Sam. 5:6–9; Ps. 2:6; 132:13–18). If "Zion" refers to the earthly capital, then this passage teaches that God has preserved the 144,000 from physical death and that they will be with Christ when He returns to Jerusalem after the seven years of Tribulation.

If "Zion" refers to the heavenly city, then the passage teaches that the 144,000 have gone to be with Christ after their physical deaths, possibly caused by the rise of the Antichrist. Since they are before the throne of God the Father (14:3), they apparently are in heaven. Their seal is further described as the Father's name upon their foreheads

(14:7). In addition, they are singing a song that no other group can sing (14:3).

They are further identified as male virgins, obedient followers of Christ, redeemed as the possible first converts of the Great Tribulation period, guileless spokesmen, and without fault before God.

Robert G. Gromacki

WRATH

Anger and wrath are assigned to both God and people in the Bible. The Greek terms *thumos* (anger) and *orge* (wrath) are used in the LXX and the NT normally without any distinction of meaning (Eph. 4:31; cf. Col. 3:8). Each can mean anger, wrath, or rage.

Human Anger

Human anger and wrath are always spoken of in a negative sense (cf. James 1:20), with the exception of those occasions where anger is aroused because the holiness of God has been offended (cf. Moses in Exod. 32:19; David in 2 Sam. 12:5; Jesus in Mark 3:5; all believers in Eph. 4:26). Anger is viewed as a characteristic of fallen human nature that, if not kept in check, becomes the root of interpersonal bitterness by which many become defiled (Heb. 12:15). Further, James reminds us that human wrath does not produce the righteousness of God (James 1:20).

Divine Anger

Of much greater significance is the role of divine anger. The anger/wrath of God is the personal manifestation of His holiness in judgment against sin. Unlike human anger, God's wrath is not irrational or fitful; it is not vindictive or malicious. God's wrath is provoked by ungodliness (cf. Exod. 4:14; 2 Sam. 6:7; Rom. 1:18).

The Bible teaches that all unbelievers stand under the wrath of God (John 3:36), are by nature children of wrath (Eph. 2:3); are vessels of wrath prepared for destruction (Rom. 9:22), and that there are present manifestations of God's wrath upon the ungodly (cf. Rom. 1:18ff). In contrast, believers, because of their justification by the blood of Christ, are assured they shall be saved from wrath through Him (Rom. 5:9): "As forgiven men and women, we are outside the sphere in which God's wrath operates" (L. Richards, *Expository Dictionary of Bible Words*, 50).

There is also eschatological significance to God's wrath. The establishment of Messiah's kingdom and the events attendant to it are described by Zephaniah as a day of wrath (1:15), and a day of the Lord's wrath (1:18). These expressions correspond to the wrath of the Lamb (Rev. 6:16), Jesus Christ, that will come upon the ungodly in association with His Second Advent. This future expression of the wrath of God (cf. Rom. 2:5,8; 9:22; 1 Thess. 1:10) follows the removal of the church to heaven (cf. 1 Thess. 4:15–17), an event that delivers church-age believers from that wrath (1 Thess. 5:9; Rev. 3:10). The last great judgment of human history, taking place at the Great White Throne (Rev. 20:11), represents the final manifestation of God's wrath against the ungodly, even though the terms *anger* or *wrath* are not used.

See also TRIBULATION, THE GREAT.

G. Harry Leafe

Bauer, Arndt, and Gingrich, eds., *A Greek-English Lexicon of the New Testament and Other Early Christian Literature* (Chicago: The University of Chicago Press, 1957); *Exegetical Dictionary of the New Testament*, eds. Horst Balz and Gehard Schneider, vols. 1–3 (Grand Rapids: Eerdmans, 1994); *The New International Dictionary of New Testament Theology*, ed. Colin Brown, vols. 1–3 (Grand Rapids: Zondervan, 1975); Lawrence O. Richards, *Expository Dictionary of Bible Words* (Grand Rapids: Zondervan, 1991).

Z

ZECHARIAH, ESCHATOLOGY OF

The author of the book is stated to be Zechariah the prophet, the son of Berechaiah, the son of Iddo. Zechariah was a postexilic prophet and a contemporary of Haggai. He was part of the almost fifty thousand Jewish exiles that returned from Babylon at the decree of Cyrus in 538 B.C. under Zerubbabel. He was both a prophet and a priest. When the exiles had returned to the land they had built an altar, renewed the burnt offerings (Ezra 3:1–6), and only a few years later they had completed the foundation of the temple (Ezra 3:8–13; 5:16). The building was stopped as a result of pressure from the poples of the land and the temple work was idle for sixteen years. Then God raised up Haggai in 620 B.C. to encourage the exiles to continue the building. Haggai preached four messages to the people over a period of about four months. Then Zechariah started his prophetic ministry in the same year.

Merrill Unger gives a helpful outline for the book of Zechariah.

I. Foregleams of the Future Kingdom (1:1–8:23)
  A. An Introductory Call to Repentance (1:1–6)
  B. Vision 1: The Rider Among the Myrtles (1:7–17)
  C. Vision 2: The Four Horns and Four Smiths (1:18–21)
  D. Vision 3: The Surveyor (2:1–13)
  E. Vision 4: The Cleansing of the High Priest (3:1–10)
  F. Vision 5: The Golden Lampstand and Two Olive Trees (4:1–14)
  G. Vision 6: The Flying Scroll (5:1–4)
  H. Vision 7: The Woman in the Ephah (5:5–11)
  I. Vision 8: The Four Chariots (6:1–8)
  J. The Crowning of the High Priest (6:9–15)
  K. The Question of the Fasts (7:1–8:23)
II. Two Prophetic Burdens—The Great Messianic Future (9:1–14:21)
  A. The First Burden: The First and Second Advents of the Messiah (9:1–11:17)
  B. The Second Burden: The Second Advent of the Messiah (12:1–14:21).

I. Foregleams of the Future Kingdom (1:1–8:23)

An Introductory Call to Repentence

Zechariah begins the book by dating the introductory call to repentance as occurring in the eighth month of the second year of Darius, or October–November 520 B.C. Zechariah's first message to the exiles was to repent. He reminded them of the chastisement that had been brought on their fathers. Although the Lord had said to them, "Return to ME . . . that I may return to you," they had ignored Him until it was too late (1:3, 6). Although they realized their need for punishment, their repentance was too late and they were taken into exile (1:6). This reminded the exiles of what was required of them if they were to experience God's blessing in this endeavor of rebuilding the temple and renewing their covenant commitment.

The series of eight visions spanning from 1:7–6:8 are dated at the twenty-fourth day of the eleventh month (Shebat) in the second year of Darius (1:7) or February 15, 519 B.C. This would be five months after the work on the temple had resumed.

Vision 1: The Rider Among the Myrtles

The vision of the rider among the myrtles (1:3–17) begins with the details of the vision. Zechariah saw a man riding a red horse standing in a ravine among some myrtle trees. Behind the man were other horses of red, sorrel, and white (1:8). An angelic interpreter was sent along to help Zechariah understand the vision (1:9). The man riding the red horse standing among the myrtle trees is identified as the Angel of the Lord, or the preincarnate Christ (1:11–12; cf. 3:1–2). The other riders were sent to patrol the earth (1:10). Lindsey points out that the term used here "seems to be used in the military sense of patrolling or reconnoitering." The report was that all the earth is peaceful and quite (1:11). The report that all the nations were at peace when Israel was in captivity angered the Lord (1:15). His response was, "I am exceedingly jealous for Jerusalem and Zion." The Lord proclaimed, "My house will be built in it [Jerusalem]" and the cities would be rebuilt and be prosperous and during that time the Lord will again comfort Zion and again choose Jerusalem (1:16–17). Although this prophecy certainly had its place in encouraging the returned exiles to complete work on the temple and assured them of the Lord's support in that, there seems to be a more far-reaching aspect. The temple was completed in 516 B.C. (Ezra 6:15–16). Verses 16–17 will have their ultimate fulfillment in the millennial kingdom when the city and temple will be rebuilt and the nation will experience great prosperity (Ezek. 40–43:9; Isa. 2:2–3; Jer. 31:38–40; Amos 9:13–15; Isa. 14:1).

Vision 2: The Four Horns and Four Smiths

The second vision involves Zechariah seeing four horns and four smiths, or artisans. The angelic interpreter said that the four horns represented horns that have scattered Judah, Israel, and Jerusalem. As Unger states, "The four horns must symbolize the four great world powers of the times of the Gentiles (Luke 21:24) seen by Daniel in his colossus vision (Dan. 2:37–45) and beast vision (7:2–8, 17–28)—Babylon, Medo-Persia, Greece, and Rome, the last one to be revived in the end time (2:42–44; 7:7–8, 20; Rev. 13:1)." Thus, the smiths are to throw down the horns by bringing God's judgment on them. These would then correspond to Medo-Persia, Greece, Rome, and the millennial kingdom set up by the Messiah at His Second Advent (Rev. 19:16–20:6). The literal fulfillment of the majority of the vision to this point insures that the millennial kingdom set up by the Messiah will be literal also.

Vision 3: The Surveyor

In the third vision Zechariah saw a man measuring Jerusalem, indicating that Jerusalem would be rebuilt (2:1–2; Ezek. 40:2–3). This would have been a tremendous encouragement to the returned exiles who saw the city in ruins. Then Zechariah was told that the city would experience a prosperous expansion (2:3; Isa. 2:2–3; 49:19–20). The Lord revealed that He would provide divine protection (2:5) and that His people should flee Babylon because judgment was to come on it (2:6–8; Rev. 17–18). He also states that Israel's former captors will become their slaves and all this is done so that they will acknowledge their Lord (2:9). Israel was encouraged to sing for joy and be glad because the Lord will dwell in their midst and He will claim Judah and Jerusalem as His again (2:10–12). All flesh is called on to be silent because the Lord is aroused from His holy habitation (2:13). Although much of this vision would apply directly to Zechariah's generation, there is some of the vision that is obviously looking to a time yet future. In the millennial kingdom the temple will be rebuilt (40:2–30) and Jerusalem will expand and experience great prosperity (Isa. 2:2–3; 49:19–20). Many nations will come to Jerusalem and become followers of the Lord (Gen. 12:3; Isa. 2:2–4, 60:3; Zech. 8:20–23). The Lord will rule from Jerusalem (Zech. 14:9; Isa. 60:19; Ezek. 43:1–5, 48:35) and protect them.

Vision 4: The Cleansing of the High Priest

The vision of the cleansing of the high priest presents Joshua as the high priest with filthy garments standing before the Lord. Satan is at God's right hand accusing Joshua (3:1–3). The Lord rebukes Satan for accusing His chosen city and people (3:2). The Lord calls on those standing before Him to remove the filthy garments from Joshua. Since Joshua was the high priest, he represented the entire nation and thus the nation is seen to be cleansed by the Lord. The filthy garments were replaced with festal robes and a clean turban (3:4–5). The symbolism is clearly that of Israel's sinful state and future spiritual restoration and national conversion (Rom. 11:26; cf. Zech. 12:10–13:1). The lesson for Joshua was that if he would walk in the ways of the Lord then he would be blessed. But the angel also states that they represented future events for Israel. In the future God will send His servant, the Branch. As Lindsey points out, "As the Servant of the Lord, Christ is the One who comes to do the will of the Father (Isa. 42:1; 49:3–4; 50:10; 52:13; 53:11). As the Branch of David, Christ is the Davidic Descendent who will rise to power and glory of the humiliation into which the line of David had fallen (Isa. 4:2; 11:1; Jer. 23:5; 33:15; Zech. 6;12–13)." The vision concludes with the mention of a stone with seven eyes (Isa. 11:2–5) that is set before Joshua. The inference is that God will use this stone to remove the iniquity of the land in one day. The stone (Ps. 118:22; Matt. 21:42; 1 Peter 2:6), which is Christ, will at His Second Coming set up His kingdom and restore Israel. He will also bring peace to the earth that will allow everyone of Israel to "invite his neighbor to sit under his vine and under his fig tree" (3:10).

Vision 5: The Gold Lampstand and the Two Olive Trees

Zechariah's fifth vision, the golden lampstand and two olive trees, involves the angelic messenger showing Zechariah a golden lampstand with it's bowl on top, with seven lamps with spouts, as well as two olive trees on either side of the bowl (4:1–3). When Zechariah asked what this all meant the angel said, "This is the word of the Lord to Zerubbabel" (4:5–7). The message to him was that it was not by might nor by power that the temple would be completed but the power of the Spirit of God would be the force that would bring it to pass (4:6). The task that seemed like a mountain, with so much opposition, would be as a plain, and the task would be accomplished and be a witness of the Lord's presence with them 4:7, 9). The seven lamps represent the eyes of the Lord which range to and fro throughout the earth (4:10), assuring them that God is constantly aware of their plight. The two olive trees represent "the two anointed ones," Zerubbabel and Joshua, king and priest. At the Second Coming Christ will take on both of these roles. The lampstand would then represent Israel as a light to the Gentiles (Isa. 42:6; 49:6). As Walvoord states, "All of this encouraged the returning captives to rebuild the temple. The abiding truth for all was that what was accomplished for God must be accomplished in the power of the Spirit." Again the vision foreshadows the future millennial kingdom when the King-Priest, Christ Jesus, will reign from Jerusalem and the nation of Israel will truly be a light to the Gentiles.

Vision 6: The Flying Scroll

Zechariah saw a scroll thirty feet long and fifteen feet wide flying through the air. The scroll was unrolled and could be read on both sides. Since this is the same dimensions as the tabernacle, some have suggested that the judgments proceeding from it were in harmony with God's holy presence in the midst of the Israel. A curse or punishment will go out against those who violate His law, symbolized here by those who steal (Exod. 20:15) and swear falsely (20:7). All those involved in such things will be purged from the covenant people (5:4). The severity and totality of the judgments suggests a fulfillment in the millennial kingdom when the Messiah will rule with a rod of iron (Ps. 2:9–12; Rev. 12:5; 19:15).

Vision 7: The Woman in the Ephah

In Zechariah's seventh vision, the angelic messenger showed Zechariah a vision of an ephah that was said to represent "their appearance in all the land" (Zech. 5:6). The ephah was covered with a lead cover and when lifted up it revealed a woman sitting in the ephah. The woman, in 5:8, is said to be wickedness personified, which represented the civil, ethical, and religious evil. The angel threw the woman down in the middle of the ephah and cast the lead weight on its opening, securing the content. The ephah was lifted between the earth and heaven by two women with the wings of a stork. These unidentified women transported the ephah to Shinar (in Babylon). Unger believes these women are demonic forces that seek to protect the woman of wickedness and enshrine her in Babylon, but they could also represent agents of divine power or providence. Since the tower of Babel, Babylon has been the source of much evil and has become a symbol of evil. This shows us that in the days before Christ's return to the earth to set up His kingdom, evil will be removed from Israel and returned to Babylon where a false religious system will exist. Then the evil in Babylon will be judged (Rev. 17–18), followed by the bringing in of the righteous kingdom of Christ (Rev. 19–20).

Vision 8: The Four Chariots

Zechariah's final vision involved four chariots with horses of red, black, white, and dapple coming from between two bronze mountains (6:1–2). The angelic messenger stated that these four chariots were the four spirits of heaven which go forth to patrol the earth (6:1–7). The horses are seen going north and south, which are the directions one must travel in and out of Israel by land. Lindsey suggests, "If the colors are significant, perhaps red symbolizes war and bloodshed, black designates death and famine, white speaks of triumph and victory, and dappled denotes pestilence and plagues" (cf. Rev. 6:1–8)." Bronze, the material of the two mountains, is a symbol of divine judgment (Rev. 1:15; 2:18). The four spirits stood before the Lord of all the earth (cf. Micah 4:13) and the "He" whose wrath is appeased by the judgments is that same Lord (6:7–8). The judgments would be on Babylon, the north country, and Egypt, the south country. After God's wrath is poured out on Babylon His wrath is said to be appeased in the land of the north. As Lindsey points out, "God's wrath, after being executed on the wickedness transplanted to Babylon (Zech. 5:5–11; cf. Rev. 18:2, 10, 21; 19:1–3) will then come to rest. In the first vision God was angry with the nations that felt secure (Zech. 1:15); in this vision He was satisfied with their just judgment (cf. Rev. 19:2, 15–19)."

The Crowning of the High Priest

The eight night visions were followed by the Lord's instruction to take an offering and from it to make an ornate silver and gold crown and place it on the head of Joshua the high priest (6:9–11). This historical event had prophetic symbolism, as the Lord states in 6:12–13. In the future there would be a man named Branch who would branch out from where He is, and He will build the temple of the Lord. The fact that Joshua was crowned (becoming king-priest) instead of Zerubbabel (an heir of the Davidic dynasty) makes the symbolism clear. This is symbolic of the time shortly after the nations are judged when Christ will become King and Priest (Ps. 110:4; Rev. 19:12). He will also build the temple of the Lord (6:13), that is, the millennial temple (Isa. 2:2, 4; Ezek. 40–42). That the crowning of Joshua was symbolic of a future event is borne out by the fact that the crown that Joshua was crowned with was not left on his head but placed in the temple as a reminder of the Lord (6:14). In that future millennial reign the nations will come and "build in" (Heb.) the temple of the Lord by bringing their wealth into it (Ps. 127:1; cf. Isa. 56:6–7).

The Questions of the Fasts

The next prophetic message came almost two years later on December 7, 518 B.C. The four messages covering 7:4–8:23 are in response to a question posed by a delegation from Bethel (7:2). The Jews had instituted a fast in the fifth month, soon after arriving in Babylon during the captivity, to commemorate the destruction of Jerusalem and the temple. The question was, "Shall I weep in the fifth month and abstain, as I have done these many years?" (7:3). The Lord's answer was a rebuke that they observed the fast in the fifth month and seventh month (both instituted by people, not by God) for themselves and not for God. They were doing the same thing that the earlier prophets had warned against, eating and drinking for themselves (6:6).

The next message was another reminder of how those who had come before this generation had failed. Though the Lord made it clear that His desire for them was to dispense justice, to practice kindness and compassion to each other; not to oppress the widow or the orphan, the stranger or the poor, and not to devise evil against one another, they refused to pay attention (7:9–11). Thus God had scattered them like a storm wind and the land was left desolate behind them (7:12–14).

The third message was a message of encouragement. In contrast to the destruction discussed in 7:14, in the future there would be a time of ultimate restoration. The restoration would come because of the Lord's exceeding jealousy for Zion (8:1; cf. Zech. 12:1–9; 14:1–7; Rev. 19:11–20:3). The period will be characterized by the Lord dwelling in the midst of Jerusalem and as a result it will be called the City of Truth and Zion will be called the Holy Mountain (8:3, 21–23; 14:16–21; Isa. 2:2–3; Jer. 50:5). Jerusalem will be characterized by peace, security, and prosperity (8:4–9–14; cf. Isa. 65:20). The Jews will be restored by the Lord's sovereign hand (8:6–8). The same Sovereign Lord who promised and brought judgment on the previous generation will also bring to fruition His promise of restoration and blessing to a future generation (8:14–15). The Lord's final instruction in this message was that they speak the truth, judge with truth, do not devise evil, and do not love perjury (8:16–17). This, as opposed to the meaningless fast, was what He desired of them for His blessing. This regathering and restoration to blessing will occur at the Second Coming of Christ as He establishes His millennial reign.

In Zechariah's fourth and final message he returns to the subject of the fasts. He speaks of a time when all the fasts (fourth month, fifth month, seventh month, and tenth month) would turn to feasts of joy and gladness (8:18–19). During this time people will come from other cities saying, "Let us go at once to entreat the favor of the LORD, and to seek the LORD of hosts; I will also go" (8:20–21). This pilgrimage will involve "many peoples and mighty nations [who] will come to seek the Lord of hosts in Jerusalem (8:21)." And during this time the peoples of the nations will recognize God's blessing on the Jewish people (8:23). This will occur in the millennial reign of Christ, as described by Isaiah 2:2–3.

Two Prophetic Burdens— The Great Messianic Future (9:1–14:21)

In this section the overriding theme is the great messianic future for the Jews.

The First Burden: The First and Second Advents of the Messiah

This division starts with a pronouncement of judgment on the nations that surround Israel. The Lord's judgment was declared on Hadrach, Damascus, Hamath, Tyre, Sidon, and four of the Philistines' major cities. These judgment were carried out by Alexander the Great as God's instrument, during his conquest throughout the area of Palestine after the battle of Issus in 333 B.C. The Lord says during this campaign "I will camp around My house because of an army, because of him who passes by and returns." The Macedonian armies of Alexander the Great passed by Jerusalem without laying seige to it—another literal fulfillment of prophecy. The text also says that no oppressor will pass over them anymore (9:8). This foreshadows the Lord's divine protection during the millennial kingdom (cf. Joel 3:16–17).

From 9:9–10:12 Zechariah deals with the blessing of the Messiah. In 10:9, we have a very clear prophecy related to the Messiah's first coming (cf. Isa. 9:5–7; Micah 5:2–4; Luke 1:32–33). The Messiah would come, humble and riding on a donkey, even the colt, the foal of a donkey (9:9; cf. Matt. 21). One verse later Zechariah leaps to the future in describing the rule of Christ in the millennial kingdom. During that time He will end all wars and speak peace to the nations (9:10; cf. Isa. 2:4, Micah 4:3). Zechariah then switches from messianic prophecy to encourage his contemporaries. In 9:11 he refers to "the blood of My covenant with you." This is probably a reference to the Mosaic covenant (Exod. 24:3–8), and because of the Lord's covenant with them He will deliver them and restore double to them [probably the remaining exiles in Babylon (9:11–12)]. Verse 13 probably refers to the Lord's delivering the Jews in the struggle of the Maccabees against Greek paganism between 175 and 163 B.C. It is possible that the rest of chapter 9 describes the same time period, but it is also at least a foreshadowing of Christ's deliverance of Israel before His kingdom is established. Unger states, "Then they will be 'saved' (Rom. 11:26), regenerated spiritually, when they accept the Messiah–Redeemer at His Second Advent (Zech. 12:10-13:1), and they will be delivered nationally from their foes, when the Lord really becomes 'their God,' and they become the flock of his people (Psalm 23:1–6)." There is a transition in 10:1. The Lord is recognized as being the source of the blessings of rain and vegetation (10:1), as opposed to the false shepherds who are seeing lying visions and false dreams and not shepherding the people (10:2–3). The Lord's response will be to punish these "male goats" and then restore and strengthen the house of Judah (10:3–5). In verses 6–12 we see that because of the Lord's compassion on them (10:6), He will carry out a massive regathering of His people from all the world (10:7–12). As Lindsey points out, "Their regathering will be accompanied by redemption and multiplication (10:8b; cf. Hosea 1:10)."

In chapters 9–10 we see a glorious future for the Lord's covenant people, but chapter 11 is a stark contrast to the two previous chapters. In chapter 11 is recorded the future rejection of the Good Shepherd and the resulting consequences on the nation. First we see a prophecy of the devastation that will come on the land. Fire will consume the cedars of Lebanon, the cypress and the oaks of Bashan. The pastures also are denuded because the shepherds wail and even the young lions roar because their habitation is destroyed. But why the destruction? This question is answered in the following verses. Zechariah, in a parable showing the rejection of the Good Shepherd, played the role of a shepherd holding two staffs in his hands called "Favor" and "Union." This flock was doomed to slaughter already (11:4). Their own shepherds buy them and slay them and have no pity on them (11:5). Even the Lord says, "I will no longer have pity on the inhabitants of the land" (11:6) and thus He would cause the men to fall, and they [the Romans] will strike the land, and He will not deliver them from their power. So Zechariah (symbolizing the Messiah) pastured the flock. The three leaders of Israel—prophet, priest, and king—were discarded (11:8) and they rejected the shepherd (11:8). As a result, the shepherd responded by rejecting them (11:9). The staff Favor was destroyed as a sign of the shepherd's covenant being broken and he asked for his wages, a mere thirty shekels. The price was thrown into the house of the Lord for the potter (11:13). This was prophetic of Judas's betrayal of Christ for thirty pieces of silver. Then the other staff, Union, was destroyed symbolizing the break in the relationship between Judah and Israel. Zechariah was next asked to play the role of a "foolish shepherd" (11:15). This foolish shepherd would not care for the perishing, seek the scattered, heal the broken, or sustain the one standing, but will devour the flesh of the fat sheep and tear off their hoofs (11:16; cf. Rev. 13:7). But a woe is announced on this foolish shepherd who will have his power (the arm) and his intelligence (his eye) destroyed (11:17). The Jews rejected the Good Shepherd at His first coming; when the Antichrist comes on the scene (the foolish shepherd) they will accept him. But Christ will destroy him at His Second Coming (Rev. 19:20). Unger, commenting on verse 16 states the following, "The false shepherd (the Antichrist) is described in salient contrast to the true Shepherd (the Christ). Israel's rejection of the Good Shepherd was judicially punished by their accepting the bad shepherd (John 5:43)."

The Second Burden: The Second Advent of the Messiah

The remaining chapters deal predominantly with the Second Advent of Christ. In 12:1–9, Zechariah deals with the future deliverance of Israel from its enemies. After reminding his readers of the Lord's divine sovereignty in the affairs of the universe

(12:1), he proclaims that the Lord will make Jerusalem "a cup that causes reeling." The Lord will gather all the nations against Jerusalem (12:3) and then He will protect His holy city by striking the horses blind and thier riders with madness (12:4). He will protect the house of Judah and His protection of Jerusalem will cause Judah to recognize that "A strong support for us are the inhabitants of Jerusalem through the Lord of hosts, their God" (12:5). In that day the Lord will divinely protect Judah and Jerusalem (12:4–6). Thus, at Christ's Second Coming He will first physically deliver Israel from their enemies.

Zechariah next deals with the spiritual repentance that will occur in that day (the Day of the Lord). The Lord will divinely bring about repentance in Israel by pouring out His Spirit on the remnant that He physically delivered in 12:1–9. The result will be a national repentance at Christ's Second Coming when they will be able to see the scars on Him from crucifixion and realize they rejected and crucified their Messiah. The Lord says, "They will look on Me whom they have pierced; and they will mourn form Him" (12:10). The repentance will be so widespread that it will involve every individual Jew (12:11–14).

The physical deliverance of Israel (12:1–9) and the spiritual repentance of Israel (12:10–14) will be followed by a spiritual cleansing of the nation (13:1–6). In that day, at Christ's return, a fountain will be opened for the house of David and for the inhabitants of Jerusalem, for sin and for impurity (13:1). There will be a purge of the idols as well as the false prophets at this time (13:2). The people will be so committed to the Lord that even if their own children should speak a prophecy falsely they will kill them (13:3). In fact the purge will be so severe that former false prophets will do every thing they can to not be identified as having given false prophecies. To explain the scars from cutting their breasts (a common practice in idol worship) they will say, "I was wounded in the house of a friend" (13:4–6).

Verse 7 starts a prophecy that speaks of a stricken Shepherd (13:7), His scattered sheep (13:8), and then a refined remnant (13:9). The difficult phrase, "My Associate," is from a Hebrew word used in only one other book in the OT, Leviticus (6:2; 18:20; etc.). There it refers to a "near relative." Thus the Lord is referring to this Shepherd as a near relative. This is a strong affirmation of His deity. This Shepherd will sovereignly bring a third of the scattered sheep and refine them as a pure remnant. Then He will be their God and they will be His people (13:9).

Chapter 14 speaks of a time when the nations will be gathered against Jerusalem and the city will be penetrated by the enemy forces. The city will be plundered and the armies will exile half of the people and leave half (14:1–2). This will occur just before the Second Coming and is the battle referred to in Revelation 16:14, 16. Then the Lord will return and go forth and fight against those nations (Rev. 19:11–21). This will occur on the same day when the Lord returns and there are some interesting geographical changes. The Mount of Olives will be split in two by a very large valley as the Lord returns visibly and physically, just as He left (Acts 1:11). Those trying to escape Jerusalem will flee down this valley running from Jerusalem to Jericho (14:5). At this time Christ will return with the "holy ones" (angels or departed saints) with him. This will also be a unique day in that it will be a day without night (Isa. 13:10; Jer. 4:23; Ezek. 32:7–8; Joel 2:30–31; Acts 2:16, 19–20). There will be no need for luminaries since the Light of the world will be present, so even in the evening there will be light (14:7). Apparently Jerusalem will be physically elevated where half of the water flow, from the living waters, will go to the east and half to the west (14:8). At this time the Lord will be the King of all the earth and the curse will be taken away and the inhabitants of Jerusalem will live securely (14:9–11).

Chapter 14:12–15 is a section Lindsey calls a parenthetical flashback referring to the phrase "the peoples *who have gone* to war against Jerusalem" (14:9, italics mine). Unger comments: "The destruction of Israel's foes will be accomplished by the Lord through the use of the following three weapons unleashed against the godly remnant's enemies, who will be bent on annihilating them and thus defeating God's purpose for His people and the earth: (1) a deadly plague (vv. 12, 15); (2) a frightful consternation, producing mutual annihilation (v. 13), and (3) superhuman valor divinely instilled in the remnant (v. 14)."

After the nations are defeated and Christ sets up His millennial reign, those left from among the nations will be required to come to Jerusalem each year to worship the King, the Lord of hosts and to celebrate the Feast of Booths (14:16). The penalty for non-compliance will be that the Lord will withhold the rain from them (14:17). Even Egypt, which depends on the floods of the Nile rather than the annual rain, will experience the drought if they do not comply (14:18–19).

Finally life will be characterized in the millennial kingdom by holiness. From the bells of the horses to the "cooking pots" in the newly constructed millennial temple (Ezek. 40–43), holiness will be the norm (14:20–21). Here "Canaanite" probably is used symbolically of anyone unclean and unholy. The millennial reign of Christ will be characterized by holiness.

See also DAY OF THE LORD; THEOCTIC KINGDOM; TRIBULATION, THE GREAT.

Russell L. Penney

Gleason L. Archer, *A Survey of Old Testament Introduction* (Chicago: Moody Press, 1994); Kenneth L. Barker, "Zechariah" in *The Expositor's Bible Commentary*, ed. Frank E. Gaebelein, vol. 7 (Grand Rapids: Zondervan, 1985); F. Duane Lindsey, "Zechariah" in *The Bible Knowledge Commentary,* eds. John F. Walvoord and Roy B. Zuck (Wheaton: Victor Books, 1988); Merrill F. Unger, *Unger's Commentary on the Old Testament,* vol. 2 (Chicago: Moody Press, 1981); John F. Walvoord, *The Prophecy Knowledge Handbook* (Wheaton: Victor Books, 1990).

ZEPHANIAH

The theme of Zephaniah's prophecy is found in the phrase, "the day of the LORD." This phrase is mentioned throughout the book no less than nineteen times (1:7–10, 14–16, 18; 2:2–3; 3:11, 16). However, to employ a theme referencing judgment alone is too limited. It fails to describe the full content of the Day of the Lord that includes both judgment and regathering, or restoration. A fuller theme must include both of these aspects, such as "the interruption of sinful human activity by Yahweh through judgment and restoration." Although Zephaniah is one of the most ignored books in the Bible, it remains the key book for gathering a full description of what is involved in the Day of the Lord.

The Day of the Lord is a divine interruption of or intrusion into human affairs for the purpose of bringing about purification (1:17) and maintaining a realization of God's sovereignty. It is imminent by nature (1:7,14) and thorough in purpose (1:15–18). The Lord will exact punishment upon the earth that can be either local (1:4–13; 2:4–15) or universal (1:2–3,18; 3:8). The ultimate end of this punishment is not annihilation, but restoration of a remnant (2:1–3; 3:8–13), especially of His beloved nation, Israel (2:1–3; 3:11–20), to whom the threat of an impending Day of the Lord is initially given. This personal involvement of the Lord is meticulously proclaimed by the continual use of the first person pronoun in contexts of judgment and restoration (1:2–4, 8–9, 12, 17; 2:5; 3:3, 8–9, 11–12, 19–20).

The prophecy was articulated to Judah during the reign of King Josiah, prior to the finding of the Law in the temple by Hilkiah in 622 B.C. Josiah, age eight at the time of his inauguration in 640 B.C., was influenced by royal court officials of questionable integrity (3:3). Prior to Josiah's spiritual awakening in 632 B.C. (2 Chron. 34:3), the nation had gone through a systematic elimination of their covenant responsibilities to the Lord under the leadership of Manasseh and his son, Amon (686–632 B.C.), a time known as Judah's "Dark Ages." The land was full of idolatry and selfish ambition that led to sexual perversity, astrological worship, human sacrifice, and social injustice (2 Chron. 33:2–9). The earliest date for Zephaniah's insertion into Judean culture would therefore be just prior to Josiah's awakening, assuming that it was Zephaniah's ministry that challenged Josiah's upbringing. It should be noted that other scholars claim that the dating of the prophecy must occur after the discovery of the Law, although all agree that the prophecy preceded the destruction of Assyria in 612 B.C. because Zephaniah describes Assyria's present existence and imminent demise (2:13–15). The overall range given by scholars for the writing of Zephaniah is from 635–612 B.C.

The prediction of the Day of the Lord is both a historical event and an eschatological event. To the Judean nation and their idolatrous neighbors, Zephaniah gives a clear warning of impending judgment (1:4–13; 2:3–3:7). These passages are clearly historical and find their fulfillment for Assyria in 612 B.C. and for Judah in 605 B.C. under the tide of Babylonian expansion ("he has consecrated those he has invited" 1:7). The other nations mentioned also became vassals of the Babylonian Empire. It is interesting to note that this visitation of the Lord, although avoidable through repentance (2:1–2; 3:7), was so certain that the few who do repent and are faithful are admonished to seek the Lord, righteousness, and humility while passing through the judgment against the nations. Believers experience the consequences of judgment against unbelievers. It is from surviving believers, a remnant, that God begins to initiate His objectives again. Daniel and Ezekiel are two examples from the believing remnant, whom God had deported to Babylon for the purpose of bringing the nation of Judah back to Him.

To the Judeans, this prophecy appeared to be universal in character. Had they believed the words of Zephaniah, no doubt they would be expecting a judgment that would bring worldwide catastrophe (1:1–3, 15–18; 3:8), as well as raining specific devastation on Judah and Jerusalem (3:1–5). Their ultimate hope would be everlasting peace for the people of the world and greatness to Israel, the people of God (3:9–20). Today's students of the Bible have the benefit of history to realize that Zephaniah was providing descriptions of the Day of the Lord not only to his immediate audience, but to audiences throughout history as well. The terrifying portrait of the Day of the Lord in 1:14–18 describes the extremities of any disaster connected with a visitation or intrusion of the Lord into the affairs of humankind. The passage characterizes the terror of Day of the Lord that was implemented by God through the Babylonians, all future "days" or intrusions, and a final eschatological Day of the Lord. The punishment and restoration of the people of the world and Israel in 3:8–20 is so complete and final that it can only have reference to the Great Tribulation and millennial kingdom. The idea of a universal judgment as first mentioned in 1:2–3 is revisited in 3:8. The prophet states that all the nations of the earth will be gathered together and devoured as a result of the Lord's indignation. This isn't a local destruction of Judah and Jerusalem (1:4–2:3; 3:1–7) or a judgment against Judah's immediate enemies (2:4–15). It is a description of an eschatological devastation that will affect the entire earth, a destruction reminiscent of Zechariah's and John's great gathering of the nations that takes place at the end of the Great Tribulation at Armageddon (Zech. 14:2; Rev. 16:14–16). The blessings that follow this great conflagration describe a moral and spiritual restoration of the surviving Gentile world (3:9–10), and a complete cleansing and restoration of Israel (3:11–20) that has as its supreme leader the King of Israel, the Lord Jesus Christ (Isa. 9:7; Zech. 14:9; 1 Tim. 6:14–15; Rev. 19:16) to protect her forever (3:15–17). The eschatological "Day of the Lord" begins with punishment for sin, which is always the provocation for God's intervention (1:17), and ends with the restoration of a remnant under the direct counsel and leadership of the Lord Himself in the person of Jesus Christ during the Millennium.

The historical judgment and restoration of ancient Judah foreshadows all interventions that God may exact upon the world at any time, anywhere, including the eschatological Day of the Lord. The fact that they are imminent (1:7, 14) is essential to the fear they are intended to induce upon people who question the sovereignty of God and, therefore, lack motivation for repentance.

Gary P. Stewart

Paul. N. Benware, *Understanding End Times Prophecy: A Comprehensive Approach* (Chicago: Moody Press, 1995); Arnold G. Fruchtenbaum, *Israelology: The Missing Link in Systematic Theology* (Tustin, Calif.: Ariel Ministries Press, 1989); John D. Hannah, "Zephaniah" in *The Bible Knowledge Commentary,* eds. John F. Walvoord and Roy B. Zuck (Wheaton: Victor Books, 1985); Greg A. King, "The Day of the Lord in Zephaniah" in *Bib Sac,* 152:16–32 (January–March 1995); R. D. Patterson, "Nahum, Habakkuk, Zephaniah" in *The Wycliffe Exegetical Commentary,* ed. Kenneth Barker (Chicago: Moody Press, 1991); Charles C. Ryrie, *Come Quickly, Lord Jesus* (Eugene, Oreg.: Harvest House, 1996); Larry L. Walker, "Zephaniah" in *The Expositor's Bible Commentary,* ed. Frank E. Gaebelein (Grand Rapids: Zondervan, 1985); John F. Walvoord, *Prophecy Knowledge Handbook* (Wheaton: Victor Books, 1990)

INDEX

INDEX

NOTES

NOTES

NOTES

NOTES